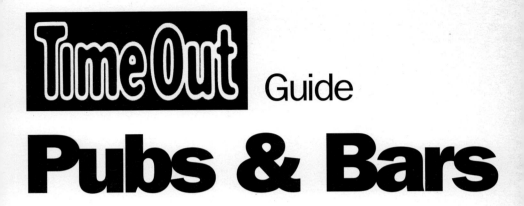

TimeOut Guide

Pubs & Bars

ABSOLUT POWER.

CHARGE YOUR GLASSES. THERE IS NO PURER VODKA. SERVE IT NEAT AT 0°C.

Contents

About the Guide 7
The chain gang 9
Advertisers' index 238
Where to go for... 239
A-Z index 249

Published by
Time Out Guides Ltd
Universal House
251 Tottenham Court Road
London W1P 0AB

Tel + 44 (0)20 7813 3000
Fax + 44 (0)20 7813 6001
e-mail guides@timeout.com
http://www.timeout.com

Editorial
Editor Andrew White
Consultant Editor Jim Driver
Copy Editors Lily Dunn, Will Fulford-Jones, Angela Jameson, Nick Rider
Reviewers Frank Broughton, Rhonda Carrier (*Hammersmith ghosts*) James Christopher (*Beer market*;
Southern comfort), Ian Cunningham, Guy Dimond (also *A Hoxton hike*) Jim Driver, Charlie Godfrey-
Faussett, Peter Fiennes, Cara Frost, Danny Fryer, Will Fulford-Jones (also *EastEndings*; *Moonlighting*;
Musical lairs; *On the Waterfront*), Sarah Halliwell, Will Hodgkinson, Dean Irvine, Phil Jones, Jenny Knight,
Patrick Marmion, Rachael Philipps, Cath Phillips, James Pretlove, Vanessa Raison, Nick Rider, Lisa Ritchie
(*Lobby fodder*) Helen Roshier, Davis Rowley, Nicholas Royle (also *Postman's round*), Rachel Sawyer, NJ
Stevenson, Rebecca Taylor, Andrew White.
Listings Researcher Rachel Sawyer
Proofreader Tamsin Shelton
Indexer Jackie Brind
Editorial Director Peter Fiennes

Design
Art Director John Oakey
Art Editor Mandy Martin
Senior Designer Scott Moore
Designers Benjamin de Lotz, Lucy Grant
Picture Editor Kerri Miles
Deputy Picture Editor Olivia Duncan-Jones
Picture Admin Kit Burnet
Scanning/Imaging Chris Quinn, Dan Conway

Advertising
Group Advertisement Director Lesley Gill
Sales Director/Sponsorship Mark Phillips
Sales Manager Alison Gray
Advertisement Sales James Coulbault, Thea Pitcher, Andrew Williams
Copy Controller Angela Davis

Administration
Publisher Tony Elliott
Managing Director Mike Hardwick
Financial Director Kevin Ellis
General Manager Nichola Coulthard
Production Manager Mark Lamond
Production Controller Samantha Furniss
Marketing Director Gill Auld
Marketing Manager Christine Cort
Marketing Executives Mandy Martinez, Jo Tomlin, Sandie Tozer
Marketing Designer Paul Reed
Marketing Assistant Beki Morris
Accountant Catherine Bowen

Photography Frank Bauer, Georgie Scott, Paul Salmon, Dominic Dibbs, Luca Zampedri
Cover & openers photography Paul Avis
Maps Lucy Grant

The editors would like to thank: Guy Dimond, Sarah Guy, Ruth Jarvis, Caroline Taverne.

Repro by Precise Litho, 34-35 Great Sutton Street, London EC1.
Printed and bound by Southernprint, Factory Road, Upton Industrial Estate, Poole, Dorset BH16 5SN.

Copyright © Time Out Group Limited 2000

ISBN 0 903446 52 9

Distributed by Seymour Ltd (020 7396 8000)

About the Guide

The Guide is arranged by area because that's how most people drink. If you're after something more specific than a good pub or a groovy bar in your area, then turn to page 239 for a rundown on different types of drinking establishments, from those with great gardens to the ones with the best cocktails.

Opening times
We only list the opening times of the bar or pub. We do not list the opening times of any attached restaurant, brasserie or shop (although these may be the same). Note that opening times and food-serving times in particular may change. It is also worth noting that most City pubs and bars are closed at the weekend.

Food served
As above, we only list the times that food is served in the bar or pub, not in any attached restaurant or brasserie. 'Food served' can mean anything from cheese rolls to a three-course meal. When the opening times and food-served times are run together (Open/food served), it means that food is served until shortly before closing time. We haven't included any establishment that requires you to eat in order to be allowed to drink.

Admission
In some cases, particularly in central London, pubs and bars charge admission after a certain hour. Where there is a regular pattern to this, we have listed the details. And you may not be able to get into the hipper bars at all, as during busier times the doorman might send you packing simply because you don't look the part. Note that there are more and more venues that become members-only after a certain hour, although the rules are often blurred.

Credit cards
The following abbreviations are used: **AmEx** American Express; **DC** Diners Club; **MC** MasterCard; **V** Visa.

Babies and children admitted
Under 14s are only allowed into the gardens, separate family rooms and the restaurant areas of pubs and wine bars, unless the premises has a special 'children's certificate'. If the establishment has a certificate, children can go in as long as they're with an adult. Those aged 14-17 can go into a bar, but only for soft drinks. It's an offence for a licensee to serve alcohol in a bar to anyone under 18. Unless drinkers can prove they're at least 18, the licensee can refuse to serve them and can ask them to leave the premises. In our listings look out for *Babies and children admitted* as a guide to whether your children are welcome or not.

Disabled: toilet
If a pub claims to have a toilet for the disabled, we have said so; this also implies that it's possible for a disabled person to gain access to the venue. However, we cannot guarantee this, and no matter how good the arrangements appear, we recommend phoning in advance to check feasibility.

Function room
Means the pub or bar has a separate room that can be hired for meetings or parties; some do not charge for this.

Late licence
We have listed any pub or bar that is open until midnight or later as having a late licence.

Music
Unless otherwise stated, bands play in the evening. The same goes for any other form of entertainment listed.

No-smoking room/area
Very few pubs or bars have a no-smoking room or area (the JD Wetherspoon chain is an exception to this rule); we've listed the ones that do. But note that a separate no-smoking area is not necessarily much protection from the usual smoky pub or bar.

Vegetarian dishes
Be warned that this may mean no more than a cheese sandwich or a plate of chips, although some pubs (particularly gastropubs) and bars do make more of an effort.

Websites
If a pub or bar has a website address we have listed it after the telephone number in the listings.

Sponsors and advertisers
We would like to thank our sponsor Perrier for their involvement in this Guide. We would also like to thank the advertisers. However, we would like to stress that they have no control over editorial content. No bar or pub has been included because its owner has advertised in the Guide; an advertiser may receive a bad review or no review at all.

The chain gang

The growth of the pub and bar chain continues unabated, with many of the established players extending their portfolio still further, and still more starting up. Having bought up old pubs, banks and shop premises, these corporate giants have found a recipe for success: the formula generally includes large, pine-drenched premises, a few beers on tap and still more by the bottle, MOR music and a menu on which everything is usually served with rocket and fries.

Of course, the formula varies from chain to chain, as does the size – **Davys** has over 40 London outlets, **Edward's** only five at present – and there are undoubted reasons for their success. Some – such as the longer-established City-centred **Corney & Barrow**, **Balls Brothers** and **Davys** wine bar chains – have a fine reputation for their wine and food, and the venues themselves are often highly individual; others, such as **All Bar One**, **Slug & Lettuce** and **Pitcher & Piano** are more homogenised, and have become the natural meeting – and picking-up – points for young Londoners. **Wetherspoons**, however, cannot be so readily recognised from their appearance,

but from features such as cheap drinks and no-smoking areas. Other chains have their own idiosyncratic distinctiveness. **Babushkas** are a vodka aficionado's dream, **Po Na Na** have a lively Moroccan spirit, while the **Tups** aren't sheepish in encouraging a cheerful spirit to prevail. The **Firkins** have converted interesting premises with imagination, but with their ownership having recently changed, how they will evolve in the future is uncertain. Unfortunately, the microbreweries are disappearing, a sad loss to fans of real ales and diversity.

And, yes, they are all popular, albeit for different reasons. But also partly because of their reliability, efficiency and predictability. You can make an educated guess at the decor, ambience, food and drink before you've even stepped through the door, and therefore to some degree, you can predict the sort of evening you have in store.

All this is by way of explaining this guide's policy towards these chains. We have not reviewed every outlet, but we offer, instead, a review of at least one from each chain, and have listed the rest in the **Also in the area...** postscript for each area.

▶

espresso that tastes
as good as it looks

PIAZZA
D'ORO
ESPRESSO

Here is where to find the reviews:

●**All Bar One** (branches, at time of writing
– 39; see p155 for review)
Stripped pine, big tables, huge food,
decent beer.

●**Babushka** (4; see p105)
Flavoured vodkas are the chief attraction
here, but don't discount dancing and
dating.

●**Balls Brothers** (17; see p123)
Deeply trad wine bars (with a hefty list
majoring in French wines), particularly big
in the City.

●**Café Flo** (12; see p61)
Brasserie food, with a few
tables set aside for
drinkers.

●**Café Med** (7; see p76
and p142)
Good-time venues with
fair (yep, Mediterranean)
food, and a new bar
opened up in Notting Hill.

●**Café Rouge** (39; see p52)
Reliable food in French-
flavoured cafés, often with real
French people serving. Usually
child-friendly.

●**Corney & Barrow** (12; see p62
and p127)
Lavish wine cellars, smart interiors,
good-quality food and smooth service.

●**Davys** (41; see p21, p30 and p195)
Sawdust on the floor, barrels of ale, and
some fine wines by the glass. See page 15
for details of the offer of a free glass of
wine in Davys' outlets.

●**Dôme** (12; see p101)
The French food's fair enough, but you can
drink too.

●**Edward's** (5; see p209)

Breakfast, lunch and tea all available in
the build-up to a pacey evening scene.

●**Fine Line** (8; see p50)
A colourful mix of sofas, armchairs and
barstools in this Fuller's chain.

●**Firkins** (33; see p48, p172, p187
and p231)
Some stunning buildings, and excruciating
wit, but some changes ahead?

●**Jamies** (12; see p40 and p125)
Bottled beers and wines head the drinks
list in these popular, friendly bars.

●**Pitcher & Piano** (18; see p90)
Noisy, unpretentious, up-for-it.
And yet more pine.

●**Po Na Na** (4; see p48)
Drink cocktails and
dance in these upbeat,
late-night bars.

●**Puzzle** (4; p155)
Proudly presents itself
on the cusp of the
pub/bar divide.

●**Ruby in the Dust** (5; see
p229)
Bottled lagers and decent international
food in a colourful, comfortable setting.

●**Slug & Lettuce** (16; see p134)
The original, bright and breezy, pine-with-
everything chain.

●**Tup Inns** (10; see p45, p67, p154
and p236)
Large, spacious and cheerful – a
welcoming home for their flock.

●**JD Wetherspoon** (see p103, p109,
p124, p125, p129, p178, p182, p196,
p204, p216 and p221)
There are numerous Wetherspoons
throughout the capital. Distinguishing
features are cheap ales, acceptable food
and no-smoking areas.

Windows Restaurant

CENTRAL

Bayswater, Paddington, W2

Archery Tavern
4 Bathurst Street, W2 (020 7402 4916). Lancaster Gate tube. **Open** 11am-11.30pm Mon-Sat; noon-10.30pm Sun. **Food served** noon-3pm, 6-9.30pm daily. **Credit** AmEx, DC, MC, V.
Given that the few pubs in Bayswater tend to be filled with tourists, the Archery is a good spot to know about: a colourful, cosy little place with a hearty, unpretentious feel appreciated by the local workers who frequent it. The genteel front room sticks to the most traditional of pub formulae – plates on the walls, hanging baskets, ageing man in a flat cap on a bar stool – while the more rowdy back room has a dartboard and a TV screen for all the big matches. Within this down-to-earth domain is a suitably traditional menu – steak and ale pie (£6.25), shepherd's pie (£5.50), gammon steak (£5.50) – and Badger bitters, including Golden Champion (£2.20), Tanglefoot (£2.20) and Blackadder III (£2.25).
Babies and children admitted. Games (board games, darts, fruit machine). Quiz (Sun). Satellite TV. Tables outdoors (pavement). Vegetarian dishes.

Fountains Abbey
109 Praed Street, W2 (020 7723 2364). Edgware Road tube/Paddington tube/rail. **Open** 11am-11pm Mon-Sat; noon-10.30pm Sun. **Food served** 11am-10pm Mon-Sat; noon-10pm Sun. **Credit** AmEx, DC, MC, V.
The Fountains Abbey is unique among Paddington pubs in that it's pretty similar to a generic West End bar. Huge, noisy, and packed with a twenty- and thirtysomething after-work crowd of both sexes, its proximity to Paddington Station makes it popular with commuters fending off the journey home. Huge clear-glass windows, a long central bar, a high red ceiling and oak panelling give it an old ale house feel. The crowd acts accordingly, happy to shout over the loud rock music and even make a few misguided attempts to dance to it as the night wears on: you won't find anyone popping in for a quiet pint and a read of the paper. Food is bog-standard pub grub – Yorkshire pudding (£4.45), burgers (£3.45) and the like – while on draught there's Courage Directors (£2.28), Theakston Best (£2.14), Foster's (£2.32) plus guest ales such as Old Speckled Hen.
Babies and children admitted (until 6pm). Function room. Games (fruit machines). Tables outdoors (pavement). Vegetarian dishes.

Leinster
57 Ossington Street, W2 (020 7243 9541). Bayswater tube. **Open** noon-11pm Mon-Sat; noon-10.30pm Sun. **Food served** noon-3pm, 5-9pm daily. **Credit** MC, V.
The Leinster has been refurbished as a modern-style pub, and the renovation suits its large space well. With its cream walls, deep sofas, orange lamps and spiral staircase (leading to a first floor built around a gallery that looks down on to the bar below), it feels light and airy, yet manages to be both welcoming and laid-back. Situated halfway between Notting Hill and Bayswater, the pub hosts a young, well-heeled but not excessively style-conscious clientele, and bar staff tend to be pretty and foreign. There are TV screens almost everywhere; on the night we went, they were showing classic episodes of *Fawlty Towers*, which made a pleasant change from football. The food is unremarkable, straight-from-the-freezer stuff (burgers £3.25, fish and chips £3.95), while beers include Guinness (£2.50) and Caffrey's (£2.30).
Function room. Games (chess, fruit machine, quiz machine). Satellite TV (big screen). Tables outdoors (patio). Vegetarian dishes.

Leinster Arms
17 Leinster Terrace, W2 (020 7723 5757). Lancaster Gate or Queensway tube. **Open** 11am-11pm Mon-Sat; noon-10.30pm Sun. **Food served** 11am-8pm Mon-Sat; noon-8pm Sun. **No credit cards**.
This former coaching inn has an attractive façade; step through the door, however, and you'll find a fairly ordinary, low-ceilinged pub filled with tourists and a few construction workers. The long bar, attended by staff in white shirts and black ties, is decorated with all the usual pub ornaments: plates, old ale pumps and prints of scenes from Victorian London. There's usually football on the wide-screen television and the music is about as bad as it gets – Bryan Adams, Celine Dion and other motorway service station favourites – but the atmosphere is generally low-key, and this inoffensive though unremarkable tourist stop-off is fine for a quick pint of Tetley's (£2.10), Young's Special (£2.20) or Carlsberg (£2.25) if you're in the area.
Babies and children admitted (until 8pm). Games (backgammon, darts, fruit machine). Jukebox. Satellite TV (big screen). Tables outdoors (pavement). Vegetarian dishes.

Mitre
24 Craven Terrace, W2 (020 7262 5240). Lancaster Gate tube/Paddington tube/rail. **Open** 11am-11pm Mon-Sat; noon-10.30pm Sun. **Food served** noon-9.30pm daily. **Credit** MC, V.
This well-kept Edwardian-style pub, like so many of its neighbours, makes few concessions to the modern age. Set on a quiet residential street, it's large and labyrinthine, with hanging baskets and etched glass windows. Parts of the pub are separated by screens that work their way around a large central bar, leading to a low-lit room at the end. Attracting a mixed crowd of locals, tourists and workers, the Mitre sticks to tradition in its menu, offering such hearty favourites as roast beef and Yorkshire pudding (£5.95) and gammon steak (£5.55), which can be washed down with a pint of Wadworth (£2.20) or Abbot (£2.25). The pub has its own raised pavement area filled with tables that stretch along the side of a mews street, making this a good place to come on a summer's day.
Babies and children admitted (separate room). Games (darts, fruit machines, pool table, table football). No-smoking area. Satellite TV. Tables outdoors (patio, pavement). Vegetarian dishes.

Planet Organic
42 Westbourne Grove, W2 (020 7221 7171/ www.planetorganic.com). Bayswater tube. **Open** 9am-8pm Mon-Sat; 11am-5pm Sun. **Unlicensed**. **Credit** MC, V.
As organic food continues to break out of its health-nut ghetto and into the mainstream, the original organic superstore goes from strength to strength. If you find yourself on Westbourne Grove in need of some positive stimulation, it's good to know there's a sit-down juice bar within the shop, selling juices, frozen yoghurts and smoothies made from whichever fruits are in season (£1.50-£2.50). The giant juicer will knock up cocktails like Red Planet (carrot, celery and beetroot £1.99), and there are also organic coffees and teas (with soya milk, naturally) on offer. It's not licensed for drinking alcohol on the premises, but there are ten organic beers to choose from in the shop for about £2 a bottle.
Babies and children admitted. No smoking.

Ranoush Juice
43 Edgware Road, W2 (020 7723 5929/ www.ranoush.com). Marble Arch tube. **Open** 8.30am-3am daily. **Food served** 10am-3am daily. **Unlicensed**. **No credit cards**.

Time Out Free glass of wine for every reader

We have linked up with the **Davy's wine bar outlets** to offer readers of the **Pubs & Bars Guide** a free glass of wine. Choose from over **40 outlets** and simply present the voucher printed on the card at the back of this guide and you can claim your **free wine**. Readers can choose from either a Davy's Bordeaux Claret or a Bordeaux Sauvignon.

Simply present your voucher from the back of this guide at any of the Davy's outlets below to claim your free glass of wine:

WC1
Bung Hole Wine Rooms, Bung Hole Cellars (see p51 for address); Truckles at Pied Bull Yard, Truckles Bar Café (see p21 for review); Champagne Charlie's, Tappit Hen Wine Rooms & Tappit Hen Cellars (see p36); Crusting Pipe (see p30 for review).

W1
Davy's Bar-Café-Bar, Dock Blida (see p69 for addresses); Chopper Lump (see p76); Lees Bag (see p42).

EC1
Bottlescrue, City Pipe, City Vaults, Colonel Jaspers (see p123 for addresses).

EC2
Bangers, The Bishop of Norwich, Bishops Parlour, Davy's at Russia Court, City Boot, Pulpit (see p127 for addresses).

EC3
Bangers Too, City Flogger, City FOB, Habit & New Waterloo (see p130 for addresses).

EC4
Davy's at Creed Lane (see p134 for address).

E1
Docks & Co, Grapeshots, Vineyard, Vineyard Coffee House (see p123 for addresses).

SE1
Cooperage, Mughouse, Skinkers (see p168 for addresses).

SW1
St James's, Tapster (see p101 for addresses).

E14
Davy's at Canary Wharf (see p195 for review).

Also
Davy's Wine Vaults, 161 Greenwich High Road, SE10; Gyngleboy, 27 Spring Street, Paddington, W2; Davy's in the Avenue, 3 Beacon House, Queen's Avenue, Clifton, Bristol; Colonel Jaspers, 15B Longbridge Road, Barking, Essex; Spotted Dog, 15 Longbridge Road, Barking, Essex; The Wine Vaults, 122 North End, Croydon.

Offer valid until November 30, 2000.

Everybody should visit Ranoush Juice at least once for a taste of affordable exotica. This mainstay of that strange strip of the Middle East that is the Edgware Road is filled with chrome furnishings, mirrored walls, and white-capped, moustachioed staff serving fruit juices, falafels and sticky sweets to a predominantly Arab crowd. Pay first, and present your ticket to the man at the juice bar: he'll then make you a delicious drink from the piles of fruit behind the glass display cabinets. Recommended favourites include the banana milkshake (£1.90), and the Ranoush Juice Cocktail (£1.75). This place is something of a Lebanese family favourite, so don't be surprised if you see small children accompanying their parents here late into the evening.
Babies and children admitted. Vegetarian dishes.

Royal Exchange
26 Sale Place, W2 (020 7723 3781). Edgware Road tube.
Open/food served 11am-11pm Mon-Fri; noon-3pm, 7-11pm Sat; noon-3pm, 7-10.30pm Sun. **Credit** MC, V.
A rarity, this: a true local in an area largely made up of hotels, shops and offices. It's a tiny corner pub along a small street, with a tiled exterior and an ornate, colourful, slightly rough-around-the-edges interior with a few tables lining the corridor-like room. On our visit it was packed with a raucous but amiable crowd, who could have done with a piano to make their singing a little sweeter, and who clearly appreciated the landlord's resolve to keep the prices down: roast rib beef, roast turkey and steak sandwiches are £4, double shots of house spirits are £2, and bitters such as Wadworth 6X and Brakspear cost £2-£2.30 a pint. The Royal Exchange is worth seeking out, if only because it offers a little character in an area that doesn't really have one.
Jukebox. Satellite TV. Tables outdoors (pavement). Vegetarian dishes.

Swan
66 Bayswater Road, W2 (020 7262 5204). Lancaster Gate tube. **Open/food served** 10am-11pm Mon-Sat; 10am-10.30pm Sun. **Credit** AmEx, DC, MC, V.
Looking out across Hyde Park and shadowed by hotels from every other direction, the Swan is hardly a local. As touristy pubs go, however, it's quite a pleasant one: there's a beer garden (heated in winter), a lively interior decorated with paintings of ships that look like they've been bought straight off the park railings opposite, and a genuine air of history to the olde-worlde style. Although the present building dates from the nineteenth century, it is reputedly the site of the last watering hole for seventeenth-century villains before they went off to be hung at Tyburn. Meals are served school-dinner style from a canteen (jacket potatoes £3.95, Burgundy beef £6.95), along with English teas and other refreshments. For a truly strange experience, head to the back room in the evening, when coachloads of Swedes and Germans join a chirpy Cockney character in a 'traditional' British singalong. Draught beers include Theakston Best (£2.19), Courage Directors (£2.25) and Foster's (£2.33).
Babies and children admitted (high chairs). Games (fruit machine). Jukebox. Music (trad pianist Mon-Sat). Satellite TV. Tables outdoors (forecourt). Vegetarian dishes.

Victoria
10A Strathern Place, W2 (020 7724 1191). Lancaster Gate tube/Paddington tube/rail. **Open** 11am-11pm Mon-Fri; noon-11pm Sat; noon-10.30pm Sun. **Food served** noon-2.30pm, 6-10pm Mon-Sat; noon-4pm, 6-9pm Sun. **Credit** MC, V.
The Victoria is a remarkably ornate pub: globe lamps along the bar, frosted glass windows etched with Britannia insignias, wood panelling, a large fireplace with a portrait of

the Royal Family (c1900) over it, caricatures of politicians, and, outside, fake gaslights. The effect of all this Victoriana is somewhat destroyed by the enormous wide-screen TV in the downstairs bar, however, so if it hasn't been pre-booked, head for the upstairs room: with its tiny staircase and bijou bar, it's a far nicer place for a drink. The pub is in a quiet, residential area and, since the only people who can afford to live nearby tend to be fabulously wealthy, the clientele tends to be the young and posh. Prices, though, are the usual, with Fuller's ESB at £2.25.
Babies and children admitted (until 4pm). Function room. Jukebox. Satellite TV. Tables outdoors (pavement). Vegetarian dishes.

Also in the area...

Café Rouge Unit 209, Whiteleys, Queensway, W2 (020 7221 1509).
Fettler & Firkin 15 Chilworth Street, W2 (020 7723 5918).
Slug & Lettuce 47 Hereford Road, W2 (020 7229 1503).

Belgravia SW1

Antelope
22-24 Eaton Terrace, SW1 (020 7730 7781). Sloane Square tube. **Open** 11.30am-11pm Mon-Sat; noon-10.30pm Sun. **Food served** 11.30am-3pm Mon-Sat. No food Sun. **Credit** AmEx, MC, V.
What with the photo of the pub cricket team on the wall and the drawling accents at the counter, this is one of the more patrician of Belgravia pubs, though one that wears its faintly scruffy look with the aplomb of a country gentleman sporting an old set of tweeds and a loosely knotted cravat. The Antelope's atmosphere of quiet contemplation is enhanced by its relaxing yellow decor and pleasing lack of music; the only jarring note is from two spectacularly ugly games machines, which, to paraphrase Raymond Chandler, are about as in-keeping as a tarantula on a fairy cake. There's a reasonable range of beers (Guinness £2.50, London Pride £2.30, Adnams Bitter £2.25), though the food is strictly routine (lasagne, chips and salad or chilli con carne, both £5.95).
Function room. Games (quiz machine, fruit machine). No piped music or jukebox. Vegetarian dishes.

Grenadier
18 Wilton Row, SW1 (020 7235 3074). Hyde Park Corner tube. **Open** noon-11pm Mon-Sat; noon-10.30pm Sun. **Food served** noon-3pm, 6-10pm Mon-Fri; noon-10pm Sat, Sun. **Credit** AmEx, MC, V.
The Grenadier is one of the capital's most delightful pubs. The cheerful red, white and blue livery and (genuine) sentry box outside the door herald the pub's military associations: not only was the Duke of Wellington a regular here, but the place is said to be haunted by the ghost of one of his men, flogged to death for cheating at cards (for some reason, he is particularly active in September). The interior of this mews-set pub is dark, snug and music-free, and behind the 200-year-old pewter bar, unsnooty staff dispense a decent selection of ales (Marston's Pedigree £2.34, Courage Best £2.26) and magnificent Bloody Marys (£4.25). The restaurant in the back offers pricier versions of the unpretentious, rib-sticking fare on offer in the bar (Grenadier burger £5.75, sausage and mash £4.50). It's a tiny place and is usually crowded, though at weekends it's less of a male preserve. Visit on a summer weekday afternoon after the suits have trundled back to the

London crawling

Moonlighting

'Same again,' says the man to the bartender, handing his glass across the bar. The bartender nods, and pours another pint of bitter. Having paid, the man takes his drink and returns to his friends, who sit chatting, drinking and smoking.

So far, so ordinary. The kind of scene played out in thousands of London pubs every day of the year. So much so, in fact, that we need to look at our watches just to confirm what our sleepy bodies are telling us. Sure enough, we're in the pub. And sure enough, it's 6.18 in the morning.

This isn't the result of a night out gone horribly wrong, either. Rather, this is part of an ill-advised plan to drink in London for 24 hours on the trot. But for the denizens of Borough Market, this is just part of a regular day.

We're in the **Market Porter**, a charming olde-worlde watering hole. It fills up during the evening with besuited city types, but early in the morning, the few drinkers are refugees from the market: the pub's early licence has been maintained with them specifically in mind. For some punters, this is their equivalent of lunchtime – whereas we're still rubbing the sleep out of our eyes.

At 8am, fresh air is beginning to seem like a very good idea, and a stroll over Blackfriars Bridge is a bracing thrill. The Smithfield Market meatpackers, though, have been up for hours already, and a few of them are already tucking into their third or fourth pint as we enter London's most notorious early-opening pub on the other side of the market. Sandwiched between the British Philatelic Society and a saucy underwear shop, the **Fox & Anchor's** eccentric choice of neighbours complements its esoteric opening hours perfectly. The full English breakfast and a pint of Guinness sounds appealing, but we fear we may not be able to move afterwards. Double sausage, bacon, egg, toast and a lager suffice. And we still can't move afterwards.

But by now it's 11am, and most of London's pubs are opening their doors. Up to this point, any 24-hour pub crawl is dependent upon the few early-openers. But from here on in, it can become a freeform alcoholic odyssey, taking in whichever pubs you fancy. We spend the next few hours wending our way through Holborn and into Bloomsbury, starting at the trad **Bleeding Heart Tavern** and continuing on to the mildly kooky **Three Cups** and the vibrant **Point 101**.

By 10pm, Soho beckons: handy as it's chocka with late-night bars. The legendary **Coach & Horses** seems as good a place to start as any, but when it calls last orders just before 11pm, we try to beat the night-owls' rush and get to the not-as-trendy-as-it-used-to-be **O Bar** before it starts charging for admission. However, conversation proves impossible above the music, and it's soon off to **Freedom**. Ostensibly a gay bar, its clientele is actually very mixed, and it's a decent bar in which to while away a couple of hours.

After 3am, it all gets a little more difficult. In fact, there aren't any non-members' bars in Soho that are legally entitled to serve alcohol beyond three in the morning. That's not to say that there aren't drinking possibilities in the area, of course. Just that we can't tell you exactly how or exactly where they are. Suffice to say, though, that we were able to carry on drinking for another three hours.

At 6am, we emerge, bleary-eyed, into the first light. Mission accomplished. The idea of one for the road back at the Market Porter crosses our minds. But we decide against it. Bed seems like a far better idea.
Will Fulford-Jones

Bleeding Heart Tavern *(p112)* Bleeding Heart Yard, 19 Greville Street, EC1 (020 7404 0333).
Coach & Horses *(p83)* 29 Greek Street, WC2 (020 7437 5920).
Fox & Anchor *(p115)* 115 Charterhouse Street, EC1 (020 7253 4838).
Freedom *(p84)* 60-66 Wardour Street, W1 (020 7734 0071).
Market Porter *(p166)* 9 Stoney Street, SE1 (020 7407 2495).
Point 101 *(p21)* 101 New Oxford Street, WC1 (020 7379 3112).
O Bar *(p89)* 83 Wardour Street, W1 (020 7437 3490).
Three Cups *(p50)* 21-22 Sandland Street, WC1 (020 7831 4302).

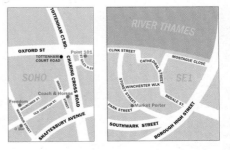

office, though, and you'll experience the place at its quiet, timeless best, providing, of course, you're not wearing soiled clothing (they won't serve you).
Babies and children admitted. Dress code. No piped music or jukebox. Restaurant. Tables outdoors (pavement). Vegetarian dishes.

Grouse & Claret
14 Little Chester Street, SW1 (020 7235 3438). Hyde Park Corner tube/Victoria tube/rail. **Open** 11am-11pm Mon-Fri. **Food served** noon-2pm Mon-Fri. **Credit** AmEx, DC, MC, V.
A refit would make all the difference to the Grouse & Claret's main bar. Encased in Winchester Club panelling, the only concessions to decoration are a token stuffed grouse and a stopped clock. It's not as if they don't try to get the punters in – 'Smile! You've just found an excellent pub!' exhorted the pavement blackboard – but the strong smell of furniture polish suggested they weren't expecting visitors. The food, though, is imaginative and inexpensive (pork in cider, minted lamb and apricot casserole, both £4.75), and there's a nice range of ales, among them Badger Tanglefoot (£2.20). The first-floor restaurant specialises in meaty English dishes, and is aimed squarely at the expense-account fraternity.
Babies and children admitted (dining area only). Games (board games). Function rooms. Vegetarian dishes.

Library
Lanesborough Hotel, Hyde Park Corner, SW1 (020 7259 5599/www.infoatlanesborough.com). Hyde Park Corner tube. **Open/food served** 11am-11pm Mon-Sat; noon-10.30pm Sun. **Credit** AmEx, DC, MC, V.
Hidden away inside one of London's most imposing hotels (formerly St George's Hospital, now the Lanesborough), the Library is very luxurious, very intimate and very expensive-looking. What it is not, despite all appearances to the contrary, is snooty – the Italian staff are far too busy and efficient for that – so if you're prepared to dress up, you'll be free to enjoy the dark, smoky atmosphere and try to identify the Hollywood actors and Tory MPs through the cigar-infused haze. Best known for its range of Vodka Martinis (£9), the prices are generally expensive but not piss-takingly so (house red £5, Glenmorangie £7.50).
Disabled: toilet. Function rooms. Music (pianist Mon-Fri; jazz Sat, Sun). Vegetarian dishes.

Plumbers Arms
14 Lower Belgrave Street, SW1 (020 7730 4067). Victoria tube/rail. **Open/food served** 11am-11pm Mon-Fri; noon-3pm Sat. **Credit** AmEx, DC, MC, V.
The Plumbers Arms has earned itself a footnote in criminal history: yellowing newspaper articles on the wall describe the night in November 1974 when Lady Lucan burst in screaming for help after her husband, as legend has it, had bludgeoned the nanny. These days, it's popular as an after-work unwinding zone: the large windows admit plenty of natural light giving it a soothing appearance. The plumbers may have gone, but the burr of male voices at the bar and the decorous Edwardian porn in the gents' suggest that this is still very much a man's pub. Food is standard pub fare, but the beer is reasonably priced (Courage Best £2.16, Bombardier £2.34).
Function room. Games (fruit machine, darts). Satellite TV. Tables outdoors (pavement). Vegetarian dishes.

Star Tavern
6 Belgrave Mews West, SW1 (020 7235 3019). Knightsbridge or Sloane Square tube. **Open** 11.30am-11pm Mon-Fri; 11.30am-3pm, 6.30-11pm Sat; noon-3pm,

7-10.30pm Sun. **Food served** noon-2.30pm daily; 6-9pm Mon-Fri; 6.30-9pm Sat; 7-9pm Sun. **Credit** MC, V.
The mews setting suggests another **Grenadier** (*see p16*) and, though appearances can be deceptive – the Star has a more mixed clientele, in terms of both age and class – the Star can stake an equal claim to be the best pub in the area. You'll need to be careful as you make your entrance, mind: the bar is immediately behind the door, which, if opened too abruptly, is liable to pitch a couple of regulars over the counter. The long, narrow lounge, with its real coal fire and sensible, well-worn wooden chairs, gives an endearing impression of a 1950s living room. There's no music or games machines, but the quality of the conversations going on around us – the use of parasols in hot countries, collectable car number plates – suggested neither was needed. Beers are the usual Fuller's range (London Pride £2.20, ESB £2.26), the food plain and affordable (potato with beans £2.75, ham and chips £4.50).
Babies and children admitted. Function room. No piped music or jukebox. Vegetarian dishes.

Talbot
1-3 Little Chester Street, SW1 (020 7235 1639). Hyde Park Corner tube/Victoria tube/rail. **Open** 9am-11pm Mon-Fri. **Food served** 9am-9.30pm Mon-Fri. **Credit** AmEx, DC, MC, V.
Though it's yet to acquire a distinctive atmosphere, this large, modern pub improves on acquaintance. It's a comfortable place with plenty of quiet nooks and crannies, particularly in the raised, corralled area at the back. The friendly staff are clearly keen to establish a reputation for both the food – an extensive menu includes rump steak (£7.45) and cod and chips (£5.75) – and the wines: Merlot Vin de Pays (£2.80) and a fruity Argentinian Tempranillo (£2.20) are among the entries on a lengthy and occasionally eclectic list. Bottled beers (Beck's £2.46, Holsten Pils £2.35) and Courage Best (£2.10) on tap are among the standard offerings. The huge seating area outside has heaters for nippy evenings.
No-smoking area. Satellite TV. Tables outdoors (patio). Vegetarian dishes.

Bloomsbury WC1

Duke of York
7 Roger Street, WC1 (020 7242 7230). Russell Square tube. **Open** noon-11pm Mon-Fri; 6-11pm Sat. **Food served** noon-3pm, 6-10pm Mon-Sat. **Credit** MC, V.
With its pockmarked lino floor, unco-ordinated chairs and cheerful red formica tables, you'd be forgiven for thinking the Duke of York had been left unchanged for decades. In fact, it's been made-over – to great effect – only in the last couple of years. Once a well-kept secret (it's tucked away at the end of a longish mews) and frequented mainly by elderly men, the Duke of York now attracts a mixture of bohemian mews-dwellers – the huge, unframed paintings and moody background jazz are presumably for their benefit – and discerning local office workers. It's still primarily a beer-drinker's pub (Burton's £2, Tetley's £2.40), though the food is not as cheap and cheerful as the decor would suggest (leek and pork sausage £8, blackened salmon fillet £8.50).
Babies and children admitted. Function room. Restaurant. Tables outdoors (pavement). Vegetarian dishes.

Enterprise
38 Red Lion Street, WC1 (020 7269 5901). Holborn tube. **Open** 11am-11pm Mon-Fri. **Food served** noon-3pm, 5-9pm Mon-Fri. **Credit** AmEx, MC, V.

mybar. *See page 20.*

The Enterprise was originally named after a celebrated ship, though these days there's nothing in the long, darkish, determinedly soulless bar to suggest it ever had a history. Not that this deters the young, locally employed clientele: when we visited on a Friday night, the place was a solid wall of heaving flesh, the suits had to bellow into their mobile phones to make themselves heard, flashbulbs were going off everywhere and the resident transvestite was dancing with an inflatable doll. And it wasn't yet 6pm. Being very much a group venue, the Enterprise has a strong line in four-pint pitchers (Bass, Carling, Worthington all £8, Grolsch £9), while the food is mainly routine fare (bangers and mash, gammon and eggs both £5.75).
Tables outdoors (garden). Vegetarian dishes.

Glass Bar & Solution
Marlborough Hotel, Bloomsbury Street, WC1 (020 7636 5601/www.radissonedwardian.com). Tottenham Court Road tube. **Open/food served** 11am-1am Mon-Sat; 11am-midnight Sun. **Credit** AmEx, DC, MC, V.
What were once the Brasserie Bar and the Duke's Head have been reinvented as the Glass Bar and Solution, but they still represent two welcome options in a relative desert for drinking venues. The Glass Bar is the cosier of the two: olive green walls hold huge wood-framed mirrors and ruched curtains help to dim the light, while leather armchairs provide homely comfort, enhanced by the buzz of bonhomie. Cocktails (£7.50), Grolsch and Worthington on tap (both £3) and a range of bottled beers (£3 to £3.50) constitute the main attractions on the drinks list, and a bar menu lists sandwiches of more or less flamboyance for £5 to £9. Across the lobby lies the larger open plan Solution, a bar of clean lines and ample light, square armchairs and state of the art lighting, which is the more public venue, as it looks out onto the street from the corner of the hotel. The drinks list is similar to that of the Glass Bar. Whichever you visit, you are likely to meet a mix of ages and nationalities, as you'd expect from hotel bars.
Babies and children admitted (daytime only). Disabled: toilet. Function rooms. Late licence. No-smoking area. Restaurant. Vegetarian dishes.

Grape Street Wine Bar
224A Shaftesbury Avenue, WC2 (020 7240 0686). Holborn or Tottenham Court Road tube. **Open** 11am-11pm Mon-Fri. **Food served** noon-10pm Mon-Fri. **Credit** AmEx, MC, V.
Tucked away at the quiet northern end of Shaftesbury Avenue, the Grape Street Wine Bar is simply but pleasingly decorated in cream and green, and run by cheerful, welcoming staff. Perhaps inevitably for a small basement bar, the atmosphere tends to be close and crowded on busy nights, though there are a few quiet nooks and crannies. Taken over and redecorated in late 1997, the place has yet to acquire a truly distinctive atmosphere, though the little bookcase at the bottom of the stairs ('Grape Street Library: feel free to browse and borrow') is a nice touch. A gloss of wine costs £2.40-£3.70, though the house speciality is champagne (11 varieties, £12.50-£80 a bottle). If you're feeling peckish, there's a salad bar (£2.75-£6.50) and a daily specials menu.
TV. Vegetarian dishes.

King's Bar
Hotel Russell, Russell Square, WC1 (020 7837 6470). Russell Square tube. **Open** 10am-11pm Mon-Sat; 2-10pm Sun. **Food served** noon-5pm daily. **Credit** AmEx, DC, MC, V.
One of the last great Victorian hotels – it opened in 1900 – the massive, terracotta-coloured Russell has lost some of its grandeur, though it continues to make a decent living as a tourist hotel. The King's Bar is a reminder of its former glory:

with its high ceiling, large fireplace (with a cunningly disguised gas fire) and capacious armchairs and sofas, it resembles a sitting room in a stately home. Though the drinks themselves are unremarkable (bottled beer £2.75-£3.50, cocktails £5.95-£7.95), a waiter will bring them to your table, together with free nibbles on a silver salver. An excellent place in which to relax on a winter's afternoon.
Babies and children admitted. Function room. No piped music or jukebox. Vegetarian dishes.

Lamb
94 Lamb's Conduit Street, WC1 (020 7405 0713). Russell Square tube. **Open** 11am-11pm Mon-Sat; noon-10.30pm Sun. **Food served** noon-2.30pm daily. **Credit** MC, V.
This is one of the best Young's pubs in central London – a traditional Victorian pub with some handsome features. As an ex-regular noted: 'It is substantially unchanged since my last visit in 1947. The nooks and crannies and unevenly shaped bar, and the quick service, are just as I remember them. It is now equipped with its own lavatories: in our day, there were none, and customers were obliged to use the public conveniences at the end of the street.' And its popularity hasn't waned over time either, as a loyal collection of pub-lovers enjoy its leather benches or small rear yard on summer days. For the record, a pint of Young's Special is £2.08. The daily changing menu includes roast lamb (£5.75) and steak and kidney pudding (£5.25). Both were excellent.
Function room. No piped music or jukebox. No-smoking area. Tables outdoors (patio). Vegetarian dishes.

Museum Tavern
Great Russell Street, WC1 (020 7242 8987). Holborn or Tottenham Court Road tube. **Open/food served** 11am-11pm Mon-Sat; noon-10.30pm Sun. **Credit** AmEx, DC, MC, V.
A truly authentic London pub, with a solid, shiny wood-and-glass bar, red, brown and butterscotch walls, and hefty hanging lights. Over the years, many a scholar has dropped in from the British Museum across the road, including the novelist George Gissing, taking refuge from his unhappy home life, and Karl Marx, who's reputed to have broken one of the mirrors. Nowadays, it's more of a tourists' venue, but the smallish, oblong bar itself is substantially unchanged and unspoilt by games machines. Food, too, is on the traditional side (steak and kidney pie £5.75, fish and chips £6.95) and the beers are reliable stalwarts (Theakston Best £2.18, Old Peculier £2.49).
Babies and children admitted (until 4pm). Tables outdoors. Vegetarian dishes.

mybar
11-13 Bayley Street, WC1 (020 7667 6000/ www.myhotels .co.uk). Tottenham Court Road/Goodge Street tube. **Open** 11am-11pm daily. **Food served** 11am-11pm daily. **Credit** AmEx, DC, MC, V.
'A vibrant place to relax and socialise' is how mybar describes itself. Well, yes and no: it's too obviously a place in which to be seen to be truly relaxing, though as a thoroughly modernist take on the traditional hotel bar, it's well worth a visit. Dominated by a large picture window, the smallish, tidy bar has a goldfish-bowl look, an impression reinforced by the built-in tropical fish tank. The moneyed young party animals who frequent the place tend to gather around the glittering, bathroom cabinet-like bar, where the relentlessly high-spirited young staff dispense a steady stream of fruit, Martini and champagne cocktails (£4.50, £6.50 and £7 respectively). Appropriately minimalist dishes include sushi (natch) and goat's cheese salad (both £4).
Babies and children admitted. Disabled: toilet. Function rooms. Jukebox. No-smoking area. Restaurant. Vegetarian dishes.

Old Crown

33 New Oxford Street, WC1 (020 7836 9121). Holborn or Tottenham Court Road tube. **Open** 11am-11pm Mon-Sat. **Food served** noon-3pm, 5.30-9.30pm Mon-Sat. **Credit** AmEx, MC, V.

Not to be confused with the more traditional Crown a few doors down, the misleadingly named Old Crown is a likeable place that doesn't take itself too seriously despite the in your face decor (cream and green distressed walls, with huge bronze crowns and painted twisty branches hanging from the ceiling). Someone's clearly been having fun naming the cocktails (£4-£5), notably Pirates of Men's Pants (blue curaçao, Cointreau, lemon), and Wet Patch (Because Somebody's Got To) (Galliano, Kahlua, cream). Among the dishes are chicken ciabatta (£5.50) and potato skins (£3.50), which may or may not go well with some wine (£2.10-£2.50 a glass, £9.50-£21.50 a bottle). The cheerful staff, healthily mixed clientele – both suits and bohemian types – and piped jazz help make this an excellent venue, especially if you arrive in the early evening when it's neither too empty nor too crowded.

Function rooms. Tables outdoors (pavement). Vegetarian dishes.

Plough

27 Museum Street, WC1 (020 7636 7964). Tottenham Court Road tube. **Open** 11am-11pm Mon-Sat; noon-10.30pm Sun. **Food served** noon-7pm daily. **Credit** AmEx, MC, V.

Somewhat overshadowed by the **Museum Tavern** (*see above*) at the other end of the road, the Plough is one of those pubs that seems authentic-Victorian as you go in but resolves itself into authentic pub-Victorian – all empty bottles and Pickwickian scenes – as you get to work on your first pint. However, one original thing about the Plough is the fact that it doubles as a coffee bar, either drink-in or take-out. Otherwise, it's more predictable: Tetley's (£2.10) and Stella (£2.70) on tap, fish and chips and steak and kidney pie (both £5.75) on the menu, and a truly authentic pub apostrophe ('Wine's to suit your palate') on the blackboard.

Babies and children admitted (separate room). Function room. No-smoking area. Pub quiz monthly. Satellite TV. Tables outdoors (patio). Vegetarian dishes.

Point 101

101 New Oxford Street, WC1 (020 7379 3112). Tottenham Court Road tube. **Open/food served** 10am-2am Mon-Thur; 10am-2.30am Fri, Sat; noon-midnight Sun. **Credit** AmEx, MC, V.

Nestling under Centre Point in an area almost devoid of decent bars, Point 101 comes as a pleasant surprise. Its appearance is 1970s-municipal – huge concrete pillars and floor-to-ceiling windows – but thankfully it falls short of brutalist, and even on weekday afternoons there are usually enough customers, mainly from the wealthier end of the student market, to mitigate against the bus depot effect. The long, well-stocked bar is especially strong on cocktails (most of them £3.95) and liqueur coffees (£2.85-£3.95); bottled beers include Asahi and Staropramen (both £2.70). The menu offers the usual fare of soup (£3.25), club baguette (£3.50) or dish of the day (£5.25).

Babies and children admitted (until 5pm). Function room. Late licence (Mon-Sat). Music (DJs Mon-Sat). Tables outdoors. Vegetarian dishes.

Queen's Larder

1 Queen Square, WC1 (020 7837 5627). Holborn or Russell Square tube. **Open** 11am-11pm Mon-Sat; noon-10.30pm Sun. **Food served** noon-3pm, 6-9.30pm daily. **Credit** MC, V.

The unusual name of this pub commemorates one of the more poignant episodes during the now well-documented madness of King George III: while he was being treated by Dr Willis on the other side of the square, Queen Charlotte arranged to have some of his favourite food stored in the cellar. These days, the tiny, cosy bar is usually crowded with middle-aged to elderly locals, who tuck into the traditional pub food (chicken and mushroom pie, scampi and chips, gammon steak, all £5.75) and familiar beers (Wadworth £2.26, Boddingtons £2).

Babies and children admitted. Jukebox. Restaurant. Tables outdoors (pavement). TV. Vegetarian dishes.

Swan

7 Cosmo Place, WC1 (020 7837 6223). Holborn or Russell Square tube. **Open/food served** 11am-11pm Mon-Sat; noon-10.30pm Sun. **Credit** AmEx, DC, MC, V.

The Swan has been around since the middle of the eighteenth century, and inside there's a rough-wood, saloon-like feel that seems pleasantly devil-may-care until you start to notice all the generic pub touches (empty bottles and bought-by-the yard sepia photos showing English taverns in days of yore). What the Swan has retained, though, is a real-ale pub, with a frequently changing list of guest ales such as Abbot and Bombardier (both £2.26); for devotees, the three-beers deal (three third-pint tasting glasses £2.22) is recommended. The menu also offers variety: dishes include salmon tagliatelle (£5.35) and mushroom, red pepper and Stilton casserole (£5.95), as well as more conventional pub grub.

TV. Tables outdoors (pavement). Vegetarian dishes.

Truckles of Pied Bull Yard

Off Bury Place, WC1 (020 7404 5338). Holborn or Tottenham Court Road tube. **Open/food served** 11.30am-10pm Mon-Fri; 11.30am-3pm Sat. **Credit** AmEx, DC, MC, V.

Situated in a quiet courtyard and surrounded by art shops, this esteemed Davys wine bar consists of two entirely dissimilar bars. The orange-painted ground floor is bright, well lit and favoured by after-work groups, while the basement bar is much darker and generally more sparsely populated, though useful for tête-à-têtes. There's as varied a range of wines as you'd wish for, plus a few surprises (Amontillado £2.30, Old Vintage Port £3.50), while typical dishes include Caesar salad (£7.95) and a cheese board (£4.50). The tables in the courtyard offer a rare central London opportunity to sit in the open air without ingesting traffic fumes.

Function rooms. Restaurant. Tables outdoors (courtyard). Vegetarian dishes.

Vats

51 Lamb's Conduit Street, WC1 (020 7242 8963). Russell Square or Holborn tube. **Open** noon-11pm Mon-Fri. **Food served** noon-2.30pm, 6-9.30pm Mon-Fri. **Credit** AmEx, MC, V.

This narrow wine bar gets better and better as time goes on. The main bar is pleasant but unremarkable, done out in bank manager's-office panelling and decorated with grotesque Ronald Searle prints. Next is a quiet cloakroom-like area, but beyond that, behind an unlikely floral curtain, is an enticing rear bar, decorated with *trompe l'oeil* murals and often colonised by private parties. Vats is the archetypal locals' and regulars' wine bar, so much so that entering it is a little like intruding on a family gathering. However, the young bar staff and raffish middle-aged clients offer an equally enthusiastic welcome. House white is £2.95 a glass; the guest clarets on our visit were £16.95 and £17.95 a bottle. Food is the usual wine bar stuff (haddock and salmon £8.95).

Function room. Tables outdoors (pavement). Vegetarian dishes.

Vespa Lounge

Under Centre Point House, St Giles High Street, WC2 (020 7240 1860). Tottenham Court Road tube. **Open** 6-11pm daily. **No credit cards.**

Woven into the Centre Point complex and sat atop the Conservatory, the Vespa Lounge proved a baffling location for us on our first visit, though judging by the hordes of gay women who head inside it isn't a problem shared. A long overdue alternative to the **Candy Bar** (*see p83*) for West End drinking lesbians, the Vespa's popularity must be due largely to its easy air and approachability: particularly friendly bar staff see to it that ordering a round (Stella £2.80 a pint) is a straightforward affair and not the tiresome attitude-laden event it often can be. Arrive early or prepare to make do with back-to-back seating on its austere foam cushions - a useful ploy if you and a mate want to 'de-couple' yourselves for the benefit of would-be cruisers, but a certain flaw if you're on a first date. Men are admitted as guests.

Comedy night (Sun £5/£4 advance). Games (pool table). TV (big screen). Music (DJs Thur-Sat; indie night Mon).

Also in the area...

All Bar One 108 New Oxford Street, WC1 (020 7307 7980).

Chelsea SW3, SW7, SW10

Anglesea Arms

15 Selwood Terrace, SW7 (020 7373 7960). South Kensington or Gloucester Road tube. **Open** 11am-11pm Mon-Sat; noon-10.30pm Sun. **Food served** 6.30-9.30pm Mon-Sat; 6.30-9pm Sun. **Credit** MC, V.

This very pleasant pub is where the haute bourgeoisie slip into their rugby shirts and sup beer. And good beer it is, too: try not to let the quotient of braying boozers put you off, and sample an Adnams Broadside (£2.20), Brakspear's Bitter (£2) or draught Budvar (£2.60). The place itself is an old-fashioned Victorian-style pub, complete with requisite William Morris wallpaper, dark wood furnishings and darker ceilings. Enticing food is served in the back of the pub, and, from around £6.50 for bangers and mash, it's more reasonable than most.

Babies and children admitted (before 6pm). No piped music or jukebox. Tables outdoors (terrace). Satellite TV. Vegetarian dishes.

Big Easy

332-334 King's Road, SW3 (020 7352 4071). Sloane Square tube, then 11, 19, 22 or 49 bus. **Open/food served** noon-midnight Mon-Thur; noon-12.30am Fri, Sat; noon-11.30pm Sun. **Happy hour** noon-midnight Mon; 4-7.30pm, 10-11pm Tue-Fri. **Credit** AmEx, MC, V.

Oh dear. The British try to 'do' an American-style Southern bar; no prizes for guessing what's happened. The point about American bars is that the drinks are dirt-cheap, the snacks are free and they sell weak beer all night long. This place falls at the first hurdle: cocktails start at £4.95, house wine starts at £2.50 and moves up quickly, and Lone Star beer comes in at £2.75. The food, too, is pricey, humdrum stuff. A real American bar would sell Pabst and Schaeffer, some of the weakest and worst beers known to mankind, and make very strong cocktails at a proper price. Must try harder.

Babies and children admitted (children's menu, high chairs). Music (country/soul bands 9pm nightly). No-smoking area. Restaurant. Satellite TV. Vegetarian dishes.

Bluebird

350 King's Road, SW3 (020 7559 1000/www.bluebird-store.co.uk). Sloane Square tube, then 19, 22 bus/49 bus. **Open** noon-11pm Mon-Fri; 11am-11pm Sat; 11am-10.30pm Sun. **Credit** AmEx, DC, MC, V.

Part of the Conran empire, the Bluebird is housed in a converted 1930s garage on the King's Road, and comprises a restaurant, a scandalously expensive food hall, a flower shop and a mini Conran shop. The bar, though, is in the perfect spot for watching the people of Chelsea stroll by. As you'd expect from Conran, the bar itself is sleek and stylish, with tables outside and in, and bar stools for those who prefer to perch. Cocktails start at £5.25, with beers from £3.25, and there's also a good list of wines from around the world. The atmosphere, though, isn't great, and is hardly helped by the fact that the bar connects directly to the Bluebird 'supermarché'. In the summer, though, the crowds expand out to the concourse and bring more of a buzz to the place.

Babies and children admitted (restaurant only). Disabled: toilet. Function room. Music (pianist nightly; lunch Sat, Sun). Restaurant. Satellite TV. Vegetarian dishes.

Builder's Arms

13 Britten Street, SW3 (020 7349 9040). South Kensington or Sloane Square tube. **Open** 10am-11pm Mon-Sat; 11am-10.30pm Sun. **Food served** noon-2.30pm, 7-10pm Mon-Sat; noon-3pm, 7-9.30pm Sun. **Credit** DC, MC, V.

Not a builder in sight, of course – this is Chelsea, after all – but the pashminas and rugger buggers who drink here are diffused by the odd normal person, too. With its schizophrenic feel – hunting lodge meets *fin de millennium* urban living room – the Builder's Arms is the very definition of a postmodern pub, with evidence of a split personality including weird Freudian pictures invoking genitalia, bonsai trees under the topiary treatment and Chris de Burgh blaring out of a cheap cassette deck. Wine starts at £2.40 a glass and Adnams Southwold at £2.10 a pint, but this is the kind of place where more people are drinking Veuve-Clicquot.

Babies and children admitted. Disabled: toilet. Tables outdoors. Satellite TV. Vegetarian dishes.

Cadogan Arms

298 King's Road, SW3 (020 7352 1645). Sloane Square tube, then 11, 19, 22 bus. **Open/food served** 11am-11pm Mon-Sat; noon-10.30pm Sun. **Credit** AmEx, MC, V.

Dark and creaking, with a Tudor-style bar, the Cadogan Arms feels a bit like an old ship's galley. Sky TV burbles in the corner, the upholstery is well worn and dirty, and the young clientele represents, in comparison to other nearby pubs, a healthy mix. The draught lagers are all the usual staples, ales include Theakston XB (£2.33) and Courage Best (£2.15), and food is of the classic pub grub variety (chicken kiev, fish and chips and the like). Ultimately, though, the one selling point of this pub is that it offers some sanctuary from screeching Sloanes and their Tim Nice-But-Dim hubbies. *Babies and children admitted (until 8pm). Jukebox. Pool tables. Satellite TV (big screen). Vegetarian dishes.*

Café Milan

312 King's Road, SW3 (020 7351 0101). Sloane Square tube, then 11, 19, 22 bus. **Open/food served** noon-3pm, 6-11pm daily. **Credit** AmEx, DC, MC, V.
Another modern bar-cum-café, with neutral tones and window tables affording a good view of the passing shoppers. One of the increasing welter of watering holes that offer a more European way of drinking; that is, with food, and in moderation rather than excess. When we visited, the wine list was rather truncated due to 'restructuring', and was entirely made up of Italian and Spanish bottles; it's not cheap, either, with glasses starting at £3.50, although the array of bottled beers makes for better value, starting at £2.50. *Babies and children admitted. Function room. Restaurant. Vegetarian dishes.*

Cahoots

2 Elystan Street, SW3 (020 7584 0140). Sloane Square tube. **Open/food served** 11am-11pm Mon-Sat; noon-10.30pm Sun. **Credit** AmEx, DC, MC, V.
It's quite amazing that a place as poorly decorated as this could have the cheek to locate itself right down the street from the Conran Shop, but Cahoots seems to do pretty well, especially on weekends. The bar looks strangely like a breakfast buffet room in a chain hotel, and serves the usual array of bog-standard food. Wine starts at £2.40 a glass, and cans of Red Bull are stacked alluringly in pyramids behind the bar. One of the bar's attractions is that it offers some relief from the King's Road shoppers; it doesn't, sadly, allow an escape from the people who live around here. *Babies and children admitted (until 6pm). Vegetarian dishes.*

Chelsea Ram

32 Burnaby Street, SW10 (020 7351 4008). Sloane Square or Fulham Broadway tube, then 22 bus/C1, 11, 31 bus. **Open** 11am-3pm, 5.30-11pm Mon-Thur, Sat; 11am-11pm Fri; noon-10.30pm Sun. **Food served** noon-2.30pm, 7-9.45pm Mon-Sat; noon-3pm, 7-9.30pm Sun. **Credit** MC, V.
A pleasant gastropub, extremely well located for all those who work at nearby Chelsea Wharf. It's a Young's house, so beers are good: Young's 'ordinary' (£2.05) is always worth a go, and on our visit this was one of only ten Young's pubs offering AAA (£2.35). The interior is decked out in familiar Young's style – pine tables and chairs coupled with church pews – and the food looks most alluring: fish specials, daily meaty treats from Smithfield market, and a yummy puddings menu. *Babies and children admitted. Function room. Tables outdoors (pavement). Vegetarian dishes.*

Cooper's Arms

87 Flood Street, SW3 (020 7376 3120/ www.thecoopers.co.uk). Sloane Square or South Kensington tube. **Open** 11am-11pm Mon-Sat; noon-10.30pm Sun. **Food served** 12.30-3pm daily. **Credit** AmEx, MC, V.

Café Milan

Another Young's pub, the Cooper's Arms has a bar-cum-pub ambience that strikes exactly the right note for the area. Plenty of pine furniture and a smattering of cushions make the nicely lit bar physically and aesthetically comfortable, and even the pub grub is a notch above the usual standard, with gastropub-type offerings such as pan-fried scallops (£5.50). Young's Ordinary (£2.05), Special (£2.15) and Winter Warmer (£2.40) were all present on our visit, with Stella Artois and Hoegaarden providing variety. As you'd expect, the clientele is generally well heeled, although a slightly funkier element also comes along for the ride. *Babies and children admitted. Function room. No piped music or jukebox. Vegetarian dishes.*

Cross Keys

1 Lawrence Street, SW3 (020 7349 9111). Sloane Square tube. **Open** noon-midnight Mon-Sat; noon-10.30pm Sun. **Food served** noon-3pm, 7-11pm Mon-Fri; noon-4pm, 7-11pm Sat; noon-4pm, 7-10.30pm Sun. **Credit** AmEx, MC, V.
The first things that hit you when you walk into the Cross Keys are the lovely roaring fire (good) and the disgusting chimney fashioned out of stone, which depicts a Bacchanalian-looking monk lifting his robes and warming his 'vitals' (bad). Once you've got over this affront on the senses, you'll find a modern pub with a dark front bar and a starker, well-lit inner room. It was designed by the people who brought us Beach Blanket Babylon in Notting Hill, so at least we all know who the culprits are. Swanky fusion food makes up the menu, and prices overall aren't too bad (Foster's £2.30 a pint, house wine £2.30). If you're roaming along the Thames, it's a fine place for a quick pint before peak time.

Babies and children admitted (children's menu, high chairs). Function rooms. Restaurant. Vegetarian dishes.

Fox & Hounds

29 Passmore Street, SW1 (020 7730 6367/ www.theestablishmentltd.co.uk). Sloane Square tube. **Open** 11am-3pm, 5.30-11pm Mon-Fri; 11am-3pm, 6-11pm Sat; noon-3pm, 6.30-10.30pm Sun. **Food served** noon-2.30pm, 5.30-8.30pm Mon-Fri. **Credit** MC, V.

Part of London life changed for ever in August last year when the capital's last remaining 'beer only' pub served its first measure of Laphroaig whisky. Despite the name, which conjures up all sorts of images of the Sloane Square Hunt, the Fox & Hounds is actually a fairly modern pub, not least following a recent makeover after its acquisition by Young's brewery. Light walls, pine tables and pews for the younger clientele make it nicely airy. However, although it does have the feel of a pub populated by the sedate (Chelsea pensioners, resting actors) and the privileged (locals), previous reviews suggest a serious pest problem with the rugby crowd if you don't time your visit right. On a good day, though, you can sit peaceably and enjoy the usual range of Young's fare ('ordinary' Bitter £2.05), or tuck into dishes such as marinated seafood (£5.95) or bangers and mash (£4.95).

Babies and children admitted. No piped music or jukebox. Vegetarian dishes.

Front Page

35 Old Church Street, SW3 (020 7352 2908). Sloane Square tube. **Open** 11am-11pm Mon-Sat; noon-10.30pm Sun. **Food served** noon-2.30pm, 7-10pm Mon-Sat; noon-3pm, 7-9.30pm Sun. **Credit** AmEx, MC, V.

The rather genteel-looking Front Page offers all the trappings you'd expect from a modern watering hole, and is reasonably characterful to boot. Its wood panelling makes it resemble a a city pub, but the mood and decor are lightened with church pews and pine tables. The reasonable selection of beers (Theakston Best £2.30, Courage Directors £2.30) and good wine list are complemented by an interesting menu that includes such treats as carrot, sweet potato and chive soup (£3.45) and Jamaican crab cakes (£6.75).

Babies and children admitted (until 5pm). Function room. Satellite TV (big screen). Vegetarian dishes.

Henry J Bean

195-197 King's Road, SW3 (020 7352 9255). Sloane Square tube. **Open/food served** 10am-11pm Mon-Sat; 10am-10.30pm Sun. **Happy hour** 5-7pm Mon-Fri. **Credit** MC, V.

Who is Henry J Bean? We're not sure, but according to the hoarding, 'his friends all call him Hank'. We'll stick to Henry, if it's all the same. Mr Bean has been busy milking our love of the USA for several years now, but has recently undergone something of a makeover. However, it doesn't really offer us anything new. This is yet another bar with a schizophrenia problem: the main bar is done out in *Cheers* style, but the nooks and crannies are decked out with black leather sofas and big pictures of Mr and Mrs JFK in their '60s prime; an odd mix. Otherwise, it's the same old American-style bar snacks such as loaded potato skins (£3.95), bottles of Budweiser and Budvar (£2.70) and – a redeeming feature – a happy hour offering two drinks for the price of one.

Babies and children admitted (except Friday evenings). Disabled: toilet. Music (DJs Fri). Restaurant. Tables outdoors (garden). TV (sport). Vegetarian dishes.

Lomo

222 Fulham Road, SW10 (020 7349 8848). Fulham Broadway, South Kensington or Earls Court tube. **Open/food served** noon-12am daily. **Credit** AmEx, MC, V.

A perfect bar for the accident-prone: Lomo is situated just opposite Chelsea and Westminster Hospital. This is also a bar that should be applauded by the rest of us, for doing something different and doing it well. A Spanish-style design bar, Lomo is modish and hip – think early '80s airport lounge chic – and offers an excellent choice of Spanish brandies, liqueurs and sherries and a refined international wine list; the food menu features sophisticated tapas-style dishes (mostly around £5-£6) using superb-quality Spanish ingredients. Also, the range of bottled beers (from £2.50) is decent, the freshly squeezed OJ is nice, staff are congenial, and the olives faintly addictive. Aside from the slightly awkward stools – with matt orange vinyl covers that must be an acquired taste – this is a great little spot.

Babies and children admitted. Disabled: toilet. Restaurant. Vegetarian dishes.

Moore Arms

61-63 Cadogan Street, SW3 (020 7589 7848). Sloane Square tube. **Open** noon-11pm Mon-Sat; noon-10.30pm Sun. **Food served** noon-3pm, 6-9pm Mon-Thur; noon-3pm Sat, Sun. **Credit** AmEx, DC, MC, V.

With its dark, dank atmosphere, fading oil paintings and shabby furniture, you might mistake this pub for an authentic Victorian anachronism. Strangely, though, the grey drabness of the place has all the unmistakable trappings of a chain pub makeover, made all the more apparent by the dearth of customers. Still, at least there's an open fire to bring some colour to an otherwise lifeless local, along with a small selection of wines (£2.35) and a respectable range of real ales (Marston's Pedigree £2.30, London Pride £2.35).

Babies and children admitted (until 7pm). Games (pool table, quiz machine). Jukebox. Satellite TV. Tables outdoors (patio, pavement). Vegetarian dishes.

Orange Brewery

37 Pimlico Road, SW1 (020 7730 5984). Sloane Square tube. **Open/food served** 11am-11pm Mon-Sat; noon-10.30pm Sun. **Credit** AmEx, DC, MC, V.

Milling masses of rugby boys, fruit machines and a turn of the century feel can at first sight make this place seem pretty indistinguishable from any other Victorian-style pub in the area, but the thing that marks it out is the hole in the floor that reveals a microbrewery in the basement. And, once you've settled down to a pint of its award-winning ales, the difference is clear (even if the brewery is ultimately owned by Scottish & Newcastle). The potent 6% Sloane Danger Winter Warmer (£2.32), Pimlico Porter (£2.16) and SW2 (£2.16) all live up to the locale's tradition (there's been a pub on this site since 1776), and offer pleasant respite from all the hoorays around you.

Tables outdoors (pavement). Vegetarian dishes.

Phene Arms

9 Phene Street, SW3 (020 7352 3294). Sloane Square or South Kensington tube. **Open** 11am-11pm Mon-Sat; noon-10.30pm Sun. **Food served** noon-3pm, 6-10.30pm Mon-Fri; noon-4pm, 6-10.30pm Sat, Sun. **Credit** AmEx, DC, MC, V.

A very interesting pub, this, not least because it draws a healthy mix of punters despite a location in a very affluent area. The paint was barely dry when we visited, but the carpet had been worn to the floor tiles. The pub is small and friendly,

Lomo

CONTEMPORARY SOUTHWESTERN CUISINE

Named as one of London's Best Cocktail Bars by Time Out, November 1999

- Lunch
- Dinner
- Drinks
- Function Rooms
- Children are most welcome
- Conference and meeting facilities

Restaurant & bar open 11am–12 midnight (last food orders 10.30pm)

75 Upper Street, Islington,
London N1 0NU
Telephone: 020 7288 2288

with a tiny real fire and an old-fashioned, central bar that wouldn't look out of place at a seaside bed and breakfast, given its wrought-iron fittings and cheesy red lanterns. In the summer the garden comes into its own, where alfresco salads are served from the restaurant upstairs. Meanwhile, smart bar snacks, such as Thai green chicken goujons (£2.95), are available inside. The beers are reasonably priced (Courage Best, Directors, both £2.30), although the real treat here is the convivial atmosphere.

Babies and children admitted. Function room. No piped music or jukebox. Restaurant. TV (sport). Tables outdoors (garden, roof terrace). Vegetarian dishes.

PJ's Bar & Grill

52 Fulham Road, SW3 (020 7581 0025/ www.maxwells.com). South Kensington tube. **Open/food served** noon-12am daily. **Credit** AmEx, DC, MC, V.

The decor at this smart South Ken bar-restaurant suggests something between an American gentlemen's club and a planter's retreat. There are two floors, with a solid mahogany bar counter jutting out to the centre of the ground-floor bar, with a hole cut through the ceiling into the upstairs dining room through which a huge ceiling fan rotates. The clientele are a mixed bunch, with smartly dressed local estate agent types hobnobbing with Fulham models and (when we dropped by) a table of TV execs discussing the next big project – it's about an Irish detective and it's set in Camden Town, apparently. The extensive wine list kicks off at £3.35 a glass (£11.50 a bottle), with bottled Budvar and Beck's at £3.15. Former Harvey's chef David Tamlyn is in charge in the kitchen, adding a new dimension to the eating experience. Pavé of asparagus risotto is £5.95; peppered fillet of beef £7.45; and daube of beef with wild mushrooms and celeriac mash £13.95.

Babies and children admitted (high chairs). Tables outdoors (pavement). TV (sport). Vegetarian dishes.

Sporting Page

6 Camera Place, SW10 (020 7376 3694/ www.frontpagepubs.com). Bus 11, 14, 19, 22, 328. **Open** 11am-11pm Mon-Sat; noon-10.30pm Sun. **Food served** noon-2.30pm, 7-10pm Mon-Fri; noon-7pm Sat, Sun. **Credit** AmEx, MC, V.

Perhaps inevitably, this bar dedicated to British sporting glories is decorated with tableaux dating back to the days of WG Grace. The clientele seems to be of a similar age: lots of old soaks in suits and their secretaries, and even someone sporting a monocle when we visited. The posh aura is exacerbated by garish red walls and bar stools, and the black-and-white tiled floor, which makes it feel like a poorly designed brasserie in Paris. There's Bollinger (£6 a glass), of course, but also a decent wine list (from £2.60) – this venue is from the same stable as the **Front Page** (*see p24*) – and Wadworth 6X (£2.20) for the hoi polloi who mistakenly stumble in.

Babies and children admitted. No piped music or jukebox. Satellite TV (big screen). Vegetarian dishes.

Surprise

6 Christchurch Terrace, off Flood Street, SW3 (020 7349 1821). Sloane Square tube. **Open** noon-11pm Mon-Sat; noon-10.30pm Sun. **Food served** noon-3pm, 6.30-10pm Mon-Sat; 1-4pm Sun. **Credit** MC, V.

This pub has a colour theme: green, green and more green. But when you see a man wearing spats and smoking a fat stogie going into a pub called the Surprise, you know you're in for a good evening. Beneath the sea of green, the Surprise is a classy refurbished pub with polished wood floors and stained-glass windows; hidden in a maze of quiet, residential

streets, it's very much a locals' pub, but outsiders get a decent welcome, too. The fairly adventurous food menu is complemented by ales such as Bass (£2.20), London Pride (£2.30) and Robinson Best Bitter (£2.20).

Babies and children admitted. Satellite TV. Tables outdoors (pavement). Vegetarian dishes.

Also in the area

Café Flo 25-35 Gloucester Road, SW7 (020 7589 1383).
Café Rouge 390 King's Road, SW3 (020 7352 2226).
Dôme 354 King's Road, SW3 (020 7352 2828).
Ferret & Firkin 114 Lots Road, SW10 (020 7352 6645).
Pitcher & Piano 316-318 King's Road, SW3 (020 7352 0025).
Po Na Na Souk Bar 316 King's Road, SW3 (020 7352 7127).

Covent Garden, Strand, WC2

Africa Bar, Calabash

The Africa Centre, 38 King Street, WC2 (020 7836 1976). Covent Garden tube. **Open/food served** 5.30-11pm Mon-Thur; 5.30pm-3am Fri, Sat. **Credit** AmEx, DC, MC, V.

Non-stop African music, red velvet bench seats and stools, carpeted walls and posters showing Kenya's and Zimbabwe's tourist hotspots make this an ideal bar for expats and those who hanker after the Africa experience without too much travelling. The bar's in the basement of the Africa Centre, (where regular events promote the continent's cultural wealth), and across the corridor from the Calabash restaurant – which specialises in African delicacies (chicken gizzards starter, Malawi beef stew with sweet pepper and potato, anyone?) – with a balconied dancehall (in use every weekend) upstairs on the ground floor. The ideal beer to have here is Tusker Premium Lager from Nairobi, at £2.10 a bottle.

Babies and children admitted (restaurant only). Function room. Music (DJs nightly, live music Fri, Sat.) Satellite TV. Restaurant. Vegetarian dishes.

AKA

18 West Central Street, WC1 (020 7836 0110). Holborn tube. **Open** 6pm-1am Tue; 6pm-3am Wed-Fri; 7pm-3am Sat. **Food served** 6pm-midnight Tue-Fri; 7pm-midnight Sat. **Credit** AmEx, DC, MC, V.

Round the corner from New Oxford Street, this fashionable warehouse-sized bar-restaurant attracts a young and stylish media crowd, including the odd famous actor we've encountered. The bar area is large and square-shaped with a metal serving area running down the right-hand side, and a scattering of chrome tables and chairs opposite. Upstairs is the Mezzanine restaurant where you can order dishes such as creamed Jerusalem artichoke soup (£4), spicy duck pancakes with celeriac (£6) and char-grilled marinated lamb rump with spinach and scorzonera gratin (£15). Back down in the bar, standard bottled beers are £2.95, Hoegaarden £3.10 a pint, and spirits £3 with mixer, £3.50 with juice. A glass of champagne is £6, a bottle of Belle Epoque 1990 £180; cocktails can be had for a tad under £6, rising to £8.50 for a Jayne Mansfield. Service is efficient and friendly.

Disabled: toilet. Late licence (Tue-Sat). Music (DJs Thur-Sat). Restaurant. Satellite TV. Vegetarian dishes.

American Bar

Savoy Hotel, Strand, WC2 (020 7836 4343/
www. savoygroup.co.uk). Charing Cross tube/rail. **Open**
11am-11pm Mon-Sat. **Food served** noon-2.30pm Mon-
Sat. **Credit** AmEx, DC, MC, V.
Head barman Peter Dorelli runs a tight ship at the American
Bar where, it is said, the first-ever Martini cocktail in Britain
was served. These days the drink will cost you £9.90, but
people say that it's the best this side of the Algonquin. And
lest imbibers get the idea that there's no originality in WC2,
the well-known White Lady cocktail (£8.50) was devised in
this very room. Malt whiskies are another speciality, and
decent stuff starts at around £10. The decor is understated
art deco, with muted colours and a gleaming mirrored bar
fronted with bottles. There's usually a pianist inserting
twiddly bits around a wide variety of cocktail classics, but
that's exactly what the target clientele want. As the signed
and framed pictures of faded film and TV stars on the walls
indicate, the bar attracts more than its fair share of celebrities
and we were pleased to spot a prominent exponent of the
American Rifle Association when we last popped in for a
champagne cocktail (£10.50). If only we'd had a gun…
Dress code. Function rooms. Music (pianist 7-11pm Mon-
Sat). No-smoking area.Vegetarian dishes.

Angel

61 St Giles High Street, WC2 (020 7240 2876).
Tottenham Court Road tube. **Open** 11am-11pm Mon-Sat;
noon-10.30pm Sun. **Food served** noon-3pm, 5.30-9pm
Mon-Sat; noon-3pm Sun. **Credit** MC, V.
Built on the site of a leper colony and reputedly a staging post
on the last journey to Tyburn, this is a pub with something
of a history. Although it was taken over a couple of years ago
by Samuel Smith's Tadcaster brewery and now offers Old
Museum Ale and Ayingerbrau lager (£1.78), the decor's not
changed much in the last couple of decades – barring the odd
lick of paint, new carpet and occasional reupholstery of the
sagging settles. The well-designed fireplace that heats both
small bars is still there, and you still have to dodge darts to
get to the gents toilet. Like an old dog, it may not be beautiful,
but it's good to have around.
Games (darts, fruit machine, quiz machine). No piped
music or jukebox. Tables outdoors (garden).
Vegetarian dishes.

Axis Bar

One Aldwych Hotel, 1 Aldwych, WC2 (020 7300 0300/
www. onealdwych.co.uk). Covent Garden or Charing Cross
rail/tube. **Open/food served** noon-3pm, 6-11.30pm, Mon-
Fri; 6-11.30pm Sat. **Credit** AmEx, DC, MC, V.
Overlooking the trendy Axis restaurant, this small smart bar
occupies a vaguely semicircular balcony with a handful of low-
slung tables and stools dotted in front of a gracefully curved
serving area. The style is 1930s Poirot, with a colour scheme
that's a relaxing mix of black and pastel colours. A small band
of high-profile media types seem to have made Axis their own,
so expect to see pairs of men discussing mega-deals in hushed
tones. Drinks, as expected, are upmarket: Camux XO Superior
cognac is £27 a shot, most bourbons £6.25, rums £5 and
cocktails £7.50, although it is possible to get a bottle of Beck's
or a Guinness for £3.25. Food in the restaurant is adventurous
European, and includes starters like poached haddock and
cheese soufflé tart (£5.50-£8.25), and mains like hay-baked leg
of lamb, or mushroom duxelle (£12-£18). The same hotel also
contains the similarly chic **Lobby Bar** (*see p32*).
Babies and children admitted. Disabled: toilet.
Function rooms. No piped music or jukebox. Restaurant.
Vegetarian dishes.

Bank

1 Kingsway, WC2 (020 7234 3344). Covent Garden or
Holborn tube. **Open** 7am-11pm. **Food served** 7.30am-
10.30am, noon-2.45pm, 5.30-11pm Mon-Fri; 11.30am-3pm,
5.30-11pm Sat, Sun. **Credit** AmEx, DC, MC, V.
The bar here is large, metal and designed to suck you in from
the street. Once ensnared, you can try a cocktail for around a
fiver, a glass of wine from £4 or a bottled beer of the Bud type
for £3. Your fellow customers will probably be middle-
management types in tailored suits and designer dresses. To
the right of the serving area, just past the open kitchen, is the
restaurant, where you can breakfast on Beluga caviar, potato
waffle and crème fraîche for £330 (or a quarter of that if you're
a cheapskate and don't mind Sevruga) or lunch on the likes
of fishcake (£9.90), macaroni with smoked chicken (£8.50 as
starter/£11.50 main) and langoustines (£16.50). The serving
staff are efficient and polite, but stop a little way short of
being friendly.
Babies and children admitted (high chairs). Disabled: toilet.
Restaurant. Vegetarian dishes.

Bar des Amis

11-14 Hanover Place, WC2 (020 7379 3444/
www. cafedesamis.co.uk). Covent Garden tube.
Open/food served 11.30am-11pm Mon-Sat.
Credit AmEx, DC, MC, V.
This small basement wine bar below the stylish Café des
Amis has recently been renovated to accommodate the young,
stylish crowd that use it. An oval serving area sits in the
centre of the room, with seating arranged tightly around. The
decor is Left Bank black, beige and light wood. Wine is what
it's all about here, and the predominantly French selection
should satisfy most tastes, from around £3 a glass, or just
over £10 a bottle. The enlightened bar menu includes the likes
of baked cod hollandaise with basil mash (£7.95), Thai
fishcakes with coriander (£5.50) and assiette of charcuterie
with cornichons and silverskin onions (£6.25).
Restaurant. Tables outdoors (terrace). Vegetarian dishes.

Bar Aquda

13-14 Maiden Lane, WC2 (020 7557 9891).
Charing Cross or Covent Garden tube. **Open** noon-11pm
Mon-Sat; noon-10.30pm Sun. **Food served** noon-7pm
daily. **Credit** MC, V.
Aquda, the latest bar on this site (the third in a decade), is a
brewer's idea of a gay style bar, with sleek lines and a watery
theme. The walls are painted in wet blues and greens, with a
beard of quirky lamps hanging from the ceiling at the rear.
The backlit bar runs along one side of the long thin room,
selling standard beers such as Grolsch and Carling Black
Label at non-standard prices – £3.04 and £2.84 a pint,
respectively. Food is of the cajun chicken (£6.95), nachos and
dips (£4.95) variety. Most of the customers when we visited
were thirtysomethings in suits, and research revealed that the
name is meant to be pronounced like 'barracuda', although
this didn't come from the bar manager, since he was dancing
to the overly loud dance music that thuds around the room.
Disabled: toilet. Function room. Games (trivia).
Restaurant. Vegetarian dishes.

Bar 38

1-3 Long Acre, WC2 (020 7836 7794). Covent Garden or
Leicester Square tube. **Open** 10am-11pm Mon-Sat; noon-
10.30pm Sun. **Food served** 10am-10.30pm Mon-Sat;
noon-10pm Sun. **Credit** AmEx, DC, MC, V.
There's something about style bars owned and run by pub
companies, and whatever it is, Bar 38 has plenty of it. It's a big,
brash bar-diner with plenty of light wood and glass, which

Axis Bar

Brasserie Max

Covent Garden Hotel, 10 Monmouth Street, WC2 (020 7806 1000/www.firmdale.co.uk). Covent Garden tube. **Open/food served** 7.30am-11pm Mon-Sat; 8am-10.30pm Sun. **Credit** AmEx, MC, V.

The five-star Covent Garden Hotel is a haunt of the fashion industry, and this stylish cocktail bar attracts more than its fair share of 'beautiful people'. The decor is a cross between a dark-wood-dominated gentlemen's club and a chromed Groucho, but both elements coexist quite harmoniously. The staff are helpful and efficient without being too sniffy, and the soundtrack is usually low-key, cool jazz. Prices aren't outrageous – beers are £3 a bottle, reasonable wines kick off at £3.50 a glass, and Martini cocktails are £8.50 – and each table comes with a bowl of juicy olives and a glass of cinnamon sticks, so you can't complain. The bar menu includes the likes of curried crab spring rolls (£6.96), miso-glazed halibut (£14.95) and roast tomato risotto cake (£6.95). *Babies and children admitted. Function room. Restaurant. Tables outdoors (pavement). Vegetarian dishes.*

Café Baroque

33 Southampton Street, WC2 (020 7379 7585/ www. cafebaroque.co.uk). Covent Garden tube/Charing Cross tube/rail. **Open/food served** noon-midnight Mon-Sat. **Credit** AmEx, DC, MC, V.

This unassuming little bar downstairs from the popular Café Baroque restaurant is practically corridor-like, and it's wise to grab a seat at one of the cloth-covered tables as soon as you get in, unless you want to cause a pile up with waitresses and other arriving customers. The food and wine tend to be above average, and the atmosphere is friendly and relaxed, almost matronly. On the back of the menu are two recommended wine options for each dish on the menu. Thus you learn that a warm tart of smoked chicken and asparagus (£5.30/£9.50 main) goes well with 1997 Sillogi Lafazani (£2.95) or 1998 Verdicchio Casal di Serra (£3.40) and that confit of leg of lamb with aubergine caviar, roast garlic and brandy jus (£15.50) is perfect with 1996 Château Haut-Gueyrot St Emilion Grand Cru or 1997 Pouilly-Fuissé Chevrières (both £4.95). Snacks start at £3.50 for soup of the day, and bottled beers are £2.50. *Babies and children admitted. Games (backgammon, chess). Tables outdoors (pavement). Restaurant. Vegetarian dishes.*

Café Pacífico

5 Langley Street, WC2 (020 7379 7728). Covent Garden tube. **Open/food served** noon-11.45pm Mon-Sat; noon-10.45pm Sun. **Credit** AmEx, MC, V.

More of a restaurant with a bar, the food here is Mexican-influenced and can get pretty dandy at times, what with the likes of lobster and papaya quesadillas with mango cream starter (£8.50) and fillet of beef in chipotle cracked-pepper gravy (£11.95). But the basis is the usual mess of tacos, burritos and refried beans we all know and love. This is a virtual reality Mexican cantina, where groups of officefolk and tourists combine to drink litres of Margaritas (from £4.25 a glass, £24.45 a pitcher), Mexican beers (Pacífico, Corona, Negra Modelo, £2.80-£2.90) and draught lager (£1.85 a half – that's £3.70 a pint) until they either have to eat something or else fall into a passing cab. The decor is what you'd expect, with stone and chunky wood dominating, and the walls are studded with 'typically Mexican' pictures and posters. The kitchen is open-plan and faces you as you walk in; service is friendly and efficient. *Babies and children admitted (children's menu, high chairs). Restaurant. Vegetarian dishes.*

can't quite work out whether it would rather sell you a beer, a cocktail or a meal. The range of beers is what you'd find in any Courage pub – John Smith's Extra Smooth, Kronenbourg (£2.69) – but no handpumps, and the food consists of the usual global fry-ups relying heavily on a bastardised Southwest American 'cuisine': guacamole, tortilla chips and the like. Prices are standard for the area (that is, more than you'd want to pay) and most of their regular post-work clientele tend to congregate in the more intimate basement, away from the tourists upstairs. *Disabled: toilet. Function room. Vegetarian dishes.*

Box

32-34 Monmouth Street, WC2 (020 7240 5828). Covent Garden or Leicester Square tube. **Open** 11am-11pm Mon-Sat; noon-10.30pm Sun. **Food served** 11am-5pm daily. **Credit** MC, V.

This gay bar has been recently refurbished, converting the basement into open-plan, beautiful (for now) unisex toilets à la *Ally McBeal*; they look so plush that you might do as we did and mistake them for part of the bar. However, the ground-floor bar now seems about three times its previous size, leaving enough room for it to be half-covered by tables, even at night, with the other half a stand-around-and-chat space. The crowd is predominantly male, largely attractive, mostly young and, by the looks of it, all about to go on clubbing. The picture is completed by the clean-cut, muscular bar staff, one of whom was serving Goldschlager (£1.50 a shot) through an ice sculpture in the shape of a torso: pouring it down a tube in the neck, with the drink emerging at the other end in a place that required you to kneel down to get the most of your shot. A friendly, non-threatening atmosphere makes the Box well worth coming to, and well worth returning to as well. *Babies and children admitted (daytime only). Tables outdoors (pavement). Vegetarian dishes.*

Chez Gérard at the Opera Terrace

First Floor Opera Terrace, Covent Garden Central Market, WC2 (020 7379 0666/www.sante-cgc.com). Covent Garden tube. **Open** 11am-11pm Mon-Sat; noon-10.30pm Sun. **Food served** 11am-5pm daily. **Happy hour** 5-7pm Mon-Wed, Sun. **Credit** AmEx, DC, MC, V.
The Opera Terrace isn't all the name might suggest. A long zinc counter runs down one side of the bar, while on the other tables and chairs are arranged in a long line. Outside, a further row of tables looks down over the edge of the market towards Bow Street. Service is welcoming and friendly, and the all-French wine list starts at £2.50 for a glass; Kronenbourg is £3 a bottle and there's a long list of flavoured vodkas at under £3 a shot. As with other branches in the chain, the food is centred around steak and frites, with excellent fillets costing around £15.
Babies and children admitted (before 5pm). Restaurant. Tables outdoors (terrace). Vegetarian dishes.

Club Bar

Le Meridien Waldorf, Aldwych, WC2 (020 7836 2400/ www.fortehotels.co.uk). Covent Garden or Temple tube. **Open** 11am-11pm Mon-Sat; noon-10.30pm Sun. **Credit** AmEx, DC, MC, V.
Unusually, this is a hotel bar with cask-conditioned beer and a less than snooty attitude. Nevertheless, it does expect patrons to be reasonably dressed, and prices that start at £3.20 for a pint of Bass and £5 for one of its rather fine whiskies do tend to exclude the riff-raff. It stocks 12 cognacs and ten champagnes, and there's a cellar-full of wine by the glass from £4. Relax in the gargantuan leather and velvet sofas and armchairs, luxuriate in the waiter service and think about ordering a meal from the bar menu. We were very tempted by the spicy seafood linguine, which at only £3.95 was almost £13 cheaper than in the adjoining Palm Court restaurant.
Dress code. Function rooms. Music (harpist 1-5pm, pianist 6-11pm, daily).

Coach & Horses

42 Wellington Street, WC2 (020 7240 0553). Covent Garden tube. **Open** 11am-11pm Mon-Sat; noon-10.30pm Sun. **Food served** noon-2.30pm daily. **Credit** MC, V.
A small one-bar Irish-run pub in the centre of Covent Garden that's famous for its giant lunchtime baps of hot salt beef, lamb and ham (£4 a throw) and imported Dublin Guinness at £2.45. Its Irishness stems from the personality of landlord Jim Ryan, whose face adorns most of the sporting pictures scattered around the walls. The atmosphere (despite the lack of seats) is laid-back and mellow, and your fellow customers are likely to be staff from other pubs, local office workers and theatrical types. The best Coach & Horses in the West End.
Dress code. TV.

Coal Hole

91 Strand, WC2 (020 7836 7503). Embankment tube/ Charing Cross tube/rail. **Open** 11am-11pm Mon-Sat; noon-10.30pm Sun. **Food served** noon-6pm daily. **Credit** MC, V.
Baroque-style pennants, fancy plasterwork, stained glass and (fake) period beams add style to what can be a scrum of a pub when the offices and theatres turn out. There's a good selection of real ales (its Marston's Pedigree at £2.35 remains the best in the area) and the largely Antipodean staff manage to cope good-naturedly with one of the liveliest crowds of drinkers in London. Downstairs there's a cellar bar that's often closed for private parties. The food is standard pub grub, reasonably priced and served with a smile.
Babies and children admitted (until 6pm). Function room. Tables outdoors (pavement). Vegetarian dishes.

Columbia Bar

69 Aldwych, WC2 (020 7831 8043). Covent Garden or Holborn tube. **Open** 11am-11pm Mon-Fri. **Food served** 11am-10pm Mon-Fri. **Credit** AmEx, DC, MC, V.
Young's rather fine brewery has gone out over a barrel (so to speak) by opening this stylish two-floor bar – and yes, the handpumps on the bars are real. Special bitter is £2.25, Young's own Pilsner lager £2.40, and as well as the full range of Young's beers and lagers there's a wide-ranging selection of wines, spirits and cocktails and an ever-changing menu of well-prepared meals – Modern European food such as fresh basil risotto (£4.25), or duck, bacon and pork sausage cassoulet (£7.50). The walls are covered in contrasting pastel shades, and the furniture is comfortable-but-stylish, in a chrome and glass way.
Disabled: toilet. Function room. Games (quiz machine). No-smoking area (restaurant). Restaurant. Vegetarian dishes.

Cross Keys

31 Endell Street, WC2 (020 7836 5185). Covent Garden tube. **Open** 11am-11pm Mon-Sat; noon-10.30pm Sun. **Food served** noon-2.30pm daily. **Credit** MC, V.
This is a good place to come and wait for someone who is invariably late, because the amount of reading matter on the walls will keep you occupied for hours. Along the canopy of the medium-sized oblong bar on the ground floor it's Beatles, Elvis and general pop paraphernalia, while the rest of the place is dripping with brass and copper kettles, kitchen utensils and horse brasses. There's also a small function room upstairs that's open at lunchtimes. The food is pretty standard pub fare, but you can eat reasonably well and get change from a fiver; beers include Marston's Pedigree (£2.20 a pint) and Guinness (£2.40).
Function room. Tables outdoors (pavement). Vegetarian dishes.

Crusting Pipe

27 The Market, The Piazza, WC2 (020 7836 1415). Covent Garden tube. **Open/food served** 11am-11pm Mon-Sat; 11am-6pm Sun. **Credit** AmEx, DC, MC, V.
This underground branch of the Davys wine bar chain used to be a vegetable store, and the multiple stone arches and flag-stone floor came in pretty handy when the designers moved in. The addition of upended barrel tables, a wide range of wines (from £3.30 a glass, or just over £10 a bottle), good-value Manzanilla sherry (£2.30 a glass) and a regular supply of fine Havana cigars pretty much guarantee a full house of local businessfolk and office workers, not to mention tourists after a genuine olde-worlde experience. As usual in Davys branches the food is solid stuff, mostly British and meat-based with hefty snacks like Cumberland sausages in a baguette with mustard (£3.50), together with some lighter fare like poached salmon salad (£7.50).
Babies and children admitted. Function room. No-smoking area. Restaurant. Tables outdoors (courtyard). Vegetarian dishes.

Detroit

35 Earlham Street, WC2 (020 7240 2662/ www.detroit.uk.com). Covent Garden tube. **Open** 5pm-midnight Mon-Sat. **Food served** 6-11pm Mon-Sat. **Credit** AmEx, MC, V.
There's something womb-like about Detroit, a cellar bar-diner of linked capsules containing various permutations of modern furniture, a DJ and a busy serving area. As you make your way down the all-enclosing spiral staircase with its brown concrete walls, you'll know whether it's your kind of place or not by the ever-swelling dance music and young arty

types you meet on your journey; Detroit isn't really for middle-aged beer drinkers with their shirt tails hanging out, or even women who lunch. There's table service all round, and food is limited to a dozen dishes, which are pricey but good: starters such as organic squash soup (around £5) and main courses (pan-fried salmon, Thai beef) around £10-£12. Wine begins at £4 a glass, £12 a bottle, and cocktails are in the £4-£6.50 range.

Function rooms. Late licence (Mon-Sat). Music (DJs Thur-Sat). Restaurant. Vegetarian dishes.

Fire & Water

1 The Piazza, WC2 (020 7836 6369). Charing Cross tube. **Open** noon-11pm Mon-Sat; noon-4pm Sun. **Food served** noon-3.30pm, 6-10.30pm Mon-Sat; noon-3pm Sun. **Credit** MC, V.

This new addition to the Covent Garden drinking and dining scene seems to aim for the area's more stylish crowd. On the first floor, reached via very classy marble stairs, is the tidy little modern bar, and a series of small, alcove dining areas filled with light wood and steel furniture. The colour scheme blends beige, cream, pale blue and sand, and the staff do their best to make you feel welcome. Down in the basement there's a similarly laid-out dining room (without bar). Drinks are what you'd expect in this kind of venue: bottled beers cost from £3.25, a Bloody Mary £4.50 and wine from £2.95 a glass or £11.95 a bottle. Food is satisfyingly enjoyable, with a brunch menu of staples such as eggs Florentine (£4.25) and roast cod with mustard mash (£8.95) and a set-lunch and pre-theatre (available 6-7pm) menu at £11.50 for two courses or £15.50 for three. Usual starters include sauté of baby squid and ravioli of roast pheasant, while mains might be braised onglet of beef or breast of guinea fowl. Be warned, though: standard issue vegetables (new potatoes, Vichy carrots) are treated as 'side orders', at £2.50 each.

Babies and children admitted. Function rooms. Restaurant. Tables outdoors (balcony). Vegetarian dishes.

First Out

52 St Giles High Street, WC2 (020 7240 8042). Tottenham Court Road tube. **Open/food served** 10am-11pm Mon-Sat; 11am-10.30pm Sun. **No credit cards.**

There's something delightfully old-fashioned about the basement bar at First Out. Despite many makeovers, it's still the only gay bar in London with any sense of community about it. Unlike most central London gay venues, First Out serves up a night for the women, and not any old night either: it's women-only (and their male guests) downstairs every Friday. The prices are also those of a community centre: all spirits are £1 every night from 5pm (a mixer costs an extra 50p), while beers cost from £1.90 (Clausthaler) to £2.70 (Sol). Combine all this with the basement noticeboard and the selection of flyers on the ground floor, and First Out has the edge for people of all ages who don't like the over-coolness of neighbouring Soho. The potato and red onion salad (£3.80) – there's a restaurant and coffee shop on the ground floor – isn't half bad either.

Babies and children admitted. Music (DJs 8.30pm Fri). No-smoking area (upstairs). Vegetarian dishes.

Freedom Brewing Company

41 Earlham Street, WC2 (020 7240 0606/www. freedombrew.com). Covent Garden tube. **Open** 11am-11pm Mon-Sat; noon-10.30pm Sun. **Food** noon-3pm, 6-11pm, Mon-Sat; noon-6pm Sun. **Credit** AmEx, MC, V.

Originally the Soho Brewing Company and among the first of London's new-breed 'brew-bars', this is a stylishly minimalist basement with a long metal bar along one side, copper brewing vessels beside it and a scattering of wooden

benches. Nearer the main staircase there are some fancy high-tech toilets, and an eating area where starters like tartlet of smoked haddock, poached egg and bitter leaves (£6.50), followed by mains such as rump of lamb with mint yoghurt and curried potato (£11), are served. Beers are brewed on the premises (although absolute purists may frown at the gas pressure that propels them into the glass) and cost £1.50-£1.60 a half; among them are a toothsome wheat beer (yes mother, it's meant to be cloudy), a crisp, hoppy pale ale and the smooth Soho red. To try them out ask for a sampler, of five small glasses for £1.50. Wines are typically £2.75 a glass, or from £11.75 a bottle. The customers reflect the area, a mix of upmarket office workers and style-seeking tourists.

Babies and children admitted. Restaurant. Vegetarian dishes.

Freud

198 Shaftesbury Avenue, WC2 (020 7240 9933). Covent Garden or Tottenham Court Road tube. **Open** 11am-11pm Mon-Sat; noon-10.30pm Sun. **Food served** 11am-4.30pm daily. **No credit cards.**

This smallish square room is accessed down a clanky metal staircase, which adds to a feeling of adventure that the young and largely arty crowd must appreciate. A sign on the pavement says 'basement café, bar and gallery', and just about sums up this venue. There's a padded bench around most of the room, modern art on the walls, slate-topped tables and a slate-topped bar, which dispenses cocktails (from £4.95), bottled beers (Budvar, £2.40) and energy drinks. Food is soup-, sandwich- and salad-based, with the odd cake with cream thrown in to show that Freud people needn't worry about diets.

Babies and children admitted. No-smoking tables (11am-4.30pm). Vegetarian dishes.

Fuel

21 The Market, Covent Garden, WC2 (020 7836 2137). Covent Garden tube. **Open/food served** 10.30am-2am Mon-Sat; 10.30am-11.30pm Sun. **Happy hour** 6-8pm Fri, Sat £5. **Happy hour** 6-8pm Mon-Fri. **Credit** AmEx, MC, V.

Removed upstairs – its former site is now the basement crêperie of the parent Market Café – but still slap in the middle of Covent Garden market, Fuel is a bar worth getting to know. Given new space and deprived of their earlier maze-like cellar location, the designers have incorporated the best of the old – surprising features like mock-leopardskin settles, striking African art – with lush new sofas, red velvet banquettes and eye-catching lighting effects. The move appears to have increased the ratio of young, arty types over European backpackers, helped no doubt by the unobtrusive clubby-style music. Bottled beers are £2.95, wine starts at £3.25 for a glass of house red/white, rising to £42.95 for a bottle of Perrier Jouet Blason de Rosé; tea is £1.75 a pot, double espresso £2. Food comes from the kitchens of the Market Café and centres around wood-burned pizzas, priced from £6.95 to £7.95, plus such things as roasted tomato and basil soup (£3.75) and savoury crêpes for under £8.

Babies and children admitted. Function rooms. Late licence. Tables outdoors (piazza).

Kudos

10 Adelaide Street, WC2 (020 7379 4573). Embankment tube/Charing Cross tube/rail. **Open** 11am-11pm Mon-Sat; noon-10.30pm Sun. **Happy hour** 4-6pm daily. **Food served** noon-5pm daily. **Credit** AmEx, MC, V.

Kudos is looking a little tired these days, but parts of this two-level gay bar are still bumping and grinding. Head into the basement and you'll probably find a crowd mesmerised by the

sights and sounds emanating from two large screens, which play a constant stream of music videos and give the folk an excuse, if one were needed, to shake their stuff. Up on the ground floor all is calmness and tranquillity by comparison. Half the L-shaped room is given over to tables and chairs, with the rest a standing (and cruising) space. The crowd here is very cosmopolitan – if you had a wall map and some tacks, you'd soon have most of the globe covered – and drinks include Carling for £2.60 a pint or bottled Bud for £2.75.
Music (video, DJs nightly). Vegetarian dishes.

Lamb & Flag

33 Rose Street, WC2 (020 7497 9504). Covent Garden or Leicester Square tube. **Open** 11am-11pm Mon-Thur; 11am-10.45pm Fri, Sat; noon-10.30pm Sun. **Food served** 11am-3pm daily. **No credit cards**.
The former Bucket of Blood is still one of Covent Garden's most popular boozers, 377 years after it was built. Although now more likely to attract hordes of office workers and tourists than playwrights and novelists, it was much mentioned by Dickens, and in 1679 John Dryden was duffed up in the alleyway outside. These days it serves Young's Special (£2.30), guest ales such as Charles Wells Bombardier (£2.45) and around 30 fine whiskies. The ground-floor bar is a rickety wooden-floored affair stuffed with mementos such as the 'Coutts is in/out' slider sign and metal plaques for current regulars, while a staircase leads up to the Dryden restaurant on the first floor. Food is fairly basic and British-based, with roasts for £5.95. The bar menu specialises in well-stuffed sandwiches, including Cumberland sausage on French bread (£2.50) and roast beef and horseradish (£3.95).
Babies and children admitted (upstairs bar only). Music (jazz Sun). No piped music or jukebox. Satellite TV. Vegetarian dishes.

Livebait Bar

21 Wellington Street, WC2 (020 7836 7161). Covent Garden tube. **Open** noon-11.30pm Mon-Sat. **Food served** noon-3pm, 5.30-11.30pm Mon-Sat. **Credit** AmEx, DC, JCB, MC, V.
The theme here is fish, and this small, wedge-shaped bar in the entrance to the Covent Garden branch of the celebrated fish restaurant is a pleasant place to while away an hour or two, or wait while your table's being prepared. The walls are decorated in cool, fishmonger-like ceramic tiles, in a chequerboard theme that continues on the lino floor. The cocktail list begins at £5 a throw, the 20-odd wines available by the glass cost from £3 and a very presentable selection of bottled British beers (including Freedom lager and Black Sheep bitter) will set you back £3-£5. The bar menu includes rock oysters from around £1.10 each (prices vary according to the market), a piscatorially rich fish soup at £4.50 and half a lobster at a seasonally adjustable price of around £17. The clientele varies enormously, although typically will be a thirty-something couple with a decent income.
Babies and children admitted. No-smoking area. Restaurant. Vegetarian dishes.

Lobby Bar

One Aldwych Hotel, 1 Aldwych, WC2 (020 7300 1000). Covent Garden tube/Charing Cross tube/rail. **Open** 9am-11pm Mon-Sat; 10am-10.30pm Sun. **Credit** AmEx, DC, MC, V.
A classy bar that's in the lobby to the hotel that is One Aldwych, so no prizes for originality when it comes to naming. The design, however, shows much greater imagination: high-backed chairs that make you think you've had one Martini too many and tall, graceful sculptures and flower arrangements on glass plinths all point up to a lofty, vaulted ceiling. The staff, impeccably attired in sharp shirts,

are more friendly than you'd expect, and we were surprised to find a young, casually dressed crowd mixing in with the inevitable suits. Cocktails are where it's at here, and start at £6.50, or £7.50 for a Martini; champagne (Heidsieck Monopole) cocktails cost from £8.25. Wines begin at £4 a glass, and bottled beers at £3. Expensive but quality modern food is available from the adjoining Indigo and **Axis** restaurants and bar (*see p28*).
Babies and children admitted. Disabled: toilet. Function room. Restaurants.

Lyceum Tavern

354 The Strand, WC2 (020 7836 7155). Embankment, Covent Garden or Temple tube/Charing Cross tube/rail. **Open** 11.30am-11pm Mon-Sat; noon-10.30pm Sun. **Food served** 11.30am-8.30pm daily. **Credit** MC, V.
The ground floor of this brash Sam Smith pub is where local publishers come to sneer at authors, and groups of office workers hold after-work leaving parties. There's a row of wooden alcoves on one side of the room, with a long raised bar opposite and a small games area with dartboard. Tourists and the bosses of the downstairs workforce gravitate to the first-floor bar and dining area, where leather sofas and low tables are on offer. Food is the usual fish in beer batter/steak and kidney pie/lasagne stuff. A plate and a pint of Old Brewery bitter (reasonably priced at £1.52) or Ayingerbrau lager (£1.78) will give you change from £10.
Babies and children admitted. Games (darts). No-smoking area. Tables outdoors (pavement). Vegetarian dishes.

Maple Leaf

41 Maiden Lane, WC2 (020 7240 2843). Covent Garden tube. **Open/food served** 11am-11pm Mon-Sat; noon-10.30pm Sun. **Credit** AmEx, DC, MC, V.
Canadians in London will need no introduction to the Maple Leaf. Even if you wander in by accident, the CD soundtrack, flags, crossed hockey sticks, framed sports shirts, fake totem poles and carved native warrior should put you right. A recent makeover added more bare wood, but deducted none of the Canadian-ness. The menu is dedicated to the gods of North American fast food, with the likes of Hudson Bay cod and chips or cajun chicken salad from £3.50 to £7.65 a plateful – and expect more than a soupçon of a Quebec French accent. Molson is available on draught (£2.44 a pint) and in bottle, with the artfully de-tastified Ice at £2.60 a go. Amazingly, they also still sell proper British beer, and cask-conditioned Courage Directors is £2.36. The multi-screen TV is sports obsessed, although soccer from Middlesbrough often takes a back seat to ice hockey from Montreal.
Music (9pm Thur). Satellite TV. Vegetarian dishes.

Marquess of Anglesey

39 Bow Street, WC2 (020 7240 3216). Covent Garden tube. **Open** 11am-11pm Mon-Sat; noon-10.30pm Sun. **Food served** noon-10pm Mon-Sat; noon-9pm Sun. **Credit** AmEx, DC, MC, V.
The first floor at this busy Young's pub houses a small bar and restaurant that's one of Covent Garden's more relaxing beer-friendly experiences. This is where the orchestra members from a nearby theatre come for their interval pints, so it's best to stock up with drinks in advance of the short 9pm rush; the decor is reminiscent of a planter's front terrace, with cane chairs and swirling ceiling fans. The restaurant's food is Modern European, while the bar menu centres around the likes of fish and chips (beer batter, natch) for the tourists and tomato and basil risotto for veggies. Expect to spend upwards of £10 a head for starter and main course without drinks. These are led by Young's Special (£2.30), Young's Pilsner (£2.35) and a good selection of wines from £2.45 a

glass. The ground-floor bar is much more of an after-office/tourist hang-out, with the usual wooden alcoves, chunky furniture and bare floorboards.

Babies and children admitted (restaurant only). Function room. Games (fruit machines). No-smoking area (in restaurant). Restaurant. Vegetarian dishes.

Marquis of Granby

51 Chandos Place, WC2 (020 7836 7657). Charing Cross tube/rail or Covent Garden tube. **Open** 11am-11pm Mon-Sat; noon-10.30pm Sun. **Food served** 11am-9pm Mon-Sat; noon-7pm Sun. **Credit** AmEx, DC, MC, V.

Although it was rebuilt in 1845, there's been a pub on this site behind the Coliseum since Oliver Cromwell was a sparkle in his dad's eye. Originally called the Hole in the Wall, this was where the notorious highwayman Claude Duval was arrested in 1670. These days it's a remarkably well-preserved, wedge-shaped old boozer with three tiny ground-floor bars separated by intricately carved wooden partitions, crowned with glorious glasswork and fitted out with wooden bench seats. Hanging from the ceiling are two massive Heath Robinson-type gas heating contraptions, and at the bar there's now an espresso machine, so there's café au lait as well as the usual pints. The cask-conditioned beers include Adnams bitter, Marston's Pedigree and at least one guest ale (all £2.10). Food is served in the first-floor dining room (check out the giant mirror), and includes adventurous dishes such as Thai fishcakes with wild rice salad (£6.95) next to a humble but tasty own-made cottage pie (£5.50). Customers tend to be a complete cross-section of Covent Garden life, with a leaning towards theatrical types.

Babies and children admitted (upstairs). Function room. Satellite TV. Restaurant. Vegetarian dishes.

Navajo Joe's

34 King Street, WC2 (020 7240 4008). Covent Garden tube. **Open/food served** noon-11pm daily. **Happy hour** all day Mon-Wed; 5.30-8.30pm Thur; 5.30-7.30pm Fri, Sat. **Credit** AmEx, DC, MC, V.

An ornate door leads into a big room that's high-ceilinged, spacious and quite stylish, with a long copper bar decorated with back-lit bottles along one wall, and a double deck of alcoved drinking areas opposite. Walls are bare brick, peppered with video displays and modern sculpture, the suggestion being that this is an upmarket New Mexico bar, c2005. Further back is a dining area, and there's another bar in the basement. The Southwestern theme slips into the drinks menu, with 250 different tequilas and mescals (from £2.25, to £75 a shot for very good stuff), around 30 bourbons and rye whiskies (from £2.50), 40 rums and a fridge full of beers, with Budweiser at £2.85. The above-average food menu includes tomato and tomatillo risotto with rocket and goat's cheese salad (£8.95) and smoked chicken and Monterey Jack quesadilla (£4.95). Staff are slick but friendly, and their customers a cut above the usual Covent Garden barflies.

Function room. Restaurant. Satellite TV. Vegetarian dishes.

Neal's Yard Café Society

13 Neal's Yard, WC2 (020 7240 1168). Covent Garden tube. **Open/food served** 10am-8.30pm daily. **Credit** DC, MC, V.

This small, brightly lit modern café is one of the friendliest in the area, and a good place to stock up on minerals and essential vitamins – as well as death-by-chocolate thick shakes, beer, wine and pizza. The juice bar part of the operation includes 'cocktails' like Detox (carrot, apple and ginger), Body Cleanser (spinach, carrot, celery and apple) and smoothies of the Energiser (melon, pineapple, banana, apple, grapes and berries) and Blue Banana (banana, blackcurrant

sorbet, grapes and blueberries) type. All are £2.75 for a regular size, £3.75 large. There's also room on the menu for beer (Beck's £2.65), wine (house white/red £2.95), cappuccinos (£1.30/£1.90) and upmarket milkshakes (£2.75/£3.75). The food is predominantly vegetarian, although the odd chicken and tuna dish sneaks in. The organic soups (around £4) can be recommended, as can the aubergine, pepper, olive, tomato and mozzarella pizzas (£4.95/£5.65).

Babies and children admitted. Tables outdoors (pavement). Vegetarian dishes.

Opera Tavern

23 Catherine Street, WC2 (020 7836 7321). Covent Garden tube. **Open** 11am-11pm Mon-Sat; noon-10.30pm Sun. **Food served** noon-3pm, 6-9pm Mon-Sat. **Credit** AmEx, MC, V.

Built in 1879 and retaining its Victorian good looks, this is a modest-sized, friendly pub with a real fire in winter, a comfortable patterned carpet and enough reds, yellows and golds to cast a warm glow even in the brightest summer months. The drinks stretch from real ale (Adnams is always a good bet, at £2.25) to the usual lagers, wines (from £2.45 a glass, £9.50 a bottle) and spirits. The theme is, er, opera, so walls are peppered with playbills, mementos and sheet music, much of it featuring the nearby Royal Opera House. Food is reliable but largely unexciting pub grub, enlivened by the occasional special.

Satellite TV. Vegetarian dishes.

PJ's Grill

30 Wellington Street, WC2 (020 7240 7529). Covent Garden tube. **Open/food served** noon-midnight Mon-Sat; noon-4pm Sun. **Credit** AmEx, DC, MC, V.

Not unlike an upmarket American gentlemen's club in style – all seasoned wood panelling, leather seats and golfing paraphernalia – PJ's manages to combine a certain elegance with a friendly welcome and efficient service. A haunt of the area's theatrical fraternity, as well as the hipper end of the local office crowd, it has a small bar area with seating at the front, leading on to a much larger sunken dining room, which exits on to Catherine Street. The sole draught beer is Miller Lite (£3.25 a pint), but there's a fair selection of bottled lagers at £2.95, wine from £2.95 a glass/£9.95 a bottle and house champagne at £4.25/£17.95. The food menu is impressive, and starters come in between £3.95 for New England corn chowder and £6.95 for seared scallops (£12.95 as a main), with mains specialities such as roast rump of lamb, roast halibut and saffron risotto from £8.95 to £14.95, or £22.95 if you want to order chateaubriand for two. The atmosphere is good, especially when the bar is buzzing after work, and it's a great place to star spot; just remember that it's rude to stare.

Babies and children admitted. Music (pianist Tue, Thur, Fri). Restaurant. Vegetarian dishes.

La Perla

28 Maiden Lane, WC2 (020 7240 7400/www.pacifico-laperla.com). Covent Garden tube/Charing Cross tube/rail. **Open/food served** noon-midnight Mon-Sat; 4-10.30pm Sun. **Happy hour** 5-7pm daily. **Credit** AmEx, MC, V.

A Mexican-style restaurant/cantina with a lively bar at the front that's invariably crammed with a young crowd, guzzling Margaritas (£4.25) and Mexican beers (£2.60-£2.85). There are over 40 types of tequila and mescal, a big choice of bourbons and whiskies and an impressive number of cocktails (from £4). The atmosphere is frenzied but good-natured, and staff seemed to have turned up the throttle slightly since we last visited, so expect friendly and speedy service. The colour scheme is beige/sand, with plenty of bare wood around, and walls are flecked with colourful prints.

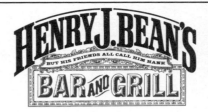

Cooking can be variable, but good bets are the stuffed jalapeño peppers (£3.95), grilled swordfish (£8.95) and coletas de cordero (lamb chops with jalapeño mint jelly, £9.75).
Babies and children admitted (restaurant only). Restaurant. Vegetarian dishes.

Porters Bar
16 Henrietta Street, WC2 (020 7836 6466/ www.porters.co.uk). Covent Garden tube. **Open** noon-11pm Mon-Sat; noon-10.30pm Sun. **Food served** noon-10pm daily. **Credit** AmEx, DC, MC, V.
The decor here is crisp, predominantly lilac and white, with modernist murals of flowers opposite the ground-floor bar and wooden recliner seats scattered around low-slung tables. In the basement there's a more formal line-up of tables and chairs in what is supposed to be a dining area (but which you have to pass through to use the toilet). The food is a junior version of the British menu served at Porters restaurant next door, and you can fill up any empty corners for around a fiver. Unusually for a modern-ish bar like, this there are five real ales on offer at £2.50 (we sampled palatable, if a little too well chilled, Old Speckled Hen and Boddingtons), and cocktails (from £3.50) are a speciality. Most of the customers wear suits and work locally.
Restaurant. Vegetarian dishes.

RamPage
32 Great Queen Street, WC2 (020 7242 0622). Holborn or Covent Garden tube. **Open** 11am-11pm Mon-Sat. **Food served** noon-5pm Mon-Sat. **Credit** MC, V.
This new sports bar between Covent Garden and Holborn attracted a committed crowd within minutes of opening, and seems not to have had an empty moment since. The emphasis is on 'the lads', and the dark blue walls are strewn with extravagantly framed pictures of 'great' historic battles. The floor is bare wood, and tables litter the medium-sized ground-floor (there's another similar bar downstairs). Beers are standard (Foster's £2.40, Miller £2.50), but food is more imaginative than you'd maybe expect: we were surprised to find char-grilled lamb steak (£9) and spiced chicken sandwich with cucumber raita (£5). The punters appear to be young, suited and macho, but with a surprisingly high proportion of twentysomething females in attendance.
Function room. Restaurant. Satellite TV. Tables outdoors (pavement). Vegetarian dishes.

Retro Bar
2 George Court, off the Strand, WC2 (020 7321 2811). Embankment tube/Charing Cross tube/rail. **Open** noon-11pm Mon-Fri; 5-11pm Sat; 5-10.30pm Sun. **Credit** MC, V.
The very antithesis of the stereotypical idea of the gay bar, Retro is an offshoot of the **Popstarz** (*see p54*) empire, and consequently is full of people who are gay but obviously feel different from the majority of other gay people. After all, where else would you find three punks sitting in the corner of a gay bar, near an ad for the monthly Eurovision nights where the customers are the jury, choosing between Dana and Dana International, and beneath posters of Suede album covers on the ceiling? Promoted as the only gay alternative, the Retro Bar is a place to head if you feel out of synch with the rest of the gay world. Drinks include the usual suspects, such as Carling for £2.35 or bottled Bud for £2.85.
Games (fruit machine, quiz machine). Jukebox. Music (DJs most nights; karaoke Wed). Quiz (Tue).

Roadhouse
Jubilee Hall, 35 The Piazza, WC2 (020 7240 6001/www.roadhouse.co.uk). Covent Garden tube. **Open** 5.30pm-3am Mon-Sat; 5.30-10.30pm Sun. **Happy hour**

5.30-10.30pm Mon-Wed; 5.30-8.30pm Thur, Sat; 5.30-7.30pm Fri. **Food served** 5.30pm-1am Mon-Sat; 5.30-10pm Sun. **Credit** AmEx, MC, V.
This roomy, neon-decorated basement is where a large proportion of the area's young things hang out until the wee hours. Love it or loathe it, Roadhouse is a phenomenon: the atmosphere's loud and breezy, it's inevitably packed (queues run literally around the block at weekends) and it all comes with a soundtrack of the bounciest hits of the last four decades. There's at least one live band a night – mostly playing good quality covers, although original artists like Rufus Thomas and Limahl crop up – plus a DJ or two. Prices are fluid, depending on whether happy or crazy hours are in force, but bottled lager (including Freedom and Rolling Rock) will set you back anything from £1.90 to £3.10, cocktails are £2.90-£4.90, and wine is £1.90-£2.90 a glass (sometimes there's a 2 for 1 promotion on). Food is served in an American railroad-car-style space, and includes burgers and quesadillas from around £5. Other rock 'n' roll imagery includes a couple of Harley-Davidsons, a mini-helicopter over the stage and more US diner and roadhouse signs from the 1950s-60s than you'd find south of the Mason-Dixon line.
Games (pinball machines). Late licence. Music (bands nightly). TVs. Vegetarian dishes.

Round House
1 Garrick Street, WC2 (020 7836 9838). Covent Garden tube. **Open** 11am-11pm Mon-Sat; noon-10.30pm Sun. **Food served** 11am-10pm Mon-Sat; noon-9.30pm Sun. **Credit** AmEx, DC, MC, V.
This being a TJ Bernard ale house, you'll find an impressive selection of cask-conditioned beers from around £2.30 a pint, as well as bottled exotic brews such as German wheat beers, Czech Pilsners and Belgian Trappist ales (around £3 a bottle) and the usual lager and nitro-keg stuff. More of a semicircle than a round house, it has big curved windows looking out on to Tesco shoppers and Covent Garden-bound revellers, plus plenty of chunky wood furniture and the now obligatory bare board flooring. It's a busy place, and customers tend to be a mix of office folk and tourists; the rushed staff's attitude reflects their heavy workload. Food is of the order of burgers, sandwiches and 'all-in-one' pies, and you'd be hard-pressed to spend more than a fiver.
Games (fruit machine). Vegetarian dishes.

Speakeasy at Christopher's
18 Wellington Street, WC2 (020 7240 4222). Covent Garden tube/Charing Cross tube/rail. **Open/food served** 11.30am-11pm Mon-Fri; 5-11.30pm Sat. **Happy hour** 8.30-9.30pm Mon-Sat. **Credit** AmEx, DC, MC, V.
This pleasantly distressed bar is situated in the basement of the classy Christopher's restaurant, where haute American cuisine seldom comes hauter. The stairs leading to Speakeasy, though, are frankly tatty, and once you get there the floor is simply tiled and the furniture, apart from the odd leather sofa, is minimalist but comfortable. The stone walls are decorated with odd little framed pictures, and a mural of caricatures of some more renowned customers of recent years. Cocktails start at £5.60, beers £3, and there's an extensive range of rare whiskies and bourbons from around £5. It wouldn't do here to turn up in jeans and sneakers, so dress up and enjoy an atmosphere that's a cross between an exclusive cocktail bar and a public school dinner hall. Bar food is served all day, and includes pasta or risotto of the day (£6), tomato, mozzarella and basil salad (£3.75) and grilled swordfish (£9.75).
Babies and children admitted (restaurant only). Function room. Restaurant. Vegetarian dishes.

Spot

29 Maiden Lane, WC2 (020 7379 5900).
Covent Garden tube/Charing Cross tube/rail.
Open noon-1am Mon-Sat; 5pm-1am Sun. **Admission** £5
Fri, Sat. **Happy hour** noon-7pm Mon-Sat. **Food served**
noon-8pm Mon-Sat. **Credit** AmEx, MC, V.
This popular bar is really a set of different spaces lumped
together into one club-like venue – the smart gold and red
main bar on the ground floor contrasts with its smaller, tattier
cousin to the right, while the aptly named Oval Room is where
the 'cool' people hang out. Here the music is louder and
clubbier, the lights lower and the big screen, er, bigger. Drinks
are pretty standard but less expensive than you'd expect:
draught Guinness is £2.40, bottled lagers from £2.50, and
cocktails start at under £5. Expect to have to talk your way
in at weekends, when some of the area's heftiest bouncers
loom menacingly at the door.
Babies and children admitted (restaurant only). Function
room. Late licence. Music (DJs Thur-Sun, live music Sun).
Restaurant. Satellite TV (big screen).

La Tartine

14 Garrick Street, WC2 (020 7379 1531).
Covent Garden tube/Leicester Square tube.
Open noon-11pm Mon-Fri. **Food served** noon-10.45pm
Mon-Fri. **Credit** AmEx, MC, V.
This comfortable cellar wine bar is accessed by a sturdy
wooden staircase, inside the entrance to the swanky
L'Estaminet French restaurant. Once downstairs you'll find
a smallish room with salmon-pink walls, simple furniture and
a compact serving area, dispensing pretty decent wines from
£2.50 a glass. Bottled beers begin at £2.90. The walls are
dotted with rugby pictures, which gives a clue to the typical
customer: he's mid-30s, fit and wears a hand-tailored suit;
she's younger and squeezes effortlessly into an expensive
short skirt. The food also has a French flavour and includes
the likes of fricassée de fruits de mer and vegetable terrine
(both £5); simple bar snacks like olives or peanuts are £1.50.
Restaurant. Vegetarian dishes.

TGI Friday's

6 Bedford Street, WC2 (020 7379 0585). Covent Garden
tube/Charing Cross tube/rail. **Open/food served** noon-
11.30pm Mon-Sat; noon-11pm Sun. **Credit** AmEx, MC, V.
You know what to expect: outrageously bubbly red-and-white
striped waiting staff serving big plates of 'appregeous' Tex-
Mex towers (quesadillas, nachos and suchlike in a three-tier
arrangement, £10.50), crayfish gumbo (£10.95), Philly steak
wrappers (£8.25) and so on to 'gangs' of sozzled twentysomething office workers and families in town for a treat and
determined to enjoy themselves. The bar resembles the one
in *Cheers*, with the serving area a blur as barmen throw
bottles around (it's called flairing), producing cocktails such
as Frozen Friday's Freeze (orange and vodka) and Lynchburg
Lemonade (JD-based) for £4.65 a throw, or £7.25 for an
'ultimate'. Bottled beers (Bud, Labatt's and similar) are £2.75.
Babies and children admitted (children's menu, high
chairs). Disabled: toilet. No-smoking area. Restaurant.
Vegetarian dishes.

Wellington

351 The Strand, WC2 (020 7557 9881). Embankment
tube/Charing Cross tube/rail. **Open** 11am-11pm Mon-Sat;
noon-10.30pm Sun. **Food served** noon-9.30pm daily.
Credit AmEx, MC, V.
As might be expected, this split-level, wooden-floored pub is
decorated with pictures of the Iron Duke himself, and other
reminders of army life circa the time of Waterloo. Then there

are pseudo gas lamps, the odd mirror and as much glass and
wood as the decorators thought they could cram in without
giving away their fetish. Expect to be surrounded by post
office crews, and tourists looking askance at the pints of
draught Bass and London Pride (both £2.20) they thought
they'd better ask for, this being London and all. Upstairs
there's another bar with comfortable armchairs and a carpet,
but keg beer and lager only. Food is standard pub grub, filling
and good value at around £5 a plateful.
Babies and children admitted (restaurant only). Satellite
TV (big screen). Tables outdoors (patio). Vegetarian dishes.

Also in the area...

All Bar One 19 Henrietta Street, WC2
(020 7557 7941); 84 Cambridge Circus, WC2 (020
7379 8311).
Café Rouge 34 Wellington Street, WC2
(020 7836 0998).
Dôme 32 Long Acre, WC2 (020 7379 8650).
Champagne Charlie's (Davys) 17 The Arches, Villiers
Street, WC2 (020 7930 7737).
Faun & Firkin 18 Bear Street, WC2 (020 7839 3252).
Flyman & Firkin 166-170 Shaftesbury Avenue, WC2
(020 7240 7109).
Savoy Tup 2 Savoy Street, WC2 (020 7836 9738).
Tappit Hen (Davys) 5 William IV Street, WC2
(020 7836 9839).

Earl's Court SW5

Blackbird

209 Earl's Court Road, SW5 (020 7835 1855). Earl's
Court tube. **Open** 11am-11pm Mon-Sat; noon-10.30pm
Sun. **Food served** noon-9pm daily. **Credit** AmEx, DC,
MC, V.
The din from the bar never quite drowns out the traffic
outside, but no matter: the Blackbird is a locals' local,
favoured by the permanent residents of Earl's Court rather
than by the area's famously transient population. As a
result, workmen and OAPs rub shoulders with office
workers and young bohemians. With its massive windows
and dark wood fittings, it's a handsome place, solid
partitions offering privacy not only in the body of the pub
but along the bar as well. The cave-like back bar, guarded
by two Cerberus-like games machines, offers further
seclusion. A long menu includes Blackbird pie with lamb,
tomato and rosemary (£5.95) and chicken, bacon and
spinach pie (£6.50), while Fuller's London Pride (£2.15) and
Honeydew (£2.20) are among the real ales.
Games (fruit machine). Satellite TV. Vegetarian dishes.

King's Head

17 Hogarth Place, SW5 (020 7244 5931). Earl's Court
tube. **Open** noon-11pm Mon-Sat; noon-10.30pm Sun.
Food served noon-3pm, 5-8pm Mon-Thur; noon-6pm
Fri-Sun. **Credit** DC, MC, V.
Tucked away around the back of the Earl's Court Road, the
King's Head largely steers clear of the lairy Australian theme
that blights a couple of its neighbours. Much like the nearby
Blackbird *(see above)*, it's basically a nice, slightly old-
fashioned English boozer, a fact appreciated by the daytime
crowd made up mostly of local office workers and journalists
from nearby *TNT* magazine; in the evenings, particularly on
Fridays, it gets altogether louder. The recent refurbishment
seems to have been largely limited to the banishment of the
misted and stained-glass windows that gave the pub an

escapist charm; in their place are the now standard plate-glass windows, which let in more light and take away some of the cosiness of before. Still, the best seats in the house – the two massive sofas, tucked away in one corner – have survived, and the pub remains a pleasant spot for a pint of London Pride (£2.30) or Guinness (£2.40). The menu offers tasty burgers, sandwiches and the like, with most mains costing under £5.

Babies and children admitted (until 5pm). Games (fruit machines, video game). Satellite TV (big screen). Vegetarian dishes.

Prince of Teck
161 Earl's Court Road, SW5 (020 7373 3107). Earl's Court tube. **Open** 11am-11pm Mon-Sat; noon-10.30pm Sun. **Food served** 11am-3pm, 6-9pm Mon-Sat; noon-3pm Sun. **Credit** MC, V.

'Prince of Tack, more like,' muttered one of our party as he surveyed the Aussie paraphernalia – Sydney Opera House posters, Outback road signs, stuffed 'roo – that festoons the raucous, carpetless ground-floor bar. The much quieter upstairs lounge seems to have been transplanted from a different pub altogether, although perhaps the combination of Christmas decorations – in mid-November – and stifling heat was supposed to remind the predominantly Antipodean clientele of Crimbo Down Under. Food is standard British Empire stuff (roast lamb £5.50, shepherd's pie £4.50), Young's 'ordinary' is £1.75 and a pint of Foster's – but of course – costs £2.30.

Babies and children admitted (upstairs bar). Games (fruit machine). Jukebox. Satellite TV (big screen). Restaurant. Vegetarian dishes.

Troubadour
265 Old Brompton Road, SW5 (020 7370 1434). Earl's Court tube. **Open** 9am-midnight daily. **Admission** (performances in basement) from £4. **Food served** 9am-11.30pm daily. **No credit cards.**

Part bar, part café, part coffee house, the dark, candlelit Troubadour comes as close to the atmosphere of a Parisian bar as you're likely to find in London, although there are plans afoot to expand the premises in the months ahead. Opened in the 1950s, it has regulars who range from ballet dancers to latter-day existentialists. Bob Dylan once gave an impromptu performance of *Blowin' in the Wind* here, while Charlie Watts of the Rolling Stones used to be the resident drummer; it still offers live jazz and comedy. Bottled beers include Budvar (£2.45), and there's a selection of wine (£2.20 a glass, £7.65 a half-litre carafe), but you can just as easily order tea (English breakfast, Earl Grey, Darjeeling or Builders, all £1.50) or sit down to an all day breakfast (£4.50). A treasureable one-off.

Babies and children admitted (high chairs). Function room. Games (board games). Late licence. Music (jazz Thur, folk & blues Fri). No-smoking area (restaurant only). Poetry (every other Mon). Satellite TV. Restaurant. Tables outdoors (garden, pavement). Vegetarian food.

Warwick Arms
160 Warwick Road, W14 (020 7603 3560). Earl's Court or Kensington High Street tube. **Open** noon-11pm Mon-Sat; noon-10.30pm Sun. **Food served** noon-3pm, 6-10pm, Mon-Fri; noon-3pm Sat. **Credit** AmEx, MC, V.

'A smart appearance,' a sign on the door informs us, 'is required to obtain service in this bar.' It's unfortunate, then, that first appearances here – a games machine performing an epilepsy-inducing pyrotechnic display – are not exactly promising. Stick around, though: the long, quiet, wood and brick bar, hermetically sealed behind frosted glass, and easy-going Irish staff seem to exist in a different dimension to the murderous Warwick Road traffic outside. It's the sort of place where you confidently leave your goods and chattels behind when you go to the loo. A Fuller's pub, it charges £2.30 for ESB and £1.95 for Chiswick, and has an extensive menu (home-made pies £6.50, steaks £12.95-£14.95).

Games (fruit machine). No-smoking area. Restaurant. Tables outdoors (courtyard, pavement). TV. Vegetarian dishes.

Also in the area...

Dôme 194-196 Earl's Court Road, SW5 (020 7835 2200).

Fitzrovia W1

Bar Madrid
4 Winsley Street, W1 (020 7436 4649/www.latenightlondon.co.uk). Oxford Circus tube. **Open/food served** 4.30pm-3am Mon-Sat. **Credit** AmEx, MC, V.

They certainly encourage you to build up a thirst here: when we arrived minutes after opening time, a gruelling Brazilian dance session was already in full swing. Located in a cavernous basement off Oxford Street, Bar Madrid is a groover's paradise, with themed, organised dancing sessions (Spanish, salsa and so on) every night. As a result, it's not exactly a drinker's joint – there's very little seating, for a start – though the bar staff do their best to get you into the spirit of the place: the barman flings bottles of beer about like a majorette. Cocktails (£3.95) and beers (£2.80 a bottle) are the house specialities, though there's a disappointing dearth of Spanish/Latin American brands. Food, inevitably, is chiefly tapas, some disconsolate examples of which are displayed under glass in the central bar.

Function room. Late licence. Music (DJs & live nightly). Restaurant. Satellite TV. Vegetarian dishes.

Bertorelli's
19-23 Charlotte Street, W1 (020 7636 4174). Goodge Street or Tottenham Court Road tube. **Open/food served** noon-11pm Mon-Sat. **Credit** AmEx, DC, MC, V.

Situated at the front of the ground-floor restaurant, the bar at Bertorelli's is frequented mainly by people waiting to eat, but it's open to all and there's nothing to stop you from sitting and lingering. Courteous staff and cheerful decor – mirrors, colourful neon, and candy-coloured chairs and tables – make it well worth a visit for its own sake, and it's a useful place to know about for when the pubs are heaving. House wine is £2.70; a good range of bottled beers includes Peroni (£2.75).

Babies and children admitted. Function rooms. Restaurant. Vegetarian dishes.

Bradley's Spanish Bar
42-44 Hanway Street, W1 (020 7636 0359). Tottenham Court Road tube. **Open** 11am-11pm Mon-Sat. **Food served** 11am-10pm Mon-Sat. **Credit** MC, V.

Light on space but heavy on atmosphere, Bradley's is a Fitzrovia institution, its tiny ground-floor bar crammed with bullfight memorabilia, Barcelona FC pennants and fading *cerveza* ads, its all-vinyl jukebox yielding the likes of Sam Cooke and Gene Pitney. The dark basement tends to be more popular with Spaniards – perhaps because it's less kitsch – but both bars are liable to be thronging by 6pm as the local shops and offices begin to empty. Inevitably, the accent is on Spanish beer, with Sol, Dos Equis and San Miguel all at £2.50 a bottle, and the food is strictly tapas.

Jukebox. Vegetarian dishes.

Bradley's Spanish Bar.
See page 37.

Bricklayer's Arms

31 Gresse Street, W1 (020 7636 5593). Tottenham Court Road tube. **Open** 11am-11pm Mon-Sat; noon-10.30pm Sun. **Food served** noon-2.30pm, 5.30-8.30pm Mon-Fri. **Credit** AmEx, DC, MC, V.

The Bricklayer's Arms is a rambling, highly popular pub tucked into a notch between Oxford Street and Tottenham Court Road. The small, panelled ground-floor bar looks as if it was built for a small provincial hotel; the much bigger upstairs bar, with its dark green wallpaper and big fireplace, resembles a hotel lounge. If you get a seat on the sofas by the windows, though, the panoramic view of the nearby Royal Mail depot, complete with toiling workers, suggests a Marxist version of Hitchcock's *Rear Window*. The pub's good, inexpensive food and drink continues to pack in the customers, with the former including breaded plaice (£4.95) and roast chicken (£5.50), and Samuel Smith Old Brewery Bitter (£1.52) among the latter. *Games (darts, fruit machine). Tables outdoors (pavement). Vegetarian dishes.*

Champion

12-13 Wells Street, W1 (020 7323 1228). Oxford Circus tube. **Open** 11.30am-11pm Mon-Sat; noon-10.30pm Sun. **Food served** noon-2.30pm, 6-9pm daily. **Credit** MC, V. The Champion's dominating feature is its huge stained-glass windows depicting Victorian sporting heroes such as WG Grace and Captain Webb (the first man to swim the Channel), and a few others, such as Florence Nightingale. With its solid central horseshoe bar and Tiffany ceiling lamps, the ground-floor bar comes tantalisingly close to perfection; over-loud music and distracting games machines are the inevitable flies in the ointment. Still, there's no faulting the friendliness of the (mainly Australian) staff and the keenness of the prices (Sovereign and Old Brewery, Sam Smith's brews, are both £1.52), though food is not exactly a major selling point (assorted burger variations £4.95-£5.90). *Games (darts). Function room. No-smoking area. Restaurant. Tables outdoors (pavement). TV. Vegetarian dishes.*

Cock Tavern

27 Great Portland Street, W1 (020 7631 5002). Oxford Circus tube. **Open** 11am-11pm Mon-Sat; noon-10.30pm Sun. **Food served** noon-2.30pm, 6-8.30pm Mon-Fri; noon-6pm Sat, Sun. **Credit** MC, V.

Edwardian makeovers are two a penny these days, but with its chocolate-coloured ceiling, tiled floor and Gothic fireplace, the Cock's is more convincing than most; one can't help feeling that Patrick Hamilton, principal chronicler of pre-war Fitzrovia pub life, would still feel at home here. Prices, if not exactly pre-war, are still competitive (Samuel Smith Old Brewery Bitter £1.52, Extra Stout £1.88), and the huge ploughman's lunches – with no fewer than ten cheeses to choose from – are a house speciality. Incidentally, thanks to its lack of lighting, this has to be one of the darkest pubs in London, although the upstairs room is lighter, and quieter. *Tables outdoors (pavement). Vegetarian dishes.*

Crown & Sceptre

86 Great Titchfield Street, W1 (020 7307 9971). Oxford Circus tube. **Open** 11am-11pm Mon-Fri; noon-11pm Sat; noon-10.30pm Sun. **Food served** 11am-3pm Mon-Fri; noon-4pm Sat, Sun. **Credit** MC, V. Hard to miss at the busy end of Foley Street, the Crown & Sceptre is large and, thanks to recent refurbishments, attractive: the pleasant yellow walls are complemented by dark panelling and an attractive range of London prints that, unusually for a pub in the capital, actually seem to have been chosen with care. The comfortable armchairs and sofas are another inducement to stay for a while. Wine is the main attraction (£2.50-£3.50), with London Pride (£2.20) the pick of the beers. The place isn't big on main meals, but there's a good range of bar snacks (chicken dippers £2.75, sesame prawn toast £3.25). *Satellite TV. Vegetarian dishes.*

Cyberia

39 Whitfield Street, W1 (020 7681 4200). Goodge Street tube. **Open/food served** 9am-9pm Mon-Fri; 11am-7pm Sat; 11am-6pm Sun. **Credit** AmEx, DC, MC, V. This being an Internet café-bar, the one thing you don't get at Cyberia is the hum of pub conversation; instead, it's the clickety-click of keyboards and, on our visit, some impassioned R&B over the tannoy. The clientele is as varied as you'd expect – that is, as varied as the people who use computers – and the decor as plain: the tables in the middle of the room are a pleasant lilac shade, but more or less represent the beginning and the end of the decoration. With much of its income coming from the use of the computers, the bar prices are very reasonable (bottled Beck's £2, Jack Daniel's £1.40), though the menu consists of snacks rather than main meals (soup of the day £2, toasted sandwiches £2.50). Recommended for synchronised sipping and surfing. *Babies and children admitted. Function room. Vegetarian dishes.*

Fitzroy Tavern

16 Charlotte Street, W1 (020 7580 3714). Goodge Street tube. **Open** 11am-11pm Mon-Sat; noon-10.30pm Sun. **Food served** noon-2.30pm, 6.30-9.30pm Mon-Thur, Sat, Sun; noon-2.30pm Fri. **Credit** DC, MC, V. Originally a nineteenth-century coffee house, the Fitzroy now trades heavily on its glory days as Fitzrovia's leading bohemian hangout from the 1920s to the '50s. Dylan Thomas was thrown out more than once for practising his 'cats and dogs' ankle-biting trick on unsuspecting ladies, while other regulars included Augustus John and Albert Pierrepoint, the last hangman. The plethora of black-and-white photos on the walls showing the place in its heyday – all decorous high jinks, glassy smiles and pints of wallop – now seem to belong to another world, but the place still has a relaxing, introspective feel that partly compensates for the plasticky seats and ugly games machines. The competitively priced

---

beers include Ayingerbrau lager (£1.78) and Sam Smith's Sovereign (£1.52), while food consists of reliable pub grub (seafood basket £5.75, jumbo cod £5.95).
Games (fruit machine). Tables outdoors (pavement). Vegetarian dishes.

Flutes Wine Bar & Brasserie
61 Goodge Street, W1 (020 7637 0177). Goodge Street tube. **Open** 11.30am-11pm Mon-Fri. **Food served** noon-10pm Mon-Fri. **Credit** DC, MC, V.
Wooden floorboards, romantic lighting and chalkboards give this long, narrow basement a classic wine bar feel. Other distinguishing features are the rows and rows of signed photos (a gallery of luvvies, from Leslie Howard to Kenneth Williams); a varied and inexpensive wine list (£9.95-£19.95 a bottle), including a truly outstanding house white that's fragrant, not too woody and perfectly chilled (Les Pallisages, £2.50 a glass); a good line in cocktails (£3); and chef's specials such as hare terrine (£3.95) and red snapper (£8.95). All in all, an excellent wine bar.
Restaurant. Vegetarian dishes.

Hope
15 Tottenham Street, W1 (020 7637 0896). Goodge Street tube. **Open** 11am-11pm Mon-Sat; noon-10.30pm Sun. **Food served** noon-2.30pm Mon-Fri. **Credit** MC, V.
The Hope's reputation rests squarely on its food: more than a dozen varieties of sausage and a variety of meat pies (all £5.50) are served in the upstairs room. Otherwise, it's a pretty unremarkable place, dominated by a murky oversized TV screen at one end, and by the large empty space in front of the bar that fills with standing after-work drinkers in the early evening. The seating is confined to the perimeter. Hoegaarden (£3.36) and Boddingtons (£2.07) are among the beers on tap.
Comedy (Tue). Function room. Games (fruit machine). Jukebox. No-smoking area. Satellite TV (big screen). Tables outdoors (pavement). Vegetarian dishes.

Jamies
74 Charlotte Street, W1 (020 7636 7556). Goodge Street tube. **Open** 11am-11pm Mon-Fri. **Food served** noon-2.45pm, 6-9.15pm Mon-Fri. **Credit** AmEx, DC, MC, V.
A cavernous wine bar in the heart of TV Land, Jamies is a popular haunt among wealthy young media types. The acres of floor space – with functional wooden tables and zestily painted walls – make Jamies more suitable for groups than couples. Beer comes in the bottle here, not on tap, but there's no faulting the wine list. In addition to the 11 champagnes on offer, there are some 50 varieties of wine (Wolf Blass Chardonnay £3.80 a small glass/£5.45 a large glass, House Rioja £3.95/£5.65). There's also a large selection of club and hot sandwiches, while among the more substantial dishes are charburger (£8.50) and roast cod (£8.95), which may be had in the mezzanine restaurant.
Function rooms. Restaurant. Satellite TV. Tables outdoors (patio). Vegetarian dishes.

Jerusalem
33-34 Rathbone Place, W1 (020 7255 1120). Tottenham Court Road tube. **Open/food served** noon-2am Mon-Thur; noon-3am Fri; 7pm-3am Sat. **Admission** after 10.30pm Mon-Thur £3; Fri, Sat £6. **Credit** AmEx, MC, V.
Walk down the easy-to-miss steps and you'll find yourself in an enormous basement bar done up like a baronial hall, complete with vast refectory tables and settles that seem to have been constructed from the timbers of the Ark. The blood-red velvet curtains and wrought-iron candle holders complement the Dracula's Castle effect, but despite its size,

the bar is surprisingly cosy and the staff disarmingly friendly. The long bar is spectacularly well stocked: the chilled draught Leffe (£2.20 a half, £8 a two-pint pitcher) is particularly recommended, though there are huge arrays of bottled beers, wines and cocktails (£5.50). Given the atmosphere, a roast boar on a spit wouldn't look out of place, though the bar food is generally on the light side (nachos with salsa £7.50, Caesar salad £3.50). A separate restaurant serves up Modern European dishes for those with heartier appetites.
Late licence (Mon-Sat). Music (DJs Mon-Sat). Restaurant. Vegetarian dishes.

King & Queen
1 Foley Street, W1 (020 7636 5619). Goodge Street tube. **Open** 11am-11pm Mon-Fri; 11am-3pm, 7-11pm Sat; noon-3pm, 7-10.30pm Sun. **Food served** 11.30am-2.30pm Mon-Fri. **Credit** MC, V.
Tucked away at the quiet end of Foley Street in Fitzrovia, the King & Queen is that increasingly rare beast: a central London pub that looks as if it has never been – nor, indeed, ever will be – made-over for modern times. Instead, what you see is what you get: a completely straightforward, entirely unpretentious pub – never, in a million years, a bar – although a pub with a history. According to the friendly staff, the upstairs function room hosted Chartist meetings during the movement's heyday in the 1840s, Karl Marx used to drink here, and Bob Dylan played gave one of his earliest London performances when it was a popular folk music venue in the early '60s. It still hosts a monthly folk evening, and serves a good range of beers (Ruddles Best £2.30, Adnams Broadside £2.40) and pub food (pork chops £4.95, steak and Guinness pie £4.30).
Function room. Jukebox. Music (folk club, monthly). Tables outdoors (pavement).

Mash
19-21 Great Portland Street, W1 (020 7637 5555). Oxford Circus tube. **Open** 11am-2am Mon-Sat; 11am-4pm Sun. **Food served** 11am-11pm Mon-Sat, 11am-4pm Sun. **Credit** AmEx, DC, MC, V.
Taking its name from the mixture of grain and water used for brewing rather than the stuff you eat with bangers, Mash is the glitziest of the new bars that have brightened up dreary old Great Portland Street over the last few years. The far end is dominated by Mash's own microbrewery, all gleaming metal behind glass; a sunken alcove to the right is furnished with comfortable leatherette seating and decorated with huge, cunningly doctored photos from the '70s. Own-brand beers (£2.90-£3.20) take pride of place at the bar, with Mash lager even available in an eight-pint mini-keg (£14, takeaway only). Power quenchers (fruit cocktails, basically) are £3.50 a go, and there's a full wine list. Seldom empty, Mash is thronged in the evenings with a mixture of off-duty suits and leisured bright young things. A pricey menu includes eggs Benedict (£8.50) and confit duck pizza (£9.50).
Babies and children (until 8pm). Disabled: toilet. Late licence (Mon-Sat). Music (DJs Wed-Fri). Restaurant. Vegetarian dishes.

Mortimer
37-42 Berners Street, W1 (020 7436 0451). Goodge Street tube. **Open** noon-11pm Mon-Sat. **Food served** noon-3pm, 6-11pm Mon-Sat. **Credit** AmEx, DC, MC, V.
With its vast empty space, sheet-metal bar and almost complete lack of decoration, the Mortimer is impersonality personified. Fortunately, the bar staff are pleasant enough for this not to matter, and the roominess of the place becomes welcome once it starts to fill up – usually with staff from the

London crawling

Postman's round

A Blue Posts crawl is a way of getting from Tottenham Court Road tube to Oxford Circus without suffering one of London's most dismal experiences – Oxford Street. Start facing the entrance to Boot's on the corner of Hanway Street and Tottenham Court Road. Breathe in. Can you smell it? Try again.

On the spot where the chemist stands, there was, until 1998, a shack of a pub called the Blue Posts. It would be a shame to think it has left no trace on the air, no bar towel scent or tang of ghostly spirits. But it's gone, so let's move on. Turn left down Stephen Street, pass the British Film Institute, right into Gresse Street, right again into Rathbone Place. Opposite is **Jerusalem**, a basement bar serving draught Leffe and sustaining meals. Another time: we're working up a thirst. Where Rathbone Place hits Percy Street, take a look at the newsagent on the corner. If you've seen Michael Powell's *Peeping Tom*, it and the rest of the building will be familiar to you. As will Newman Passage, halfway up Rathbone Street on the left. The **Newman Arms** here serves excellent home-made pies, but keep walking. Turn left into Newman Street and our first still-standing **Blue Posts** is on the corner with Eastcastle Street.

You'll note with interest that it's a Sam Smith's pub. Let's be kind and say that Sam Smith's beers are distinctive and unusual. Still, imbibe the dark-wood, leaded-windows, leather-upholstered atmosphere. Karl Marx drank here before you and survived. The Silent Three, a group of novelists led by the hugely talented Robert Irwin, who number considerably more than a trio, meet in the upstairs room once a month. They don't have to put up with the piped music that unsettles the ambience in the main bar. Never mind, press on.

Along Eastcastle Street, right down Berners Street, dashing over Oxford Street into Wardour Street (the Movie Café on the left looks interesting; the Prêt, on the right, doesn't), right into Broadwick Street and our second **Blue Posts** is on the corner with Berwick Street. The contrast between Marx's haunt and this tangerine assemblage of velour benches and formica tables is striking. This working-class local is packed with Soho residents and market traders. The relaxed atmosphere lulls you. Ditto the draught John Smith's and Kronenbourg 1664. It's as good a place as any to lose yourself in contemplation of nomenclature. How did five pubs so near to each other come by the

Blue Posts name? (There's a sixth on Bennet Street off Piccadilly, which we'll leave to one side since it's away from Soho.) Were the Blue Posts what Henry VIII tied his horse to when he came here chasing after animals, crying 'So, ho!'? Did they mark the corners of his hunting ground? Surely not: the present location would have been right smack in the middle.

It gets easier now. Walk south down Berwick Street, running the Walkers Court porno gauntlet, cross Shaftesbury Avenue and enter the **Blue Posts** on the corner of Rupert Court, 'the best pub in the West End' according to a sign. Well, it used to be before its refurbishment several years back, when it attracted a young crowd with its tatty carpets, orange seats and neon signs. Now it's all wooden shelving, Belgian beers (Hoegaarden on tap, others bottled) and the upstairs room only open in the evening, and even then closed for private parties two nights or so a week.

Exit into Rupert Court and go left past PizzaExpress (if you're in need of beer-soakage materials, you could not do better) back on to Wardour. Cross Shaftesbury Avenue and go left down Brewer, turning right into Lexington. If you

didn't grab a pizza, Andrew Edmunds (No.46) is a cosier, costlier alternative. Crane your neck for a nosey in the first-floor offices of Auberon Waugh's *Literary Review* (No.44). Left on to Broadwick, right into Marshall, pausing outside William Blake House; the visionary poet and artist was born on 28 November 1757 in a house on this site. Walk down Ganton Street, crossing Carnaby Street as quickly as you forded Oxford Street's tide of tack. On the corner of Ganton and Kingly is our final **Blue Posts**. It's the least prepossessing of the four, but by now who cares?

The Blue Posts are not about fixtures and fittings but the triumph of imagination over humdrum reality. You make up your own myth, write your own story and maybe, like Blake, glimpse an angel at the bar – especially if you've had a few.
Nicholas Royle

Blue Posts (*p80*) 22 Berwick Street, W1 (020 7437 5008).
Blue Posts (*p80*) 28 Rupert Street, W1 (020 7437 1415).
Blue Posts (*p80*) 18 Kingly Street, W1 (020 7734 1170).
Blue Posts (*no review*) 81 Newman Street, W1 (020 7637 8958).
Jerusalem (*p40*) 33-34 Rathbone Place, W1 (020 7255 1120).
Newman Arms (*p42*) 23 Rathbone Street, W1 (020 7636 1127).

Middlesex Hospital, the pink brickwork of which dominates the view through the huge plate-glass windows. The emphasis is on wine rather than beer (£2.50-£3.60 a glass, £9.20-£27.50 a bottle), with a restaurant-style menu offering the likes of marinated lamb (£8) and rib-eye steak (£12.50). *Babies and children admitted. Disabled: toilet. Restaurant. Tables outdoors (patio). Vegetarian dishes.*

Newman Arms

23 Rathbone Street, W1 (020 7636 1127). Goodge Street tube. **Open** 11.30am-11pm Mon-Fri. **Food served** noon-3pm Mon-Fri; 6-9pm Mon-Thur. **Credit** MC, V.
The Dickensian location – under an archway in a well-worn flagstone alley – and the view through the window of the snug, dark bar suggest a truly outstanding pub. In fact, the place is pretty unremarkable once you're inside, though it's a popular and frequently thronging haunt of predominantly middle-aged businessmen. Given its dull range of beers (Carling £2.20, Stella £2.60), the Newman Arms' real claim to fame is its pies, served in a sedate, panelled upstairs restaurant that was one of the locations for the cult film *Peeping Tom.*
Function room. Restaurant. Vegetarian dishes.

Office

3-5 Rathbone Place, W1 (020 7636 1598). Tottenham Court Road tube. **Open/food served** noon-3am Mon-Fri; 9.30pm-4am Sat. **Admission** after 6pm Wed £5; after 8.30pm Fri £5; Sat £7. **Happy hour** 5-7.30pm Mon-Fri. **Credit** AmEx, MC, V.
Originally named for the benefit of after-work boozers who could quite truthfully ring their spouses to inform them 'I'm at the Office', this is a cavernous basement bar that bears a passing resemblance to the one Jack Nicholson visits in *The Shining.* The effect here, though, is one of cheerful eccentricity, thanks to the spaced-out but welcoming staff, the semi-concealed multicoloured neon lighting (it's curiously relaxing), and the large bunches of pink straws arranged along the bar. Unsurprisingly, the punters are generally on the youthful side; indeed, the place doubles as a nightclub late in the evening. Bottled beers include Beck's (£2.40) and Budweiser (£2.60), while among the lurid-sounding cocktails are Dune Bug Annihilator, Sloe Comfortable Screw and Walking on the Peaches (£3.95 a glass, £11.95 a pitcher).
Babies and children admitted (until 6pm). Late licence (Mon-Sat). Music (DJs Thur-Sat). Vegetarian dishes.

Rising Sun

46 Tottenham Court Road, W1 (020 7636 6530). Goodge Street or Tottenham Court Road tube. **Open/food served** 11am-11pm Mon-Sat; noon-10.30pm Sun. **Credit** AmEx, DC, MC, V.
The dark furnishings and – in the afternoon, at least – quiet hum of conversation suggest that the Rising Sun has been unchanged for decades. Not so: in the 1980s, the place served time as Presley's, an Elvis theme bar. However, times have moved on, and the pub is now 'traditional' again, with the short end of the L-shaped bar your best bet if you want a bit of peace and quiet. The clientele, a mix of office workers and students from the nearby University of London, are well served by an impressive selection of bottled beers, a more familiar draught ales (Theakston Best £2.14, XB £2.28), and a weekly changing selection of four or five guest ales – Thomas Watkins and Three Sheets were among those on tap the night we visited. The food is a cut above standard pub fare: smothered pepper chicken and vegetable and stilton casserole were both £5.95.
Tables outdoors (pavement). TV. Vegetarian dishes.

Sevilla Mía

22 Hanway Street, W1 (020 7637 3756). Tottenham Court Road tube. **Open/food served** 7pm-1am Mon-Sat; 7pm-midnight Sun. **Credit** AmEx, DC, MC, V.
Despite the unprepossessing corridor down to this tiny bar, this is a real escape from central London's mayhem. A flamenco bar with no pandering to modern design, the basement room, with its arches, bull fight posters and scrolled metalwork, houses £3 bottles of San Miguel, Cruz Campo or Amber, or a £12.90 jug of sangria with which to wash down the tapas. Bench seating and chairs surround small wooden tables set on marble patchwork floors, while a drunken crowd recall past moments in the bar with raucous nostalgia. Clearly popular with homesick Spaniards, its late licence also draws those in the know after closing time. Very basic and totally charming.
Late licence. Vegetarian dishes.

Ship

134 New Cavendish Street, W1 (020 7636 6301). Goodge Street or Oxford Circus tube. **Open/food served** 11am-11pm Mon-Fri. **No credit cards.**
An oasis of good cheer in the lee of the Telecom Tower, the Ship comes complete with Jolly Roger signboard and acres of nautical paraphernalia. The neon-lit bar has an excellent range of beers (Bass £2.40, Carling £2.50), dispensed by a largely Irish staff to a loyal and local clientele: there's little passing trade at this subterranean end of New Cavendish Street. The only disappointment is the food, which consists mainly of pre-wrapped sandwiches in a glass case disturbingly reminiscent of a British Rail snack bar. That apart, the Ship is a good, modest pub that's worth making a detour for.
Function room. Games (fruit machine). Tables outdoors (pavement). TV. Vegetarian dishes.

Social

5 Little Portland Street, W1 (020 7636 4992). Oxford Circus tube. **Open/food served** noon-midnight Mon-Sat; 5-11pm Sun. **Credit** MC, V.
At last there's a decent indie music bar in the Portland Street area. And the Social lives up to its name without being horribly self-conscious about it. On the ground floor a narrow pine-panelled room with tables fixed diner-style along the wall is usually crammed with resting clubbers. Draught and bottled beers are expensive (draught Guinness is £2.70 and Miller £2.60, a bottle of Budvar is £2.80, although you can buy eight of them for the price of six if you're in a party mood) and there's usually a blond beer, a real ale and cider on draught as well. Cocktails are better value, all at £4.80: our Margarita was the real McCoy and the Jamaican Mule (rum, ginger beer and lime) also deserved some respect. Bar food includes sandwiches (£2.70) and student standbys like eggy bread (£2) and fish fingers with baked beans (£3). Downstairs there's another darker, slightly less cramped bar where the decor gets more industrial and the DJ-driven sounds that bit harder and louder. All in all, well worth a visit.
Function room. Jukebox. Music (DJs Mon-Sat, live music £3 Wed). Vegetarian dishes.

Also in the area...

Fitz & Firkin 240 Great Portland Street, W1 (020 7388 0588).
Flintlock & Firkin 108A Tottenham Court Road, W1 (020 7387 6199).
Ha! Ha! Bar & Canteen 43-51 Great Titchfield Street, W1 (020 7580 7252).
Lees Bag (Davys) 4 Great Portland Street, W1 (020 7636 5287).

Social

Fulham SW6, SW10/Parsons Green SW6

Atlas

16 Seagrave Road, SW6 (020 7385 9129/www.theatlas-fulham.co.uk). West Brompton tube. **Open** noon-11pm Mon-Sat; noon-10.30pm Sun. **Food served** 12.30-3pm, 7-10.30pm Mon-Sat; noon-3pm, 7-10pm Sun. **Credit** DC, MC, V.

Formerly a run-of-the-mill local, the Atlas has recently blossomed into a first-class foodie pub under the aegis of two brothers, one of whom was once chef at Farringdon's **Eagle** (*see p115*). The Mediterranean/Iberian-influenced menu, listed above the fireplace, changes daily. Choices might include Catalan beef casserole, or a tempting Moroccan lamb tagine (both £9), while desserts include exotic cheese dishes, such as one featuring Spanish sheep's milk cheese (£5). Wooden wall benches, school chairs and well-spaced tables create an informal ambience, and regulars rub shoulders with a young, well-heeled crowd, and a smattering of visitors from Earl's Court Exhibition Centre. Beers include Theakston Best and Greene King IPA (both £2.10), and there's a pedigree wine list with a strong selection of European wines (average £11), a smattering of New Worlders and an interesting Argentinian option (£14.50). Come to enjoy fine food and wine, as well as the lovely garden with outside seating in the summer.
Babies and children admitted (until 7pm). Function rooms. Tables outdoors (heated courtyard). Vegetarian dishes.

Bardo

196-198 Fulham Road, SW10 (020 7351 1711). West Kensington tube/14 bus. **Open** 5pm-midnight Mon-Sat. **Food served** 5-10.30pm Mon-Sat. **Credit** AmEx, DC, MC, V.

Sleek and minimalist, with a pick 'n' mix smattering of Asian artefacts, Bardo gives a rather muddled nod to the Eastern aesthetic. Still, there are nice touches, such as the elegant bronze hands on the door handle and Japanese-style pebble-dash decoration around the bar. The Eastern theme is also reflected in the menu, with pan-Asian titbits – vegetable spring rolls (£6.50), a ten-piece sushi box (£8.50) – as well as fuller evening meals. The warm saké (£3) is a perfect antidote to a cold winter evening; apart from that, as well as beer (£3), there's an extensive drinks list with everything from regular spirits to champagne cocktails (£6.50) and Bardo specials, such as a heavenly peach and apple schnapps concoction (£6.50). Seating is limited, so if you're with a party go early and grab a seat in the rear alcove, decked out in (decidedly Western) shocking-pink walls with red sofas. Otherwise, join the young, yuppie-ish crowd at the bar. More like a private club than a cosy local, this is nevertheless a good place for splashing out with friends with something to celebrate.
Games (backgammon). Vegetarian dishes.

Beach Bar

351 Fulham Road, SW10 (020 7351 2939). Earl's Court or South Kensington tube. **Open/food served** 8am-midnight Mon-Fri; 9am-midnight Sat, Sun. **Credit** AmEx, DC, MC, V.

Surfer culture comes to Fulham courtesy of this delightful, unpretentious bar-restaurant and its waiter-posse of bleached-blonde Australian guys. For those interested in surfing of another kind, the Beach also bills itself as an Internet café – although there's only one funky blue iMac available at present. The bar offers draught beers (Budvar, Beck's) at a pricey £2.75, but it shakes up excellent cocktails, such as the mouth-wateringly moreish Mango Splice (£5.95). Behind the

Atlas

bar area is the restaurant, which offers beachside-style bites such as Thai fishcakes (£3.95), potato skins (£2.45), main courses (from around £8), as well as an all day breakfast menu. Snacks can also be ordered at the bar. Go for the cocktails, friendly service and an ambience so mellow you can practically hear the waves lapping at the kerb.
Babies and children admitted. Restaurant. TV.

Blue Bar Café

451 Fulham Road, SW10 (020 7352 8636). Fulham Broadway or Sloane Square tube. **Open** 10am-midnight daily. **Food served** 10am-3pm, 6pm-midnight daily. **Credit** AmEx, DC, MC, V.

With wooden flooring and furniture and inviting sofas, Blue Bar Café offers a more intimate take on the All Bar One concept: pleasant enough to resemble your own sitting room, but also bland enough to resemble everyone else's. The combination of bar drinks and café beverages (herbal tea £1.50) lends a genial air to the place, and both of its two floors seem to fill up quickly with a lively, but not overwhelming, young professional crowd. Choose from a good selection of bottled beers (£2.40), or splash out on cocktails (from £5) that are so generously portioned you might think twice before heading for the upstairs seating. A comfortable, functional venue, but, in the words of one discerning punter, 'a little dull'.
Babies and children admitted. Disabled: toilet. Function room. Restaurant. Tables outdoors (garden). TV. Vegetarian dishes.

Deco

294 Fulham Road, SW10 (020 7351 0044). Earl's Court or Fulham Broadway tube. **Open** 5.30-11pm Mon-Sat. **Food served** 10am-3.30pm, 6-11pm Mon-Sat. **Happy hour** 5.30-7pm Mon-Sat. **Credit** AmEx, DC, MC, V.

All the cod art deco trademarks are here in this dimly lit basement bar: lampshades supported by nubile naked maidens, marble columns and mirrored walls. Tacky and fun rather than tasteful, it's a good escape from the relentless trendyness of the rest of the Fulham Road, and the clientele (young and old) make for mellow drinking companions. But the main reason to come here is the cocktails. If you simply can't decide between a gorgeous frozen-fruit Daiquiri (£5.50) or a white chocolate Martini (£4.50), invent your own mix. Attentive bartenders are on hand to cater to your every whim. If you insist on something simpler, bottled Beck's are £2.50. Snacks such as fried calamari (£3.95) or Thai spring rolls (£4) are available, as well as steaks, baguettes and burgers. Alternatively, the restaurant upstairs has set dinners from £9.95, and an à la carte menu.
Function room. Restaurant. Satellite TV. Tables outdoors (pavement). Vegetarian dishes.

Duke of Cumberland
235 New King's Road, SW6 (020 736 2777). Parson's Green tube. **Open** 11am-11pm Mon-Sat; noon-10.30pm Sun. **Food served** noon-2.30pm, 7-9pm, Mon-Fri; noon-2.30pm Sat; 1-3.30pm Sun. **Credit** MC, V.
On a Friday night the front half of this ornate Edwardian pub was wall-to-wall testosterone, without a woman in sight. A popular haunt for Fulham FC supporters, it can seem a little daunting at first, and if you're looking for something mellower, head for the bistro-style back room. Here, a more subdued professional crowd jostles for space around large wooden tables while downing beers (Young's Special £2.10, or the deliciously rich Young's Winter Warmer for £2.16). There's also a basic wine list (Chardonnay £2.95), but more adventurous (or sweet-toothed) punters should check out the infamous Young's Double Chocolate Brew (£2.29).
Babies and children admitted. Games (fruit machine, table football). Satellite TV (big screen). Tables outdoors (pavement). Vegetarian dishes.

Eight Bells
89 Fulham High Street, SW6 (020 7736 6307). Putney Bridge tube. **Open** 11am-11pm Mon-Sat; noon-10.30pm Sun. **Food served** noon-2.30pm, 6-8pm, daily. **No credit cards**.
Small, snug and kitted out with antique furniture and dark wood panelling that's cosy rather than oppressive, this is a real pubbers' pub. Friendly bar staff enhance the down to earth atmosphere, while an older local crowd mix with strangers and out-of-towners. Come to savour the fine Guinness, as well as Kronenbourg and Foster's (both £2.25). Traditional, hearty pub fare includes cottage pie, steak, and a fabulous sticky toffee pudding (£2) that will have you ditching your fat-free diet in an instant.
Games (fruit machine). Satellite TV. Tables outdoors (pavement). Vegetarian dishes.

Fox & Pheasant
1 Billing Road, SW10 (020 7352 2943). Fulham Broadway tube. **Open** 11am-11pm Mon-Sat; noon-10.30pm Sun. **Food served** noon-2.30pm Mon-Sat. **No credit cards**.
Apart from the TV in the corner, this tiny old pub seems like a throwback to a time when Chelsea really was a village, and to get to London proper involved a schlep via mud track, horse and cart. Traditionally kitted out with a low ceiling, wood panelling and china crockery, the pub is divided into two by a small mullioned bar in the centre. Quiet nights might only see a handful of old-timers knocking back their pints, but Chelsea's ground is a stone's throw away, and during a big game one half of the bar is packed with fans watching the

footie on TV. Fine, lip-smacking Abbot Ale (£2.10) is available on tap, alongside a robust IPA (£2). Traditional home-cooked lunch is available, with nothing over £5.
Games (darts). No piped music or jukebox. Satellite TV. Tables outdoors (garden, pavement). Vegetarian dishes.

Front Room
246 Fulham Road, SW10 (020 7823 3011). Fulham Broadway or South Kensington tube. **Open/food served** noon-11pm Mon-Sat; noon-10.30pm Sun. **Happy hour** 5.30-6.30pm daily. **Credit** AmEx, DC, MC, V.
Although not quite home-from-home, this is definitely an appealing chill-out option after the rigours of a Saturday night. Tuck into the all day breakfast (£5.95) from the comfort of a leather armchair, and if you really want to get into the spirit, there's even a cigar list (from £6). With its huge, blue Matisse-style mural on one wall, and bright, light space, this is a very cosy place to spend a Sunday afternoon. At night it takes on an altogether more frenetic edge, as it fills with a loud, hearty crowd who come for the friendly ambience, TV sports and happy-hour drinks (beer and Margaritas are £1.90). At other times beers cost from £2.60 (draught Stella), cocktails around £3.60. A fun, upbeat local haunt, it's popular with Chelsea rugger types and with doctors and nurses from the Chelsea and Westminster Hospital, just a bleeper call away down the road.
Vegetarian dishes.

Fulham Tup
268 Fulham Road, SW10 (020 7352 1859). Fulham Broadway tube. **Open** noon-11pm Mon-Sat; noon-10.30pm Sun. **Food served** noon-3pm, 6-10pm Mon-Thur; noon-3pm, 6-9pm Fri, Sat; noon-9pm Sun. **Credit** AmEx, MC, V.
On Saturday nights this airy, spacious pub is packed to bursting with a raucous twentysomething crowd 'tubthumping' along to the likes of Chumbawumba and other chart toppers. There are no surprises in the beer department: Marston's Pedigree is £2.20, Guinness and Stella both £2.50. Come Sunday afternoon, calm is restored, as Saturday's revellers nurse their hangovers with a glass of decent Australian red wine (£2.40) and roast lamb (£8.50). Alternatively, you can choose one of several tasty vegetarian options (around £6) and enjoy the decor with a clear conscience: as in other Tup pubs sheep are everywhere, and soft-toy sheep lounge on shelves behind the bar, food is chosen from a 'menewe', the busy staff are kitted out in 'Baa staff' T-shirts, and there's even a sheep clock on the wall.
Babies and children admitted. Disabled: toilet. Satellite TV (big screen). Tables outdoors (pavement). Vegetarian dishes.

Havana
490 Fulham Road, SW6 (020 7381 5005). Fulham Broadway tube. **Open/food served** noon-2am Mon-Sat; noon-10.30pm Sun. **Admission** after 10pm Wed £3; after 11pm Thur £5; after 1pm Fri, Sat £5 after 10pm Fri, Sat £7. **Happy hour** 6-8pm daily. **Credit** AmEx, DC, MC, V.
You half expect to see Carmen Miranda sashaying her way round the dancefloor at this homage to Latin glam and '50s retro kitsch. Fabulously ornate on the outside, opulently tacky on the inside, this is a fun and funky place to drink and dance Latino style. Fake zebra and leopard skins adorn the intimate curved booths, while paper lanterns suffuse the place with a cosy, orange hue. True salsa aficionados give it short shrift, but there's plenty of space to dance, and on weekends the place is bumping to Latin vibes and '70s disco. A couple of Daiquiris or refreshing fruit Caipirinhas (both £4.95) will soon have you swinging along with the best of them. Dos Equis, Bohemia and Hatuey bottled beers are £2.85. Nosh takes the form of tapas (£3.50 a plate) or more substantial fare such as

the smoked chicken and goat's cheese wrap (£6.50) or swordfish in herbs (£9.45). On the night we visited service was slow, and many choices were unavailable; still, for a burst of Latin energy Havana is hard to beat.

Babies and children admitted (until 6pm). Late licence (Mon-Sat). Music (Latin bands Fri, Sat; DJ's nightly; Flamenco guitarist Sun). Restaurant. Vegetarian dishes.

Hollywood Arms

45 Hollywood Road, SW10 (020 7349 9274). South Kensington or Earl's Court tube. **Open/food served** noon-11pm Mon-Sat; noon-10.30pm Sun. **Credit** DC, MC, V.
A traditional Edwardian pub, with a pretty, frosted-window exterior and charming, comfortably frayed insides. Friendly staff, down-to-earth regulars and the rambling layout, extending to a pool room and extra bar upstairs, all contribute to its laid-back, slightly studenty ambience. There's a good range of beers, including Guinness (£2.49) and Beck's (£2.60 on tap, £2.50 a bottle), and a wide range of spirits. There's also a jukebox, wide sports screen (upstairs) and an attractive beer garden at the back. The pub will be closed for a few months for refurbishment from about May 2000.

Function room. Games (fruit machines, pool table). Jukebox. Satellite TV (big screen). Tables outdoors (garden, pavement).

Ifield

59 Ifield Road, SW10 (020 7351 4900). Earl's Court, Fulham Broadway or West Brompton tube. **Open** noon-11pm Mon-Sat; noon-10.30pm Sun. **Food served** noon-11pm Mon-Sat; noon-8pm Sun. **Credit** AmEx MC, V.
A lively, Sloaney pub-restaurant divided into a bar area at the front with a more formal restaurant behind. Decor, with candles, dark wood and subdued furnishings, is restrained and tasteful, but it's the upbeat dance music and bustling staff that give the place its bounce. The well-heeled, slightly cliquey crowd lounges across low leather sofas swigging back Mexican bottled beers (from £2.60), supping Rebellion IPA (£2.30) or sipping Margaritas (£4.25). Alternatively, you can also sit in more intimate curved booths. There's a sizeable wine list, featuring a smattering of Californians alongside European offerings (from around £2.50 a glass), and dessert wines (£4.25 a glass). Food is served in the restaurant and bar area and includes tapas-type offerings (£2.95) as well as Modern European-style larger dishes (around £10). A high-quality hangout.

Babies and children admitted. Function room. Restaurant. Satellite TV. Vegetarian dishes.

Imperial

577 King's Road, SW6 (020 7736 8549/ www.imperial@fulham.co.uk). Fulham Broadway tube. **Open** 11am-11pm Mon-Sat; noon-10.30pm Sun. **Food served** noon-2.30pm, 7-9.30pm Mon-Fri; noon-2.30pm Sat; 12.30-3pm Sun. **Happy hour** 5.30-7pm Mon-Fri (except Chelsea FC home games days). **Credit** AmEx, DC, MC, V.
Blue mermaid-like creatures swim across the wall in a fantasy mural, and flying-saucer light fittings hang from the ceiling, but the bizarre interior decorations here seem to be rather lost in the combined cacophony of blaring MTV rock and the noisy, jeans and T-shirt set that makes up the Imperial's customers. Among its real ales, the malty Imperial (£2.30), brewed by the owners at their brewery in Battersea, is the one to go for, although many of the crowd opt for bottled lagers (Beck's £2.60). There's also a well-stocked wine list, including a better-than-average Chardonnay (£2.50), as well as vodka jelly shots. A rowdy, boozy, studenty atmosphere prevails.

Babies and children admitted (until 3pm). Function rooms. Games (board games). Satellite TV. Tables outdoors (patio/pavement). Vegetarian dishes.

Ink Bar

541A King's Road, SW6 (020 7610 6117). Fulham Broadway tube. **Open/food served** 11am-midnight daily. **Credit** MC, V.
A delightful new bar-restaurant, decked out with ethnic bric-a-brac, bunches of dried flowers hanging from the ceiling, atmospheric lighting and scented candles. Sweet if slightly spacey bar staff serve a wide range of drink such as Freedom Lager (£3) and Stella (£2.50), while spirits include a choice of absinthe shots (£6). The Ink is also one of the few venues in London to offer a variety of organic wines. The enticing food menu also headlines things organic, with dishes ranging from the sublime – butternut pumpkin and saffron risotto (£4.95) – to the earthy, as in Toulouse sausage, mash and onion gravy (£7.95). Downstairs there's another bar, sofas and a DJ booth. Despite a few teething problems (among them manky loos and a phone that didn't work), this place is a colourful, imaginative and welcome antidote to the usual anodyne chain-bar drinking options.

Disabled: toilet. Function rooms. Music (DJs Thur-Sat). Restaurant. Vegetarian dishes.

Jim Thompson's

617 King's Road, SW6 (020 7731 0999/ www.jimthompsons.com). Fulham Broadway tube. **Open** 11am-11pm Mon-Sat; noon-10.30pm Sun. **Happy hour** noon-11pm Mon-Thur, Sun; noon-7pm Fri, Sat. **Food served** noon-11pm Mon-Sat; noon-10.30pm Sun. **Credit** AmEx, DC, MC, V.
Oriental bric-a-brac, Asian artefacts and silk drapes spill from every surface in this branch of a popular bar-restaurant chain. Seating at the bar is limited and food is only served there up to 7pm, so go early. Alternatively, head for one of the tables in the main dining area and choose from an extensive pan-Asian food menu. Lowenbrau (£2.70) and Hoegaarden (£3.50) are among the draught beers on offer. We chose a zesty Woo Woo cocktail (£4.50) and a glass of house white wine. But be warned: wines come in small or large glasses (£2.50, £3.50 respectively), and our waiter ordered and charged us for the more expensive one without giving us the option. When we complained, he told us this was usual practice.

Babies and children admitted. Restaurant. Tables outdoors (garden). Vegetarian dishes.

Legless Ladder

1 Harwood Terrace, SW6 (020 7610 6131). Fulham Broadway tube. **Open** noon-11pm Mon-Sat; noon-10.30pm Sun. **Food served** noon-3pm, 7-10pm Mon-Thur; noon-9pm Fri, Sat; noon-9pm Sun. **Credit** MC, V.
A traditional, down-to-earth drinking hole just off the New King's Road. On a winter Sunday the inviting circular bar, old-fashioned wooden decor and log-burning fire provided welcome respite from the cold. On weekdays, a mellow, local posse comes here for top-notch Boddingtons or a decent pint of Courage Directors (both £2.40). Unfortunately, the pub no longer has its formerly superb Theakston bitter. Sustaining and tasty pub fare is available in the week, and brunch is served on Sunday. On a busy Saturday night, though, the Ladder can fill to bursting with a young, vivacious crowd – and the villagey weekday mood feels a million miles away.

Babies and children admitted (until 6pm). Function room. Music (DJs nightly). Satellite TV. Tables outdoors (garden, marquee). Vegetarian dishes.

Mixology

108-110 New King's Road, SW6 (020 7731 2142). Parsons Green or Putney Bridge tube. **Open** noon-11pm Mon-Sat; noon-10pm Sun. **Food served** noon-3pm,

Kiss a nerd today.

-It's good practice for tonight.

5-9pm, Mon-Thur; noon-3pm, 5-8pm Fri, Sat; noon-8pm Sun. **Credit** DC, MC, V.

At weekends, this recently opened bar buzzes with thumping beats and a young, effervescent crowd. Sofas and bar seats are provided, but most of the action takes place around the bar, where suits rub shoulders with a T-shirts-and-trainers crew. Draught John Smith's Extra Smooth and Foster's are £2.50, bottled beers £2.60. Vodka shots in a variety of flavours (including toffee) are other popular faves (£2). The food menu features pizza (£5) and soups (£2.80), but this is more a place to party (and pull) than to eat.
Tables outdoors (pavement). Satellite TV. Vegetarian dishes.

La Perla

803 Fulham Road, SW6 (020 7471 4895). Parsons Green tube. **Open** 5-11pm Mon-Thur; noon-11pm Fri, Sat; noon-10.30pm Sun. **Food served** 5-10.15pm Mon-Sat; noon-9.45pm Sun. **Credit** AmEx, MC, V.

With over 60 different tequilas (from £2.50 a shot, £4.25 for a Margarita), cocktails galore (around £5) and Modelo Especial and Sol (both £2.75) among the bottled beers, this is the place to come for an authentic Mexican drinking experience. Of the shots, the fruit-flavoured tequilas (£2.75) are the way to go, while on the cocktail front the Divine 'La Perlita' is a winner. If you're a tequila beginner, don't fret – helpful staff will point you in the right direction. There's also a restaurant that serves up modern Mexican cuisine as well as generous snack-sized portions (£3-£9). Bright and airy, with ceiling fans, Mexican-style murals and Latin beats, this is a fun and popular hangout, and on a weekday night it filled quickly with a mix of officefolk and a youngish, easygoing local crowd.
Babies and children admitted (high chairs). Restaurant. Vegetarian dishes.

Pharaoh & Firkin

90 Fulham High Street, SW6 (020 7731 0732). Putney Bridge tube. **Open** noon-11pm Mon-Sat; noon-10.30pm Sun. **Food served** noon-10pm Sun-Thur; noon-8.30pm Fri, Sat. **Credit** AmEx, DC, MC, V.

Everything is a little larger than life at this recently revamped member of the Firkin family. The soaring ceiling looks down on a spacious, drinking area that encompasses both a mezzanine level and a split-level lounge complete with huge, plush sofas and art deco-style windows. Despite the country-club trappings, this place aspires to be part of the gastropub scene, and a lively and noisy twentysomething crowd competes to be heard over the stream of unflinchingly loud '80s compilation hits. Standard chain-pub food (chicken/Thai curry £5.45, broccoli pasta bake £4.60) is ordered at the bar and brought to your table. Since the pub's own Firkin brew became history the main draught ales are Green King IPA (£1.95) and Marston's Pedigree (£2.20), and the house wine (red or white Elm Grove) is fine at a reasonable £6.50 a bottle.
Disabled: toilet. Games (football table, fruit machine). Jukebox. Music (live Fri). Satellite TV (big screens). Vegetarian dishes.

Po Na Na Fez

222 Fulham Road, SW10 (020 7352 5978/ www.ponana.com). Earl's Court or Fulham Broadway tube/14 bus. **Open/food served** 8.30pm-2am Mon-Sat. **Admission** after 10pm £3-£5. **Credit** AmEx, MC, V.

Hip young things gather to drink, eat and dance in this characterful late-night basement club, which looks as if it's been airlifted from the set of *Casablanca*. Exotic neo-Moroccan decor, low lighting and hideaway-grotto seating make it a

perfect choice for a romantic date, but there are also nightly DJs and space aplenty to shake your booty during those less intimate moments. The enclosed seating areas also make it a great place to come with a group of friends who want to party, play pool and compare cocktails (£6). Be sure to try the Fez speciality shot, the fruity and colourful One-Eyed Parrot (£3). Beck's and Tiger are among the bottled beers (all £2.50). But note, there's an entrance charge after 10pm.
Games (pool table). Late licence. Music (DJs Mon-Sat). Vegetarian dishes.

Shoeless Joe's

555 King's Road, SW6 (020 7610 9346/ www.shoelessjoes.co.uk). Fulham Broadway tube. **Open/food served** 10am-midnight Mon-Wed; 10am-1am Thur-Sat; 10am-5pm Sun. **Admission** (club) after 9pm Fri, Sat, £5. **Happy hour** 5-8pm Thur. **Credit** AmEx, DC, MC, V.

Shoeless Joe's is trying to shed its sports bar image, but when Chelsea play away this is still the destination of choice for fans who cram into the blue-painted downstairs bar to follow the game on the wide-wall screen. Otherwise, the place heats up around 11pm most nights, with a little help from DJs (Thur-Sat). According to one barman, weekends here 'get pretty crazy'. Apart from the sports crowd, the downstairs bar attracts a clean-cut, mild-mannered lot (some of whom look like they've not long had their first-ever drink), while the bar and restaurant above cater to the smart-suit and briefcase brigade. There's a good range of bottled beers, such as San Miguel (£3). Shooters are £4 and cocktails, served with panache by very sociable bar-people, £5. The jaw-droppingly potent Flaming Lamborghini (£5) certainly perked us up. This could be because only double shots are served.
Babies and children admitted (until 9pm). Disabled: toilet. Function room. Late licence. Music (club downstairs Thur-Sat). No-smoking area. Restaurant. Satellite TV (video wall). Vegetarian dishes.

White Horse

1-3 Parsons Green, SW6 (020 7736 2115/ www.whitehorse@breworld.com). Parsons Green tube. **Open** 11am-11pm Mon-Sat; 11am-10.30pm Sun. **Food served** noon-3pm, 5.30-10pm Mon-Fri; 11am-10pm Sat, Sun. **Credit** AmEx, MC, V.

An eclectic, slightly arty crowd of all ages (plus the occasional Dalmatian) pack this warm and welcoming pub, something of a Chelsea institution. The main bar area has recently been extended to create a new dining space, which, with its original timber beams, candles and quirky, wooden furniture, makes a charming addition to an already atmospheric drinking hole. Food can be served in either area, and the menu is worth perusing: portions are generous, and on a cold winter night the chicken noodle soup (£3.50) came like manna from heaven. There is a 100-strong wine list, featuring Ridge and Cloudy Bay wines (from £2.50 a glass), and a fair selection of dessert wines (£3.50 a glass). The pub's real *raison d'être*, though, is its beers. There are 57 different bottled beers in stock (Belgian Trappist beers feature strongly), and over 300 draught ales are served in the course of a year, including, among the 'regulars', the excellent Harvey's Sussex Bitter (£2.20). Every November the pub hosts an Old Ales Festival, when over 60 traditional ales can be sampled, and if you can't wait until then, the White Horse also holds 'mini-beer festivals' every couple of months, with themes such as 'the beauty of hops' or wheat beers. Helpful, friendly staff enhance the bonhomie.
Babies and children admitted. Function room. Games (fruit machine). No-smoking area (restaurant only). Restaurant. Tables outdoors (garden). Vegetarian dishes.

Na Zdrowie.
See page 50.

Also in the area...

All Bar One 587-591 Fulham Road, SW6
(020 7471 0611); 311-313 Fulham Road, SW10
(020 7349 1751).
Café Flo 676 Fulham Road, SW6 (020 7371 9673).
Café Med 2 Hollywood Road, SW10 (020 7823 3355).
Café Rouge 855 Fulham Road, SW6
(020 7371 7600).
Fine Line 236 Fulham Road, SW10
(020 7376 5827).
Pitcher & Piano 214 Fulham Road, SW10
(020 7352 9234); 871-873 Fulham Road, SW6
(020 7736 3910).
Ruby in the Dust 53 Fulham Broadway, SW6
(020 7385 9272).
Slug & Lettuce 474 Fulham Road, SW6
(020 7385 3209).

Holborn WC1, WC2

Cittie of Yorke

22 High Holborn, WC1 (020 7242 7670). Chancery Lane or Holborn tube. **Open** 11.30am-11pm Mon-Sat. **Food served** noon-9.30pm Mon-Sat. **Credit** AmEx, DC, MC, V.
Three bars in one, the Cittie of Yorke attracts a lively crowd of legal eagles and office types, plus a smattering of tourists. There's been a pub on this site since Chaucer was a lad, but the present Gothic pile was built only a century ago and spent much of its life as the original Hennekeys wine bar. The main room houses what is reputedly the longest bar in the world. Running across the opposite wall are some interesting partitioned booths: designed specially for legal conferring, each has just enough room for four people and their briefs. There's a smaller bar at the front, plus a vaulted wine bar downstairs. Food is standard pub grub at around a fiver, with bar snacks (olives, chips, garlic bread) from £1.50 to £4. Being a Sam Smith pub, the draught beer is theirs and a lot cheaper than you'll find in rival pubs (Old Brewery Bitter £1.52).
Babies and children admitted (downstairs). Function rooms. Games (darts, fruit machine). No-smoking area. Tables outdoors (pavement). Vegetarian dishes.

Fine Line

77 Kingsway, WC2 (020 7405 5004). Holborn tube. **Open** noon-11pm Mon-Fri. **Food served** noon-10pm Mon-Wed; noon-9pm Thur, Fri. **Credit** AmEx, DC, MC, V.
Fine Line is Fuller's answer to the modern theme bar, à la All Bar One and Pitcher & Piano, and being at heart a regional brewery, it does a pretty good job. The decor is typically polished pine, pale peach walls, with splashes of bold reds, blues and purples to remind you that you're in a bar. Most of the space is taken up by restaurant-style tables, but there's seating at the bar – which can be annoying if you're trying to squeeze in to get served – and on very comfortable sofas and armchairs. We've yet to find a discourteous server in a Fine Line (which is more than you can say for most of its rivals) and customers tend to be twenty- and thirtysomethings who like a little style with their Sauvignon. Wines start at £2.70 for a 175ml glass, £3.60 for 250ml and £10.50 a bottle; house cocktails are £4.25 and London Pride is £2.50 a pint. The food tends towards Modern European and includes delights such as ricotta, spinach and nutmeg tortelloni (£6.50), field mushroom, Gryère and red onion tart (£6) and beef and applewood burger with chips (£6.50).
Babies and children admitted (noon-3pm). Disabled: toilet. Music (DJ Thur). Restaurant. Vegetarian dishes.

King's Arms

11A Northington Street, WC1 (020 7405 9107). Chancery Lane or Russell Square tube. **Open** 11.30am-11pm Mon-Fri. **Food served** noon-2.30pm Mon-Fri. **Credit** AmEx, DC, MC, V.
In the winter, the coal fire is as welcoming as the bar staff at this unpretentious old-style pub, in the northern fringes of the Holborn legal area. There are a couple of well-kept real ales – Marston's Pedigree and Wadworth 6X (both £2) – as well as the usual lagers and a reasonable choice of wines. The decor is strictly old school: hanging drapes, regimentally patterned carpets and clusters of table-and-stool nests. Upstairs are two function rooms that are available to drinkers if they've not been hired out, while the lunchtime bar food covers familiar ground (filled jacket potatoes from £2, sausage and mash £3.75, lasagne £3.50).
Babies and children admitted (separate room). Function rooms. Games (darts). No-smoking area. Satellite TV. Tables outdoors (pavement). Vegetarian dishes.

Na Zdrowie

11 Little Turnstile, WC1 (020 7831 9679). Holborn tube. **Open** noon-11pm Mon-Fri; 6-11pm Sat. **Food served** noon-9pm Mon-Fri; 6-9pm Sat. **Credit** MC, V.
Lovers of vodka and all things Polish will love this small bar tucked away in the little rat-run that links High Holborn with Kingsway. The drinks list includes Luksusowa (clean-tasting potato vodka), Sliwowica (dry plum spirit), kosher vodkas, tea rum (to drink with tea) and EB Polish lager. Spirits are priced £1.50-£2 a shot, beers £2-£3. The menu is similarly ethnic and changes on a regular basis; expect plenty of stews, priced at under £5 a plate. The service is fast and friendly, and drinkers cover the spectrum of Holborn boozers: film people slumming it, messengers pretending to be MDs, office workers out on the razzle and students from the LSE.
Tables outdoors (pavement). Vegetarian dishes.

Princess Louise

208 High Holborn, WC1 (020 7405 8816). Holborn tube. **Open** 11am-11pm Mon-Fri; noon-11pm Sat. **Food served** noon-9pm Mon-Sat. **Credit** AmEx, DC, MC, V.
If Victorian pub interiors turn you on, prepare for an orgasm at this wonderful old pub in the British Museum section of High Holborn. The tall, engraved glass mirrors, dark red and gold moulded ceiling, intricately carved and fixed woodwork and magnificent horseshoe-shaped bar resemble a set from *Nicholas Nickleby*. The Princess Louise used to be a freehouse, but since it has been taken over by Samuel Smith the choice of beers is now more limited. However, with Old Brewery Bitter at just £1.52 and Ayingerbrau at £1.78, objections from the drinkers – a scrum of office workers and their admirers – are muted. Typical pub food is available for lunch (soup £1.25, to steak at £10.25), with snacks on offer in the evening.
Function room. No piped music or jukebox. Tables outdoors (pavement). Vegetarian dishes.

Three Cups

21-22 Sandland Street, WC1 (020 7831 4302). Chancery Lane or Holborn tube. **Open** 11am-11pm Mon-Fri. **Food served** noon-3pm Mon-Fri. **No credit cards.**
The Three Cups was recently given a bit of a facelift, but don't worry: it's still the same friendly pub under the new cream and deep red paint, the tasteful drapes and the patterned carpet. The clientele is an eclectic mix: solicitors, barristers and their staff (this is the heart of Holborn's legal area, after all), students from the nearby art school, and a smattering of

posties and blue-collar workers. This being a Young's pub, the beer is good (bitter £1.95) and there's a fine array of decent wines to look through (from £2.50 a glass). Lunchtime food is above average: expect dishes such as Cumberland sausages, potatoes and gravy for under a fiver.
Function room. No piped music or jukebox. Tables outdoors (pavement). TV. Vegetarian dishes.

Also in the area...

All Bar One 58 Kingsway, WC2 (020 7269 5171).
Bung Hole (Davys) Hand Court, 57 High Holborn, WC1 (020 7831 8365).
Fulmar & Firkin 51 Parker Street, WC2 (020 7405 0590).
Jamies 50-54 Kingsway, WC2 (020 7405 9749).
Pitcher & Piano 42 Kingsway, WC2 (020 7404 8510).

Holland Park W11

Academy
57 Princedale Road, W11 (020 7221 0248). Holland Park tube. **Open** noon-11pm Mon-Fri; 7-11pm Sun; noon-3.30pm, 7-10.30pm Sun. **Food served** noon-3.30pm, 6.30-10.30pm daily. **Credit** MC, V.
Attracting well-heeled, middle-aged casuals, this school of good food and drink is a modest, unpretentious bistro-bar. Wooden Venetian blinds shut out the street, and whitewashed walls are relieved by a handful of oil paintings, with only a framed England rugger shirt to remind you of the Sloaney culture hereabouts. Courage Best is served alongside five kegged beers, and a huge bar-side basin chills a popular and well-priced collection of white wines to go with their red counterparts (house wines £2.35 a glass). There is a deceptively simple food menu, which changes weekly, offering such mains as chilli con carne and seafood paella for around £8. There are a host of nibbly, deli-like starters, and salads. Business is unsurprisingly brisk, and service highly solicitous.
Babies and children admitted (until 9pm). Tables outdoors (garden, pavement). Vegetarian dishes.

Castle
100 Holland Park Avenue, W11 (020 7313 9301). Holland Park tube. **Open** 11am-11pm Mon-Sat; noon-10.30pm Sun. **Food served** 12.30-3pm, 6.30-10pm Mon-Fri; 11am-10pm Sat; noon-10pm Sun. **Credit** MC, V.
With a polo-necked DJ playing 1960s car-chase music, the Castle is a wannabe hip and groovy joint attracting flash cats about town. However, its site on this unglamorous thoroughfare works against it, as do the cumbersome chain-pub furniture and overly bright lighting, which extinguishes the glow of scattered candles. This and the fact that three of the beers (Pride, Bass and Staropramen) were off on the night of our visit mean it may be some time before it fulfils its hipster ambitions. Perhaps at lunch the standard gastropub menu (lamb shank, battered cod, bangers and mash, all £6-£10) draws more interest, but this is one Castle that needs to fortify its ideas.
Function room. Music (DJs Thur-Sat). Tables outdoors. Vegetarian dishes.

Julie's Wine Bar
137 Portland Road, W11 (020 7727 7985). Holland Park tube. **Open/food served** noon-11.30pm Mon-Sat; noon-10.30pm Sun. **Credit** AmEx, MC, V.

In the heart of sleepy residential Holland Park, this is a quiet, intimate retreat for local residents and an ideal venue for conducting extra-marital affairs. The wine bar has a pretentiously sophisticated café-bistro atmosphere, and is spread over two floors prettily decorated with a jumble of antiques, fine oriental fretwork and assorted hanging plants. The *sotto voce* atmosphere is cradled by a wine list of simple global classics (from £2.95 a glass) and the food is à la mode with sushis and salads. It's never exactly crowded, as customers trickle in and out all day for morning coffee, afternoon tea and evening champagne.
Babies and children admitted (crèche Sun). Function rooms. Restaurant. Tables outdoors (pavement). Vegetarian dishes.

Ladbroke Arms
54 Ladbroke Road, W11 (020 7727 6648). Holland Park tube. **Open** 11am-11pm Mon-Sat; noon-10.30pm Sun; *winter* 11am-3pm, 5.30-11pm Mon-Fri; 11am-11pm Sat; 11am-10.30pm Sun. **Food served** noon-2.30pm, 7-9.45pm Mon-Sat; noon-3pm, 7-9.45pm Sun. **Credit** MC, V.
Extensively refurbished, this is a great pub cleansed of all its former character. Done up to look like a country-hotel lounge, it has a green tartan carpet, cream-coloured woodwork, gilt-framed mirrors and inoffensive watercolours, plus a display of olive oil and other condiments to complete the Chiantishire look. The idea is to make better use of the space, with a broad front room spanning the width of the handsome building, but, with the bar tucked in a corner and a narrow, airless corridor squeezed in by the loos, the rethink seems only partially successful. Well-kept ales (Tiger, Directors, Abbott, all £2.20), like the wine selection, remain top-notch and food is at the upper end of the gastropub spectrum with risottos, pastas, seafood and char-grills from £6 to £12. The gas-heated outside terrace can be adopted by those who want to turn their back on the refurbishment and pretend that time has stood still.
Tables outdoors (terrace). Vegetarian dishes.

Prince of Wales
14 Princedale Road, W11 (020 7313 9321). Holland Park tube. **Open** noon-11pm Mon-Wed, Fri, Sat; noon-1am Thur; noon-10.30pm Sun. **Food served** 6-9.30pm Mon-Sat; noon-3pm Sun. **No credit cards**.
It may seem like a miracle that such an unpretentious local could survive in such an exclusive area, but there is more to Holland Park than toffs with a taste for high security and organic butchers. Run by a good-humoured Spanish lady, the PoW satisfies a variety of different needs with a pool table, satellite TV and wholesome pub grub, served to the three sectors round the central bar. Although the decor is a rather tacky faux-Victoriana, it attracts a wide, chatty social spectrum. Standard pub beverages (London Pride £2, Grolsch £2.40) refresh the palate, and there's a large beer yard in which kids can exhaust themselves by running round in circles.
Babies and children admitted. Disabled: toilet. Games (fruit machines, table football, pool table). Jukebox. Late licence (Thur). Satellite TV (big screen). Tables outdoors (garden). Vegetarian dishes.

Kensington W8

Abingdon
54 Abingdon Road, W8 (020 7937 3339). High Street Kensington tube. **Open** noon-11pm Mon-Sat; 12.30-10.30pm Sun. **Food served** 12.30-2.30pm, 6.30-11.30pm, Mon-Sat; 12.30-2.30pm, 6.30-10.30pm Sun. **Credit** AmEx, MC, V.

This uncluttered antechamber to the ever-popular Abingdon restaurant, on the other side of two swooping glass doors, is a short-stay wine bar. Decoration is in uncontroversial shades of cream, with a couple of chequered sofas and high stools – plus the odd bit of art to break up the walls rather than expand the mind. The choice of 30 wines for £2.75 a glass is as attractively varied as the bottled-beer selection is minimal. Patronising this bar in more ways than one are rubicund old duffers, permed wives, a smattering of four-wheel drive casuals and assorted suits. Also a pleasant stop for a tea or coffee after a hard day's shopping on the High Street.
Babies and children admitted (high chairs). Restaurant. Tables outdoors (pavement). Vegetarian dishes.

Britannia

1 Allen Street, W8 (020 7937 1864). High Street Kensington tube. **Open** 11am-11pm Mon-Sat; noon-10.30pm Sun. **Food served** noon-3pm, 6.30-9.30pm daily. **Credit** MC, V.
A peculiar mix of the old and the new, this pleasant little pub is still redolent of the old English class structure, with a place for everyone and everyone in their place. Hence the smart, white-shirted bar staff observe proper decorum for both the red-faced old colonels reminiscing about Rommel and the tradesmen working for local gentry. The bar divides up similarly between two original 1930s wood-panelled front bars, and a modern extension to the rear that hosts functions and quiz nights. The price of house bitter (Young's) also reflects the class divide; £1.87 a pint in the public bar, £1.92 in the saloon.
Babies and children admitted (conservatory). Games (fruit machine, video game). No-smoking conservatory (lunch only). TV. Vegetarian dishes.

Café Rouge

2 Lancer Square, Kensington Church Street, W8 (020 7938 4200). High Street Kensington tube. **Open** 10am-11pm Mon-Sat; 10am-10.30pm Sun. **Food served** 10am-11pm Mon-Sat; 10am-10.30pm Sun. **Credit** AmEx, MC, V.
This odd-shaped building has been described as 'brutish', but we find it rather agreeable in a grotesque kind of way. Inside the central motif appears to be a spiral and the peculiar shape of the space means that there are plenty of curved edges and circular features. As with many of the chain's other branches, blonde wood is much in evidence; add to this a mock yellow marble floor and cream walls and you've got a light and airy space with a vaguely Gallic flavour. The beers are mainly bottled (Stella, Beck's and Heineken, all £2.60) and a rather more extensive wine list gets going at £2.50 a glass, £9.45 a bottle. The menu is the usual mix of well-chosen French-Mediterranean dishes – moules marinière (£5.25/£9.25), penne au pesto rouge (£3.95/£6.50) and poulet Méditerranéenne (£8.95) – and the core clientele appear to be solvent thirtysomethings in couples and groups.
Babies and children admitted (children's menu, high chairs). Disabled: toilet. Function room. No-smoking areas. Restaurant. Tables outdoors (pavement, terrace). Vegetarian dishes.

Churchill Arms

119 Kensington Church Street, W8 (020 7727 4242). High Street Kensington or Notting Hill tube.
Open 11am-11pm Mon-Sat; noon-10.30pm Sun.
Food served noon-2.30pm, 6-9.30pm Mon-Sat; noon-2.30pm Sun. **Credit** DC, MC, V.
Seldom in the field of west London drinking have so many owed so much to one pub. Heavily themed around the orator statesman, the Churchill has long set the standards among Kensington's traditional pubs. Aside from the Churchill

memorabilia and traditional pub trappings (mullioned windows, copper knick-knacks and a roaring fire), there are respectable wines, lovingly tended ales (London Pride £2.05, Chiswick £1.80) and service that is a model of libatory performance. However, for all of the pub's proclaimed Englishness, posters of Irish football teams serve to remind us that like many of England's finest institutions this Fuller's pub is Irish-run. Not only this, there is another multicultural twist in the conservatory's Thai restaurant. Here sardonic oriental wit spices the service as much as their chillis spice the classic Thai dishes, for around £5.50 each.
Babies and children admitted. Games (fruit machine). No piped music or jukebox. Restaurant. Satellite TV. Vegetarian dishes.

Cuba

11-13 Kensington High Street, W8 (020 7938 4137). High Street Kensington tube. **Open/food served** noon-2am Mon-Sat; 2-10.30pm Sun. **Happy hour** noon-8.30pm Mon-Sat; 2-8.30pm Sun. **Credit** AmEx, DC, MC, V.
Cuban colour schemes of ochre and turquoise, not to mention Havana drinking habits of rum and cocktails, have once more come back into fashion and so ensured the survival of this long-standing Latin cocktail bar. The formula hasn't changed down the years, although the Latin club offering salsa lessons downstairs goes from strength to strength. Both wine and bottled beers are faithful to their Latin American roots, but Cuba is best exploited for its cocktail list (generally £4.50/£4.95) and its happily extended happy hours. However, since Cuba also serves tapas and other Latin dishes in the dining area at the back, its late licence makes it handy after-hours, too.
Babies and children admitted (restaurant only). Dance class (Salsa Mon-Wed; Samba Thur). Late licence (Mon-Sat). Music (Latin nightly). Restaurant. Vegetarian dishes.

Devonshire Arms

37 Marloes Road, W8 (020 7937 0710). High Street Kensington or Gloucester Road tube. **Open** 11am-11pm Mon-Sat; 11am-10.30pm Sun. **Food served** noon-3pm, 6-9pm daily. **Credit** AmEx, DC, MC, V.
Although it's a uniform Nicholson's pub with standard fittings, the big windows of this handsome local in a Kensington terrace keep it bright and high ceilings keep it airy, while a small, hedged-off, gas-heated terrace is still brighter and airier. For the more activity-minded there's darts, fruit machines and bar billiards. A basic pub-grub menu of pie and chips is being supplemented with a range of French, Italian and vegetarian dishes, all reasonably priced at around £5-£6. So all in all, with alcoved seating inside and a snug bar with its own period fireplace, this is a commendably diverse retreat. Apart from basic wines, the star attractions are the four real ales (including Burton Ale and Adnams Southwold for £2.20, and London Pride at £2.30).
Babies and children admitted (until 6pm). Games (fruit machine, pool, video golf). Satellite TVs. Tables outdoors (garden). Vegetarian dishes.

Goolies

21 Abingdon Road, W8 (020 7938 1122). High Street Kensington tube. **Open** 12.30-3pm, 6-11pm daily.
Food served 12.30-3pm, 6-10.30pm daily.
Credit AmEx, DC, MC, V.
It has to be Antipodean, because no Englishman would ever name a wine bar after his gonads. But far from being a ballsy, macho environment, soft lighting takes the edge off the potentially harsh postmodern design, mixing stone, metal, wood and fabrics. On the night of our visit, the clientele were largely at the sales end of suitdom, but an ambient

atmosphere prevailed. This was fuelled by a robust list of New World wines (house white £2.75). Suitable for either quiet quaffing or aperitifs before tackling the menu in the sedate restaurant on the upper level at the back, which centres on kangaroo and Pacific Rim delicacies.
Babies and children admitted. Restaurant. Vegetarian dishes.

Hillgate
24 Hillgate Street, W8 (020 7727 8543). Notting Hill Gate tube. **Open/food served** 11am-11pm Mon-Sat; noon-10.30pm Sun. **Credit** MC, V.
Don't be deceived: this lively bar prettified with potted plants on the outside and books, illustrations and elderly crockery within may look like a cosy snug, but this is just a cover for its rowdier and more eccentric regulars. Also, the TV in the small back bar and big screen in the front bar, not to mention its regularly busy-ness, make it difficult to seal yourself off for a meditative pint or a quiet read. Wines are fair and beers include Abbot Ale (£2.30) and Webster's Yorkshire Bitter (£1.90), while food centres on pies, chips and sandwiches. But this is not a destination for ceremonious eaters or drinkers.
Babies and children admitted. Disabled: toilet. Satellite TV (big screen). Vegetarian dishes.

Scarsdale
23A Edward Square, W8 (020 7937 1811). High Street Kensington tube. **Open** noon-11pm Mon-Sat; noon-10.30pm Sun. **Food served** noon-3pm, 6-9.45pm daily. **Credit** AmEx, DC, MC, V.
Now that it's been refurbished with the good sense to preserve its qualities and improve its shortcomings, the Scarsdale is perhaps the best pub in Kensington – if you can accept the hoity-toity casuals who compose the clientele. With gilt-framed mirrors and oil paintings around a coal-effect fire, along with modest bits of statuary and fake topiary, the management has created an England-en-Provence feel – after all, Edward Square was built as barracks during the Napoleonic wars. The colour scheme has been updated, too, while the handsome bar remains illuminated by broad, cut-glass windows overlooking a pretty, gas-heated terrace. The dining area inside has been smartened up along with the menu (particularly strong on Sunday lunch). With bar snacks (ciabatta rolls, nachos and baked spuds) for £5 or less, good ales (Courage Best, Directors and 6X) and a worldwide wine selection, this pub is better than ever.
Babies and children admitted (restaurant only). Restaurant. Tables outdoors (garden). Vegetarian dishes.

The Tenth Bar
Royal Garden Hotel, 2-24 Kensington High Street, W8 (020 7937 8000/www.royalgdn.co.uk). High Street Kensington tube. **Open** noon-2.30pm, 5.30-11pm Mon-Sat. **Credit** AmEx, MC, V.
From this bar on the tenth floor of the Royal Garden Hotel, on a clear day, you can see as far as the Millennium Dome. This is surely one of the most spectacular views in London, covering everything from Kensington Palace, below left, around to Primrose Hill, the Telecom Tower and the Albert Hall, on the right. However, unless you have a taste for anonymous hotels, there's little else to recommend it. Done up in a jazzy, modernist style with syncopated colours in the carpet and furnishings, it offers service that's impeccable to the point of being timid. Meanwhile, a pianist is condemned to play the world's blandest tunes on a grand piano, and drinks centre on classic English cocktails (from £7.50).
Disabled: toilet. Music (live jazz 8pm Sat in restaurant). Restaurant. Vegetarian dishes.

Windsor Castle
114 Campden Hill Road, W8 (020 7243 9551). Kensington High Street or Notting Hill Gate tube. **Open** noon-11pm Mon-Sat; noon-10.30pm Sun. **Food served** noon-10.30pm Mon-Sat; noon-10pm Sun. **Credit** AmEx, MC, V.
A once-great pub, but many of its greatest characteristics have been eroded by time and redevelopment. Even the quality beers, wines and food that once marked it out among pubs in the area have fallen behind the times. A calorific menu, relieved by the odd salad, offers better value than quality, but a bowl of chips or cold sausage and mustard makes an ideal bar snack. The beer (London Pride £2.25, Bass £2.20) is usually up to scratch, and the Sloaney clientele are honoured with a decent set of wines (house wine £2.90 a glass). Meanwhile, the handsome garden is still good, but making room for a bigger kitchen has shorn it of much of its character. Inside, at least the fabulous 1930s oak panelling connecting the three snug bars remains.
No piped music or jukebox. No smoking area (lunchtime). Satellite TV. Tables outdoors (garden). Vegetarian dishes.

Also in the area...

Café Flo 127-129 Kensington Church Street, W8 (020 7727 8142).
Dôme 35A Kensington Court, Kensington High Street, W8 (020 7937 6655).
Po Na Na Souk Bar 20 Kensington Church Street, W8 (020 7795 6656).

King's Cross N1, WC1/ Euston NW1

Backpacker
126 York Way, N1 (020 7278 8318/www.thebackpacker. co.uk). King's Cross tube/rail. **Open** 7pm-2am Fri, Sat; 3.30pm-midnight Sun. **Happy hour** 8-10pm Fri, Sat. **No credit cards**.
If you don't know what to expect from this infamous Antipodean booze-dunnie, the doormen soon put you in the picture: 'People in there are seriously smashed. You will get knocked into and drinks will probably be spilled. Are you okay with that?' We were. The place doesn't look like much: it's basically a barn for hearty partiers. Booze-sodden straw covers the floor in clumps, and there's very little to sit or lean on; music – anything from Meatloaf to Tavares – is extra loud, and booze dirt-cheap. Pints of Foster's, Kronenbourg, Stella and Holsten cost £2, bottles cost £2.50. Sawdust, dancing, drinking and spillage: the Backpacker is so specific in its image of fun, it could almost be a fetish.
Late licence. Music (DJs Fri-Sun). Tables outdoors (courtyard).

Head of Steam
1 Eversholt Street, NW1 (020 7383 3359/ www.headofsteam.co.uk). Euston tube/rail. **Open** noon-11pm Mon-Sat; noon-10.30pm Sun. **Food served** noon-2.30pm, 5-8pm Mon-Fri; noon-3pm Sat. **Credit** MC, V.
Just outside Euston Station, with a pleasant view of Euston Square, the Head of Steam is a bolthole for commuters, office workers, tourists, football fans and anyone seeking solace from all that 'wrong kind of leaves' malarkey. As you'd expect, it's plastered with all kinds of railway memorabilia, including station signs, lamps, uniforms and signals. It's a proper pub too, though, and one that respects its beers, to the extent that it has become one of the London pubs most esteemed by ale

fans. There are two regulars, Shepherd Neame's Master Brew (£1.80) and Hop Back Summer Lightning (£2.10), as well as Biddenden Cider (£2.20) and six guest ales at any one time. It even holds regular beer festivals and art exhibitions.
Babies and children admitted (separate area). Games (fruit machine, bar billiards). No-smoking area. Satellite TV. Vegetarian dishes.

Popstarz Liquid Lounge
257 Pentonville Road, N1 (020 7837 3218).
King's Cross tube/Thameslink. **Open** 5.30pm-2am Mon-Thur; 5.30pm-1am Fri; 5.30pm-3am Sat; 5.30pm-1am Sun.
No credit cards.
Many moons ago this was the Bell, home to infamous gay indie bash, Pop Tartz. It's now come full circle, through several incarnations, to become Popstarz, a gay indie-and-alternative bar brought to you by the crew of the club night of the same name. It's a strange brew: multicoloured and garish, yet low-lit, subdued and comfy. It offers the gamut of alcopops (£2.50) and promotes cheap cans of Breaker lager (£1 or £2 depending on the night). This is a club-bar, so spinning silver balls are de rigueur. Both of its two lounges have wooden seating, although one is small with tables and faux-leather sofas, while the other boasts purple velvet settees. The natives are friendly, and the music is always loud.
Games (football table, pool). Late licence. Music (DJs nightly).

Ruby Lounge
33 Caledonian Road, N1 (020 7837 9558).
King's Cross tube/rail. **Open** noon-11pm Mon-Sat.
Food served noon-4pm Mon-Fri. **Credit** MC, V.
As its name suggests, the Ruby has a laid-back vibe, aided by the deep red decor and a funky-chunky sofa that lines the length of one wall; the whole is offset by a huge, ornate designer lampshade hanging over the central bar. It tends to pull quite a crowd on any night, but DJs do their stuff at weekends. Staropramen (£2.50) and Hoegaarden (£3.60) are on tap, and there's an extensive range of cocktails, including the Absolut Ruby for £3.50. Sadly, it's a small place, and one that can get all too intimate all too quickly: apart from the sofa, there's little by way of seating.
Music (DJs Fri, Sat). Vegetarian dishes.

Smithy's Wine Bar
Leeke Street, WC1 (020 7278 5949). King's Cross tube/ rail. **Open** 11am-11pm Mon-Fri, 11am-6pm Sat.
Food served 11am-10pm Mon-Fri; noon-5pm Sat.
Credit AmEx, MC, V.
Tucked down a cobbled side street, this wine bar, itself possessed of a large cobblestone floor, is the last word in dark, candlelit intimacy. There are plenty of cosy alcoves and high-backed benches, where you can relax and sift through a selection of over 200 wines, about 120 of which are available by the glass (£2-£8.50), or draw from the draught selection (London Pride £2.10, Flowers IPA £2). The Modern European menu changes daily, but features the likes of seafood pie (£6.50) and grilled lamb steak (£8). And, should your attention start to wander, Tarot readers make the rounds on Mondays; there's live jazz on Tuesdays, and comedy on Wednesdays.
Babies and children admitted. Cabaret (Thur). Comedy (Wed). Function rooms. Music (jazz Tue). Restaurant. Tables outdoors (pavement). Vegetarian dishes.

Waterside
82 York Way, N1 (020 7837 7118). King's Cross tube/rail. **Open** 11am-11pm Mon-Fri; noon-11pm Sat; noon-10.30pm Sun. **Food served** 11.30am-10pm Mon-Fri; noon-10pm Sat; noon-8pm Sun. **Credit** MC, V.

Formerly a Berni Inn, this bar now has the oddly discordant distinction, proudly displayed by a large sign outside, of containing a Pizza Hut within the pub. The establishment itself is all mock-Tudor charm: brickwork walls, an open fireplace, low-beamed ceilings, leaded windows and rustic wooden benches and tables. There's a small, red baize pool table in a cramped side room. Its biggest draw, however, is the beer garden, which overlooks a sedate stretch of Regent's Canal. There's a regular selection of guest ales available from £2.35, as well as Flowers IPA (£2.05) and Boddingtons (£2).
Games (pool table, table football). Jukebox. No-smoking area. Restaurant. Satellite TV (big screen). Tables outdoors (canalside terrace). Vegetarian dishes.

Also in the area...

Babushka 125 Caledonian Road, N1 (020 7837 1924).
Friar & Firkin 120 Euston Road, NW1 (020 7387 2419).

Knightsbridge SW3

Australian
29 Milner Street, SW3 (020 7589 6027). Sloane Square tube. **Open** 11am-11pm Mon-Sat; noon-10.30pm Sun.
Food served noon-3pm, 6-8.30pm Mon-Thur; noon-3pm Fri-Sun. **Credit** AmEx, DC, MC, V.
Surely the one place where you'd expect to find a couple of our Antipodean friends behind the pretty central copper-topped bar, but the only thing that's Australian about this pub is its name. Small but friendly, this is the kind of Knightsbridge establishment that unites the classes in their common love of drinking. Backgammon, chess, draughts, darts and pool are all available, but most people were too busy propping up the bar. Wadworth 6X (£2.30) Marston Pedigree (£2.25) or Adnams Southwold (£2.20) were in keeping with the trad feel of the place, although new management might change the range of ales on tap. Edible offerings include grilled lamb cutlet and veg, pork escalope in mustard sauce, and smoked haddock bake (all around £5.45).
Babies and children admitted. Function room. Games (board games, darts). No piped music or jukebox. Satellite TV. Vegetarian dishes.

Popstarz Liquid Lounge

Bunch of Grapes

207 Brompton Road, SW3 (020 7589 4944).
Knightsbridge or South Kensington tube. **Open/food**
served 11am-11pm Mon-Sat; noon-10.30pm Sun.
Credit AmEx, DC, MC, V.
Proof that it ain't all brass-buttoned doormen and women
on the verge of spending a fortune on the Harrods stretch,
the Bunch of Grapes provides a view of the world from the
bow window at the front, which is actually a separate
semicircular booth, and an excellent refuge from the
horrors of sale-time shopping. The rest of the pub is in keeping with
the olde-worlde façade (the Grapes dates from 1770), with
high ceilings and a central bar and the traditional hot food
counter displaying quiche and pies. There's a restaurant
upstairs, although the menu doesn't get any more exotic, but
if it's a good honest pint you're after, John Smith's (£2.24).
Guinness (£2.51) and Foster's are just some of those
available on tap.
Babies and children admitted (restaurant only). Games
(fruit machine). Restaurant. Vegetarian dishes.

Chelsea Bar

Chelsea Hotel, 17 Sloane Street, SW1 (020 7235 4377).
Knightsbridge tube. **Open/food served** 11am-11pm Mon-
Sat; 6.30-10.30pm Sun. **Credit** AmEx, DC, MC, V.
Chelsea girls may prefer hipper hangouts, but this hotel bar
shouldn't be overlooked as a place to kick up your heels if
you prefer a less posey environment. A swishy staircase
lined with mirrors leads up to leather sofas and a killer
cocktail list (from £7), which all have appeal, although the
all-day food menu reveals a little trying-too-hard
pretentiousness: hoi-sin fillet of pork on a lychee salsa,
anyone? Still, it's not hard to make yourself at home, and
there must be a fair few tourists who've innocently started
on the afternoon tea (£15 per head) only to find themselves
dazed and confused on Negronis at 11pm. The restaurant is
worth a visit, too.
Babies and children admitted. Disabled: toilet. Function
rooms. No piped music or jukebox. No-smoking area.
Restaurant. Satellite TV. Vegetarian dishes.

Enterprise

35 Walton Street, SW3 (020 7584 3148). Knightsbridge
or South Kensington tube. **Open** noon-11pm Mon-Sat;
noon-10.30pm Sun. **Food served** 12.30-2.30pm,
7-10.30pm Mon-Thur; 12.30-2.30pm, 7-11pm Fri;
12.30-3.30pm, 7-11pm Sat; 12.30-3.30pm, 7-10.30pm Sun.
Credit AmEx, MC, V.
'We're not a pub,' we were told rather firmly by staff at this
nice little earner, 'we're a bar-restaurant.' Well, excuse us.
They are right, though. It may look like a pub from the
outside, but there are only three taps, hot and cold in the loo,
and Stella on the bar, which isn't even served in pints (£2 for
250ml). Champers is the order of the day at this gastro-
enterprise Walton Street-style, and the place is literally lined
with bottles of the stuff. No scrubbed rescued oak here, the
tablecloths are linen, as are the napkins waved to summon
the waiters. But just as the Eagle is hugely popular in
Farringdon, so is the Enterprise on its home turf, and it's
down-to-earth in its own way – venison and merguez sausages
are 'bangers', and lemon sole comes with mash, albeit made
with saffron. But, at £9.65 and £14.45 respectively, they ain't
cheap, and the fact that the bottles of Chablis being drained
like Whites' Lemonade are £23 a pop should put anyone on
the right track.
Babies and children admitted (until 6pm).
Restaurant. Satellite TV. Tables outdoors (pavement).
Vegetarian dishes.

Fifth Floor Bar

Harvey Nichols, 109-125 Knightsbridge, SW1 (020 7235
5000). Knightsbridge tube. **Open** 11am-11pm Mon-Sat;
noon-6pm Sun. **Food served** noon-3.30pm, 5-11pm Mon-
Sat; noon-3.30pm Sun. **Credit** AmEx, DC, MC, V.
It surprised us to find that a bar housed in the capital's
shopping mecca isn't really a good place for a woman to sit
on her own. You'll either be suspected of trying to pick people
up or people will try to pick you up. This is not an easy place
to try and fade into the background (they don't hold fashion
parties regularly for nothing), so if you don't fancy the
attention, turn up with a friend or two to check out the fifth-
floor flash. The popularity of this high-flying watering hole
adjoining the main restaurant hasn't waned over the years,
and the lack of square feet around the large central bar
ensures that the place is nearly always heaving. Bottled beers
(Stella, Beck's) are £3.25, and there's a prix-fixe lunch served
in the bar for £23, or snacks and sandwiches – tuna with
cherry tomatoes on olive bread £7.50 – but only corn chips
with salsa (£5) are available in the evening. It's worth
propping yourself on a well-upholstered bar stool,though, for
the Fifth Floor Smash, a posh-totty confection of champagne,
strawberries, Cointreau and wild strawberry liqueur (£7.50).
Disabled: toilet. Restaurant. Vegetarian dishes.

Gloucester

187 Sloane Street, SW1 (020 7235 0298). Knightsbridge
tube. **Open/food served** 11am-11pm Mon-Sat; noon-
10.30pm Sun. **Credit** AmEx, DC, MC, V.
When we visited last year, the Gloucester was a one-stop grot
shop, but it's had a much-needed facelift since then, and the
Victorian-look wallpaper and brass give this Sloane Street
pub a much cosier feeling. It still has its corporate identity,
but what a difference the welcome makes. It's a pub on Prozac,
and the long room was full of punters chatting happily rather
than staring gloomily into their drinks. Pints start at £2.18
for John Smith's, and a Famous Grouse whisky is £1.70. The
menu includes all the usual crowd-pleasers – fish and chips
are £5.95, ham and eggs £5.24, and, when you're done, they'll
point out the short cut to Harrods down Basil Street opposite.
Games (fruit machine). Jukebox. No-smoking area.
Vegetarian dishes.

Le Metro

L'Hôtel, 28 Basil Street, SW3 (020 7591 1213).
Knightsbridge tube. **Open** 7.30am-midnight Mon-Sat;
8am-noon Sun. **Food served** 7.30am-10.30pm Mon-Sat;
8am-noon Sun. **Credit** AmEx, DC, MC, V.
There's nothing showy about this intimate little wine bar in
the basement of a small hotel on Basil Street, but the
impression is one of selective good taste. The designer of Le
Metro has used white, chrome and mirrors to make the place
as light as possible, but it seems far from cold or clinical. The
separate bar area has tables situated far enough apart for
private conversation, and the extensive wine list has 55 wines
by the glass from the house red and white at £2.50 to a
Sancerre or Côte Bon Villages at £4.75, so it's easy to sample
more than one. The friendly staff are happy to serve you
snacks here, a croque monsieur and chips is £5.50, a club
bagel £4.95, or you can sample from the larger menu in the
restaurant area at the back.
Babies and children admitted (high chairs). Tables
outdoors. Vegetarian dishes.

Nag's Head

53 Kinnerton Street, SW1 (020 7235 1135). Hyde Park
Corner or Knightsbridge tube. **Open/food served** 11am-
11pm Mon-Sat; noon-10.30pm Sun. **No credit cards.**

Le Metro

Anyone fussy about the quality of their drinking environment should sample the Nag's Head – as aesthetically pleasing an inn as any imbiber could wish for. A blazing fire in the grate welcomes you as you step into the higgledy-piggledy bar, where the local old devils prop themselves up and gaze lovingly at the Irish barmaid. Down a couple of mouse-size steps there's a tiny snug where hot food, salads and sandwiches are served at lunchtime. Museum-piece slot machines on the walls add to the Beatrix Potter feel, and the only things missing are pewter tankards and a man with a hurdy-gurdy in the corner. Adnams is £2.20 a pint, and Bells is £1.50 a shot.
Tables outdoors (pavement). Vegetarian dishes.

Osteria

145 Knightsbridge, SW1 (020 7838 1044). Knightsbridge tube. **Open/food served** noon-3pm, 6-10.30pm Mon-Fri; noon-4pm, 6-10.30pm Sat; noon-4pm, 6-9pm Sun.
Credit AmEx, DC, MC, V.
Just three months old when we visited, Oliver Peyton's Italian Osteria is the newest swanky eaterie on the block, and certainly knocks spots off anywhere else around Knightsbridge looks-wise, including the legendary **Fifth Floor** across the road (*see p56*). All very Gucci, the chrome, white and glass design leaves the competition resembling dowdy old Sloanes or overdressed Mayfair mules. The formal dining room, Osteria d'Isola, is on the ground floor; the bar is downstairs, running along one wall of the less formal basement restaurant and furnished with low-slung black leather sofas. The backlit cocktail bar serves up a mean champagne cocktail (£8.50) or Martini (£7.50). Behind the sofas the entire contents of the extensive Italian (of course) wine list are available for you to sample by the glass, and bar snacks include tasty bruschetta (£5). We spotted a distinguished designer and artist or two, but Posh and Becks were nowhere to be seen – has no one told them yet?
Babies and children admitted (high chairs). Disabled: toilet. No-smoking area (downstairs). Restaurant. Vegetarian dishes.

Paxton's Head

153 Knightsbridge, SW1 (020 7589 6627). Knightsbridge tube. **Open** 11am-11pm Mon-Sat; noon-10.30pm Sun.
Food served noon-9pm daily. **Credit** AmEx, MC, V.
A sparkling example of an Edwardian boozer: you could imagine the various locals suddenly jumping up on the bar for a dance routine from *My Fair Lady* in the Paxton's. Huge mirrors, etched glass, curlicues, what-nots and a blazing fire hark back to the days when you could have a knees-up down the old Bull and Bush and still have a shilling to take a bottle of stout home to the missus. In fact, if it wasn't for the tikka masala with nan (£5.75) on the menu, Hoegaarden on tap (£3.90 a pint) and Steps on the sound sytem you could easily forget which century you were in.
Babies and children admitted (until 6pm). Function room. Jukebox. Satellite TV. Vegetarian dishes.

Swag & Tails

10-11 Fairholt Street, SW7 (020 7584 6926). Knightsbridge or South Kensington tube. **Open** 11am-11pm Mon-Fri. **Food served** noon-3pm, 6-10pm Mon-Fri. **Credit** AmEx, MC, V.
Deep in a warren of mewses, hidden behind a horticultural display that could grace the Chelsea Flower Show, lies this upmarket pub-cum-restaurant. Studied ranks of Bollinger stand guard over a bar serving well-kept Pedigree (£2.40), Konig Pils (£2.95) and a fine hand-pumped Bombardier (£2.40). The light oak furniture, burnt sienna walls and dried flower frieze ensure the public bar is as handsomely appointed

as the surrounding houses. The menu is suitably grand and changes regularly, with Moroccan spiced lamb shank and panfried salmon fillet (both £9.75) typical dishes. The staff may be uniformed, the wine list extensive, but the relaxed atmosphere created by the stripey-shirted crowd makes the Swag & Tails that strange thing, a real local in mews-land.
Babies and children admitted (separate area). Restaurant. Vegetarian dishes.

Tea Clipper

19 Montpelier Street, SW7 (020 7589 5251). Knightsbridge tube. **Open/food served** 11am-11pm Mon-Sat; noon-10.30pm Sun. **Credit** AmEx, DC, MC, V.
The fact that come lunchtime and after work this little pub is always bustling means that those in the know have sought the Tea Clipper out as an unpretentious place for a pie and a pint. It's a million miles from the chi-chi little pâtisseries that line the Brompton Road, and worth the few steps away from the madding crowd if you need refreshment to warm the cockles rather than tug at your purse strings. There's a fine array of old faves on tap, including Courage Best (£2.12) and Theakston Best (£2.60), and the bar menu provides pub grub staples including crispy haddock (£3.95).
Babies and children admitted (not after 6pm Sat). Games (fruit machine). Quiz. Satellite TV. Tables outdoors (pavement). Vegetarian dishes.

Also in the area...

Café Rouge 27-31 Basil Street, SW3 (020 7584 2345).

Leicester Square, Piccadilly Circus, W1, WC2

10 Room

10 Air Street, W1 (020 7734 9990). Piccadilly Circus tube. **Open** 6pm-3am Mon-Sat. **Food served** 6pm-2.30am Mon-Sat. **Credit** AmEx, DC, MC, V.
Entry to the 10 Room seems to be a very hit-and-miss affair but, if you are one of the lucky few without membership who manage to get in, be prepared for palatial purple splendour: deep purple walls, lilac drapes, matching ceilings, with contrasting red and blue chaise longues and sofas. The chairs are enormous and much coveted for their comfort, especially on a Sunday, when there's a film club. Sadly, the toilets weren't much cop. There are three premium beers to choose from: Sleemans, Sapporo and EB, all £3, several champagnes and a very well-mixed line in cocktails (£5.50-£6.50).
Games (backgammon, chess). Function room. Late licence. Music (DJs Fri-Sat, live Mon-Thur). Vegetarian dishes.

10 Tokyo Joe's

85 Piccadilly, W1 (020 7495 2595). Green Park tube. **Open/food served** 5pm-4am Tue-Sat. **Credit** AmEx, DC, MC, V.
The folk behind the 10 Room recently revamped and re-opened Tokyo Joe's. And what a makeover it has had. Descending the stairs of the Clarges Street entrance to this basement bar is like walking into God's waiting room: a celestial, tranquil lounge of airport proportions. A bright, white minimalist-chic space has been created with punters' needs and comfort very much in mind. Clusters of mellow yellow organic pod-like seating scatter the floor, while private booths dominate the far end. Ambient lighting can be changed at whim, from golds and greens to sapphires and soft, soft reds. State-of-the-art, wafer-thin speakers are built

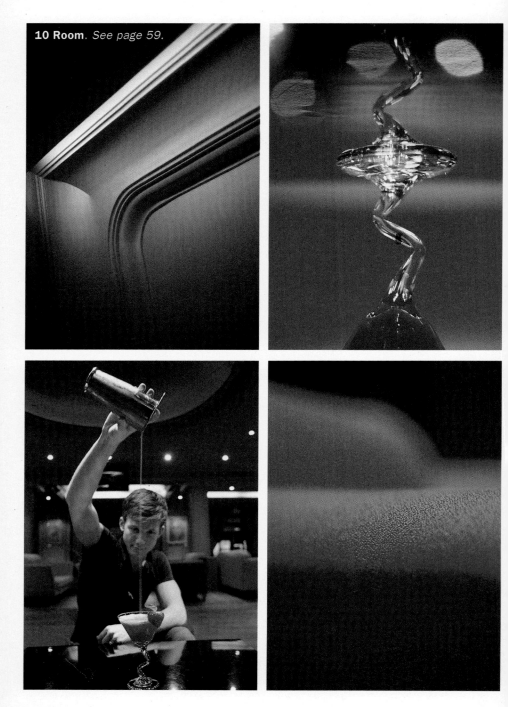

10 Room. *See page 59.*

into the ceiling, while the private booths have their own personal light-setting and speaker controls, so that the mood can be dictated by you. To secure one of these, though, you must promise to spend £500 while in there. To quench your thirst there are cocktails and bottled beers; the cocktails appear colour co-ordinated in the menu and start at £5.50. The Long Island Iced Tea, like the surroundings, is absolute heaven. The platters are a global mix – crostini, sushi, chicken satay, Caribbean mullet, Thai green shrimps, and Mongolian beef – each for £5.75.
Late licence. Restaurant. Vegetarian dishes.

79CXR

79 Charing Cross Road, WC2 (020 7734 0769). Leicester Square tube. **Open/food served** 1pm-2am Mon-Thur; 1pm-3am Fri, Sat; 1-10.30pm Sun. **Happy hour** 8-10pm daily. **No credit cards.**
This shotgun shack of a gay bar could really do with a make-over. The off-putting blacked-out windows give way to a rather dim and grubby interior, done out in shades of tatty brown and drab magnolia. That said, both bar staff and door security are welcoming, and the mature crowd the bar attracts is low-key and amiable, although the place seems to draw more than its fair share of lone drinkers. A few chairs and tables adorn a raised dais to the rear, and there are more on the cruisey mezzanine area above. The main attraction of 79CXR is its late licence, which makes it perfect for those who aren't ready to go home, but don't want to pay for a club to extend their drink time. Drinks include Foster's (£2.30), Kronenbourg (£2.50) and John Smith's Extra Smooth (£2.20).
Games (fruit machines, pinball, quiz machine). Late licence (Mon-Sat). Music (DJs Thur-Sat). Tables outdoors (patio).

Atlantic Bar & Grill

20 Glasshouse Street, W1 (020 7734 4888/www.pompeii-atlantic.com). Piccadilly Circus tube. **Open** noon-3am Mon-Sat; 6-10.30pm Sun. **Food served** noon-2.30am Mon-Sat; 7-10.30pm Sun. **Credit** AmEx, DC, MC, V.
Its glory may have faded, but the grandeur hasn't: from the sweeping staircase and ornate chandelier by the entrance, to the fake leopardskin and wood panelling in Dick's Bar and through to the marble-columned glory of the main bar and restaurant – the Atlantic has always been the last word in polished panache. The impossibly high ceilings are a claustrophobe's answered prayer. Still, at the end of the day, you can expect to pay no less than £6 for a rum and coke, £4.60 for a glass of house wine, and they play Wham! Bottles of Czechoslovakian Kozel and Foster's own-produced Mash cost £3, and Leffe Blonde and Hoegaarden are also available. Grand snacks such as oak-smoked salmon sandwiches and wild mountain leaf salad come in around the £7 mark.
Function room. Late licence (Mon-Sat). Restaurant. Vegetarian dishes.

Browns

82-84 St Martin's Lane, WC2 (020 7497 5050). Leicester Square tube. **Open/food served** noon-11pm Mon-Sat; noon-10.30pm Sun. **Credit** AmEx, DC, MC, V.
The Olympian and eternal flaming torches outside belie the old-style pub decor within. Warm browns and pale creams dominate, as does foliage in the form of many a potted plant. It's better known – by the West End glitterati and nearby Covent Garden literati at least – for its restaurant, but the bar proper nonetheless throbs to the sound of a dozen expense accounts at any given time. Seating is a very precious commodity. Cocktails start from £3.95, but Browns is also big on its bourbons and Martinis, with your classic Bond

Vodka Martini costing a cool £4.55. The menu includes dishes such as pan-fried fillet of sea bass (£13.95) and roast rump of lamb with broccoli (£14.95).
Babies and children admitted. Disabled: toilet. Function rooms. Restaurant. Satellite TV. Vegetarian dishes.

Café Flo

11 Haymarket, SW1 (020 7976 1313). Piccadilly Circus tube. **Open/food served** 10am-11.30pm Mon-Sat; 10am-11pm Sun. **Credit** AmEx, MC, V.
The Café Flo brasserie-style bar chain is similar in looks to rivals Café Rouge and Dôme, but has retained its own French identity, with waiters combining just the right amount of aloofness and dark Gallic looks to thrill the post-shopping clientele. Surprisingly, for a central London chain, the bar has a wide selection of beers (for instance, St Omer £1.60 a half-pint, bottled Budvar £2.70) and wines (12 available by the glass, starting at £2.75), with a champagne bar in the evening. Reasonably priced food (garlic and herb bread £2, chocolate brûlée £3.95) makes this the perfect place to take your mother before *Cats*.
Babies and children admitted (until noon). Function room. No-smoking area. Restaurant. Tables outdoors. Vegetarian food.

Chandos

29 St Martin's Lane, WC2 (020 7836 1401). Leicester Square tube/Charing Cross tube/rail. **Open** 11am-11pm Mon-Sat; noon-10.30pm Sun. **Food served** 11am-7pm Mon-Wed; 11am-6pm Thur-Sat; noon-6pm Sun. **Credit** AmEx, DC, MC, V.
A pub with two distinct floors this. Downstairs seems, on first impression, to be rather austere: all plain walls and bare wooden floors. Its saving grace, however, are the many private alcoves that come with bench tables and coat hooks. The upstairs Opera bar is a much warmer affair, carpeted, and with some rather plush leather sofas. Due to its location, Chandos draws a mix of suits, tourists and theatregoers, although they may find the choice of drinks quite limiting. There are Samuel Smith's ales and lagers, including Old Brewery Bitter (£1.52) and Ayingerbrau lager (£1.78), and standard pub grub (steak and ale pie £6.50, baguettes £5.95) are available upstairs in the Opera Room.
Babies and children admitted (upstairs bar). Games (fruit machine). Vegetarian dishes.

Cheers

72 Regent Street, W1 (020 7494 3322). Piccadilly Circus tube. **Open** noon-3am Mon-Sat; noon-10.30pm Sun. **Food served** noon-11pm Mon-Sat; noon-10.30pm Sun. **Happy hour** 3-8pm Mon. **Credit** AmEx, MC, V.
Life does indeed mimic art with this tribute to that well-known Bostonian comedy. It's a barn-sized place, with episodes of *Cheers* running on the many built-in TV screens; character *bon mots* and photographs line the walls, as do sports-playing projector screens. The staff are good at showing off their bottle-flipping skills, but a little slow to serve. And they'll never know your name, as they'll never hear it over the din. This place heaves on any given night and, sad to say, not just with tourists. There are DJs on every night except Sundays, and patrons can choose to sup the likes of Miller, Coors and Boston Beer (all £1.30 a half-pint, £4.90 a pitcher jug). If cocktails are more your thing, try the Bostonian (Southern Comfort, vodka, amaretto and grenadine, with orange, pineapple and lemon juice, £3.50). Food includes Norm's Big Burgers, from £6.95, and Sammy's Sandwiches, from £7.50.
Babies and children admitted (high chairs). Disabled: toilet. Late licence. Music (DJs Mon-Sat). No-smoking area. Restaurant. Satellite TV (big screen). Vegetarian dishes.

Cork & Bottle

44-46 Cranbourn Street, WC2 (020 7734 7807). Leicester Square tube. **Open/food served** 11am-11.30pm Mon-Sat; noon-10.30pm Sun. **Credit** AmEx, DC, MC, V.

A sane haven just off the garish nightmare that is Leicester Square, and one that, unless you know exactly where to look, can be a little hard to find. The rickety street-level stairway leads to this fair-sized basement wine bar, replete with candlelit tables and cosy alcoves, and a simple and informal atmosphere that has proved popular for over 25 years now. They don't serve beers or spirits here, but there's a 200-strong wine list that particularly favours the New World (£3-£5.25 a glass); champagne (bottles £25-£150) and some dessert wines supplement the cellar. The menu includes things such as raised ham and cheese pie (£5.25) and Australian sirloin steak sandwich (£9.95).

No-smoking area (daytime). Restaurant. Satellite TV. Tables outdoors. Vegetarian dishes.

Corney & Barrow

116 St Martin's Lane, WC2 (020 7655 9800/www.corney-barrow.co.uk). Leicester Square tube/Charing Cross tube/rail. **Open/food served** 11am-midnight Mon, Tue; 11am-2am Wed-Sat. **Credit** AmEx, DC, MC, V.

A more-chic-than-thou wine bar in a to-die-for location, the Corney & Barrow is a lesson in minimalist limestone and granite, with steel stools and leather chairs. Even the cigarette machines here are stylish. And, while the downstairs bar isn't exactly the last word in comfort, the clientele tends to linger, hooked, perhaps, by a selection of over 50 wines and 20 champagnes. Bottled beers start from £2 and include Kirin, Bishop's Finger and Bittburger, while a lengthy cocktail list includes a range of fruit flavoured champagne cocktails,. Upstairs is a brasserie, serving up Modern European grub along the lines of pan-seared Scottish salmon in chermoula, with bulgar wheat salad, tsatsiki and preserved lemon for £10.75, and there's now a late night menu featuring the likes of mezze platter (£10.50) to coincide with the late licence.

Disabled: toilet. Function room. Restaurant. Vegetarian dishes.

De Hems

11 Macclesfield Street, W1 (020 7437 2494). Leicester Square or Piccadilly Circus tube. **Open/food served** noon-midnight Mon-Sat; noon-10.30pm Sun. **Credit** AmEx, MC, V.

We've had it on good authority, from someone who knows both pubs and architecture, that this really does look like an eighteenth-century Netherlands ale house. But, then, this is London's one and only Dutch boozer. Not only does the bar have a high ceiling and long, heavy wood tables, Vermeer prints and Delft pottery, but all the signs are in Dutch (making the loos a bit tricky to locate), as is the menu, which includes such things as Bitterballen (deep-fried meat in béchamel sauce, £2.50) and Vlammetjes (a spicy meat spring roll, £2.95). Beers include Oranjeboom (£2.75) and Witte Raaf (£3.60). There's an upstairs bar that also plays host to the Oranjeboom Boom comedy club on a Wednesday night.

Comedy (Wed). Dutch night (every other Thur). Function room. Games (fruit machine). Vegetarian dishes.

Denim

4A Upper St Martin's Lane, WC2 (020 7497 0376). Leicester Square tube. **Open/food served** noon-2am Mon-Sat; 3.30pm-12.30am Sun. **Credit** AmEx, DC, MC, V.

Denim's lurid red pop art design, so innovative when the bar was opened in October 1998, is starting to look dated, particularly since *Changing Rooms* popularised curvy MDF across the land. Stained seats and overflowing ashtrays add to the disappointment in this once-trendy drinkerie. That said, the bar staff are friendly and clued-up, and the local Covent Garden types still cram Denim's two floors every weekend. Beer is expensive (Red Stripe and Michelob are £3.50), but there's an extensive cocktail list – a fruit Daiquiri costs £6.50 – to compensate. There's a restaurant upstairs, with a wide range of bar snacks, such as fat chips with mayo and chilli jam for £3, available on the ground floor.

Dress code (Sat). Function rooms. Late licence (Mon-Sat). Music (DJs nightly). Restaurant. Vegetarian dishes.

Dive Bar

48 Gerrard Street, W1 (020 7437 5858). Leicester Square tube. **Open** 5.30-11pm Mon-Sat; 7-10.30pm Sun. **No credit cards**.

Located beneath the King's Head in Chinatown's Gerrard Street, the no-frills Dive Bar lives up to every image the name conjures up. Tatty film posters line the dark and dingy walls, while the floor tends to stick to the shoes. Womb-like tunnels house long tables and benches suitable for political discourse, drunken ramblings and, if you're lucky, a snog. DJs cater to a not-always appreciative audience on Saturday nights and, perhaps unsurprisingly, this place is a favourite with students. The beer choice is limited, with only Foster's and Kronenbourg on tap, but no one seems to mind in this boozer that stills plays to the old seedy Soho ideal.

Music (DJs Fri, Sat).

Down Mexico Way

25 Swallow Street, W1 (020 7437 9895). Piccadilly Circus tube. **Open/food served** noon-midnight Mon-Sat; noon-10.30pm Sun. **Credit** AmEx, DC, MC, V.

A Latin-inspired bar-restaurant that's a little more stylish and a little less predictable than most. The downstairs bar is decorated in shades of tasteful blue, edged with ornate tiling and topped by a gorgeous blue glass ceiling. There are 11 different tequilas to choose from (£3.75-£5.50), and the bottled beers include Sol, Tecate, Iguazu, Brahma and San Miguel (all £2.75) and Dos Equis and Bohemia (£3). There's a small dance area and DJ booth; piped Latin music plays when they're not in use. Warning: there will be singing to accompany your meal in the restaurant upstairs; be jolly.

Babies and children admitted. Function room. Late licence. Music (DJs Fri, Sat). Restaurant. Vegetarian dishes.

Global Café

15 Golden Square, W1 (020 7287 2242). Piccadilly Circus tube. **Open/food served** 8am-11pm Mon-Fri; 10am-11pm Sat; noon-10.30pm Sun. **Credit** MC, V.

A light and airy, cosmopolitan café-bar for Internetters this, with around a dozen workstations, a licensed bar and basic menu. It's a cream-walled and wooden-floored affair, populated by cheery blue-topped tables. The bottle-only beers include Grolsch (£2) and Budvar (£2.50), but there are also cocktails, hot toddies, wines, absinthe, coffees, organic teas and other beverages. The light Mediterranean menu includes pastries, croissants, soups, salads, sandwiches and quiches. DJs are a regular feature, as are art exhibitions. Altogether a fine and funky place in which to chill and e-mail your global companions.

Babies and children admitted. Function rooms. Music (DJs). Tables outdoors (pavement). Vegetarian dishes.

Imperial

5 Leicester Street, WC2 (020 7437 6573). Leicester Square or Piccadilly Circus tube. **Open/food served** 11am-11pm Mon-Sat; noon-10.30pm Sun. **Credit** AmEx, DC, MC, V.

Given its location, the fact that the Imperial has managed to remain a rather down-to-earth and no-nonsense boozer can only be marvelled at. Here you will find neither hordes of sheep-like tourists, nor foul-mannered door staff. And, while the decor may not be all that slick – it's done up in varieties of traditional pub brown, with plenty of large antique mirrors for good measure – there's a fair selection of wines on offer, from £2.40 a glass, and beers include Beck's (£2.70 a pint), Courage Best (£2.19), Foster's (£2.40) and John Smith's Extra Smooth (£2.28).
Games (fruit machine, video golf game). Tables outdoors (pavement). Vegetarian dishes.

Ku Bar
75 Charing Cross Road, WC2 (020 7437 4303/ www.kubar.co.uk). Leicester Square tube. **Open** noon-11pm Mon-Sat; 1-10.30pm Sun. **Happy hour** noon-7pm daily. **No credit cards.**
This pleasant, unpretentious gay bar is just a couple of doors down from **79CXR** (*see p61*); it, too, has blacked-out windows, but there the similarity ends. The decor is modern and comfortable, with dark blue-grey walls adorned with wrought-iron candelabra and photographs of such pop luminaries as Boy George, the Human League, Kylie and Mariah Carey. It's a two-level bar with minimum seating downstairs, but more upstairs. The crowd is young, fashionable and sceney, no doubt drawn by the loud, disco-tastic jukebox. It can get packed, but still people bump and grind, despite or perhaps because of the dense crowd. All drinks are in bottles as there are no taps, but you can select from Budweiser, Beck's, Rolling Rock and Grolsch (all £2.60) or Metz, Rigo and Bacardi Breezer (£2.50). Cocktails seem popular, too, especially during happy hour.
Tables outdoors (pavement).

L'Odéon
65 Regent Street, W1 (020 7287 1400). Piccadilly Circus tube. **Open** 11am-1am Mon-Sat. **Food served** noon-1am Mon-Sat. **Credit** AmEx, DC, MC, V.
Regent Street's best-kept secret; L'Odéon's curvaceous lines, attentive staff and soft armchairs give London's bar scene a much-needed shot of immaculate taste. Attracting an upwardly mobile thirtysomething crowd, it has drinks that are pricey, but provide value for money: champagne cocktails (£7), mint julep (£6) and a stunning wine list. The bar menu has the likes of Caesar salad (£4.50) and cod and chips (£10.50), but you can move upmarket and upstairs to the restaurant, which offers such indulgences as white truffles, venison and oysters. Unrivalled views over Regent Street make this the perfect place to impress clients, or indulge those Mafia-don fantasies.
Babies and children admitted. Disabled: toilet. Function room. Late licence (Mon-Sat). No-smoking area. Restaurant. Vegetarian dishes.

Oxygen
17-18 Irving Street, WC2 (020 7930 0907). Leicester Square tube. **Open** 4pm-1am Mon-Wed; 4pm-2am Thur; 4pm-3am Fri, Sat; 4-10.30pm Sun. **Credit** AmEx, MC, V.
Oxygen, at ground-level, is an industrial-Gothic affair: dark, brooding, atmospheric and heavy on the metal. The stuff is used everywhere – for tables and chairs, the bar, the bar top, even the flooring. And while there are spotlights in the bar, lighting elsewhere comes from candles. A couple of large, metal-framed mirrors are used to open the place up a tad. The mood changes upstairs, towards earthier, more natural colours. Warm browns and wooden features prevail, although the candles are still there. There are two working open

fireplaces, and wrought-iron gates line the wall behind the bar. There's a basement bar area, too, available for private hire. Bottled beers, such as San Miguel, Beck's, Corona Extra and Red Stripe cost £2.90, while all the usual suspects make up the cocktail menu at £4.25 each, or £10.95 for a two-pint jug. And for those of you looking for invigoration, you can buy canisters of oxygen (25-30 puffs £8; 70-80 puffs £12) for that natural high.

Function rooms. Late licence. Music (DJs Thur-Sat). Satellite TV. Tables outdoors (pavement).

Saint

8 Great Newport Street, WC2 (020 7240 1551). Leicester Square tube. **Open/food served** 5pm-2am Mon-Thur; 5pm-3am Fri; 7.30pm-3am Sat. **Admission** after 9pm Thur £5; Fri, Sat £7. **Credit** AmEx, DC, MC, V.

The once-brusque doormen here appear to have adopted a more charming if slightly unsettling approach: one of them required a kiss from a friend if we were to gain entry on the night we visited this blink-and-you'd-walk-straight-past-it basement bar. Once inside we were greeted by a throbbing, nouveau-riche crowd, many – if they were to be believed – record producers and bar owners, all eager to splash the cash on champagne with wild abandon (Perrier Jouet £6). Some rather plush alcove seating lined the packed dancefloor, and an interesting green glass ensemble spread around the top of the bar added some nice touches to an interior that, otherwise, wasn't much to shout about. A number of cocktails are available (around £7), and beers include Budvar, Corona (both £3), and Leffe (£3.20). A small but exotic bar menu offers, among others, chicken skewers with a peanut sauce, or duck on chilli fried noodles (both £5).

Disabled: toilet. Dress code (Fri, Sat). Late licence (Mon-Sat). Music (DJs Tue-Sat). Restaurant. Vegetarian dishes.

Salisbury

90 St Martin's Lane, WC2 (020 7836 5863). Leicester Square tube. **Open/food served** 11am-11pm Mon-Sat; noon-10.30pm Sun. **Credit** AmEx, DC, MC, V.

The Salisbury has only recently undergone refurbishment but, thankfully, has kept its original Victorian charm. The wooden plaque outside still details its history: it was leased to the third Marquis of Salisbury in 1892, a period reflected by the decor within. The double-door entrance can be a little difficult to negotiate, and the original cut-glass mirrors that seem to line every available wall are offset by red velvet banquettes, marble-topped bar, mahogany wood detail and gold statuette lighting. A truly splendid pub in every way, it has Theakston Best (£2.24), Marston's Pedigree (£2.38) and Guinness Extra Cold (£2.60) on draught, and a menu featuring such dishes as Chicken Wellington, with Burgundy sauce (£9.25) and a traditional British pie for £5.75.

Babies and children admitted (in separate area). Function room. Games (fruit machine). Tables outdoors (pavement). Vegetarian dishes.

Sound

Swiss Centre, Leicester Square, W1 (020 7287 1010). Leicester Square or Piccadilly Circus tube. **Open/food served** noon-1am Mon-Thur; noon-3am Fri, Sat; noon-midnight Sun. **Admission** (except for diners) after 11pm Mon-Thur £3.50; after 11pm Fri, Sat £5. **Happy hour** 5-8pm daily. **Credit** AmEx, MC, V.

The combination of a happy hour, giant video screens and industrial/pseudo-glam interior left us confused and delirious within 20 minutes of arriving at Sound, the erstwhile Sound Republic. For what is essentially a music theme bar, the atmosphere is welcoming enough, although the bar staff take the rock star stroppiness a little far. House spirits at £2

(including mixers) in happy hour draw a lively crowd o shoppers and young tourists, but this isn't a bar to linger ir just somewhere to fuel up before moving elsewhere. Foo (such as chicken Caesar salad or 'bang bang' chicken fo £4.95) is served in the central bar area.

Babies and children admitted (until 7pm). Disabled: toilet. Dress code. Function room. Late licence. Music (DJs nightly). Restaurant. Tables outdoors (terrace). Vegetarian dishes.

Sports Café

80 Haymarket, SW1 (020 7839 8300). Piccadilly Circus tube. **Open/food served** noon-2am Mon-Fri; noon-3am Fri-Sat; noon-10.30pm Sun. **Credit** AmEx, DC, MC, V.

A huge TV screen-strewn temple to the great god sport Screens are everywhere: behind the bars, above the bars an hanging from the ceilings. Small screens are built into th dining booths and into the walls of the toilets, where, if that' not enough to distract you, the latest sports news from th papers has also been pinned up on notice boards. The rest o the bar is dark wood and, over all, has a very American fee There are purple baize pool tables upstairs, and table footbal downstairs; dirt bikes are strung from the ceiling and an F race car hangs from a wall. A small selection of sports-base video games are on offer, and there's even a small basketbal cage in the far right-hand corner. Kronenbourg is served o tap (£2.80), bottles include Beck's and Foster's Ice (both £2.60 and cocktails start at £3.95. Strangely, given the emphasis o sport, it's pretty female-friendly. The restaurant is popular a lunchtime and early evening but, if you're under 21, don't tr getting in after 9pm.

Babies and children admitted (children's menu, play areas). Disabled: toilet. Dress code. Function room. Games (PlayStations, pool tables, table football, video games). Late licence (Mon-Sat). Music (DJs nightly). No-smoking area. Restaurant. Satellite TV (big screens). Vegetarian dishes.

Studio Lounge, Waterstone's

203-206 Piccadilly, W1 (020 7851 2400). Piccadilly Circus tube. **Open/food served** 10am-11pm Mon-Sat; noon-6pm Sun. **Credit** AmEx, MC, V.

How can we be dumbing down culturally, when Waterstone's has this thriving Goliath dedicated to all things literate and not so literate (well... the Geri Halliwell autobiography wa on prominent display)? On the fifth floor, the Studio Lounge cordially invites you to sit and chat or peruse potentia purchases in an à la mode minimalist bar with tiled wooder floors, low-backed leatherette seating, comfy sofas and a splendid window view. Wines start at £2.75 a glass champagnes at £5.75 and bottled beers include the likes o Budvar, Tiger and Sapporo, all at £2.75, St Peter's Golden Ale at £3.25 and Schneider Weisse at £3.50. Don't peruse for too long, as your printed words could become a bit blurred.

Babies and children admitted (until 5pm). Function rooms. Restaurant. Tables outdoors (balcony). Vegetarian dishes.

Tiger Tiger

29 Haymarket, SW1 (020 7930 1885/ www.tigertiger.co.uk). Piccadilly Circus tube. **Open/food served** noon-3am Mon-Sat; noon-11.30pm Sun. **Admission** after 10pm Mon-Wed £3; after 10pm Thur £5; after 10pm Fri, Sat £8. **Happy hour** 5-7pm daily. **Credit** AmEx, MC, V.

This place is hangar-huge, with many stairs and many levels containing a club, cocktail bar and lounge bar. The mishmash decor – vaguely Far East ethnic in parts, almost Moroccan in others, with no taste at all in places – is all bizarrely offset by an escalator to lift you between floors. Expect to park your

...ottom on anything from huge comfy, curvy sofas to bamboo
...nd wicker stools or fake zebraskin seats. While it may not
...e as upmarket and trendy as it likes to think, Tiger Tiger is
...aughably naff and a good place in which to quaff. Bottled
...eers include Tiger (no surprise there), Budweiser, San
...Miguel, Corona and Miller (all £2.95), shooters cost £3.95 and
...he snack menu is as eclectic as the upholstery.
...Babies and children admitted (until 5pm). Disabled: toilet.
...Dress code. Late licence (Mon-Sat). Music (DJs 9pm Mon-
...Sat). Restaurant. Vegetarian dishes.

Titanic

...81 Brewer Street, W1 (020 7437 1912).
...Piccadilly Circus tube. **Open/food served** noon-3am
...Mon-Sat; 5.30-11.30pm Sun. **Credit** AmEx, MC, V.
...Having such an infamous name was always going to be a bit
...of a jinx, but the Titanic has bravely weathered the initial
...critical lashings and proudly borne the brunt of the occasional
...bureaucratic iceberg. Its current licence restricts numbers to
...350 (the restaurant alone holds 300); it is hoped this number
...will be increased early in 2000. That said, those who get in are
...greeted by a spacious bar with plenty of elbow room for diners
...nd seating for barflies. All maroon art deco, Titanic's one
...major drawback is its nine enormous spinning mirrored balls,
...which can induce headaches, if not epilepsy. Drinks served at
...he sumptuous oval bar include cocktails for £7.50, Martinis
...rom £6.50, a modest selection of wines and champagnes and
...bottled beers by the likes of Kirin, Budvar and Hoegaarden all
...or £3.20. Aside from the restaurant menu, bar snacks range
...rom poached egg Benedict with hollandaise sauce (£6.50) to
...a scalope of calf's liver and bacon, with pommes purée and
...onion gravy (£13.50).
...Disabled: toilet. Late licence (Mon-Sat). Music (DJs 11pm
...Mon-Sat). Restaurant. Vegetarian dishes.

West Central

29-30 Lisle Street, WC2 (020 7479 7980).
Leicester Square tube. **Open** *main bar* noon-11pm daily;
theatre bar 5-11pm Mon-Sat; 5-10.30pm Sun; *basement bar*
10.30pm-11pm daily.
Admission (basement only) from £3. **Credit** MC, V.
West Central is a place where the party never seems to stop.
This permanently packed-to-the-hilt gay pub-cum-club
appears to host some sort of event nearly every night. It's
a pub of three parts, each with its own opening times and
atmosphere. If the raucous behaviour and camp disco hits
in the long, narrow main bar are not to your liking, you can
always seek sanctuary in the more subdued, living-room-
like theatre bar upstairs. If you want to party on, or haven't
got homes to go to, then head for the small but clubby
basement bar and dancefloor. Drinks are at basic pub
prices, with Grolsch at £2.67, Caffrey's £2.65 and
Worthingtons £2.32.
*Disabled: toilet. Late licence (Wed-Sat). Music (DJs
Wed-Sat).*

Zinc Bar & Grill

*21 Heddon Street, W1 (020 7255 8899). Oxford Circus or
Piccadilly Circus tube.* **Open/food served** noon-11pm
Mon-Sat. **Credit** AmEx, DC, JCB, MC, V.
Zinc is a small, but nonetheless popular Conran effort that,
crowd aside, is thankfully thin on pretension. Most of the area
is taken up by the restaurant, although the small bar area –
with its industrial-style bar, all gunmetal grey and pop rivets
– remains crowded throughout the evening. The chefs can be
seen going about their business in the open-plan kitchen, and
various crustacea line the far wall. This watery theme of the
menu is echoed by the scallop-imprinted glass partitions that
separate the rows of tables. Cocktails (from £6) dominate, and

Zinc Bar & Grill

there's a fine selection of champagnes, ranging from £32.50 to £120 a bottle, and beers include Freedom, Peroni, Budvar and Sapporo (all £2.75). A small selection of post-prandial cigars is also available.
Babies and children admitted (restaurant only). Disabled: toilet. Function room. Restaurant. Tables outdoors (terrace). Vegetarian dishes.

Also in the area...

All Bar One 48 Leicester Square, WC2 (020 7747 9921).
Café Flo 51 St Martin's Lane, WC2 (020 7836 8289).
Moon Under Water 28 Leicester Square, WC2 (020 7839 2837).
Slug & Lettuce 14 Upper St Martin's Lane, WC2 (020 7379 4880).

Marylebone W1, NW1

Atlantis
114-117 Crawford Street, W1 (020 7224 2878). Baker Street tube. **Open** 5-11pm Mon-Sat. **Food served** 7-10.30pm Mon-Sat. **Credit** AmEx, MC, V.
An aquatically themed and intimate basement bar, and one that's acquired another new fish tank. The owner said it housed genetically mutated sea bass, but they looked like goldfish to us. Other tanks, meanwhile, are home to blue zebras, silver dollars and, normally, freshwater sharks. But, when we paid a visit to the latter, it had escaped, passed on, and was yet to be replaced. Decor is green, aquamarine and all shades in between, with funky blue tubular lighting and a light-projected clock that beams out on to one wall. It's a popular place, with friendly staff who know how to mix their cocktails, including a pretty sharp Long Island Iced Tea (£6), while the more deranged among you may succumb to absinthe's bohemian charms for £4. Bottled beers start at £2.50.
Games (Connect 4, Jenga, Twister). Music (DJs). Vegetarian dishes.

Barley Mow
8 Dorset Street, W1 (020 7935 7318). Baker Street tube. **Open** 11am-11pm Mon-Sat. **Food served** 11.30am-3pm Mon-Sat. **Credit** AmEx, DC, MC, V.
Tatty it may be, what with its old wooden benches and well-worn maroon leather upholstery, but the Barley Mow is a warm and cosy place all the same. Having been around since 1791, it qualifies as the granddaddy of pubs, and deserves an award for never having had a trendy makeover. Near-original features include wooden snugs (little more than cubby holes opening up to the bar), remnants of a bygone era when Marylebone was a small village and people came here to celebrate the barley harvest. Nowadays these things serve only to add privacy for those who want it. For the rest, there are newspapers to read and real ales to be drunk. Choose from a fine selection, including Pedigree (£2.25), Addlestone's SP (£2.35), London Pride (£2.30) and Young's Special (£2.30). Food tends towards the basic, and a traditional ploughman's lunch costs £3.95.
Games (fruit machine, quiz machine). Satellite TV. Tables outdoors (pavement). Vegetarian dishes.

Beehive
7 Homer Street, W1 (020 7262 6581). Edgware Road tube. **Open** 11am-3.30pm, 5.30-11.30pm Mon-Thur; 11am-11pm Fri, Sat; noon-10.30pm Sun. **Food served** noon-2.30pm Mon-Fri. **Credit** MC, V.

To say this is a small pub would be an understatemen there's room for just six tables, and 20 people would fill i Effects such as the sepia-toned photographs arrange around the bar only add to the feeling that this could almo be someone's living room. It's about as unpretentious as the come, and get here early, as punters tend to stay for th duration. Be warned, the stairs to the gents are perilou especially after a bottle or two of Stella (£2.30) and a pint Young's Best Bitter (£2.20).
Tables outdoors (pavement). Vegetarian dishes.

Carpe Diem
28 Paddington Street, W1 (020 7935 0556). Baker Stree tube. **Open/food served** 10.30am-11pm Mon-Sat; noon-10.30pm Sun. **Credit** AmEx, MC, V.
It's name means 'seize the day', which, though a positiv platitude, is something that's hard to do while watching th world go by from inside a pub. Still, this is a pleasant enoug place, if a little too in love with the ubiquitous pine. Here it coloured for that matured and aged look, but it cover everything. Some of the tables are quite large, handy for th raucous after-work crowd that this place seems to attrac There are newspapers on sticks and a snack menu, and beer include Carlsberg (£2.30), Calders and Stella (both £2.55 while its much-touted but limited selection of wines starts a £2.50 a glass. Music here is constant, but unintrusive making this a good place if you actually want conversatio with your booze.
Babies and children admitted (high chairs). No-smoking area. Restaurant. Tables outdoors (pavement). Vegetarian dishes.

Chapel
48 Chapel Street, NW1 (020 7402 9220). Edgware Road tube. **Open** noon-11pm Mon-Sat; noon-4pm, 7-10.30pm Sun. **Food served** noon-2.30pm, 7-10pm daily. **Credit** AmEx, MC, V.
The Chapel is a bright and roomy place, but one that's onc again heavy on the pine. Upmarket and trendy, it draws an unpretentious, lively crowd of techno-kids and media types Drinks include Hoegaarden (£3.60), Staropramen (£2.80) Grolsch (£2.60), London Pride (£2.40) and Greene King IP (£2.40) on tap, and there's a large open-plan kitchen, so yo can see your food being rustled up. There's an eclectic an interesting if heftily priced menu that includes such things a watercress and feta tart (£8) and roasted parrot fish with di mash and grilled aubergines (£12.50). Light and airy whe empty, the Chapel can quickly become crammed, especiall on Fridays. There's a small terrace outside, with heater thoughtfully provided for those winter sessions.
Babies and children admitted. Function room. Tables outdoors (pavement, garden). Vegetarian dishes.

Churchill Bar & Cigar Divan
Churchill InterContinental, Portman Square, W1 (020 7486 5800). Marble Arch tube. **Open/food served** 11am-11pm Mon-Sat; 5-10.30pm Sun. **Credit** AmEx, DC, MC, V.
This grand and stately bar resides behind the rather blanc façade of the five-star Churchill InterContinental Hotel. Al rich wood panelling and highly polished floors, it's replet with leather armchairs and memorabilia related to th legendary war leader. Appropriately, then, the ba specialises in malt whiskies: there are over 70 to choose from, ranging in price from £7 to £16. You can also selec a cigar to go with your malt, from a generous range tha includes full-flavoured Bolivars, medium Montecristos, a well as Cohibas, Cuabas and Davidoffs. Prices are prett steep, with wines starting at £4.50 a glass, and a pint o

Grolsch will set you back £4.60, but drinks do come with such nibbles as spicy nuts, crackers and olives. Other snacks include chicken satay and dim sum, and there's a modest main menu, too.
Babies and children admitted (until 7pm). Disabled: toilet. Function room. Music (pianist Mon-Sat). Restaurant. Satellite TV. Vegetarian dishes.

Devonshire Arms
21A Devonshire Street, W1 (020 7935 8327). Baker Street tube. **Open** 11am-11pm Mon-Fri; noon-11pm Sat. **Food served** noon-10pm Mon-Sat. **Credit** AmEx, MC, V.
A sister-pub to the nearby **O'Conor Don** (*see below*), with the same kind of laid-back charm, although for different reasons. Here, it's a combination of bare wood floors, patterned tiles, frosted windows and friendly service, together with a gorgeous open-plan curved, bronzed and futuristic art deco-ish style bar to lean on, that make this a very warming place in which to sup. Drinks include Abbott Ale (£2.20), Greene King IPA (£2) and Guinness Extra Cold (£2.25). There are plenty of stools and high tables, some with the Guinness harp built into the stands, and the day's newspapers are available to read. The modest menu includes things such as home-cured salmon platter with bread and dill mayonnaise, £5.55, and mozzarella and aubergine bake for £5.65.
Function rooms. Tables outdoors (pavement). Vegetarian dishes.

Dover Castle
43 Weymouth Mews, W1 (020 7580 4412). Regent's Park tube. **Open** 11.30am-11pm Mon-Fri; noon-11pm Sat. **Food served** noon-2.30pm, 6-9.30pm Mon-Fri; noon-2.30pm Sat. **Credit** MC, V.
We arrived at the Dover Castle just in time to be included in an impromptu singalong of *Perfect Day*, led by former Squeeze frontman Glenn Tilbrook. All of which served to embellish further the reputation of this excellent pub, tucked away in a West End mews. The delightfully cheap beer comes courtesy of Samuel Smith, so there's Old Brewery (£1.52), Extra Stout (£1.88) and cider (£2.02) served up by friendly bar staff who seem up to speed on the usual football and politics banter, making this the ideal refuge from the All Bar Ones and Pitchers & Pianos of this world.
Function room. Games (quiz machine). TV. Vegetarian dishes.

Feathers
43 Linhope Street, NW1 (020 7402 1327). Marylebone tube/rail. **Open** 11am-11pm Mon-Sat; noon-10.30pm Sun. **Food served** noon-3pm Mon-Fri. **Credit** MC, V.
An unashamedly shabby bar that claims to be the second-smallest pub in London, and with good reason. It is tiny. Twelve people can and do make for a crammed, shoulder-rubbing crowd; the landlord claimed to have had 80 people in here once for an Ireland-England match, and while we couldn't help but wonder how they managed it, we were silently glad not to have been part of the experience. Carling (£2.25) and Stella (£2.40) are on draught, as well as Flowers Original (£2.05) and a regular selection of guest ales (from £2.10).
Jukebox. Tables outdoors (garden, pavement). Vegetarian dishes.

Henry Holland
39 Duke Street, W1 (020 7629 4426). Bond Street tube. **Open** 11am-11pm Mon-Sat; noon-8.30pm Sun. **Food served** 11am-3pm Mon-Sat. **Credit** MC, V.
The Henry Holland is a most pleasant find, all dark wood and, thanks to the low lighting, quite glowing with warmth. Here you can sit and watch the suits out for a post-work sup, or

cast an eye over the shoppers resting their wearies after having blitzed Selfridges opposite. The styling has a very 1920s feel, aided by the art deco prints lining the walls, which, in turn, are offset somewhat by the PlayStation ads on the walls in the toilets. Beers include Wadworth 6X (£2.25), Boddingtons (£2.10) and Flowers Original (£2.02). Bench seating is available outside.
Function room. Jukebox. Satellite TV. Tables outdoors (pavement). Vegetarian dishes.

Marylebone Tup
93 Marylebone High Street, W1 (020 7935 4373). Baker Street tube. **Open** 11.30am-11pm Mon-Sat; noon-10.30pm Sun. **Credit** AmEx, DC, MC, V.
'Oves Optimae Sunt' (sheep are best) is the Tup chain motto, emblazoned across the staff T-shirts, and, as if to push the point home, toy sheep adorn the bar area. This is a fine example of a Tup: large and spacious, catering to a polite and comfortably affluent crowd. The pale cream walls are decorated with lamps, a bronzed ram's head on a plaque and art generally depicting pub crowd scenes, although at least four pieces contained women revealing their breasts. There's Courage Best and Marston's Pedigree on tap (both £2.40) and the bottled selection includes Smirnoff Ice (£2.60).
Games (pool table). Satellite TV. Tables outdoors (pavement).

Oceana
Jason Court, 76 Wigmore Street, W1 (020 7224 2992). Bond Street tube. **Open/food served** noon-3pm, 5.30-11pm Mon-Fri; 5.30-11pm Sat. **Happy hour** 5.30-7pm Mon-Sat. **Credit** AmEx, DC, MC, V.
People do actually come just to drink here in this bar-restaurant (with the emphasis on the latter) tucked away off Wigmore Street. The walls are done out in lime green and aquamarine, and the bar area consists of half a dozen or so tables with chairs. The choice of beers is limited to bottles of San Miguel and Beck's (both £2.75), but there's a reasonable selection of wines, from £3 a glass, and cocktails from £5.50. You can order bar food if you don't want to dine proper, choosing from a selection of snacks such as goat's cheese, asparagus and red onion spring roll or deep fried halloumi sticks with spiced tomato jam, each for £3.75.
Babies and children admitted. Restaurant. Vegetarian dishes.

O'Conor Don
88 Marylebone Lane, W1 (020 7935 9311). Bond Street tube. **Open** 11am-11pm Mon-Fri; noon-11pm Sat. **Food served** noon-10pm Mon-Sat. **Credit** AmEx, MC, V.
This is an utterly charming place, if a little overenthusiastic with the Irish- and Guinness-related paraphernalia: it's on the walls, in and around the tables and even makes it into the tiling on the floor. Unsurprisingly, there's Guinness and Guinness Extra Cold (£2.30), Guinness Bitter and Harp lager (£2.30). On the first floor there's a country house-style dining room where a menu of hefty Irish-based dishes is served, and you can have a dozen fresh oysters for £6.75 and Irish Coffee for £3.30, but it's not a patch on the downstairs bar, which is a timeless place in which to sup. The bar staff are great, and more than happy to bring your pint to your table; they even come over and politely inform you when last orders are being called.
Function room. Restaurant. Tables outdoors (pavement). Vegetarian dishes.

The Street
58 Crawford Street, W1 (020 7724 4991). Baker Street, Edgware Road or Marylebone tube. **Open** 11.30am-11pm Mon-Fri; 10am-11pm Sat; 10am-

10.30pm Sun. **Food served** 11am-3pm, 6-10pm Mon-Fri;
10am-4pm Sat, Sun. **Credit** MC, V.

The young and trendy crowd that flock to this café-cum-bar-cum-restaurant are attracted, perhaps, by the cheery blue and yellow decor. Bamboo sofas predominate and, in the winter, there's a most welcoming, roaring open fire. The Street is Moroccan-owned, and this is reflected in the prints of North African street scenes on the walls and the food on the menu, which includes lamb tagine (£7.95) and, as a snack, houmous with pitta (£2.75). Games such as Jenga and Monopoly are available, and beers include Carling (£1.80) and Staropramen (£2.40).
Games (board games, Jenga). Restaurant. Tables outdoors (pavement). Vegetarian dishes.

Tsar's Bar

*Langham Hilton, 1 Portland Place, W1 (020 7636 1000).
Oxford Circus tube.* **Open** noon-11pm Mon-Fri; 6-11pm
Sat. **Food served** noon-3pm, 6-11pm Mon-Fri; 6-11pm
Sat. **Credit** AmEx, DC, MC, V.

Hotel bars are not everyone's immediate or regular choice of drinking hole, but, if vodka is your thing, then Tsar's Bar is really worth a look-in. Just tune out from the over-formal decor and the silly-frilly faux-Russian costumes the staff have to wear, and take your pick from over 80 different vodkas, including flavoured vodkas, vodka cocktails, vodkas from around the world and vodka combinations. Most, such as the Smirnoff Black, come in 50ml glasses that sit in frosted stands and cost around £6.50. The frosting means the vodka stays ice-cold all the way to the bottom, which just makes it that much easier to drink. If you're feeling frivolous, then peruse the selection of caviars, from Sevruga to Beluga (£34-£140). Note, though, that only guests and diners can stay after 11pm.
*Babies and children admitted (high chairs). Disabled: toilet.
Function rooms. Restaurant. Vegetarian dishes.*

Wigmore

*36 Wigmore Street, W1 (020 7487 4874).
Bond Street tube.* **Open** 10am-11pm Mon-Fri; 5-11pm Sat;
10am-10.30pm Sun. **Food served** noon-2.30pm,
6-10.30pm Mon-Fri; 6-10.30pm Sat; noon-2.30pm,
6-10.30pm Sun. **Credit** AmEx, MC, V.

Hard to find – we had to ask in a basement bar where we thought we should be, to be told that, yes, we were in the Wigmore, beneath the Wigmore Hall. The place was dead when we arrived, but we're assured that it had just been packed out, especially during the intermission from the auditorium. Nonetheless, it's a lovely place, more café than bar, but still a relaxing place to drink. The floors are tiled in wood, and the non-working open fireplace was stuffed with pine cones. The general ambience of the place inclines toward the French, with a menu listing such lunch options as filled baguettes (about £3) and croque monsieur (£3.30), and bottled beers include Stella as well as Beck's (both £2.50), but the cans of Coke appeared to have come from Spain.
*Function room. Music (live nightly). Restaurant.
Vegetarian dishes.*

William Wallace

*44 Blandford Street, W1 (020 7935 5963). Baker Street
or Bond Street tube.* **Open** 11am-11pm Mon-Sat; noon-
10.30pm Sun. **Food served** noon-3pm, 6-9pm Mon-Fri;
noon-8pm Sat, Sun. **Credit** AmEx, DC, MC, V.

The William Wallace is just like lots of other London pubs in every respect, except the crucial one, betrayed by its name: it's vigorously Scottish, down to the provenance of its beers and of the landlady, Frances. Both are worth travelling to find. The award-winning Deuchars IPA (£2.10) is on draught, along with other Scottish brews like McEwans 80 shilling

(£2), while Frances and English landlord Ray are more than happy to tell tales of home, even if you're from the south. If that happens to be the case, it might be best to avoid the place when England-Scotland sporting internationals are being broadcast. It's sister pub is the Rob Roy in Sussex Gardens.
*Babies and children admitted (upstairs). Jukebox. Music
(live Scottish, Sat). Restaurant. Satellite TV. Tables
outdoors (pavement). Vegetarian dishes.*

Windsor Castle

*29 Crawford Place, W1 (020 7723 4371).
Edgware Road tube.* **Open** 11am-11pm Mon-Sat;
noon-10.30pm Sun. **Food served** 11am-3pm, 6-11pm
Mon-Fri; 6-11pm Sat. **Credit** MC, V.

The Castle was opened in July 1990 by *EastEnders*-actress Wendy Richard – it says so on a plaque outside. And if that doesn't hint at the nature of the place, then the overwhelming amount of royal paraphernalia, memorabilia and general bric-a-brac in the form of pictures, postcards, glasses, figurines and other assorted souvenirs should. Every available surface is well and truly covered, and even the tables do not escape unscathed, inscribed as they are with the names of various royal houses. As if that were not enough, the bar is also the regular haunt of the Handlebar Club, a group of tufty-'tache fans who have been meeting since 1947. Drinks on offer include Hancock's HP and Bass, both for £2.10, and Caffrey's at £2.40. A charming, otherworldly, if somewhat surreal place in which to sup.
*Babies and children admitted. Restaurant. Tables outdoors
(patio). Vegetarian dishes.*

Windsor Castle

98 Park Road, NW1 (020 7723 9262). Baker Street tube.
Open 11am-11pm Mon-Sat; noon-10.30pm Sun.
Food served noon-2pm daily. **Credit** MC, V.

An impressive three-storey edifice, and one that claims to have been the first Brakspear pub in London. It should come as no surprise then to find that Brakspear Bitter (£2.10), Special (£2.20) and OBJ (£2.30) are all on draught, as are such staples as Stella and Heineken. It's a bright and well-lit, Georgian-style place, with cream-coloured walls and pale green ceilings. Huge gilt-edged mirrors dominate the downstairs bar, and carpeted stairs lead first to a small one-table bar decorated with brewing-related paraphernalia, and then on to a carpeted lounge bar that contains a pool table. Sadly, the sofas have been passed over in favour of extra tables, perhaps to allow space for the standard bar food (all around £5). A fine bar indeed.
*Function room. Games (fruit machines, pool table).
Jukebox. Satellite TV. Tables outdoors (pavement).
Vegetarian dishes.*

Zoe

*3-5 Barrett Street, St Christopher's Place, W1
(020 7224 1122). Bond Street tube.* **Open** 11.30am-
11.30pm Mon-Sat. **Food served** noon-3.30pm, 6.30-
11.15pm Mon-Sat. **Happy hour** 5.30-7.30pm Mon-Sat.
Credit AmEx, DC, MC, V.

Despite its over-designed façade, Zoe is an unpretentious cocktail bar of Spanish influence done up in a vaguely '70s style with music to match, and with a restaurant round the back. It's popular with shoppers from the local boutiques and its happy hour is particularly good value: from 5.30pm to 7pm all its classic cocktails (from Bellinis to Slow Comfortable Screws, £5-£6) are half price. On our visit, many of the punters seemed to know the bartender, which made for a jolly atmosphere enhanced by the bar's intimate scale.
*Babies and children admitted (high chairs). Disabled: toilet.
No-smoking area (restaurant). Restaurant. Tables
outdoors (courtyard). Vegetarian dishes.*

All Bar One 5-6 Picton Place, W1 (020 7487 0161); 289-293 Regent Street, W1 (020 7467 9901); 7-9 Paddington Street, W1 (020 7487 0071).
Café Flo 14 Thayer Street, W1 (020 7935 5023).
Café Rouge 46-48 James Street, W1 (020 7487 4847).
Davys 92 Wigmore Street, W1 (020 7224 0169).
Dock Blida (Davys) 50-54 Blandford Street, W1 (020 7486 3590).
Farrier & Firkin 74 York Street, W1 (020 7262 1513).

Mayfair W1

American Bar
Connaught Hotel, 16 Carlos Place, W1 (020 7499 7070).
Bond Street or Green Park tube. **Open** 11am-3pm, 5.30-11pm Mon-Sat; noon-2.30pm, 7-10.30pm Sun.
Credit AmEx, DC, MC, V.
Early Thursday evening, and most of the clientele here are busy deciding what to eat in the deservedly famous dining room next door. The bar itself is also famous, as the one-time haunt of jaded aristos and American *arrivistes*, but precious little of their glamorous aura remains. The stately home-style decor of oak panelling, stuffed stags' heads and equestrian oil paintings looks like an expensive but tacky refit. On our visit, one inscrutable crimson-blazered waiter was having difficulty understanding a request for potato vodka from the senior member of a mixed group of garrulous guests from the Deep South. Cocktails are expensive (£10.50 for a Kir Royale, £8 for a Gin Fizz), although the shorts are better value.
Disabled: toilet. Dress code. Function rooms.
Vegetarian dishes.

Audley
41-43 Mount Street, W1 (020 7499 1843).
Green Park tube. **Open** 11am-11pm Mon-Sat; noon-10.30pm Sun. **Food served** 11am-9.30pm Mon-Sat; noon-9pm Sun. **Credit** AmEx, DC, MC, V.
The Audley is a grand old Mayfair corner pub with the atmosphere and furnishings of a slightly tatty gentlemen's club: chandeliers, studded red leather high-backed benches and high ceilings, and a large clock hanging above the bar in a beautifully carved bracket. In short, it's somewhat smarter than your average watering hole. Weekday lunchtimes and after work the place rapidly fills up with office workers in suits talking shop, but later gives way to a more relaxed local crowd. The service is courteous, the beers are strictly standard (Directors £2.32, Courage Best £2.10), but the Audley's decor does at least give it some individuality.
Babies and children admitted (dining area only). Function room. Tables outdoors (pavement). Vegetarian dishes.

Château Bar
Mayfair InterContinental Hotel, Stratton Street, W1 (020 7629 7777/www.interconti.com). Green Park tube.
Open/food served 11.30am-11pm Mon-Fri; 6-11pm Sat; 6-10.30pm Sun. **Credit** AmEx, DC, MC, V.
A Manhattan-style piano-cocktail bar par excellence, this small, dimly lit place is a surprising find in the otherwise fairly characterless Mayfair InterContinental. Fine champagnes and cocktails are served up by reliable-looking, uniformed old-timers, while on our visit the piano in the corner was being tunefully fingered by a beautiful blonde. Martinis (all £11) are a speciality, including the famous Silver Bullet (with whisky) and not-so-famous Bitch on Wheels (with

Claridge's Bar. *See page 71.*

Pernod and crème de menthe). For the same price you can also try a Green Fairy or a Casino, absinthe-based concoctions involving gin and lemon and champagne and brandy respectively. More traditional numbers like a Sea Breeze or Margarita are £8.50, and worth every penny. Signed photos of assorted musos and minor celebs who have visited over the years beam down on the escapist scene.
Disabled: toilet. Function rooms. Music (pianist 6.30pm-12.30am Mon-Sat). No-smoking area. Restaurant. Satellite TV. Vegetarian dishes.

Chocolate Bar
59 Berkeley Square, W1 (020 7499 7850). Green Park tube. **Open** 11am-3am Mon-Fri; 10am-3.30pm Sat. **Food served** 11am-6pm Mon-Fri. **Credit** MC, V.
The Chocolate Bar has already earned a reputation for its Ucci club nights on Saturdays downstairs, while the upstairs space is a music café-bar that's refreshingly straight-forward, given that it's in Berkeley Square. Decorated in a vaguely '70s style, with chunky chocolate-coloured high-back benches and sofas, poinsettias on the zinc-topped tables and mellow lighting, it's generally pretty laid-back in mood, even if the window displays make it feel a bit like a car showroom. Staff are laid-back, too, although it was a pity they couldn't be bothered to change the ashtrays. Drinks costs as much as you might expect for the area: bottles of Beck's, Red Stripe or Carling are £3, as are spirits, while a Kir Royale clocked in at a regal £7. The food menu, available until 6pm, looks better value, offering baked potatoes for £3 or a salmon steak for £7.50. A handy place to know about if you happen to be in the area.
Babies and children admitted (until 6pm). Function room. Late licence. Music (DJ Tue, Fri). Tables outdoors (pavement). Vegetarian dishes.

WAIKIKI WHEN YOU CAN TRADER VIC'S

Trader Vic's is the legendary cocktail bar and restaurant for tropical-minded urbanites, a mood lagoon tucked away beneath th London Hilton in Park Lane. It is the home of the Mai Tai and sets standards for Island cuisine. It is delicious and exotic in the extreme. Make a reservation for dinner or book our private functio room and we are sure you will soon agree, that it's the bee's-knees

ADVENTURES IN CUISINE

TRADER VIC'S AT THE LONDON HILTON ON PARK LANE
22 PARK LANE, LONDON W1Y 4BE TEL: 020 7208 4113 FAX: 020 7208 4050

Claridge's Bar

Claridge's Hotel, Brook Street, W1 (020 7629 8860/ www.info@claridges.co.uk). Bond Street tube. **Open/food served** 11am-11pm Mon-Sat; noon-10.30pm Sun. **Credit** AmEx, DC, MC, V.
When it was redecorated in 1998 to celebrate the hotel's centenary, this august bar was voted one of the world's best by hi-chic *Wallpaper** magazine. It's not difficult to see why: the art deco interior (by David Collins) manages to be both a thing of beauty and somewhere in which you feel immediately at home. The bar stools alone are almost too lovely to put your bum on; the polite and unhurried service is impeccable, as you would expect in the bar of one of the capital's most exclusive hotels. No real surprises on the drinks front, which offers a classic selection of cocktails (Martinis £7.50), and an extensive range of wines and spirits. The bar snacks, though, are extraordinary: spring rolls (£6.50) took the form of six exquisite little finger morsels. As elegant a place for a tipple as Mayfair can provide.
Disabled: toilet. Function rooms. Restaurant. Vegetarian dishes.

Coach & Horses

5 Bruton Street, W1 (020 7629 4123). Bond Street or Green Park tube. **Open** 11am-11pm Mon-Fri; 11am-8pm Sat. **Food served** noon-10.30pm Mon-Fri; noon-7.30pm Sat. **Credit** AmEx, DC, MC, V.
It's hard to miss the Coach & Horses' small olde-worlde timber-framed building amid the smart offices and boutiques of Bruton Street. Once inside things are just as out-of-keeping with the area: a bog-standard little pub that owes its charm to its tiny size and friendly bar staff. Understandably, it's very popular with an affable crowd of after-work office wallahs and cheery locals. The unflappable landlord has perfected the art of keeping a cool head and his customers happy, even at the busiest times, which probably explains why the atmosphere doesn't seem rowdy. Later on in the evening the quiet of the place comes as a blessed relief from some of the area's more pretentious hangouts. Standard beers on offer are Courage Best at £2.15 and Directors at £2.34, and a variety of pies (£5.75), fish and chips (£6.95) et al fill the menu.
Babies and children admitted (restaurant only). Function room. Games (fruit machines). Restaurant. Vegetarian dishes.

Dorchester Bar

Dorchester Hotel, 53 Park Lane, W1 (020 7629 8888). Hyde Park Corner tube. **Open** 11am-12.30am Mon-Sat; noon-10.30pm Sun. **Food served** noon-11.45pm Mon-Sat; noon-10.30pm Sun. **Credit** AmEx, DC, MC, V.
The bar at one of the poshest hotels in town certainly achieves the kind of showbiz magic you might expect, but not without considerable effort. A corridor of tinted mirrors leads into a sunken room sparkling with reflective tiles stuck all over the walls, ceiling and even the piano. There's plenty of opportunity to sneak glances at other guests enjoying the deep yellow armchairs and comfortable banquette-booths. The atmosphere is not at all stuffy, and the service is smiling and efficient. Prices are also as high as you would expect (£8.50 for most cocktails, £4.50 for the bottled beers) but our Singapore Sling and Long Island Iced Tea were so uncannily and perfectly concocted they might well have been done with mirrors, too. The food is traditional Italian – the pasta is home-made – at equally home-made prices (£12-£15).
Disabled: toilet. Function rooms. Music (pianist Sun-Tue; jazz band Wed-Sat). Restaurant. Vegetarian dishes.

Guinea

30 Bruton Place, W1 (020 7409 1728). Bond Street or Green Park tube. **Open** 11am-11pm Mon-Fri; 6.30-11pm Sat. **Food served** noon-2.30pm Mon-Fri; 6.30-11pm Sat; 6.30-10pm Sat. **Credit** AmEx, DC, MC, V.
Tucked away off Berkeley Square, the Guinea Grill restaurant behind this old-fashioned Young's pub has been a reliable Mayfair institution since the 1950s. Its menu of traditional British fare – which is quite expensive – can also be enjoyed in the tiny pub out front, unless the place is packed. As in many Mayfair pubs the clientele is dominated by male office-dwellers, who quickly occupy the little available seating. The beer is as good as you'd expect from Young's, and if you pick your time right this makes a lovely place for a pint (bitter £2) and, if you're feeling hungry, a pie.
Function room. No piped music or jukebox. Restaurant. Tables outdoors (pavement). Vegetarian dishes.

Hanover Square Wine Bar

25 Hanover Square, W1 (020 7408 0935). Oxford Circus tube. **Open** 11am-11pm Mon-Fri. **Food served** 11am-10.30pm Mon-Fri. **Credit** AmEx, DC, MC, V.
A basement wine bar on the corner of Hanover Square (its entrance is actually on George Street) that has a long-standing reputation for the quality of its wines and the warmth of the welcome it offers all-comers. The layout is pitched just right between bar and restaurant, the dark red colour scheme and low ceilings making for a pleasingly louche atmosphere. Reasonably priced bistro-style food (two courses for roughly £15) is served to tables at either end of the S-shaped room, while the bar, wine racks and kitchen occupy centre stage. A typical house white might be a Listel Sauvignon Blanc (£9.95) and the extensive list is particularly strong on the New World.
No-smoking area. Restaurant. Satellite TV. Vegetarian dishes.

Havana Square

17 Hanover Square, W1 (020 7629 2552). Oxford Circus tube. **Open/food served** noon-2am Mon-Wed; noon-3am Thur-Sat; 5pm-1am Sun. **Admission** after 11pm Mon, Tue £3; after 10pm Wed £5; after 11pm Thu £5; after 9pm £5, after 10pm Fri, Sat £10; after 8pm Sun £3. **Happy hour** 5pm-2am Mon; 5-7pm Tue-Sun. **Credit** AmEx, DC, MC, V.
We stumbled into an open salsa class here of a Wednesday night, and the place was packed with hip-swinging twentysomethings. This is the first in a lively stretch of bars catering for a youngish crowd that rounds the corner into Dering Street, and like some others manages to be a club, bar and kind-of restaurant all at the same time. The decoration of its basement space is appropriately wild, with misshapen metal plates snaking along the ceiling, crumpled-looking lampshades and a lurid colour scheme. There's a marginally quieter area at the bottom of the stairs as you enter, but otherwise this is a place for partying, not a dinner à deux. A couple of the classic cocktails that we tasted (Margarita £4.75) could have been better mixed, but then sophistication here is not the name of the game.
Dress code. Late licence. Music (DJs 9pm nightly, Brazilian band 8pm Sun, Salsa band Thur). Restaurant. Vegetarian dishes.

Hogshead in St James's

11-16 Dering Street, W1 (020 7629 0531/ www.hogshead.co.uk). Bond Street or Oxford Circus tube. **Open** 11am-11pm Mon-Sat. **Food served** noon-9pm Mon-Thur; noon-8pm Fri, Sat. **Credit** DC, MC, V.

Hush

A large corner pub in Mayfair – not St James's as the name suggests – this place may be part of Whitbread's burgeoning Hogshead chain but it doesn't lack character. Open-plan and woody, its main asset is size: three floors make finding a seat no problem, even when everyone else also seems to have congregated here to sit out the rush hour. There's an impressive choice of drinks, from real ales to Belgian lagers (Wadworth 6X £2.15, Hoegaarden £1.75 a half-pint), as well as a respectable wine list and an appetising, if standard, pub menu (fish and chips £4.80, sausage and mash £4.65).
Disabled: toilet. No-smoking area. Vegetarian dishes.

Hush

8 Lancashire Court, Brook Street, W1 (020 7659 1500). Bond Street. **Open** 11am-11pm Mon-Sat. **Food served** 11am-10pm Mon-Sat. **Credit** AmEx, MC, V.
What makes the atmosphere at Hush live up to its name? Perhaps it's the deadening acoustics of the padded chocolate wall hangings, more likely it's the glam clientele being far too busy looking over each others' shoulders to actually converse. Bar snacks tend towards the penne, risotto and Hush club variety (£6.50-£8), and there are only a few beer options (Pils £3, St Peter's Organic Ale £4.25). It's best to stick to champagne cocktails (£7), Martinis (£6.50) or shorts as refreshment between bouts of celebrity spotting – whispers of Madonna, sightings of Posh – and ostentatious draws on your cigar (Montecristo joyitas £7, Trinidad fundadores £22). All good clean fun, but shouldn't the beautiful people be told that bald-headed businessmen perched on piles of brown velour scatter cushions is just a little too redolent of tired hotel lounge bars. "Hush," they'd reply, "it's ironic, silly."
Disabled: lift, toilet. Tables outdoors (courtyard). Restaurant. Vegetarian dishes.

The Loop

19 Dering Street, W1 (020 7493 1003/ www.theloopbar.co.uk). Oxford Circus tube. **Open/food served** noon-1am Mon-Wed; noon-3am Thur-Sat. **Happy hour** 5-7pm daily. **Credit** AmEx, MC, V. Over-25s only.
Just along the road from the late and surprisingly lamented telephone bar Caspers, this massive new venture boasts four different bars and a restaurant. The cavernous basement is the main party area, and on busy Friday and Saturday nights it's a veritable Bermuda Triangle for cocktail jugs (£11.25-£16). Upstairs is usually a quieter place to enjoy something like a Long Beach Iced Tea (or a Long Island with cranberries instead of cola, £3.95) and interesting bar snacks like crispy Chinese barbecue duck with beanshoots, snow peas and oyster mushrooms (£5.25), a smoked salmon and cream cheese bagel for £4.25, or if you prefer something a little more straightforward, chunky chips with ketchup are £2.50. A good value happy hour offers bottles of wine at half price, and cocktails at £2.50.
Dress code. Music (DJs Thur-Sat). Late licence. Restaurant. Vegetarian dishes.

Metropolitan Bar

Metropolitan Hotel, 19 Old Park Lane, W1 (020 7447 1000/www.metropolitan.co.uk). Hyde Park Corner tube. **Open/food served** 11am-6pm daily. **Credit** AmEx, DC, MC, V.
The Met Bar's popularity with celebrity bohos continues unabated, largely because of its glittering (and full) membership list. Don't expect to get in here after 6pm unless you happen to be staying at the hotel, know the manager or are on the guest list. Sadly, the bar is like death warmed up during the day and surprisingly small in the light of its widespread fame. At night its scarlet colour scheme receives the benefit of some sophisticated lighting, as do its clientele.

They're likely to be knocking back any one of 40 vodkas, 27 Martini cocktails or an absinthe (£9 a shot). Bar snacks include the Met Club sandwich with chips (£10), which is big enough for two.
Disabled: toilet. Function rooms. Music (DJs Mon-Sat). Restaurant. Vegetarian dishes.

Mulligans of Mayfair

13-14 Cork Street, W1 (020 7409 1370). Green Park or Piccadilly Circus tube. **Open** 11am-11pm Mon-Sat. **Food served** noon-3pm, 5.30-9.30pm Mon-Sat. **Credit** AmEx, DC, MC, V.
Now part of the Balls Brothers chain, the basement oyster bar and restaurant at Mulligans was providing a taste of the old country in Mayfair long before Oirish theme bars were a twinkle in a marketing man's eye. The ground-floor bar, done up in dark green and looking a little tatty, is popular with suited devotees of the dark stuff and with post-private viewers from the galleries on Cork Street. A pint of Guinness comes in at £2.60, served up patiently by amiable bar staff who also do a good job of keeping the tables clean. No bitters, but a good selection of draught lagers, and a superb collection of Irish whiskeys, including Red Breast (£3.80) and Middleton Very Rare (£7.50).
Function room. Jukebox. Restaurant. Vegetarian dishes.

Nicole's

158 New Bond Street, W1 (020 7499 8408). Bond Street or Green Park tube. **Open/food served** 10am-10.45pm Mon-Fri; 10am-6pm Sat. **Credit** AmEx, DC, MC, V.
The appropriately stylish, minimalist restaurant beneath Nicole Farhi's New Bond Street store also has a long bar area with tables for drinkers overlooking the eaters. At seven o'clock of an evening it was practically deserted, and an ideal place for some meditative whisky sours (£5), listening to mellow strains of the likes of Sinatra and Fitzgerald. As you'd expect, there's also an impressive wine list (from £3.25 a glass) and service at the bar is unfailingly polite and attentive, which probably explains the service charge automatically added to the bill, even though we were sitting at the bar. The charge proved to be purely optional, which enhanced our impression of a smooth operation that must be a sophisticated treat when it's busy, either at lunchtimes or later in the evening. The bar menu is equally sophisticated, with the likes of pan-fried swordfish (£11.50), or cornmeal blini with smoked salmon and crème fraîche (£10.50).
Babies and children admitted. No-smoking area. Restaurant. Vegetarian dishes.

Polo Bar

Westbury Hotel, New Bond Street, W1 (020 7629 7755). Green Park or Oxford Circus tube. **Open/food served** 11am-11pm daily. **Credit** AmEx, DC, MC, V.
Not the mint with the hole, but the game with the ponies is the theme here, albeit in a pretty understated style. If polo pitches have pavilions, maybe this is what they're like: all masculine burgundy and dark green with large windows, although in this case they overlook the boutiques and rarified streetlife of Conduit Street. It's the service that sets this place apart from some more supercilious five-star establishments in the area. Laddered your tights? No problem, a helpful Australian barmaid is at hand with some nail varnish to stop it going further. Wondering how to take your Martini (£7)? How about trying one 'dirty', splashed with a dash of olive brine and tasting much better than it sounds, which could equally well be said of the Westbury's style in general. They only do bottled beers here (Beck's, Michelob, both £3.50), and fine, if expensive, snacks (Westbury Club £9.25, croque monsieur £7.25).
Function room. Music (pianist Fri-Sat). No-smoking area. Satellite TV. Restaurant. Vegetarian dishes.

Punch Bowl

41 Farm Street, W1 (020 7493 6841).
Green Park tube. **Open** 11am-11pm Mon-Fri;
noon-6pm Sat. **Food served** 11am-9.30pm Mon-Fri;
noon-5pm Sat. **Credit** AmEx, DC, MC, V.
After a hard day reviewing Mayfair bars and dodging the
Range Rovers and Rolls-Royces emerging smoothly from
behind their electric garage doors, it came as something of a
relief to find this bog-standard boozer happily doing business
at the end of Farm Street. On a Monday night it was pretty
quiet, but a few regulars were propping up the bar and
chatting to some surprisingly casual-looking local office
types. Drinks are nothing special (Guinness £2.27, Courage
Best £2.02) and nor are the furnishings, but the friendly
service and clientele make for a pleasingly unassuming
atmosphere. Upstairs you'll find pool tables and a dartboard.
*Function room. Games (darts, fruit machine, pool tables,
video golf). Jukebox. Vegetarian dishes.*

Q Bar

*12 New Burlington Street, W1 (020 7434 3949). Oxford
Circus or Piccadilly Circus tube.* **Open** 5pm-3am Mon-Sat.
Food served 6-10.30pm Mon-Sat. **Happy hour**
5-8pm Mon-Fri. **Credit** AmEx, DC, MC, V.
First and foremost this is a music bar, but when we visited it
was unusually quiet: the DJ had gone home early because
someone awash with festive spirit had poured their drink into
the amp. Kosovar barman Afrim seemed unfazed, though, if
a little less busy than he might like, and mixed up a couple of
very fine Martinis (£6, or £3 in happy hour). The decor of the
long thin room is vaguely Moorish/Graeco-Roman in
inspiration, and attracts wealthy Europeans and besuited
men and women. Italian food is available in the evenings.
*Function room. Late licence (Mon-Sat). Music (DJs
nightly). Restaurant. Vegetarian dishes.*

Red Bar

Grosvenor Hotel, Park Lane, W1 (020 7499 6363).
Marble Arch tube. **Open** noon-11pm Mon-Sat;
7-11pm Sun. **Credit** AmEx, DC, MC, V.
Somehow the Red Bar, in one of Park Lane's poshest hotels,
sounds as if it ought to be either very trendy or dangerously
decadent. In fact it's neither: the name is nothing if not
accurate, as it's decorated throughout in deep reds in an old-
fashioned way, but it has all the style of an executive lounge
at an international airport. On our visit mid-evening of a
Friday, the radio provided background music and chat
beside a couple of muted TVs, while an odd assortment of
dressed-up individuals chatted at the bar. Otherwise the
place was almost empty. All the drinks you would expect of
a smart hotel are available, at a price (Martinis £8.50, double
whisky £5.50). The feeling that you're an extra in an episode
of *Twin Peaks* is free.
*Babies and children admitted. Disabled: toilet. Late licence.
Satellite TV.*

Red Lion

1 Waverton Street, W1 (020 7499 1307).
Green Park tube. **Open** 11.30am-11pm Mon-Fri;
6-11pm Sat; noon-3pm, 6-10.30pm Sun.
Food served noon-2.30pm, 6-9.30pm Mon-Sat; noon-
2.30pm, 6-9.30pm Sun. **Credit** AmEx, DC, MC, V.
More country-pub than most pubs in the country, even on a
cold winter's night the Red Lion was popular enough with
the local after-work suits to have a crowd of them standing
around drinking outside. Inside, once they've departed for
home and left room to breathe, you'll find a delightfully snug
set of panelled rooms with wooden high-backed benches and

diamond-shaped lead-latticed windows. Standard but well-
kept beers include Greene King IPA (£2.30) and Guinness
(£2.48). In a back room there's a restaurant, which offers
what must be some of the most expensive traditional fish
and chips in London, for £14.50. Another option might be
best end of lamb (£18). These prices might reflect the quality
of the food, or just the pub's popularity with wealthy tourists
in search of a genuine English pub tucked away in the heart
of the capital.
*Babies and children admitted (children's menus). No piped
music or jukebox. Restaurant. Vegetarian dishes.*

Running Footman

5 Charles Street, W1 (020 7499 2988). Green Park tube.
Open 11.30am-11pm Mon-Fri; 11.30am-3pm, 7-11pm Sat;
noon-3pm, 7-10.30pm Sun. **Food served** 11.30am-10pm
Mon-Fri; 11.30am-2.30pm, 7-10pm Sat; noon-2.30pm,
7-9.30pm Sun. **Credit** AmEx, DC, MC, V.
Just around the corner, traffic hurtles around Berkeley Square
at speeds that would have staggered this place's namesake, the
man who used to trot along in front of automobiles with red
flags to warn pedestrians and equestrians of the approaching
machine. The pub itself isn't quite so stuck in olden times, but
offers a pleasantly down-to-earth and friendly place to enjoy
the usual selection of beers (Theakston Best £2.18, Directors
£2.32), or maybe a snack like a baked jacket potato, sausage
and beans for £2.65, or a filled baguette for £2.95, exceptionally
good value for the area. Upstairs there's a small dining room
that's busy at lunchtimes, and a function room.
*Babies and children admitted. Function room. Games
(fruit machine, quiz machine). Jukebox. TV. Tables
outdoors (pavement). Vegetarian dishes.*

Scotts

*20 Mount Street, W1 (020 7629 5248). Bond Street or
Green Park tube.* **Open/food served** noon-3pm, 5-11pm
Mon-Fri; 5-11pm Sat; noon-3pm, 6-10.30pm Sun. **Happy
hour** 5-7pm, 10-11pm Mon-Fri. **Credit** AmEx, DC, MC, V.
The restaurant on the ground floor here is a traditional
Mayfair institution (starched white tablecloths and waiters
in well-pressed jackets) while down a spiral staircase that
twists round a column of bubbling water there's a small,
smart cocktail bar. It's a cocktail bar par excellence, where
some superb concoctions are confidently put together by head
barman Celso and his impeccable staff. All cost £6.50, and

Critics' choice
internet bars

Buzz Bar (p76)
Surf the net or sup on the sofa (7 terminals).

Cyberia (p39)
Synchronised sipping and surfing (18).

Global Café (p62)
Even die-hard technophobes will be tempted by
this fine and funky café (12).

Vibe Bar (p204)
Loud and hyper-cool in an old brewery (4).

Webshack (p95)
Hot food and plenty of terminals (20).

---

include the likes of Scotts No.1 (gin, Cointreau and orange juice) or the Sidecar (brandy, Cointreau, and lemon juice). Stylish, comfortable Pierre Chareau sofas and low coffee tables surround the bar, and there's also a discreet dining area that can be specially booked. Service is polite and attentive and to cap it all the pianist played like she was in love.
Babies and children admitted. Function rooms. Music (jazz Sat, pianist 6-10pm Mon-Fri). No-smoking area. Restaurant. Tables outdoors (pavement). Vegetarian dishes.

Shepherd's Tavern
50 Hertford Street, W1 (020 7499 3017). Green Park or Hyde Park Corner tube. **Open** 11am-11pm Mon-Sat; noon-10.30pm Sun. **Food served** 11am-10pm Mon-Sat; noon-9.30pm Sun. **Credit** AmEx, DC, MC, V.
A small corner pub conveniently close to the Curzon Mayfair cinema, this Scottish and Newcastle house is a pleasant if unremarkable refuge from the weather in winter or the tourist crowds in summer. Brightly coloured chalkboards and fruit machines set the slightly impersonal tone, but when it's busy the place is perfectly snug. The standard Courage beers are available: Courage Best £2.10, Directors £2.29, Sky TV provides the sporting entertainment, and trad English pub food (fish and chips £5.45, sausage and mash £4.95) the kitchen's offerings.
Babies and children admitted (dining area only). Function room. Games (fruit machines). Jukebox. Restaurant. Satellite TV. Vegetarian dishes.

Trader Vic's & Windows
Hilton Hotel, Park Lane, W1 (020 7493 8000). Hyde Park Corner tube. **Open** 5pm-1.30am Mon-Sat; 5-10.30pm Sun. **Food served** 6pm-12.30am Mon-Sat; 6-9.45pm Sun. **Credit** AmEx, DC, MC, V.
The transformation of the basement of the Hilton into a South Island beach bar back in the 1970s might have cost a bomb, but it's certainly paid off. As an exercise in sophisticated kitsch the place now has a timeless charm, and looks none the worse for wear. Low lighting, piped samba music and bamboo complete a perfectly escapist atmosphere. Elegant waitresses in oriental costume still glide around with practised efficiency, serving up deservedly famous cocktails from a list of more than 100; some, like Black Stripe, a reviving hot skull-mug of rum, honey and cinnamon (£5.50), and Buttered Rum (also £5.50), a sickly sweet hot drink, are prepared at your tableside with bizarre ceremony. The whisky sours (£6.25) were not the strongest we've ever tasted, but still packed a punch. Flame-roasted food can be had from the Chinese red clay ovens. The **Windows** bar up on the 28th floor offers spectacular views across London, and although it is extremely popular, it has a faintly seedy atmosphere, and a £6 cover charge to non-guests after 11pm. The drinks list is again extensive, but so are the prices (bottled beers £4), but it does have the added advantage of being open at lunchtimes during the week. It is however closed Sunday evenings.
Babies and children admitted (restaurant only). Function rooms. Late licence (Mon-Sat). Music (Latin 10.30pm Mon-Sat). Restaurant. Vegetarian dishes.

Vendôme
20 Dover Street, W1 (020 7629 5417). Green Park tube. **Open/food served** noon-11pm Mon-Fri. **Food served** noon-2.30pm, 6-10.45pm Mon-Fri. **Credit** AmEx, DC, MC, V.
Popular with smart business men and women, and adjacent to a swanky restaurant, this is a thoroughly Frenchified cocktail bar. The accessories that accompany the drinks, from stirrers down to the beautiful glasses, have a certain style,

and our French waiter was wonderfully solicitous without being overbearing. The decor is classy and colourful (gold, vermilion, maroon and black), with the bizarre exception of what looked like ranks of framed artichoke hearts hanging on the wall, and the seats are achingly comfortable. Late in the evening, the place was a welcome retreat from some of the area's brasher joints, even though it comes at a price: cocktails start at £5.50 and the bottled beers are all £3.
Babies and children admitted. Function room. Music (pianist 6pm Mon-Fri). Restaurant. Vegetarian dishes.

Windmill
6-8 Mill Street, W1 (020 7491 8050). Oxford Circus tube. **Open** 11am-11pm Mon-Fri; noon-4pm Sat. **Food served** noon-3pm Mon-Fri; 12.30-3pm Sat. **Credit** AmEx, DC, MC, V (minimum charge £10).
Another Young's pub like the **Guinea** (*see p71*), the Windmill has considerably more space and is consequently less cosy or crowded, but makes up for that with the no-nonsense jolliness of the staff, its award-winning sandwiches and pies (£3-£7), and, of course, its beer. 'Nothing fancy' might well be the motto here, making the place feel vaguely as if it belongs in the north of England rather than Mayfair. It's an attitude clearly appreciated by a loyal local following of lunchers and after-work drinkers, who don't mind the fact that the furnishings have become a bit tatty round the edges and the carpet rather stained. Both can be taken to reflect a preoccupation with a pub's important qualities, its beer (Young's Special £2.15, Pilsner £2.25) and its atmosphere, so often overlooked in other central London drinking holes.
Function room. Games (fruit machine). No-smoking area (lower bar). No piped music or jukebox. Restaurant. Vegetarian dishes.

Woodstock
11 Woodstock Street, W1 (020 7408 2008). Bond Street tube. **Open/food served** 11am-11pm Mon-Sat; noon-10.30pm Sun. **Credit** MC, V.
A pretty average pub in many respects, the Woodstock is worth knowing about as somewhere quiet and decent to go for a pint just off Oxford Street, even at lunchtime. There's usually no problem getting a seat, and the back room is lit by an attractive wooden lantern skylight. Reasonable pub grub is served all day and their draught bitters are above average, with Theakston Old Peculier (£2.43), Abbot Ale and Directors (£2.28) the mainstays, plus a regularly changing guest ale. The bar staff are friendly, and service is prompt and efficient.
Tables outdoors (pavement). Vegetarian dishes.

Ye Grapes
16 Shepherd Market, W1 (020 7499 1563). Green Park or Hyde Park Corner tube. **Open** 11am-11pm Mon-Sat; noon-10.30pm Sun. **Food served** 12.30-2.30pm daily. **Credit** MC, V.
Nestling amid the rather twee environs of Shepherd Market, Ye Grapes looks tiny from the outside, but inside puts on a passable imitation of a grand Edwardian shooting lodge. Well-worn red plush velvet seating, green flock wallpaper, stuffed animals in glass cases and a real coal fire make for a cosy but faintly seedy atmosphere, in keeping with the market's former reputation for ladies of the night. Despite its size, the pub is so popular with tourists that it can become very crowded, testing the Australian bar staff's patient efficiency to the limit. Good draught ales include 6X (£2.40) and Flowers Original (£2.40).
Babies and children admitted (until 2.30pm, dining only). Function room. Games (fruit machine). No-smoking area (dining). Vegetarian dishes.

Zeta

35 Hertford Street, W1 (020 7208 4067). Green Park or Marble Arch tube. **Open** noon-3am Mon-Sat; noon-10.30pm Sun. **Food served** 6pm-3am Mon-Sat 6-10pm Sun. **Credit** AmEx, DC, MC, V.

The third and most recent wining-and-dining venue at the Hilton International is a good-looking ground-floor bar and restaurant in a long, narrow space with a screen of little metal tubes strung on wires down the windows, comfortable leather seats and a blonde-wood floor. The place is also home to a fruity philosophy expounded on the menus about the health-giving properties of their various cocktails, which we weren't sure was wholly ironic. Sticking with a reliable favourite, we tried their Singapore Sling (£6), which was delicious, but didn't have much kick. On the place's first full day in operation, the staff were being over-fussy in their attentions, and the dress sense of the clientele – mainly American preppies and international businessmen – let the style of the place down. The restaurant offers a variety of interesting dishes from the Pacific Rim. *Late licence. Music (DJs nightly). Restaurant. Satellite TV. Vegetarian dishes.*

Also in the area...

All Bar One 3-4 Hanover Street, W1 (020 7518 9931).
Balls Brothers 34 Brook Street, W1 (020 7499 4567).
Chopper Lump (Davys) 10C Hanover Square, W1 (020 7499 7569).
Pitcher & Piano 1 Dover Street, W1 (020 7495 8704); 10 Pollen Street, W1 (020 7629 9581).
Slug & Lettuce 19-20 Hanover Street, W1 (020 7499 0077).

Notting Hill W11

192

192 Kensington Park Road, W11 (020 7229 0482). Ladbroke Grove or Notting Hill Gate tube. **Open** 12.30-11.30pm Mon-Sat; 12.30-11pm Sun. **Happy hour** 5.30-7.30pm Mon-Fri. **Food served** 12.30-3pm, 6.30-11.30pm Mon-Fri; 12.30-3.30pm, 6.30-11.30pm, Sat; 12.30-3.30pm, 7-11pm Sun. **Credit** AmEx, DC, MC, V.

Notting Hill's top media wine bar may be open to the public, but as an offshoot of Soho's Groucho Club, it might as well be a members' club, too. You won't find much else here but media tarts, air-kissing friends and enemies as a prelude to professional blood-letting. For those not throwing themselves on to the bonfire of vanities, a wine list in excess of 80 from all over the world makes this a fine place for quaffing quality plonk (£2.65-£6.40 a glass). However, it is principally a café-cum-Modern European restaurant, and it's hard-edged, soft-furnished interior with chic colour schemes makes it unsuitable for mob drinking (bottled beers only, Budvar and San Miguel, all £3). Food is fashionably global in its influences, and might include sea bass with spicy couscous or scallops with stir-fried vegetables, for around £7-£15. *Babies and children admitted. Restaurant. Tables outdoors (pavement). Vegetarian dishes.*

Beat Bar

265 Portobello Road, W11 (020 7792 2043). Ladbroke Grove tube. **Open** 11.30am-11pm daily. **No credit cards**. This must be one of the very few bars in London not to do food of any kind. Nothing, not even a pickled egg, although they are looking into the possibilities, but only 'if we can do it properly'. Just drink, including draught Grolsch (£2.60), Extra Cold Guinness (£2.80) for those who like their stout tasteless, and a range by the bottle (Red Stripe, Beck's, Hoegaarden, all £2.50). And plenty of cool, cool vibes. Beat Bar is decorated in contrived, cold colours, with blue stone flooring, bare blue and orange walls, dotted with original art and projected pictures. Down at the end away from the bar is a clutch of sofas where ultra-cool Portobello types swap tattoo stories and practice their English. *Babies and children admitted (until 6pm).*

Belgo Zuid

124 Ladbroke Grove, W10 (020 8982 8400/ www.belgo-restaurant.co.uk). Ladbroke Grove tube. **Open/food served** noon-3pm, 6-11pm Mon-Fri; noon-11pm Sat; noon-10.30pm Sun. **Credit** AmEx, DC, MC, V.

The small balcony overlooking the hangar-like soundbox that is the latest addition to the Belgo empire may not be quite right for an all-nighter, but it is worth a visit. There are more than 100 beers (blonde, amber, dark, fruit and wine-beers, mostly for around £1.90-£3.50 a bottle, plus Trappist ales and some weird beer cocktails), eight red and eight white wines from across the world, and flavoured schnapps for those who can take neither beer nor wine. Service from the habited staff is usually instructive, and there are tasty bar snacks from frites to seafood platters from £3 or so. However, if the fine ales sharpen the appetite to a keener hunger, the restaurant will surely satisfy your every need: crab has clawed its way to pole position on the crustacean menu, and there are the usual buckets of moules and top sausages as well as a number of veggie dishes (£6.95-£15). *Babies and children admitted (children's menus, high chairs). Disabled: toilet. Restaurant. Vegetarian dishes.*

Buzz Bar at Portobello Gold

95 Portobello Road, W11 (020 7460 4906/ www.portobellogold.com). Notting Hill Gate tube. **Open/food served** 10am-midnight daily; *Buzz Bar* 10am-9pm Mon-Fri; 10am-7pm Sat; noon-7pm Sun. **Happy hour** 5.30-7pm daily. **Credit** DC, MC, V.

Home to Notting Hill's older antiquarian roués from surrounding shops and stalls, the Portobello Gold is also popular with more separatist local trustafarians. The decor is distinctive, with tiled floors and pea-green walls touting photos for sale, and there's a conservatory-style bistro (with sliding roof) at the back. Bar food includes oysters, sashimi, and baroque ciabatta sandwiches for around £5-£6, and a house speciality is seafood, with mixed platters for £25 (starters from £4, or mains from £8). This is accompanied by a couple of real ales (Directors and Pedigree), bottled lagers such as Budvar (£2.50), a decent wine list starting at £8.75 and assorted cocktails. A sign over the bar also warns of the dreaded absinthe. The Buzz Bar, upstairs, is an Internet café in a concrete mausoleum painted in aquamarines and burnt orange, with a warm, youth-club atmosphere enjoyed by twentysomething students drifting round Portobello Market or warming up for a night's clubbing. Drinks can be brought up while you surf the Net on one of seven computers. *Babies and children admitted (except bar). Function rooms. No-smoking area. Restaurant. Satellite TV. Tables outdoors (roof conservatory, pavement). Vegetarian dishes.*

Café Med

184A Kensington Park Road, W11 (020 7221 1150). Ladbroke Grove tube. **Open** 10am-midnight Mon-Sat; 10am-10.30pm Sun. **Food served** noon-11.30pm Mon-Sat; noon-10.30pm Sun. **Credit** AmEx, DC, MC, V.

Tall green leatherette benches and low-slung wooden tables form strong perspectival lines down this handsome corridor of a cocktail bar adjacent to the Café Med restaurant proper. The log-effect gas fire in a brick fireplace is the main decorative feature in an otherwise softly lit, minimalist interior with an atmosphere most suitable for aperitifs, dating and intimate gossips. The tasteful chic of the design is matched by gently funky music, bottled beers (Stella £2.60), cocktails for around a fiver and spirits served in 50ml measures – although the full range of nine scotches wasn't available the night of our visit. Bar snacks include potato skins, chicken wings, pâté and houmous all for under £5, while healthy breakfasts (muesli, eggs, smoothies) are available from 10am.

Babies and children admitted (children's menu, high chairs). Games (board games). Restaurant. Tables outdoors (pavement). Vegetarian dishes.

Ground Floor

186 Portobello Road, W11 (020 7243 8701).
Ladbroke Grove tube. **Open** 11am-11pm Mon-Sat; noon-10.30pm Sun. **Happy hour** 6.30-8.30pm daily. **Food served** 11am-9pm Mon-Fri; 11am-4pm Sat, Sun. **Credit** AmEx, DC, MC, V.

The Ground Floor has slowly become one of the hipper haunts of choosy W11 socialites. The basic decorative combinations of khaki green and red ochre paint with gold trimmings and chandeliers have been supplemented by groovier music, fitted furnishings, canopied seats on the street and a greatly improved but simple menu (starters of soup and bruschetta £4, mains of sausage and mash, salad or pasta £6-£7). As a result, this corner-sited goldfish bowl, which until recently was a soulless rendezvous for disoriented Euro-trash, is now all abuzz with local hipsters. There is a fair selection of wine, while beer drinkers must be satisfied with Belgian bottles (from £2.50), Kirin and the now-common Leffe Blonde on tap – but this is no place for beardy beer bores anyway.

Babies and children admitted (high chairs). Function rooms. Restaurant. Tables outdoors (pavement). Vegetarian dishes.

Ion Bar & Restaurant

161-165 Ladbroke Grove, W10 (020 8960 1702).
Ladbroke Grove tube. **Open/food served** 5pm-midnight Mon-Fri; noon-midnight Sat, Sun. **Happy hour** 5-7pm daily. **Credit** AmEx, DC, MC, V.

1999 saw a major refurbishment here, with Ion closed down for several weeks only to open looking exactly the same as it did before. In other words, it retains the '60s airport departure lounge aesthetics with the same chrome finish, op art mobiles and leatherette puff-benches on a geometric parquet floor. Meanwhile the overhead motorway and the bar's proximity to Ladbroke Grove tube lend the air of transience that has become its hallmark. Beneath Ion's mezzanine restaurant, the drinking arena serves cocktails (£4.65-£5) and a handful of wines, plus the inevitable stock of bottled beers (Grolsch, Budweiser, Asahi, all around £2.70), and there's reduced prices before 8.30pm early in the week. DJ nights ensure a mixed and dedicated following of young groovers, and the only distinctive innovation is the muscular concierge in the gents, pushing towels and inviting you to spray yourself with Hugo Boss toilet water. Could he by any chance be an undercover security guard?

Babies and children admitted (crayons, high chairs). Disabled: toilet, lift. Function room. Games (board games). Music (DJs nightly; live Wed, Sun). No-smoking area (restaurant). Restaurant. Tables outdoors (terrace). Vegetarian dishes.

Market Bar

240A Portobello Road, W11 (020 7229 6472). Ladbroke Grove or Notting Hill Gate tube. **Open** noon-11pm Mon-Fri; noon-midnight Sat; noon-10.30pm Sun. **Credit** MC, V.

Things come and go in Notting Hill, but the Market Bar stands aloof. When the floor fell in one year, they might have taken this as a cue to refurbish, but even then the management stuck to the winning formula celebrated by two Indonesian horses rearing over the bar, and echoed by the thick, tasselled curtain dividing the joint in two. Elsewhere, curly iron furniture and candelabras heavy with mops of waxy dreadlocks complete the Transylvanian schtick. Although this is one of the few remaining bars in the area with a good racial mix, the atmosphere can get as heavy as the music is loud. Things get saucy at the weekend with punters warming up for nearby Subterania. Drinks major on cocktails (from £3.50), but there is a decent set of other beverages, while upstairs, the Market Thai restaurant is average of its kind, but blessed with similar mod-Gothic decor, and has starters for around £4, mains for about £7.

Babies and children admitted (until 7pm). Music (DJs Tue, Sat; live jazz Sun).

Pharmacy

150 Notting Hill Gate, W11 (020 7221 2442).
Notting Hill Gate tube. **Open** noon-3pm, 6pm-1am Mon-Thur; noon-3pm, 6pm-2am Fri, Sat; 11.15am-3pm, 6-10.30pm Sun. **Food served** noon-3pm, 6-11pm Mon-Sat; noon-3pm, 6-10pm Sun. **Credit** AmEx, DC, MC, V.

The novelty value of Damien Hirst's medical-theme bar may have worn off, but it's still a swanky dispensary of both food and alcohol. Despite attempts to purloin or deface fittings, medical display cabinets, aspirin-shaped stools and glass urinals stuffed with swabs and syringes all remain in surprisingly good shape. There is a great range of fruity cocktails (from £6.50), good house wines (£3 per glass), standard bottled beers (£3) and the deadly artists' ruin, absinthe. Table service adds a sophisticated note, and only a small supplement on the bills. The slowly expanding bar menu includes Welsh rarebit (£4.50) and pasta dishes, but the Pharmacy burger and fries with gherkins and Gruyère (£6.50) is good value. Be wary of turning up late to take advantage of the licensing hours: there are queues outside, and a door policy. Try also the deli next door, wryly named Outpatients.

Babies and children admitted (until 10pm; high chairs). Disabled: toilet. Music (DJs Fri, Sat). Restaurant. Vegetarian dishes.

Portobello Star

171 Portobello Road, W11 (020 7229 8016). Ladbroke Grove or Notting Hill Gate tube. **Open/food served** 11am-11pm Mon-Sat; noon-10.30pm Sun. **No credit cards**.

In a postal district renowned for pretentious bars, this is one good old boozer where it is possible (nay, de rigueur) to abandon your dignity entirely. Despite recent refurbishments, neither the folding front giving access to the street, nor the wood flooring that replaced the lino, nor the floral stencilling between mock-Tudor effects can change the bright and feisty atmosphere. This pub is also famous for its jukebox, which punctuates modern chart sounds with aged and dead crooners like Tom Jones and Frank Sinatra, just as weather-beaten market traders punctuate the ranks of the pub's newer recruits. Flowers Original (£1.94), strong lager and standard pub libations dominate the drinks, and you are encouraged to quaff dangerously cheap house vodka. When fully tanked up, tuck into the toasted sandwiches (£1.30-£1.75).

Games (fruit machine). Jukebox. Satellite TV. Tables outdoors (pavement).

Also in the area...

All Bar One 126-128 Notting Hill, W11
(020 7313 9362).
Café Rouge 31 Kensington Park Road, W11
(020 7221 4449).
Frog & Firkin 96 Ladbrook Grove, W11 (020 7229
5663).
Ruby in the Dust 299 Portobello Road, W10
(020 8969 4626).

Pimlico SW1

Gallery

1 Lupus Street, SW1 (020 7821 7573). Pimlico tube.
Open/food served 11am-11pm Mon-Sat; noon-10.30pm
Sun. **Credit** MC, V.
Pimlico is home to the kind of pen-pushing, white-collar office
life that inspired the Bristow cartoon strip in the *Evening
Standard*, and this local was buzzing quite contentedly at 5pm
on a Monday evening. The homely interior is a comfy spot
for Joan from accounts to meet Mike from IT for a clandestine
Archers and lemonade. American tourists may well indeed
wonder how we ever get anything done, as half the civil
service seemed to be in this pub. They could do worse, though
– the seating area is well spaced and the staff are amenable.
The usual sandwiches and chips are served at lunchtime:
chicken and Cheddar or bacon and Cheddar (£4.50), as well
as traditional hot dishes and puds. Beer on tap includes
Young's Bitter (£2.10), Foster's and Caffrey's and a wine list
is available for the pint-shy (a glass of Chenin Blanc is £2.50).
Tables outdoors (pavement). Vegetarian dishes.

Morpeth Arms

58 Millbank, SW1 (020 7834 6442). Pimlico tube.
Open 11am-11pm Mon-Sat; noon-10.30pm Sun.
Food served 11am-6pm Mon-Sat; 11am-3pm Sun.
Credit AmEx, MC, V.
An ideal spot for dreamers: you can settle down in the cosy
snug in winter with a pint to mull over the Turners at the
nearby Tate or sit outside in summer and wistfully dream of
a 'shaken not stirred' as you sip your Martini overlooking the
river where Bond raced his boat from MI6 in The World is
not Enough. In reality, the clientele is mostly made up of suits
from Millbank (although there is always a possibility that one
of them may be a spy) and old guys enjoying a pint of Young's
'ordinary' (£1.94) or Special (£2.10) while their dogs nap on
the floor. There's a wooden booth at the back of the pub (ideal
for a rendezvous with a secret agent) and the food won't
disappoint the more refined of palate: wild boar sausages with
onion gravy and mash is £5.95.
*Babies and children admitted. Function room. Games
(fruit machine). Satellite TV. Tables outdoors (riverside
terrace). Vegetarian dishes.*

Pimlico Wine Vaults

*12-22 Upper Tachbrook Street, SW1 (020 7834 7429).
Pimlico tube/Victoria tube/rail.* **Open** noon-11pm Mon-Fri.
Food served noon-3pm, 5.30-9.30pm Mon-Fri.
Credit AmEx, MC, V.
You could be forgiven for thinking that you'd strayed into
Vinopolis on the other side of the river, as the entrance to this
wine bar resembles Ye Olde Wine Vault theme park with a
Dickensian jolly wassailing vibe. Indeed, the atmosphere is
jolly: fruity voices and red noses abound as the drinkers enjoy
the extensive wine list and eclectic menu. The price range is
comprehensive: Merlot is £3.50 a glass or £12.90 a bottle;

Sauvignon £3 a glass or £11.90 a bottle; and scales up to a
Nuits St Georges '93 at £39.90. The New World is well
represented and there is a separate champagne list. Bar
snacks served in the main area looked imaginative and
generous: houmous, roast garlic, olives and freshly baked
bread are £4.50, Thai fishcakes with sweet chilli sauce are
£5, and diners in the smaller bar seemed more than happy
with their angel hair pasta with prawns and green lip mussels
(£11.50) from the globally inspired carte.
Function room. Restaurant. Vegetarian dishes.

White Swan

*14 Vauxhall Bridge Road, SW1 (020 7821 8568).
Pimlico tube.* **Open/food served** 11am-11pm Mon-Sat;
noon-10.30pm Sun. **Credit** AmEx, DC, MC, V.
We reported on the refit of the White Swan last year, and 12
months have done nothing to tarnish its appearance. The
exposed beams still looked spanking new in their corporate-
distressed way and the barmen in their little burgundy aprons
are still squeaky clean and eager to please. The Swan is a long
barn of a place but fills easily after six with local workers, who
want to avoid the dingy drinking holes that you find on every
corner in Pimlico. Indeed, the little touches of exotica such as
the St Peter's wheat beer and coriander and cracked pepper in
the chicken salad are barely needed to lure drinkers in, so
scarce are light, welcoming bars in the area. Leffe Blonde
(£2.46) and Schneider Weisse (£2.45) are speciality beers, and
the wine list starts with a glass of South Chilean Chardonnay
for £2.50. The menu also includes lamb and rosemary pie
(£4.65) and tomato and basil soup (£2.25), but for all their
striving for gentrified rustication, T&J Bernard have produced
a pub that isn't a million miles from a Harvester.
*Games (fruit machine, quiz machine). No-smoking area.
Tables outdoors (pavement). Vegetarian dishes.*

Also in the area...

Slug & Lettuce 11 Warwick Way, SW1
(020 7834 3313).

Soho W1, WC2

Admiral Duncan

*54 Old Compton Street, W1 (020 7437 5300). Leicester
Square or Piccadilly Circus tube.* **Open** 11am-11pm Mon-
Sat; noon-10.30pm Sun. **Credit** AmEx, DC, MC, V.
Following its bombing in summer 1999, this quiet social for
gay men of a certain age turned, understandably, into
something of a cause célèbre: it was particularly poignant that
one of the most unobtrusive of London's gay pubs should be
singled out for a homophobic attack. Now it has been restored
in much the same style as it always was, albeit with a bouncer
on the door, who will probably search your bag before entry,
and it remains a place for a chat and a drink rather than a
cruise, with show tunes on the stereo and cheaper drinks than
other central London gay bars: pints (Foster's, Kronenbourg)
are around £2.50.
Games (fruit machines). Jukebox.

Alphabet

*61-63 Beak Street, W1 (020 7439 2190).
Oxford Circus tube.* **Open/food served** noon-11pm Mon-
Fri; 5-11pm Sat. **Credit** MC, V.
Since its opening a couple of years ago this design bar has
remained the favoured haunt of the more fashionable
inhabitants of the ad agency world, with part-time DJs, trendy
shop assistants and a few models adding to the throng that

inevitably packs into the place on most evenings. On the ground floor the bartenders hold court, serving double measures of spirits for around £5, bottled beers for £2.75, and a huge list of cocktails from £3.50 to £6, while the more laid-back basement has big sofas and remodelled car seats to sink into, DJs playing jazzy house and hip hop, and a map of London printed on to the floor. Alphabet embodies the spirit of West Soho: smarter and more materialistic than its more bohemian neighbour, but just as style-conscious.
Babies and children admitted (until 5pm). Function room. Games machines. Music (DJs occasionally). Restaurant. Vegetarian dishes.

Amalfi

29-31 Old Compton Street, W1 (020 7437 7284). Leicester Square or Piccadilly Circus tube. **Open** 9am-11.15pm Mon-Sat; 10am-10pm Sun. **Food served** noon-11.15pm Mon-Sat; noon-10pm Sun. **Credit** AmEx, DC, MC, V.
The café-bar to this long-standing Italian restaurant always seems out of step with the Soho of today: while more and more designer bars and restaurants fill Old Compton Street and beyond, Amalfi remains resolutely unreconstituted, looking like it belongs in a provincial seaside town rather than at the city's throbbing epicentre, and its '60s-style op art ceiling, tiled bar and mishmash of wicker, plastic, and wooden chairs and tables give a healthy dose of design consultancy-free irregularity. There are only half a dozen tables, but it makes for a cosy place to come for a cappuccino (£1.30) or a Peroni (£2.30) before moving on elsewhere. The restaurant, which serves heavy pizza and pasta dishes, isn't quite as charming.
Babies and children admitted. Restaurant. Tables outdoors (pavement). Vegetarian dishes.

Argyll Arms

18 Argyll Street, W1 (020 7734 6117). Oxford Circus tube. **Open** 11am-11pm Mon-Sat; noon-9pm Sun. **Food served** 11am-9.30pm Mon-Sat; noon-4pm Sun. **Credit** AmEx, DC, MC, V.
Just off Oxford Street is this attractive, ancient pub: it opened in 1716, and the frosted-glass sections, oak-panel sections, deep red ceiling and flock wallpaper all suggest that it wants to keep within tradition as much as possible. As a result it is usually packed with tourists and a mostly male, often rowdy after-work clientele. Unless you come in the day, it's not a place for a quiet drink: most of it, including a long corridor at the back, is given over to standing space, and the frenetic atmosphere and loud music discourage quiet contemplation. Better to come here for a hefty bite (traditional roast beef £6.95, steak and ale pie £5.50), and a quick pint (Tetley's £2.20), before moving on elsewhere.
Babies and children admitted (restaurant only). Dress code (in restaurant). Function room. Games (fruit machines). No-smoking area (until 4pm in restaurant). Restaurant. Satellite TV. Tables outdoors (pavement). Vegetarian dishes.

Bar Code

3-4 Archer Street, W1 (020 7734 3342). Piccadilly Circus tube. **Open** 1pm-1am Mon-Sat; 1-10.30pm Sun. **Admission** after 11pm Fri, Sat £3. **Happy hour** 5-7pm daily. **Credit** MC, V.
This is one of the rougher gay bars, more in keeping with the clandestine spirit of the Soho of old – hidden down a quiet street, its painted front gives few clues as to what goes on inside. It's a spit and sawdust place, with virtually no tables and chairs, and bare floorboards providing standing space around the makeshift bar, from which a young and rowdy crowd order pints of Guinness and Kronenbourg for around

£2.70. Downstairs is a dark and unfurnished room, where DJs play loud techno and men in bomber jackets check each other out around the pool table. This is a place for heavy drinking, lots of cruising, and, of course, regrets the following morning.
Games (fruit machines). Late licence (Mon-Sat). Music (DJs Thur-Sun).

Barra

12A Newburgh Street, W1 (020 7287 8488). Oxford Circus tube. **Open** noon-midnight Mon-Sat. **Food served** noon-10.30pm Mon-Sat. **Credit** AmEx, MC, V.
The best thing about Barra is its location: halfway down quiet, pedestrianised, cobbled Newburgh Street, there are no exhaust fumes or crowds of people to make sitting outside more of a chore than a pleasure. Essentially a wine bar with a modish, continental and rather expensive menu (pappardelle and mixed seafood, moules marinière and chips, both £11), it has a bright, clean interior and young, good-looking staff, attracting a smartly dressed crowd of local ad agency and film company types. The minimal decor and huge, clear glass windows help curb a rather claustrophobic feel: it is very popular, and the small tables are too close together. But the wine list is good: most wines are available by the glass at £3/£5, and we enjoyed a very good bottle of Domaine Subremont Colombe Blanc – reasonable at £11. Come in the evening to see it loosen up into a bar.
Babies and children admitted (high chairs). Function room. Tables outdoors (pavement). Vegetarian dishes.

Bar Rumba

36 Shaftesbury Avenue, W1 (020 7287 6933/ www.barrumba.co.uk). Piccadilly Circus tube. **Open/food served** 5pm-3.30am Mon-Thur; 5pm-4am Fri; 7pm-6am Sat; 8pm-2am Sun. **Admission** after 9pm Tue-Thur, after 8pm Sun, £3; after 9pm Mon £4; after 11pm Wed, after 10.30pm Thur, £5; after 9pm Fri, Sat £6; after 11pm Fri, Sat £10; after midnight Sat £12. **Happy hour** 5-9pm Mon-Fri. **Credit** AmEx, DC, MC, V.
It's always surprising that Bar Rumba continues to have such a good vibe. It could be one of the naffest places in London: it's in the basement of the tacky Trocadero Centre, it has a Latino theme, and it's a stone's throw from tourist-trap Piccadilly Circus, but some very good club nights here have helped establish it as a reliably fun place to spend an evening. The long-running Monday nighter, Gilles Peterson's That's How It Is, continues to play classic jazz and modern breakbeats to an appreciative crowd, and there are other innovative nights worth checking out. It's a normal bar before the clubs start, with bottled beers at £2.90 and cocktails at around a fiver, but less than scintillating food (Tex-Mex) and a lack of light or places to sit make this a better place to come to later on.
Dress code (Sat). Late licence. Music (DJs nightly). Vegetarian dishes.

Bar Soho

23-25 Old Compton Street, W1 (020 7439 0439). Piccadilly Circus tube. **Open/food served** 4pm-1am Mon-Thur; 4pm-3am Fri, Sat; 3-10.30pm Sun. Admission after 11.30pm, £5. **Credit** AmEx, DC, MC, V.
Subtle it ain't: from the enormous sign announcing itself to the world to the pumping house music, huge TV screen and crowds of after-work parties getting plastered on jugs of sangria, Bar Soho is a raucous hangout for the kind of people who don't like clubs, but fully intend to avoid heading back home until the early hours. The clipboard-wielding doorman gives the place a pretence of exclusivity, and there's a late licence and an entrance fee past 11.30pm, but the glass façade

and crowds that come here for cocktails (around £5) and two-pint jugs of Kronenbourg (£6) belie that. There is a lot of money floating around here, with Armani-clad businessmen toasting their success with champagne cocktails, and there's certainly a buzz about the place, but avoid it if you fancy an intimate drink.
Dress code. Late licence (Mon-Sat). Vegetarian dishes.

Bar Sol Ona
17 Old Compton Street, W1 (020 7287 9932). Leicester Square tube. **Open/food served** 5pm-3am Mon-Sat; 5-10.30pm Sun. **Happy hour** 5-10pm Mon-Thur; 5-8pm Fri, Sat; 5-7pm Sun. **Credit** AmEx, DC, MC, V.
Squeezed in between the different bits of the expanding Cafe Bohème empire is this almost-secret little place. Head down a corridor lined with Goya prints and down the narrow staircase, and you'll come to two low-ceilinged rooms with big wooden tables and small alcoves that make for a good place to meet an old friend early in the evening, or to come with a group later on, when the Latin music gets louder and the dancing begins. It's popular with groups of girls drinking cocktails at £3.50-£4.50 or jugs of Margarita at £6.95/£10.95, and all the tapas are £3.
Late licence. Music (DJs nightly). TV. Vegetarian dishes.

Blue Posts
18 Kingly Street, W1 (020 7734 1170). Oxford Circus or Piccadilly Circus tube. **Open** 11am-11pm Mon-Sat. **Food served** noon-4pm Mon-Sat. **Credit** DC, MC, V.
This corner boozer is as unpretentious as they get: with locals predominantly being middle-aged men, sports on the giant television screen, U2 on the stereo and beers including London Pride (£2.10), Guinness and Stella (both around £2.40) being passed from one side of the bar to another, the Blue Post is resolutely normal. It is slightly rough around the edges, its octagonal room having worn oak panelling and dusty floorboards, but this makes it a bit of a respite after the many designer bars springing up in the area. Upstairs it is quieter, and the usual pub-grub suspects include fish and chips (£4.95) and chicken and mushroom pie (£4.15). Not the most exciting of pubs, but it's good to know it's there.
Function room. Games (football games, fruit machine). Jukebox. Satellite TV. Tables outdoors (pavement). Vegetarian dishes.

Blue Posts
28 Rupert Street, W1 (020 7437 1415). Leicester Square or Piccadilly Circus tube. **Open** 11am-11pm Mon-Sat; noon-10.30pm Sun. **Credit** MC, V.
Recently refitted and now with very new-looking wood panelling, floorboards and a wooden bar, this is still an ale house in the old tradition, with lots of real ales on tap including London Pride, Timothy Taylor Landlord, Flowers and Wadworth 6X (from £2.10-£2.30), although these change regularly. Unsurprisingly, it attracts a mostly male mix of blue- and white-collar workers, who appreciate the straightforward menu that includes steak and ale pie (£4.95) and bangers and mash (£3.95). There isn't much space downstairs and it tends to get crowded; head upstairs for a bit of peace and quiet.
Games (fruit machine). Jukebox.

Blue Posts
22 Berwick Street, W1 (020 7437 5008). Oxford Circus or Tottenham Court Road tube. **Open** 11am-11pm Mon-Sat. **Food served** 11am-9pm Mon-Sat. **No credit cards.**
One of the less salubrious of Soho's pubs, this place is popular with old men and thirtysomethings who wish to escape from the medialand around them. The small room has a warm feel,

with its worn, soft furnishings and swirly carpet, wood panelling, dark frosted glass and an ageing landlord who seems to be on first name terms with many of the patrons. Food sticks to fish and chips, steak and ale pie and other traditional pub fare, and on our visit, almost everyone was drinking pints (Directors £2.40, Guinness is £2.50).
Function room. Games (fruit machine). Vegetarian dishes.

Blues Bistro and Bar
42-43 Dean Street, W1 (020 7494 1966). Piccadilly Circus or Tottenham Court Road tube. **Open** noon-midnight Mon-Thur, Sun; noon-1am Fri, Sat. **Food served** noon-11pm Sun-Thur; noon-midnight Fri, Sat. **Credit** AmEx, MC, V.
There's nothing particularly bluesy about this sophisticated, bijou bar at the front of a well-respected restaurant: it is an upmarket hangout with an art deco style in the heart of medialand, attracting a thirtysomething crowd in suits and designer labels. There isn't much space, but come here early in the evening and you might be able to sink into one of the deep sofas and enjoy a double measure of a spirit for around £4-£5, or a cocktail for £5-£6. On Fridays and Saturdays there is a late licence with DJs playing rare groove and jazz, and with friendly staff and a usually easygoing atmosphere, this slightly yuppie-ish hangout makes for a good place to begin or end a night out on the town.
Babies and children admitted. Function room. Late licence (Fri, Sat). Restaurant. Satellite TV. Vegetarian dishes.

Café Bohème
13-17 Old Compton Street, W1 (020 7734 0623). Leicester Square tube. **Open/food served** 8am-3am Mon-Thur; 24 hours Fri, Sat; 8am-midnight Sun. **Admission** after 10pm £3, after 11pm £4, Fri, Sat. **Credit** AmEx, DC, MC, V.
Recently expanded with a Bohème Kitchen & Bar a couple of doors down, Café Bohème was the original 1980s Parisian bistro-style hangout, selling Gallic sophistication to a style-conscious moneyed clientele who went there to discover their bohemian side. It's much the same today, and is notable for being one place in Soho where those no longer young won't be made to feel their age. Most of the space is given over to tables and a very good restaurant, but if you come here early in the evening you can catch a stall by the bar and enjoy a large measure of a spirit (£4-£5) or a French lager (around £2.80), and bar snacks that include crab cake with guacamole (£5.50), croque monsieur (£5.25) and roasted red pepper and tomato salad with whitebait (£3.95). Sunday afternoons are the best time to come, when there is live jazz and a laid-back atmosphere that wouldn't be out of place along the Left Bank.
Late licence. Music (jazz 3.30-5pm Tue-Fri). Restaurant. Tables outdoors (pavement). Vegetarian dishes.

Café Lazeez
21 Dean Street, W1 (020 7434 0022). Leicester Square or Tottenham Court Road tube. **Open/food served** 11am-1am Mon-Sat; noon-10.30pm Sun. **Credit** AmEx, DC, MC, V.
This huge new place is essentially an Indian restaurant, but you wouldn't guess to look at it: it has a sloping ceiling covered by a hanging piece of fabric, a clear glass façade, a very long bar, walls made of staggered blocks of orange lit from behind, and burly staff in suits. Downstairs is a restaurant proper, but upstairs is a brasserie where you can have a drink and some delicious lighter meals, such as a fish Amritsar (£8.75), which is a cod fillet fried in a spicy chickpea batter, or ginger-suffused lamb chops with Indian spices (£8.75). A Cobra or Kingfisher beer is £3, and a large measure of a spirit is £4.50-£5. Taking up where **Soho Spice** (*see p93*)

Lobby fodder

Why go to a hotel bar? Time was anyone after a decent Martini in London had to seek satisfaction there. No longer, now that the capital is bursting with bars boasting lengthy cocktail lists and master 'mixologists'. While they have an indulgently luxurious appeal, the plush lounges around Park Lane tend to be a bit impersonal. The latest crop of 'boutique hotel' bars, however, have distinct identities, making them hip hangouts in their own right. A crawl in the area radiating out from Covent Garden provides plenty of variety.

To soothe after-office nerves, start at the feng shui-ed **mybar** in the Conran-designed myhotel off Tottenham Court Road. Despite the irritatingly trendy lower-case name and gimmicky menu concepts such as 'mysandwich', this is a laid-back place buzzing with Euro-chic tourists and style-conscious local workers. Lounge in the back, where sculptural sofas grouped around a fireplace look like a Conran Shop room display. Fashionably shorn staff shake up interesting concoctions, from a Hurricane Marilyn (rum, Canadian Club, Cointreau and fruit juice, £6.50) to a Brain Shooter (Baileys, Frangelico and Southern Comfort, £5).

Cross Bedford Square to Bloomsbury Street and on to the recently refurbished **Glass Bar** in the terribly English Marlborough Hotel. A rich brown colour scheme incorporating animal prints, distressed leather chairs and squashy sofas add up to a stylish atmosphere that attracts a casually dressed crowd. Cocktails (£6.25) and substantial snacks are on the menu, but the mainstream music keeps it just short of groovy.

Heading south, cut across New Oxford Street to Monmouth Street, where **Brasserie Max** is accessed through the lobby of the impeccably designed Covent Garden Hotel. A slick zinc bar set against dark panelling and upholstered chairs create an updated country house style somewhat incongruous with the sharply dressed clientele. While this large bar provides a good chance of getting a seat in a busy area, the odd choice of music (heavy metal on Saturday night), expensive drinks (cocktails from £8) and a slightly sterile air may spur you on to your next port of call.

A left-hand turn at Seven Dials on to Earlham Street and then a right at Endell Street will take you down to the Aldwych. The capacious **Lobby Bar** of One Aldwych is in complete contrast to the rustic-chic cosiness you've left behind. Amid the vast arched windows, enormous pillars and monumental artwork in this Edwardian former newspaper premises, besuited drinkers are dwarfed by outsize *Alice in Wonderland* chairs. Subdued lighting, friendly young bar staff in violet shirts and a jolly after-work crowd counteract any coldness of decor. Sample from the list of 19 Martinis (£7.50), including the inky, liquorice-flavoured Gotham.

Your crawl wouldn't be complete without a visit to the hotel that introduced cocktails to London, importing American barman Harry Craddock in the '20s. Although the pseudo art deco theme looks a bit dated, the **American Bar** at the Savoy retains its glamour. Polite white-coated staff and silver baskets of nibbles make you feel pampered as you sip Craddock's invention, the White Lady (gin, lemon

juice and Cointreau, £8.90), or the suitably decadent Savoy Royale (champagne, crushed peaches and strawberries, £10.50). A resident pianist reinforces the retro sophistication.

Last stop St Martin's Lane, the hotel of the same name has a bar open until 3am. Walk purposefully through the sweeping white lobby to the **Light Bar**. While priority is given to residents, if it's not too packed and you look the part, they'll let you in. The multicoloured ceiling 'light wells' give a surreal quality to the small, Philippe Starck-designed space. There is no actual bar – drinks are served by waitresses in strapless black dresses – but a long, thin central table with high stools encourages a fashion and media crowd to mingle. If you're feeling peckish there's a good choice of late-night nibbles, such as sushi (from £5.50). Round off the excesses of the evening with a Detto Shooter (vodka, peach schnapps and cranberry juice, £5).
Lisa Ritchie

mybar (*p20*) myhotel, 11-13 Bayley Street, WC1 (020 7667 6000).
Glass Bar (*p20*) Marlborough Hotel, Bloomsbury Street, WC1 (020 7636 5601).
Brasserie Max (*p29*) Covent Garden Hotel, 10 Monmouth Street, WC2 (020 7806 1000).
Lobby Bar (*p32*) One Aldwych Hotel, 1 Aldwych, WC2 (020 7300 1000).
American Bar (*p28*) Savoy Hotel, Strand, WC2 (020 7836 4343).
Light Bar (*no review*) St Martin's Lane Hotel, 45 St Martin's Lane, WC2 (020 7300 5500) – *ring before 4pm to book your name on the guest list.*

left off, Café Lazeez is combining typical elements of a smart London bar and a supposedly very traditional Indian cuisine (Pathan, from North-West India) to good effect.
Babies and children admitted. Disabled: lift, toilet. Function room. No-smoking area. Restaurant. Vegetarian dishes.

Candy Bar
4 Carlisle Street, W1 (020 7494 4041).
Tottenham Court Road tube. **Open/food served** 5-11.30pm Mon-Thur; 5pm-2am Fri, Sat; 5-11.30pm Sun. **Admission** after 10pm Fri, Sat £3 (members), £5 (non-members); £1-£3 (downstairs) Sun. **No credit cards**.
London's best women-only, predominantly gay bar is about as far from the old lesbian cliché as you could get: always packed and raucous, it's trendy, image-conscious, and positively encourages bad behaviour from its patrons. It occupies a space that used to be a members' bar, and still has that feel about it: upstairs is a corridor-like room with a long bar, from which cocktails (around £5) and bottled beers (around £3) are ordered in abundance; downstairs there are DJs playing anything from hard house (long-standing favourite of gay nights Princess Julia is on Fridays) to '20s tea dance music. Unaccompanied men won't be admitted, although the friendly door staff make occasional exceptions.
Games (pool table). Late licence (Fri,Sat). Music (DJs Fri-Sun).

Circus
1 Upper James Street, W1 (020 7534 4000/ www.circusbar.co.uk). Oxford Circus or Piccadilly Circus tube. **Open/food served** noon-1.30am Mon-Sat. **Credit** AmEx, DC, MC, V.
The basement of this sleek, expensive restaurant is a buzzy bar, replete with young and good-looking staff in white, a tropical patio, soft lighting and lots of sleek, modern armchairs to sink into. That's if you get past the bouncer and the glamorous young women on the door. It attracts a wealthy rather than fashionable crowd, with groups of smartly dressed men drinking spirits (around £5 for a double measure) and taking clients out on their expense accounts, and you get the impression that the management would prefer it if there were more beautiful women about the place. It does feel a bit ostentatiously flashy, but it makes for a great place for a romantic rendezvous and a bit of '80s Hollywood film-style fantasy.
Disabled: toilet. Late licence (Mon-Sat). Music (DJs nightly). Restaurant. Vegetarian dishes.

Clachan
34 Kingly Street, W1 (020 7734 2659). Oxford Circus or Piccadilly Circus tube. **Open** 11am-11pm Mon-Sat; noon-6pm Sun. **Food served** 11am-8.30pm Mon-Sat; noon-6pm Sun. **Credit** AmEx, DC, MC, V.
Just off Regent Street is this traditional, very beautiful pub, replete with frosted-glass snob screens with floral etchings, brilliant gilt edges, chandeliers, an oak-panelled bar and raised cubby holes at the back. The original fittings have all been very well kept, and the blackboard announcements of pub grub and special deals are misplaced in so ornate a setting. Despite its proximity to Oxford Circus, Clachan attracts few tourists, and has a predominantly after-work crowd from nearby Liberty and surrounding offices. It's a place to come and drink pints of Guinness (£2.40) and Addlestone's bitter (£2.45), and enjoy some very good cod and chips (£8.95), cooked on the premises.
Babies and children admitted (until 4pm). Function room. Games (fruit machines). Satellite TV. Vegetarian dishes.

Coach & Horses
29 Greek Street, W1 (020 7437 5920). Leicester Square or Tottenham Court Road tube. **Open/food served** 11am-11pm Mon-Sat; noon-10.30pm Sun. **Happy hour** 11am-4pm Mon-Fri. **No credit cards**.
The beer is overpriced (Guinness is now £2.60), the rickety formica tables look like they are hardly ever cleaned, and the landlord, Norman Balon, prides himself on his tag as the rudest in London, but this is still Soho's greatest drinking den. Perhaps because, in an area dominated by generic chain pubs and pretentious designer bars, this is the real thing: an eccentric, genuinely bohemian throwback to the Soho of the 1950s, with an always entertaining mix of failed writers, part-time gangsters, art school students and bombastic ageing alcoholics. Jeffrey Bernard made a career from going to seed by his stool at the bar, and the many cartoons about him by Heath, which fill the walls, show how justly proud Norman is of his departed customer's loyal patronage. School trip-style sandwiches are still only £1, and house spirits are only £2 for a double measure.
No piped music or jukebox. No-smoking area. Tables outdoors (pavement). Vegetarian dishes.

Comptons of Soho
51-53 Old Compton Street, W1 (020 7479 7961). Leicester Square or Piccadilly Circus tube. **Open** noon-11am Mon-Sat; noon-10.30pm Sun. **Credit** MC, V.
In an attempt to shake off its former sleazy past, Soho's oldest gay pub had a major refit about a year ago, replacing secret cubby holes with open spaces, but it is still pretty clear why people come here. It's famous for being the place to come for what is known as the briefcase encounter: men in suits come here after work, order a pint (Staropramen £2.80, Grolsch £2.70) and hang around until they're given an offer that means they don't have to order another one. Loud techno and house keeps conversation down to a minimum; don't ask for a light unless you're really asking for something more. The carpeted room upstairs is quieter and more sociable, but this isn't really the place to catch up with old mates.
Games (fruit machines).

Crown & Two Chairmen
31 Dean Street, W1 (020 7437 8192). Tottenham Court Road tube. **Open/food served** 11am-11pm Mon-Sat; noon-10.30pm Sun. **Credit** AmEx, DC, MC, V.
This loud, scruffy boozer seems to attract the detritus from any nearby student unions: on our visit there were few people out of their early twenties, and a roughly equal measure of young men and women drinking youthful favourites like snakebite and Hooch, and singing along to the indie hits blasting out of the loudspeakers. You can only put their enthusiasm down to low standards: the blackboard art, posters for various drinks promotions and bland pub grub (steak and ale pie £5.95) give the place a lack of character made up for only by the raucousness of its clientele. A pint of Marston Pedigree is £2.35 and Guinness is £2.60.
Function room. Games (fruit machines). Vegetarian dishes.

Dog & Duck
18 Bateman Street, W1 (020 7437 4447). Piccadilly Circus or Tottenham Court Road tube. **Open** noon-11pm Mon-Fri; 6-11pm Sat; 7-10.30pm Sun. **No credit cards**.
This ornate, tiny pub is an essential part of the area's history. In existence since 1734, it is on the site of the one-time home of the Duke of Monmouth, who used to go hare-coursing on the other side of Oxford Street with the rallying cry of 'So-ho', from which came the name we use today. It's so small that it

is invariably packed in the evenings, usually with rough-hewn thirty- and fortysomething men, so the best time to come here is on a winter's day, when the rickety chairs around the tiny fireplace at the back are particularly welcoming. It's a pint-drinking place (Addlestone's bitter £2.35, Guinness £2.40), with a range of ales that changes regularly, and there is a colourful mosaic of a dog chasing a duck on the floor of one of the entrances.
Function room.

Dog House

187 Wardour Street, W1 (020 7434 2116/2118).
Tottenham Court Road tube. **Open/food served** 5-11pm Mon-Fri; 6-11pm Sat. **Happy hour** 5-7.30pm Mon-Fri; 6-7.30pm Sat. **Credit** AmEx, DC, MC, V.
It's easy to miss this basement bar: its entrance is a doorway with only the smallest of signs to announce itself. But head down the narrow staircase and you'll discover a neat little multicoloured hideaway, which has little alcoves marked off by thick, curving stone walls, and as the bar is rarely crowded, these make for a good place to come with a group. With nothing on tap, it was mostly bottled beers being drunk on our visit (San Miguel, Heineken and Budvar, all £2.60) with spirits served in double measures at around £4. The clientele is mostly young and vaguely trendy, although a fair few businessmen also escape from the rat race down here.
Dress code. Function room. Satellite TV.
Vegetarian dishes.

Downstairs at the Phoenix

1 Phoenix Street, Charing Cross Road, WC2
(020 7836 1077). Leicester Square or Tottenham Court Road tube. **Open/food served** 5pm-1am Mon-Wed; 5pm-3am Thur, Fri; 2pm-3am Sat. **Happy hour** 5-8pm Mon-Thur. **Credit** AmEx, MC, V.
Although its late licence means that it is increasingly operating as a members' bar, you can still get into the Phoenix before 8pm, and once you're in you can stay until closing time. It's a baroque, cavernous place that looks a lot like a Bavarian drinking hall, with all manner of ephemera (including a small, stuffed crocodile) hanging from the rafters and posters from famous plays framed on the walls. It's a lot of fun, but beware of bad service: expensive malt whiskies might well be served in half-pint glasses, and God forbid you should sit at the wrong table (there is a members-only section) – you're likely to be thrown out. The restaurant serves unsubtle dishes like steak Roquefort (£12.95) and salmon steak (£8.95), and draught beers are £2.60 a pint.
Babies and children admitted. Function room.
Late licence (Mon-Sat; members only after 8pm).
No-smoking area. Restaurant. Theatre. Vegetarian dishes.

Edge

11 Soho Square, W1 (020 7439 1313/
www.theedge-group.com). Tottenham Court Road tube.
Open/food served noon-1am Mon-Sat; noon-10.30pm Sun. **Credit** AmEx, MC, V.
This long-standing Soho institution is a huge gay bar, usually crowded and known by everyone on the London scene, but generally attracting conventional-looking gay men. There are four floors connected by a warehouse-like metal staircase; the candlelit, pastel-shaded ground floor is the most relaxed; head upstairs and you'll find a headier party atmosphere, with bouncers on every floor, hard house pumping out of the speakers, and industrial spaces with few concessions to comfort. If you want to enjoy cocktails (a long list, from £4.50 to £6) or have a bite to eat (warm chicken and watercress salad

£3.50, cheeseburgers £5.80), stay on the ground floor; above, it's de rigueur to swig from bottled beers (most are £2.80).
Function room. Late licence (Mon-Sat). Music (DJs Fri, Sat). Tables outdoors (pavement). Vegetarian dishes.

Ego

23-24 Bateman Street, W1 (020 7437 1977).
Tottenham Court Road or Leicester Square tube.
Open/food served 6pm-1am Mon-Sat. **Happy hour** all night, Mon Tue. **Admission** after 10pm Fri, Sat £3.
Credit AmEx, DC, MC, V.
Try and ignore the appalling name if you can, and you might find this simply designed, but bright and colourful bar a good place for a rendezvous. Its two floors are decorated almost entirely in blocks of red and white, and the clear windows that look out on to Bateman and Greek Streets stop the small upstairs room, which is filled with big red sofas and chairs, from getting too claustrophobic. It draws in a young, trendy and often foreign crowd (it's popular with the French, for some reason), who come here to drink bottled beers that include Grolsch and Staropramen (£2.80), double measures of spirits (£4-£4.50) and to listen to funk and disco classics and even have a little boogie on busy nights downstairs.
Dress code. Late licence (Mon-Sat). Music (DJs Wed-Sat). Tables outdoors (pavement). Vegetarian dishes.

est

54 Frith Street, W1 (020 7437 0666). Tottenham Court Road tube. **Open/food served** noon-1am Mon-Sat; noon 10.30pm Sun. **Credit** AmEx, MC, V.
This smart, clean little brasserie, popular with well-dressed, thirtysomething women, who use it to escape from the dingy Soho streets and the hordes that fill them, has a very downtown New York feel, with its spotlit bar, wood-veneered beige interior and clean-cut, occasionally frosty staff. The little wooden tables are too small, but it's still a good place for Italian dishes like grilled squid (£8.80) and gnocchi lazio (£6.80) and a drink or two – although, with bottled beers at around £3 and cocktails at £5-£7, it's quite a pricey place to make an evening of. Better to come here for a long, slow, generous spirit measure (around £5), grab a seat by the bar, and watch the visiting celebs staying low-key (Cameron Diaz was spotted by us on a recent visit).
Babies and children admitted. Late licence (Mon-Sat). Tables outdoors (pavement). Restaurant.
Vegetarian dishes.

Freedom

60-66 Wardour Street, W1 (020 7734 0071). Leicester Square tube. **Open/food served** 11am-3am Mon-Sat; noon-midnight Sun. **Admission** after 11pm Mon-Wed £3; after 10.30pm Thur-Sat £5. **Credit** MC, V.
Another major redesign for a place that started life as an intimidatingly trendy gay bar and has slowly become more and more straight. Now it is more colourful and softer than before, with flowers along the bar, contemporary art on the walls, and the once-open space broken off into different levels. It's as popular as ever, although the fickle fashion set has long since moved on, and these days a mixed crowd of all ages come here for the famous champagne cocktails (£7-£7.50); other cocktails are £6-£7, an Asahi or Grolsch is £3.30, or large measures of spirits are £4.50-£6. The crowd gets younger as the night wears on, while the clubby music gets louder and the doorman gets pickier. Head downstairs to find the action, although it is often closed for sections of the evening for private functions.
Dress code. Function room. Late licence (Mon-Sat). Music (DJs nightly). Vegetarian dishes.

Freedom Brewing Company.
See page 86.

Gold Bar Café

Freedom Brewing Company

14-16 Ganton Street, W1 (020 7287 5267/
www.freedombrew.com). Oxford Circus tube. **Open** 11am-
11pm Mon-Sat. **Food served** noon-3pm, 5-10pm Mon-Sat.
Credit AmEx, MC, V.
Recently opened by Fulham's Freedom Brewery, London's
only microbrewery, this is a bar where the beer is brewed on
the premises, and it tastes great (at £3.10 a pint for Pilsner,
£3.20 for wheat beer). Huge silver vats dominate much of the
large space, which has a spartan, no-nonsense look:
unadorned beige walls, large, brand-new wooden tables, tiled
seating areas and huge, clear glass windows looking out on
to the tourist-filled side street outside. In keeping with the
main reason for coming here, there is a healthy, organic menu,
featuring such straightforward dishes as pan-fried cod (£10)
and salmon fishcakes (£9.50). It was very quiet on the night
we went, but it had only just opened: with more and more
people wanting a healthier, more natural diet, it's easy to see
that this place could be a big success.
Restaurant. Satellite TV. Tables outdoors (pavement).
Vegetarian dishes.

French House

49 Dean Street, W1 (020 7437 2799). Leicester Square
or Piccadilly Circus. **Open** noon-11pm Mon-Sat;
noon-10.30pm Sun. **Food served** 12.30-3pm, 6.30-10pm
Mon-Sat. **Credit** AmEx, DC, MC, V.
Now here's a true Soho institution. This tiny pub, whose
history is displayed proudly on every available inch of wall,
became the meeting place for the French Resistance in
London during WWII; then, in the 1950s, under the auspices
of its famously charming French landlord Gaston, it was the
watering hole of Britain's most celebrated bohemians,
including Francis Bacon, Lucian Freud, Dylan Thomas and

Brendan Behan. With the recent death of the second Gaston
(son of the founder) that era is now firmly in the past, but its
spirit lives on with a noisy theatrical crowd, who do their
best to honour the stylishly dissolute behaviour of their
famous forebears. As a resistance to British boorishness, the
French still refuses to serve pints: a half is £1.50, but most
people drink wine, from £2.20 a glass. A separate restaurant
upstairs serves very good Modern European food, but you
must book in advance.
No piped music or jukebox. Restaurant. Vegetarian dishes.

Garlic & Shots

14 Frith Street, W1 (020 7734 9505). Leicester Square
or Tottenham Court Road tube. **Open** 5pm-midnight
Mon-Wed; 6pm-1am Thur-Sat; 5-11.30pm Sun.
Food served 5-11.15pm Mon-Wed; 6pm-12.15am Thur-
Sat; 5-10.45pm Sun. **Credit** MC, V.
London's only garlic restaurant has a strange cellar bar that,
with a view to the vampiric associations of the potent bulb,
looks like the lair of the undead. Entrances into catacombs
are in the shape of coffins, walls are painted black, and only
candles lodged into wax-encrusted wine bottles break the
darkness. Unsurprisingly, London's few remaining goths
have made this place their own, and they come here to gorge
on over 100 shots made up of Black Death vodka (naturally)
and all manner of noxious ingredients for £2.50 each. The
extremely strong Bloodshot (garlic, Tabasco, chilli, tomato
juice and vodka) is a favourite, and there are also garlic
brandies (£4), garlic Martinis (£2.50), garlic beer (£1.80), and
six-times pickled garlic at £3.80. The smiling, flaxen-haired
Swedish barmaid broke the ghoulish spell somewhat, but
otherwise it's doomladen fun all round.
Babies and children admitted. Late licence (Mon-Sat).
Restaurant. Vegetarian dishes.

George

1 D'Arblay Street, W1 (020 7439 1911). Oxford Circus or Tottenham Court Road tube. **Open** noon-11pm Mon-Sat; 3-10.30pm Sun. **Credit** AmEx, MC, V.

One of the shabbier of the area's pubs, with ornate fittings including frosted glass etched with floral patterns and a moulded burgundy ceiling looking a little rough around the edges, as do the clientele: generally musicians and music industry types, who pack into the small square rooms and have long and loud arguments about who sucks and who rocks out of today's bands. Beer is most commonly drunk (Tetley's £2.30, London Pride £2.40), but there's a good wine list with a nice Australian Chardonnay at £12.25 a bottle, and the jukebox sticks to indie rock favourites plus a few Rolling Stones and Beatles classics.

Games (fruit machine). Satellite TV.

Gold Bar Café

23A Ganton Street, W1 (020 7434 0109). Oxford Circus tube. **Open/food served** 11am-11pm Mon-Sat. **Happy hour** 5-8pm Mon-Sat. **Credit** MC, V.

The name is misleading: this West Soho brasserie-bar is decked out in the boldest of reds, with a 1960s-style design of a long bar with small red stalls, red plastic menu boards, and a great downstairs room that looks like the rest quarters of the *Starship Enterprise*. It is stylish, the young staff are friendly, and there are always piles of newspapers and magazines to help pass the time here, and after a slow start it is beginning to build up a buzzy atmosphere. The straightforward menu includes Californian wraps (£6.50), pizzas (£6.95), and Chicago dogs (£6), while there are bottled beers (Becks, Budvar) at £2.60-£2.70 and house spirits at £4. Relaxed, reasonably priced, and open all day, the Gold Bar is West Soho's best new hangout.

Babies and children admitted. Function room. Music (DJs nightly). Restaurant. Tables outdoors (pavement). Vegetarian dishes.

Intrepid Fox

99 Wardour Street, W1 (020 7287 8359). Leicester Square, Oxford Circus or Piccadilly Circus tube. **Open** noon-11pm Mon-Sat; 3-10.30pm Sun. **No credit cards**.

The last bastion of greasy rock 'n' roll rebellion in the West End is like every roadie's spiritual home: heavy metal, punk and grunge coming through the loudspeakers, tattooed and pierced bar staff in sleeveless T-shirts selling pints of snakebite and blackcurrant at £2.60, and the walls and ceiling covered in all of your typical adolescent boy's favourite things: band posters, broken guitars, skulls, car chassis, skeletons and motorbike parts. It used to be the home of London's postcard punks; these days it's a predominantly heavy metal crowd, with a smattering of European punks and even a few businessmen reliving the wild days of their youth.

Function room. Games (fruit machine, pool table, video games). Music (DJs Tue-Sun).

Jazz After Dark

9 Greek Street, W1 (020 7734 0545). Tottenham Court Road tube. **Open/food served** noon-2am Mon-Thur; noon-3am Fri, Sat. **Credit** AmEx, DC, MC, V.

This small, narrow music bar is a bit like a mini-disco: it has a Copacabana-like neon sign outside, small spotlights built into the ceiling, walls adorned with glitter, a bouncer on the door, and plenty of private parties to make sure that you have to shout to order a drink and be pretty assertive to find somewhere to sit. On quieter nights, however, the soundtrack – mostly mainstream or smooth jazz, attracting a thirty- to

fortysomething crowd – makes a change from pounding house music, and the drinks are reasonable: cocktails are £5 each or £16 for a jug, and you can get shots of absinthe for £5. Food sticks to reliable brasserie faves like steak frites (£9.50) and fillet of salmon (£9.50), and service can be a little rushed.

Babies and children admitted. Late licence. Music (live jazz nightly). Restaurant. Vegetarian dishes.

Kettners

29 Romilly Street, W1 (020 7734 6112). Leicester Square tube. **Open** 11am-11pm Mon-Sat; noon-10.30pm Sun. **Food served** noon-midnight Mon-Sat; noon-10.30pm Sun. **Credit** AmEx, DC, MC, V.

Kettners is a slice of grandeur that is open to all. Most of the proud, white-walled Victorian building, opened in the 1860s by Napoleon III's chef Auguste Kettner, is given over to a restaurant serving very affordable steaks and pizzas, but turn left after the bright chandeliered entrance and you'll come to a champagne bar that looks like it belongs in a stately home: historic portraits, Regency furnishings and wicker armchairs create a sense of aristocratic splendour. In spite of all this, champagne prices are reasonable: all 32 marques are represented, and a bottle of house bubbly at £24.75 or £3.60 a glass. The clientele is made up of expense account businessmen taking their clients out, romantic couples treating themselves, and well-heeled ladies. At the back is a brandy bar with a more modern, art deco style, but it lacks the sophistication of the champagne bar.

Music (live pianist, nightly). Restaurant. Vegetarian dishes.

Lab

12 Old Compton Street, W1 (020 7437 7820/ www.lab-bar.co.uk). Tottenham Court Road tube. **Open** 10am-midnight Mon-Sat; 5-10.30pm Sun. **Food served** 5pm-midnight Mon-Sat. **Credit** AmEx, DC, MC, V.

Seemingly finding the one small stretch of Old Compton Street that didn't have a bar on it, this hip hangout is the latest addition to a street where drinkers are spoilt for choice. The interiors of the two floors are very '70s-*Superfly* hip, with a bar made up of curving wood veneers, walls and windows decorated with multicoloured rainbow designs and space age bachelor-pad furniture. A young, fashion-conscious and (notably, for the area) straight crowd pile into the small space in the evenings, nod their heads to the DJ's hip sounds, and drink bottled beers like Budvar and Beck's at £2.80, big measures of spirits at £4.50, and, especially, some very fruity cocktail creations. The best include Queen of Bahia (fresh strawberries, lime, sugar, cachaça and crème de fraise, £6.50); and Very Berry (Absolut, lime, blue- and blackberries, £6.50).

Games (board games, Sun). Music (DJs Tue-Sun). Vegetarian dishes.

Little Italy

21 Frith Street, W1 (020 7734 4737). Leicester Square or Tottenham Court Road tube. **Open/food served** noon-4am Mon-Sat; noon-10.30pm Sun. **Credit** AmEx, MC, V.

The sister restaurant to the famous Bar Italia a couple of doors down is a smart, sleek, modern place with small silver tables, a chrome bar, and lots of photographs and portraits of famous Italians on the walls. The front bar area only has six tables and drinks are expensive, so this isn't the place for a boozy night out, but it's perfect for a romantic tête-à-tête. Appreciated touches like olives, nuts and flowers on every table and attentive waitresses justify the higher prices – Beck's beer is £3, grappa (from a long list) is from £3 to £7.50, and whiskies start at £4.50.

Babies and children admitted. Late licence (Mon-Sat). Restaurant. Tables outdoors (pavement). Vegetarian dishes.

Lab. *See page 87.*

Lupo

50 Dean Street, W1 (020 434 3399). Leicester Square, Piccadilly Circus or Tottenham Court Road tube. **Open** noon-midnight Mon; noon-1am Tue; noon-2am Wed; noon-3am Thur-Sat. **Food served** noon-3pm, 6.30-11.30pm Fri; 6.30-11.30pm Mon-Thur, Sat. **Credit** AmEx, MC, V.

The small front bar of this labyrinthine Italian restaurant feels like something of a hideaway: despite its perfect location, it's often quiet on weeknights, and the dark walls illuminated by candles, creaking floorboards and low-key Italian waitresses dressed in black make for a good place to come and escape from it all for a while. Other sections of the restaurant can be noisier, however, with the red velvet curtained downstairs room often being given over to DJs and dancing, and the various boltholes taken over by after-work gangs. Bottled beers are £3, but the best bet is to choose something out of the long list of spirits, as the measures, mostly at £4.50, tend to be generous.

Function rooms. Late licence (Mon-Sat). Music (DJs Wed-Sat). Restaurant. Tables outdoors (pavement). Vegetarian dishes.

Mezzo

100 Wardour Street, W1 (020 7314 4000). Tottenham Court Road tube. **Open/food served** noon-1am Mon-Thur, Sun; noon-3am Fri, Sat. **Credit** AmEx, DC, MC, V.

It's tacky, trashy and flashy, but it's still packing in a twenty- to fortysomething, moneyed, dressed-up, mostly out-of-town crowd, who come here because, for all its rather phoney grandeur, Mezzo does have the ability to make you feel special. In contrast to what happens in more cutting edge but equally expensive places in the area, staff here are always professional and treat customers well, so you won't get ignored when you order a drink, and your table will be kept clean. Upstairs there's usually a throng around the bar and nowhere to sit; if you want to stay awhile, head down the 1920s-style spiral staircase to find a comfortable leather armchair to sink into, and chances are there'll be light jazz coming from the grand piano, a cigarette girl plying her wares, and plenty of entertaining conversations you can't help but eavesdrop on. Spirits are around £5, (and the measures last for ages); cocktails are £5-£7, and bottled beers (Corona, Foster's Ice) from £2.50-£3. As long as you don't take it too seriously, Mezzo is a great place to drop into once in a while.

Babies and children admitted. Function room. Late licence. Restaurant. Satellite TV.

Minty

50 Old Compton Street, W1 (020 7439 4130). Tottenham Court Road tube. **Open** noon-11pm Tue-Sun. **Happy hour** 5-7.30pm Tue-Fri. **Credit** MC, V.

Don't come to this mixed/gay bar if you want a bit of peace and quiet. The small square room with its bright red interior, pounding techno, and, on our visit, young woman who seemed to be employed solely to dance about and whip everyone up into a frenzy of club culture hedonism – we found the power to resist – all give the impression of this being a pre-largin' it hangout. But the clear glass windows cause self-consciousness rather than wild abandon, and a less frantic approach on the part of the staff might improve the atmosphere. The bar at the back is more secluded, however, and features measures of deluxe spirits at £6 (Tanqueray, Myers rum), while they also stock the lethal absinthe (£8). During happy hour beers (Beck's, Budweiser, Budvar and Labatt Ice) are two for the price of one (£3). Bar food include beef udon (noodles), Caesar salad and toasted ciabattas (all £4.50-£7).

Function room. Tables outdoors (pavement).

Mondo

12-13 Greek Street, W1 (020 7734 7157). Piccadilly Circus tube. **Open/food served** 6pm-3am Mon-Sat. **Admission** after 10pm Mon-Sat £5. **Credit** MC, V.

It was once famous for its intimidating and elitist door policies, but those days are long gone, and Mondo has settled in to being a smart late-night bar that fills up with a more flashy than trendy crowd as the night wears on. It's surprisingly large inside, and before 11pm it is easy to find an empty alcove on most evenings, making this a good place to come with a crowd, while on Friday nights the music is surprisingly good: a mix of classic funk, modern hip hop and even a bit of rock. Food is straightforward and inexpensive – assorted dim sum, steak and salsa in pitta, £4.50 – and double measures of spirits are £4.50-£5.50, while bottled beers, which most people seem to drink here, are around £3.

Late licence (Mon-Sat). Music (DJs from 10.30pm Wed-Sat). Vegetarian dishes.

Moon Under Water

105-107 Charing Cross Road, WC2 (020 7287 6039). Tottenham Court Road tube. **Open** 11am-11pm Mon-Sat; noon-10.30pm Sun. **Food served** 11am-10pm Mon-Sat; noon-9.30pm Sun. **Credit** AmEx, MC, V.

Formerly the Marquee, this is now popular with large groups of single-sex, after-work parties, which try to chat each other up, often with disastrous consequences as the night wears on. This enormous barn-like place is a real people's palace, offering low-priced drinks (Beck's £1.49, double vodka and Red Bull £3.49) and bland meals with which to mop it up (burgers £4.25, chicken balti £5.65). It gets packed from 6pm onwards, and by the end of the evening you're sure to find snogging couples, girls in tears, and, on the street outside, at least one fresh-faced young junior clerk regretting he had that last pint of Tetley's. By the Greek Street entrance there's a relatively quiet, self-contained little bar, which opens out on to the raucous main room.

Disabled: lift, toilet. Games (fruit machines). No-smoking area. Vegetarian dishes.

N20

187 Wardour Street, W1 (020 437 7770). Oxford Circus, Piccadilly Circus or Tottenham Court Road tube. **Open/food served** 1-3pm, 6-11pm Mon-Thur; 1-3pm, 6-1am Fri; 6pm-1am Sat. **Credit** AmEx, DC, MC, V.

It looks more like a café than a bar, with its small wooden tables and stalls and stark, clean interior made up of sheets of metal and a tiled floor, but frosted windows create a bit of intimacy and a fairly regular throng of people most evenings (it's a youngish, working crowd) give the otherwise cold surroundings warmth. Drinks aren't too expensive, either – a pint of Stella is £2.50, a vodka and cranberry £3.15, not bad for Soho – and the dishes are good if a little slight: ricotta and spinach tortelloni (£5.50) and a salmon and broccoli cake with tartare sauce (£6) were both tasty. It doesn't really have the buzz about it that the interior suggests the owners had hoped for, but being easygoing and friendly isn't a bad consolation prize for them.

Late licence. Music (occasional DJs). Restaurant. Vegetarian dishes.

O Bar

83 Wardour Street, W1 (020 7437 3490). Leicester Square or Piccadilly Circus tube. **Open/food served** 3pm-3am Mon-Sat; 4-10.30pm Sun. **Happy hour** 3-8pm Mon-Sat. **Admission** after 11.30pm Mon-Thur £3; after 10pm £3, after 11pm £5, Fri, Sat. **Credit** AmEx, MC, V.

One of the original club-bars, the O Bar continues to straddle that line, although these days for a crowd of tourists, teenagers and whoever else happens to wander in. It has wisely forsaken the former stripclub look of the ground floor for more sedate cream walls and bare floorboards, while the basement has clubby dark shades, flashing lights, and DJs on most nights playing commercial house and garage. The opulent, book-furnished upstairs room looks like it belongs in a private club and, as such, is often closed off for private functions. But this is not a place for uptown sophistication: most people drink bottled beers like Budweiser and Michelob (£3) and do their best to pick each other up.
Function room. Late licence (Mon-Sat). Music (DJs 9pm nightly). Satellite TV. Tables outdoors (pavement). Vegetarian dishes.

Old Coffee House
49 Beak Street, W1 (020 7437 2197). Oxford Circus or Piccadilly Circus tube. **Open** 11am-11pm Mon-Sat; noon-3pm, 7-10.30pm Sun. **Food served** noon-3pm Mon-Sat. **No credit cards.**
Not a place to drink coffee at all, rather a heavily furnished, darkly lit pub, which, with its stuffed animals, maritime illustrations and vaguely erotic portraits of nineteenth-century strumpets, has the rough, masculine charm of a hunting lodge. Resolutely down-to-earth in comparison to the increasing number of fashionable bars along Beak Street, it is always filled with a mix of stallholders from Berwick Street Market, tourists and shop assistants, who appreciate the pub's low prices (house spirits are £2.10 a double, a large glass of house wine is £2.50, Pedigree £2.40 a pint) and unpretentious bonhomie.
Function room. Games (fruit machine). Restaurant. Vegetarian dishes.

Pillars of Hercules
7 Greek Street, W1 (020 7437 1179). Tottenham Court Road tube. **Open** 11am-11pm Mon-Sat; noon-10.30pm Sun. **Food served** 11am-10pm Mon-Sat; noon-10pm Sun. **Credit** AmEx, MC, V.
Since its refit of a couple of years ago, this age-old Soho favourite sadly feels more like a chain pub – beige walls and shiny wooden fittings have replaced the grubby old Dickensian ale house-style furnishings – but it is still a lively place, drawing in a mixed crowd, from groups of businessmen to noisy students to Japanese tourists. Most people come here to drink pints of real ale (Marston's Pedigree £2.30, Theakston Best £2.10, with guest ales changing regularly), watch the big matches, and escape from Soho's mayhem at the raised area at the back of the bar.
Games (fruit machine). Vegetarian dishes.

Pitcher & Piano
69-70 Dean Street, W1 (020 7434 3585). Leicester Square or Tottenham Court Road tube. **Open** noon-11pm Mon-Sat. **Food served** noon-9pm Mon-Sat. **Credit** AmEx, MC, V.
One of the success stories of the last decade, this chain of pubs has cornered the *Ally McBeal*-watching market by being a little more sophisticated than its rivals, but keeping its prices in line with theirs, thereby making it the ideal place for the aspirational thirtysomething to enjoy a pint. This branch captures the chain's ethos perfectly: it looks like a members' bar from the outside, it has affordable champagne (£25 for a Canard Duchene), and the huge space is divided into areas with large sofas waiting to be taken over by a group of friends meeting after work. The mainstream crowd that pack into the place drink pints by

the bar (Guinness £2.50, Marston's Pedigree £2.40), enjoy the slightly Mediterranean meals at the tables (salmon fillet on mash £7.25, char-grilled chicken and roast vegetables £6.25), and even start dancing before closing time to disco classics and Abba.
Babies and children admitted (until 5pm). Function rooms. Vegetarian dishes.

Pop
14 Soho Street, W1 (020 7734 4004). Tottenham Court Road tube. **Open/food served** 5pm-3.30am Mon-Thur; 5pm-4am Fri; 8pm-5am Sat. **Credit** AmEx, MC, V.
London's newest designer bar is a huge and extremely flashy place that has gone for a colourful 1960s look and a nightclub ambience. As you walk down the curtained staircase you know this isn't the Rat & Parrot; carry on and you will find a huge room with a forest scene on one wall, circular sofas and formica tables, a VIP area behind a velvet rope and decor of the most vibrant oranges and blues. The young, enthusiastic staff struck out dance moves to the lounge music playing over the loudspeakers on our visit, and kept asking us if we were alright. All of this doesn't come cheap: sprits start at £5.80, cocktails are £5.50-£7 and beers are £3, but it's certainly poptastic.
Function room. Late licence. Music (DJs nightly). Vegetarian dishes.

Rupert Street
50 Rupert Street, W1 (020 7292 7141). Piccadilly Circus tube. **Open** noon-11pm Mon-Sat; noon-10.30pm Sun. **Food served** noon-6pm daily. **Credit** MC, V.
The success and style of this large gay bar is very much a sign of the times: with its massive, clear glass windows, a mixed crowd of both sexes who come here to pose and socialise rather than cruise, and upbeat, unintimidating atmosphere, it wouldn't have been possible in an age when London was less willing to accept different choices of lifestyle. It is probably Soho's trendiest gay bar, with the emphasis on spending money and looking good. Prices are high (a pint of Grolsch is £2.90, a double shot of spirits is £6), bar snacks are tasty (Italian chicken wrap £4.55), and the design is all important here, from the deep red sofas to the wood panelling behind the bar to the floral arrangements along the window sills. It's very easy to meet people here, although it's maybe not the best place for an in-depth conversation: the stereo and the general hubbub get very loud.
Disabled: toilet. Vegetarian dishes.

Sak
49 Greek Street, W1 (020 7439 4159). Leicester Square or Tottenham Court Road tube. **Open/food served** 5.30pm-2am Mon, Tue; 5.30pm-3am Wed-Sat. **Happy hour** 5-7pm daily. **Admission** after 11pm Fri, Sat £5. **Credit** AmEx, DC, MC, V.
On our visit last year, Sak's staff had more attitude than the doorman of Studio 54 after a line of coke; this time they were far more pleasant, perhaps having since realised that in the fickle world of Soho's trendy bars, pride comes before a fall. Without such an aggressive edge Sak is in fact a far nicer bar than most. The design is very sleek – brown leather sofas, huge floral arrangements, art deco bar – and the cocktails are expensive (£8-£9) but very good; try In The Sak (Vermouth, vodka, chambord, blood-orange juice). Alternatively, come here at happy hour for an entire jug of cocktail for £8, and some Thai fishcakes with mango dressing at £3.
Dress code. Late licence (Mon-Sat). Music (DJs Wed-Sat). Vegetarian dishes.

Pop

Salsa!
96 Charing Cross Road, WC2 (020 7379 3277).
Leicester Square or Tottenham Court Road tube.
Open 5.30pm-2am Mon-Sat. **Food served** 6pm-1.30am
Mon-Sat. **Admission** after 9pm Mon-Thur £4; 7-9pm Fri,
Sat £2; after 9pm Fri, Sat £8. **Happy hour** all day Mon;
5.30-8pm Tue-Sat. **Credit** AmEx, DC, MC, V.
The success of Salsa! is proof that the average inhibited Briton
secretly yearns to break out and live life like a hot-blooded
Latino. Coming here on a Friday night, it's not hard to see why:
while the groups of girls on hen nights and smart-casual lads
chasing after them get full marks for effort, their enthusiastic
jerks and thrusts were sadly not a scratch on the fluid grooving
of the bona fide Brazilians who took to the stage with such
grace. With bands on most nights and a restaurant, however,
even the most rhythmically challenged can make a night of it
here. Drinks are cheap (a glass of draught beer is £1.40,
cocktails are £3.95), there is unimaginative but edible food
(paella, tortilla chips, guacamole), and the energy is addictive.
On weekends the huge space gets crammed, and it's best to get
here before 10pm if you want to avoid the slow-moving queues.
*Dress code. Games (fruit machines). Late licence (Mon-
Sat). Music (DJs, Latin bands, salsa classes, nightly).
Restaurant. Satellite TV. Vegetarian dishes.*

Shampers
*4 Kingly Street, W1 (020 7437 1692). Oxford Circus or
Piccadilly Circus tube.* **Open/food served** 11.30am-11pm
Mon-Sat. **Credit** AmEx, DC, MC, V.
This bijou wine bar is reminiscent of the late '70s restaurant-
set comedy *Robin's Nest*: with its dripping candles, starched
white tablecloths and inoffensive paintings on the walls, it
has a dated, provincial air that isn't in keeping with its central
location. This is no criticism: it provides a welcome relief to
the generic chain pubs and designer bars that dominate the
area, and it's certainly popular. New World wines are well
represented here, with ones from California starting with a
Mondavi at £11.75 a bottle and a Lindauer from New Zealand
at £13. There are wine bar staples like goat's cheese salad
(£4.35) and lemon tart (£4.50) to soak it up with, as well as a
tasty pan-fried salmon at £10.95.
*Babies and children admitted (downstairs). Function room.
Restaurant. Satellite TV. Vegetarian dishes.*

Signor Zilli
*41 Dean Street, W1 (020 7734 3924). Tottenham Court
Road tube.* **Open/food served** noon-3pm, 5.30-11.30pm
Mon-Fri; 5.30-11.30pm Sat. **Credit** AmEx, DC, MC, V.
The popular Italian restaurant has an adjacent bar that is
almost as big as the restaurant itself, so you won't be made
to feel conscious of your non-eating status should you wish
to meet people for a drink here. It's a popular place for young
people with money and aspirations, older businessmen with
mobile phones, and loud Italians, and it has a sleek design
with a curving bar of wood veneer and colourful frescoes on
the walls. The Italian beers (Peroni, Dreher) are bottled and
cost from £2.50 to £2.90, double measures of spirits are
£4.50-£5, and you can order from the superior menu should
you get peckish: grilled calamari with Mediterranean
prawns is £9.50, capellini with spring vegetables is £6.90.
*Babies and children admitted. Restaurant.
Vegetarian dishes.*

Si Señor
*2 St Anne's Court, off Dean Street, W1 (020 7494 4632).
Tottenham Court Road tube.* **Open/food served**
noon-midnight Mon-Sat. **Happy hour** 5-7pm daily.
Credit AmEx, MC, V.

While all theme bars have an inescapable whiff of naffness
about them, this massive Mexican cantina is more eccentric
and colourful than most. Just like in Mexico, there's
something going on in every available bit of space, from the
comicbook-style skeletons on motorbikes, grinning devils
and bunches of fruit hanging from the ceiling to the
enormous murals of ageing men with their faithful hounds
on the walls. Hidden down a small alleyway, the large space
thrives late into the night these days with Mexican expats
and drunken girls trying to make the waiters dance (it's part
of their job). Find a tin table here and enjoy good Mexican
beers (Negra Modelo, Corona, both £2.75), huge Margaritas
(£5), a plate of tostadas (£3.10), upbeat Latin music from the
DJs and friendly if a little frantic service.
*Babies and children admitted (children's high chairs).
Music (Latin DJs Mon-Sat). No-smoking area. Restaurant.
Satellite TV. Vegetarian dishes.*

Six Degrees
*56 Frith Street, W1 (020 7437 2723/www.six-
degrees.co.uk). Piccadilly Circus or Tottenham Court
Road tube.* **Open/food served** noon-1am Mon-Sat.
Credit AmEx, DC, MC, V.
Taking over the site of former ultimate 1990s hangout
Dell'Ugo, Six Degrees is a recent venture that is far more in
keeping with the modern mood. Downstairs there's a sleek,
minimalist bar that attracts a well-heeled crowd of
thirtysomethings; it gets packed quite early on most nights.
The first floor is given over to a restaurant, but if you can,
blag your way into the upstairs bar. Currently operating a
vague members' policy, this is by far the nicest part: deep red
leather sofas, polished floorboards and panelled walls give it
the classic feel of a gentlemen's club, and the staff are very
friendly. Bottled beers like Sapporo or Tiger are £2.80; most
large measures of spirits are £5.50.
*Dress code. Function rooms. Late licence. Tables outdoors
(pavement). Vegetarian food.*

Soho Soho
*11-13 Frith Street, W1 (020 7494 3491/www.sante-
gcg.com). Leicester Square, Piccadilly Circus or Tottenham
Court Road tube.* **Open/food served** noon-11pm Mon-
Sat; noon-10.30pm Sun. **Credit** AmEx, DC, MC, V.
Bars come and go at a rate of knots round here, but this
quintessential 1980s yuppie hangout is becoming a bit of an
institution. It's still attracting a very mainstream, suited and
moneyed after-work crowd, who are content to stand up
around the bar and drink glasses of house wine at £3.50,
bottled beer (San Miguel, Moretti) at £2.70, and order bottles
of champagne from around £25. Its appeal remains
unfathomable to us, particularly considering the less than
welcoming service and huge stone statue of a pigeon (or
skyrat as they are more commonly known), but even we have
to admit that the omelettes (£6.50) are pretty good.
*Babies and children admitted (high chairs). Function
room. Music (pianist 9.30pm nightly). No-smoking area
(lunchtime only). Restaurant. Tables outdoors (patio).
Vegetarian dishes.*

Soho Spice
*124-126 Wardour Street, W1 (020 7434 0808). Oxford
Circus or Tottenham Court Road tube.* **Open/food
served** 11.30am-midnight Mon-Thur; 11.30am-3.30am
Fri, Sat; 12.30-10.30pm Sun. **Happy hour** 5.30-7pm Mon-
Sat. **Credit** AmEx, DC, MC, V.
The success of Soho's only decent Indian restaurant has
stretched to its downstairs bar; come here late on a Friday
night and you can't move. Veering sharply away from the
traditional Indian restaurant approach, Soho Spice has gone

for the theme-bar look, with waiters in acid-coloured kurtas and walls in colours that match. It's popular with a rowdy after-work crowd who come here for the Kingfisher on tap (£3 a pint) or cheap cocktails like Brandy Alexander and Margarita (£4).

Disabled: toilet. Function room. No-smoking area. Restaurant. Satellite TV. Vegetarian dishes.

Spice of Life

37-39 Romilly Street, W1 (020 7437 7013). Leicester Square or Tottenham Court Road tube. **Open/food served** 11am-11pm Mon-Sat; noon-10.30pm Sun. **Credit** AmEx, DC, MC, V.

Being right next to *Les Misérables*, this massive place is invariably filled with tourists, but as tourist pubs go it is a pretty good one. Frosted-glass windows, deep-red moulded ceilings, small gas-lamp-style sidelights and heavy flock furnishings add up to a fairly agreeable slice of Victoriana, and it is big enough usually to have a table free. The uniformed staff pull a lot of real ale pints from Hertford-based independent McMullen brewery: Original AK is £2.10, Gladstone is £2.25. A word of warning: do not touch, feed or make faces at the apes on the door under any circumstances – they are not known for their sense of humour.

Function room. Games (fruit machines). Tables outdoors (pavement). TV. Vegetarian dishes.

Sugar Reef

42-44 Great Windmill Street, W1 (020 7851 0800/ www.sugarreef.co.uk). Piccadilly Circus tube. **Open/food served** noon-3pm, 6pm-12.30am Mon-Sat. **Credit** AmEx, DC, MC, V.

Occupying the sleaziest, most unreconstituted strip of Soho, the Sugar Reef is following in the tradition of places like **The Atlantic** (*see p61*) in being an exclusive bar-restaurant where you have to look the part to get in. It is all rather grand: as soon as you get past the frosted-glass doors that the bouncer guards, there's a woman inside who will guide you towards the coat check; from there it's a short stroll across an underlit, gilded room with modern art on the walls to the bar, which is lined with huge floral displays and tended by affable young Spaniards and Italians. Drinks are prices typical for such places, with cocktails from £6.50 and a large measure of spirits from around £5 (a J&B whisky was £5.50). But on the night of our visit the Sugar Reef was just too empty to feel that special. Perhaps there are just too many exclusive bars in Soho these days.

Disabled: toilet. Function room. Late licence. Music (DJs nightly). Restaurant. Vegetarian dishes.

Sun & Thirteen Cantons

21 Great Pulteney Street, W1 (020 7734 0934). Oxford Circus or Piccadilly Circus tube. **Open** noon-11pm Mon-Fri; 4-11pm Sat. **Food served** 12.30-3pm Mon-Fri. **Credit** AmEx, MC, V.

This small West Soho corner boozer is an unusual phenomenon: a traditional pub that has turned itself into a pre-club hangout. Hordes of youthful groovers pack into the narrow walls of the front room, hassling the DJs about what records they're playing and misguidedly attempting to break out into some dance moves while holding a pint in one hand and a cigarette in the other (disaster inevitably ensues). For a safer bet, head to the pleasant back room: wood panelled, lined with mirrors, more subtly lit and quiet enough that you don't have to shout. Which you will have to do to order a pint of London Pride (£2.45) and Stella (£2.65). Note that food is only a lunchtime phenomenon.

Function room. Music (DJs Fri, every other Thur). Satellite TV. Vegetarian dishes.

Tactical

26-27 D'Arblay Street, W1 (020 7287 2823). Oxford Circus tube. **Open/food served** 11am-11pm Mon-Fri; noon-11pm Sat; noon-10.30pm Sun. **No credit cards.**

This two-roomed hangout for modern beatniks has a slightly pseudo-intellectual vibe – lots of hipsters pretending to read Burroughs while nodding their heads to the cutting edge sounds being mixed up by the DJ – but it's still fun and friendly. There are shelves of books and piles of magazines, a few battered sofas, and lots of small tables softening the harshness of the stone interior. Art students come here by day to discuss the burning issues of the hour (old skool trainers: are they still acceptable?) and drink lattes (£1.30); in the evenings a pre-club crowd orders large measures of spirits at £4.50 and bottled beers at around £2.50. With the added bonus of good snacks (try waffles with maple syrup, £3.50) and young, laid-back staff, it makes for a cool place to pose.

Babies and children admitted. Music (DJs Sun). Tables outdoors (pavement). Vegetarian dishes.

Taylors of Soho

11-13 Soho Street, W1 (020 7287 7103). Tottenham Court Road tube. **Open** noon-midnight Mon-Sat. **Food served** noon-11.45pm Mon-Sat. **Admission** after 7.30pm Mon £3.50. **Happy hour** 5-7pm Mon-Fri; 5-9pm Sat. **Credit** AmEx, MC, V.

Taylors still looks like a provincial 1980s wine bar with its wrought-iron tables, blue neon and Athena-style framed photographs of muscular hunks staring at babies in a rather confused manner, but come here on a Saturday night and you can catch some good jazz bands. The rest of the time it's the home for a strictly mainstream after-office crowd, who drink cockails like Sea Breeze, Blue Note (Bacardi, curaçao, cream and orange juice), and Margarita at £4.50, dip into the bottled beer selection (for instance Beck's £2.47, Budvar £3) and order tapas at £3.95.

Babies and children admitted (until 5pm). Music (new songwriters Mon). Tables outdoors (pavement). Vegetarian dishes.

Three Greyhounds

25 Greek Street, W1 (020 7287 0754). Leicester Square or Piccadilly Circus tube. **Open** 11am-11pm Mon-Sat; 3-10.30pm Sun. **Food served** noon-3pm Mon-Sat. **No credit cards.**

This tiny corner pub certainly has its own character – rough and ready – but it always seems to be overshadowed by its neighbour, the more bohemian **Coach & Horses** (*see p83*). It gets packed very quickly, and it feels very much a winter pub with its heavy beamed ceiling, Victorian photos, rough stone walls and wood panelling. It gets rowdy, but the formidable flame-haired landlady is too much of an opponent for any potential troublemaker, and drinking anything other than a pint (Adnams Bitter, Marston's Pedigree, both £2.35) would just seem silly in a place like this.

No piped music or jukebox. Vegetarian dishes.

Toucan

19 Carlisle Street, W1 (020 7437 4123). Tottenham Court Road tube. **Open/food served** 11am-11pm Mon-Fri; 1-11pm Sat. **Credit** AmEx, DC, MC, V.

This tiny Guinness bar has become so successful that the only civilised time to come here is in the afternoon, or on a Sunday evening – otherwise expect it to be rammed to the rafters, and the crowds spilling out on to the street. You can see why: this is no naff Irish theme pub, rather the real thing, with a cellar bar crammed with war-era tin advertisements, rickety tables and plastic toucans from a bygone advertising age. The

creamiest imported Guinness (£2.60 a pint) or Irish whiskey (from £2 to not far off £100) are the only things to drink here, and you can also get tasty bar snacks like Guinness pie and chilli con carne at £2-£3. Upstairs there is a similarly decorated, but less cosy, ground-floor bar.
Satellite TV. Vegetarian dishes.

Two Floors
3 Kingly Street, W1 (020 7439 1007). Oxford Circus or Piccadilly Circus tube. **Open** 11am-11pm Mon-Sat. **Food served** 11am-5pm Mon-Sat. **Credit** MC, V.
This was the first bar to put West Soho on the cool hangout map; it continues to do a brisk trade, attracting a crowd of youthful hipsters who come here for its relaxed, European-style ambience. With its piles of magazines, Arne Jacobson-style furniture, foreign bar staff and clean geometric lines, it looks like a bar you might find in Copenhagen. Bottled beers like Heineken, Red Stripe and Rolling Rock are £2.50; better to order a large measure at £4.50 and make it last. The downstairs bar is often hired out for fashionable private functions, but the upstairs room has a better vibe.
Babies and children admitted. Function room. Games (backgammon). Vegetarian dishes.

Two Thirty Club
23 Romilly Street, W1 (020 7734 2323). Leicester Square or Piccadilly Circus tube. **Open** 5.30pm-1am Mon-Sat. **Food served** 5.30-11pm Mon-Sat. **Credit** AmEx, MC, V.
In the basement of a new members drinking club, 23 Romilly Street, lies this tiny public bar. It's a short thin room, with grey velour seating round the edges, against wood-panelled walls, all leading to the bar at the end (although table service is the order of the day here. There is a list of classic coctails, Margaritas and Martinis (all £6 –), plus shooters (£4.50) and champagne cocktails (£7.50). When we went, it was refreshingly attitude-free and the drinks were lovingly made (the Singapore Sling was particularlyfine), but it was curiously empty mid evening on a Saturday. However, such a situation is unlikely to last long, so sample it while you can.
Late licence. Music (DJs Thur-Sat). Vegetarian dishes.

Village Soho
81 Wardour Street, W1 (020 7434 2124). Piccadilly Circus tube. **Open/food served** 4pm-1am Mon-Sat; 4-10.30pm Sun. **Credit** AmEx, DC, MC, V.
Gay standby the Village is a bar on two levels. Downstairs is a small and tastefully decorated L-shaped bar that runs around the back side of the **O Bar** (*see p89*), courtesy of entrances on both Wardour Street and Brewer Street. It's a low-lit, private affair, with added intimacy supplied by the dozens of altar-style candles strewn around with careful abandon. They come in earthenware pots, jugs, candelabra and, on one occasion, shining out from under what looks like a Victorian birdcage. There's a teeny-tiny courtyard thing that looks out on to the neon glare of a stripclub when the doors are open, adding a note of tack to an otherwise stylish environment. Upstairs is a smaller, more private affair with a few tables and chairs and an excellent view of Old Compton Street. Drinks include Foster's and Kronenbourg on tap (£2.80) and Pure Six and Miller in bottles (£2.90). A friendly and unpretentious place.
Function room. Late licence. Vegetarian dishes.

Webshack Internet Café
15 Dean Street, W1 (020 7439 8000/www.webshack-cafe.com). Tottenham Court Road tube. **Open/food served** 10am-11pm Mon-Sat; noon-8pm Sun. **Happy hour** (Internet) 8-11pm £1. **Credit** DC, MC, V.

The latest of the crop of Internet bars popping up across London feels more like a student computer club than a real bar: virtually all of the clientele are young, male and spotty, staring intently into flashing screens, and even the ones taking a break from the monitors at the sofas didn't seem that interested in talking to each other. The people along the bar, meanwhile, were watching MTV. Not the best place to socialise, then, but it isn't expensive: surfing the Internet costs £4 an hour, a cappuccino is £1.50, a bottled beer £2.60, and a range of hot food (from antipasto and Greek salad to jacket potatoes, sandwiches and burgers) starts at £1.95.
Babies and children admitted. No-smoking area. Satellite TV. Vegetarian dishes.

Yard
57 Rupert Street, W1 (020 7437 2652). Piccadilly Circus tube. **Open** noon-11pm Mon-Sat. **Credit** AmEx, DC, MC, V.
One of Soho's best, most down-to-earth gay bars, the Yard is large enough to feel like a community unto itself. It is indeed built around a courtyard, which is set down an alleyway off from the street and gives the impression of a hotel patio. The downstairs bar is upbeat, trendy and loud, while the upstairs bar, a barn-like affair with exposed brick walls, is more relaxed and sociable. Unlike most of Soho's gay dives, it's not male-dominated and there is no particular scene: lots of women of both sexual persuasions come here, too. Grab a pint of beer (Grolsch and Staropramen, both £2.80) and make some friends; this is a place to sit and have a chat rather than come to for cruising.
Function room. Tables outdoors (courtyard).

Yo! Below
52 Poland Street, W1 (020 7439 3660/www.yosushi.co.uk). Oxford Circus tube. **Open** noon-1am Mon-Sat. **Food served** noon-11pm Mon-Sat. **Credit** AmEx, DC, MC, V.
It isn't going to be to everyone's taste, but if you're in the mood, this long-planned addition to the restaurant where the bar staff are robots and the food comes on conveyor belts can be a fun break from the norm. It's a large, white, space age-style split-level basement room with tables and stalls so low that you must sit cross-legged, while serving yourself beer from the pumps that are under every table. It's £1 a glass (roughly a third of a pint); alternatively there are bottled beers (Asahi, Kirin, Sapporo) at £3, a range of sake from £3 to £11, and spirits at £2.50 an oversize measure. Be warned: perky staff might jump up and shout 'Yo! Is everything OK?' or even attempt to give you a free massage – it all feels a bit like being part of an MTV video. We've had mixed experiences from previous visits (wrong drink and food orders taken), but having a drink here is a true 21st-century experience, and with a surprisingly mixed crowd.
Function room. Late licence (Mon-Sat). Music (DJs Thur-Sat). Restaurant. Vegetarian dishes.

Also in the area...

All Bar One 36-38 Dean Street, W1 (020 7479 7921).
Café Flo 103 Wardour Street, W1 (020 7734 0581).
Café Med 22-25 Dean Street, W1 (020 7287 9007).
Café Rouge 15 Frith Street, W1 (020 7437 4307).
Dôme 55-59 Old Compton Street, W1 (020 7287 0770).
Fanfare & Firkin 38 Great Marlborough Street, W1 (020 7437 5559).
Slug & Lettuce 80-82 Wardour Street, W1 (020 7437 1400).

South Kensington SW3, SW5, SW7

Admiral Codrington
17 Mossop Street, SW3 (020 7581 0005).
South Kensington tube. **Open** 11am-11pm Mon-Sat;
noon-10.30pm Sun. **Food served** noon-2.30pm, 7-11pm
Mon-Fri; noon-3.30pm, 7-11pm Sat; noon-3.30pm, 7-10pm
Sun. **Credit** AmEx, MC, V.
The Admiral Codrington is one of the new breed of drinking
establishments, seamlessly blending pub and bar: the ladies of
the area feel happy to drop their pashminas and quaff a glass
of wine, while there are still enough pub-like qualities to entice
the local gents to take up residence at the bar. All in all, it's a
very comfortable place, although the clientele might get a bit
overbearing on a busy night. Beers include Boddintons (£2.20),
while the excellent wine list comes courtesy of esteemed wine
merchant Berry Bros & Rudd: the fine house wines start at
£2.50 a glass, £10 a bottle. The Codrington is also something
of a gastropub, although, to be honest, the fairly expensive food
served in the rear dining area is nothing to write home about.
*Babies and children admitted. Restaurant. Tables outdoors
(garden). Vegetarian dishes.*

Bar at 190
190 Queensgate, SW7 (020 7581 5666).
Gloucester Road tube. **Open** 11am-1am Mon-Sat; 11am-
midnight Sun. **Credit** AmEx, DC, MC, V.
Hidden away in one of the area's many hotels, this elegant
little bar serves as a retreat for the local gentry. The
Kensington leisure class can while away their afternoons here
surrounded by old oil paintings, weathered wood panelling
and the hip young things behind the bar. By night, locals
looking for respite from the tourist throngs and office outings
come here to exchange mobile phone numbers and boogie in
their armchairs to Take That. And all the while they can
select from an extensive drinks list – over twenty Martinis at
£7.50, shooters at £5, ten or so bottled beers (Ritter First
£3.50, San Miguel £3.95 and St Peter's Ale £4.50), and
absinthe at £9.50 – that also serves to attract those in the
know about this charming hideaway.
*Babies and children admitted (high chairs). Function
room. Late licence. Restaurant. Vegetarian dishes.*

La Belle Epoque
*151 Draycott Avenue, SW3 (020 7460 5000). South
Kensington tube.* **Open** 5.30pm-midnight Mon-Sat.
Credit AmEx, DC, MC, V.
La Belle Epoque seems to be over for this vast restaurant: it
has the feel of an upmarket American restaurant in the late
'80s, in part architecturally and in part because it's empty
most evenings. It's therefore a good place to go if you don't
want to be overwhelmed by the braying, über-rich inhabitants
of the area and just fancy a quiet drink. You do have to be
pretty flush to drink here, though: champagne cocktails start
at £7, with gin and tonics a pricey £3.50. Those who would
rather drink than eat are placed right by the window, so you'll
also be afforded a good view of the C-grade celebs falling out
of Daphne's just over the road.
*Babies and children admitted (restaurant only). Function
room. Restaurant. Tables outdoors (courtyard).
Vegetarian dishes.*

Blenheim
27 Cale Street, SW3 (020 7349 0056).
South Kensington tube. **Open** 11am-11pm Mon-Sat;
noon-10.30pm Sun. **Food served** noon-3pm, 6-9.30pm
daily. **Credit** AmEx, DC, MC, V.

In this area of high-concept, high-design bars, the Blenheim
makes a refreshing change. Put simply, it's a no-nonsense pub
that sells proper beers: no pine, not a whiff of a church pew
and all the better for it, although it has obviously had a
tasteful refit in the not-too-distant past. The food isn't too
high-falutin' either (chips and mayo are a very reasonable
£1.60), but the demands of the modern pubgoer mean that
Sky TV burbles in the background. Beer drinkers should take
advantage of the fine range of Dorset's Badger Brewery beers
(Dorset Best £2.12, Tanglefoot £2.25).
*Babies and children admitted. Function room. Games (bar
billiards, fruit machines). Jukebox. Quiz (Tue). Satellite
TV. Vegetarian dishes.*

Cactus Blue
86 Fulham Road, SW3 (020 7823 7858).
South Kensington tube. **Open/food served**
5.30pm-12.45am Mon-Fri; noon-midnight Sat; noon-11pm
Sun. **Happy hour** all day Mon; 5.30-7.30pm
Tue-Sun. **Credit** AmEx, DC, MC, V.
A vast atrium of a bar-restaurant with something of a
schizophrenic personality: decor-wise, Cactus Blue has
attempted to fuse New Mexican, Mexican and Native American
ephemera in a bid to borrow an 'ethnic' identity for its metal-
and-glass building. On a busy night, it's not much more than a
zoo. However, at quieter times Cactus Blue is a good place to
tuck into the quesadillas (£5.25) and quaff a couple of beers
(Budvar, Corona, both £3.15-£3.50): particularly if you hit the
happy hour, when beers drop from their usual £3.15 to £2.20,
and cocktails are a very reasonable £3.50. On our visit, both the
Bloody Marys and gin and tonics were good, ballsy numbers
with, pleasingly, no stinting on the booze part of the equation.
*Babies and children admitted (high chairs). Function
rooms. Music (live jazz Tue, Wed). No-smoking area.
Restaurant. Vegetarian dishes.*

The Collection
*264 Brompton Road, SW3 (020 7225 1212). South
Kensington tube.* **Open** noon-11pm Mon-Sat; noon-
10.30pm Sun. **Food served** noon-3pm, 7-11pm Mon-Sat;
6-10.30pm Sun. **Credit** AmEx, DC, MC, V.
The entrance to the Collection is remarkable: the
multicoloured glass walkway is a mixture of a catwalk, the
yellow brick road and the illuminated pavement in Michael
Jackson's *Billie Jean* video. Inside, the decor is rather more

toned down: the muted browns are set off with diplomatic lighting, and there's a suggestion of comfortable wealth everywhere. Although the Collection may have gone out of fashion with the 'it' crowd, if you're looking to impress someone it's a good place to go, while the suede chairs are very comfortable for a post-work slump. Sample the champagne cocktails (£7.50), though note a trip at happy hour will save you precious pennies. And if you're concerned about your spending, then it is probably best to steer clear of the menu, which offers the likes of veal and mash for £13.50.
Babies and children admitted (high chairs). Disabled: toilet. Dress code. Music (DJs 8pm nightly). Restaurant. Vegetarian dishes.

Crescent
99 Fulham Road, SW3 (020 7225 2244). South Kensington tube. **Open/food served** 11am-11pm Mon-Fri; 10am-11pm Sat; 11am-10.30pm Sun. **Happy hour** 5-7pm Mon-Fri. **Credit** AmEx, DC, MC, V.
A modern café-bar, Crescent is a more laid-back and pleasant place to visit than many of the local establishments. Bright and clean, it offers a wine list that will sate even the most curious oenophile: it even offers tutored wine tastings (two Mondays a month, from £30), while on Sundays and Mondays, you get a free glass of wine for every one you buy. Food is of the Modern British variety (chicken satay £3.25, leak and potato cake with goat's cheese £6.95, confit of duck's leg £9.50) – and we've heard mixed reports on its quality. The clientele is largely made up of post-Brompton Cross shoppers, so expect to find Prada and Joseph bags strewn around with gay abandon.
Function room. Vegetarian dishes.

Crown
153 Dovehouse Street, SW3 (020 7352 9505). South Kensington tube. **Open** 11am-11pm Mon-Sat; noon-10.30pm Sun. **Food served** noon-3pm, 7-10pm Mon-Thur. **Credit** MC, V.
Situated right next to Brompton Hospital, this pub would probably be called the Recovery Room if it weren't such a predictably classy establishment. A corner pub, it's been given the requisite revamp in a bid to capture the Pitcher & Piano market, but still hasn't quite rid itself of the rugby boy/businessman-on-the-way-home-from-work feel. However, the pub offers small rewards for those who decide to visit: a decent array of beers (London Pride £2.20, Adnams Southwold £2.20, Hoegaarden £3.40), plus the now-commonplace gastropub-style menu (sausages and mash £7.95, club sandwich £5.95).
Babies and children admitted. Tables outdoors (pavement). Vegetarian dishes.

Drayton Arms
153 Old Brompton Road, SW5 (020 7835 2301). Earl's Court or Gloucester Road tube. **Open** 11am-11pm Mon-Sat; noon-10.30pm Sun. **Food served** noon-3pm, 6-9pm Mon-Fri; noon-8pm Sat, Sun. **Credit** MC, V.
This mammoth place has combined the best features of a traditional pub with those of an American bar. Situated in a lovely Victorian building with towering windows, the Drayton Arms looks like a pub from the outside. However, the interior has been stripped bare, leaving room for both sofas and mingling space: come the weekend, the place is a bit of a meat market. But for all the improvements in social dynamics, the Drayton Arms can't entirely escape its roots: the food, for example, is the standard pub fare (steak and chips £5.75), and the drinks offer few surprises (Carling £2.30, Staropramen £2.70), and bottled beers are around the £2.80 mark.
Games (fruit machine). Tables outdoors (pavement). Vegetarian dishes.

Eclipse
113 Walton Street, SW3 (020 7581 0123). South Kensington tube. **Open** noon-midnight Sun-Wed; noon-1am Thur-Sat (members only after 7pm). **Food served** noon-4pm daily. **Credit** AmEx, DC, MC, V.
A pleasant new bar, Eclipse is clearly hoping to catch passing trade from Joseph or the Conran Shop. It may succeed, too, for aside from a limited selection of bottled beers, there's a fine cocktail list: try the excellent Mojito (£5.50) or the Cosmopolitan (£5.25); and simple but reasonably priced Italian lunchtime fare (soups, salads £4.75-£7.25). Decorated in standard 'good taste' brown-and-cream neutral '90s tones, it has comfy seats at the back, and enthusiastic young bartenders at the front doing half-decent Tom Cruise impressions, jiggling your drinks for all they're worth. The trick mirrors in the toilets are worth checking out, too.
Babies and children admitted (until 6pm). Dress code. Late licence (members only). Vegetarian dishes.

Hereford Arms
127 Gloucester Road, SW7 (020 7370 4988). Gloucester Road tube. **Open** 11am-11pm Mon-Sat; noon-10.30pm Sun. **Food served** 11am-10pm daily. **Credit** AmEx, DC, MC, V.
The Hereford Arms is one of the more 'ordinary' pubs in the South Kensington area: for one, the drinkers aren't all trust funders and public schoolers. Unfortunately, this mixed clientele doesn't manage to make it especially worthwhile: it's a bog-standard boozer churning out pints and deep-fried foods. As its name suggests, the Hereford Arms has been designed to bring the country pub to the city: the interior is made from hulking lumps of wood and has a vaguely 'rural' feel. Beerwise, it's the usual selections of cider, bitter (Theakston Best £2.14), and lager (Kronenbourg, Foster's, both £2.50); the food available ranges from sandwiches (£2.95) to steaks and the like at around £9. The selections playing on the jukebox during our visit – Smokie and Terry Jack's horrific *Seasons in the Sun* – suggest this place could successfully transform itself into a '70s theme pub with little or no effort.
Babies and children admitted (dining area). No-smoking area (dining). Restaurant. Tables outdoors (pavement). Vegetarian dishes.

itsu
118 Draycott Avenue, SW3 (020 7584 5522). South Kensington tube. **Open/food served** noon-11pm Mon-Sat; noon-10pm Sun. **Credit** AmEx, MC, V.
Although the restaurant at itsu (you gotta love that lower-case 'i') is all steel, glass and burgeoning modernity, the upstairs bar is rather more traditional. Dark furnishings and spot lighting help create an intimate feel, but do all you can to grab one of the sofas here: the stools are of the bum-numbing variety. Depending on your alcoholic politics, the cocktail list is either daringly iconoclastic or the worst kind of fusion drinking; certainly, the saké cocktails (from £6.50), such as saké Martini or Caipirinha, sound like a pavement pizza waiting to happen. You may be better off with the house wine (£2.95) or champagne (£6.95) instead. A limited version of the restaurant's sushi menu is available up in the bar, although without the conveyor belt display.
Babies and children admitted (children's menus). Function room. No-smoking area (restaurant). Restaurant. Vegetarian dishes.

Oratory
232 Brompton Road, SW3 (020 7584 3493). South Kensington tube. **Open/food served** noon-11pm Mon-Sat; noon-10pm Sun. **Credit** MC, V.

Situated just across the road from the Brompton Oratory, this restaurant-wine bar is a pleasant little place, with far fewer pretensions than many of the other local watering holes. It's basically a restaurant (mains £7-£11), but staff are quite happy for customers to sit and booze during the day and up to 8pm at night. The Oratory's main selling point is its wine list. The wines here seem to be sold at pretty much retail price – from Brinkley's Wines, incidentally – and there are some corkers at very reasonable prices: try the Guigal Côtes de Rhône at £9, or a bottle of Lindauer fizz at £10. All beers are bottled, with the usual suspects (Beck's, Michelob, Budvar) at around £2.50.
Babies and children admitted. Restaurant. Tables outdoors (pavement). Vegetarian dishes.

Also in the area...

All Bar One 152 Gloucester Road, SW7 (020 7244 5861).
Café Flo 89 Sloane Avenue, SW3 (020 7225 1048)..
Café Rouge 102 Old Brompton Road, SW7 (020 7373 2403).

St James's SW1

Avenue

7-9 St James's Street, SW1 (020 7321 2111). Green Park tube. **Open** noon-11pm Mon-Sat; noon-10pm Sun.
Food served noon-3pm, 5.45pm-midnight Mon-Thur; noon-3pm, 5.45pm-12.30am Fri, Sat; noon-3pm, 5.45-10pm Sun. **Credit** AmEx, DC, MC, V.
For those that seek solace from warts-and-all Soho, this salubrious St James's establishment could be just the ticket. Settle down in the slouchy bar seating at the front and watch the bartenders as they mix you up a Godfather (J&B and amaretto, £5.50), an Irish Monk (Kahlúa, Frangelico, Bailey's, £5) or pour you out a Polish potato vodka (yum, £6.50). Bar snacks can be obtained, too, so that you don't have to feel your way down to the main restaurant with its scary mirrored wall. Chips (£2.75) and mini-hotdogs (£3.50) come under 'small eats' and the more serious section carries Avenue fishfingers (£11.75) and the intriguing-sounding Italian delicacies. It might be wise to sample some of these as a few too many killer cocktails could see you trying to exit through the plate-glass front instead of the door.
Babies and children admitted. Disabled: toilet. Late licence. Music (pianist 8pm Mon-Sat). Restaurant. Vegetarian dishes.

Buckingham Arms

62 Petty France, SW1 (020 7222 3386).
St James's Park tube. **Open** 11am-11pm Mon-Sat; noon-5.30pm Sun. **Food served** noon-2.30pm, 6-9pm Mon-Sat; noon-2.30pm Sun. **Credit** MC, V.
There's a very good reason for knowing about this pub – it's only a few doors down from the Passport Office in Petty France. Even on the winter's day when we visited, there were backpackers staring into their pints, waiting to pick up the necessary before they could go off and find themselves. During the summer rush, the place is indispensable. The staff are well aware of this, and the bar is well stocked with vital refreshment: there's Young's Bitter (£1.94) and Special (£2.10), and bites include hot sausage and onion sandwiches (£2.20) and fish and chips (£4.50) for your last taste of home before you spread your wings.
Games (fruit machine). No piped music or jukebox. Satellite TV. Vegetarian dishes.

Che

23 St James's Street, SW1 (020 7747 9380).
Green Park tube. **Open/food served** 11am-11pm Mon-Sat. **Credit** AmEx, DC, MC, V.
Situated between Davidoff and JJ Fox, purveyors of fine hand-rolled Cubans, St James's Street is the ideal home for Che, for which cigars are the whole point. Central American Marxists aside, the huge humidor would have been Groucho Marx's dream – it's a kind of cigar library. But if you don't smoke, there's still something to keep you entertained: back-lit, coloured glass cubby holes hold the bottles of spirits to make up the cocktails on the menu, a Martini is £7.50, and there are man-sized bar snacks including club sandwiches (£12.25) and burger and chips (£8) if you want to make it a night with the boys, although on our visit most of the besuited couples were having a pre-date drink before making their way to the restaurant upstairs.
Babies and children admitted. Disabled: lift, toilet. Games (board games). Restaurant. Satellite TV. Vegetarian dishes.

Chequers

16 Duke Street, SW1 (020 7930 4007).
Green Park or Piccadilly Circus tube. **Open** 11am-11pm Mon-Fri; 11am-8pm Sat. **Food served** 11am-10pm Mon-Fri; 11am-8pm Sat. **Credit** V.
A cosy little hidey-hole amid the gentlemen's realm of St James's, Chequers reinforces the trad atmosphere of the area, so you'll find no outlandish cocktails or fancy foreign snacks here. Etchings of the PM's country residence hang on the wall and the decor is far more Winston C than Tony B with its heavy oak, warm dark colours and solid fittings. Pints available include Kronenbourg (£2.28), Guinness and Theakston Best (£2.14) and food is along the lines of pies and chips-with-everything pub grub (£2-£4.95). Those who can't get away from town to make the match would find Chequers a welcoming place to catch the sport on TV.
Games (fruit machine). Satellite TV. Tables outdoors (pavement). Vegetarian dishes.

Dukes Hotel Bar

Dukes Hotel, 35 St James's Place, SW1 (020 7491 4840/ www.dukeshotel.co.uk). Green Park tube.
Open noon-11pm Mon-Sat; noon-10.30pm Sun.
Food served noon-2pm, 6-9.45pm Mon-Fri, Sun; 6-9.45pm Sat. **Credit** AmEx, DC, MC, V.
Once you've managed to find this hotel embedded in the seemingly impenetrable heart of St James's, you'll be glad you did. In winter it's the cosiest place imaginable, and if you arrive early you'll be hard-pushed to wait till six o'clock for a cocktail, although you could while away the time with the Dukes' rather splendid afternoon tea. It's the Martinis that are celebrated, though, and we were very impressed by an American couple who had stayed here especially to taste one again. The trolley was ceremoniously wheeled to their table – the vermouth, in its tiny vinegar decanter, was 'shown' to the gin and finished with a twist, although the couple from Iowa had obviously been dreaming of olives, so olives were duly produced. We were happy to sit in the easy chairs and contemplate the snug great uncle's library of a bar and munch the salted almonds with a sparky Kir Royale (£7.50) – a welcome refuge from the 21st century.
Dress code. Function rooms. No piped music or jukebox. Restaurant. Vegetarian dishes.

Golden Lion

25 King Street, SW1 (020 7930 7227). Green Park or Piccadilly Circus tube. **Open** 11am-11pm Mon-Sat. **Food served** noon-2.30pm Mon-Fri. **Credit** AmEx, MC, V.

This pub has an extremely historic-looking façade, and the interior has been decorated accordingly with not altogether authentic-looking results, but the punters seem pretty content. This is the buzzy regular for the workers in the area – Christie's is across the road – and lunchtime and after-work stints are busy and jolly. Adnams Bitter, Theakston Best, Tetley's and Marston's Pedigree were all being quaffed with enjoyment on our visit, and the usual sandwiches are on offer as well as the speciality of the house – chilli at £3.95. There's a seated area at the back where food is served, but this is generally the kind of place where regulars prefer to stand three deep at the bar to get in maximum lunch-hour drinking time. *Function room. Games (fruit machine). Restaurant. Satellite TV. Tables outdoors (pavement). Vegetarian dishes.*

Quaglino's

16 Bury Street, SW1 (020 7930 6767/www.conran.com). Green Park tube. **Open** 11.30am-1am Mon-Thur; 11.30am-2am Fri, Sat; noon-11pm Sun. **Food served** 11.30am-midnight Mon-Sat; noon-11pm Sun. **Credit** AmEx, DC, MC, V.

Yes, Quags has a reputation for posh flash, attracting customers who look like the cast of *EastEnders* up west for the night, but on our visit to the Conran flagship, staff couldn't have been friendlier or more willing to please. People around us were enjoying champagne with a late lunch of Mr C's signature bivalves and crustaceans in the bar, which overlooks the giant cruise liner of a restaurant. We could have gone for standard bottled beers (Beck's, Miller, Kirin, all £3.50), but we opted to blow the cobwebs away with a Cowboy Martini (Plymouth gin, fresh mint and sugar, £6.25) and munched a delicious Caesar salad (£6.95) from the bar menu when we got peckish. On the whole, our visit was extremely pleasurable, and we'd recommend the afternoon as the time when the place really does seem to have a bit of 1930s glamorous magic, before the hordes arrive. *Babies and children admitted (restaurant only; high chairs). Disabled: lift, toilet. Function room. Late licence (Mon-Sat). Music (jazz Fri, Sat; pianist nightly). Restaurant. Vegetarian dishes.*

Red Lion

23 Crown Passage, off Pall Mall, SW1 (020 7930 4141). Green Park or St James's Park tube. **Open/food served** 11am-11pm Mon-Sat; noon-10.30pm Sun. **Credit** AmEx, MC, V.

A tavern from another time, the Red Lion calls itself 'the oldest village pub in London', and it certainly looks like it's been around for a while. In fact, the windows that look out on to the little cobbled passage are so ancient that you can't even see through them. On entering, you'll still be glad you've checked this one out – it's a comfy place to while away a few hours – and for pub connoisseurs the Red Lion is a hostelry oasis in a town of theme bars. Old dogs snooze on the floor, and old boys sit on the rickety, dark wood benches with a pint of Adnams Extra (£2.20) or a single malt. On a busy night there's a warm fug and the kind of atmosphere that makes for easy supping. If you're making an evening of it, Ye Olde Village Restaurant upstairs does steak and sole and other dishes that have been staples since St James's really was a village. *Babies and children admitted. Function room. No piped music or jukebox. Restaurant. Vegetarian dishes.*

Red Lion

2 Duke of York Street, SW1 (020 7930 2030). Piccadilly Circus tube. **Open** 11.30am-11pm Mon-Sat. **Food served** noon-3pm Mon-Sat. **No credit cards.**

There are a couple of places to drink on this street – this pub and a lap-dancing bar a few doors down. We chose the former, and our fellow drinkers didn't look as if they had other things on their minds either. The Red Lion is a pretty straightforward kind of a place, still fitted with its original oak furnishings and mirrors and popular with older office workers in the area for an after-work drink. If you prefer to sit and sip, there is wooden seating lining the room, or tables outside on the sloping pavement in the summer, but then there's always a 'just a quick one before I get off home' crowd standing around for a chat. There's a good choice of malts and beers on tap, Adnams Bitter is £2.20 a pint and Guinness is £2.40, and the usual range of snacks and sandwiches is offered. *No piped music or jukebox. Vegetarian dishes.*

Ritz

Ritz Hotel, Piccadilly, W1 (020 7493 8181/www.theritzhotel.co.uk). Green Park tube. **Open** 11.30am-11pm Mon-Sat; noon-10.30pm Sun. **Credit** AmEx, DC, MC, V.

Be careful what you choose to wear if you're intending to drink here: one would-be visitor was obliged to leave because she was wearing designer denim. Even her plaintive cries of 'But they're Chloé!' fell on heard-it-all-before ears. The Ritz doesn't really have a bar as such, but rather a series of elegant floral sofas set in recesses on either side of a hall. Drinks are served on the small tables, by staff who conjure them up magically from a hidden bar. As you'd expect, it all comes at a price, and you'll have to part with over a tenner for a cocktail, and £4.90 for a bottled beer, but they are accompanied by a inexhaustable supply of nuts and the crunchiest crisps in London. Don't wear trainers of any description, and men shouldn't wear open-necked shirts either. *Disabled: toilet. Dress code. Function rooms. Music (pianist 11pm Mon-Sat; harpist 2-7pm Sat, Sun). No-smoking area.*

Texas Embassy

1 Cockspur Street, SW1 (020 7925 0077/ www.texasembassy.com). Charing Cross tube. **Open/food served** noon-11pm Mon-Wed; noon-midnight Thur-Sat; noon-10.30pm Sun. **Happy hour** 5-7pm Mon-Fri. **Credit** AmEx, DC, MC, V.

A huge building in a fairly stuffy part of town just off Trafalgar Square has been converted into a bit of a tourist trap, amid the airline offices and bank headquarters. This Tex-Mex hotspot tries to look like a rugged cantina, where chicas and bandidos share Margaritas under a starry sky. It's a pretty family-oriented place; early evening means kids tucking into tacos while their parents enjoy a well-earned sit-down, but the pitchers of beer and cocktails on offer mean that it gets pretty rowdy later, and it's an office-outing favourite. Wooden tables and chairs are grouped under makeshift balconies from which sombreros hang, and the *High Chaparral* bartenders keep the beers (Mexican in bottles £2.60) coming with cheerful banter above the steady backbeat of the music. Authentic Tex-Mex food (among the best in London) includes enchiladas (£9.50) and quesadillas (£5.20). *Babies and children admitted (children's high chairs, balloons, crayons, menus). Disabled: toilet. Function room. Restaurant. Tables outdoors (pavement). Vegetarian dishes.*

Two Chairmen

39 Dartmouth Street, SW1 (020 7222 8694). St James's Park tube. **Open/food served** 11am-11pm Mon-Fri. **Credit** AmEx, DC, MC, V.

It's always easier to convince people that a stroll through the park is a good idea if there's a pub at the end of it. The Two Chairmen is just such a location to head for after you've fed the ducks in St James's Park, and a good deal more congenial than the lousy tea room next to the lake. Just at the bottom of Queen Anne's Gate, this pub dates from the seventeenth century and

was the place where you could pick up a sedan chair if you didn't want to get your feet dirty. These days you still have to dodge the horse shit (the Horse Guards' barracks is nearby), the cab drivers don't wear livery, and you're more likely to be enjoying a pint of Guinness or Kronenbourg (£2.30) and a plate of calamari and lime (£3.95) than cakes and ale. There's still a mural of the chair-carriers from bygone times, though, which makes a nice change from sepia pictures of Olde London Town or rustic beams and rusty pieces of farm machinery.
Function room. No piped music or jukebox. Vegetarian dishes.

Also in the area...

Balls Brothers 20 St James's Street, SW1 (020 7321 0882).
Davys at St James's Crown Passage Vaults, 20 King Street, SW1 (020 7839 8831).
Tapster (Davys) 3 Brewers Green, Buckingham Gate, SW1 (020 7222 0561).

Temple WC2

George IV
28 Portugal Street, WC2 (020 7831 3221). Holborn or Temple tube. **Open** 11am-11pm Mon-Fri. **Food served** 11am-3pm, 5-9pm Mon-Fri. **Credit** MC, V.
This high-ceilinged Edwardian pub used to be the haunt of students from nearby LSE; indeed, Mick Jagger is reputed to have trapped his finger in the door way back when. These days, though, they prefer their own subsidised hangouts, leaving the George free to be colonised by packs of office slaves and builders. Food is heavily advertised and tends towards the fish and chips/pasta bowl/chicken tikka masala scheme of things (£3.95-£4.75), while beers include Bass and London Pride (both £2.10). The large TV screen can bring the worst out of the assembled throng, especially when England are losing to whoever they're losing to this week.
Function room. Games (fruit machines, pool tables, video game). Satellite TV (big screen). Vegetarian dishes.

Seven Stars
53-54 Carey Street, WC2 (020 7242 8521). Chancery Lane, Holborn or Temple tube. **Open/food served** 11am-11pm Mon-Fri. **Credit** MC, V.
A little gem of a pub that gives the impression that it's not been altered since it was built in the early 1600s. It has, of course - mainly around the turn of the last century, by the looks of it - but the cream plaster and thin, dark wood beams point to a bygone era, and there's no TV, music or fruit machine. The bar area is accessed through a door marked 'General Counter', while the small, crowded room at the end of the pub is entered via a 'Private Counter' door. Beers are good, with four real ales - including, on our visit, a perfect Charles Wells' Bombardier (£2) - and a fridge full of bottled beers. The landlord cooks the lunchtime food: expect the likes of corned beef hash and 'special' curry for under £4.
No piped music or jukebox.

Shoeless Joe's
Temple Place, WC2 (020 7240 7865). Temple tube. **Open** noon-1am Mon-Wed; noon-3am Thur-Sat. **Admission** after 9pm Fri £5, after 11pm £10; after 9pm Sat £5. **Food served** noon-3pm, 6-10pm Mon-Sat. **Credit** AmEx, DC, MC, V.
This branch of Victor Ubogu's chain - named after Joe Jackson, the baseball player immortalised in *Field of Dreams* - is housed in what looks like a disused toilet near the river.

Sports are high on the agenda, and the picture quality on the large screens is impressive. So, too, is the food: the raised restaurant area promises above-average bar nosh. The interior is cavernous (not a toilet, then), decor is bright and colourful, and you're likely to find a live DJ pumping out dance and jazz tracks. Bottled beers are the thing - Beck's and Budweiser are around £3 - with cocktails and tall drinks setting you back a fiver or more. A suit and tie is a good idea, especially on busy nights when the doorman picks a little more carefully.
Disabled: toilet. Dress code (no trainers). Late licence. Music (jazz Tue, Wed; live band, Thur, Fri; DJs Thur-Sat). Restaurant. Satellite TV. Vegetarian dishes.

Trafalgar Square WC2, SW1/ Charing Cross WC2

Dôme
8-10 Charing Cross Road, WC2 (020 7240 5556). Leicester Square tube/Charing Cross tube/rail. **Open** 8am-11.30pm Mon-Sat; 9am-11pm Sun. **Food served** 9am-11.30pm Mon-Sat; 9am-11pm Sun. **Credit** AmEx, MC, V.
More brasserie than bar - although the option of dropping in for a glass or two is there - this branch of the Dôme chain is typical of the light and airy French café style they've made their own: beige walls, wood floor and furniture, topped off with two plastic-looking chandeliers. The clientele is generally a mix of tourists, shoppers and office workers partial to the semi-Gallic experience. Cocktails start at £3.95 for a Sea Breeze, house wine is £2.35 a glass and beer prices are average for the area, at £2.60 for Beck's. As you'd imagine, the menu has something of a French accent, so expect dishes like baguette au poulet (fancy chicken roll, £5.95) and steak frites (£10.95).
Babies and children admitted (high chairs). No-smoking area. Restaurant. Vegetarian dishes.

Gordon's
47 Villiers Street, WC2 (020 7930 1408). Embankment tube/Charing Cross tube/rail. **Open** 11am-11pm Mon-Sat. **Food served** noon-9pm Mon-Sat. **Credit** MC, V.
Ignore the unwelcoming exterior and follow the steep steps down until you come to the food serving area (offering simple hot and cold food for around £5), then turn left to the heart of this slightly tatty wine bar. This used to be a wine cellar, and the low arches, nooks and cobwebby corners add a charm rare for the area. The customers tend towards the besuited office worker, with a definite leaning to Rumpoles and ruddy-faced thirtysomethings who assure you that their spare time is spent engaged in dangerous sports. Gordon's serves nothing but wine, in all its various forms, with sherry, Madeira and port coming from barrels behind the small bar. Prices start at around £2.60 a glass, or £8.25 a bottle, for the house stuff.
Tables outdoors (terrace). Vegetarian dishes.

Phillip Owens @ The ICA
The Mall, SW1 (020 7930 2402/www.ica.org.uk). Charing Cross or Piccadilly Circus tube. **Open** noon-1am Tue-Sat; noon-10.30pm Sun; noon-11pm Mon. **Food served** noon-10.30pm Mon; noon-11pm Tue-Fri; noon-4pm, 5.30-11pm Sat; noon-4pm, 5.30-10pm Sun. **Credit** AmEx, DC, MC, V.
The newly refurbished bar and restaurant at the ICA are popular with members dropping in to view an exhibition or film, but it's worth noting that for non-members, one-day membership costs £1.50 on top of your bill. The bar is on a

Gordon's.
See page 101.

mezzanine floor, with modern metal furniture and a fancy, chrome-and-glass backlit bar. They only serve keg beer on draught (including Bombardier and Red Stripe, both £2.70), which would seem to be at odds with the 'only the best and freshest' philosophy of the café, although bottled beers and cocktails seem to be what the young arty customers want. The eating area – self-service at lunchtime, waiter service after 5.30pm – has an adventurous modern-Italian menu that changes daily. Expect the likes of lasagne al forno (with organic meat) and stuffed cabbage leaves for around £5 at lunch. Although it's enjoyed great reviews, our experience didn't inspire: the sole vegetarian dish had sold out within 40 minutes of opening, and in lieu we were offered what would have made an inadequate starter, and charged £6.95 for the privilege.
Function room. Late licence (Tue-Sat). No-smoking area. Restaurant. Vegetarian dishes.

Queen Mary

Victoria Embankment, WC2 (020 7240 9404).
Embankment or Temple tube. **Open** noon-11pm daily (summer); noon-6pm daily (winter). **Food served** noon-9pm daily (summer); noon-6pm daily (winter).
Credit AmEx, DC, MC, V.
Ahoy! Or not, as the case may be. It would be easy simply to dismiss this floating pub as a nautical nonsense for tourists, but in warmer months, the open deck provides an ideal place to sun and sip. If the river breeze is too much for you, nab a window seat inside and enjoy the view across the Thames to the South Bank. Except for the views, however, the interior of leatherbound seats and dark wood furnishings could be in any similarly tourist-oriented enterprise on land; not much jolly rogering here – at least we didn't notice any. There are five bars on board, some

doubling up as a nightclub, but in winter the bulk of them are resolutely closed. There's a range of beers (Beck's £2.50) and basic pub grub unremarkable in anything but price. *Babies and children admitted. Function rooms. Games (quiz machine). Tables outdoors (deck). Vegetarian dishes.*

Sherlock Holmes

10 Northumberland Street, WC2 (020 7930 2644).
Embankment tube/Charing Cross tube/rail. **Open** 11am-11pm Mon-Sat; noon-10.30pm Sun. **Food served** noon-10pm daily. **Credit** MC, V.
Friendly and cosy, arranged around a central serving area, this is a small, old-style pub that's invariably busy, so getting a seat can be tricky. Still, standing gives an excuse to peruse the Sherlockia (as it's called) that practically hold the walls together and if a Sherlock Holmes mug or ashtray is your thing, then buy one at the bar. There's also a good selection of beers, including an exclusive Sherlock Holmes bitter (which wasn't on when we visited), and Abbot Ale which was, but hardly cheap (even for the area) at £2.34 a pint.
Babies and children admitted. Games (fruit machine). Restaurant. Tables outdoors (pavement). Vegetarian dishes.

Tattershall Castle

King's Reach, Victoria Embankment, SW1 (020 7839 6548). Embankment tube/Charing Cross tube/rail.
Open 11am-11pm Mon-Sat; noon-10.30pm Sun. **Food served** noon-10pm daily. **Credit** AmEx, DC, MC, V.
As on the **Queen Mary** (*see above*), the interior here owes more to Berni Inns than Horatio Nelson, and the drinks (Foster's £2.40, bottled Bud £2.71) are considerably more expensive than they are ashore. Meals – with a leaning towards seafood – are overpriced for what's on offer (fish and chips £5.95, chicken

kiev £5.65). They seem immeasurably proud here of the separate Steamers nightclub (open Wednesdays to Saturdays, with a cover charge), which gives some idea of the clientele they're seeking at this floating pub. But catch a summer's day, and the deck bar still offers a refreshing breeze and river views. *Function room. Games (fruit machine, quiz machine). Jukebox. Tables outdoors (decks). Vegetarian dishes.*

Two Chairmen

1 Warwick House Street, SW1 (020 7930 1166). Charing Cross tube/rail. **Open** 11am-11pm Mon-Sat. **Food served** noon-2.30pm Mon-Sat. **No credit cards.**
A small, narrow one-bar pub just off Trafalgar Square that remains an unspoilt gem. The Two Chairmen (the sign outside showing two men hefting a sedan chair explains all) dates back to the 1680s and has that cosy, lived-in feel that only genuinely old pubs have. The walls are wood panelled and the furniture is solid and comfortable, if not particularly new. The only concession to modern life is a discreetly placed wide-screen TV. There are usually three real ales on offer: Courage Best (£1.80), Directors and Marston's Pedigree (£2.30), although we've never found them all on at once. House spirits are particularly good value at £2 for a double measure. Food is basic and limited to Scotch eggs, meat pies and suchlike, for around £4-£5.
Babies and children admitted. Games (quiz machine). Vegetarian dishes.

Also in the area...

Pitcher & Piano 40-42 William IV Street, WC2 (020 7240 6180).

Victoria SW1

Boisdale

13-15 Eccleston Street, SW1 (020 7730 6922/ www.boisdale.co.uk). Victoria tube/rail. **Open** noon-1am Mon-Fri; 7pm-1am Sat; noon-10.30pm Sun. **Food served** noon-2.30pm, 7-10.30pm Mon-Fri; 7-10.30pm Sat; noon-5pm, 7-10pm Sun. **Credit** AmEx, DC, MC, V.
A little bit of Belgravia stranded close to Victoria Station, Boisdale attracts a posh, successful-looking clientele. A Scottish theme predominates, with a big range of whiskies, and haggis on the menu at the adjoining restaurant. Tartan is used throughout, but this traditional touch is matched with a long zinc bar and red walls, which emphasise that the place is about fun, too. House whisky, Famous Grouse, is a reasonable £3.50 for a double shot, and also popular is the Macallan malt at £3.50. For a real treat try the Royal Lochnagar malt, 25 years old, at £12.50 a shot. This is no whisky bores' bar, though, for chilled white wine at £3.50 a glass is equally popular. You'll also find a large range of cigars in a long humidor, and a fine and extensive bar menu (Rannoch Moor wild smoked venison sandwich £7.50, home-made pie of the day £9.90) that comes from the same kitchen that serves the restaurant. Highly recommended.
Babies and children admitted. Function room. Late licence. Music (live jazz 9pm-midnight Mon, Tue; 10pm-midnight Wed-Sat). Restaurant. Tables outdoors (conservatory). Vegetarian dishes.

Cardinal

23 Francis Street, SW1 (020 7834 7260). Victoria tube/ rail. **Open** 11.30am-11pm Mon-Sat; noon-10.30pm Sun. **Food served** noon-4pm, 5-9pm Mon-Fri; noon-3pm Sat. **Credit** AmEx, DC, MC, V.

A great example of the loving restoration Samuel Smith's have brought to Victorian some of London's pubs. Dining areas in pubs are usually an apology for a picnic, but here a large space has been neatly partitioned off; meals range from an Italian salad (£5.10) to ostrich steak and fries at £8.25. Elsewhere the dimly lit pub with its deep red colour scheme and central bar has numerous pictures of cardinals from the nearby Catholic cathedral. Despite the classy mansion blocks opposite, this pub has long attracted a working-class clientele. Good Samuel Smith's Cider is served at £2.02 a pint, and the new Ayingerbrau Bavarian white lager Hefe Weisse is £2.24, and comes in its own special wavy-shaped glass.
Babies and children admitted (except Fri; children's menu). Function room. Games (fruit machine). No-smoking area. Quiz (Tue). Vegetarian dishes.

Tiles

36 Buckingham Palace Road, SW1 (020 7834 7761). Victoria tube/rail. **Open** 11am-11pm Mon-Fri. **Food served** noon-2.30pm, 6-10pm Mon-Fri. **Credit** AmEx, DC, MC, V.
Using only the simplest props of large mirrors, candles, small round tables for two and the old tiled floor of a Victorian shop, Tiles wine bar creates a classy, intimate atmosphere, and it was packed on the Thursday night we visited; healthy acoustics help, too. Its broad range of wines is good, glasses cost upwards of £2.75 (Pinot Grigio at £3.25 was smooth, the Montelpulciano d'Abruzzo a little dull, £2.75), and bottles start at £10.95. There are bar snacks such as potato skins and nachos for £3-£5.50 and good larger meals from £4.95 to £8.95, such as mussels and bangers and mash or cajun chicken.
Function room. Restaurant. Tables outdoors (pavement). Vegetarian dishes.

Wetherspoons

Unit 5, Victoria Island, Victoria Station, SW1 (020 7931 0445). Victoria tube/rail. **Open** 11am-11pm Mon-Sat; noon-10.30pm Sun. **Food served** 11am-10pm Mon-Sat; noon-9.30pm Sun. **Credit** AmEx, DC, MC, V.
Many station pubs try in vain to shut out the rush and stress outside their doors. Here relative calm is created by allowing you to watch the hordes outside from within an insulated glass-sided room above WH Smith on the station concourse. There's a great range of bitters (Boddingtons, Theakston, London Pride) and guest ales (such as Hook Norton, for £2.10). Wine is from £2.20 a glass. A studiously bland interior emphasises that this is a handy pub, more than a good one. Much of the seating is given over to diners, who can choose from a wide range of meals around a fiver, including chicken tikka masala and chicken pasta alfredo (both £5.55).
Disabled: toilet. Tables outdoors (balcony). No piped music or jukebox. No-smoking areas. Vegetarian dishes.

Also in the area...

Café Rouge Victoria Place Shopping Centre, 115 Buckingham Palace Road, SW1 (020 7931 9300).

Waterloo SE1

Archduke

Concert Hall Approach, South Bank, SE1 (020 7928 9370). Embankment or Waterloo tube/rail. **Open/food served** 11am-11pm Mon-Fri; noon-11pm Sat. **Credit** AmEx, DC, MC, V.

Twenty years since it formed as a gleam in the eye of Liz Philip, who wanted somewhere to drink before the concerts next door, the unassuming Archduke is set to outlast the House of Lords. It's a brick-and-metal cavern, crouching in a railway arch within a stone's throw of the Royal Festival Hall. A handsome spiral staircase connects the restaurant, bar and no-smoking area in the middle with the all-day snack bar on the ground floor. You can avoid the concert crush or dodge the early-closing South Bank bars with San Miguel on tap (£1.75 a half, £6.75 a two-pint jug) and a large choice of wines such as Montepulciano (£2.90 a glass, £11.75 a bottle). The neon signs and live jazz won't be to everyone's taste, but the rumble of trains overhead brings the bubbles to the top of your glass in a charming way.
Babies and children admitted. Function rooms. Music (jazz 8.30-11pm Mon-Sat). No-smoking area. Restaurant. Tables outdoors (pavement). Vegetarian dishes.

Auberge
1 Sandell Street, SE1 (020 7633 0610). Waterloo tube/ rail. **Open/food served** 11am-midnight Mon-Fri; noon-11pm Sat. **Credit** AmEx, DC, MC, V.
An Islington-style remix of a monastery refectory – all wood floors and chapel chairs – Auberge is a stylish venue for both drinkers and diners. Chunky white candles on every table and lights fitted into the deep blue ceiling like stars create a warm ambience. There's not a monk in sight, although pleasant staff do serve Trappist beers: the tasty Kwak (£3.45) comes in a giant hourglass with wooden stand. The wines cost from £9.95 for a bottle of Collingbourne Cape White to £19.95 for Chablis Brocard. The same range of delicious French food – including large bowls of moules paysanne (£8.95) and magret de canard (£9.95) – is served upstairs as downstairs, but the mezzanine restaurant boasts a late licence. A great hideaway.
Babies and children admitted. Function room. No piped music or jukebox. Tables outdoors (roof terrace). Vegetarian dishes.

Bar Citrus
36 The Cut, SE1 (020 7633 9144/www.barcitrus.co.uk). Southwark tube. **Open** 8.30am-11pm Mon-Fri; 10am-11pm Sat; 10am-9pm Sun. **Food served** 8.30am-10pm Mon-Fri; 10am-10pm Sat; 10am-8pm Sun. **Credit** AmEx, DC, MC, V.
Bedford brewers Charles Wells have converted the former Anchor & Hope into an upmarket two-room bistro-style bar, big on clean lines, light wood and glass. The ceiling and pillars are dark emerald green, the walls the customary creamy beige and decorated with hand-painted notices: 'wines of the world', 'real ales', 'speciality hot drinks', etc. The wine list, wrapped around bottles holding (when we were last there) a single daffodil, is comprehensive, with a large glass of the house white or red at £2.50. Two real ales are kept, Bombardier and Eagle IPA (£1.82 a pint), as well as other Charles Wells products such as Kirin, Red Stripe and Fargo (geddit?). Food is cooked in the open-plan kitchen, beginning at 8.30am with breakfast (£5.95 for a Full On Waterloo), through to lunch and dinner of speciality sausage and mash (£4.95), or baby corn and snow pea stir-fry (£6.60). Customers tend towards the young professional type, either grabbing a quick drink before heading down the nearby Young Vic or on the way home from work.
Babies and children admitted (restaurant only). Disabled: toilet. No smoking area. Restaurant. Tables outdoors (pavement). Vegetarian dishes.

Cubana
48 Lower Marsh, South Bank, SE1 (020 7928 8778/ www.cubana.co.uk). Waterloo tube/rail. **Open** noon-midnight Mon-Sat. **Food served** noon-3pm, 5.30-11pm

Mon-Fri; 6-11pm Sat. **Happy hour** 5-6.30pm Mon-Sat. **Credit** AmEx, DC, MC, V.
From a ruddy paint daub of Castro's head on the brick wall, through a poster advertising that 'I'll See You in Cuba', to the statue of the Virgin Mary, everything here is Cuban. Cristal (£2.55), billed as Cuba's top beer, is served here, along with tap beers such as San Miguel (£2.45) and cocktails including Margaritas and Daquiri Cubanas (both £4.75). Attentive staff serve a menu of cheap Cuban country cooking (£5.95 for two courses at lunch), such as an over-salty chicken soup (£3.45), and great bread and salsa (95p). By day, only the 'two for a pound' cries from the nearby market stalls and the techno music remind you that you're in London. By night, though, the place fills up and becomes a vibrant hangout. On Wednesdays, live salsa music ensures the city folk can Havana breeze.
Babies and children admitted. Disabled: toilet. Restaurant. Tables outdoors (pavement). Vegetarian dishes.

Fire Station
150 Waterloo Road, SE1 (020 7620 2226). Waterloo tube/ rail. **Open** 11am-11pm Mon-Sat; noon-10.30pm Sun. **Food served** noon-11pm Mon-Sat; noon-9.30pm Sun. **Credit** AmEx, DC, MC, V.
Fancy a drink in an old fire station? Try this spacious, high-ceilinged venue. While we couldn't find a fireman's pole, there are hoses, metal lamps and two large red-and-gold phoenixes (rising from the ashes?) on a small balcony. The building's split in two. In one half is a bar where you can sup Adnams Best (£2.20), Hoegaarden (£3.15) and Caffrey's (£2.50) at heavy pine tables; in the other, a restaurant area serving delicious and well-presented food, such as Fire Station fishcake (£5.50), seared tuna (£11.95) and a set menu (£10 for two courses, £13.50 for three). Staff are friendly, and the location – by Waterloo and the Cut – makes this a good place in which to hose down at any time of day.
Babies and children admitted (children's menu at weekends, high chairs). Function room. Restaurant. Satellite TV (big screen). Vegetarian dishes.

King's Arms
25 Roupell Street, SE1 (020 7207 3986). Waterloo tube/ rail. **Open** 11am-11pm Mon-Sat; noon-4pm, 8-10.30pm Sun. **Food served** noon-2.45pm Mon-Fri. **Credit** MC, V.
Tucked away in the Victorian backstreets between the National Theatre and the Cut, the King's Arms is a friendly, old-fashioned local. The circular bar serves both the public and saloon rooms, but the two are divided by a wood and glass partition. The public bar is all wood and decorated with old black-and-white photographs of the area, while the saloon bar has plush red velvet curtains and plants. If neither takes your fancy, you can drink your Adnams or Ushers (both £2.10) and eat your cod and chips or all day breakfast (both £3.95) out the back in a Mediterranean-style conservatory, which can also be hired for functions.
Function room. Tables outdoors (courtyard). Vegetarian dishes.

Laughing Gravy
154 Blackfriars Road, SE1 (020 7721 7055). Southwark or Waterloo tube. **Open** noon-midnight Mon-Fri; 7pm-midnight Sat. **Food served** noon-11pm Mon-Fri; 7-11pm Sat. **Credit** AmEx, DC, MC, V.
The Laughing Gravy takes its name from a dog in a Laurel and Hardy short film. A black-and-white photograph of the comedy duo hangs obligingly on the cream walls, but otherwise, the Laughing Gravy is a serious affair. A champagne-and-wine bar (all beer is bottled), specialities include New Zealand Jackson Estate Sauvignon Blanc (£28.25) and Medot et Cie

champagne (£4.75 a glass, £25 a bottle). The more upmarket restaurant area has an upright piano – which, if you're feeling musical, you're welcome to have a tinkle on – a Tiffany lamp on the dark sideboard, and posh dishes such as wild boar (£12.25). Given its proximity to the new Southwark tube and Shakespeare's Globe, it's surprising that it's shut on weekends and that it was closed at 10.30pm on a Monday due to lack of customers.

Babies and children admitted (high chairs). Games (board games). Restaurant. Tables outdoors (pavement). Vegetarian dishes.

Mulberry Bush

89 Upper Ground, SE1 (020 7928 7940). Waterloo tube/rail. **Open** 11am-11pm Mon-Sat. **Food served** 11am-9pm Mon-Sat. **Credit** AmEx, DC, MC, V.

Despite the romantic name, this is in fact a modern, orangey-brick Young's pub, with an interior of new pine and red carpets and three separate rooms. The Family Room runs along the end of the bar and has a red tiled floor, on to which you can drop your chips and ketchup, and adjacent nappy-changing facilities, while the traffic-free Gabriel's Wharf opposite also offers some child-friendly cvorting area. The Bar Bistro and the Café-Bar are frequented by office workers in search of sustenance. Food is pubby – chilli con carne (£3.50), jacket potatoes (£3.20) – and the ales are from Young's familiar range. Wines include Jalousie Vin de Pays des Côtes de Gascogne (£2.35 a glass, £9.35 a bottle) and El Coto Crianza Rioja 1996 (£2.35/£11.95). A useful place to know about if you have kids or work in the area, but hardly one to seek out otherwise.

Babies and children admitted (separate room). Disabled: toilet. Function rooms. Games (fruit machine, quiz machine). No-smoking area. Restaurant. Satellite TV. Tables outdoors (pavement). TV. Vegetarian dishes.

Oxo Tower

Riverside, Oxo Tower Wharf, Barge House Street, SE1 (020 7803 3888). Blackfriars or Waterloo tube/rail. **Open** 11am-11pm Mon-Sat; noon-10.30pm Sun. **Credit** AmEx, DC, MC, V.

Great views of London, of course, but at great prices. The menu offers an extensive list of cocktails (from £7), although we settled for a Budweiser (£3.20) and, perched on silver stools, sipped it slowly in front of the smart waiters. The leather-topped indigo-and-chrome bar divides the eaters from the drinkers. The former, sadly, get the riverfront views, leaving the latter to peer over their heads at the lights or check out the warehouse walls and latest installation at the Museum Of… while humming along to piped Billie Holiday. Otherwise, try and adopt a friend in the neighbouring IPC tower and get the views for free.

Babies and children admitted. Disabled: lift, toilet. Music (jazz/blues nightly). Restaurant. Tables outdoors (terrace). Vegetarian dishes.

Paper Moon

24 Blackfriars Road, SE1 (020 7928 4078). Blackfriars or Southwark tube. **Open** 11am-11pm Mon-Sat; noon-10.30pm Sun. **Food served** noon-2.30pm Mon-Fri. **Credit** AmEx, DC, MC, V.

The Paper Moon's rectangular room holds a long, thin bar down one side, leaving plenty of room for its broad choice of draught lagers and ales: Staropramen and Grolsch (both £2.40), Hoegaarden (£1.85 half-pint), London Pride (£2.15) and Caffrey's (£2.35), to name but a few. Along the other wall are some high tables and stools under fringed lamps and old black-and-white prints of London. The raised area at the back, with its green bannister and half-curtain, is a no-smoking spot

at lunchtimes, with cheap and wholesome food served on the marble tables: lamb chops and mash (£3.95), toasties (£1.95) and the like. Welcoming and helpful staff help ensure there's always a warm hubbub here.

Function room. Games (darts, fruit machine). No-smoking area. Quiz (monthly). Satellite TV. Tables outdoors (pavement). Vegetarian dishes.

Studio Six

Gabriel's Wharf, 56 Upper Ground, SE1 (020 7928 6243). Waterloo tube/rail. **Open/food served** noon-11pm Mon-Sat; noon-10.30pm Sun. **Credit** AmEx, DC, MC, V.

Situated at the end of the pedestrianised toy town that is Gabriel's Wharf, this bright blue-and-yellow glass-fronted bar-restaurant is like a glamorous beach hut. Popular with office workers at lunchtimes, Studio Six attracts a mix of theatregoers and good-time drinkers during the evenings, the latter drawn by the glitterball, loudish music and the range of beers and wines (Hoegaarden £4 a pint, Boddingtons £2.50). The menu has a continental flavour, and includes a hearty bouillabaisse with a chunk of slightly tired snapper (£7.95) and tender gigot of lamb with aubergines (£8). Outside, blue benches and tables, surrounded by a matching fence, are popular with riverside revellers in summer.

Babies and children admitted. Tables outdoors (pavement). Vegetarian dishes.

Waterloo Bar & Kitchen

131 Waterloo Road, SE1 (020 7928 5086). Waterloo tube. **Open** 11am-11pm Mon-Sat. **Food served** noon-2.30pm, 5-10.30pm Mon-Sat. **Credit** AmEx, MC, V.

Funky and cheery – colourful flowers decorate every table – the Waterloo is a welcome addition to the Cut. Delicious aromas waft from the wood-fired oven in the café section, from where you can watch your free range chicken (£10) being flame-roasted in the chrome kitchen. Divided by a light pine partition, the bar offers a mix of wines and beers including Staropramen (£2.50), with a stack of newspapers ensuring that lone drinkers can feel relaxed. With its wall ledges and high stools, it's the perfect place to people-watch without being noticed, but if you are caught, you can stare at yourself in one of the googly mirrors on the sunny yellow walls.

Babies and children admitted. Restaurant. Vegetarian dishes.

Also in the area...

All Bar One 1 Chicheley Street, SE1 (020 7921 9471).

Westbourne Grove W2, W11

Babushka

41 Tavistock Crescent, W11 (020 7727 9250). Westbourne Park tube. **Open** 5-11pm Mon-Fri; noon-11pm Sat; noon-10.30pm Sun. **Food served** 5-10.30pm Mon-Fri; noon-10.30pm Sat; noon-10pm Sun. **Credit** AmEx, MC, V.

Devotees of *Withnail and I* will be saddened to hear that the pub used in the 'perfumed ponce' scene is now a completely unrecognisable link in this vodka-bar chain. But the good news is that it's one of the grooviest bars in the area, rocked by DJs nightly (send demo tapes first for Tuesday's trial night). If that all sounds too energetic, earlier in the day deep red walls, soft wood panelling and low-level lighting with

funky music create a coolly intimate vibe. As for the vodka, that all sits in a back-lit line behind the mirrored bar, like a long, spacey hallucination. Different flavours include savoury garlic, chilli and white chocolate, but those who don't need their drink tarted up can stick to lager (Stella £2.50) or wine (£2.50).

Babies and children admitted. Function room. Music (DJs Wed-Sun). Tables outdoors (garden). Vegetarian dishes.

Beach Blanket Babylon
45 Ledbury Road, W11 (020 7229 2907). Notting Hill Gate tube. **Open** 11.30am-11pm Mon-Sat; 10.30am-10.30pm Sun. **Happy hour** 4-7pm Mon-Sat. **Food served** noon-3pm, 6.30-11pm Mon-Thur; noon-3pm, 6.30-11.30pm Fri; 11am-4pm, 6.30-11.30pm Sat; 11am-4pm, 7-10.30pm Sun. **Credit** AmEx, DC, MC, V.
Once upon a time BBB was a cool hangout for Notting Hill's chic set, drawn by the Gaudi-esque interior and pretty garden topiary. Those days seem increasingly remote and, although the interior is as attractive as ever with its mosaic walls and fire in the mouth of a great roaring gargoyle, it is now an (unintentional) singles cocktail bar for 18-30s suits and empty headed Eurocrats. Prices are levied at nightclub rates: £2.95 for fresh orange juice, £4.20 for a vodka and orange, and a minimum £5 for a 50ml shot of whisky. Daytimes still draw a more sophisticated crowd, especially for the brunch or breakfast (£8.50), and it's OK for a quick aperitif if you're booked into the inconsistent Mediterranean restaurant beyond a labial doorway and over a tiny drawbridge.
Babies and children admitted. Function room. Music (DJs nightly). Restaurant. Tables outdoors (garden/pavement). Vegetarian dishes.

Cow
89 Westbourne Park Road, W2 (020 7221 5400). Royal Oak or Westbourne Park tube. **Open** noon-11pm Mon-Sat; noon-10.30pm Sun. **Food served** 12.30-3pm, 6.30-10.30pm Mon-Fri; 12.30-4pm, 6.30-10.30pm Sat; 12.30-4pm, 6.30-10pm Sun. **Credit** AmEx, MC, V.
An Irish bar in theory only, Tom (son of Terence) Conran's HQ features hand-woven Irish lace curtains and is dominated by a huge painting depicting a subterranean scene from Irish folklore. However, it draws its clientele from the arty, public-schooled classes. Even with a 'Cow Special' of half a dozen oysters and a pint of Guinness for £8, you're as likely to find native Irishmen here as you are to find Ian Paisley in the Vatican. Instead, there is a typically Conranesque Parisian feel reflected in high-quality food and very drinkable wine (£2.75 a glass). The changing menu majors on the banks of seafood racked up on ice by the bar, but also features hearty stews or salads. To go with this, surprisingly, there's also London Pride (£2.20), and you'll be hard-pressed to find a better one anywhere in town. The cosy eating area at the back fills up quickly and is too smoky for some, but it's still a great place to pitch up for the night.
Babies and children admitted. Function room. Restaurant. Satellite TV. Vegetarian dishes.

Durham Castle
30 Alexander Street, W2 (020 7229 4043). Westbourne Park tube. **Open** 5-11pm Mon-Fri; noon-11pm Sat; noon-10.30pm Sun. **Food served** 7-10pm Mon-Fri; 12.30-3pm, 7-10pm Sat; 12.30-3pm, 7-9.30pm Sun. **Credit** MC, V.
A new pub-cum-wine-bar of great loveliness, this is the unofficial overspill bar for the **Westbourne** (*see p108*) and the **Cow** (*see above*), and the spiritual home of Notting Hill's shawl-wearing, neo-bohemian media darlings. It's

prettily decorated in pastel shades with sweet rococo trimmings and furniture assembled from upmarket bric-a-brac shops, ameliorated with throws on sofas and rubberised snakeskin on tables. Booze includes Belgian and other bottled beers (Stella £2.70, Beck's £2.50), plus the expected range of wines to go with a limited but unusually good menu – pasta with ragout was homely and authentically Bolognese (£6). Decorations in the gents have been wackily improvised with marker pens along with 'fly-check' mirrors to create a 'fun' vibe. Though it sometimes feels like you're crashing a private party, this is a pleasant alternative off the beaten track.
Babies and children admitted. Vegetarian dishes.

Elbow Room
103 Westbourne Grove, W2 (020 7221 5211/ www.elbow-room.co.uk). Bayswater or Notting Hill Gate tube. **Open/food served** noon-11pm Mon-Sat; noon-10.30pm Sun. **Credit** MC, V.
Age has not withered nor custom staled London's pioneering, unisex pool hall, now in its fifth year. The purple baize has been a triumph, spread over seven full-size American tables in a classy post-industrial design of steel, glass and sand-blasted wood with a Cuban colour scheme. Tables are bookable by the hour, for £6 before 7pm Monday through Friday, or before 5pm Saturday and Sunday; and for £9 after then. Waitress service means you don't have to interrupt your game except to top up on food and drink. Nachos, satays, sandwiches and burgers are all freshly prepared on an open grill, and the well-stocked bar with separate carousing space means you don't have to come just to play pool. Good news for Islingtonians is that a brand-new, bigger, late-licenced, million pound, all singing and dancing Elbow Room is cued up to roll into their back pockets in Chapel Market.
Games (pinball machines, pool tables). Vegetarian dishes

Liquid Lounge
209 Westbourne Park Road, W11 (020 7243 0914). Westbourne Park tube. **Open** 5pm-midnight Mon-Fri; 10am-midnight Sat; 10am-11.30pm Sun. **Food served** 6.30-10.30pm Mon-Fri; 10am-9.30pm Sat, Sun. **Credit** DC, MC, V.
With its distinctive and overwhelmingly blue interior, leatherette banquette seating and garishly co-ordinated pop art work, the Liquid Lounge is well established as one of trendy Notting Hill's flagship destinations. It's especially popular with twentysomething hedonists for its late-ish licence, but to take advantage of this they must order food. However, this is no great hardship with a menu offering French toast, bacon, banana and maple syrup (£4.50) among breakfast options, and super models' salad (£5.50) or fish and chips (£7.50) among other things for dinner. Late evening it's usually rammed and the music becomes deafening, so its suitability for dining is somewhat tenuous. There are, however, decent wines, an adequate line-up of beers (Staropramen £2.50), standard shots and cocktails (£4.50).
Babies and children admitted (eating area only). Satellite TV. Tables outdoors (pavement). Vegetarian dishes.

Prince Bonaparte
80 Chepstow Road, W2 (020 7313 9491). Notting Hill Gate or Royal Oak tube/7, 28, 31, 70 bus. **Open** noon-11pm Mon, Wed-Sat; 5-11pm Tue; noon-10.30pm Sun. **Food served** 12.30-3pm, 6.30-10.30pm Mon, Wed-Sat; 6.30-10.30pm Tue; 12.30-3pm, 6.30-10pm Sun. **Credit** MC, V.
Although this good, ordinary gastropub was chosen for filming the Johnny Vaughan Strongbow ad, there's nothing particularly remarkable about its design. Decor is the usual

Lord Moon of the Mall

stripped floors matched by wooden benches and blackboards displaying wines, beers and dishes of the day. Most nights of the week the bright and basic surroundings are heaving with its younger, studenty clientele, lured by a good beer (London Pride £2.30), lagers (Grolsch £2.55) and global wines served from behind a spacious central bar. These help wash down a strong menu ranging from hearty British grub to more slimline Mediterranean fare (around £8). In the broad, carpeted eating area at the rear you can watch your dishes being prepared in the open kitchen.
Babies and children admitted (until 9pm).
Vegetarian dishes.

Westbourne

101 Westbourne Park Villas, W2 (020 7221 1332).
Royal Oak or Westbourne Park tube. **Open** 5-11pm Mon; noon-11pm Tue-Fri; 11am-11pm Sat; noon-10.30pm Sun.
Food served 7-10pm Mon; 1-3pm, 7-10pm Tue-Fri; 12.30-3.30pm, 7-10pm Sat; 12.30-4pm, 7-10pm Sun.
Credit DC, MC, V.
Few can match the Westbourne for quality of food or drink, but even fewer can match its overcrowding. Things recently got so bad that the young style fascists who flock here began spilling on to the road, making potential traffic sacrifices of themselves. Eventually a cordon was set up around the heated front terrace, patrolled by big blokes with lots of muscles but few GCSEs. One of the best times to come therefore is for lunch or early evening: at these times you can get served more easily at the chrome bar, enjoy the beatnik decor and steal into the sofa-ed snug at the back. Meanwhile, the Anglo-Med menu sustains unusually high and inventive standards. Customised fish soup consorts with polenta dishes and all manner of roasted flesh and veg (mains are around £6-£12). Alongside this

the bar has a couple of real ales (Old Speckled Hen £2.20), Belgian beers (Duvel £3 a bottle), as well as good wines and very fine Bloody Marys.
Babies and children admitted. Tables outdoors (pavement).
Vegetarian dishes.

Also in the area...

All Bar One 74-76 Westbourne Grove, W2 (020 7313 9432).

Westminster, Whitehall, SW1

Adam & Eve

81 Petty France, SW1 (020 7222 4575). St James's Park tube. **Open/food served** 11am-11pm Mon-Sat; noon-3pm Sun. **Credit** AmEx, DC, MC, V.
The main attraction at the Adam & Eve, a roomy pub centred around a main bar studded with cosy little alcoves and a couple of spacey drinking areas around pillars, is the regularly changing selection of guest ales, although the otherwise pleasant and helpful staff had difficulty in pouring to anywhere near the top of the glass when we visited. Eventually, we were lucky enough to get well-kept pints of Gale's HSB and Brakspear's Special, although the price (£2.31) was a little steep, even for the area. Wine is better value, starting at £2.20 a glass or £8.35 a bottle for Chenin Blanc or Merlot. This is a T&J Bernard branch of the Scottish & Newcastle conglomerate, so food is the usual burgers, filled Yorkshire puds and beer-battered cod (£4.75): good value, but nothing special. Only the overly loud music grated.
Games (fruit machines, video games). TV. Vegetarian dishes.

Albert Tavern

52 Victoria Street, SW1 (020 7222 5577).
St James's Park tube/Victoria tube/rail. **Open/food
served** 11am-11pm Mon-Sat; noon-10.30pm Sun.
Credit AmEx, DC, MC, V.
A glorious Victorian pub that attracts a diverse range of
customers, including – the night we last visited – a couple
of Chelsea Pensioners, a pair of vicars, a former cabinet
minister and party, a malevolence of off-duty bouncers
(although they could have been coppers from nearby
Scotland Yard), a gaggle of secretaries and a gang of noisy
office workers. The decor is opulent Victorian inside and
out, highlighted by extravagant engraved windows,
stunning flower displays in summer and, inside, a staircase
rich enough to play a major part in a TV chat show. Indeed
photos of past (and present) Prime Ministers line the
stairway, while poltical cartoons and caricatures can be seen
in both the upstairs in the carvery-type restaurant and in
the downstairs bar area. In the roomy bar, there are hot and
cold food counters and a separate bar menu that includes
such delights as deep-fried scampi, BLT and vegetable
lasagne, all under a fiver. The beer's good, too, and includes
Marston's Pedigree (£2.30) and Theakston Best (£2.16).
*Babies and children admitted (weekends only). Restaurant.
Vegetarian dishes.*

Clarence

*53 Whitehall, SW1 (020 7930 4808). Embankment tube/
Charing Cross tube/rail.* **Open** 11am-11pm Mon-Sat;
noon-10.30pm Sun. **Food served** 11am-10.30pm Mon-Sat;
noon-10pm Sun. **Credit** AmEx, DC, MC, V.
This is a pub you'll either love or hate: tourists go mad for
the ancient wood beams (said to be timber from a
demolished Thames pier), scrubbed wooden tables and

alcoves, the stripped floorboards framed by carpet, not to
mention the Victorian artefacts that litter the walls. Less
endearing points include piped music that can be too loud
at times, and a food menu that offers reasonable food at
pretty high prices (fish and chips, sausage and mash, three
cheese pasta bake and shepherd's pie are all around the
£6.25 mark). The beer is standard mix from Scottish &
Newcastle – guest ales were Theakston Best (£2.10), Old
Peculiar (£2.43) and Greene King's Abbot Ale (£2.28) on
our last visit, while there's Guinness, lagers and a wine list
for the not-too-discerning.
*Function room. Games (billiards, fruit machine). Jukebox.
Satellite TV. Vegetarian dishes.*

Lord Moon of the Mall

*16-18 Whitehall, SW1 (020 7839 7701). Embankment
tube/Charing Cross tube/rail.* **Open** 11am-11pm Mon-Sat;
noon-10.30pm Sun. **Food served** 11am-10pm Mon-Sat;
noon-9.30pm Sun. **Credit** AmEx, DC, MC, V.
Formerly the principal branch of Cock's & Co (Bankers),
then Martins, then Barclays, this gigantic, high-ceilinged
banking hall is now a busy Wetherspoon pub: it's rumoured
the portrait of the gallant Regency gentleman on the wall is
actually none other than Wetherspoon founder Tim Martin.
You get all the usual Wetherspoon perks of a no-smoking
area, reasonably well-cooked food at bargain prices (two
meals for £5.95 when we visited), no music and a wide
selection of keenly priced drinks, including bottled Beck's
(£1.89) and draught Theakston XB (around £1.70), It all
seems pretty popular with the besuited brigade, probably
civil servants from the various departments of state that line
Whitehall, and, of course, tourists.
*Disabled: toilet. Games (fruit machine). No piped music or
jukebox. No-smoking area. Vegetarian dishes.*

Marquis of Granby

41 Romney Street, SW1 (020 7227 0941). Westminster tube. **Open** 11am-11pm Mon-Fri. **Food served** 11.30am-3pm Mon-Fri. **Credit** AmEx, MC, V.

This traditional-style pub is near enough to the seat of government to attract the odd politician, BBC journo and suchlike, without politics becoming the central attraction, such as seems to be the case at the **Red Lion** *below*). The ground floor has an oblong-shaped bar in a room daubed with plenty of dark brown paint, with doors at either end, oak pews, and shelves for resting your glass when the post-work crowds fill the place up. Food is only available at lunchtimes, and is of the pub-grub type, with fish and chips(£5.25) and jacket potatoes (£4.20) typical examples. and plenty of dark brown paint. Upstairs is a smaller room with its own bar. Among the beers are Bass (£2.10), London Pride (£2.20) and Staropramen (£2.65).

Function room. Games (fruit machines). Satellite TV (big screen). Vegetarian dishes.

Old Shades

37 Whitehall, SW1 (020 7321 2801). Embankment tube/ Charing Cross tube/rail. **Open** 11am-11pm Mon-Sat; noon-10.30pm Sun. **Food served** noon-3pm, 5-8.30pm Mon-Fri; 11am-8.30pm Sat, Sun. **Credit** DC, MC, V.

The exterior of this neo-Gothic Victorian pub is well worth a look: you'll have to go a long way to see such a quaintly ornate pile. Inside, it's all wooden floors, prints of a bygone London, an old stone fireplace and well-upholstered chairs, a sweet little cupola above the bar and stained glass windows – you can see why it's such a popular haunt for both office workers and tourists. The pub itself is shaped like a dumbbell, with a long, wooden bar occupying the handle. Beers include draught Bass (£2.20), London Pride (£2.25) and Caffrey's (£2.50); connoisseurs of British-brewed lager will enjoy their Grolsch (£2.55) and Carling Black Label (£2.30). The food aims at the upper end of the pub-grub spectrum, with well-filled doorstep sandwiches (around £3) and Caffrey's and beef pie (£6.95).

Function room. Games (fruit machines). Satellite TV (big screen). Vegetarian dishes.

Page's Bar

75 Page Street, SW1 (020 7834 6791/www.rednet.co.uk). Pimlico or St James's Park tube. **Open** 11am-11pm Mon-Fri; 5-11pm Sat. **Food served** noon-2pm Mon-Fri; 6-10pm Sat. **Credit** AmEx, DC, MC, V.

Any bar that features a massive model of the *Starship Enterprise* zooming over a blue-baize pool table has to be worth a visit. The decor here may be modern and airy, with hidden lighting, comfortable semi-armchairs, a stylishly decorated serving area, and two cabinets of futuristic memorabilia, but the atmosphere seems very pub-like; not that there's anything wrong with that, of course. The welcome at the bar couldn't have been friendlier, and both the Bass (£2.05) and the Grolsch (£2.35) were in fine shape. Customers are the usual office types, although they seemed a more cosmopolitan mix than in other bars in the area. The food is good value, if basic, ranging from cheese, tomato and pickle baguettes (£2.75) to vegetable kiev and chips (£4.25) and 8oz rump steak (£5.25). Sci-fi theme nights are every Saturday night, when episodes of *Dr Who, Blake's Seven* or, of course, *Star Trek* might be shown; it is also the time to be seen with one of the more colourful cocktails (£4.75) – a Romulan (blue) or a Klingon Bloodwine (red), whose ingredients are a closely guarded secret. Vulcans welcome.

Games (fruit machine, pool table). Music (DJs Sat). Satellite TV. Sci-fi night (Sat). Vegetarian dishes.

Paviours Arms

Page Street, SW1 (020 7834 2150). Pimlico or St James's tube. **Open** 11am-11pm Mon-Fri. **Food served** noon-2.30pm, 5.30-9.30pm Mon-Fri. **Credit** AmEx, DC, JCB, MC, V.

A deliciously quirky art deco pub with an ostentatious red neon sign outside and one of London's most pleasing 1930s interiors. The long black bar stretches through three linked rooms, themed in chrome, glass, beige and black (check out the ceiling in the main bar). This is a Fuller's house, so the beers are good and the wines are worth trying: D'istinto Sangiovese is a crisp Italian red (a snip at £2.40 a glass, £9.45 a bottle), and the house white (Gascogne Vin de Pays, £2.30/£8.50) went down all too easily. The food is Thai, and costs from £3-£5.95. The clientele is chiefly office workers, although evening-class students make up the numbers once the suits start going home.

Babies and children admitted (until 7pm). Function room. Games (darts, fruit machine, pool table). Restaurant. Satellite TV. Vegetarian dishes.

Red Lion

48 Parliament Street, SW1 (020 7930 5826). Westminster tube. **Open** 11am-11pm Mon-Sat; noon-7pm Sun. **Food served** 11am-3pm Mon-Sat; noon-2pm Sun. **Credit** MC, V.

Much intrigue has been sniffed out at this politico's den practically in Big Ben's shadow (at least it would be if Big Ben were the clocktower and not the name of the bell) – it was reputedly the setting for an indiscreet phone call that unleashed the press onto a story that brought about a minister's resignation – so if you don't spot a familiar face or two during termtime, you're really not trying. The upstairs restaurant and J-shaped ground-floor bar are dominated by TVs carrying the BBC Parliamentary channel. Don't be alarmed if a bell sounds during the evening: it's not last orders, just a division (vote) being called across the road. The place is much as it was when last rebuilt 100-odd years ago, and the clutter that lines the walls – photos of MPs, the odd historic document – has accumulated since. There's usually a handful of real ales on offer (including Directors, £2.35) and the food is pleasant pub grub. The cellar bar is nicely cosy.

Babies and children admitted (in dining area). Function room. No-smoking area (dining only). TV (parliamentary channels, sport). Restaurant. Tables outdoors (pavement). Vegetarian dishes.

Westminster Arms

9 Storey's Gate, SW1 (020 7222 8520). St James's Park or Westminster tube. **Open** 11am-11pm Mon-Sat; noon-6pm Sun. **Food served** 11am-9pm Mon-Fri; noon-5pm Sat, Sun. **Credit** AmEx, DC, MC, V.

A small but busy Edwardian freehouse serving six or seven real ales (we tried Bass, £2.20), as well as the usual suspects in the lager and bottled beer departments (Beck's £2.50) and 20 wines. The decor on the ground floor is minimal but authentic: bare floorboards, dark wood panelling and plenty of glass. The downstairs wine bar – with a separate entrance – boasts stone flags and wooden benches, and there's an unpretentious restaurant upstairs, serving traditional British delights such as roast beef (£6.95). Being so near to the Palace of Westminster, the presence of two MPs (Labour and Lib-Dem) came as no surprise, but the clientele mostly consists of local office workers and spillage from the Queen Elizabeth Conference Centre across the way.

Babies and children admitted (restaurant only). Function room. Games (fruit machine). No-smoking area (in wine bar). Restaurant. Satellite TV. Tables outdoors (pavement). Vegetarian dishes.

Barbican, Clerkenwell, Farringdon, EC1

19:20

19-20 Great Sutton Street, EC1 (020 7253 1920).
Farringdon tube/rail. **Open** noon-11pm Mon-Fri; 6-11pm
Sat. **Food served** noon-3pm, 6.30-10pm Mon-Fri; 6.30-
10.30pm Sat. **Credit** AmEx, DC, MC, V.

19:20 certainly gives sleepy old Great Sutton Street a kick up
the backside. Busy practically from the day it opened, this is
another of those modern bar-restaurants currently springing
up like mushrooms after a thunderstorm. The restaurant
occupies the ground floor and the basement bar is accessed
down a staircase leading past a water feature in the tall front
window. The walls are red and orange plastic upholstery,
there are low tables and sofas opposite a long curved metal
bar underneath the customary open metal ducting.
Hoegaarden and Leffe Blonde are on draught (£1.80 a half-
pint), and, on our visit, *Withnail and I* was showing silently
on TV screens, which perhaps says something about the
proprietors' aspirations. Customers tend to be local arty types
and besuited advertising and media workers trying to look
creative. The restaurant menu has an oriental feel to it but
could hardly be described as cheap: mains like stuffed
chargrilled squid with clams and sweet chilli and roast fillet
of beef with wasabai pesto stretch from £8-£13.
Babies and children admitted (dining area only). Disabled:
toilet. Function room. No piped music or jukebox (in
restaurant). Restaurant. Satellite TV. Vegetarian dishes.

Abbaye

55 Charterhouse Street, EC1 (020 7253 1612). Chancery
Lane tube/Farringdon tube/rail. **Open/food served**
noon-10.30pm Mon-Fri. **Credit** AmEx, MC, V.

Run by the same company that controls Café Rouge and
Dôme, Abbaye, packed with office workers on the midweek
night we visited, offers the corporate slant on the Belgian bar
theme. You trot up some steps to a wooden-floored bar
scattered with tables and chairs, with a serving area and more
of the same beyond. Most beers are obscure, but those who
prefer can opt for draught Stella (£2.50) and Hoegaarden (£4).
The more adventurous are better off with the proper gubbins:
Chimay, Leffe, Orval, various fruit beers, costing £3-£4 per
small bottle. Beers are served at your table in the appropriate
glass, and we thought the level of friendliness might be linked
to how often you go in. Food is mostly what you'd expect
(think Belgo), but includes moules madras (curried mussels
£4.95/500g,£8.75/1kg) and sausage of the day with stoemp
(Belgian mash) and red wine jus (£7.75).
Babies and children admitted. Disabled: toilet. Function
room. No-smoking area. Restaurant. Vegetarian dishes.

Al's Bar Café

11-13 Exmouth Market, EC1 (020 7837 4821). Angel/
Farringdon tube/rail or King's Cross tube/rail/19, 38 bus.
Open 8am-midnight Mon, Tue; 8am-2am Wed-Fri;
9.30am-2am Sat, Sun. **Food served** 8am-midnight Mon-
Fri; 9.30am-midnight Sat, Sun. **Credit** AmEx, DC, MC, V.
What Exmouth Market has been waiting for. The medium-
sized room is illuminated by big picture windows, with a
sliding door arrangement opening on to a clutch of pavement
tables. Inside the look is minimalist, with small, tightly
packed tables and low-backed chairs. There's a good selection
of European beers, including draught Hoegaarden, Leffe
Blonde/Brune, Gambrinus and Budvar; it's always cheaper
to buy pints (except with Leffe, which only comes in halves),
as the price ratio is usually £1.60/£2.60, with Hoegaarden

£2/£3. Wines cost £2.70 a glass or from £10 a bottle, and
bottled beers are £2.50-£3.50. Food begins with a breakfast
menu that runs from builder's (big, £5.50) to super veggie
(£6.50); carries on with lunch centred around burgers and
fajitas (£6.50-£8.50, although there is a £5 menu, served noon-
3pm); and on to dinner, which is more of the same plus added
starters of the warm breaded brie, char-grilled vegetables type
(£3.50-£4.50). Customers tend to be young and earnest, with
a fondness for black polo necks and thick rimmed glasses.
Babies and children admitted. Function room. Late licence
(Wed-Sun). Music (DJ Fri). Tables outdoors (pavement).
TV. Vegetarian dishes.

Barley Mow

50 Long Lane, EC1 (020 7606 6591). Barbican tube.
Open 11am-11pm Mon-Fri. **Food served** noon-3pm
Mon-Fri. **Credit** MC, V.
With Hendrix coming at you out of the jukebox and a sign
promising that you'll pay nothing if you manage to drink a
yard of ale (record at the time, 22 seconds), you get the idea
that this is no ordinary City boozer. It comes as something of
a surprise to learn that this is part of the Hogshead chain, and,
apart from the decor, which is distressed wood with typically
gaudy signs, you wouldn't know it. The regular cask-
conditioned beers include London Pride (£2.20), Flowers IPA
(£2.40) and Wadworth 6X (£2.30), with at least four guest ales
on tap. Food is the kind of pub fry-up they refer to as a
'sizzler', and includes steaks from £5.45 and hot cajun chicken
sandwiches. Service is friendly and efficient (a pint with an
overly large head was 'topped up' without complaint) and the
customers range from office workers to nurses, postmen, a
smattering of real ale buffs and foreign visitors.
Babies and children admitted (restaurant only, lunchtime).
Function room. Games (fruit machine, quiz machine).
Jukebox. Restaurant. Vegetarian dishes.

Bleeding Heart Bistro

Bleeding Heart Yard, off Greville Street, EC1 (020 7242
2056). Farringdon tube/rail. **Open** noon-11pm Mon-Fri.
Food served noon-3pm, 6-10.30pm Mon-Fri. **Credit**
AmEx, DC, MC, V.
A welcoming brick-lined room with bare wood floor, high
ceiling and a wonderful selection of wines from a cellar of
some 9,000 bottles. In price they range from around £10 a
bottle (or £3.95 a glass) to well over £100; buffs say that the
1982 Noble One Sémillon dessert wine (£125 a bottle) is to die
for – especially when the bill arrives. As reflected in the
framed posters that line the walls, most wines are French, but
producers like New Zealand, Hungary and Italy get a look in.
Food is good here, and reasonably priced, although
vegetarians would be hard-pressed to overeat: starters such
as roasted pepper soup and crab gateaux are £3.50-£5.95, and
main courses (omelette of smoked salmon, confit of rabbit leg,
grilled black pudding) £6.95-£12.50. As an added bonus,
there's no piped music, a perk appreciated by the mixed
office/arty crowd who flock here after work.
Function room (crypt). No piped music or jukebox.
Restaurant. Tables outdoors (terrace). Vegetarian dishes.

Bleeding Heart Tavern

Corner of Bleeding Heart Yard, 19 Greville Street, EC1
(020 7404 0333). Farringdon tube/rail. **Open** 11.30am-
11pm Mon-Fri. **Food served** 11.30am-3pm, 5.30-
10.30pm Mon-Fri. **Credit** AmEx, DC, MC, V.
Recently restored to a contemporary version of its original
1746 glory, with sturdy wooden flooring and furniture, raised
bar and plenty of glass and stone, this is a London flagship
for Southwold's Adnams brewery. The Suffolk ales are well
kept (Broadside is £2.20 a pint), even though many of the

London crawling

A Hoxton hike

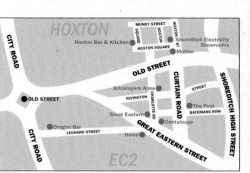

Despite what you might think if you read style magazines, the area around Hoxton Square in Shoreditch is still a dodgy cockney neighbourhood. This was the manor of the Krays during the 1960s, and it's still the archetypal breeding ground of boxers and topless models; there are plenty of strip clubs, pugilist gyms and dodgy boozers in the area. But it's that very unfashionability that has given Shoreditch new life; low property prices have made it the centre of a flourishing arts scene over the last few years. Photographers, artists, fashion stylists, post-production companies and graphic designers have come to Shoreditch to stay the night as well as work; and in the evenings they want to party…

One of the first bars on the scene was **Cantaloupe**, which has decent draught beer, an excellent wine list, great food – usually still the best in the area – and a friendly atmosphere in a bare-boards pub. It's the least posey of the new crop; you even see City suits in here, and on some evenings the number of pinstripes matches the number of trouser side pockets. It's a labyrinthine place with a DJ bar and good restaurant at the back, while out front it's more pubby.

Others have followed, with each new bar hipper than the ones before. Venture into somewhere like the **Shoreditch Electricity Showrooms** and the dress code is the latest trainers, cargo pants, fleecies, pristine workwear (US or Australian – carhartt and Blundstone are a favourite combination). Required reading includes *Wallpaper**, *Dazed and Confused*, the *Guardian*'s Space supplement and just about any photographic or architectural journal. The average age is 20-35, and you're more likely to bump into conceptual artist Tracey Emin than secretary Tracy from Essex.

The music has, of course, got to be right, and ambient music is likely to range from Kruder & Dorfmeister to LTJ Bukem. In the bars where DJs play in the evenings, such as **Dragon**, it's more likely to be big beat, speed garage or anything else that sounds housey. Be warned that although these bars have relaxed door policies when compared to the West End, they can become a crush later in the week; queues are not unknown for places like **Home**. This is a basement bar that has been filled with every kind of knackered sofa retrieved from skips, then had a few breakbeats thrown in. The spirits, draught beers and the cocktails are mediocre, but it's a friendly kind of place that has become deeply groovy, for no particular reason. The food is decent, though – global, Pacific rim stuff – which is why they've recently expanded the dining area to the ground floor.

Home is part of the aesthetic that is uniquely Shoreditch: the semi-derelict basement look, exemplified by places such as **Hoxton Square Bar and Kitchen**. It seems to be a reconstruction of a bunker – a concrete basement with a concrete bar and not much else. There's not even a sign to indicate the toilet door: you're left to seek it out using your on-board homing system.

If you prefer a finer dining environment, stride out for the **Great Eastern Dining Room**. Set up by Australian Will Ricker, this former garment factory has been stunningly modernised in a slick but retro 1950s kind of way. The menu is ostensibly rustic Italian, but owes as much to Melbourne as to Umbria. Food is variable, but it's undeniably slick.

Of course, you might simply want a game of pool, in which case make a beeline for **The Pool**. It's a curious mixture of stark (the plate-glass frontage gives unrelenting exposure to heavy traffic) and elegant design (the basement bar has a striking use of colour and lighting). The food's OK and there are the usual nitrokegs on draught.

If it's just a normal, old-fashioned boozer you want, the finest is the **Bricklayer's Arms**, which the local bohos have adopted as their own but which still retains an ageless charm – and, unusually for the area, serves good cask-conditioned ales (almost everywhere else sells nitrokeg or badly-made cocktails).
Guy Dimond

Bricklayers' Arms (*p134*) 63 Charlotte Road, EC2 (020 7739 5245).
Cantaloupe (*p135*) 33 Charlotte Road, EC2 (020 7613 4411).
Dragon (*p137*) 5 Leonard Street, EC2 (020 7490 7110).
Great Eastern Dining Room (*p137*) 54-56 Great Eastern Street, EC2 (020 7613 4545).
Home (*p137*) 100-106 Leonard Street, EC2 (020 7684 8616).
Hoxton Square Bar and Kitchen (*p138*) 2 Hoxton Square, N1 (020 7613 0709).
The Pool (*p138*) 104-108 Curtain Road, EC2 (020 7739 9608).
Shoreditch Electricity Showrooms (*p138*) 39A Hoxton Square, N1 (020 7739 6934).

office crowd and jewellers who descend on the place, especially in the early evening, seem to prefer swigging bottled lagers. Since Adnams are also noted wine merchants, the wine list is recommended (from £2.50 a glass), even though there's a better choice at its sister bar the **Bleeding Heart Bistro** (*see p112*). The food has a high reputation, and the small menu includes starters like curried parsnip soup for around £4 and meaty mains such as ale-fed pork (from their own farms in Suffolk) and Billingsgate-fresh fish for £6-£12.
Babies and children admitted (restaurant only).
Function room. No piped music or jukebox. Restaurant.
Vegetarian dishes.

Café Kick
43 Exmouth Market, EC1 (020 7837 8077). Angel tube/ Farringdon tube/rail. **Open** noon-11pm Mon-Sat.
Food served noon-10pm Mon-Sat. **Happy hour** 4-7pm Mon-Sat. **No credit cards.**
This rough-edged but classy version of a continental football bar has a charm that washes away bad memories of London's other sport-as-theme drinking dens. The bare wood floor is painted with garish colours – presumably to do with football teams – and the three table football machines by the entrance can get some rough treatment on a Friday night. But the atmosphere is of the Nick Hornby (with an Eric Cantona accent) sort, and the predominantly male clientele suck at their bottled beers (San Miguel, Stella, around £2.50 each) with style. A limited lunchtime menu is supplemented by bar snacks of pistachio nuts and olives for around £1.50.
Games (table football). Tables outdoors (pavement).
Vegetarian dishes.

Cicada
132-136 St John Street, EC1 (020 7608 1550). Farringdon tube/rail. **Open** noon-11pm Mon-Fri; 6-11pm Sat. **Food served** noon-3pm, 6-11pm Mon-Fri; 6-11pm Sat. **Credit** AmEx, DC, MC, V.
A big glass-fronted bar-restaurant with leather sofas, parquet flooring and a horseshoe-shaped bar around which the world seems to revolve. About a third of the tables are set aside for dining, which has seemed an unnecessarily high proportion whenever we've visited. This aims to be a trendy bar, although most customers look to be office workers in suits and short skirts, albeit of the handmade and expensive sort. Drink centres around a pretty standard mix of draught beer (Guinness, Kronenbourg) for slightly above local prices (£2.50), with a fridge-full of the bottled stuff and a fairly typical range of spirits and wines. The pan-Asian food is impressive, with starters like chilli salt squid from £4.50 to £6, and main courses of Thai green curry and Japanese-style ramen for under £10. A cicada, incidentally, is a chirping insect, and there's a depiction of one (silent) outside.
Babies and children admitted (restaurant only; high chairs). Function room. No-smoking area (restaurant). Restaurant. Tables outdoors (piazza). Vegetarian dishes.

Clerkenwell House
23-27 Hatton Wall, EC1 (020 7404 1113). Chancery Lane tube/ Farringdon tube/rail. **Open** noon-11pm Mon-Fri; 5-11pm Sat; 1-10.30pm Sun. **Food served** noon-3pm, 6-10pm Mon-Fri; 6-10pm Sat; 1-9pm Sun. **Credit** MC, V.
You can see the neon glow from this open-plan, glass-fronted bar-restaurant for miles, and it seems to work as a beacon that draws in the trendier end of Hatton Garden and Clerkenwell's arty crowd. Inside, it's a clean white space dotted with sofas and low tables, with a small drinking area devoted to pool-playing in the basement. The open-plan food bar-kitchen can be a hiss and flash of action, although usually it's occupied by a chef wiping down the stainless steel and

tapping along to the prominent club music; this is no reflection on the quality of the food, listed on a huge blackboard above drinkers who seem to resent you for invading their space. Expect the likes of bruschetta of roast oyster mushrooms (£4.95), porcini linguine (£7.95) and char-grilled meat with Mediterranean names and fancy sauces. Drinks are the usual mix of draught keg beer (around £2.50), bottles (£2.50-£3), wine (from £2.50 a glass) and spirits.
Games (pool tables). Music (DJs Fri-Sun). Restaurant.
Vegetarian dishes.

Crown Tavern
43 Clerkenwell Green, EC1 (020 7250 0757). Farringdon tube/rail. **Open** 11am-11pm Mon-Fri; noon-5pm Sat. **Food served** noon-3pm Mon-Sat. **Credit** AmEx, DC, MC, V.
A typically large, two-room corporate-run pub that looks as if it hasn't been made-over since Disraeli was a lad, although the newness of the furnishings dispels that myth. The atmosphere is conducive to a quiet pint (Adnams or Tetley's bitters are a tad over £2), although we've known it get a little brash and exciting when the white-wine-and-lager brigade are in. This is the sort of place where the office manager will come for lunch ('hearty' pub grub like beef stew and chilli, mostly under £5), where groups congregate after work, and where Clerkenwell dwellers come once they've washed off the corporate grime.
Function room. Games (fruit machine). Satellite TV.
Tables outdoors (pavement). Vegetarian dishes.

Dovetail
9 Jerusalem Passage, EC1 (020 7490 7321). Farringdon tube/rail/55 bus. **Open** 11.30am-11pm Mon-Fri; noon-6pm Sun. **Food served** 11.30am-10pm Mon-Fri; noon-6pm Sun. **Credit** MC, V.
The latest hatching from Hackney's **Dove Freehouse** (*see p197*) is another variation on the Belgian-style bar, with bare-brick walls, shiny metal fixtures and plenty of framed Tintin posters to emphasise the theme. The medium-sized space is divided up into several small drinking and eating areas, each crammed with slightly more furniture than is really comfortable. The space in front of the small serving area was heaving with local office folk when we visited, and the combination of gourmet Belgian beers (Chimay, Westmalle, Grimbergen, from £3.20-£3.70 per small, potent bottle) and food seems to go down well. Oddly, a Spanish flavour has

---

Critics' choice
wine bars

Albertine (p152)
A friendly place to refine your knowledge of the wine world.

Bleeding Heart Bistro (p112)
Extensive wine list in welcoming brick-lined room.

Odette's (p213)
Quirky nooks and crannies for tasting romance.

Truckles of Pied Bull Yard (p21)
A courtyard retreat from the Bloomsbury bustle.

Willie Gunn (p190)
Fine food and wine in easygoing Earlsfield bar.

crept in: the usual mussels might be served in a paella-style sauce (£5.95), and as well as various types of sausage and mash (duck with chilli and St Louis Pêche, or wild boar with De Koninck, both £7.50) there are some tapas for £4.95 each. *Disabled: toilet. No-smoking area. Vegetarian dishes.*

Dust

27 Clerkenwell Road, EC1 (020 7490 5120). Farringdon tube/rail. **Open/food served** 11am-11pm Mon-Wed; 11am-midnight Thur; 11am-2am Fri, Sat. **Credit** AmEx, DC, MC, V.

Dust is possibly the typical Clerkenwell bar. With its low, comfortable sofas, original wood floors, silvered walls and basic, square tables, all shrouded in warm, yellowy-gold lighting, it offers a home from home to a young, predominantly trendy crowd. Service varies from keen and knowledgeable to vague and gum-chewing, so pick your bar-person carefully. The music is too loud, and interesting beers from Belgium and elsewhere (mostly £2.50) are served too chilled for our taste. The food is European in style and hardly a bargain: roasted peppers and aubergine, feta cheese and couscous is £7.75, and sausage (Toulouse) and mash is no snip at £8.25. *Disabled: toilet. Function room. Late licence (Fri, Sat). Music (DJs Thur-Sat). Vegetarian dishes.*

Eagle

159 Farringdon Road, EC1 (020 7837 1353). Farringdon tube/rail. **Open** noon-11pm Mon-Sat; noon-5pm Sun. **Food served** noon-2.30pm, 6.30-10.30pm, Mon-Fri; 12.30-3.30pm, 6.30-10.30pm Sat; 12.30-3.30pm Sun. **No credit cards**.

With the current fad for watching cooks at work, it's hardly surprising that this big, square, open-plan green and white-painted pub is busy practically all the time. Its position next to the *Guardian/Observer* offices also helps, as does the good selection of beers (Eagle IPA £2, Bombardier £2.20), but what really makes the difference is that you can stand at the bar and watch chefs toil away in the half of the wall-long servery that's now the kitchen. One of the prime movers behind the gastropub trend, the Eagle has kept ahead as one of the best places for food in the City. Most sauces are kept in large pans at the back of the stove, and main ingredients are heaved out of under-counter fridges and char-grilled or pan-fried in front of your eyes – 'We're such showoffs,' explained one of the chefs as he flambéed a pan of guinea fowl. Specials change daily, but expect the likes of potato and butternut squash soup (£4) and 'Bife Ana' (marinated steak in a bap, £8.50), accompanied by pleasantly discreet latino music. *Babies and children admitted. Tables outdoors (pavement). Vegetarian dishes.*

Fluid

40 Charterhouse Street, EC1 (020 7253 3444/ www.fluidbar.com). Barbican tube or Farringdon tube/rail. **Open** noon-midnight Tue, Wed; noon-2am Thur, Fri; 7pm-2am Sat; all day Sun £3. **Admission** after 11pm Fri, Sat £3; all day Sun £3. **Food served** noon-11pm Tue-Fri. **Credit** AmEx, DC, MC, V.

You'll either feel at home in this cool designer bar, or you won't, and you'll know which way the fluid tumbles the minute you open the door. It's a great concept – trendy sushi and trendy bottled beers (Japanese lagers from £2.40, Leffe £2.80) and cocktails – served by keen if slightly supercilious bartenders in modern surroundings. The buzzing mix of arty locals and smart suits enjoy the low-slung sofas and chic decor, and seem to like taking up as much room as they can. Order your sushi from the sushi bar (where else?) and expect to pay between £6 and £10 for mixed sets, with vegetarian and seafood options available. Individual sushi portions are priced between £2 and £3.

Babies and children admitted (until 9pm). Disabled: toilet. Games (retro video games). Function room. Late licence (Thur-Sat). Music (DJs Thur-Sun). Vegetarian dishes.

Fox & Anchor

115 Charterhouse Street, EC1 (020 7253 4838). Barbican tube/Farringdon tube/rail. **Open** 7am-11pm Mon-Fri. **Food served** 7am-9pm Mon-Fri. **Credit** AmEx, MC, V.

Despite the claims of its rivals, this is regarded as *the* Smithfield pub, and representatives of our stricken meat industry are as loyal to it as they are to rib-eye and bags of fatty mince. The downstairs bar is well-preserved Edwardian, with walls covered with original tiling below the dado rail and fine glass and woodwork. At the rear are some small, wood-panelled rooms, which can be booked. Breakfasts, served from 7am, are legendary and include just about every animal part known to man, plus a few not generally encountered. Drinks are also served from 7am, but apparent sobriety and the right attire will help – not everyone gets served (to avoid disappointment, wear a blood-spattered white coat and attach a rasher of bacon to your lapel). The beers are good, with Pedigree and Adnams bitter on tap (both £2.20), plus a couple of guest ales. Post-breakfast nosh includes home-made beef burgers (£3.50) and cajun chicken (£4.50). Vegetarian dishes are available, but veggies could well be put off by a place so full of meat-market odours. *Babies and children admitted (lunchtime). Function room. Games (fruit machine). Vegetarian dishes.*

Hand & Shears

1 Middle Street, EC1 (020 7600 0257). Barbican tube. **Open/food served** 11am-11pm Mon-Fri. **Credit** AmEx, DC, MC, V.

Although this cosy, wood-panelled pub first saw the light of day in the sixteenth century, it has the look of a recently renovated bar. The two wood-floored rooms at the Hand & Shears are centred around the serving area, where Courage draught bitters (Best £2.05) and Foster's lager are served to the office workers and medical types (from nearby St Bart's) who frequent the place. The walls are scattered with interesting nineteenth-century cartoons and pictures of old Smithfield; the atmosphere is relaxed and pleasant, and the efficient, friendly serving staff hard to fault. Food (described as 'sizzling red hot value') includes a half chicken, chips and gravy for £3.49, vegetarian oriental rice bowl for £2.99 and burgers from £1.99. *Function room. Games (pool table, quiz machine). No piped music or jukebox. Vegetarian dishes.*

Hope

94 Cowcross Street, EC1 (020 7250 1442). Farringdon tube/rail. **Open** 6-10.30am, 11.30am-9pm Mon-Fri. **Food served** noon-2pm Mon-Fri. **Credit** AmEx, DC, MC, V.

Like the **Fox & Anchor** (*see above*) the Hope opens early, and serves up a breakfast that would appeal to anatomists: bacon, sausage, black pudding, lamb's liver and kidney, plus fried bread, beans, tomatoes and mushrooms, all for £7.50, presented in its Sir Loin (or Sir Lion, depending which sign you read) upstairs restaurant. Some meat workers swear by the Hope; others swear inside it. Downstairs there is a well-preserved Edwardian bar painted pale green, with modest crystal chandeliers. Sadly, the original wall tiles are mostly obscured by modern seating. Beers include Webster's Yorkshire bitter (£2) and Young's Special (£2.20). Its early opening time inevitably leads to early closing during the week and throughout the weekend. *Function room. No-smoking area. Restaurant. Tables outdoors (patio). Vegetarian dishes.*

Jacomo's

88 Cowcross Street, EC1 (020 7553 7641). Farringdon tube/rail. **Open** noon-11pm Mon-Fri. **Food served** noon-2.30pm Mon-Fri. **Credit** MC, V.
Decoratively speaking, Jacomo's appears to downplay its status as a mixed gay bar – it's IKEA come to life in icy pastels and pine, delivered in a cool and uncluttered design. Perhaps it's playing to the passing straight trade of Farringdon; it doesn't, after all, have a Soho postcode to buoy its gay appeal. That said, we arrived to a hi-energy version of *Boys of Summer*, so its intentions were quite clear and for an early weekday night it was impressively busy. Food is simple lunchtime fare; baguettes £3.75, jacket potatoes £3.50 and standard beers at £2.80 (Beck's, Grolsch). A sufficiently pleasant place to drink and inoffensive enough to hire out for an office do (with your straight work mates, of course).
Babies and children admitted (until 6pm). No-smoking area. Vegetarian dishes.

Jerusalem Tavern

55 Britton Street, EC1 (020 7490 4281). Farringdon tube/rail. **Open** 9am-11pm Mon-Fri. **Food served** noon-3pm Mon-Fri. **Credit** AmEx, MC, V.
Tucked away with barely a light to guide you in at night (but invariably packed with a mixture of suits and arty types), this is the sole London outpost for Suffolk's rather fine St Peter's Brewery. Inside it's a snug Georgian parlour, with wooden floors, cosy panelled cubicles and sturdy furniture. Not too long ago it was a Turkish-coffee house, and a meeting place for St Peter's executives; the owner was retiring, he'd kept on a full licence and so the Jerusalem was born – or rather reborn, as a pub of the same name stood around these parts up to a century ago. Around 15 beers come in dinky green bottles with five on draught for £2.25 a pint, and they seasonally include Old Style Porter, Wheat Beer, Best Bitter, Lemon and Ginger Spiced Ale and Suffolk Gold. There's a welcome lack of background music. The food, available only for lunch, is top-end Modern European pub fare, with a smattering of pies, sausages, mash and suchlike for around £5.
Babies and children admitted (until 6pm). No piped music or jukebox. Vegetarian dishes.

L.e.d.

171 Farringdon Road, EC1 (020 7278 4400). Farringdon tube/rail. **Open** 10am-midnight Mon-Fri; 6pm-midnight Sat. **Happy hour** all day Mon; 4-8pm Tue-Sat. **Food**

Critics' choice
spirits

291(p197)
Gallery, restaurant and a fine stock of spirits.

Boisdale (p103)
Malts and cigars in a wee back bar.

Brixtonian Havana Club (p168)
Lots of Yo-ho-ho and bottles of rum.

Navajo Joe's (p33)
Tequilas, mescals, whiskies, rums ...

Tsar Bar, Langham Hilton (p68)
Vodka expertise in faux Russian setting.

---

served noon-3pm, 6-10pm Mon-Fri; 6-10pm Sat. **Credit** DC, MC, V.
Captain Scarlet graphics, comfy sofas and low lights in the groovier basement; bare walls, amplified club music (DJs at weekends) in the bright and airy ground floor – L.e.d. provides a contrast that seems to suit most twentysomething moods. An integral part of the buzzy Exmouth Market scene, it now also offers an early (and all day) breakfast and brunch list incorporating organic ingredients, including field mushrooms on toast (£4.50) and eggs Florentine (£5). Emptier bellies may go for the veggie or meat chilli (£5.50) and home-made seasonal soups for £3. There's a whole range of drinks prices, with special low prices at happy hour, but generally speaking the usual 'premium' bottled beers are £2.40-£2.60, and cocktails are priced between £2.50 and £5.
Babies and children admitted (until 6pm). Disabled: toilet. Function room. Games (Sony PlayStation). Music (DJs Fri, Sat). Vegetarian dishes.

Leopard

33 Seward Street, EC1 (020 7253 3587). Barbican tube/Old Street tube/rail. **Open** 11am-11pm Mon-Fri. **Food served** noon-9.30pm Mon-Fri. **Credit** AmEx, MC, V.
The arty depiction of the eponymous beast on the sign outside hints that this is no ordinary pub. It's a modern conversion with a narrow, bare-boarded space in front of the long serving area, leading into a tall-ceilinged conservatory-style room at the back, and with a balcony upstairs reached via a curling, cast-iron staircase. There are usually four real ales on offer (all £2 a pint), and we were impressed by the Nethergate bitter, which was all but perfectly kept. Wines start at £2.45 a glass/£7.25 a bottle, and house champagne is just £3.95/£14.95. The pub was in the process of employing a new chef when we visited, but typically the menu will include pan-fried salmon (£6.95), vegetable lasagne with chunky bread (£4.75) and a pasta dish for around a fiver.
Babies and children admitted (separate area, daytime only). Disabled: toilet. Function room. Tables outdoors (conservatory-patio). Vegetarian dishes.

Match

45-47 Clerkenwell Road, EC1 (020 7250 4002). Farringdon tube/rail. **Open/food served** 11am-midnight Mon-Fri; 6pm-midnight Sat. **Credit** AmEx, MC, V.
A hangout for a smart, arty crowd, who don't seem to mind sharing the place with after-office groups in the early evening. The overriding colour is blue, with Atlantic blue walls and blue velvet seats complementing frosted glass panels, steel pillars and subtle, low lighting. The food menu is based around pan-American favourites (Cuban burger £6.50, quesadilla of the day around £6) as well as more basic dishes like spiced lamb sausages with yam mash (£6.25), steamed mussels (£5.75) and vegetarian pithivier of Jerusalem artichoke, pepper and Monterey jack cheese (£6.50). The drinks list is dominated by cocktails of the order of White Russian, Vodka Espresso and Manhattans (from around £5) and bottled beers at £2.50-£2.70 a go.
Babies and children admitted. Disabled: toilet. Music (DJ Sat). Tables outdoors (pavement). Vegetarian dishes.

Mint

182-186 St John Street, EC1 (020 7253 8368). Farringdon tube/rail. **Open/food served** 11am-midnight Mon-Fri; 1pm-midnight Sat; 1-10.30pm Sun. **Happy hour** 5-7pm Mon-Thur. **Credit** AmEx, MC, V.
The former Bar Rock premises have been taken over by new owners and completely revamped, and now attract a young, upmarket crowd. As you walk in, the long, curving glassy bar – backed by striking blue neon – is to your right, with a

Three Kings of Clerkenwell.
See page 120.

raised seating area opposite; predominant colours are deep pink, green and red, with clever blue lighting imparting a modern but relaxing vibe. Arty-clubby music pumps from high quality speakers at medium volume. The high-tech toilets and another room – available for hire – are in the basement. The staff know what they're about and even manage to smile: Italian house wine is £2.50 a glass (£10 bottle), beers kick off at £2.60 and cocktails are all under £6 – including a wicked Bombay Sapphire Martini at £5.40. Food is good value, too, stretching from bread and olives (£2.40) to wild mushroom and Gorgonzola tartlet (£5.20) and char-grilled rump steak with roasted vegetables and truffle Béarnaise at £8.60.
Disabled: toilet. Function room. Music (DJ Fri). No-smoking area. Restaurant. Tables outdoors (pavement). Vegetarian dishes.

The Peasant

240 St John Street, EC1 (020 7336 7726/ www.thepeasant.co.uk). Angel tube/Farringdon tube/rail.
Open/food served noon-11pm Mon-Fri; 6.30-11pm Sat.
Credit AmEx, DC, MC, V.
Formerly a boozer known as the George and Dragon, this place only retains from those days a magnificent mahogany bar, the mosaic flooring in front of it and a spectacular tiled depiction of George battering the giant reptile. Today the battering is confined to crêpes, and The Peasant has been transformed into a gastropub of some note and style. Sadly the gastro doesn't stretch to the draught beers, and only keg is available, including Boddingtons and Hoegaarden (both £2.20), Murphy's (£2.40), and Stella (£2.50). Bottles offer better options, including La Trappe, Westmalle and a tasty Schneide Weisse at a pricey £3.50 for 50cl. The food's the thing, though, and while the menu is short, it does promise goodies such as lentil, spinach and chilli soup (£3.80), Italian sausages, cavolo nero and borlotti beans (£9) and a white chocolate tiramisù dessert to die for. The customers – mostly middle/upper management and entourage – tend to be territorial (be prepared to ask for a coat or a briefcase to be moved to get a seat) and more snobby than the staff, who offer friendly and efficient service.
Babies and children admitted. Function room. Restaurant. Tables outdoors (conservatory, garden terrace). Vegetarian dishes.

Rising Sun

38 Cloth Fair, EC1 (020 7726 6671). Barbican tube/ Farringdon tube/rail. **Open** 11.30am-11pm Mon-Fri; noon-3pm, 7-11pm Sat; noon-3pm, 7-10.30pm Sun. **Food served** noon-2pm, 5.30-8pm Mon-Fri; noon-2pm Sat, Sun.
Credit AmEx, MC, V.
A pub with a long and chequered past that recently found itself part of the Samuel Smith tied chain, and was given a typically wooden (bare boards, alcoves and chunky furniture) mock-Victorian makeover. The street, Cloth Fair, was the home of London's largest cloth market, Bartholomew Fair, from the twelfth century until 1855. Beers are at the brewery's usual bargain prices (Old Brewery Bitter £1.52 a pint, Ayingerbrau lager £1.78) and the customers – predominantly local office folk, although we found four members of a moderately well-known indie band in there once – seem to appreciate it. Modest pub grub is served at lunchtimes only.
Function room. Games (fruit machine, quiz machine). Quiz (Tue). Restaurant. Vegetarian dishes.

St John

26 St John Street, EC1 (020 7251 0848/ www.stjohnrestaurant.co.uk). Farringdon tube/rail.
Open 11am-11pm Mon-Fri; 6-11pm Sat. **Food served**

noon-3pm, 6-11pm Mon-Thur; 6-11.30pm Fri, Sat.
Credit AmEx, MC, V.
As the racks high above the bar hint, this used to be a meat smokehouse, but its transformation into a comfortable and stylish bar-restaurant has been tastefully done. The walls of the bar are high and white, and the restaurant (on a raised area to the right as you enter) is similarly starkly decorated. The bakery at the rear manages to infuse the air with a comforting whiff of baked bread, no mean feat when 50 sets of lungs are pumping nicotine at each other. The clientele comes predominantly from local offices, although the odd group of journalists or – on our last visit, at least – well-known visual artist and friends, manage to raise the tone. Food and drink are robustly British, with Wadworth 6X (£2.35) and Welsh rarebit on the menu (formidably priced at £4.50). Other delicacies include potted pig's head (£5) and potato soup and foie gras (£6.50).
Babies and children admitted. Function room. No piped music or jukebox. Restaurant. Vegetarian dishes.

Sekforde Arms

34 Sekforde Street, EC1 (020 7253 3251). Farringdon tube/rail. **Open** 11am-11pm Mon-Fri; 11am-6pm Sat; noon-4pm Sun. **Food served** noon-9.30pm Mon-Fri; noon-6pm Sat; noon-2.30pm Sun. **Credit** MC, V.
Named after a lawyer who retired to Clerkenwell in times past, this is a small, wedge-shaped corner local just off the Green. There's a restaurant upstairs where the local Rotary Club meets, but most of the action takes place in the ground-floor bar, which is carpeted and old-pub-style cosy. It helps getting served if the bar staff know you, and they seem to know practically everybody by name anyway, be it postmen, bankers, students or a senior lecturer in law from nearby City University. Being a Young's pub the beer's fine (Special is £2.05, lagers are £2.25-£2.50) and food always seems in demand, even though it's just burgers, sausage, mash and peas (£3.95), whitebait and salad (£4.25) and similar pub favourites. There's no jukebox, but TV football tends to take over if there's a match on.
Babies and children admitted (eating area only). Function room. Games (fruit machine). Quiz (football quiz, during season). Restaurant. Tables outdoors (pavement). Vegetarian dishes.

Sir Christopher Hatton

4 Leather Lane, EC1 (020 7831 3241). Chancery Lane tube. **Open** 11am-11pm Mon-Fri. **Food served** 11am-3pm, 5-9pm Mon-Fri. **Credit** MC, V.
Named after Elizabeth I's chancellor – whose Hatton House stood where Hatton Garden is now – this is a distinctly modern boozer built to appeal to the white-collar crowds who flock here in droves to play pool in the downstairs sports bar, listen to loud pop and drink. London Pride is £2.30 a pint, wine from £3 for a 350ml glass. The floors are flagstone, the furniture wooden and chunky and the lighting brash; food comes in large portions and is based around burgers and such delights as bangers and mash (£5.75), rump steak and chips (£6.50) and tagliatelle carbonara (£5.50).
Function room. Games (pinball machine, pool tables, quiz machine, video games). No-smoking area. Satellite TV. Tables outdoors (patio). Vegetarian dishes.

Sutton Arms

16 Great Sutton Street, EC1 (020 7253 2462). Barbican tube/Farringdon tube/rail. **Open** 11am-11pm Mon-Fri. **Food served** noon-3pm Mon-Fri. **Credit** MC, V.
Two small connecting rooms culminating in a compact bar at the rear of this friendly little pub create an impression of it being one long, thin room. Someone has had fun with

colours here: the carpet's a red pattern, the paintwork's emerald green and upholstery is a mix of Aztec-psychedelic and sea green – but it works. A handful of handpumps offer well-kept cask-conditioned beers such as Everards Tiger or Greene King IPA, all for around £2; bottled Beck's and Stella are £2.20; and house vodka and whiskies are £1.70 a double. Lunchtime bar food is simple and sandwich-based but well received – hot salt beef sandwiches for £2.20 (£3.50 with salad), or gammon on crusty bread for £1.90. The clientele on the Thursday evening we visited were exclusively male, and ranged in age from late teens to middle-age. There's a small restaurant on the first floor, which doubles as a function room. *Disabled: toilet. Function room. Satellite TV. Vegetarian dishes.*

Three Kings of Clerkenwell
7 Clerkenwell Close, EC1 (020 7253 0483). Farringdon tube/rail. **Open** noon-11pm Mon-Fri; 7.30-11pm Sat. **Food served** noon-3pm Mon-Sat. **No credit cards**.
Anyone interested in puppetry or papier-mâché modelling should make a beeline for this small, intimate pub. Its walls are bright red and yellow, and out of them pop three-dimensional creations, framed in heavy wood. Many of the models work with a pull of a cord or a twist of a handle, and some are even for sale, although you're talking pretty big money. A large rhino's head overlooks the bar, where beers on tap include Old Speckled Hen (£2.10) and London Pride (£2.05). Food is of the macaroni cheese and chilli con carne type, and you can feed reasonably well for under £5. The crowd is a mix of arty types and students, with a smattering of suited office soldiers, and on busy balmy evenings they all spill out onto the steps of St James church opposite. *Satellite TV. Vegetarian dishes.*

Vic Naylor
38-40 St John Street, EC1 (020 7608 2181). Barbican tube/Farringdon tube/rail. **Open** noon-midnight Mon-Fri; noon-midnight Sat. **Food served** noon-11pm Mon-Fri; noon-4pm, 7pm-midnight Sat. **Credit** AmEx, MC, V.
A pioneer on St John Street, this is a good place for meeting up or for solo relaxation. The main room has bare boards and clean white tablecloths over wooden tables with matching chairs; lighting comes from well-positioned perforated metal fittings. Wines start at £2.50 a glass for French house red and white (£10 a bottle), rising to £95 for a bottle of Krug grande cuvée brute; bottled beers include Leffe Blonde (£2.75) and Yorkshire's Black Sheep Ale (£3), and there are several interesting ciders, led by Kopparbergs pear cider from Sweden and South Africa's Savuti dry (both £2.50). The food is a cut above much of the competition – reflected in prices – with starters like pasta roulade or wild mushroom soup (both £5) and mains such as roasted pheasant, smoked haddock or char-grilled cured salmon (£9-£14). *Babies and children admitted. Music (DJs Fri). Restaurant. Vegetarian dishes.*

Also in the area...

All Bar One 93A Charterhouse Street, EC1 (020 7553 9391).
Betjeman's (Jamies) 44 Cloth Fair, EC1 (020 7600 7778).
Burgundy Ben's (Davys) 102-108 Clerkenwell Road, EC1 (020 7251 3783).
Café Med 370 St John Street, EC1 (020 7278 1199).
Dôme 57-59 Charterhouse Street, EC1 (020 7336 6484).

City E1

Bolt Hole Bar
8A Artillery Passage, E1 (020 7247 5056). Liverpool Street tube/rail. **Open** 11am-9pm Mon-Fri. **Food served** 11am-5pm Mon-Fri. **Credit** AmEx, DC, MC, V.
Down a Dickensian alley that links the East End to the City, is this cute and modern hideaway. With crimson walls and a small range of seats, it could fit around 25 people at a tight squeeze. Since it is aimed more at sophisticated drinkers, there is only Bitburger on tap; otherwise Peroni, Budvar and Beck's (£2.50) come by the bottle. There are 25 wines from £10 a bottle and a good range of spirits with nine whiskies, cognac, armagnac, calvados, port, sherry and Madeira. The menu is extensive – snacks of panini with fillings such as char-grilled vegetables and chicken, cheese and avocado, home-made pies, curries, pasta and sandwiches – and all from £3.75 to £5.25. *Babies and children admitted. Vegetarian food.*

City Limits
16-18 Brushfield Street, E1 (020 7377 9877). Liverpool Street tube/rail. **Open/food served** 11.30am-3pm, 5-11pm Mon-Fri. **Credit** AmEx, DC, MC, V.
A wine bar of the old school that attracts a loyal following, and is especially popular with middle managers and ageing execs. This crowd creates a relaxed, clubby atmosphere that many of the flashier pubs in the area must envy. The bar is simply bare wood floors and wooden stools, and conspicuously lacks music, fruit machines or gimmicks, although satellite TV does find a home here. Up to 60 wines are served, with a bias towards French and vintage wines; very reasonable house red and white wines are £10 each, while wines by the glass are from £2.95. All the beers are bottled, but there's some breadth to the choice (Beck's, Peroni, John Smith's, Victorian Bitter, all £2.50 to £2.90). Downstairs is a shady restaurant that serves the likes of veal escalope (£15.50) and T-Bone steak (£18.95). *Babies and children admitted (restaurant). Function room. Restaurant. Satellite TV. Vegetarian dishes.*

Dickens Inn
Marble Quay, St Katherine's Way, E1 (020 7488 2208). Tower Hill tube/Tower Gateway DLR. **Open** 11am-11pm Mon-Sat; noon-10.30pm Sun. **Food served** noon-4pm Mon-Fri; noon-6pm Sat, Sun. **Credit** AmEx, DC, MC, V.
A converted warehouse now usually means somewhere slick and minimalist, but this grand old spice warehouse was done up in 1976 when an olde-English pub style was considered the vogue. The bare wooden floors and exposed beams appeal to tourists and traditionalists alike. Its location, among the yachts in St Katherine's Dock with Tower Bridge in the distance, is also one of the most scenic in London. The dining room has window views of the dock and on Sunday serves a tasty-looking Sunday roast with Yorkshire pudding (£5.95). There is an uninspired range of drinks such as John Smith's Extra Smooth (£2.25) and Beck's (£2.65). Upstairs there is a choice of a pizza restaurant and an English restaurant. *Babies and children admitted (high chairs, nappy-changing facilities). Disabled: toilet. Function room. Games (fruit machine). Jukebox. Quiz (Tue). Restaurants. Satellite TV. Tables outdoors (garden). Vegetarian dishes.*

Hogge's Bar & Brasserie
East India House, 109-117 Middlesex Street, E1 (020 7247 5050). Liverpool Street tube/rail. **Open** 10am-10pm Mon-Fri. **Food served** 11am-8pm Mon-Fri. **Credit** AmEx, DC, MC, V.

London crawling

Beer market

The cobweb of pubs and wine bars in the Square Mile comprises the highest concentration of alcohol and money on the planet. A pub crawl here is a deliberate act of madness. It must be treated with genuine reverence. These venues have played unfeeling witness to the making and breaking of men's souls. Have a care when you elbow your way to the bar that you don't spill a doomed man's last drink.

Gather your troops at the **Hoop & Grapes**, across the road from Aldgate tube. Reputedly the City's oldest pub, its foundations date from the thirteenth century. But it's too well scrubbed and touched by theme for much Falstaffian sleaze. Sup deep on the seasonal ales: Wild Thing and Hair of the Dog are dreadful names, but they are yeasty delights.

The first long walk (12 minutes) along Fenchurch Street brings you to the lovely squash of pubs near Leadenhall Market. A minute up Gracechurch Street is the **New Moon**, an airy lozenge in Leadenhall Market. This is wide-boy territory, but the bar is long and well stocked. Four sets of double doors open on to the arcade where braces of grouse hang off ornate metal racks. The beautiful ceiling and happy stretch of beers (IPA, Boddingtons, London Pride) deserve a short visit. Nearby is the **Lamb Tavern**, a grungy mix of suits and barrow boys swilling quarts of Young's in the odd-shaped public bar. A token gesture to fresh air is a roomy no-smoking upstairs bar.

Pushed up a small mews, less than a minute away, is **Simpsons Tavern**, a crusty Swiss cheese of a (Young's) pub. The public bar is a tiny wedge of space. The chop house restaurant is a small room of pews. The 'wine bar' downstairs is tiled and dressed like a public toilet. It's an odd public school venue, with few frills, but a lot of self-righteous middle-aged men and some charming eccentricities.

Three minutes away is a chic ex-bank and a large injection of sophistication, **1 Lombard Street**. Plough through the spread of restaurant tables to the comfortable bar stools, stare at the beautiful people, have a Vodka Martini and marvel at the spread of expense accounts – the schizophrenia of office playgrounds is no better demonstrated than here.

The second hike of the crawl (15 minutes) takes us through Smithfield Market to the **Fox & Anchor**, where geezers, clubbers and girls with scraped-back hair chum it from 7am on weekday mornings. It always feels like 11pm (even if you come in

for one of the legendary breakfasts). There's something Old Testament about the musty atmosphere. Fools and drunks are not suffered lightly. But strange Victorian prints, barmy East End accents and framed war medals are.

A little north lies **Jerusalem Tavern**, a Holy Grail for beer connoisseurs, and one of life's great surprises. Behind a shifty-looking door are block wooden lounges, a tiny balcony and a fabulous list of ales from the St Peter's Brewery in Suffolk. On tap: Wheat Beer, Fruit Beer, and Golden Ale at a reassuringly strong 4.7 per cent proof (all £2.25 a pint). The City formality all but melts away. Back south, past Farringdon station, you can catch the pulse again at the **Bleeding Heart Tavern**. This will always suffer in comparison to the creaky, eponymous wine bar and bistro stuffed in a courtyard around the corner. The pub is a little too varnished, airy and elegant for its own good – but it does pull a perfect pint of Adnams or the ludicrously strong Millennium Ale (7.1 per cent).

Finish in a City pub as God intended, **Ye Old Mitre**. It's within spitting distance of St Ethelreade's church, and as such, is a happy marriage of ancient ecclesiastical trappings and gloomy, self-contained snugs. This is what time warps are made of. Enjoy.
James Christopher

Hoop & Grapes (*p129*) 47 Aldgate High Street, EC3 (020 7265 5171).
New Moon (*no review*) 88 Gracechurch Street, EC3 (020 7626 3625).
Lamb Tavern (*p129*) 10-12 Grand Avenue, Leadenhall Market, EC3 (020 7626 2454).
Simpsons Tavern (*p130*) off Ball Court, 382 Cornhill, EC3 (020 7626 9985).
1 Lombard Street (*p127*)1 Lombard Street, EC3 (020 7929 6611).
Fox & Anchor (*p115*) 115 Charterhouse Street, EC1 (020 7253 4838).
Jerusalem Tavern (*p116*) 55 Britton Street, EC1 (020 7490 4281).
Bleeding Heart Tavern (*p112*) corner of Bleeding Heart Yard, 19 Greville Street, EC1 (020 7404 0333).
Ye Old Mitre (*p123*) 1 Ely Court, off Ely Place, EC1 (020 7405 4751).

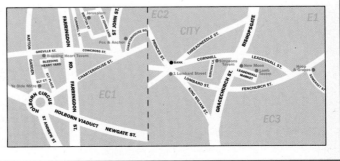

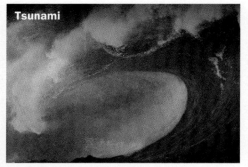
Tsunami

Designed along the lines of a Parisian brasserie, Hogge's offers an atmosphere not to be found anywhere else in the City. Its bright, welcoming, large semi-basement space with lots of formal, comfortable seating creates a warm, friendly atmosphere. Food and wine are the main attractions – particularly popular are the Chilean Chardonnay at £13.50 and the Chilean Merlot at £12.50 a bottle. The restaurant area is kept open all day, while a bar menu also offers popular snacks such as the Hogge's platter of potato wedges, sausages, chicken crostini and goat's cheese to serve several people at £12.50.

Babies and children admitted (until 4pm). Disabled: lift, toilet. Restaurant. Vegetarian dishes.

Old Dispensary
19A Leman Street, E1 (020 7702 1406). Aldgate East tube. **Open** 11am-11pm Mon-Fri. **Food served** noon-3pm daily. **Credit** AmEx, DC, MC, V.

Formerly a Victorian health centre for poor children, this is now a grand, high-ceilinged pub converted two years ago. While lacking the finery of the Victorian bank conversions in the City, its shiny bare wood floors and surfaces and abundant, comfortable seating, nooks and crannies, a galleried floor, a special no-smoking room and a cistern of an old unused loo converted to a fishtank make this the most congenial pub for streets around. A pint of Boddingtons costs £1.95; Hoegaarden £3.40; bottles of wine are from £11.40. The lunchtime menu includes sausage and mash (£5.25) and steak and oyster pie (£5.25).

Babies and children admitted. Function room. No-smoking area. Satellite TV. Vegetarian dishes.

Tsunami
1 St Katherine's Way, E1 (020 7488 4791). Tower Hill tube. **Open** 11am-11pm Mon-Fri; 6-11pm Sat. **Food served** noon-3pm, 6-10pm Mon-Fri; 6-10pm Sat. **Credit** AmEx, MC, V.

St Katherine's Dock has for too long been a pretty little theme park with not too much to do. Tsunami, with its outrageous wave-shaped bar, sea-blue uplighting and surf photos, is a welcome change. Found down the slip road next to Tower Bridge, it offers a range of cocktails created by London's top bar adviser Dick Bradsell and a fun, new Asian menu of brunch-type bites throughout the day. Popular drinks are the Berry Caphrihna (Brazilian rum, crushed limes and berries, £5.95, and

the Mango Margarita (tequila, lime and mango purée, £5.75), although Stella (£1.70 a half-pint) and Hoegaarden (£1.90 a half) are also on tap. A favourite from the menu is the Tsunami platter (for two or three people) of soy and sesame wings, chicken satay, coconut fishcakes and spring rolls (£20).
Disabled: toilet. Function room. Restaurant. Vegetarian dishes.

Water Poet

9 Stoney Lane, E1 (020 7626 4994). Aldgate tube or Liverpool Street tube/rail. **Open** 11am-11pm Mon-Fri. **Food served** 11.30am-8pm Mon-Fri. **Credit** AmEx, MC, V.
This is something of a surprise as a truly stylish, subtle and modern City pub. It boasts a long bar with split-level floors, great acoustics, tables with individual coloured spotlights, two luxury sofas, odd bits of minimalist decor and happy, helpful bar staff with their own black Water Poet branded shirts. That is not to say the place does not attract its fair share of the braying City yobs, some of whom opt for the 'liquid cocaine' cocktail, served in a pint glass and comprising champagne, vodka and Red Bull for £9.75. Others stick with the Foster's (£2.50) or Hoegaarden (£2.60) on tap, or crack open a bottle of Beck's or Budweiser (both £2.60). The pub got its name from a seventeenth-century writer of nonsense verse, who, to amuse his friends, tried to sail down the Thames in a paper boat. Lunchtime meals include steak, Guinness and mushroom pie (£6.50) and coconut and mango chicken with Jamaican rice (£7.25).
Babies and children admitted. Disabled: toilet. Restaurant. Vegetarian dishes.

Also in the area...

Docks & Co (Davys) 66A Royal Mint Street, E1 (020 7488 4144).
Grapeshots (Davys) 2-3 Artillery Passage, E1 (020 7247 8215).
Jamies Aldgate Barrs Shopping Centre, underneath Sedgwick Centre, 10 Whitechapel High Street, E1 (020 7480 7862).
Vineyard (Davys) International House, 1 St Katherine's Way, E1 (020 7480 6680).

City EC1

Ye Old Mitre

1 Ely Court, off Ely Place, EC1 (020 7405 4751). Chancery Lane tube/Farringdon tube/rail. **Open** 11am-11pm Mon-Fri. **Food served** 11am-9.30pm Mon-Fri. **No credit cards.**
London's most ancient pubs have usually survived because of their magnificent locations or grand designs. The Mitre has neither, really, and so is presumably just lucky. A pub was founded here in 1546; the present building is eighteenth-century and is an eccentric warren of little rickety rooms, the best of them the first lounge bar you enter. The pub is a bit tricky to find, located down a narrow alley between Hatton Garden and Ely Place (the crossbar at one end of the alley was put there to stop people riding down it on horseback). There are suitably old-fashioned beers such as Burtons, £2.30 a pint and Friary Meux (£2.20), although you can also get Chilean Merlot from £2.35 a glass. Food consists of basic snacks such as toasted sandwiches. The pub is a favourite of tourists and pub buffs, meaning that a good atmosphere rarely gets going.
Function room. No piped music or jukebox. Vegetarian dishes.

Terry Neill's Sports Bar & Brasserie

Bath House, 53 Holborn Viaduct, EC1 (020 7329 6653). Chancery Lane tube. **Open** 11am-11pm Mon-Fri. **Food served** noon-3pm Mon-Fri. **Credit** AmEx, DC, MC, V.
Sports bars are normally associated with blaring sound, shiny surfaces and fleecing the customers for all they are worth. Terry Neill's is much more sedate, and aimed at 30-50-year-old, unreconstructed males from nearby offices. The style is old-fashioned English pub, with added football memorabilia lining all the walls. There are TV screens at every angle and it's hard to imagine anyone not getting a good view. There's a wide range of beers, including Carling of course (£2.20), and Caffrey's, Bass, Grolsch, Guinness and Staropramen (£2.70); avoid the rather sharp Terry Neill cask ale, at £2.15. Pub grub (sandwiches and salad £2.65-£2.95, pasta dishes £5.95, scampi and chips £6.25) is served in the main bar, while the Boardroom restaurant offers an à la carte selection for lunch. Neill's also opens for major sporting events on Saturdays.
Function room. Games (darts). Restaurant. Satellite TVs. Tables outdoors (patio). Vegetarian dishes.

Viaduct Tavern

126 Newgate Street, EC1 (020 7606 8476). St Paul's tube. **Open** 11am-11pm Mon-Sat; noon-10.30pm Sun. **Food served** 11am-10pm daily. **Credit** AmEx, DC, MC, V.
A grand yet somewhat unappreciated example of a Victorian gin palace. Many of its original features – listed wall paintings, gold and silver inlay mirrors, a carved cone-shaped bar – are well preserved, and there's a debtor's prison dating from 1775 in the basement, which you might be relieved to hear is no longer in use. These kinds of details make the pub well worth a visit, but the atmosphere rarely seems to get swinging. A basically passing clientele is often made up of friends and family of those attending court cases at the Old Bailey opposite. Stella costs £2.55, London Pride £2.20, and Chilean Merlot £2.25 a glass.
Babies and children admitted (weekends only). Games (board games, fruit machine). Vegetarian dishes.

Also in the area...

Bottlescrue (Davys) Bath House, 53-60 Holborn Viaduct, EC1 (020 7248 2157).
City Pipe (Davys) Foster Lane, off Cheapside, EC1 (020 7606 2110).
City Vaults (Davys) 2 St Martin's le Grand, EC1 (020 7606 8721).
Colonel Jaspers (Davys) 190 City Road, EC1 (020 7608 0925).

City EC2

Balls Brothers

6-8 Cheapside, EC2 (020 7248 2708). St Paul's tube. **Open/food served** 11.30am-9.30pm Mon-Fri. **Credit** AmEx, DC, JCB, MC, V.
This Balls Brothers branch is brilliantly located for summer, with a circular outdoor sunken terrace providing views of St Paul's. The Balls Brothers chain, which has been trading in wine for over a century, offers a wise, unflash but not cheap range of wines (prices by the glass start at £3). Try the unique Balls Brothers' Brocard Chablis, at £18.50 a bottle, or manager Nicholas Goldsmith's recommendation, the good-value (and slightly bubbly) Varichon wine from Savoie in France, at £15.90. In line with its traditional formula, it does not bother serving beer. The branches' wooden-floored

interiors may not be fashionable in any contemporary way, but form a reliably popular setting. The food served at lunchtimes is similarly upmarket, with Scotch roast beef sandwiches and mustard (£4.25) and a smoked salmon platter with fresh lemon and black pepper (£5). Staff are enthusiastic and knowledgeable.

Function room. No piped music or jukebox. Tables outdoors (pavement). Vegetarian dishes.

Dirty Dick's

202 Bishopsgate, EC2 (020 7283 5888). Liverpool Street tube/rail. **Open** 11am-10.30pm Mon-Fri; noon-3pm Sun. **Food served** noon-2.30pm Mon-Fri. **Credit** MC, V.

An iron grille drop gate hovers over the entrance to Dirty Dick's, which has not lost its East End edge despite being enveloped by an ever-expanding City. The bar, dating back to 1870, has a curious country-pub look of bare brick walls and bare wood floors, and an even stranger history. The inn was owned by a certain Nathaniel Bentley, whose fiancée died tragically the night before the wedding. He locked up the dining room, wedding breakfast and all, and lived the rest of his life in squalor, gaining the name 'Dirty Dick'. But such maudlin misery has since departed the scene, aided by a good range of excellent Young's beers, such as the seasonal Winter Warmer (£2.20) and Young's Special at £2.10. There's an upstairs lunchtime restaurant offering standards such as fish and chips (£5.95) together with a few more complicated dishes like salmon in ginger and chilli sauce (£7.50).

Function rooms. Games (fruit machine). No-smoking area. Restaurant. Satellite TV. Vegetarian dishes.

First & Last

175 Bishopsgate, EC2 (020 7786 9251). Liverpool Street tube/rail. **Open** 11.30am-10.30pm Mon-Tue; 11.30am-11pm Wed-Fri. **Food served** 11.30am-5pm Mon-Fri. **Credit** AmEx, MC, V.

A classy bar in an unpromising location on the edge of the Broadgate development. Catering for City workers with a bit of extra cash and taste (wines start with Hardy's Chardonnay at £3.70 a glass, beers with Staropramen, £2.70 a pint), it offers a crystal-clear sound system, well-trained staff, lots of space spread over two floors, subtle lighting and table football, appreciated by a mostly twenty- to thirtysomething crowd. An open kitchen serves tempting snacks such as tuna steak melt (£4.50) and chorizo melt sandwich (£4.75), with chips extra for £2.30. There's a restaurant area upstairs, too.

Disabled: toilet. Function room. Games (football games, quiz machine). Restaurant. Vegetarian dishes.

Fleetwood

36 Wilson Street, EC2 (020 7247 2242). Moorgate or Liverpool Street tube/rail. **Open** 11am-10.30pm Mon-Thur; 11am-11pm Fri. **Food served** noon-9.30pm Mon-Fri. **Credit** AmEx, DC, MC, V.

Part of a small parade of shops off Broadgate Circle, Fleetwood looks a bit drab and featureless through its shaded glass, but inside there is much to recommend. Subtle lighting, a clear sound system, good air-conditioning, lots of handy and intimate seating and friendly, helpful bar staff all help to overcome initial impressions. Despite its location in the Broadgate Centre the interior manages a retro-'60s feel, with a sunken bar area, linear spaces and lack of gimmickry. Stella costs £2.60, Fuller's Chiswick Bitter £1.95; the food served ranges from Mexican fajitas for £5.95 to burger and chips at £5.50, with a hot special for lunch.

Function room. Games (fruit machines, video golf). Satellite TV. Tables outdoors (pavement). Vegetarian dishes.

George

Great Eastern Hotel, 40 Liverpool Street, EC2 (020 7618 7400/www.terminus-restaurant.co.uk). Liverpool Street tube/rail. **Open** 6.30am-midnight daily. **Food served** 6.30am-4.30pm, 5pm-midnight daily. **Credit** AmEx, DC, MC, V.

It's taken two and a half years to get the Great Eastern Hotel up and running and the latest of its bars is George, Conran's twist on the English pub. Made up of two rooms, the larger of the two retains the original oak panelling from 1879, including a finely carved high ceiling, and a simple bar lining one wall. The smaller marigold and beige dining room is less imposing, but when it comes to slickness and culinary expertise, George is faultless. The food centres around British classics like roast fillet of cod (£8.50) and a generous Lancashire hotpot, with a fine selection of puddings to follow (around £4). But sadly, beer gets less attention than cooking oil. Although the PR blurb promises 'the country's best beers and ciders' unless you consider John Smith's Extra Smooth and Kronenbourg the pinnacle of the brewer's art, you're out of luck. The wine list is brief, with just four whites and reds available by the glass. But service was impeccable, and if the cellar was reinforced, the George would be brimming with the City folk it inevitably attracts. And should you wish to sample different environments, the oyster bar at Fishmarket across the lobby, or the Terminus Bar & Grill towards the back of the hotel both present drinking opportunities, although it is George that the Great Eastern presents as its flagship pub.

Babies and children admitted (high chairs). Disabled: lift, toilet. Function rooms. Restaurant. Vegetarian dishes.

Green Man

1 Poultry, EC2 (020 7248 3529). Bank tube/DLR. **Open** 11am-11pm Mon-Fri; 11am-7pm Sat; noon-7pm Sun. **Food served** 11am-10pm Mon-Fri; 11am-6pm Sat; noon-6pm Sun. **Credit** AmEx, MC, V.

Another chapter in the corporate book known as Wetherspoon World Domination Enterprises Inc, the Green Man offers everything you'd expect from this now-ubiquitous chain. Those who like their pubs cheap (Boddingtons and Theakston Best are £1.70 a pint, and Carling just £1.89), cheerful and predictable will love it here, and there'll be plenty of room for them, too: the ground-level bar is a decent enough size, and the basement area is positively mammoth. The rest of us, who prefer our pubs with a little charm and character and without no-smoking areas, inconsiderate lighting and airport-pub furnishings, might choose to head elsewhere. That said, the Green Man was proving an extremely popular addition to the area when we visited, and there's no reason why it shouldn't turn itself into a local fixture.

Disabled: toilet. Games (fruit machine). No piped music or jukebox. No-smoking area. Satellite TV. Tables outdoors (pavement). Vegetarian dishes.

Hamilton Hall

Unit 32, Liverpool Street Station, EC2 (020 7247 3579). Liverpool Street tube/rail. **Open** 11am-11pm Mon-Sat; noon-10.30pm Sun. **Food served** 11am-10pm Mon-Sat; noon-9.30pm Sun. **Credit** MC, V.

What was once the ballroom of the Great Eastern Hotel has been turned into the most extravagant station pub in London – although, unlike other parts of the hotel and the **George** next door (*see above*), it is not part of the Conran empire. From a massive ceiling depicting a heavenly scene complete with gilded angels hangs an ornate golden candelabra, an incongruous canopy for the young City types who create an atmosphere closer to that of a football match than a ballroom.

It's part of the Wetherspoon organisation, and so the huge downstairs bar stocks a wide range of beers at low prices, starting at £1.70 for Theakston and £1.99 for Foster's. In the more sedate gallery bar food such as bangers and mash (£4.90) and chicken masala (£5.55) is served. In the right hands this building could make a great bar, but for the moment it remains a soulless beauty.

Disabled: toilet. Games (fruit machine, card games). No piped music or jukebox. No-smoking area. Tables outdoors (pavement). Vegetarian dishes.

Lime

1 Curtain Road, EC2 (020 7247 2225/www.limeuk.com). Liverpool Street tube/rail/Old Street tube. **Open** 8am-midnight Mon-Fri; 6pm-midnight Sat. **Food served** 8am-10.30pm Mon-Fri; 6-10.30pm Sat. **Credit** AmEx, MC, V.

Lime is the brainchild of David Vanderhook of One New Inn Square, the private dining room in Shoreditch, but despite interesting little touches like tiny TV screens looping silently through key selling points, this recently opened two-level bar-restaurant has something of the feel of an All Bar One. The customers when we visited were a very noisy crowd of suits, making it difficult to make out the pounding pop 'background' music. The decor is crisp and modern with strong lines and colours contrasting with the light wood of the floor and furniture. The prominent island bar serves Foster's and Guinness on draught, with plenty of the bottled stuff in tall see-through fridges behind. There's a dining area in front of large picture windows and downstairs is a more relaxing space with comfortable chairs and less noise. The à la carte menu is brief, based around modern bistro style dishes like tomato and cajun risotto (£5.50 starter/£7.95 main) and langoustine with garlic mayo (£11.50/£18.50). The bar menu is even briefer, with the likes of Thai fishcakes, olives with tapas and calmari, mostly around £4.

Babies and children admitted. Disabled: toilet. Function rooms. Music (DJs Thur, Fri). Satellite TV. Vegetarian dishes.

One of 2

45 Old Broad Street, EC2 (020 7588 4845). Liverpool Street tube/rail. **Open** 11am-11pm Mon-Fri. **Food served** noon-10pm Mon-Wed; noon-9pm Thur, Fri. **Credit** AmEx, DC, MC, V.

At the top of a beautifully designed, brand-new four-storey building lies this elegant new spotlit bar with a galleried floor and similarly elegant outside terrace. The atmosphere is like that of a private party (the new Basement Jaxx CD was playing loud when we came), with the spotlights turned low and smoochy corners and a three piece suite – it has a more intimate feel than its sister bar in Farringdon. Behind the bar groovy, sullenly hip staff sporting wacky hairdos look like they're itching to mix cocktails, but most of the punters were drinking wine and beer. Prices are, of course, high: a 250ml bottle of mineral water was £1.50, Hoegaarden is £3.80 a pint, Stella £2.60, and wines start at £2.70 a glass. Meals include a promising Gorgonzola and field mushroom risotto at £8, and an 8oz sirloin steak in garlic butter at £11.50.

Babies and children admitted. Function rooms. Restaurant. Satellite TV. Tables outdoors (pavement). Vegetarian dishes.

Pacific Oriental

1 Bishopsgate, EC2 (020 7621 9988). Bank tube (exit 4)/DLR/Liverpool Street tube/rail. **Open** 11.30am-11pm Mon-Fri. **Food served** 11.30-3pm, 6-9pm Mon-Fri. **Credit** AmEx, DC, MC, V.

The official description covers most eventualities – 'restaurant, brasserie, microbrewery and bar' – and PO follows in the wake of bar-brewers Mash and The Soho/Freedom Brewing Company, adding an eastern twist. The frontage is just another drab Bishopsgate office building but entering the vast bar down a tier of Hollywood-style steps beside the six copper brewing vessels is something like walking into a volcanic crater. When we last called in, it was packed with groups of upmarket twenty- and thirtysomethings, the air buzzing with conversation. The brewing here leans towards the American style and produces four draught brews: Pacific Pils (£2.70 a pint), Bishops (the nearest to a pint, £2.60), Gold (£1.75) and the welcomely light Dragon beer (£2.60). The wine list is made up of largely Aussie, New Zealand and Californian wines, while the bar snacks are oriental, upmarket and priced accordingly: temaki (Japanese rice cones with salmon and mango) is £7.95, sushi comes in at £5.95 (four pieces), and rotelle pasta with ox-tail, peas and tomato is £10.50.

Babies and children admitted. Disabled: toilet. Function rooms. No-smoking area (in restaurant). Restaurant. Satellite TV. Vegetarian dishes.

Pavilion

Finsbury Circus Gardens, EC2 (020 7628 8224). Liverpool Street or Moorgate tube/rail. **Open/food served** 11.30am-10.30pm Mon-Fri. **Credit** AmEx, MC, V.

One of the best-located bars in the City, whose large windows look out on the immaculate bowling lawns of Finsbury Circus. Since the Jamies chain took over in 1999 it has replaced the furniture and there are plans to expand so that its basement French/European restaurant can get a view, too. They only serve bottled beers (Budvar and Michelob both £2.85, Steinlager £2.75), but a visit in summer offers both the scenery and the bar's best chilled wines, the Montagny (£21.50 a bottle) and the Montmain Premier Cru Chablis (£29.50); there is a good selection of champagnes, too. Bar snacks, such as the club sandwich of corn-fed chicken and crispy bacon (£5.50), are brought up from the restaurant below.

No piped music or jukebox. Vegetarian dishes.

Railway Tavern

15 Liverpool Street, EC2 (020 7283 3598). Liverpool Street tube/rail. **Open** 8am-11pm Mon-Fri; noon-3pm Sat. **Food served** 11am-9pm Mon-Fri. **Credit** AmEx, DC, MC, V.

This unpromising-looking railway pub (opposite Liverpool Street Station) is actually a warm, characterful place, with lots of atmosphere, much of it thanks to the fact it doesn't seem to attract the brasher City types. It retains many attractive Victorian features, such as the cut-glass decorated armrests in the middle of the main bar. Upstairs there is a Pizza Hut branch, and if you order at the bar, pizzas (from £3) can be brought down to you. Beers include Heineken Export at £2.50 and Boddingtons at £2.12.

Function rooms. Music (karaoke, Fri evenings). Restaurant. Satellite TV (big screen). Tables outdoors (pavement). Vegetarian dishes.

Twentyfour

Level 24, Tower 42, 25 Old Broad Street, EC2 (020 7877 2424). Bank tube/DLR/Liverpool Street tube/rail. **Open** noon-11pm Mon-Fri. **Food served** noon-2pm, 6-9pm Mon-Fri. **Credit** AmEx, DC, MC, V.

Skyscraper bars are a rarity in London, and for ages the **Windows** bar at the Hilton (*see p75*) was the only place to go. Twentyfour easily tops it with its cinematic view of the city at night (think Chicago or New York) and an interior that's also far more welcoming, with suede-covered pouffes and easy chairs arranged so that no one gets to hog all the views. Behind the bar Marco from Rome (ex of the *QE2*) concocts fine cocktails (from £5), several of his own creation, such as

Twentyfour. *See page 125.*

the non-alcoholic, crushed-ice Fly Away of liquidised banana and strawberry with coconut cream. For big shots or wannabe-big shots there is £195 champagne, and the cheapest wine is a Californian Merlot for £15. Next door there is a similarly swish-looking restaurant that has a three-course set-lunch menu for £26.50.

Disabled: toilet. Dress code. Function rooms. Restaurant. Vegetarian dishes.

Also in the area...

All Bar One 34 Threadneedle Street, EC2 (020 7614 9931); 18-20 Appold Street, EC2 (020 7377 9671); 127 Finsbury Pavement, EC2 (020 7448 9921).
Balls Brothers 158 Bishopsgate, EC2 (020 7426 0567); 11 Blomfield Street, EC2 (020 7588 4643); 3 Kings Arms Yard, EC2 (020 7796 3049); 42 Threadneedle Street, EC2 (020 7628 3850); 5-6 Carey Lane, EC2 (020 7600 2720); Moor House, 119 London Wall, EC2 (020 7628 3944).
Bangers (Davys) 2-12 Wilson Street, EC2 (020 7377 6326).
Bishop of Norwich (Davys) 91-93 Moorgate, EC2 (020 7920 0857).
Bishops Parlour (Davys) 91-93 Moorgate, EC2 (020 7588 2581).
Chez Gérard 64 Bishopsgate, EC2 (020 7588 1200).
City Boot (Davys) 7 Moorfields Highwalk, EC2 (020 7588 4766).
City Tup 66 Gresham Street, EC2 (020 7606 8176).
Corney & Barrow 111 Old Broad Street, EC2 (020 7638 9308); 12-14 Mason's Avenue, EC2 (020 7726 6030); 19 Broadgate Circle, EC2 (020 7628 1251); 5 Exchange Square, Broadgate, EC2 (020 7628 4367).
Davys at Russia Court 1-6 Russia Row, EC2 (020 7606 7252).
Jamies 54 Gresham Street, EC2 (020 606 1755); 155 Bishopsgate, EC2 (020 7256 7279).
Orangery (Jamies) Cutlers Gardens Estate, 10 Devonshire Square, EC2 (020 7623 1377).
Pitcher & Piano 200 Bishopsgate, EC2 (020 7929 5914).
Pulpit (Davys) 63 Worship Street, EC2 (020 7377 1574).

Critics' choice
gastropubs

Duke of Cambridge (p158)
Prettily updated to a brasserie.

Duke of Cambridge (p225)
London's premier organic experience for food or drink.

Fox & Hounds (p24)
Hearty dishes in this tiny Young's outlet.

Lord Palmerston (p237)
Sparse decor, but indulgent cooking.

Salusbury (p231)
New on the scene, but the chefs are past-masters.

City EC3

1 Lombard Street
1 Lombard Street, EC3 (020 7929 6611/ www.1lombardstreet.com). Bank tube/DLR. **Open** 11am-11pm Mon-Fri. **Food served** 11.30am-3pm, 6-10pm Mon-Fri. **Credit** AmEx, DC, MC, V.
Blending innocuously into the surrounding financial institutions, the entrance to 1 Lombard Street is both understated and slightly covert; you feel you might be asked for a membership card or a password. Once inside you are greeted by a plethora of immaculately dressed and extremely attendant staff who take drink and food orders from your table. The tasteful decor in this converted bank perfectly complements the expansive and well-planned bar and dining area, with abundant seating arranged around the impressive circular bar that sits below a simply lit cupola. At £3.25 for a bottle of Rolling Rock and wine at £3.75 a glass, you get the impression that the management has a certain clientele in mind and would rather discourage the impromptu drinker. Tapas (£4.50-£7.95) are served in the bar area and there is also a restaurant.
Babies and children admitted (restaurant only). Disabled: toilet. Function room. Music (live jazz Wed). Restaurant. Vegetarian dishes.

Corney & Barrow
37 Jewry Street, EC3 (020 7680 8550/www.corney-barrow.co.uk). Aldgate tube. **Open** 9am-11pm Mon-Fri. **Food served** 9am-10.30pm Mon-Fri. **Credit** AmEx, DC, MC, V.
The entrance to the Jewry Street branch of this popular City chain is more health club than bar, with a staircase leading down to a foyer furnished with strategically placed plants and unused sofas. The exposed brickwork of the intimate, cavern-like interior makes a pleasant and unexpected contrast. However, the effect is somewhat overpowered by the black and chrome seating and outdated display cabinets that scream "80s wine bar'. The clientele seems to provide a dictionary definition of the word 'yuppie', although the extremely friendly staff and the extensive wine list including Sancerre at £19.95 a bottle make this just about bearable. Bottled beer (Kirin £2.60) and ale (Bishop's Finger £2.35) are also available and a double vodka or gin is £3.85. Mains cost around £8.50, and come from the Modern British with Mediterranean influence school of cooking.
Babies and children admitted (daytime only). Restaurant. Satellite TV. Vegetarian dishes.

Counting House
50 Cornhill, EC3 (020 7283 7123). Bank tube/DLR. **Open** 11am-11pm Mon-Fri. **Food served** noon-8pm Mon-Fri. **Credit** AmEx, DC, MC, V.
The marble walls, gilt-framed paintings and mirrors and large central bar make this Fuller's pub welcoming and atmospheric, as well as being popular with all manner of City workers. It used to be the grand entrance to a NatWest bank, and despite the change of use, the beautiful aquamarine and gold ceiling remains. Unfortunately, the loud and largely tasteless selection of music is somewhat offputting and does nothing to enhance the lavish surroundings, but there is a good selection of draught lager and real ales, including Heineken (£2.25) and London Pride (£2.15), and Hoegaarden by the pint (£4.60). There was nothing particularly enticing on the menu, although Counting House Pie (£6.95) sounded almost interesting enough to try.
Disabled: toilet. Function rooms. Satellite TV. Vegetarian dishes.

Hoop & Grapes

BADGER
I.P.A
3·6% ABV

BRAKSPEAR
SPECIAL
4·3% ABV

HEAD TOO BIG?
NO PROBLEM
WE WILL TOP
IT UP WITH
PLEASURE

RIDLEYS
2K
0% ABV

Crosse Keys

9 Gracechurch Street, EC3 (020 7623 4824). Bank or Monument tube. **Open** 11am-11pm Mon-Sat; noon-10.30pm Sun. **Food served** 11am-10pm Mon-Sat; noon-10.30pm Sun. **Credit** AmEx, MC, V.

Yet another Wetherspoon venture descends on London's already chain-saturated drinking scene. This mammoth pub, which until recently was the Hong Kong Shanghai Bullion bank, features the standard cheap and cheerful value-for-money drinks (Theakston £1.80, Guinness £2.31) that are synonymous with the Wetherspoon logo. Slightly out of its depth in this ornate Grade II-listed building, it is nonetheless an interesting stop-off point, as many original features remain. The menu offers the usual fare, such as rump steak and onion bap (£4.25), but it is one of the few pubs in the area open on a Sunday, when roast dinner is available for £4.95. *Disabled: toilet. Games (fruit machine, quiz machine). No-smoking area. No piped music or jukebox. Vegetarian dishes.*

Hogshead

1 America Square, EC3 (020 7702 2381). Tower Hill tube/Tower Gateway DLR. **Open** 11am-11pm Mon-Fri. **Food served** 11am-8pm Mon-Fri. **Credit** AmEx, DC, MC, V.

This sprawling pub, occupying the arches beneath Fenchurch Street Station, is more drinking abyss than drinking hole: it has huge vaulted ceilings, flagstone floors and copious amounts of tables. The railway memorabilia is tasteful as opposed to tacky and the general impression is that the pub is quite in keeping with the space that it occupies. There are plenty of special offers, such as Boddingtons at £1.60 a pint and wines from £2.40, with a 'try before buy' deal on all guest wines. The guest ale is £2.10 a pint and they also serve food (mushroom, chestnut and stilton bake costs £5.30). *Disabled: toilet. Function room. Games (fruit machine). No-smoking area. Vegetarian dishes.*

Hoop & Grapes

47 Aldgate High Street, EC3 (020 7265 5171). Aldgate tube. **Open** 11am-10pm Mon-Wed; 11am-11pm Thur, Fri. **Food served** noon-3pm Mon-Fri. **Credit** AmEx, DC, MC, V.

Part City pub and part local boozer, the Hoop & Grapes is perched precariously on the boundary that separates the financial centre of London from the East End. Bankers and builders can be seen happily drinking together in this amicable but mediocre drinking hole. The pub itself is deceptively large, with wooden beams, wood and brick floors and a number of different seating areas. Reputedly built in the 1500s, there is an historic element to the pub that adds another dimension, in contrast to many of the newer pubs and bars in the area. Real ales change weekly, with London Pride and Timothy Taylor Landlord (both £2.25) among the more regular draught beers, and a double spirit and mixer is £3. *Games (video games). Satellite TV. Vegetarian dishes.*

Jamaica Wine House

12 St Michael's Alley, EC3 (020 7626 9496). Bank tube/DLR. **Open** 11am-11pm Mon-Fri. **Food served** noon-3pm Mon-Fri. **Credit** AmEx, DC, MC, V.

Originally opened as a coffee house in 1652, destroyed in the Great Fire of London in 1666, then reopened on the same site between 1674 and 1680, this pub is steeped in history and looks as though it has remained much the same throughout its various incarnations. Wood panelling and partitions add to the anachronistic mood and nicotine provides the finishing touches to the interior design. It has a quiet, unpretentious ambience, suiting its modest decor and its small location off the beaten track. Bottled beers start at £2.35 (Beck's, Budvar, Michelob) and bottles of wine from £9.50. Port is £2.25 and sandwiches are £3.75. *Babies and children admitted. Function room. Games (fruit machine). Vegetarian dishes.*

Lamb Tavern

10-12 Grand Avenue, Leadenhall Market, EC3 (020 7626 2454). Bank or Monument tube/DLR. **Open** 11am-9pm Mon-Fri. **Food served** noon-2.30pm Mon-Fri. **Credit** AmEx, DC, MC, V.

This is not the place to go for a quiet drink, yet despite being crowded and extremely noisy, the trained eyes of the bar tenders seem to be able to spot anyone waiting to be served anywhere along the bar. A cast-iron staircase leads to an upstairs level and there is also a downstairs bar that is hired out as a function room. A bottle of Budweiser is £2.50 and a pint of Young's Bitter is £2.04. Food is served and is centred around lunchtime fare, such as beef in French bread (£4.50) and a selection of toasted sandwiches (£1.50-£1.60). *Babies and children admitted. Function room. Games (darts, lunchtime only). No-smoking room.*

Leadenhall Wine Bar

27 Leadenhall Market, EC3 (020 7623 1818). Monument or Bank tube/DLR. **Open** 11.30am-11pm Mon-Fri. **Food served** 11.30am-10pm Mon-Fri. **Credit** AmEx, DC, MC, V.

Tucked away in the centre of Leadenhall market, this small wine and tapas bar provides a welcome retreat from the noisy and often overcrowded pubs that surround it. The stairs are a bit of an endurance test, but if you persevere you'll be glad you made the effort, as the friendly staff and intimate surroundings make this an ideal location for a relaxing drink. There is, as the name would imply, a large selection of wines including a number of champagnes. Try a glass of La Serre (£3.40) and settle by the windows for a great view of the market. The hot and cold tapas range from £1.25 to £5.50 and if you're spending the evening here, then try a litre of Pimms and lemonade (£13.50) to accompany your food. *Babies and children admitted. Function rooms. Restaurant. Vegetarian dishes.*

Market Bar & Restaurant

1-2 Crutched Friars, EC3 (020 7480 7550). Aldgate or Tower Hill tube. **Open** 11am-11pm Mon-Fri. **Food served** 11am-9pm daily. **Credit** AmEx, MC, V.

A spacious, comfortable bar with a separate restaurant behind, the Market Bar is a popular venue for business lunches and after-work drinks. With its luxurious leather sofas and wooden floors, it appeals to the more discerning drinker. However, the numerous TV screens geared up for Sky Sports hint at a slight reluctance to fully commit to just one section of the City's drinking fraternity. Pints of lager start at £2.30 and spirits at £3.20, but each drink's prices decrease as more is drunk. The all day bar menu includes a meze plate for £5. The restaurant menu is Mediterranean and is reasonably priced, including dishes such as wild boar and calvados sausages with mash, gravy and chutney (£7). *Babies and children admitted. Disabled: toilet. Restaurant. Satellite TV. Vegetarian dishes.*

Poet

20 Creechurch Lane, EC3 (020 7623 2020). Aldgate tube/Liverpool Street tube/rail. **Open/food served** 11am-11pm Mon-Fri. **Credit** AmEx, MC, V.

Poet has gone for the modern, natural look, but has ended up as a Slug & Lettuce/All Bar One hybrid, with a sleek, but extremely predictable wood and glass theme running throughout. Obviously aimed at the gap that is not being filled by pubs or wine bars in the City, Poet tries to break the mould created by stereotypes, but seems to endorse them further. In its favour, it is a pleasant environment to drink in and it offers a broad and reasonably priced menu, including six oysters for £7.80 or roast salmon with chive butter sauce for £12.50. There is a good selection of wines starting at £3 a glass, as well as real ales (Adnams Broadside, Directors both £2.30), bottled beers and champagne (Veuve-Cliquot £37.95 a bottle). *Babies and children admitted. Disabled: toilet. Function room. Restaurant. Satellite TV. Vegetarian dishes.*

Prism
147 Leadenhall Street, EC3 (020 7256 3888). Bank or Monument tube/DLR. **Open** noon-11pm Mon-Fri. **Food served** noon-3pm, 6-10pm Mon-Fri. **Credit** AmEx, DC, MC, V.
This new restaurant and bar is a Harvey Nichols venture and it shows. With a 130-seat restaurant and bar on the ground floor, a basement bar and a mezzanine area above, Prism is an immaculately turned-out establishment that is sure to stake a rightful claim to a flawless reputation in the area. The downstairs bar adds a sophisticated, modern twist to a subtle 1920s theme, with abundant seating and subdued lighting running the whole length of the long rectangular bar. The drinks menu is comprehensive, with a particularly impressive selection of cocktails, cognacs and champagnes, including house champagne at £32.50 a bottle. A variety of bottled beers is available (Asahi £3.25), as well as the usual spirits (Tanqueray £5). There is also a bar menu that includes the usual chips and olives, as well as more sophisticated snacks such as duck spring rolls with Hoi-sin sauce (£8). *Babies and children admitted (restaurant only). Disabled: toilet. Function rooms. No piped music or jukebox (in restaurant). Restaurant. Vegetarian dishes.*

Simpsons Tavern
Off Ball Court, 382 Cornhill, EC3 (020 7626 9985). Bank or Monument tube/DLR/Cannon Street tube/rail. **Open/food served** 11.30am-3pm Mon-Fri. **Credit** AmEx, DC, MC, V.
Simpsons is difficult to visit and unless you work right in the centre of the City and take your lunch break at the traditional lunchtime, then you won't be frequenting this tavern. Despite all that, it is popular with the suited and booted City gents, who arrive en masse for a pint of ale (Bass is £2 a pint) or a litre of wine (£10.50) and particularly to tuck into the appetising traditional roast lunch. There are two bars, both of which are extremely small, and a restaurant. Decor is basic, comprising of bare walls and wood panelling, but this is a strictly functional pub with no frills and no fuss. *Babies and children admitted. No piped music or jukebox. Restaurant.*

Swan
Ship Tavern Passage, 77-80 Gracechurch Street, EC3 (020 7283 7712/www.swanec3.co.uk). Monument or Bank tube/DLR. **Open** 11am-11pm Mon-Fri. **Food served** noon-2.30pm Mon-Fri. **Credit** AmEx, DC, MC, V.
This tiny pub, arranged over two floors, is well worth a visit if you are in the vicinity. The ground-floor bar is a miracle of spacial planning, with the bar area taking up most of the room and customers strategically arranged alongside it. Upstairs the mirrors on the far wall give a sense of space, but it is actually no bigger than a small living room, with an unashamed chintz theme to match. The cosy atmosphere reflects the size of the pub, although the geographical limitations mean that it can take a while to get your pint

(Heineken £2.20, London Pride £2.05). Lunchtime snack such as coronation chicken ciabatta (£2.95) are available. *No piped music or jukebox. Satellite TV. Vegetarian dishes.*

Also in the area...

19th Hole (Jamies) 13 Philpot Lane, EC3 (020 7621 9577).
All Bar One 16 Byward Street, EC3 (020 7553 0301).
Balls Brothers 22 Mark Lane, EC3 (020 7623 2923) 52 Lime Street, EC3 (020 7283 0841); 2 St Mary at Hill, EC3 (020 7626 0321).
Bangers Too (Davys) 1 St Mary at Hill, EC3 (020 7283 4443).
City Flogger (Davys) Fenn Court, 120 Fenchurch Street, EC3 (020 7623 3251).
City FOB (Free On Board) (Davys) Lower Thames Street, EC3 (020 7621 0619).
Corney & Barrow 1 Leadenhall Place, EC3 (020 7621 9201); 2B Eastcheap, EC3 (020 7929 3220); 16 Royal Exchange, EC3 (020 7929 3131).
Fine Line 124-127 The Minories, EC3 (020 7481 8195); Equitable House, Monument Street, EC3 (020 7623 5446).
Habit (Davys) 65 Crutched Friars, Friary Court, EC3 (020 7481 1131).
Jamies 107-112 Leadenhall Street, EC3 (020 7626 7226); 119-121 The Minories, EC3 (020 7709 9900).
Number 25 (Jamies) 25 Birchin Lane, EC3 (020 7623 2505).
Pitcher & Piano The Arches, 9 Crutched Friars, EC3 (020 7480 6818); 28-30 Cornhill, EC3 (020 7929 3989).

City EC4

Bar Under The Clock
74 Queen Victoria Street (entrance on Bow Lane), EC4 (020 7489 9895). Mansion House tube. **Open** 11am-11pm Mon-Fri. **Food served** 11am-2.30pm, 5.30-9.30pm Mon-Fri. **Credit** AmEx, DC, MC, V.
The Bar Under The Clock doesn't seem to have picked up many punters since our visit last year, when it was just starting out. This is both a shame, since its modern, funky vibe makes for a welcome change from all the olde-worlde boozers around this area, and a treat: the last thing fans of this bar want is an invasion of the suited rabble. As it is, this is a refreshingly quiet and relaxed place for a drink, with an impressive beer list: aside from Beck's (£2.50), Budvar and Corona (£2.60), there are fine Belgian beers such as Leffe Blonde, Leffe Brune and Duvel, at £3.50 a bottle. The food menu offers 'main meals' and 'light bites', such as spinach and ricotta cannelloni (£5.95) and Thai fishcakes with a sweet chilli sauce (£4.25). Add to this excellent service and the fact that the pumpin' dance music that so blighted our visit last year has gone, and you have a bar definitely worth seeking out if you're nearby. Please, don't anybody ruin it... *Babies and children admitted. Vegetarian dishes.*

Bar Bourse
67 Queen Street, EC4 (020 7248 2200). Mansion House tube/Cannon Street tube/rail. **Open** 11.30am-11pm Mon-Fri. **Food served** 11.30am-3pm Mon-Fri. **Credit** AmEx, MC, V.

The Rolls-Royce of EC4 bars, if only because of its cheekily interlinked 'BB' logo. Bar Bourse exudes class in its decor, too: a stunning mix of red-and-gold banquettes and huge, tilted mirrors that doubtless gives the moneyed punters a buzz as they flash their cash for expensive bottled beers and spirits. On the night we visited, though, it was almost empty despite the fact that it had barely turned 8pm, and it appears that Bar Bourse may suffer from the same problem as its near-neighbour **Bar Under The Clock** (*see above*): it's just too nice for its own good. The TVs in the corner do not show sport but rather financial headlines on Ceefax. Food includes spicy calamari with lemon crema (£5.50).
Disabled: toilet. Restaurant. Vegetarian dishes.

Black Friar
174 Queen Victoria Street, EC4 (020 7236 5650). Blackfriars tube/rail/City Thameslink. **Open** 11.30am-11pm Mon-Fri. **Credit** AmEx, DC, MC, V.
A thoroughly peculiar, entirely charming bar whose name gives its location away, the Black Friar marks itself out as a characterful establishment even before you're through the door: it's in a cheese-wedge-shaped building right at the junction of two main roads, standing out a mile amid the bland architecture that surrounds it. Inside, it's even better: busy, but usually with sedate, middle-aged City folk having a quickie before the train home, as opposed to their younger, more hearty-voiced colleagues. The decor is ace, too: art nouveau monastery isn't too far off the mark, with cosy corners providing a lovely setting for an evening's drinking and chattering, all made easier by the lack of piped music. Wines are £2.35-£2.90 a glass or £9.60-£12 a bottle, while ales include 6X and Marston's Pedigree, both £2.20 a pint.
Games (fruit machine). Satellite TV. Tables outdoors (garden). Vegetarian dishes.

Cartoonist
76 Shoe Lane, EC4 (020 7353 2828). Blackfriars tube/ rail/City Thameslink. **Open/food served** 11am-11pm Mon-Fri. **Credit** AmEx, DC, MC, V.
Providing 'organised' competition to the cartoon-dominated **Punch Tavern** nearby (*see p133*) – the Cartoonist acts as official HQ for the Cartoonists' Club of Great Britain – this modern-looking pub is a bit of a mixed bag. Maybe it's just us, but thanks to the prevalence of All Bar Slug & Pianos we're a little sick of light wood in pubs, even if – as is the case here – the Cartoonist was there before the chains. Perhaps more universally annoying are the extremely bright lights: they help to illuminate the cartoons that line the walls, but they hardly foster an atmosphere of intimacy and cosiness. Still, the punters and staff were all charming, the pub wasn't too busy, and the downstairs room (sometimes closed for functions) has a bar billiards table, for which they deserve a hearty slap on the back. The bitter range is short and sweet: Courage Best is £2.24, Directors £2.38.
Function room. Games (fruit machine, bar billiards). Tables outdoors (terrace). Vegetarian dishes.

Castle
26 Furnival Street, EC4 (020 7404 1310). Chancery Lane tube. **Open** 11am-11pm Mon-Fri. **Food served** 11am-2.30pm Mon-Fri. **Credit** MC, V.
The Castle is one for those City suits for whom the modern pub world is decidedly unimpressive. An old-fashioned local, replete with pally bar staff, dim lighting and decent ales (Adnams Bitter £2.20, Pedigree £2.30, when we visited), this corner pub hums with conversation in the early evenings, a welcome change from the shouty racket found in some of its neighbours. Huge windows provide ample views of an unremarkable stretch of road, but the Castle is not the sort of pub where you gaze out of the window; rather, it's a place to slump over a table, sup on good beers and shoot the shit with a mate or three for a few hours. Two well-kept red pool tables and a dartboard upstairs take care of those punters for whom old-style boozy conversation isn't entertainment enough.
Function room. Games (fruit machine, pool tables, quiz machine). Quiz (music, Thur). Satellite TV. Vegetarian dishes.

Coolín
2-3 Creed Lane, EC4 (020 7248 7799). Blackfriars or St Paul's tube. **Open** noon-11pm Mon-Fri. **Food served** noon-2.30pm, 6-9.30pm Mon-Fri. **Credit** AmEx, DC, MC, V.
The King has gone; long live the Coolin? This Irish bar moved into EC4 after the demise of Bier Rex, previous occupant of this Creed Lane site. And while we were sad to see its predecessor go, Coolin seems to have picked up the slack quite nicely. It's a modish sort of a place, so the furniture is the usual turn-of-the-century light wood tables and chairs, although the black-and-chrome bar and humungous windows appeal slightly more. Punters? Well, this is the City, so don't expect a great social mix. Still, everyone seemed quite amiable, many munching on an intriguing food menu that includes a range of salads (£3.10-£8.25), assorted sandwiches (£2.95-£3.35) and some more substantial fare. The beer selection isn't a patch on Bier Rex, but does include Freedom Lager on tap (£2.60) in among the Foster's (£2.30) and Kronenbourg (£2.50) and a range of bottled options. Guinness is £2.54.
Babies and children admitted (until 6pm). Function room. Vegetarian dishes.

El Vino
47 Fleet Street, EC4 (020 7353 6786/www.elvino.co.uk). Blackfriars, Chancery Lane or Temple tube. **Open/food served** 11.30am-9pm Mon-Fri. **Credit** AmEx, MC, V.
A slice of old-fashioned Blighty in thoroughly modern Laahndaahn, El Vino is stuck in a timewarp and proud of it – it has the feel of a gentleman's club-cum-public school common room. That said, the dress code has been relaxed: women are now allowed to wear trousers, although quite why any woman would want to drink in a place filled with stuffy, besuited (another rule: jacket-and-tie-only for men) Gentlemen Of A Certain Age is entirely beyond us. However, there's something strangely charming about such an ill-mannered, 'politically incorrect' place, not least the predictably excellent range of wines available either on the premises (20 listed by glass, from £2.65, or 180 sold by the bottle, from £10.95) or to take away from its on-site off-licence.
Dress code. Function room. No piped music or jukebox. Vegetarian dishes.

La Grande Marque
47 Ludgate Hill, EC4 (020 7329 6709). Blackfriars tube/rail. **Open** 11.30am-9.30pm Mon-Fri. **Food served** 11.30am-3pm Mon-Fri. **Credit** AmEx, DC, MC, V.
La Grande Marque is a wine bar, sure, but it's an entirely different prospect to its near-neighbour **El Vino** (*see above*). As the name suggests, this Ludgate Hill bar is going for a French wine bar theme (imagine a massively poshed-up version of a Dôme café), and for the most part pulls it off. A well-chosen wine list helps, with wines available by glass (from £2.50) and by bottle (from £11.50). The most pleasing aspect of our visit, though, was that the clientele were no longer the brash lot we remembered, but an altogether more welcoming crowd. Expect minor luxury – and come with the wallet to match – and you won't be disappointed.
Vegetarian dishes.

Mucky Duck

*108 Fetter Lane, EC4 (020 7242 9518). Chancery Lane
tube.* **Open** 11am-11pm Mon-Fri. **Food served** noon-
2.30pm Mon-Fri. **Credit** MC, V.

Nothing more and nothing less than an entirely pleasant local,
in an area profoundly lacking in homely boozers. Don't expect
anything spectacular, mind: just a familiar mix of dark woods,
dim lighting, decent ales (Greene King IPA £2.10, London
Pride £2.20) and lagers (Staropramen £2.50) and the
ubiquitous Sky Sports on the TV (with the sound turned right
up when we went, despite the show having moved on to dull
post-match analysis). The Mucky Duck, though, pulls it all
off with some aplomb, for an appreciative small crowd of
relaxed and seemingly well-lubricated locals. As you're
supping quietly away in the gloom, take some time out to look
at the pictures on the wall: a selection of saucy postcards that
you certainly won't find in the **Slug & Lettuce** (*see p134*).
Function room. Satellite TV. Vegetarian dishes.

Old Bank of England

*194 Fleet Street, EC4 (020 7430 2255). Chancery Lane or
Temple tube.* **Open** 11am-11pm Mon-Fri. **Food served**
noon-8pm Mon-Fri. **Credit** AmEx, MC, V.

A Fuller's ale and pie house has taken over from a bank (doh!)
at the Aldwych end of Fleet Street, and they've certainly made
the most of the space. It's a startling, daunting room: ceilings
that seem to stretch up forever, a balcony ringing the central
bar and massive windows looking out on to the street all help
create a remarkable first impression. It's only after you've
been in there a while that the drawbacks begin to become
apparent: despite the lack of piped music, it's an extremely
noisy pub (perhaps due in part to the size of the room, and
the natural echo that results), and its popularity among the
moneyed moneymen of the area means it can take three
minutes short of forever to get served. However, beardies will
doubtless love the well-kept beers (London Pride £2.15, ESB
£2.25, Chiswick £1.75) and the pub grub menu.
*Babies and children admitted. Function rooms. No-
smoking area. Vegetarian dishes.*

Old Bell Tavern

*95 Fleet Street, EC4 (020 7583 0070). Blackfriars tube/
rail/City Thameslink.* **Open** 11.30am-11pm Mon-Fri; noon-
4pm Sat. **Food served** noon-3pm Mon-Fri; noon-4pm Sat.
Credit AmEx, DC, MC, V.

Although soft souls used to the airy comforts of the modern
chains would doubtless see it as unacceptably cramped, the
Old Bell is still a wonderfully cosy Nicholson's boozer. It's an
old-fashioned, spit-and-sawdust type place, with an excellent
selection of real ales (regularly including Timothy Taylor
Landlord for £2.25, and Brakspear for £2.10), wines by the
bottle (£9.40-£11.80), no piped music, a refreshingly pubbish
smoky fug to the air and, sadly if predictably, Sky Sports on
the TV. The clientele are suits, of course, but entirely civilised
and unfailingly polite. Recommended if you're in the area,
even though it has stiff competition from the similarly lovely
Punch Tavern (*see below*) and **Old Cheshire Cheese** (*see
below*), both less than a stone's throw away.
*Function room. Games (fruit machine). Satellite TV.
Vegetarian dishes.*

Old Cheshire Cheese

*145 Fleet Street, EC4 (020 7353 6170). Blackfriars tube/
rail/City Thameslink.* **Open** 11.30am-11pm Mon-Fri; noon-
9.30pm Sat; noon-4pm Sun. **Food served** noon-9pm Mon-
Sat; noon-4pm Sun. **Credit** AmEx, DC, MC, V.

The Cheese might look closed from Fleet Street, but it
probably isn't: its dark frontage conceals the entrance,

Old Bank of England

located down the alley at the side of the pub. You'll be in good company when you finally walk through the door, however: both Dickens and Dr Johnson boozed here in their time, even if nowadays it's mainly the haunt of the few remaining journalists who work in the area. The renovations and extensions executed on the old pub have been largely sympathetic, so it's probably almost as spartan and under-developed as it was a century or more ago, although it's doubtful Dickens benefited from the pagers given to anyone ordering food such as sandwiches (£2.95-£3.95) or nachos (£4.25). Thrillingly, they light up and vibrate when your food's waiting at the counter. It's a Sam Smith's pub, with Old Brewery Bitter for £1.52, and Ayingerbrau lager at £1.78.
Babies and children admitted (restaurant only). Function rooms. No piped music or jukebox (until 5.30pm). Restaurant. Vegetarian dishes.

Hogshead

12 Ludgate Circus, EC4 (020 7329 8517). Blackfriars tube/rail/City Thameslink. **Open** 11.30am-11pm Mon-Fri. **Food served** noon-9pm Mon-Thur; noon-8pm Fri. **Credit** MC, V.
Slap bang on Ludgate Circus, this used to be called Old King Lud, but it is in fact a Hogshead pub, and, following a refurb last May, is barely distinguishable from other members of the chain in its pine wood furnishings and slightly niffy bar staff. However, it's not as obnoxious as many pubs in the area, even if it is pretty noisy despite a refreshing lack of piped music. The food menu is decent enough (scampi and chips £4.95, Irish stew and dumplings £5.25) and the beer list excellent: the five resident ales, including 6X (£2.30), Pedigree (£2.20) and Old Speckled Hen (£2.39), are usually joined by a guest brew or two, as well as plenty of lagers.
Disabled: toilet. Function room. Games (fruit machine). No-smoking area. Vegetarian dishes.

Ye Olde Watling

29 Watling Street, EC4 (020 7653 9971). Mansion House tube. **Open** 11am-11pm Mon-Fri. **Food served** 11am-10pm Mon-Fri. **Credit** AmEx, DC, MC, V.
While other pubs make fraudulent claims to heritage in their names, Ye Olde Watling is entirely justified in the ancient schtick employed in its moniker: the pub was built in 1666, and has been preserved remarkably sympathetically ever since. This is a lovely old pub: quiet, relaxed and, in an area increasingly dominated by the chain pubs, extremely characterful: dark wooden beams line the ceilings, a yellow haze passes as lighting, and the staff go about their business with quiet efficiency. London Pride and Bass are among the ales (both £2.20), while the food downstairs – there's also a grill restaurant above the main bar – is typical pub nosh (sandwiches £4.25, burgers £5.75).
Function room. Games (darts, fruit machines, pool table). Restaurant. Satellite TV. Tables outdoors (courtyard). Vegetarian dishes.

Punch Tavern

99 Fleet Street, EC4 (020 7353 6658). Blackfriars tube/rail. **Open** 11am-11pm Mon-Fri; noon-5pm Sat, Sun. **Food served** noon-3pm daily. **Credit** AmEx, DC, MC, V.
Thankfully, not a boxing theme pub, but a boozer that takes its name from the satirical magazine that was founded here in 1841, cartoons from which line the walls of the impressive main room. The decor is Victorian extravagant, although not overly so: the Punch manages to be both welcoming and comfortable, due no doubt in good part to the friendliness of the staff and the sedateness of the requisitely besuited punters. The decent beer selection includes Staropramen

(£2.50), London Pride (£2.20) and Greene King IPA (£2.10). Two main changes from last year: all-pervading piped music (bad), and the introduction of fridge-frosted glasses for the lagers (very, very, very good indeed).
Babies and children admitted (restaurant area; weekends only). Function room. Vegetarian dishes.

Samuel's

80 Farringdon Street, EC4 (020 7353 8808). Blackfriars or Farringdon tube/City Thameslink. **Open** 8am-10.30pm Mon-Fri; noon-10pm Sat. **Food served** 8am-10pm Mon-Fri; noon-10pm Sat. **Credit** AmEx, DC, MC, V.
The Samuel in question is the eminent Dr Johnson, whose ghost still haunts the character of many taverns in these parts, and a quote from whom – about how nothing in life is quite as terrific as a great boozer, or something like that – graces the menu of this dimly lit imbiberie near Ludgate Circus. Nicely decorated in dark greens and with countless rooms over its several floors (some of which can be hired out), it would ordinarily be a very nice place for a pint. The problem, as so often around here, is the clientele, rowdier than usual City slickers who, despite the preponderance of good beers (Hoegaarden for £3.50 a pint and Leffe Blonde for £2.20 a half-pint are the draught highlights) were predictably all drinking bottled Beck's (£2.40) when we visited. The upstairs Hoop & Grapes eaterie offers the likes of burgers (£6.50-£6.95), pizzas (£5.75) and steaks (£11.95-£13.95).
Babies and children admitted. Function room. Tables outdoors (terraces, two floors). Restaurant. Satellite TV. Vegetarian dishes.

Shaw's Booksellers

31-34 St Andrews Hill, EC4 (020 7489 7999). Blackfriars tube/rail/St Paul's tube. **Open** noon-11pm Mon-Fri. **Food served** noon-3pm, 6-9pm Mon-Fri. **Credit** AmEx, DC, MC, V.
What's in a name? Well, Shaw's Booksellers takes its current handle from its role as a bookshop in the 1997 movie of Henry James' *Wings of a Dove*, for which it was made over into something like its current, nicely modern-rustic style. You're unlikely to see Helena Bonham Carter in there these days, but you will find a thoroughly pleasant bar offering some nicely chosen pints on tap (Organic Honeydew – only in the summer – and London Pride both £2.20, Hoegaarden £3.55), a range of shots, shooters and cocktails (£2, £3.50 and £4.50-£5 respectively) and an inventive food menu (cajun spiced chicken with braised basmati rice £7.50, toasted steak sandwich with chips £7). We went in mid-December and found a heaving, noisy and not especially welcoming bar; another visit a month later yielded the complete opposite, and something closer, we suspect, to its true character.
Babies and children admitted. Disabled: toilet. Vegetarian dishes.

Silks & Spice

Temple Court, 11 Queen Victoria Street, EC4 (020 7248 7878). Cannon Street or Mansion House tube. **Open/food served** 11.30am-10.30pm Mon-Fri. **Happy hour** 6-9.30pm Mon-Wed. **Credit** AmEx, DC, MC, V.
Everyone's favourite Thai restaurant is now resident in the City – evidently, even the Square Mile's financial types have discovered the joys of its modish cuisine. Aside from the restaurant, though, there's also a fairly expansive bar out front. It's as modern as you'd expect: large and open-plan, the room is dominated by fishtanks, although you're not likely to be able to order the contents should you choose to eat in the restaurant at the back. Draught beers include Hoegaarden (£3.40), Stella Artois ((£2.40) and Boddingtons (£2), but the

place was full – and we mean full – of loud City types swigging arrogantly from bottles of Beck's (£2.40). Suits and Thai, if you will.
Function room. Restaurant. Vegetarian dishes.

Slug & Lettuce
25 Bucklersbury, EC4 (020 7329 6222). Bank tube/DLR/ Cannon Street tube/rail. **Open** 11.30am-11pm Mon-Fri. **Food served** 11.30am-9pm Mon-Thur; 11.30am-4pm Fri. **Credit** AmEx, MC, V.
We're not ashamed to admit that we didn't last long in here. It's a real shame, too, for the venue is an excellent one. Modern, sure, but the two-level open-plan split works well: the upstairs bit would be a particularly pleasant place for a pint of Marston's Pedigree, London Pride or Boddingtons (all £2.45) and a plate of pub grub (the usual burgers and the like, £5.50-£6.95). 'Would be' rather than 'is' because of the intolerably lairy and adolescent behaviour of the besuited brigade that led us to down our pints and leave in a hurry. Still, if you do as we didn't and go early in the week, the atmosphere might be a little better, allowing you to savour the better aspects of this particular member of the chain gang.
Disabled: toilet. Vegetarian dishes.

Tooks
17-18 Tooks Court, Cursitor Street, EC4 (020 7404 1818). Chancery Lane tube. **Open** 11.30am-11pm Mon-Fri. **Food served** noon-8.30pm Mon-Fri. **Credit** AmEx, MC, V.
For location, Tooks couldn't have it much worse: tucked away in a tiny side street, which is itself off another tiny side street, around the back of Chancery Lane tube. Not much of a position to pick up passing trade. However, maybe that's the point: judging by the thoroughly entertaining conversations we overheard on our visit, its clientele is exclusively made up of legal eagles, who perhaps value their own turf. It's quite a modern place: light woods dominate, as they seem to everywhere these days, and the atmosphere is relaxed enough. Deferential staff serve draught Bitburger (£2.80) and bottled Adnams Broadside, and a bar menu mostly made up of sandwiches (£3.95-£5.25), although there is a separate, pricier restaurant menu for those after a little more formality.
Babies and children admitted. Disabled: toilet. No-smoking area. Restaurant. Vegetarian dishes.

Also in the area...
All Bar One 103 Cannon Street, EC4 (020 7220 9031); 44-46 Ludgate Hill, EC4 (020 7653 9901).
Balls Brothers 3-6 Budge Row, Cannon Street, EC4 (020 7248 7557).
Café Flo 38-40 Ludgate Hill, EC4 (020 7329 3900).
Café Rouge Hillgate House, 2-3 Limeburner Lane, EC4 (020 7329 1234); 140 Fetter Lane, EC4 (020 7242 3469).
Corney & Barrow 44 Cannon Street, EC4 (020 7248 1700); 3 Fleet Place, EC4 (020 7329 3141).
Davys 10 Creed Lane, EC4 (020 7236 5317).
Dôme 4 St Paul's Churchyard, EC4 (020 7489 0767).
Fine Line 1 Bow Churchyard, EC4 (020 7248 3262).
Forster & Firkin 2-3 New Bridge Street, EC4 (020 7353 8852).
Heeltap & Bumper (Davys) 2-6 Cannon Street, EC4 (020 7248 3371).
Jamies 5 Groveland Court, EC4 (020 7248 5551).
Pitcher & Piano 2 Old Charing Court, EC4 (020 7248 2720).
Shotberries (Davys) 167 Queen Victoria Street, EC4 (020 7329 4759).

Old Street EC1/Shoreditch N1, EC2

Artillery Arms
102 Bunhill Row, EC1 (020 7253 4683/ www.theartilleryarms.com). Old Street tube/rail. **Open** 11am-11pm Mon-Sat; noon-10.30pm Sun. **Food served** noon-2.30pm Mon-Fri. **Happy hour** 5-6pm daily. **Credit** AmEx, DC, MC, V.
The location of the Artillery Arms, facing a grim-looking army barracks and burial ground, doesn't bode well. Once you're inside, however, it's a pretty little place that's rich in history, with green-painted walls, bare brickwork and dozens of period photographs making up the Victorian decor. Weekend nights at this Fuller's pub are somewhat cramped, but fortunately the patrons are an amiable crowd, made up mainly of locals (young and old). Perkily purple-clad bar staff serve up several ales (London Pride £2, Chiswick Bitter £1.59, ESB £2.20), as well as Grolsch (£2.35) and Stella (£2.45).
Function room. Games (darts, fruit machine). Satellite TV. Tables outdoors (pavement). Vegetarian dishes.

Barong
Units 1 & 2, 104-122 City Road, EC1 (020 7253 7356). Old Street tube/rail. **Open** 11am-11pm Mon-Fri; 11am-midnight Sat. **Admission** after 10pm, some Sats, price varies. **Food served** noon-3pm, 6-10pm Mon-Sat. **Credit** AmEx, DC, MC, V.
In retrospect, the designers of the Barong (a Malaysian name) might regret allowing an unrestricted view through a huge, arched glass frontage. Rather than transporting punters to the exotic East, it serves as a reminder of the grim reality that is the Old Street roundabout. Still, full marks for trying, and the shades of burnt ochre and sea blue do make a change from the usual minimalist decor. An upbeat crowd occupies the upstairs area, while the downstairs bar serves as a chill-out space. Both decks are spattered with Eastern artefacts and art, a theme partly echoed in the menu, a fusion of Indonesian, Malaysian and Japanese cooking. On our visit a crew of businessmen were enjoying the offer of six shots of saké for £6; Grolsch is on tap, and bottled beers include Asahi (£2.60) and Staropramen (£2.50). On Saturday nights, the venue is sometimes hired out for club events, so ring in advance.
Babies and children admitted. Disabled: toilet. Function room. Late licence (Sat). Music (DJs 6-11pm Thur, after 10pm some Sats). Restaurant. Satellite TV (big screen). Vegetarian dishes.

Bricklayer's Arms
63 Charlotte Road, EC2 (020 7739 5245). Old Street tube/ rail/26, 48, 55, 242 bus. **Open** 11am-11pm Mon-Sat; noon-10.30pm Sun. **Food served** noon-4pm, 6-11.30pm Mon-Fri; noon-11.30pm Sat; noon-9pm Sun. **Credit** MC, V.
The Bricklayer's has recently surrendered to market pressure and opened a trendy eating area in its upstairs room, serving fancified English grub. Purists believe that it's thereby lost some of its endearing eccentricity, but the fashionably shabby and unpretentious downstairs bar still attracts a very Hoxton mix of hip newcomers, art students and locals, and the dress code remains strictly stylish street gear. It's also invariably packed, and tables are few and much sought-after; ethnic lanterns and modern lighting contrast with the traditional decor, and a blackboard expounds the pub's code of behaviour. DJs playing music that ranges from nostalgic punk to soothing drum 'n' bass can be found jammed between the pool table and pinball machine. Drinks are surprisingly

Charlie Wright's International Bar

inexpensive, with a pint of Kronenbourg at £2.20, Foster's and various good draught ales all around £2.
Games (pinball machine, table football). Jukebox. Music (DJs Thur-Sun). Restaurant. Vegetarian dishes.

Cantaloupe

35-42 Charlotte Road, EC2 (020 7613 4411/ www.cantaloupe.co.uk). Old Street tube. **Open/food served** 11am-midnight Mon-Fri; 2pm-midnight Sat; noon-11.30pm Sun. **Credit** MC, V.
The first bar-restaurant to inject life into Shoreditch over three years ago, Cantaloupe now looks a little jaded next to the ultra-hip upstarts it spawned, but this cavernous place of three parts is still worth a visit. The scene that greets you on entering is one of organised chaos, with all seating taken by 7.30pm at weekends; the front bar is rowdy with large bier-keller-type communal tables, while the deep-red middle room has a cosier, more laid-back feel. Big spenders can select from a new fine wine list (bottles range from £40-£120), but settling for the house (£3 a glass) is no hardship. Stella and Budvar both £2.50) are on draught, and there's a good selection of bottled beers on offer. In the rear bar punters feed on a selection of meze/tapas-size dishes (£1.75-£3.75) while perched on tall 1950s-diner-style chairs. And, this being Shoreditch, art is for sale.
Disabled: toilet. Music (DJs Wed-Sun). Restaurant. Tables outdoors (pavement). Vegetarian dishes.

Central Bar

58 Old Street, EC1 (020 7490 0080). Old Street tube. **Open** 11am-1am Mon-Thur; 11am-2am Fri; noon-2am Sat; noon-10.30pm Sun. **Food served** noon-3pm, 5.30-10pm Mon-Fri. **Credit** DC, MC, V.
The names on the shooters drinks menu (all around £3) give an indication of what kind of pub this is – how about a Brain Haemorrhage, or maybe a Tosser is more your thing? Catering in the main for students and after-work

drinkers, this roomy horseshoe-shaped bar is a veritable hive of activity. Live jazz, theme and quiz nights, and DJs playing loud cheesy music, are among the attractions; the decor is pretty naff, with the wooden tables and bare floorboards combined, curiously, with pictures of a dairy-produce theme. Frighteningly fresh-faced bar staff serve up Absolut vodka in numerous flavours, and Stella (£2.35 a pint), Heineken (£2.15 a pint), Guinness (£2.35) and Murphy's are on tap.
Function room. Games (fruit machine, table football). Late licence. Music (DJs Tue-Sat). Satellite TV. Vegetarian dishes.

Charlie Wright's International Bar

45 Pitfield Street, N1 (020 7490 8345). Old Street tube/ rail/26, 48, 55, 242 bus. **Open** noon-1am Mon-Wed; noon-2am Thur-Sun. **Admission** after 10pm Fri, Sat, Sun £3. **Food served** noon-3pm, 6.30pm-midnight daily. **Credit** DC, MC, V.
Of all the bars in this domain, Charlie Wright's is unique in that it pulls in a genuine mix of punters. East End hardnuts, locals, wary students and foreigners get messy together, and the result is strangely compelling. Presided over by the larger-than-life Charlie Wright, a Nigerian power-lifter who's the stuff of many legends, the bar boasts a wide variety of world beers (Leffe Blonde, Hoegaarden both £3.50 a pint; Rolling Rock, Bankok Beer both £2.50 a bottle) and a Thai-inspired menu (£4.50-£6 for mains). The decor is forgettable, but this is an unpretentious establishment, and if big-screen sports, loud, late parties and alcoholically-challenged conversationalists are your thing, then Charlie Wright's won't disappoint. Ladies, watch your manners in the toilet – you have been warned.
Babies and children admitted (until 7pm). Games (fruit machine, pinball machine, pool table). Jukebox. Late licence. Music (DJs Thur-Sun). Restaurant. Satellite TV (big screen). Vegetarian dishes.

TimeOut

'THE GREATEST LONDON AUTHORITY'

Dragon

Games (fruit machine, quiz machine, pool table). Tables outdoors (garden, pavement). Satellite TV. Vegetarian dishes.

Great Eastern Dining Room

54-56 Great Eastern Street, EC2 (020 7613 4545). Old Street tube/rail. **Open/food served** noon-midnight Mon-Fri; 6.30pm-midnight Sat. **Credit** AmEx, DC, MC, V.

This warehouse turned modish bar-restaurant is proving to be a dynamic force in Shoreditch. Although the title suggests the emphasis is on eating, it's equally (or more) popular as a pre-club hangout, especially now it can brag of the addition of 'Below 54', a laid-back basement bar complete with dim lights and visuals to match. The upstairs bar, with dark wood panels, high bar stools and stainless steel tables, looks routinely minimalist by comparison. As an eating experience, the Great Eastern leans towards harsh and loud instead of intimate and quiet, but the Italian-oriented full menu is impressive, as is the shorter all day affair (seafood fritto misto or spaghetti vongole, both £5). On weekdays the place attracts a blander crowd of suits and after-work drinkers; at weekends they give way to a hipper, younger lot. There's a well-chosen wine list, but the beer on tap is limited (Kronenbourg £2.50 a pint, and Leffe £2.20 a half-pint).

Babies and children admitted (restaurant area only). Function room. Music (DJs Thur-Sat). Restaurant. Vegetarian dishes.

Griffin

93 Leonard Street, EC2 (020 7739 6719). Old Street tube. **Open** 11am-11pm Mon-Fri. **Food served** noon-3pm Mon-Fri. **No credit cards**.

Offering just the right dose of genuine rather than affected tattiness, the Griffin offers a welcome respite from the studied design bars that surround it. This is truly a pub in the traditional sense of the word. Corpulent geezers pull pints of bitter as cheap as £1.50 (Flowers IPA), and the bar snacks are veg-free Scotch eggs and pork pies – although it's not the food that attracts the Griffin's varied crowd of art students, ageing locals and office workers. Yellowing lace curtains, a gilt-edged bar and peeling paint offer just the right amount of shabby comfort. A safe place to play a quiet game of pool, have a relaxing drink and admit you do watch *Who Wants To Be A Millionaire*. Boddingtons is £1.80 a pint, and wine comes in minibar-sized bottles.

Games (darts, fruit machines, pinball machine, pool table, video games). Jukebox. Satellite TV. Tables outdoors (pavement). Vegetarian dishes.

Home

100-106 Leonard Street, EC2 (020 7684 8618). Old Street tube/rail. **Open** noon-midnight Mon-Fri; 6pm-midnight Sat. **Food served** noon-3pm, 7-11pm Mon-Fri; 7pm-11pm Sat. **Credit** AmEx, MC, V.

Home now boasts a sleek ground-floor dining area that seats 80, and serves up fashionably eclectic nosh. The main basement bar consists of three architecturally minimalist, interlocking rooms, equipped with comfy chairs and sofas in need of reupholstering. As one of the first bars to cash in on the staying-in-is-the-new-going-out trend, the place has a suitable resemblance to a lived-in living room. Decor is a mix of post- and pre-war furniture – there's even a sideboard just like granny had. Weekdays the place attracts after-work drinkers in need of winding down, but weekends it's pretty busy with hip Hoxtonites. There's a fairly extensive range of New World wines (around £3 a glass) and Heineken, Stella (both £2.60 a pint) and Boddingtons (£2.50) are on tap.

Babies and children admitted (daytime only). Restaurant. Vegetarian dishes.

Dragon

5 Leonard Street, EC2 (020 7490 7110). Old Street tube/rail. **Open/food served** 11am-11pm Mon-Sat; noon-10.30pm Sun. **Credit** MC, V.

Saunter down the dead end of Leonard Street and you'll very likely encounter young trendsters trying to locate this popular, camouflaged bar. Dragon has a plethora of streetwise sophistication, but even so attracts more suits than its prime movers would probably like. The dark ground-floor bar has bare-brick walls and chrome bar stools, while the basement is furnished with battered sofas and has an area for live bands. Climb the rickety stairs right to the top, and you'll reach a small function room. The bar's own absinthe-inspired Bomber shot is £4, but those less hedonistic can get Caffrey's (£2.50) and Staropramen (£2.60) on tap. The cooler-than-thou bar staff man the DJ decks when not serving.

Music (DJs Wed-Sat).

Eagle

2 Shepherdess Walk, N1 (020 7553 7681). Old Street tube/rail. **Open** noon-11pm Mon-Fri. **Food served** noon-10pm Mon-Fri. **Credit** AmEx, DC, MC, V.

If you can take the eardrum-bursting chart music that greets you as you walk in, the Eagle might be worth a visit. This boozer is clinging on to the cosy warmth of the more traditional pub: the carpeted floor is a rare sight in Shoreditch these days, and the pool table and etched windows and copper lanterns complete the look. Food ranges from traditional pub grub and sandwiches to slightly more adventurous dishes. The nearby university guarantees a regular crowd of students who feast on pints of Grolsch (£2.40) and Carling (£2.20), or four-pint jugs of Bass (£7.50). Staff are young and chirpy.

Hoxton Square Bar and Kitchen

2-4 Hoxton Square, N1 (020 7613 0709). Old Street tube/ rail/26, 48, 55, 242 bus. **Open** 11am-midnight Mon-Sat; noon-10.30pm Sun. **Food served** 12.30-2.30pm, 6.30-10.30pm Mon-Sat; 12.30-2.30pm, 6-9.30pm Sun. **Credit** MC, V.

Natural habitat to ludicrously fashionable youngsters and the Hoxton eskimo, this concrete basement bar has the look of a Slovakian waiting room. It's dark and smoky, but car lights flashing through the big street-level windows guide punters to shabby 1960s leather sofas. Once seated you can flirt in the customary chilled-out manner, or choose from a menu that stretches from snacks to full-on steaks. A location next to the Lux cinema and gallery ensures that works by emerging artists cover the walls, and in summer drinkers spill out into Hoxton Square. Red Stripe, Guinness and Pilsner are around £2.50 a pint, while double shot cocktails are £4.50. For first-timers there's the added thrill of playing guess your toilet.
Babies and children admitted. Disabled: toilet. Tables outdoors (pavement). Vegetarian dishes (on request).

New Foundry

84-86 Great Eastern Street, EC2 (020 7739 6900). Old Street tube (exit 3). **Open** 1-11pm Tue-Sat; 4-10.30pm Sun. **Food served** 1-6pm Tue-Fri; 6-10.30pm Sun. **No credit cards.**

Taking the lead in the crusade against calculated and excessive design, the New Foundry is a defiant accident of a bar. Located in an ex-bank, it looks pretty flash from the outside, but what greets you on entering is a combination of Steptoe & Son's gaff and an art student's bedroom. A sculpture of stacked-up security cameras stands by the door, while candles are stuffed in absinthe bottles and illuminate the mangy furniture. The uninhibited twentysomething clientele create a lively atmosphere, while monosyllabic bar-persons serve up basic food and pints of Stella (£2) or Carling (£1.50). Anything from art installations to photography exhibitions can be found in what used to be the bank's vaults, while other cultural events include poetry readings and DJs playing experimental music.
Babies and children admitted (in separate area). Music (DJs Thur-Sat). Performances (live/art, ring for details). Poetry readings (8.30pm Sun). Tables outdoors (pavement). Vegetarian dishes.

The Pool

104-108 Curtain Road, EC2 (020 7739 9608). Old Street tube. **Open/food served** noon-11pm daily. **Credit** DC, MC, V.

With its three American pool tables, jumbo-sized beanbags and resident DJs, the Pool is a romper room for trendy old (street) kids. Plate-glass windows mean the ground-floor bar is in full view of the passing commuter traffic. The cellar is larger but more intimate, with vinyl corner seats and a chocolate colour scheme. There's Red Stripe, Stella (both £2.50 a pint) and Boddingtons (£2.30) on tap; and there's also a cocktail list (£4.50-£7.50), though my vodka Martini lacked kick. The menu ranges from brunch at the weekends (when the pool tables are free), to harissa chicken breast in a sesame bagel (£6.50), or cracked pepper striploined steak (£9.50).
Babies and children admitted (until 5pm). Games (American pool tables). Music (DJs Thur-Sun). Restaurant. Vegetarian dishes.

The Reliance

336 Old Street, EC1 (020 7729 6888). Old Street tube/ rail/26, 48, 55, 242 bus. **Open** noon-11pm Mon-Thur; noon-2am Fri; 6pm-2am Sat; 3-10.30pm Sun. **Food**

served noon-3pm, 7-10.30pm Mon-Fri; 7-10.15pm Sat; 3-9.30pm Sun. **Credit** AmEx, DC, MC, V.

The Reliance is trying to place itself more in pre-club cutting edge territory with its resident and guest DJs on Friday and Saturday nights. However, punters here tend to look more like random visitors than a regular crowd, and this makes for a fairly subdued atmosphere. Still, this can be a smart and intimate place for anyone wanting to escape the rowdiness of other bars nearby. Some of its interior features are the product of the creative use of an old barge, while the part-brickwork decor edges towards mock-Tudor. There's an eclectic and enjoyable menu, and a good range of beers and lagers on tap (Hoegaarden £3.80 a pint, Staropramen £2.60). Bottled beers include Rolling Rock (£2.30) and Corona (£2.60).
Babies and children admitted (restaurant only). Function room. Jukebox. Late licence. Restaurant. Tables outdoors (balcony). Vegetarian dishes.

Shoreditch Electricity Showrooms

39A Hoxton Square, N1 (020 7739 6934). Old Street tube/26, 48, 55, 242 bus. **Open** noon-11pm Tue, Wed; noon-midnight Thur; noon-1am Fri, Sat; noon-10.30pm Sun. **Food served** noon-3pm, 7-10.30pm Mon-Sat; noon-10.30pm Sun. **Credit** DC, MC, V.

The blown-up picture postcard scene on one wall (a tropical island in winter, and a cool Alpine vista in summer) sets the hip-kitsch tone in this cleverly designed bar. There are other witty touches, too, such as the huge, floating-spaceman mural behind the bar, and the digital board flashing weather conditions. Large plate windows make it a great haunt for summer evenings, but punters come here all year round to pose, read newspapers and pick up flyers for events they'll never go to. Later in the evening the crowd ranges from Hoxtonite trendies to inebriated City boys. Aptly named cocktails such as Disorder and She's Lost Control will set you back about £6; bottled Budvar is £2.50. The small, minimalist eating area is less characterful, and attracts a more businessy crowd; the basement art space can be hired for private parties.
Babies and children admitted (until 7pm). Disabled: toilet. Function room. Late licence (Fri, Sat). Music (DJs Fri-Sun). No-smoking area. Restaurant. TV. Vegetarian dishes.

Wenlock Arms

26 Wenlock Road, N1 (020 7608 3406). Old Street tube/ rail. **Open/food served** noon-11pm Mon-Sat; noon-10.30pm Sun. **No credit cards.**

The radio tuned into Heart FM is one thing evoking feelings of nostalgia in this locals' local, tucked away in the more industrial area of Shoreditch. Ale is taken seriously, too, and a wide range of beers, including the curiously named Thrashing Tackle (£1.80) and Old Tom (£2.20) make regular appearances at very decent prices; a pint of pungent Biddenden Scrumpy cider, also, costs just £1.90. Those with a less clued-up beer palate are offered free tasters from the wide selection on offer. Weekdays, it's full of old blokes and young geezers enjoying the familiar knackered decor and friendly atmosphere; things hot up a tad towards the weekend, with jazz sessions and quiz nights. But the Wenlock is renowned for its real ales, and if you share the enthusiasm you should take time out for a visit.
Function room. Games (darts). Music (jazz Fri evenings, Sun lunch; jazz blues Sat evenings). Satellite TV. Quiz (Thur). Vegetarian dishes.

Also in the Area...

Heeltap and Bumper (Davys) 2-4 Paul Street, EC2 (020 7247 3319).

WEST

Barnes SW13/Mortlake SW14

Bull's Head

373 Lonsdale Road, Barnes, SW13 (020 8876 5241/ www.thebullshead.com). Hammersmith tube/Barnes Bridge rail/209 bus. **Open** 11am-11pm daily. **Food served** noon-2.30pm, 6-10.45pm daily. **Credit** AmEx, MC, V.
The Bull's Head claims to be the oldest jazz pub in London – bands have performed here since 1959 – and it's still a solid if no longer ground-breaking venue, with jazz and blues presented nightly (admission £6-£8). The venue is separate from the main room, a big, plain space dominated by a square central bar that kills any sense of cosiness. It's rarely crowded, and the clientele look to be mainly pot-bellied businessmen and bearded types in hand-knitted jumpers. Large, uncurtained windows let in plenty of light, but although it's on the river there's no view to speak of courtesy of a concrete parapet. Still, the staff are friendly, and Young's beers as good as ever (Special £2.15, 'ordinary' £2). There's also cheap pub food, and Young's usual impressive range of wine and whiskies (more than 80 malts).
Babies and children admitted (until 8pm). Function room. Music (live jazz, blues nightly). Restaurant. Tables outdoors (patio). Vegetarian dishes.

Coach & Horses

27 Barnes High Street, SW13 (020 8876 2695). Hammersmith tube/Barnes Bridge rail. **Open** 11am-11pm Mon-Sat; noon-10.30pm Sun. **Food served** noon-2.30pm daily. **Credit** MC, V.
This small pub tucked away off Barnes' main drag is a locals' local, attracting its fair share of the area's more elderly and eccentric citizens. Seating is arranged around the outside of the old-fashioned room, so that you can feel a bit exposed on entering, but the people behind the bar are friendly, and the Young's beers always appealing ('ordinary' £1.92). Families are also made welcome at weekends: the old inn's stable courtyard is now occupied by a children's climbing frame, and the lunches of hearty staples include a kids' menu. As in most Young's pubs, the choice of wines is more extensive than you're likely to find in pubs elsewhere.
Babies and children admitted (family area, outdoor climbing frame). Function room. No piped music or jukebox. Tables outdoors (garden). Theatre (monthly). Satellite TV. Vegetarian dishes.

Railway Tavern

11 Sheen Lane, SW14 (020 8878 7361). Mortlake rail. **Open** 11am-11pm Mon-Sat; noon-10.30pm Sun. **Food served** noon-9pm daily. **Credit** DC, MC, V.
For a train-themed pub the Railway is perfectly positioned, just down the road from Mortlake station with its busy level crossing and opposite the Budweiser brewery with its pungent malt clouds. It's a bizarre little boozer, with sauna-like brick walls and timber pitched roofs; on one side of the central bar is a draughty pool room, while on the other there's a more comfortable, carpeted lounge with a roaring fire in winter. The walls, as you might expect, are filled with photos of locomotives and train-related film posters. Service is amiable, and the food includes baguettes with speciality fillings, all day breakfast, a Sunday roast and a kiddies menu – and none dearer than a fiver. Quiet in the week, it's busier at weekends, mainly with a local, working-class, family clientele. Draught beers include the delicious Badger's Tanglefoot (£2.15) and Dorset Best (£2).
Babies and children admitted (until 7pm). Games (fruit machines, pool table, quiz machines). Jukebox. Satellite TV (big screen). Tables outdoors (pavement). Vegetarian dishes.

Sun

7 Church Road, SW13 (020 8876 5256). Barnes or Barnes Bridge rail/209, 283 bus. **Open** 11am-11pm Mon-Sat; noon-10.30pm Sun. **Food served** noon-2.45pm, 6-10pm Mon-Sat; noon-4pm Sun. **Credit** AmEx, DC, MC, V.
Sitting square in the centre of Barnes, opposite the pretty duck pond, the Sun is an attractive pub, with a dark, labyrinthine, low-ceilinged interior that's much bigger than it first appears. It's the drinking hole of choice for the noisy youth of Barnes, hence perhaps the many signs around the place banning under-21s. The bar staff are friendly enough, and the range of beers is good: Burton ale (£2.20), Wadworth 6X (£2.20), and others. A pleasant outside seating area at the front is warmed in winter by heaters, but really comes into its own when the summer crowds pour in for Sunday roasts, although the Thai food in the evenings is also proving very popular.
Games (fruit machines). No-smoking area. Satellite TV. Tables outdoors (patio). Vegetarian dishes.

Ye White Hart

The Terrace, Riverside, Barnes, SW13 (020 8876 5177). Barnes Bridge rail/209 bus. **Open** 11am-3pm, 5.30-11pm Mon-Thur; 11am-11pm Fri, Sat; noon-10.30pm Sun. **Food served** 12.30-2.30pm daily. **Credit** MC, V.
This big riverside pub is so close to the Thames the outside tables sometimes get washed by high tides, but there's also an upper-level terrace, and plenty of space in the capacious interior with its central bar. As in all Young's pubs, the beer is excellent and well priced (Special £2.05), and the wine selection impressive, with 20 wines available by the glass (from £2.20/175ml). It also offers plenty of decent if unenterprising pub food for around £4-£5 – the Sunday roasts are especially popular. For such a busy place it can be a bit lacking in atmosphere, but the clientele is pleasingly mixed in age.
Function room. Games (fruit machine). No piped music or jukebox. Satellite TV. Tables outdoors (patio, riverside terrace, towpath). Vegetarian dishes.

Also in the area...

Café Rouge 248 Upper Richmond Road, SW14 (020 8878 8897).

Critics' choice
views

Dove (p144)
Hammersmith's authentic riverside pub; also try the Old Ship (p144) or the Blue Anchor (p142).

Founder's Arms (p166)
Perched on the Thames, next to Tate Modern; the view of St Paul's is a knockout.

Marlborough (p150)
Richmond's take on the Thames.

Phoenix (p232)
Great views from north London's highest point.

Twentyfour (p125)
A cinematic panorama of the City at night.

Chiswick W4/Kew, Surrey

Railway Tavern

Bull's Head

15 Strand on the Green, W4 (020 8994 1204).
Gunnersbury tube/rail/Kew Bridge rail. **Open** 11am-11pm
Mon-Sat; noon-10.30pm Sun. **Food served** noon-10pm
daily. **Credit** AmEx, DC, MC, V.
Don't let the truly revolting brick-and-timber lobby put you
off. Carry on further inside, towards the river, and the
mishmash of beamed, butterscotch-painted, interconnecting
rooms has an unmistakably authentic feel. The raised nook
at the back makes a good hideaway from which to savour
tranquil views of the gently flowing Thames, together with
the pleasant rumble and clatter from nearby Kew railway
bridge. The bar staff are amiable, and beers well kept
(Wadworth 6X £2.25, Theakston's Best £2.01). While
partaking of the biggish menu of typical pub tucker (beef
and ale pie £5.99, jacket potatoes et al), you can also mull over
the pub's interesting historical associations: during the Civil
War, Oliver Cromwell is said to have escaped Royalist
pursuers through a secret tunnel from the pub to Oliver's
Island, in midstream.
Babies and children admitted (conservatory area).
Function room. Games (darts, fruit machines). Tables
outdoors (riverside terrace). Vegetarian dishes.

Coach & Horses

8 Kew Green, Kew, Surrey (020 8940 1208). Kew
Gardens tube/rail. **Open** 11am-11pm Mon-Sat; noon-
10.30pm Sun. **Food served** noon-2.30pm, 7-9pm Mon-Fri;
noon-2.30pm Sat, Sun. **Credit** AmEx, DC, MC, V.
This big old-fashioned pub – formerly a coaching inn (it still
offers accommodation, at £49 a double) – sits on the 'wrong'
side of Kew Green, separated from the grass and St Anne's
church by a busy road. The main, central bar is tended by
jovial staff; decor is unremarkable and in need of a revamp,
but this is probably a reason for its comfortable, well-worn
feel. For a less cluttered experience, try the big-windowed
dining room at the side. You'll find the usual range of Young's
beers ('ordinary' £1.92, Special £2.08, Pilsner £2.17, Export
£2.34) and standard pub food (gammon and eggs £4.80,
cheddar or brie ploughman's £3.70), which draws a big
Sunday crowd. There are plenty of tables outside in front of
the pub, and in a large if rather bare garden.
Babies and children (restaurant). Disabled: toilet. Function
rooms. Games (fruit machine). No piped music or jukebox.
Tables outdoors (garden, front and rear). Satellite TV (big
screen). Vegetarian dishes.

Mawson Arms

110 Chiswick Lane South, W4 (020 8994 2936).
Turnham Green tube. **Open** 11am-8pm Mon-Fri.
Food served noon-6.30pm Mon-Fri. **Credit** DC, MC, V.
Nice pub, shame about the location. It's only 200 yards from
the river, but this little boozer – the 'tap' for the Fuller's
Brewery next door – is also just yards from the busy A4, and
so any hope of a quiet drink is spoiled by the roar of nearby
traffic. Still, there's no faulting the decor – green and cream
walls, bare floorboards, leather sofas along one side and
wooden tables and chairs on the other – nor the Fuller's beer
(London Pride £1.95, ESB £2.10). It's busiest at lunchtime,
mainly with brewery staff tucking into the well-priced and
varied menu (bangers and mash, breast of lamb with celeriac
mash and rosemary and red wine sauce, both £5.25). It closes
early in the week and throughout the weekend.
Babies and children admitted. Function room.
Games (darts). No-smoking area. Pub quiz (daily).
Vegetarian dishes.

Also in the area...

All Bar One 197-199 Chiswick High Road, W4 (020 8987 8211).
Café Rouge 227-229 Chiswick High Road, W4 (020 8742 7447); 85 Strand on the Green, W4 (020 8995 6575); 291 Sandycombe Road, Kew, Surrey (020 8332 2882).
Flower & Firkin Kew Gardens Station, Kew, Surrey (020 8332 1162).
Pitcher & Piano 18-20 Chiswick High Road, W4 (020 8742 7731).

Ealing W5

Drayton Court

2 The Avenue, W13 (020 8997 1019). West Ealing rail. **Open** 11am-11pm Mon-Sat; noon-10.30pm Sun. **Food served** noon-3pm, 6-9pm Mon-Fri; 11am-11pm Sat; noon-3pm, 7-9pm Sun. **Credit** MC, V.
A really humming pub that's a good walk from central Ealing, but even so is exceptionally popular with the young and trendy who have been carrying out the gentrification of the area. It's huge, with a separate room on one side containing a vast TV screen for footie-viewing and the like. This is a Fuller's pub, so you can grab a pint of Chiswick (£1.55) or London Pride (£2.03), or opt for coffee or a decent glass of wine (from £2.35). The array of enjoyable pub grub includes such things as mushroom soup (£2.50) or vegetable fettuccini (£4.75). The Drayton also has a pool room, a wrought-iron terrace, a large well-landscaped garden for sitting outside in during summer and a theatre (the Court Room) in the basement – a real centre of activity.
Babies and children admitted (family room, playground). Disabled: toilet. Function rooms. Games (board games, fruit machines, pool room). Quiz (Sun). Satellite TV (big screen). Tables outdoors (patio, garden). Theatre. Vegetarian dishes.

The Red Lion

13 St Mary's Road, W5 (020 8567 2541). South Ealing tube. **Open** 11am-11pm Mon-Sat; noon-10.30pm Sun. **Food served** noon-2.30pm, 6-9pm daily. **No credit cards.**
The walls of this classic old pub are peppered with shots of the stars of yesteryear from Ealing Film Studios, across the road (there's also a signed pic of less-than-illustrious Little and Large). It's a wonderful place with no music, no TV, no pine and no pseudy-bourgeois food – just a pub. Enjoy a pint of Fuller's Chiswick (£1.55) or Pride (£1.98), and relax with the quiet chat of locals in the background; in the summer you can also enjoy the enclosed garden at the back. Basic pub grub is available. The Red Lion has won a Fuller's Cask Marque, awarded to pubs that pull a really good pint, and the accolade is thoroughly deserved.
No piped music or jukebox. Quiz (Mon). Tables outdoors (garden). Vegetarian dishes.

Also in the area...

All Bar One 64-65 The Mall, Ealing Broadway, W5 (020 8280 9611).
Café Rouge 17 The Green, W5 (020 8579 2788).
Edward's 28-30 New Broadway, W5 (020 8567 9438).
Photographer & Firkin 23 High Street, W5 (020 8567 1140).

Hammersmith, Ravenscourt Park, Stamford Brook, W6/ Barons Court W14

Black Lion

2 South Black Lion Lane, W6 (020 8748 2639). Stamford Brook tube. **Open/food served** 11am-11pm Mon-Sat; noon-10.30pm Sun. **Credit** AmEx, DC, MC, V.
Originally a piggery, the Black Lion became a pub some 200 years ago, and still feels like a big, old-fashioned country inn. At the western end of the Hammersmith riverside pubs, it's a friendly, unpretentious spot that makes a fine place to break a walk (it's better to get there on foot than by road, – access is off the busy A4). Larger than it first appears, this L-shaped, low-beamed hideaway is perfect for a game of billiards, a chat with the staff or a tryst behind its high-backed pews. Plates, tankards, clay pipes and meat-grinders decorate the shelves running round the rooms, and a fireplace divides the main room from a second, more private spot. Practically empty on a Saturday night in January, it's much busier in summer, when the garden is open. You'll find the usual bar food and Courage beers on tap (Courage Best £2.08, Foster's £2.28).
Babies and children admitted. Function room. Games (bar billiards, darts). Quiz (Mon). Tables outdoors (garden). Vegetarian dishes.

Blue Anchor

13 Lower Mall, W6 (020 8748 5774). Hammersmith tube. **Open** 11am-11pm Mon-Sat; noon-10.30pm Sun. **Food served** 12.30-2.30pm, 6-8.30pm Mon-Sat; noon-3pm Sun. **Credit** MC, V.
Londoners have been downing pints at this cosy, cluttered, one-roomed pub for ever – well, since 1722 – and it manages to remain totally authentic even while taking the rowing theme to extremes (oars, anchors, even whole boats abound). It's the smallest and most charming of Hammersmith's riverside pubs (and the nearest to the bridge), and the bar staff are exceedingly friendly. Holst wrote his 'Hammersmith Suite' here. Ideal for a pint of Guinness (£2.50) or Courage Best (£2.10) and some decent pub food on a dark winter evening, it's much busier and rowdier in the summer, when there's barely a space to be had at the outside seating area.
Babies and children admitted. Function room. Tables outdoors (riverside pavement). Vegetarian dishes.

Café Med

320 Goldhawk Road, W6 (020 8741 1994/ www.goldhawkw6@cafemed.co.uk). Stamford Brook tube. **Open/food served** noon-11.30pm Mon-Sat; noon-10.30pm Sun. **Credit** AmEx, DC, MC, V.
Part of the Café Med mini-chain, this spacious corner bar/restaurant is divided into two, with tables and chairs in the front restaurant area and large leather sofas, twiddly metal chairs and subdued lighting in the back bar. The enticing Mediterranean food includes the likes of merguez sausages with cumin houmous and mint (£4.50), and mackerel with lentil salad (£9.50). It is a comfortable place with a relaxed atmosphere, though it has a reputation for a somewhat predatory crowd on the weekends. Brews on tap include Courage Directors (£2.20) and Kronenbourg (£2.60), and there are also cocktails (£5), fruit smoothies (£2.75) and around 40 wines (starting at £2.75 a glass, £9.95 a bottle), including the likes of Sancerre at £5.50 a glass. A small garden opens in the summer.
Babies and children admitted (restaurant only; high chairs, children's menus). Music (live jazz Sun evenings). Restaurant. Tables outdoors (garden). Vegetarian dishes.

London crawling

Hammersmith ghosts

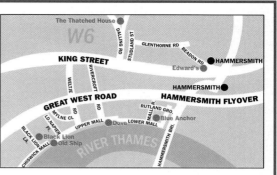

The stretch of the Thames between Chiswick Mall and Hammersmith Bridge has easygoing charms of its own, with calming river views and alluring watering holes from which to appreciate them, but it also has a number of both artistic and otherwise historical – some might even say ghoulish – associations that make a stroll by the waterside more than just a relaxing diversion.

Hammersmith Terrace, most easily reached via Chiswick Mall, is a row of sturdy waterfront houses with several claims to literary fame, having been home to Edward Johnston, calligrapher and tutor to artist Eric Gill (No.3), printer Sir Emery Walker (No.7) and MP, novelist and Thames-chronicler AP Herbert (Nos.12-13). At its eastern end you'll come to Black Lion Lane, where, in 1804, an unfortunate bricklayer by the name of Thomas Millwood was shot dead by one Francis Smith, who mistook him for the 'Hammersmith Ghost'. The cadaver was carried into the nearby Black Lion, which had been converted from a piggery into a public house not long before. Today, it's a tranquil spot from which to start your crawl, and in which to ponder Millwood's fate.

Moving on past the single brick arcade that is all that remains of the West Middlesex Water Company pumping station, you'll gain your best view of the river, with its tidal flats and moored trawlers. When thirst or bracing winds call you back to reality, proceed along Upper Mall to the **Old Ship**, another eighteenth-century pub and your second port of call. Though it's somewhat more of a beautiful people's hangout than the Black Lion, it's an undeniably inviting retreat from the cold, with a home-steeped chilli vodka that will really thaw you out.

After leaving the Old Ship, continue along Upper Mall, where you'll come across Kelmscott House, home, in its illustrious history, to Sir Francis Ronalds, inventor of the electric telegraph, poet and novelist George MacDonald (best known for *The Princess and the Goblin*) and poet, designer, craftsman and Socialist writer William Morris. Morris, who rented the house as his London base in 1877 and died there in 1896, named it after his Oxfordshire home Kelmscott Manor. Despite his love of the river, however (his two homes were both on the Thames), Morris was not entirely happy with his new surroundings, which were evidently less idyllic in his day. In an 1881 lecture he made the following outburst: 'Look you, as I sit at work at home, which is Hammersmith, close to the river, I often hear go past

the window some of that ruffianism of which a great deal has been said in the papers of late.'

He goes on to thank his stars for not having been born 'on the other side, in the empty street, the drink-steeped liquor shops, the foul and degraded lodgings'. These impressions wouldn't have been much improved by his having, in the same year, the misfortune to witness the last desperate act of one of the suicides for whom the dark waters of the Thames have long formed such a lure.

It's unlikely, given these sentiments, that Morris would have frequented the **Dove**, Hammersmith's most famous pub, but the literary theme is reprised here nonetheless. In the eighteenth century, when it was a coffee house, poet James Johnson wrote part of '*The Seasons*' and possibly also the words to '*Rule Britannia*' here; William Morris used a section of the house that stands opposite, Sussex House, for his Kelmscott Press; Morris's friend Thomas Cobden-Sanderson started the Doves book-bindery and press next door; and AP Herbert used the pub as a model for the Pigeons in his novel *The Water Gypsies*.

End your riverside walk at the atmospheric **Blue Anchor**, which rubs shoulders with the boathouses further towards the bridge. Ease your way back into the real world by finishing your crawl at the **Thatched House**, taking a leaf out of the book of that modern-day bard Shane McGowan, whose *Dark Streets of London* fondly recalls his 'dear dirty old drunken delightful old days' spent 'down Dalling Road by the dead old trees' and on the Broadway. Neither of these heavily madeover pubs would appeal to the Pogues frontman these days, but on a cold night you'll be glad of their warm welcome.
Rhonda Carrier

Black Lion (*p142*) 2 South Black Lion Lane, W6 (020 8748 2639).
Blue Anchor (*p142*) 13 Lower Mall, W6 (020 8748 5774).
Dove (*p144*) 19 Upper Mall, W6 (020 8748 5405).
Old Ship (*p144*) 25 Upper Mall, W6 (020 8748 2593).
Thatched House (*p144*) 115 Dalling Road, W6 (020 8748 6174).

Dove

19 Upper Mall, W6 (020 8748 5405). Hammersmith or Ravenscourt Park tube. **Open** 11am-11pm Mon-Sat; noon-10.30pm Sun. **Food served** noon-2pm, 6.30-9.30pm Mon-Sat; noon-4pm, 6.30-9pm Sun. **Credit** AmEx, DC, MC, V.
The Dove remains a bastion of tradition. This 300-year-old, split-level Fuller's tavern proudly eschews themed artifice – no pseudo-chesterfield upholstery, mindless muzak or one-armed banditry here. Instead, there are low, beamed ceilings, aged wood panelling, built-in wall settles, dingy lighting and an embracingly warm atmosphere, spread through a tiny front bar, a slightly larger central bar (with roaring fire) and a brick-walled area at the back. This authenticity, unfortunately, extends to the stodgy staples of the mediocre pub-grub menu (prawn salads £4.50, shepherd's pie £5.95). In summer, arrive early to grab a table on the small terrace to the rear, which overlooks a stretch of the Thames heaving with upper-class oarsmen. One other trad feature: no children are admitted at any time.
No piped music or jukebox. Tables outdoors (riverside terrace). Vegetarian dishes.

Old Ship

25 Upper Mall, W6 (020 8748 2593). Hammersmith, Ravenscourt Park or Stamford Brook tube. **Open** 10am-11pm Mon-Fri; 9am-11pm Sat; 9am-10.30pm Sun. **Food served** 10am-10.30pm Mon-Fri; 9am-10.30pm Sat; 9am-10pm Sun. **Credit** AmEx, MC, V.
With white pine panelling and high-backed lime-green banquette seating, the Ship has a lighter, more modern look than the other riverside pubs, although it still has its fair share of ships' paraphernalia, and the toilets are designated 'Ableseamen' and (groan) 'Ableseawomen'. It's quite spacious, with an attractive long bar serving beers such as Kronenbourg (£2.50) and Old Speckled Hen (£2.10), and the well-priced bar menu includes the likes of grilled swordfish (£6.95) and spicy bean burgers (£4.75). This is also a particularly good spot for families, since it offers a separate kids' menu and a nappy-changing unit.
Babies and children admitted (children's menu, high chairs, nappy-changing facilities). Disabled: toilet. Function room. Games (fruit machine). Jukebox. Satellite TV. Tables outdoors (riverside balcony, terrace). Vegetarian dishes.

Stonemason's Arms

54 Cambridge Grove, W6 (020 8748 1397). Hammersmith tube. **Open** noon-11pm Mon-Sat; noon-10.30pm Sun. **Food served** noon-10pm Mon-Sat; noon-9.30pm Sun. **Credit** AmEx, MC, V.
This large and comfortable corner pub is a big favourite with Hammersmith's fleece-wearing, combat-trousered trendies. Arrive early if you want a seat: its big wooden tables and mismatched chairs and old church pews were packed on the cold Saturday night we visited. Many punters were enjoying the excellent food, such as salmon and sweet potato fishcakes with Thai dipping sauce (£6.80) seated beneath an interesting array of artworks by local artists (all of them for sale) hung on the rough painted walls. Beers include Wadworth 6X and Brakspear's (both £2.30) – and don't be deterred by the pub sign, which misleadingly reads 'The Cambridge Arms'.
Babies and children admitted. Disabled: toilet. Vegetarian dishes.

Thatched House

115 Dalling Road, W6 (020 8748 6174). Ravenscourt Park tube. **Open** noon-11pm Mon-Sat; noon-10.30pm Sun. **Food served** noon-3pm Mon-Sat; noon-9.30pm Sun. **Credit** DC, MC, V.

Smaller than it appears from the outside, the Thatched House was originally a coppers' local, but has outlasted the local nick and was totally refurbished at the end of 1998. The decor is English-country-living-room – yellowish walls, old wooden tables, bookshelves, an assortment of unusual paintings – but looks a tad contrived, and the lighting is too bright. The clientele is more mixed in age than in some Hammersmith pubs, and the bar staff cheery. There are the usual Young's beers (Special, Winter Warmer, both £2.35), and a big selection of wines, but the real draw is the food, which is first-class. The fillet of cod with white bean purée and chorizo sauce (£9.95) and exquisite warm chocolate cake with almond ice-cream (£3.45) are heartily recommended.
Babies and children admitted (lunchtimes only). No piped music or jukebox. Satellite TV. Tables outdoors (courtyard). Vegetarian dishes.

Also in the area...

Café Rouge 158 Fulham Palace Road, W6 (020 8741 5037).
Edward's 40 Hammersmith Broadway, W6 (020 8748 1043).

Hampton Court, Surrey

Albion

34 Bridge Road, East Molesey, Surrey (020 8941 9421). Hampton Court rail. **Open** 10am-11pm Mon-Sat; noon-10.30pm Sun. **Food served** 10am-9pm daily. **Credit** MC, V.
Duck into this low-ceilinged pub hidden from the main drag of tourist chic and enter a cheery, buzzing haven, busy with locals of all shapes and sizes, ages and accents. A mishmash of tapestries, musty books and pub regalia look down from tobacco coloured walls onto leatherette armchairs in the main bar to the left, while to the right a carpeted restaurant area encourages visitors to indulge in the grand dishes on offer (rump of lamb £6.25, roasted vegetables with cream, pesto and parmesan £6). The Albion can get lively, but since it is unfailingly friendly, cosy and comfortable, and the drinks reassuringly reliable (Bass, London Pride, both £2.05), it is the always good to be worth a visit.
Babies and children admitted (until 8pm). Restaurant. Satellite TV (big screen). Tables outdoors (garden). Vegetarian dishes.

King's Arms

Lion Gate, Hampton Court Road, East Molesey, Surrey (020 8977 1729). Hampton Court rail. **Open** 11am-11pm Mon-Sat; noon-10.30pm Sun. **Food served** 11am-9.30pm Mon-Sat; noon-9.30pm Sun. **Credit** AmEx, DC, MC, V.
Sitting close to the Lion Gate of Hampton Court, the King's Arms is a pleasant retreat from the busy road outside. It is split into three distinct areas. A large wooden-floored bar mixes exposed brick and pews with old sailor types sitting below a drop-down TV screen; a cosier, dimly lit middle bar displays a series of panels depicting Henry VIII's ditched dames, and pays host to the younger more virile punter ; and beyond lies an unprepossessing buffet counter for the unenterprising food (wholetail scampi £6.95, homemade lasagne £5.95), which was rightly empty. The management has resisted the obvious possibilities for tourist kitsch, and with homely ales such as Badger's Tanglefoot (£2.25) and Frusty Ferret (£2.15) on tap, this pub somehow retains a welcoming warmth for such a sprawling mass.
Function room. Games (darts, fruit machine). Tables outdoors (patio). Vegetarian dishes.

Golborne House

Kensal W10

Golborne House
*36 Golborne Road, W10 (020 8960 6260). Westbourne
Park tube.* **Open** noon-11pm Mon-Fri; 11am-11pm Sat;
11am-10.30pm Sun. **Food served** noon-11pm Mon-Fri;
11am-4pm, 6-11pm, Sat, Sun. **Credit** MC, V.
An offshoot of the ever-fashionable **Westbourne** (*see p108*),
Golborne House is more like a Slug & Lettuce than its parent
pub. The colour schemes are an unremarkable but tasteful
mix of terracotta with khaki trimmings, plain wood floors
and chunky furniture. However, the broad windows, cowering
beneath Ernö Goldfinger's Trellick Tower, afford views of the
busy Moroccan-market throng of Golborne Road, making the
bar bright and lively. Compared to the Westbourne the drinks
range is more limited, with only one real ale (Bass £2.40) and
a handful of lagers (Stella £2.60, Hoegaarden £3.80, Staropramen £2.70) to accompany a respectable wine list aimed at
less tutored palates. Food is good standard gastropub fare,
(steak sandwiches, risottos both £7, fishcakes £6.50).
*Babies and children admitted. Function room. Music (DJs
Fri, Sat). Vegetarian dishes.*

North Pole
*13-15 North Pole Road, W10 (020 8964 9384). Latimer
Road or White City tube.* **Open** 11.30am-11pm Mon-Sat;
noon-10.30pm Sun. **Food served** 12.30-3pm, 7-10pm
Mon-Fri; noon-3pm, 7-10pm Sat; noon-4pm, 7-9.30pm Sun.
Credit AmEx, MC, V.
There is much to admire in the casual, ageing leather sofas
and sturdy wooden furniture in the bright and broad space
of this exemplary pub, but there's also a sense that it's trying
to do too much. On the booze side, the bar has a good set of
beers (London Pride £2.30, Freedom £2.60), more than 40 red,

white and fizzy wines and assorted brandies and malts, while the kitchen serves up an exciting menu of global food. However, with table football, big screen TV and DJs banging out loud music most nights, it's not necessarily an ideal dining environment. The eclectic cuisine remains alluring, though, and usually it's your fish rather than your eardrums that'll be battered (lunch mains are around £7, rising to £7-£13 for dinner). Meanwhile, the appearance of a bouncer (albeit reading the *Daily Telegraph*) suggests that the Notting Hill fringe element and youths from the BBC on Wood Lane can sometimes get a little overexcited.
Babies and children admitted (until 6pm). Games (table football). Music (DJs Fri, Sat). Restaurant. TV (big screen). Tables outdoors (pavement). Vegetarian dishes.

Paradise by Way of Kensal Green

19 Kilburn Lane, W10 (020 8969 0098). Kensal Green tube/Kensal Rise rail. **Open** 12.30-11pm Mon-Sat; noon-10.30pm Sun. **Food served** 12.30-4pm, 7.30pm-midnight Mon-Sat; noon-4pm, noon-11pm Sun. **Credit** DC, MC, V.
Paradise recently changed hands, and although some of the austerity of the old place has been toned down, little else has changed. In keeping with a bar that took its name from the Chesterton poem about going to paradise by way of the neighbouring Kensal Green cemetery, Joe the manager continues to prowl about wearing the chilly countenance of a municipal undertaker. The hospital-green colour scheme and echoey acoustics reverberating around the pirouetting statue of Mercury in the front bar also remain. To supplement the standard range of drinks, there's a regularly changing real ale on tap (£2.10), a traditional Breton cider for £2.50, and on the night of our visit they were also optimistically pushing a bottle of Puligny Montrachet 1997 for £48. But even with the cooking in the Eurasian restaurant to the rear having picked up, it is hard to imagine spending that much on a bottle of wine anywhere, let alone in a pub.
Babies and children admitted (high chairs, menus, nappy-changing facilities). Disabled: toilet. Function rooms. Music (DJs Wed-Sat; bands Fri, Sat). No-smoking area. Restaurant. Satellite TV. Tables outdoors (garden). Vegetarian dishes.

Kingston-upon-Thames, Surrey

Boaters Inn

Canbury Gardens, Lower Ham Road, Kingston-upon-Thames, Surrey (020 8541 4672). Kingston rail. **Open** Apr-Sept 11am-11pm Mon-Sat; noon-10.30pm Sun; Oct-Mar 11am-3pm, 5.30-11pm Mon-Thur; 11am-11pm Fri, Sat; noon-10.30pm Sun. **Happy hour** 5.30-8pm Mon-Thur. **Food served** noon-2.30pm, 7-9.30pm daily. **Credit** MC, V.
A candlelit, green-pine makeover has bestowed a wine-bar look upon the Boaters, but a laid-back atmosphere pervades, and it's a good option among Kingston's glut of riverside pubs. Live jazz (every Sunday) probably accounted for the number of suburban sophisticates on our visit. Customers have an exclusive right to dock on its stretch of bank, and summer months see the patio filling up quickly and spilling into the adjoining park. The menu offers pub classics and daily specials, such as moules marinière and Cajun chicken (£5.50). Drinks are from the IPA stable, and guest ales such as Brakspear's Grim Reaper (£2) change regularly.
Babies and children admitted (children's menus, nappy-changing facilities). Games (board games, fruit machines, quiz machine). Music (live jazz Sun). No-smoking area. Restaurant. Tables outdoors (riverside patio, front balcony). Vegetarian dishes.

Canbury Arms

49 Canbury Park Road, Kingston-upon-Thames, Surrey (020 8288 1882). Kingston rail. **Open** 11am-11pm Mon-Sat; noon-10.30pm Sun. **No credit cards**.
Tucked down a suburban backstreet, the Canbury Arms should please the most devoted Camra members with the quality and breadth of its stock. As if to prove its devotion to real ale, dried hops hang over the bar. More than 420 guest ales have been pulled through the pumps by the enthusiastic, hirsute barman, and beermats to prove it are littered throughout the pub; OTT from the Hogsback Brewery in Surrey (£2.10) and Wychwood's Dog's Bollocks (£2.20) are some of the more imaginatively named beers recently on tap. Toby-jug hugging regulars make up the clientele in the refreshingly unstylish interior, although live music nights and a big-screen TV pull in a more varied bunch of local characters. During the summer months you can lounge with rabbits, guinea pigs and Baldrick the Great Dane in the beer garden.
Babies and children admitted (separate room). Games (board games, darts, fruit machines). Jukebox. Music (bands Fri, Sat). Quiz (Sun). Satellite TV (big screen). Tables outdoors (forecourt, garden).

Newt & Ferret

46 Fairfield South, Kingston-upon-Thames, Surrey (020 8546 3804). Kingston, Norbiton or Surbiton rail. **Open** 11am-11pm Mon-Sat; noon-10.30pm Sun. **Credit** AmEx, DC, MC, V.
Perched on the edge of Fairfield recreation ground, the Newt & Ferret can bring out the gamesman in you. Depending on how easily amused you are, classic board games such as chess and Scrabble will delight between trips to the bar – and a well-stocked bar it is too. Excellent Hoffbräu lagers (Export £2.20) are on tap as well as ales from the Badger Brewery (Tanglefoot ale £2.10). In summer, customers can enjoy a barbie and perhaps try their hand at boules in the garden. For the rest of the year the red interior, dotted with authentic pub props, a stuffed ferret above the bar (no newt, though), and the fire roaring in the hearth provide an enticingly cosy atmosphere.
Babies and children admitted (until 6pm). Games (board games, boules, fruit machines, pool table, pinball machine, table football). Jukebox. Quiz (Tue). Satellite TV (big screen). Tables outdoors (children's playground, garden).

Norbiton & Dragon

16 Clifton Road, Norbiton, Surrey (020 8546 1951). Norbiton rail. **Open** 11am-11pm Mon-Sat; noon-10.30pm Sun. **Food served** noon-2.30pm, 7-10.30pm Mon-Fri; noon-10.30pm Sat; noon-10pm Sun. **Credit** AmEx, DC, MC, V.
Many pubs have tried and failed to combine a decent Thai restaurant with a standard boozer, but here's one that got away with it. The Dragon restaurant serves excellent Thai dishes, and is joined to the main bar through a low arch at the back of the pub. Snacks from the menu can also be enjoyed in the bar, where Eastern-style surroundings give way to wall-to-wall Victoriana. The colour of tanned leather prevails – from the suitcases and kettles piled above the large curved bar, to the huge deer's head looming over the pool tables. Its quirkiness attracts a friendly, youngish crowd. Wadworth 6X (£2.10), Directors (£2.15) and a changing guest ale are on tap.
Babies and children admitted (restaurant only; high chairs). Function room. Games (fruit machines, pool table, video game). Restaurant. Satellite TV (big screen). Tables outdoors (garden). Vegetarian dishes.

Warrington Hotel. *See page 149.*

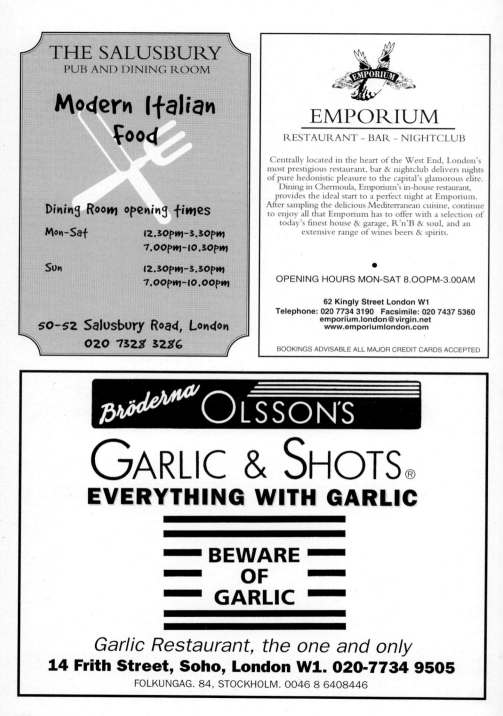

Park Tavern

*19 New Road, Kingston-upon-Thames, Surrey (no phone).
Norbiton rail.* **Open** 11am-11pm Mon-Sat; noon-10.30pm
Sun. **No credit cards.**
A brilliant little pub that rightly commands a loyal
following among appreciative locals. The kind of homely
ambience some places spend thousands to attain is here in
buckets. Walls lined with green upholstered seats and
unpretentious decor create a snugness as comforting as an
old cardigan, while taking a seat on the neat front patio
provides a delightful summer alternative. Another
attraction comes from the pub's proximity to the Kingston
Gate in Richmond Park, making it a good place to stop after
a bracing constitutional. The chipper barman and brassy
barmaids serve up pints of Foster's (£2.16 a pint) and
bitters such as Brakspear's Special (£1.98) to keep ale
enthusiasts happy.
*Games (fruit machine). Jukebox. Satellite TV (big screen).
Tables outdoors (garden, patio).*

Wych Elm

*93 Elm Road, Kingston-upon-Thames, Surrey (020 8546
3271). Kingston rail.* **Open** 11am-3pm, 5-11pm Mon-Fri;
11am-11pm Sat; noon-4pm, 7-10.30pm Sun. **Food served**
12.30-2.30pm Mon-Sat. **No credit cards.**
Owners Manuel and Janet Turnes bring a green-fingered
touch to this friendly Kingston local. The verdancy of its
hanging baskets and front patio is matched by the beautifully
tended back garden – deserved winner of a Fuller's Garden
of the Year Award in 1999. The differences in the clientele are
as distinct as the split between the saloon and lounge bars.
Darts-playing regulars and a sprinkling of codgers from a
nearby old folks' home populate the basic saloon bar, while
the second bar with its plush upholstery attracts a younger
crowd. Equality rules behind the bar, though, with a fine
selection of Fuller's ales (Jack Frost £2.20, and ESB £2.30).
Food tends towards the unremarkable pub grub variety
(pizzas, chicken casserole, steak and kidney pie), but it is all
home cooked, and costs around a fiver.
*Babies and children admitted (eating area only). Games
(darts, fruit machine). Tables outdoors (garden).
Vegetarian dishes.*

Also in the area...

Café Rouge 4-8 Kingston Hill, Kingston-upon-Thames,
Surrey (020 8547 3229).
Financier & Firkin 43 Market Place, Kingston-upon-
Thames, Surrey (020 8974 8223).
Kingston Tup 88 London Road, Kingston-upon-
Thames, Surrey (020 8546 6471).
The Puzzle 1 St James Square, Kingston-upon-
Thames, KT1 2AA (020 8549 7399).
Slug & Lettuce Turks Boatyard, Thameside, Kingston-
upon-Thames, Surrey (020 8547 2323).

Maida Vale W2, W9

Bridge House

*13 Westbourne Terrace Road, W2 (020 7432 1361).
Warwick Avenue tube.* **Open** 11am-11pm Mon-Sat;
noon-10.30pm Sun. **Food served** noon-10pm Mon-Sat;
noon-9pm Sun. **Credit** MC, V.
In 1730 the original pub on this site served ploughmen and
rustics of the locality. Today it's a good, ordinary, friendly,
carpeted local playing sports on the TV screens, dispensing
cash prizes from fruit machines and serving standard pub

grub (steak and ale pie £4.85) as well as Bass (£2.10) and
London Pride (£2.20) by way of real ale. There's a street-
side terrace for summer drinking, but a view of Regent's
canal across the road is only achieved by considerable neck-
craning. Apart from locals in the surrounding Paddington
tower block estates the pub also attracts a different, and
often younger, class of punter from the Little Venice
mansions to the Canal Café fringe theatre and long-running
comedy club, which is upstairs.
*Comedy (Thur-Sun, admission £6). Function room.
Games (fruit machine, quiz machine). Satellite TV. Tables
outdoors (terrace). Theatre. Vegetarian dishes.*

Warwick Castle

*6 Warwick Place, W9 (020 7432 1331). Warwick Avenue
tube.* **Open** noon-11pm Mon-Sat; noon-10.30pm Sun.
Food served noon-2pm daily. **Credit** MC, V.
Aside from the ghost in the cellar there's not a lot of mystery
about this good, simple Bass pub. Divided into four small
ante-rooms that afford a modicum of privacy, the decor is
fairly masculine, with traditional, unadorned wood
panelling behind a cut-glass front that opens out on to the
street – near the Regent's Canal – in summer. Otherwise, the
only features are a couple of grandfather clocks, some traces
of Victoriana, and photos of local historical interest. Food
follows the Bass pubs uber-menu, with light bites for up to
£4 and main dishes of pies, burgers and steaks for £5-£7.
Beer, meanwhile, includes Bass (£2.10) and London Pride
(£2.20), and basic house wines cost £2.40-£2.70 a glass. In
spite of the standardisation it is popular with yuppie casuals
from the mansion blocks hereabouts, and is probably one of
the more civilised bars in this poorly provided for area.
*Babies and children admitted. Games (fruit machine, quiz
machine). No piped music or jukebox. Tables outdoors
(pavement). TV. Vegetarian dishes.*

Warrington Hotel

*93 Warrington Crescent, W9 (020 7286 2929). Maida
Vale tube.* **Open** 11am-11pm Mon-Sat; noon-10.30pm Sun.
Food served noon-2.30pm, 6-10pm daily. **Credit** MC, V.
Well-known as an exceptional example of an ornate art
nouveau-style pub, serving Thai food, the handsome
Warrington has only one drawback: its excessive
popularity. The main bar, looking like an airy Edwardian
hotel lobby, glows with the red velvet upholstery of its deep
alcove seating, and decorative motifs adorn the corpulent
semi-circular bar. Off it there are also two, smaller, brighter,
more prettily decorated side bars reserved as games rooms,
with a dartboard and satellite TV. Outside, the imposing
edifice, presiding over a residential roundabout, harbours
several terrace tables, which are warmed by gas heaters
and lent a picture-postcard appearance by three red phone
boxes. Punters have been known to beach themselves
among the flowers on the roundabout as though it were a
grassy knoll, bringing their drinks from the well stocked
bar whether wine (house £2.15/£3) or one of an excellent
set of real ales (London Pride £2.10, Young's Special £2.15,
Brakspear £2.10, Greene King IPA £2). The Ben'sThai
restaurant on the upstairs floor is always bustling, too,
serving national dishes such as weeping tiger (a hot steak
dish), or grilled prawns (both £7.50).
*Babies and children admitted. Games (darts, fruit
machine). No piped music or jukebox. Restaurant.
Satellite TV. Tables outdoors (courtyard, pavement).
Vegetarian dishes.*

Also in the area...

Café Rouge 30 Clifton Road, W9 (020 7286 2266).

Richmond, Surrey/Isleworth, Twickenham, Middlesex

Cricketers

*Maids of Honour Row, The Green, Richmond, Surrey
(020 8940 4372). Richmond tube/rail.* **Open** 11am-11pm
Mon-Sat; noon-10.30pm Sun. **Happy hour** 4-7pm Mon-
Thur. **Food served** noon-8.45pm Mon-Fri; noon-6.30pm
Sat, Sun. **Credit** MC, V.

This unpretentious pub borders the green expanse of
Richmond Green and its cricket pitch, hence the cricketing
pictures (although rugby inevitably gets a look in, too). There
is a dining room upstairs, although you can also eat in the
small downstairs bar: the food is not out to win any Michelin
stars, but the menu is longer than most and prices more than
reasonable (sausage and mash £4.25, spicy bean burger
£3.75, jacket spuds from £2.40). Service was also quick, even
at a busy time. Real ale fans are given a reasonable choice,
with Abbot Ale (£2.10) and Greene King IPA (£1.85). A
pleasant place, which, thanks to the courtyard at the back
and the green, is best suited for long summer days.
*Babies and children admitted (in restaurant). Function
room. Games (fruit machines). Quiz (music, Thur).
Restaurant. Satellite TV (big screen). Tables outdoors
(courtyard). Vegetarian dishes.*

Eel Pie

*9 Church Street, Twickenham, Middx (020 8891 1717).
Twickenham rail.* **Open** 11am-11pm Mon-Sat; noon-10.30pm
Sun. **Food served** noon-2.30pm daily. **Credit** AmEx, MC, V.

This attractive pub on villagey Church Street, just off the main
roads of Twickenham, is very popular: it was heaving with
good-natured rugby types the Saturday night we visited.
Punters are no doubt drawn by its authentic and pretty decor
– dark red and cream walls, wooden floors, dried hops hanging
here and there – friendly staff and fine selection of real ales:
regulars include Badger's Dorset Best (£2) and Tanglefoot
(£2.20), and there are several more guest beers. Rugby
cartoons and pictures, inevitably, crowd every inch of wall
space. The lunchtime menu offers traditional, hearty bar food,
and this is not a place to come looking for anything much more
sophisticated than steak and ale pie (£4.50). Another great
traditional asset, though, is a bar billiards table.
*Babies and children admitted (until 7pm). Games (bar
billiards, fruit machines). Satellite TV. Vegetarian dishes.*

London Apprentice

*62 Church Street, Isleworth, Middx (020 8560 1915).
Isleworth rail.* **Open** 11am-11pm Mon-Sat; noon-10.30pm
Sun. **Food served** 11am-2.30pm, 6-9.30pm Mon-Sat;
noon-3.30pm Sun. **Credit** AmEx, DC, MC, V.

Part of Old Isleworth, the Apprentice is perhaps a bit out of
the way for many people, but its glorious location on the river
makes it worth the effort. The interior, on the other hand, is
spacious but rather dull, with some unattractive swagged
curtains and rugby memorabilia everywhere. Staff are
amiable, and the pub is best visited in summer, when you can
bask on the riverside terrace with a pint of Morland Old
Speckled Hen (around £2.40) or Courage Directors (£2.20).
Rather uninspired and overpriced bar food (Cumberland
sausage, fisherman's pie, both £6.95) is available in the
conservatory, while the upstairs restaurant (closed on the
Saturday night we visited) has more sophisticated and
expensive offerings such as grilled red snapper (£10.95), and
a respectable wine list. Although it's not always evident, past
visitors have supposedly included Henry VII, Charles I and
II, Oliver Cromwell and Dick Turpin.

White Swan

*Babies and children admitted (until 9.30pm; eating area
only; children's menus). Function rooms. Games (darts,
fruit machine, video games, bar billiards). No-smoking
area. Quiz (Tue). Restaurant. Satellite TV. Tables outdoors
(riverside terrace). Vegetarian dishes.*

Marlborough

*46 Friars Stile Road, Richmond, Surrey (020 8940 0572/
www.marlborough.co.uk). Richmond tube/rail.* **Open** noon-
11pm Mon-Sat; noon-10.30pm Sun. **Food served** noon-
3pm, 6-9pm daily. **Credit** AmEx, MC, V.

This attractive pub at the top of Richmond Hill is deceptively
large, with a sizeable front bar that leads into a long inner room
and, beyond that, a pool table. With dark wooden furniture
and floorboards, heavy green curtains and two coal fires, it
has a cosy, secluded atmosphere. Beers include Greene King
IPA and London Pride (both £2.20), and there's a decent wine
list to match (from £2.25 a glass, £8.50 a bottle). Alongside
the usual snacks and sandwiches you can find Thai chicken
curry (£6.50) and daily specials. It makes a good stop-off from
a stroll around the town or park, and the views looking down
over the Thames are stunning; the extensive walled garden is
lovely in summer, too, when they also hold weekend barbecues.
*Babies and children admitted (until 9pm; children's menu,
garden, play area). Games (fruit machines, pool table, quiz
machine). Jukebox. Music (live bands Thur, Fri). No-
smoking area. Satellite TV (big screen). Tables outdoors
(garden, patio). Vegetarian dishes.*

Orange Tree

*45 Kew Road, Richmond, Surrey (020 8940 0944).
Richmond tube/rail.* **Open** 11am-11pm Mon-Sat; noon-
10.30pm Sun. **Food served** noon-2.30pm, 7-9.30pm Mon-
Sat; noon-2.30pm Sun. **Credit** AmEx, DC, MC, V.

The Orange Tree is looking past its best. On a Sunday afternoon, one bored barmaid slouched behind the bar while a motley crew of elderly gents nursed pints of Young's Bitter (£1.93) in the corners of the large, rather shabby room. It's busier during the week with commuters from nearby Richmond station and theatregoers from the Orange Tree Theatre (recently reopened) across the road. The upstairs theatre now only hosts a comedy club on Thursday, Friday and Saturday nights. There's a standard bar menu (cod and chips, steak, ale and mushroom pie, both £5.95) but Masquerade's restaurant downstairs does better. Apparently, the pub's name derives from Britain's first orange tree, which was planted in nearby Kew Gardens 200 years ago.
Babies and children admitted (until 8pm). Function room. Games (fruit machines). No piped music or jukebox (Sun-Thur). Restaurant. Satellite TV (big screen, rugby only). Tables outdoors (garden, front and rear). Vegetarian dishes.

Racing Page

2 Duke Street, Richmond, Surrey (020 8940 1257). Richmond tube/rail. **Open** 11am-11pm Mon-Sat; noon-10.30pm Sun. **Food served** noon-3pm, 5.30-10pm Mon-Sat; noon-6pm Sun. **Credit** AmEx, DC, MC, V.
This barn-like pub was packed on the Sunday night we visited with the young and boisterous of Richmond. Most had come to down pints of Charles Wells Bombardier (£2.30), bottles of Beck's (£2.50) or flavoured vodka and schnapps shots (£2 a throw) and shout good-naturedly at their mates while the band (the wonderfully named Uncle Funk's Free Sex & Revolution) belted out Rolling Stone covers. It's yet another revamped pub, with unvarnished floorboards, pale yellow walls and wooden tables, but has a down-to-earth air that's rather appealing. Food features prominently, with a diverse, regularly changing menu that covers Thai curries and lasagne, and there is a shortish but decent wine list. Wear black, and don't come for a quiet conversation.
Babies and children admitted. Games (fruit machines). Jukebox. Music (rock bands Sun 8.30pm). Satellite TV (big screen). Vegetarian dishes.

Triple Crown

15 Kew Foot Road, Richmond, Surrey (020 8940 3805). Richmond tube/rail. **Open** 11am-11pm Mon-Sat; noon-10.30pm Sun. **Food served** noon-2pm Mon-Sat. **No credit cards.**
This small, one-roomed boozer tucked down a lane next to the Old Deer Park has an air of friendly shabbiness. It's very much a locals' local, with a smattering of regulars perched on bar stools chatting with the motherly barmaid, and a look – dark red paintwork and carpet, dark wood panelling – that's unpretentious but a tad gloomy. It's a world away from some of the more hyper drinking sheds in Richmond. The blackboards list the 30 different real ales on rotation, including Titanic, Butcombe, and London Pride, all for a reasonable £2. The pub food, such as steak and ale pie (£3.95 or £4.25), is standard but own-made.
Function room. Music (jazz Sun 2pm). Quiz (Tue). Tables outdoors (balcony). Satellite TV. Vegetarian dishes.

White Cross

Riverside, Richmond, Surrey (020 8940 6844). Richmond tube/rail. **Open** 11am-11pm Mon-Sat; noon-10.30pm Sun. **Food served** noon-4pm daily. **Credit** DC, MC, V.
A Richmond landmark, this big, attractive old pub sits proudly on the riverside. Packed to overflowing in summer, it's a different prospect in winter; a place to spend the afternoon ensconced in a window seat, a pint of Winter Warmer (£2.50) in hand, lazily watching the river flow by.

There's a central bar, gold-starred green wallpaper, patterned carpets, green and red upholstered chairs and cosy coal fires and there's also a large upstairs room. As a Young's pub it has a good selection of wine: 14 or so by the glass (from £2.35) or bottle (from £9.75). Midweek, the food is a rather dull choice of sandwiches or dishes such as hot pie and mash, but it can get busy for Sunday lunch.
Babies and children admitted (separate room; menus, nappy-changing facilities). No piped music or jukebox. Tables outdoors (garden). Vegetarian dishes.

White Swan

26 Old Palace Lane, Richmond, Surrey (020 8940 0959). Richmond tube/rail. **Open/food** 11am-3pm, 5.30-11pm Mon-Fri; 11am-11pm Sat; noon-10.30pm Sun. **No credit cards.**
This small, low-beamed pub is just off the river, hidden up a pretty street of cottages. A clutter of tables and stools, red banquette seating, coloured glass behind the bar and decorative brassware all give it a quaint, old-fashioned air. The location means it misses out on much of the passing trade on Twickenham match days, so you will tend to find only locals appreciating its selection of beers, such as Courage Directors and Marston's Pedigree (both £2.35). Food is traditional pub fare, and there is a carvery and roast on Sundays. A rather ugly modern conservatory is tacked on at the back, but the extensive gardens are lovely in summer. Note that the bottom of the road can get flooded, blocking the way and obliging you to try a longish walk around the back.
Babies and children admitted (separate conservatory). Function room. Games (fruit machine). No piped music or jukebox. Quiz (Mon). Tables outdoors (garden, pavement tables). Vegetarian dishes.

White Swan

Riverside, Twickenham, Middx (020 8892 2166). Twickenham rail. **Open** *winter* 11am-3pm, 5.30-11pm Mon-Thur; 11am-11pm Fri, Sat; noon-10.30pm Sun; *summer* 11am-11pm Mon-Sat; noon-10.30pm Sun. **Food served** noon-2.30pm, 7-9pm Mon-Thur; noon-3pm Fri-Sun. **Credit** MC, V.
The White Swan is over three centuries old, and looks it – it oozes character and atmosphere, unlike so many revamped and prettified pubs, and even the rugby memorabilia is more interesting than usual. It sits grandly overlooking Eel Pie Island, a tourist attraction for the urban poor up from London in Victorian times, and in the 1960s one of the city's first rock venues and hangouts for the 'alternative society'. The pub is raised because the river is prone to flooding (although what happens to the ground-level toilets in such an event is anyone's guess). Both staff and punters are a cheerful lot; a boisterous birthday party was in full swing in the back room the night we visited. Beers include Courage Directors and Marston's Pedigree (both £2.20), and hot food is also available. There's also a large patio area facing the river. A perfect place to start or finish a riverside stroll or a visit to Marble Hill Park.
Babies and children admitted. Music (live band, every other Wed 8.30pm). Satellite TV. Tables outdoors (balcony, riverside garden). Vegetarian dishes.

Also in the area...

All Bar One 9-11 Hill Street, Richmond, Surrey (020 8332 7141); 26-28 York Street, Twickenham, Middx (020 8843 7281).
Bull & Bush (Edward's) 1 Kew Road, Richmond, Surrey (020 8940 5768).
Café Flo 149 Kew Road, Richmond, Surrey (020 8940 8298).

Café Rouge 7A Petersham Road, Richmond, Surrey (020 8332 2423).
Dôme 26 Hill Street, Richmond, Surrey (020 8332 2525).
Flicker & Firkin 1 Duke's Yard, Duke's Street, Richmond, Surrey (020 8332 7807).
Pitcher & Piano 11 Bridge Street, Richmond, Surrey (020 8332 2524).
Slug & Lettuce Riverside House, Water Lane, Richmond, Surrey (020 8948 7733).
Twickenham Tup 13 Richmond Road, Twickenham, Middx (020 8891 1863).

Shepherd's Bush W12

Albertine

1 Wood Lane, W12 (020 8743 9593). Shepherd's Bush tube. **Open** 11am-11pm Mon-Fri; 6.30-11pm Sat. **Food served** noon-10.45pm Mon-Fri; 6.30-10.45pm Sat. **Credit** MC, V.
Albertine is a tiny, cosy space of a wine bar with old wooden seating and candles burning on every table, that concentrates its energies on the wine theme. There are over fifty wines available, many of them by the glass (£2.30-£4.10), and with a charming loyalty to the grape, no spirits, no cocktails, and only one beer (bottled Budvar £2.50). Food is also available – the menu ranges from wild boar sausages and mash (£5.50) to smoked duck salad (£5.30) – but this is not the main draw. People come back to Albertine for the friendly, informal welcome, the intimate atmosphere and the excellent choice of wines. The coffee's good, too. Grumpy BBC staff from Television Centre complaining about being stuck out in White City (as some have been doing) should count themselves lucky. *Function room. Vegetarian dishes.*

Anglesea Arms

35 Wingate Road, W6 (020 8749 1291). Goldhawk Road or Ravenscourt Park tube. **Open** 11am-11pm Mon-Sat; noon-10.30pm Sun. **Food served** 12.30-2.45pm, 7-10.30pm, Mon-Fri; 1-3.30pm, 7-10.30pm, Sat; 1-3.30pm, 7-10pm, Sun. **Credit** DC, MC, V.
People come from a lot further afield than the ultra-gentrified Brackenbury Village, where it is situated, to enjoy the many delights of the Anglesea Arms. These include Marston Pedigree and Old Speckled Hen (both £2.30), Courage Best (£2.10), strong coffee (comes in mugs), a real-effect gas fire, wood-panelling, leather settees, charming service and a mouthwatering food menu (mains such as wild mushroom risotto and venison faggots are reasonably priced at around £7). Punters sit around discussing their agents. Are they actors, writers, TV types? Doesn't matter. In some of London's local boozers you have to watch out you don't get a broken nose; the only broken noses here were fashioned on the rugby pitch. But don't let inverse snobbery put you off because this is an excellent pub, one of the best in the west. *Babies and children admitted. No piped music or jukebox. Restaurant. Tables outdoors (patio). Vegetarian dishes.*

Colton Arms

187 Greyhound Road, W14 (no phone). Barons Court or West Kensington tube. **Open** 11.30am-3pm, 5.30-11pm Mon-Fri; 11.30am-4pm, 7-11pm Sat; 11.30am-4pm, 7-10.30pm Sun. **Food served** 11.30am-3pm Mon-Fri; 11.30am-4pm Sat, Sun. **No credit cards.**
This tiny boozer tucked behind the Queen's Club tennis courts is a cosy spot for a cold winter's evening, with its three fireplaces, nicely kept beer (London Pride £2.30, Directors

£2.40) and jovial landlord. It's amazing there's space for any punters at all in the two tiny snugs and not-much-bigger front bar, so crammed are they with antique carved-wood furniture. Dating back to the 1790s, the pub is spotless – the furniture looks as if it's polished daily, and you could do your make-up in the horse brasses – and even the patrons look freshly scrubbed. We'll even forgive them the 'Sires' and 'Wenches' signs on the toilets. Standard pub food is served at lunchtime, and the pretty back garden is a delightful spot in summer. *No piped music or jukebox. Tables outdoors (garden). Vegetarian dishes.*

Havelock Tavern

57 Masbro Road, W14 (020 7603 5374). Hammersmith, Olympia or Shepherds Bush tube. **Open** 11am-11pm Mon-Sat; noon-10.30pm Sun. **Food served** 12.30-2.30pm, 7-10pm, Mon-Sat; 12.30-3pm, 7-9.30pm, Sun. **No credit cards.**
In the Brook Green hinterland between Olympia and Shepherd's Bush, the Havelock is an attractive and deservedly popular gastropub on a spacious corner site; with the usual eclectic selection of large wooden tables and chairs, dark floorboards and posh-but-hip clientele, it wouldn't look out of place in Primrose Hill. Staff are friendly, and the food is very good: we had cod fillet with grilled fennel, salsa rosso and red chilli (£9.50) and honey roast partridge wrapped in bacon with walnut mash (both £9.50). It's owned by Whitbreads; beers on tap include Marston's Pedigree and Heineken, both for £2.50, and there's an extensive (if slightly overpriced) wine list. Get there early if you want a seat. *Babies and children admitted (high chairs). Games (board games). No piped music or jukebox. Tables outdoors (garden, pavement). Vegetarian dishes.*

Vesbar

15-19 Goldhawk Road, W12 (020 8762 0215). Goldhawk Road or Shepherds Bush tube. **Open/food served** 11am-11pm Mon-Fri; 10am-11pm Sat, Sun. **Credit** AmEx, DC, MC, V.
Vesbar is a great idea – a new, stylish, friendly, attitude-free bar in a neighbourhood that is constantly being referred to as the new Notting Hill but has little choice for the discerning drinker. Seating is comfortable, a mix of old leather settees and new wooden chairs; there's a fire in the colder months and restorative fruit smoothies (£2-£2.50) that are good for hangovers. Newspapers are provided, the place is spotless and the large cappuccino is so generously proportioned you'd be wise to order it decaf. There's a changing menu of snacks and meals from the fully cooked breakfast (£5) to the likes of panfried salmon (£8). Beers include Leffe (£.90 a half-pint) and Hoegaarden (£1.80 a half-pint). The only real problem is the music, which is invariably awful and inescapable because the whole place is speakered up. A pity this, as it would be very simple to create a music-free corner (at the front left or back right, for example, if you're reading this, Vesbar). *Babies and children admitted. Disabled: toilet. Vegetarian dishes.*

Also in the area...

Café Rouge 98-100 Shepherd's Bush Road, W6 (0171 602 7732).
Edward's 170 Uxbridge Road, W12 (020 8743 3010).
Frigate & Firkin 24 Blythe Road, W14 (020 7602 1412).
Fringe & Firkin 2 Goldhawk Road, W12 (020 8749 9861).
Slug & Lettuce 96-98 Uxbridge Road, W12 (020 8749 1987).

Balham SW12, SW17

Balham Tup

21 Chestnut Grove, SW12 (020 8772 0546). Balham tube.
Open noon-11pm Mon-Sat; noon-10.30pm Sun. **Food
served** 6-10pm Mon-Sat; noon-4pm Sun. **Credit** MC, V.
Don't be sheepish, come in for a quick dip, they won't fleece
ewe! Known locally as the fuc ('fuc-tup', ya'see), this
voluminous Victorian boozer has been transformed into a
high octane chat-up zone filled with loud rave choons, lots of
eager not-quite-thirties and supershiny polyurethane varnish.
Outside it's still quite an ornate building; inside it's been
rendered brutally functional, a brightly lit single room with
a 60ft bar and a random sprinkling of stools, tables and sofas.
Bevvies include Stella (£2.50), Heineken, Caffrey's and
Guinness, along with a few ales (Flowers IPA, Bass and
Charles Wells' Bombardier, mostly for £2.20). The food (from
a men-ewe, of course) is equally bog-standard, with soup
(£3.50), sarnies (£3.50), and such mains as vegetable pasta
(£5), plus roasts on Sundays. 'All ewe ruckin' tuppers' is how
they address their clientele, and even if you don't make this
your local, you should at least check out the very fine drunken
sheep pictures on the way to the toilet.
*Babies and children admitted (until 7pm). Disabled: toilet.
Satellite TV. Tables outdoors (terrace). Vegetarian dishes.*

Bar Interlude

*100 Balham High Road, SW12 (020 8772 9021). Balham
tube.* **Open** noon-11pm Mon-Fri; 10am-11pm Sat, Sun.
Food served noon-10pm Mon-Thur; 10am-9pm Fri, Sat;
10am-10pm Sun. **Credit** AmEx, DC, MC, V.
My old uncle George, Balham wheel-tapper and copper-
riveter, would have choked on his light and bitter if you'd told
him his native soil would one day produce a bar serving five
different kinds of coffee, where the barmen give you your
change on a fancy dish. Well, such has come to pass, and
despite these pretensions being quite alien in this
Jobcentre/charity shop strip, the results are surprisingly
favourable. First impressions suggest a chain pub in the All
Bar One mould, and the proprietors here are obviously
chasing that relaxed, inoffensive, all-purpose vibe that pulls
in the all-day punters. The wide-open layout has dining tables
at the back and a few little seating areas, with the inevitable
sofas, plus some well-chosen photographic decorations.
Importantly, the food is well above average, with a full
breakfast menu, pastas, soup, paninis (posh sandwiches,
Uncle George) and delightful waffles, not to mention daily
specials of a more substantial nature. Stella (£2.60) and
Hoegaarden (£3.60) captain the lagercentric range of
draughts, with loads of bottled beers to boot and a limited
palette of wines.
*Disabled: toilet. Music (DJs Fri, Sat). Tables outdoors
(patio). Satellite TV. Vegetarian dishes.*

Bedford

*77 Bedford Hill, SW12 (020 8673 1756/
www.thebedford.com). Balham tube/rail.* **Open** 11am-
11pm Mon-Thur; 11am-2am Fri, Sat; noon-10.30pm Sun.
Food served noon-2.45pm, 7-10pm Mon-Fri; noon-
3.30pm, 7-10pm Sat; noon-3.30pm, 7-9.45pm Sun.
Credit MC, V.
For evidence of the long-awaited Balham renaissance, look
no further than the Bedford, home to the ever-popular Banana
Cabaret comedy club (where the *Mark Thomas Comedy
Product* is filmed). Taken over and revamped in February, it's
now barely recognisable as the shabby old codgers' pub it
used to be. Both the smaller Public Bar, complete with
dartboard, football on TV and a row of chain-smoking

regulars, and the spacious Saloon have been seriously
glammed up; the Saloon's walls are now a mellow gold, and
its focal point is a huge stone fireplace with a roaring fire in
front of a leather sofa. The best addition to the soft
furnishings, though, must be the owner's enormous
Newfoundland, Bedford, who shambles around the place like
a walking carpet. Despite all this dressing up, though, the
Bedford retains its lack of pretension, and the main bar is
cosy, with a good buzz. Beers include Pedigree, Young's, 6X,
Courage and Hoegaarden, plus Foster's, Stella, Heineken and
Kronenbourg, and there's an extensive wine list, with prices
ranging from £8.95 to £24.95. Food is high quality, with
offerings such as goat's cheese salad (£5.45), chicken and leek
pie with Irish champ (£8.95), and home-made burgers (£6.50).
*Banana Cabaret (£10/£7 concs Fri, Sat). Comedy (new
acts £3 Tue). Disabled: toilet. Function room. Games
(darts, fruit machines). Late licence (Fri, Sat). Line
dancing (£5 Thur). Quiz (£3 Wed). Salsa classes (£5
Wed). Satellite TV. Vegetarian dishes.*

Duke of Devonshire

*39 Balham High Road, SW12 (020 8673 1363).
Balham tube/rail.* **Open** 11am-midnight Mon-Thur;
11am-2am Fri, Sat; noon-midnight Sun. **Food served**
11am-10pm Mon-Sat; noon-10pm Sun. **Credit** MC, V.
One of the very best pubs around Balham way, because it's
happy to serve up a traditional atmosphere, on a big scale,
in a beautiful and mostly unchanged setting. The solid gold
bonus is that it regularly does so until 2am. But nobody
should call the cops, because, while it sometimes feels like a
grand lock-in, this is all, in fact, perfectly legal. An enormous
horseshoe bar is reflected in elegant patterned glass, and the
whole looks even more magical by candlelight. The scrawny
roadside terrace pales beside a vast back garden, complete
with kid-engrossing playground. Young's beers (Special
£2.05) are all present and correct, plus a fair selection of
wines and hearty food of the steak sandwich (£4.60) or
burger and chips (£4.90) variety. The kind of place that
everyone wants to claim as their very own local; luckily it's
big enough for all-comers.
*Babies and children admitted (until 7pm; separate room;
children's play area in garden). Games (darts, fruit
machines, pinball machine, table football). Late licence.
Satellite TV. Tables outdoors (garden, open May-Sept).
Vegetarian dishes.*

Point

*16-18 Ritherdon Road, SW17 (020 8767 2660).
Balham tube/rail/Tooting Bec tube.*
Open 10am-11pm Mon-Sat; 10am-10.30pm Sun.
Food served 10am-10pm daily. **Credit** MC, V.
So deep into Balham that it's darn tootin' Tooting, and
squeezed into the kind of street where all you expect is a paper
shop, the Point is quite a surprise. Daytime it's filled with
oldsters and middle-aged couples, enjoying the kind of
bright'n'airy lunch'n'coffee ambience that the blonde-wood
chain pubs have made so much money from, while at night-
time it becomes a slightly happening resort, drawing in the
area's young mortgagees (those who shun a trip up west) and
young marrieds who'd feel lost in a more traditional boozer
(assuming they can find one). You know the formula, but let's
run through it one more time: big picture windows that open
in summer, an outside terrace, lots of tables and sofas, and a
fair range of bevvies – cocktails £4.95, bottled San Miguel
and Rolling Rock £2.50, and Hoegaarden and Terken (a
French Pilsner – both £1.95 a half-pint.
*Babies and children admitted (restaurant only; children's
menu, high chairs). Disabled: toilet. Restaurant. Satellite
TV. Vegetarian dishes.*

Bar Room Bar. *See page 156.*

Puzzle
90-92 Balham High Road, SW12 (020 8265 7243).
Clapham South tube/Balham tube/rail. **Open** noon-11pm
Mon-Tue; noon-midnight Wed, Thur; noon-1am Fri, Sat;
noon-10.30pm Sun. **Food served** noon-2.30pm, 7-10pm
Mon-Thur; noon-3pm Fri; noon-5pm Sat; noon-6pm Sun.
Happy hour 5-7pm Mon-Fri. **Credit** MC, V.
The Puzzle's blurb asks 'Is it a pub or is it a bar?', when the
question you're really asking yourself is, 'Is it a chain pub or
not?' Well, yes it is – there are about ten Puzzles in all, in and
around London. This one is kept busy by youngish locals
enjoying a cosy interior with plump sofas and *Changing
Rooms*-style terracotta decor. And while more discerning
drinkers may be deterred by a place with such an identity
crisis, these folk are positively attracted by the Puzzle's
seeming aim to be all pubs to all punters, especially for the
late-opening weekend. There's giant Jenga and Connect 4
games, TV screens blaring out from every angle, music
blasting from the speakers, a tiny beer garden, and
everything has a little label on it for the hard of thinking ('Oh,
that's the dartboard!'). Beck's is £2.40 a bottle, Theakston
XB £2 a pint, and there's bangers and mash-style food with
mains starting at a fiver.
*Disabled: toilet. Games (board games, darts, fruit
machine, quiz machine, table football). Late licence (Fri,
Sat). Music (live band Thur, DJ Sat). Satellite TV. Tables
outdoors (courtyard). Vegetarian dishes.*

Battersea SW8, SW11

All Bar One
32-38 Northcote Road, SW11 (020 7801 9951).
Clapham Junction rail. **Open** noon-11pm Mon-Sat;
noon-10.30pm Sun. **Food served** noon-10pm Mon-Sat;
noon-9pm Sun. **Credit** AmEx, MC, V.

The all-conquering idea in modern pubbery is to open as
voluminous a room as you can find, dress it with as bland an
identity as possible, and make sure you have every mass-
market drinking requirement covered. From snacks and food,
to coffees and papers, All Bar One has most of them covered
in a reliable, sanitised and unspectacular way. This ABO is
no exception – it's large, the drinks range is ample (Grolsch,
Caffrey's both £2.70; bottled lagers are £2.80, and wines by
the glass start at £2.70), the design is clear, simple and plain,
and the food falls under broad headings such as Big Plates,
Small Plates and Sandwiches (all £4.45-£10.50). You might
like to know that the ABO concept is psychologically
predetermined to appeal to women: mile-long bars prevent
those scenes of male scrummaging and the bleached-blonde
pine decor, lit by blinding arc lights, banishes dark and
threatening corners. And where women go, men will follow,
with the plain predictability of, say, an All Bar One.
Disabled: toilet. Games (board games). Vegetarian dishes.

B@1
*85 Battersea Rise, SW11 (020 7978 6595/
www.beatone.co.uk). Clapham Junction rail/Clapham
Common tube, then 35, 37 bus.* **Open** 5-11pm Mon-Sat.
Happy hour 6-8pm Mon-Thur; 6-7pm Fri, Sat.
Credit AmEx, MC, V.
'Be at One, young warrior. You are the last of your kind,' says
the teacher to the eager young bartender keen on using his
trust fund to bankroll 'the perfect venue'. Not since the sixth-
form emotion of 'The Boy and The Violin' has poetry reached
the level seen in the introduction to B@1's expensively
printed cocktail menu. Does the bar reach similar heights?
Well, it depends how forgiving you are. It's a smallish lounge
with a pitched greenhouse roof over the bar, dramatic
displays of dried flowers and electric candelabras flickering
ominously. You sense an eagerness to please, but drinks don't
come cheap. Cocktails start at £3.50, shots at £3, but if you

want a beer you'll be paying club prices (a small Michelob is £2.70). There's nothing on tap. But none of the chatty after-workers (half in suits, half went home to change first) seem to mind. On one wall we spotted some great tacky pictures of an opening party, full of drunken smiles and pink eyes, the kind of thing most pubs have stuck behind the bar. At B@1, these throwaway images are individually framed.

Bar Room Bar

441 Battersea Park Road, SW8 (020 7223 7721/ www.barroombar.co.uk). Clapham Junction or Battersea Park rail/44, 49, 319, 344 bus. **Open** 11am-11pm Mon-Sat; 11am-10.30pm Sun. **Food served** noon-10.45pm Mon-Sat; noon-10.15pm Sun. **Happy hour** 5.30-7.30pm Mon-Fri. **Credit** MC, V.

Ahh, history – you won't find much left in here. Not once you're past the elegantly hulking Victorian exterior, at least, except maybe the name the Clockhouse, its previous designation (now reduced to a bit of window-glass graphics, complete with an Internet '@'). Bar Room Bar, with a mothership bar in hammy Hampstead, is a cut above the usual we-do-everything-you'll-ever-want-in-a-pub breed, thanks to a pretty sculpture-filled garden, a relaxing atmosphere centred round a magnificent fireplace that gives the minimal decor something to work with, and the ever-present possibility of ordering a delicious pizza fresh from a wood-burning oven. Pizzas start at £4.50; if you're not so hungry, have a 'pizzette' at £2.95. You'll be among a happy mix of young professionals supping the usual nitrokeg stuff – Boddingtons (£2.40) et al, plus Guinness (£2.60) and Hoegaarden (£3.90). As to the origin of the name – your guess is as good as mine.

Disabled: toilet. Music (DJs Fri, Sat). Satellite TV. Tables outdoors (garden). Vegetarian dishes.

Le Bar des Magis

7-9 Battersea Rise, SW11 (020 7738 0307). Clapham Common tube/Clapham Junction rail/ 35, 37 bus. **Open** 10am-11pm Mon-Sat; 10-10.30pm Sun. **Food served** noon-11pm Mon-Sat; noon-10.30pm Sun. **Credit** AmEx, MC, V.

Bien sûr, mesdames et monsieurs, it is as you least expect – a real Frenchie-poo hangout here in the SW11th *arrondissement*. We love the way that Le Bar is actually a real French bar/brasserie, and not just styled to resemble one: good food, genuine Gallic bartenders, poker-faced and fully matured waiters, and a bar that's relaxed enough to get pretty raucous at times. Yes, here you can order a croque monsieur (£3.40) with your Kronenbourg (£3) – in a French accent if you like – and still not feel too much of a tosser. If you're drinking on the Rise, it's good to know that this is the survivor establishment: while all around are changing their decor every second weekend in search of the perfect concept, Les Bar is happy with the one it was born with. No one even noticed the sneaky name change from Le Bar des Amis.

Babies and children admitted (children's menu; high chairs; crèche 1-3pm Sat, Sun). Function room. Satellite TV. Tables outdoors (pavement). Vegetarian dishes.

Bar Risa

49 Lavender Gardens, SW11 (020 7228 3744). Clapham Junction rail. **Open** noon-1am Mon-Thur; noon-2am Fri, Sat; noon-10.30pm Sun. **Admission** after 10pm Fri, after 11pm Sat, £3. **Food served** noon-10.30pm daily. **Credit** AmEx, DC, MC, V.

Time was when this, the bar below legendary comedy club Jongleurs, was similar in style and atmosphere to that of a provincial hotel. Now it looks like a brash, colour-saturated teenage bedroom done by *Changing Rooms*: full of zippy

graphics and dynamic-shaped bits of MDF. It's still at its busiest in the run up to shows upstairs, but has defiantly staked its claim to a separate identity, and behold, people come here as if it were just another Technicolored Battersea pub, especially when there's footy on its huge screen. Food is better than average (pizzas, sausage and mash, steaks, from £4.25), although there are few surprises in the drinks line: Stella (£2.65), Guinness (£2.60), and John Smith's Extra Smooth (£2.40). And you also have the thrill of unisex toilets to look forward to.

Comedy (Jongleurs, £14 Fri, £12 Sat). Dance classes (Ceroc Mon, Wed). Dress code. Function room. Games (board games). Late licence (Mon-Sat). Music (DJs Fri, Sat). No-smoking area. Satellite TV (big screen). Tables outdoors (garden). Vegetarian dishes.

Base

1 Battersea Rise, SW11 (020 7228 6026). Clapham Junction rail/Clapham Common tube, then 35 or 37 bus. **Open/food served** 11am-11pm Mon-Sat; noon-10.30pm Sun. **Credit** DC, MC, V.

This prime spot at the top of the Rise has seen a rapid-fire succession of bars recently, as one after the other has fallen victim to typeface obsolescence. The latest typography looks quite promising – a shiny orange and chrome sign, so futuristic you could be forgiven for thinking this is an Internet development consultancy. It's actually a pretty swank cocktail bar, complete with such pleasures as Bloody Mary-laden jazz brunch on Sundays (£3.95-£7.95), followed up by soul evenings. For the moment at least, this trendy-looking place with its stainless steel bar seems to have won the hearts of the local jeep'n'sportscar-driving fraternity, and is pleasantly packed with under-40s on most nights and especially at weekends. Cocktails cost upwards of £4.25, and Leffe Blonde (£2.50 a half) and Budvar (£1.95 a half) are on tap.

Babies and children admitted (high chairs). Restaurant. Tables outdoors (terrace). TV. Vegetarian dishes.

Beehive

197 St John's Hill, SW11 (020 7207 1267). Clapham Junction rail. **Open** 11am-11pm Mon-Sat; noon-10.30pm Sun. **Food served** noon-3pm Mon-Sat. **No credit cards**.

In a strip that's falling prey to a rash of big, dull pub 'n' clubs, the Beehive is a fine sanctuary. It's a very pretty little boozer, with a tiny frontage, and while it arguably looks more quirky from the outside than it really is, inside you'll find a nicely unchanged Fuller's pub, complete with scuffed carpet, plenty of regulars, not too many young whippersnappers and a soundtrack that's more chat than chart. A pint of ESB is £2.25, London Pride £2.15, Chiswick Bitter £2, and there's Guinness, Heineken and Grolsch to boot. Chalkboard specials add to a sandwich and chips menu, but you wouldn't rush here for the food. Nevertheless, it's a solid, cosy little pub that's holding its own against the forces of brasserie darkness.

Games (fruit machine). Satellite TV. Vegetarian dishes.

Castle

115 Battersea High Street, SW11 (020 7228 8181/ www.thecastlebattersea.co.uk). Clapham Junction rail/14, 239, 344, 345 bus. **Open** noon-11pm Mon-Sat; noon-10.30pm Sun. **Food served** noon-3pm, 7-9.45pm Mon-Sat; noon-3pm, 6-9.30pm Sun. **Credit** MC, V.

A council estate pub born in the days of Double Diamond that's since come way up in the world (just like the surrounding neighbourhood). The Castle claims to date back to 1600, but a 1965 rebuild didn't leave much in the way of Jacobean architecture, unless you count the ancient knife-

London crawling

On the waterfront

As this guide was being compiled, the Millennium Dome was, shall we say, not doing especially well. A month or so into its year-long run, its problem was a relatively serious one – no one wanted to go. And even if things pick up and the Dome does break even, it'll still prove a source of much puzzlement as to why Tony bothered spending several squillion quid on such a baffling waste of wasteground. After all, his lackeys had already arrived at a perfectly adequate way to sell London not only to the visitors, but also to us Londoners, too. Granted, it's essentially just a walk by the river, but Millennium Mile is a nice idea, if only because a stroll along it may remind a few locals what a terrific city they live in. More enticingly, it doesn't cost 20 quid to get in, it's not an absolute bugger to get to and it'll still be there in 2001, as will all of its attractions. Which, for the purposes of this guide, are, of course, the pubs and bars that can be found on the south bank of the river between Westminster Bridge and Tower Bridge, aka the official Millennium Mile.

Having said that, the pub pickings at the start of the route are pretty slim, but things begin to improve dramatically towards the South Bank Centre: by the Festival Hall is the **Archduke**, a nicely cavernous wine bar that makes a great pre-concert meeting place, while round by Waterloo East tube is **Auberge**, a pleasingly peaceful café/restaurant with a grand range of Belgian beers. Back on the riverfront, grab a pint in the colourful **Studio Six** at Gabriel's Wharf, but pass on by the **Oxo Tower**, unless you're planning on dining: those with credit card bills to run up in the expensive restaurant bit get all the best views, with drinkers forced to invest in a stepladder in order to catch anything more than a glimpse of the river. The same goes for the **Founder's Arms**: though it's been blessed with a stunning location right on the South Bank by Blackfriars Bridge, a recent redesign hasn't extended to the lighting, which is still so hideously bright as to render any attempts at looking out through the huge windows on to the river at night wastefully moot. Still, it's around here that you'll come across some of the walk's most charming

boozers, of which the first will be the **Anchor Bankside**. A local of Samuel Johnson, who wrote parts of his dictionary in one of the many rooms here, it's a charming, slightly self-consciously old-fashioned pub that's loveliest in winter. As is the **Market Porter** by Borough Market. The Porter's clientele is as mixed as you'll find in London, with market traders there first thing in the morning (literally, as it opens at 6am) and sedate suits dominating after dark. Next up should be a couple of fine ale drinkers' establishments: the **Wheatsheaf**, an endearingly shabby pub three doors down from the Porter with an excellent and ever-changing selection of obscure bitters, and the **Bunch of Grapes**, which offers a bunch of Young's ales in a room decorated with a bunch of light wood. There's then a little bit of a slow patch. However, by this time you'll probably need some fresh air: wander down the river towards Tower Bridge and, soon enough, you'll be at the **River Bar** on Tower Bridge Road, an airy café-type place with a nice food menu, before finishing up at the ace Sam Smith's pub the **Anchor Tap** for a pint of Ayingerbrau and a game of darts. Dome Schmome.
Will Fulford-Jones

Anchor Bankside (*p164*) 34 Park Street, SE1 (020 7407 1577).
Anchor Tap (*p164*) 20A Horsleydown Lane, SE1 (020 7403 4637).
Archduke (*p103*) Concert Hall Approach, SE1 (020 7928 9370).
Auberge (*p104*) 1 Sandell Street, SE1 (020 7633 0610).
Bunch of Grapes (*no review*) 2 St Thomas, SE1 (020 7403 2070).
Founder's Arms (*p166*) 52 Hopton Street, SE1 (020 7928 1899).
Market Porter (*p166*) 9 Stoney Street, SE1 (020 7407 2495).
Oxo Tower (*p105*) Oxo Tower Wharf, Barge House Street, SE1 (020 7803 3888).
River Bar (*p166*) 206-208 Tower Bridge Road, SE1 (020 7407 0968).
Royal Oak (*p166*) 44 Tabard Street, SE1 (020 7357 7173).
Studio Six (*p105*) Gabriel's Wharf, 56 Upper Ground, SE1 (020 7928 6243).
Wheatsheaf (*p168*) 6 Stoney Street, SE1 (020 7407 1514).

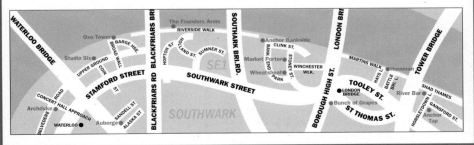

Holy Drinker

grinder in the garden. The atmosphere is warm and local, with an upmarket, over-35 emphasis – broadsheets rustle in the daytime, and a fair few wine bottles get decorked in the evenings. The food is top-notch Italian, British or French fare, with excellent weekend (organic) roasts at £7.95. The large garden is well used in warmer weather, and there's a conservatory and a sofa, too, if you can grab it. But however chatty, friendly and well-serviced a pub it is, you're still stuck in a rather joyless building. It's a Young's outlet, with 'ordinary' and Special both £2.25.
Function room. Games (board games). Tables outdoors (courtyard, garden). Vegetarian dishes.

Drawing Room & Sofa Bar

103 Lavender Hill, SW11 (020 7350 2564). Clapham Junction rail/77, 77A, 345 bus. **Open/food served** 6pm-midnight Mon-Fri; 11am-midnight Sat, Sun. **Credit** MC, V.
In a world of fawning bars doing everything they can to please, here's a lounge that really loafs. There's a wondrously relaxing shabbiness: worn red sofas and splendid bucket chairs hold you in their clutches, and once-opulent tassled drapes hang drowsily between you and the rushing world outside. This atmosphere plays best at weekends, when the Drawing Room attracts a healthy complement of skiving locals reading the papers and nibbling at coffee and croissants. It's considerably more animated in the evenings, when loud mood music permeates the smokey low-lit proceedings, but that louche feel filters through. It's hard to believe Battersea holds such a sexy downtown dive. Bottled beers predominate (Budvar £3.50, Beck's and Rolling Rock £2.65) and food from the restaurant opposite follows a Modern European menu, and is not too expensive.
Babies and children admitted (toys). Function room. Restaurant. Tables outdoors (pavement). Vegetarian dishes.

Duke of Cambridge

228 Battersea Bridge Road, SW11 (020 7223 5662). Battersea Park or Clapham Junction rail/19, 49, 344, 345 bus. **Open** 11am-11pm Mon-Sat; noon-10.30pm Sun. **Food served** noon-2.30pm, 7-9.45pm Mon-Sat; noon-2.45pm, 7.30-9.30pm Sun. **Credit** MC, V.
The Duke is a fine bewhiskered Victorian gentleman who wears a stiff frock coat and displays mutton chops so prodigious that he probably feeds them with a saucer of milk every night. His pub is a prettily updated Young's boozer with a half-covered front (heated) terrace, a spiral tree and a well-heeled clientele enjoying the early portion of middle age. There's a sofa or two and plenty of space, but rather than rip the inside to open-plan shreds, the original features have been retained and transformed with a palette of electric pinks. However, it has been irreparably transformed from pub to brasserie, with all that that implies. Food is very good (a tasty venison stew was £9.95, a classy vegetarian risotto was £6.95). Beer is the full Young's range (Special £2.20), and there's a decent wine selection.
Babies and children admitted (dining area). Disabled: toilet. Function room. Satellite TV. Tables outdoors (garden). Vegetarian dishes.

Equator

30-32 Queenstown Road, SW8 (020 7720 2442). Clapham Common tube/Queenstown Road rail/ 137 bus. **Open** noon-midnight Mon-Wed; noon-1am Thur-Sat; noon-11pm Sun. **Food served** 1-3pm, 6-11pm Mon-Thur; 1pm-midnight Fri, Sat; 1-10pm Sun. **Happy hour** 5-8pm daily. **Credit** AmEx, DC, MC, V.
A roaring trade in take-out Thai does not a cocktail bar make, and Equator can be conspicuously quiet. In fact early evening it's much more a restaurant with swank graphics than a place to enjoy a drink. But arrive, as most do, when its daily late license makes an important difference and you'll be in the crowded company of a lively bunch of young can't-go-home tipplers. Absolut has a significant presence (£2.90 with mixer), both in sponsorship terms and, alongside bottled beers (Tiger, Stella both £2.50), in what gets drunk the most. The food is above average Thai, Japanese, Indonesian and Vietnamese, speedily delivered and very affordable (set lunch is £7.50, dinner is £9.50). Happy hour is 5-8pm when cocktails are half price.
Babies and children admitted. Function room. Late licence (Thur-Sat). Music (DJs Fri, Sat). No-smoking area. Restaurant. Tables outdoors (pavement). Vegetarian dishes.

Holy Drinker

59 Northcote Road, SW11 (020 7801 0544/ www.holydrinker.com). Clapham Junction rail/35, 37 bus. **Open** 4.30-11pm Mon-Fri; noon-11pm Sat; 1-10.30pm Sun. **Credit** MC, V.
Find yourself on Northcote Road of an evening and the choice of venue is a tricky one. Do you opt to eat early and do your bevvying at one of the thoroughfare's many atmospheric restaurants, or do you grit your teeth and pitch your spot in a characterless mass-produced drinking mall? Thankfully, the Holy Drinker offers a third option – it's somewhere you can drink in the company of young and fanciable people without feeling like you're a mere digit in the chain bars' marketing strategies. A garish but nicely dimmed interior contains a curving front bar plus a split-level rear area with sofas and tables. Music is loud but not unpleasantly so and the drinking is split evenly between spirits and bottled beers, the latter drawn from a wealth of international titles (Bitburger, Budvar

both £2.50, Tiger, Summer Lightning and Froach all £2.80). Glasses of wine start at £2.40 and Guinness is on tap (£2.50). *Babies and children admitted (Sun daytime only). Music (DJ Sun). Tables outdoors (pavement). TV.*

Joe's Wine Bar
33 Lavender Hill, SW11 (020 7228 2960). Clapham Junction rail/77, 77A, 345 bus. **Open/food served** 6-11pm Tue-Fri; noon-11pm Sat; noon-10.30pm Sun. **Credit** AmEx, DC, MC, V.
Joe dropped in from New Orleans by way of the Left Bank, and what a warm and welcoming little jazzy juice joint he is. Genuinely friendly staff move around among boarded walls, ceiling fans, checked tablecloths and a gallery of mischievous black and white photos (everything from Dali's airborne cats to Ozzy Osbourne laying pipe) with a few carefully chosen Basin Street instruments thrown in. Visit in the evenings and you're doubtless here for a bottle or two of vin from their well-selected list (18 varieties on offer), but drop in at the weekend and £10 will get you Sunday lunch (any two à la carte courses), or £4.95 will provide an all day hangover brunch. All bottled beers are £2.50, and aside from San Miguel and Beck's, include the less common Barrandov.
Babies and children admitted (until 9pm; children's menus). No-smoking area. Restaurant. Tables outdoors (terrace). Vegetarian dishes.

Latchmere
503 Battersea Park Road, SW11 (020 7223 3549). Battersea Park or Clapham Junction rail/44, 49, 344, 345 bus. **Open** noon-11pm Mon-Sat; noon-10.30pm Sun. **Food served** noon-3pm, 5-8pm Mon-Fri; noon-6pm Sat, Sun. **Credit** MC, V.
Like most of the bigger pubs hereabouts, the Latchmere has been spruced up with a few up-to-date trimmings, including a new sign and a uniform graphical style. However, the bones of the place are somehow resistant to such acts of 'branding' and the atmosphere is mercifully unchanged. It still feels like the redoubtable lounge it always was, filled with locals of all stripes. Even the addition of computer terminals for surfing the web (the 'drinkernet'?) can't belittle the grand pubbiness of the place. Perhaps it's the busy upstairs theatre, or the battered old sofas that give it such authority, or maybe it's simply its position, on this busy crossroad, that keeps up its status as an old standby. Food is light but filling (baguettes and jacket potatoes, around £4), and beers include Greene King IPA (£2) and Young's Special (£2.30).
Babies and children admitted (until 8pm). Function room. Games (board games). Quiz (Tue). Satellite TV. Tables outdoors (garden). Theatre (Tue-Sun). Vegetarian dishes.

Lavender
171 Lavender Hill, SW11 (020 7978 5242). Clapham Junction rail/77, 77A, 345 bus. **Open** noon-11pm Mon-Sat; noon-10.30pm Sun. **Food served** noon-3pm, 7-11pm Mon-Fri; noon-4pm, 7-11pm Sat; noon-4pm, 7-10.30pm Sun. **Credit** AmEx, MC, V.
Although most would consider the Lavender a restaurant more than a drinks dispensary, its popular bar area often fills up to the point where the diners are rather hemmed in. Long ago a small corner pub, the glass-fronted building is now a very Battersea shade of turquoise, filled with stalked light fittings, mellow music and a cast of customers drawn from the area's more established generations of gentrifiers. What gets consumed most is wine, from a medium-sized, but well-chosen list (starting at £2.50 a glass/£8 a bottle), although there's a full range of bottled beers and spirits.

Food is very good, a brasserie-style mix of grills and salads with mains around a tenner.
Babies and children admitted (children's menus, high chairs). Tables outdoors (pavement). Vegetarian dishes.

Legless Ladder
339 Battersea Park Road, SW11 (020 7622 2112). Queenstown Road rail/44, 344 bus. **Open** noon-11pm Mon-Fri; 11am-11pm Sat; noon-10.30pm Sun. **Food served** noon-2.30pm, 7-10pm Mon-Fri; noon-9pm Sat, Sun. **Credit** MC, V.
The tiles behind the bar are filled with soldiers' songs from the World War I trenches about missing beer, mum and nookie. And while the tommies are pining for home comforts, whoever was behind the decor has been pining everything in sight. Blonde or stripped wood everywhere attempts to make this a bright and youthful drinking spot, but the remaining older elements conspire to hint at a far more dark and interesting past. Despite its split personality, you'll find a nice crowd of people here, a good mix of ages and possibly a little more down to earth than the typical Battersea drinking spot. They're enjoying Greene King IPA and Ruddle's Best at £2.20, or meals (such as fish kebabs, £6.75) that are heartier than they might sound.
Function room. Satellite TV. Tables outdoors (garden). Vegetarian dishes.

Mason's Arms
169 Battersea Park Road, SW8 (020 7622 2007). Battersea Park rail/44, 137, 344 bus. **Open** noon-11pm Mon-Sat; noon-10.30pm Sun. **Food served** noon-4pm, 6-10pm Mon-Sat; noon-4pm, 6-9pm Sun. **Credit** AmEx, MC, V.
Bang opposite Battersea Park station you'll find this spacious and lively place filled with lots of wood and a crowd of trendy young things. It's a sofas and big tables pub, an old boozer stripped and sanded to its bare bones

Latchmere

then filled with an attractive internationalist cast of staff, some of whom are nattily pierced and spiked for your entertainment. Enjoy langorous afternoons watching the footie and munching the haute grub – a global mix of homemade dishes, including breads, for between £6 and £10 (sausage and mash did the trick for us at £6.50) – or visit in the evening for an altogether more boisterous match of chat and chat-ups. Hoegaarden is £3.20, Brakspear Bitter is £2.20, Boddingtons £2.35 and Wadworth 6X is £2.25.
Babies and children admitted. Disabled: toilet. Tables outdoors (pavement). Vegetarian dishes.

S Bar & Restaurant
37 Battersea Bridge Road, SW11 (020 7223 3322). Clapham Junction rail/South Kensington tube/bus 19, 49, 219, 345. **Open** noon-11pm Mon-Wed; noon-midnight Thur-Sat; noon-10.30pm Sun. **Food served** noon-3pm, 6.30-10pm Mon-Fri; 6.30pm-midnight Sat; noon-4pm Sun. **Credit** AmEx, MC, V.
Voluminous green awnings shade a spacious corner bar that's well positioned (opposite the Royal College of Art sculpture school and very close to a big hall of residence of the London Institute) to coax in lots of arty young creative types for some good vibes and loud socialising. A big Caxtonian S is their emblem though no one could explain what it stood for. Daytimes see groups of students lounging on overstuffed sofas, sorting out the aesthetic problems of the world, in between gazing for inspiration at the central fishtank and munching on snacks like crostini and meals from around the world (mains £5.95-£7.50). Very sunny in the summer, and, when the dance classics megamix goes on, a little louder at weekends. Kronenbourg is £2.50, John Smith's Extra Smooth £2.40, and bottled beers cost from £2.50.
Babies and children admitted (until 6pm). Disabled: toilet. Games (fruit machine). Function room. Music (DJ Fri, Sat). Satellite TV. Vegetarian dishes.

South Circular
89 Battersea Rise, SW11 (020 7207 0170). Clapham Common tube, then 35 or 37 bus/Clapham Junction rail. **Open** 5.30-11pm Mon-Sat; 5.30-10.30pm Sun. **Happy hour** 5.30-8pm daily. **Credit** MC, V.

A most un-Battersea bolt-hole this, arriving as it does from the Space 1999 school of curvilinear design. Bright diffused lighting brings out the splendid colours (orange, maroon, silver and white), while a central concrete pod of a bar serves the two drinking areas. The front of the sharp hideaway has bar stools and a single window-based table; the back room is a comfy little lounge filled with neo-'70s furniture and vivid illuminated perspex. What's unusual for these parts is that South Circular (the road it's on, fact fans) actually achieves its design ambitions, rather than just giving a clueless nod to flash decor. Consequently, it attracts the trendier young pretties of hereabouts, serving them cocktails and bottled beers including Freedom (£2.20), Peroni and Budvar (both £2.40). Make what you will of the fact that its cocktail chart shows the chic Sea Breeze holding the top slot, with declassé vodka 'n' Red Bull (£5) way down at number four. Quietish music completes the picture of a relaxing Soho bar, transposed way out south-west.
Games (board games).

Tearoom des Artistes
697 Wandsworth Road, SW8 (020 7652 6526). Clapham Common tube or Wandsworth Town rail/77, 77A, 137, 345 bus. **Open** 5.30pm-1am Thur-Sun. **Food served** 5.30pm-12.30am Thur-Sun. **Credit** (in restaurant only) MC, V.
No one knows when they'll ever finish the Artesian Well bar next door, which seems to have been undergoing refurbishment for a couple of years, but judging by the obnoxious sculpture poking out from it that's not entirely a bad thing. The Tearoom itself is a bright and airy two-floored hangout attracting the hipper residents of Battersea. Not too many are actual artists, I'd wager, unless you count graphic designers and advertising creatives, but there is plenty of arty decor to merge with: pretty Catalonian colours and quirky bits of salvaged stuff, Miró-esque chairs set against a rustic interior. Bar snacks are wholesome and give a good indication of the quality of the attached restaurant (tortilla £2.50, sausage and mash £7.50, moules £5.50). There's a nice garden and, if you want to take on the smog, a terrace overlooking Wandsworth Road. Note the limited opening hours.
Function room. Games (table football). Music (DJs Thur-Sun). Restaurant. Tables outdoors (garden). Vegetarian dishes.

Woodman
60 Battersea High Street, SW11 (020 7228 2968). Clapham Junction rail/239 bus. **Open** 11am-11pm Mon-Sat; noon-10.30pm Sun. **Food served** noon-10pm Mon-Sat; noon-9.30pm Sun. **Credit** MC, V.
You sense a little unresolved conflict here, since this admirable pub is but yards away from another hostel claiming the name of the Original Woodman. The upstart, non-original Woodman (under the emblem of a stoic groundsman wielding his chopper) is a splendid old-style pub, fronted with enamel tiles and filled with innumerable cask-based brews, interesting pub grub and no end of creaking wooden bits. A fine range of beers and ales, including offerings from Dorset's Badger Brewery (Best £2.10, IPA £2.05) plus Wadsworth 6X (£2.25) and Hofbrau lager (£2.35), is served from the old horseshoe bar. The kitchen cooks up tasty grub (try the Woodman's Original: chilli, pecuitos, mushrooms and breaded goujons, £4.95). Billiards is free 3-6pm and they've just got digital television for watching pin-sharp Chelsea games.
Babies and children admitted. Function room. Games (fruit machine, pool table, table football, video games). Quiz (Tue). Satellite TV. Tables outdoors (garden). Vegetarian dishes.

Also in the area...

All Bar One 7-9 Battersea Square, SW11
(020 7326 9831).
Bar Coast 281 Lavender Hill, SW11
(020 7924 8020).
Café Rouge 39 Parkgate Road, SW11
(020 7924 3565).
Faraday & Firkin 66A-66C Battersea Rise, SW11
(020 7801 9473).
Fine Line 33-37 Northcote Road, SW11
(020 7924 7387).
Pitcher & Piano 94 Northcote Road, SW11
(020 7738 9781).
Slug & Lettuce 4 St John's Hill, SW11
(020 7924 1322).

Bermondsey, Rotherhithe, SE16

Angel

*101 Bermondsey Wall East, SE16 (020 7237 3608/
www.famousangel.co.uk). Bermondsey tube.* **Open**
11.30am-11pm Mon-Sat; noon-10.30pm Sun. **Food served**
noon-2.30pm, 7-9.30pm Mon-Sat; noon-2.30pm Sun.
Credit AmEx, DC, MC, V.
The Angel dates back to the fifteenth century, since when
regulars have included Samuel Pepys, who mentioned it in his
diary, and Judge Jeffreys, who used it as a vantage point from
which to watch pirates being drowned at Execution Dock on
the opposite bank. These days, it's frequented during the week
by City and Docklands businessfolk, and at weekends by
residents of this socially mixed part of Bermondsey. The view
of the river, most particularly of Tower Bridge, is still arresting,
though the bar itself is pretty routine apart from its unusual
octagonal shape – it used to be five small bars – and the historic
photographs of life on the river that line the walls. Beers on
draught include Greenall's (£2), with house wine costing £3.50
a glass. The restaurant specialises in meat and fish dishes (liver
and bacon £12.95, Normandy scallops £15.50).
*Function room. Games (fruit machine). Restaurant. Tables
outdoors (riverside patio). Vegetarian dishes.*

Blacksmith's Arms

*257 Rotherhithe Street, SE16 (020 7237 1349). Canada
Water or Rotherhithe tube.* **Open** noon-11pm Mon-Sat;
noon-10.30pm Sun. **Food served** 6.30-11pm Tue-Sat; noon-
6pm Sun. **Credit** (restaurant only) AmEx, DC, MC, V.
The chances are you'll have had a long walk to get here – it's
on one of the longest streets in London – but at least you'll have
worked up a thirst for one of the draught beers (London Pride
£1.98, ESB £2.26). The Blacksmith's Arms is an old-fashioned,
wood-panelled, working-class Fuller's pub that has survived
the destruction of the old wharves and terraced dockers' houses
that once surrounded it to accommodate the expensive mock-
Georgian townhouses. It's a good place for foodies: there's
straightforward pub grub in the main bar (plaice and chips
£6.95, mackerel salad £5.95), and a separate first-floor
restaurant specialising in steaks (£11.95-£15.95).
*Babies and children admitted. Games (darts, fruit
machines, pool table). Restaurant. Tables outdoors
(garden). Vegetarian dishes.*

Mayflower

*117 Rotherhithe Street, SE16 (020 7237 4088). Canada
Water or Rotherhithe tube.* **Open** noon-11pm Mon-Sat;
noon-10.30pm Sun. **Food served** 6.30-9pm Tue-Sat; noon-
4pm Sun. **Credit** AmEx, DC, MC, V.

Mayflower

Arguably the best of the London seafaring inns, the *Mayflower* is certainly one of the most authentic, with its narrow settles, rackety wooden floors and small, dark rooms. Dating from the sixteenth century, it is rumoured that it was constructed partly from ship's timbers from the Mayflower, which moored here before sailing for America. It's a perfect all-year-round pub: they stoke up some blazing fires in winter, while summertime sees the opening-up of the open-air rear section, built on piles directly over the river. Greene King Triumph (£2.06) is one of the more unusual beers on offer, and there's a strong wine list (£6.95-£10.95 a bottle) that helps in observing the motto above the fireplace: 'A warm hearth and fine wine soothes the soul and passes time.'
Babies and children admitted (restaurant only). Games (fruit machine). Music (live bands 8-11pm Mon, Tue). Quiz (Thur). Restaurant. Tables outdoors (riverside terrace). Vegetarian dishes.

Spice Island
163 Rotherhithe Street, SE16 (020 7394 7108). Rotherhithe tube. **Open** 11am-11pm Mon-Sat; noon-10.30pm Sun. **Food served** noon-9pm Mon-Sat; noon-5pm Sun. **Credit** AmEx, MC, V.
A local landmark – especially from the other side of the river – on the site of a spice warehouse, this is a modern, rambling and very woody bar, popular with tourists and young locals. Different areas of the ground floor cater for different needs: there are pool tables and games machines at one end, and big tables with lovely river views at the other. The huge central bar serves an unusually large selection of beers (Old Speckled Hen £2.50, Flowers Original £2.22), while sturdy wooden staircases lead to a galleried upper bar and restaurant. The menu is reasonably priced, with lasagne verdi (£4.95) and cod challenge (£6.95) typical of the dishes on offer. There's a huge terrace outside.
Babies and children admitted (until 8pm; children's menu, high chairs). Disabled: lift, toilet. Games (fruit machine, pool table, quiz machine). Music (DJs Fri, Sat). No-smoking area (in restaurant). Restaurant. Satellite TV. Tables outdoors (riverside terrace). Vegetarian dishes.

Blackheath SE3

British Oak
109 Old Dover Road, SE3 (020 8858 1082). Blackheath or Charlton rail. **Open/food served** 11am-11pm Mon-Sat; noon-10.30pm Sun. **Credit** AmEx, DC, MC, V.
A typically solid two-bar '30s pub catering almost entirely to locals: check out the hand-painted portraits in the saloon bar to see who the real regulars are. The furniture is chunky, wooden and traditional, and scattered uniformly around the bar. Food is a big thing here: there are literally dozens of bargain-priced dishes available, varying from three-cheese pasta bake and filled jacket potatoes to fish and chips and chicken jalfrezi and rice, under £3 for a sizeable dollop. The smaller public bar at the front of the pub seems the preserve of men – predominantly middle-aged and blue collar – sipping pints of Courage Directors (£2.10) and lager.
Babies and children admitted (children's menus). Games (bar billiards, board games, darts, fruit machine, quiz machine). No piped music or jukebox. Satellite TV. Tables outdoors (patio, pavement, garden). Vegetarian dishes.

Cave Austin
7-9 Montpelier Vale, SE3 (020 8852 0492). Blackheath rail. **Open** 11am-midnight Mon-Sat; 11am-10.30pm Sun. **Food served** noon-10.30pm Mon-Fri; 11am-10.30pm Sat; 11am-9.30pm Sun. **Credit** MC, V.

The decor at this trendy new watering and feeding hole for the great and good of south-east London gives it a luxurious feel that Fred and Wilma could only dream about. The walls are painted sandy beige, with false windows housing displays of twigs in vases; optic light sculptures border the large picture windows on to the street. The restaurant is lightly regimented with Scandinavian-style wood furniture, serving delights of the spiced chorizo sausage with artichoke and rosemary risotto (£11.50) variety; mussels tossed in pine nuts is one of several starters and priced around a fiver, while the £4-and-under sweets include cherry roly poly and vanilla spaghetti. To the right of the restaurant is the bar, back-lit and metal-stylish, serving a variety of bottled beers (£2.50), cocktails and wines. As might be expected, the clientele represent the younger end of Blackheath's property-owning classes.
Babies and children admitted (in restaurant). Function room. Music (DJs various evenings, live music 8.30pm Wed). Restaurant. Tables outdoors (garden). Vegetarian dishes.

Crown
49 Tranquil Vale, SE3 (020 8852 0326). Blackheath rail. **Open/food served** 11am-11pm Mon-Sat; noon-10.30pm Sun. **Credit** AmEx, MC, V.
One of Blackheath's least overwhelming pubs, yet also one of the village's oldest buildings. The Crown used to be a staging post for horse-drawn buses to the City, though there's been a pub on the site since around 1740. The walls are pleasantly wood-panelled; in winter, there's a roaring fire to warm the cockles (and the muscles). The emphasis seems to be on real ale – Theakston Best (£2.08) and Charles Wells' Bombardier (£2.22) took our fancy – and on food, which falls within strictly orthodox lines: gammon steak (£5.25), scampi and chips (£4.95) and the like. It all seems to go down well with the clientele, a mix of twentysomething rugby types, well-dressed estate agents and media gals, and ruddy-cheeked middle-aged beer-swillers.
Games (fruit machine, video game). Quiz (Tue). Tables outdoors (pavement). Vegetarian dishes.

Hare & Billet
Hare & Billet Road, SE3 (020 8852 2352). Blackheath rail. **Open** 11am-11pm Mon-Sat; noon-10.30pm Sun. **Food served** noon-7pm daily. **Credit** MC, V.
The Hare & Billet used to be a lone building on the edge of the heath, and was a staging post between London and Dover until fashionable Blackheath caught up with the pub. These days, the interior is tasteful cream and beige with wooden floors, sturdy furniture and a nifty little raised area. There's seldom a seat to be had even on midweek nights, and a good number of the twenty- and thirtysomething professionals and students who flock into Blackheath end up here. The selection of real ales at this non-regimental branch of the Hogshead chain is wide if somewhat predictable – Abbot Ale (£2.35), Marston's Pedigree and Flowers (both £2) caught our eye – though there are regular guest beers. Food is pretty decent and falls within the £4-£6 bracket.
Games (quiz machine). No-smoking area (noon-9pm). Vegetarian dishes.

Princess of Wales
1A Montpelier Row, SE3 (020 8297 5911). Blackheath rail. **Open** noon-11pm Mon-Sat; noon-10.30pm Sun. **Food served** noon-9pm daily. **Credit** MC, V.
Of all the pubs in Blackheath, this is usually the busiest and, inevitably, the noisiest. Sitting on the northern end of the heath and offering two bars and a conservatory, this Georgian pub was once the home of Blackheath RFC, the world's oldest open rugby union club. Indeed, it still retains a sporty air,

with Sky Sports beamed into the public bar. Bass and London Pride (both £2.10) top the list of real ales, with the likes of Caffrey's (£2.30) and Grolsch (£2.40) for those who like it cold and/or creamy. The seats and sofas are comfortable, though you'll usually find examples of young and probably male local humanity sprawled over most upholstered areas. Drinking on the heath is allowed – unlike at other local hostelries, though it's plastic glasses only – and hearty pub grub is available to those who desire it.

Disabled: toilet. Games (fruit machine, quiz machine). Satellite TV. Tables outdoors (garden, patio). Vegetarian dishes.

Also in the area...

Café Rouge 16-18 Montpelier Vale, SE3 (020 8297 2727).
Fairway & Firkin 16 Blackheath Village, SE3 (020 8318 6637).

Borough, London Bridge, Tower Bridge, SE1

Anchor Bankside

34 Park Street, SE1 (020 7407 1577). London Bridge tube/rail. **Open** 11am-11pm Mon-Sat; noon-10.30pm Sun. **Food served** noon-2.30pm, 6-9.30pm daily; bar snacks noon-5pm Sat, Sun. **Credit** AmEx, DC, MC, V.
This dark, labrynthine pub is extremely popular whether it's the tourist season or not. Strangely, despite its auspicious history (there has been a pub on this site for over 1,000 years), it was filled with thumping techno on the evening we visited, which made an interesting contrast with the Samuel Johnson Room – a genuinely notable site, as Johnson rented it from the then landlady, Mrs Thrale, and wrote part of his dictionary here. There's quite a bit of patronage from the staff of the nearby *Financial Times* and Lloyd's, which are both a short walk away. During the summer they battle it out with tourists at the bar for Bass and Flowers (both £2.20).
Function room. Games (fruit machine). Restaurant. Tables outdoors (riverside terrace). Vegetarian dishes.

Anchor Tap

20A Horsleydown Lane, SE1 (020 7403 4637). London Bridge or Tower Hill tube/Tower Gateway DLR. **Open** 11.30am-11pm Mon-Sat; noon-10.30pm Sun. **Food served** noon-9pm Mon-Sat; noon-6pm Sun. **Credit** MC, V.
This is a fine pub and with prices that you just can't ignore. Sam Smith's on tap is always a good sign for both taste buds and wallet, and a flavourful pint of bitter is just £1.52, while the house lager is £1.78. The pub was, sadly, rather empty on our visit, but there's no reason why it should be – staff are friendly and it has a good down-home feel. There's no pine and only basic pub food, but that's to be applauded, for this is definitely a pub and not a place to come for a meal. There's a room for families, a pool room and an extra bar upstairs, which is less characterful than the rooms below.
Babies and children admitted (high chairs). Function room. Games (fruit, pinball machine, pool table). No-smoking area (restaurant). Quiz (Tue). Restaurant. TV. Tables outdoors (garden). Vegetarian dishes.

Belushi's

161 Borough High Street, SE1 (020 7939 9700/www.st-christophers.co.uk). London Bridge tube/rail. **Open** 11am-11pm Mon-Wed; 11am-midnight Thur, Sat; 11am-12.30am Fri; 11.30am-10.30pm Sun. **Food served** 11am-3pm,

6-10pm Mon-Wed; 11am-3pm, 6-11pm Thur; 11am-3pm, 6-11.30pm Fri; 11am-midnight Sat; 11.30am-10.30pm Sun. **Happy hour** 5-8pm Mon-Fri. **Credit** MC, V (over £10).
This recently built party bar is allied with the nearby St Christopher Inn – 'the hostel with attitude', we kid you not – and aimed presumably at young visitors and resident office workers. The Wednesday night we visited it was all but deserted (a fluke, we were assured), which gave us a chance to admire the split-level aluminium and wood flooring, movie and music posters plastered to the walls, and the minor league rock 'n' roll artefacts dotted around the place. Beers of the keg Courage Best (£2.10) and Foster's (£2.20) type are on draught and bottles include Budweiser, Miller (both £2.20) and Bacardi Breezers (£2.50). If it had only been Tuesday (between 5pm and 9pm), we could have snaffled two two-pint woo woo jugs (whatever they are) for the price of one. Food includes burgers (all under a fiver) as well as the likes of caper and olive pasta (£5.95) and sausage and mash (£6.50).
Babies and children admitted. Function room. Music (DJ Fri; live bands Thur, Sat). Vegetarian dishes.

Blue Eyed Maid

173 Borough High Street, SE1 (020 7378 8585). Borough tube. **Open** 11am-11pm Mon-Fri. **Food served** noon-4pm, 5-9.30pm Mon-Fri. **Credit** MC, V (£5 minimum).
This long, thin pub was gentrified a year or so ago into a bistro-style bar. Now the large windows looking out on to Borough High Street are draped in venetian blinds and the clientele seems less suit-intensive than in most other local boozers. The stripped floorboards and chunky wooden furniture come as no surprise, and the wood feature continues with floor-to-ceiling shelving behind the serving area that is crammed with wine bottles. Other drinks include draught Grolsch and London Pride (£2), plus the usual bottled suspects. The food menu holds few surprises, but it is all fresh, GM-free and well cooked, with a lunchtime menu that includes mushroom ravioli (£5.95) and beer battered cod and chips (£6.45). They serve simpler snacks in the evening.
Function room. Games (fruit machine). Tables outdoors (pavement). Vegetarian dishes.

Cantina Vinopolis

1 Bank End, SE1 (020 7940 8333). London Bridge tube/rail. **Open/food served** noon-3pm, 6-10pm Mon-Fri; noon-5pm Sat, Sun. **Credit** AmEx, MC, V.
This vast cavern of a wine bar has a suitably encyclopaedic wine list. The only problem you may find is that the 190 wines on the list are all remarkably familiar. However, when the wine list only has one Gewürztraminer and it's from the USA, it seems like a missed opportunity. The wines all seemed to be sourced from the high street wine shops, which further adds to the feeling that this place lacks balls. Having said that, the space is fantastic – a railway arch that's been converted into a cathedral of brick – and if you love wine, at least you know that there's plenty in stock. Wines start at £2 a glass.
Babies and children admitted. Function room. No piped music or jukebox. Restaurant. Vegetarian dishes.

Cynthia's Cyberbar

4 Tooley Street, SE1 (020 7403 6777/www.cynbar.co.uk). London Bridge tube/rail. **Open** noon-11pm Mon-Sat. **Food served** noon-3pm, 5-10pm Mon-Sat. **Credit** AmEx, MC, V.
Walking into this bar is like walking into the home of a *Blake's 7* and *Blue Peter* fan – the sticky-back plastic futuristic look has a kitschy, Biddy Baxter feel to it. In a series of mirrored caverns are stools, tables, pulsing disco lights and two star attractions: Cynthia and Rastus, two huge robots that make

Cynthia's Cyberbar

your cocktails. Order from a bewildering array of 30 soft and 60 hard drinks, whether it's the appealing Martians Blood (£6.80) or the charming Alien Vomit (£6.30), and watch the robot mix it for you. The clientele is disparate to say the least – two Arran sweater-wearers amid the post-work revellers looked like fell-walkers gone awry. Serious sympathy goes out to the staff, who have to wear sub-standard Trekkie outfits. It's well worth a visit despite it all.
Babies and children admitted. Function room. Music (DJs most nights). No-smoking area. Restaurant. Vegetarian dishes.

Founder's Arms
52 Hopton Street, SE1 (020 7928 1899). Blackfriars tube/rail. **Open** 11am-11pm Mon-Sat; noon-10.30pm Sun. **Food served** noon-8.30pm Mon-Sat; noon-8pm Sun. **Credit** AmEx, MC, V.
The name might suggest an old-fashioned pub, but it was probably designed by the same firm that created your local yellow-brick schoolhouse in the 1960s. Whatever, it's not history you come here for, it's the view as the Founder's Arms is perched right on the edge of the Thames. The wrap-around windows allow a view of St Paul's that is knockout, especially at night, and during the summer there's quite a bun fight for tables outside. Its location next door to the new Tate at Bankside, a pint of Young's (£2.05) or Special Bitter (£2.20) and the panorama make for a perfect place to rest your feet.
Games (fruit machines). No-smoking area. Tables outdoors (riverside patio). Vegetarian dishes.

George Inn
77 Borough High Street, SE1 (020 7407 2056). Borough tube/London Bridge tube/rail. **Open** 11am-11pm Mon-Sat; noon-10.30pm Sun. **Food served** noon-3pm daily. **Credit** AmEx, MC, V.
If you fancy going drinking in ye olde style, then this is the place to come. It is really a series of interconnecting little rooms, which can leave you feeling like you're drinking in a corridor, and is constantly popular with locals, office workers and particularly tourists, due to its illustrious history – it is London's only surviving galleried coaching inn and once hosted the likes of Johnson, Boswell and Dickens. In the summer the courtyard outside is filled to overflowing and whatever the weather it always hosts interesting guest beers such as Abbot Ale (£2.35) and Restoration bitter (£2.30).
Babies and children admitted (high chairs). Function rooms. Games (quiz machine). No piped music or jukebox. No-smoking room. Restaurant. Tables outdoors (courtyard). Vegetarian dishes.

Market Porter
9 Stoney Street, SE1 (020 7407 2495). London Bridge tube/rail. **Open** 6-8.30am, 11am-11pm Mon-Sat; noon-10.30pm Sun. **Food served** noon-2.30pm daily. **Credit** AmEx, DC, MC, V.
This is a place to take the real ale fan in your life. With at least 30 real ales usually on offer, it's a great place to experiment with different brews and stroke your beard while you do it. This is a classic man's pub: dark, low-ceilinged and smoky. It's decorated in 'interesting' style with a variety of stuffed animals that look as though they've not seen the best taxidermist in town – a personal favourite is a stuffed goat's head complete with goatee beard. Food is pretty much standard and it's the beers people flock here for: expect to tussle for a spot at the bar to order the likes of Harvey's bitter (£2.05), Three Sheep, White Dwarf (both £2.25) or Crouch Vale Fine Pale Ale (£2.40).
Games (darts, fruit machine, quiz machine). Function room. Restaurant. Satellite TV. Vegetarian dishes.

Old Thameside Inn
Pickfords Wharf, 1 Clink Street, SE1 (020 7403 4243). London Bridge tube/rail. **Open** 11am-11pm Mon-Fri; noon-6pm Sat, Sun. **Food served** noon-2.30pm daily. **Credit** AmEx, MC, V.
Another modern bar-cum-pub with little architectural charm. In fact, it could be anywhere in the UK, but the brilliant views save it from obscurity. This is a busy, bustling place packed with tourists and local workers enjoying a pint of Adnams Bitter (£2.20) or a glass of wine (£2.30). As a punter noted as he walked in, 'It looks like a Beefeater to me.' But if you fancy a drink by the river and you can manage to fight your way past the crowds, then this is the place for you.
Babies and children admitted (in restaurant). Disabled: toilet. Games (fruit machine, pool table, quiz machine, video games). Function room. No-smoking area. Restaurant. Tables outdoors (riverside terrace). TV. Vegetarian dishes.

Ring
72 Blackfriars Road, SE1 (020 7928 2589). Southwark tube. **Open** 11am-11pm Mon-Fri; noon-3pm, 7.30-11pm Sat; noon-3pm, 7.30-10.30pm Sun. **Food served** 11am-2.30pm Mon-Fri; noon-2.30pm Sat, Sun. **No credit cards**.
The Jubilee Line has finally come to Southwark, but so far the Ring remains unchanged. As you may have guessed from its name, the Ring is a homage to boxing – it's situated across the street from the old Blackfriars Ring. An old-fashioned, no-nonsense pub, the Ring may be as anachronistic as the facial hair featured in the yellowed photos of pugilists of old, but it's all the better for it. At least until gentrification forces the landlord to bring in designer lagers from abroad, beers include Tetley's Bitter and Burton Ale (£2.20).
Satellite TV. Tables outdoors (pavement). Vegetarian dishes.

River Bar
206-208 Tower Bridge Road, SE1 (020 7407 0968). London Bridge tube/rail/Tower Hill tube/Tower Gateway DLR. **Open** 11am-11pm Mon-Sat; noon-10.30pm Sun. **Food served** noon-9.30pm daily. **Credit** AmEx, MC, V.
No real view of the river, but a great view of Tower Bridge as you cross the road to get to the bar. This brasserie lacked zip the night we visited, but that might be due to the excessively bright lights destroying any kind of atmosphere that the punters were generating – on a busy night, or lunchtime, when this place is popular with nearby office workers, things are a bit better. Hoegaarden (£3.85 a pint), Budvar (£2.60) and Kronenbourg (£2.45) are on tap, and an ample bottled beer selection is £2.55 each. Food includes steak, salmon, chicken and casseroles, all around the £8 mark. For a more earthy feel try the bar downstairs, which is darker, less polished and plays host to bands and DJs.
Function room. Music (live band 8pm Thur; live acoustic music, £3.50 8pm-midnight Tue, Wed). Satellite TV. Tables outdoors (pavement). Vegetarian dishes.

Royal Oak
44 Tabard Street, SE1 (020 7357 7173). Borough tube/London Bridge tube/rail. **Open** 11am-11pm Mon-Fri. **Food served** noon-3pm, 6-9pm daily. **Credit** DC, MC, V.
Walking down this quiet street you may think you're heading in the wrong direction for a pub, and then the Royal Oak comes into view. It's a hustling, bustling kind of place with the barmaid keeping a beady eye on proceedings and cleaning the ashtrays with alarming regularity. It's a Harvey's pub and consequently there are some decent brews on offer including

Southern comfort

There's no point beating about the bush. The Brixton pub crawl is the plaything of crooks, clubbers, geezers, posers, flakes, drifters, the interminably trendy, and the eternally bored. This is a place where serious bar-hopping has nothing to do with bonhomie, and everything to do with slipping the moorings of safe city life. The simple joy of getting trashed in these postcodes is to experience the frontier mentality of London's most unpredictable clash of cultures.

The recommended assembly points are deliberately ghastly affairs. For purely practical purposes, they are the closest pubs to the tube and rail stations, and are magnificently anonymous. The **Flourmill & Firkin** is a bland link in this ubiquitous pub chain, but, with its huge glass front, it is reassuringly impossible to miss. Directly across the road is a JD Wetherspoon pub, the **Beehive**. To spend more than an hour in either can inspire depressing thoughts (note the ominous gilt motto above the door to the Flourmill: *usque ad mortem bibendum*).

The first real stop is the **Trinity Arms**, ten minutes away, a quirky oasis in one of Brixton's eerily silent, residential squares. Misty-eyed regulars are seduced by the sense of ease, and Young's beers. Cheery prints of the Royal Family pulling pints above the bar have probably never even been noticed since the day they were hung. The truly lovely thing is that no one really notices much at all: that's the golden mean of a decent local. The atmosphere is as comfortable and old-fashioned as a hot-water bottle.

The **Z Bar & Brasserie** is less than a minute and a world away. This is a seriously creamy, soul venue. But, during happy hour (5-7pm), time, perhaps, to slip off the anorak and expose your new, matt black, leather T-shirt. Expediency is wildly in its favour: Tesco is just across the road (for tobacco, Lottery tickets...) and the brasserie serves cappuccinos, and chicken casserole dinners (£6.95). But more importantly, this is where the cocktail depth charges can be laid, flirtations can be made, and – if your evening comes off the rails – dances can be danced.

Babushka, worth every second of the eight minutes' walk, lies buried under one of Brixton's biggest housing estates. Why here? Why now? Because it's so fabulously at odds with its environment. With its long L-shaped, aluminium bar, blood-red walls, guttering candles and twinkling fairy lights, Babushka

is deliciously caught between pre-club bar, Christmas tree and local pub. Beautiful girls and men dressed, Mafia-style, in black shuffle self-consciously between the bar and a domino spread of big wooden tables. This is thirty- to fortysomething sophistication in terms of dress, testosterone and demeanour. And curiously democratic in terms of wine-, cocktail- and beer-drinkers. Again, it offers dancing opportunities, but not loud enough to spoil the adventure.

Back towards Brixton, and in the crypt of St Matthew's church lies the **Bug Bar**. Keep this visit short and simple. The novelty is entirely in the cavern-like location, inexpensive (exotic) bar nibbles, and the Ikea sofas parked in front of a DJ turntable. If you wear Joe 90 specs, and love trippy, ambient music, this is the place for you. Earlier in the evening, it's like the chill-out room in a nightclub: full of polo necks, polite icy chit-chat and meticulously hip 20-year-olds. Enjoy the lizardy feel before 10pm (when you have to pay to enter), but leave before the anaesthetised cool numbs you.

The **Fridge Bar** opposite should be treated, again, as a hitching post to better things. This is the first serious springboard to the local clubs (OK, the Fridge next door). Don't look too hard for bar stools in this wedge of yellow space. This is strictly drinks and lean-to. Treat it as do most of the people in here, as a place to gather both your wits and stray crawlers.

The real jewel is on Coldharbour Lane. This is bar clubland, where the **Dogstar** (£5 entrance after 10pm) is the place to be to gather what's left of your evening. Here, in all honesty, is the most eclectic crowd you're ever likely to meet in London. Rastas, gays and models. The large, cruisy bar helps. If you've got anything left to say at this point, the regulars – gentle as a T – will pat you on the head and tell you to kindly fuck off home.

James Christopher

Babushka (*no review*) 40 St Matthew's Road, SW2 (020 7274 3618).
Beehive (*no review*) 405-409 Brixton Road, SW2 (020 7738 3643).
Bug Bar (*p169*) The Crypt, St Matthew's Peace Garden, Brixton Hill, SW2 (020 7738 3184).
Dogstar (*p169*) 389 Coldharbour Lane, SW9 (020 7733 7515).
Flourmill & Firkin (*no review*) 450 Brixton Road, SW9 (020 7737 4892).
Fridge Bar (*p169*) 1 Town Hall Parade, Brixton Hill, SW2 (020 7326 5100).
Trinity Arms (*p171*) 45 Trinity Gardens, SW9 (020 7274 4544).
Z Bar & Brasserie (*p172*) 30 Acre Lane, SW2 (020 7501 9001).

Old Ale (£2.10) and, in season, the super strong Christmas Ale (£1.60 a half and 8.3% in strength). The food on offer is classic British pub fare and the place has a bit of a Queen Vic/SouthEnders feel to it with Victorian decor and lace curtains to spare the drinkers' blushes – a good solid pub. *Disabled: toilet. Function room. Quiz (Tue). Vegetarian dishes.*

Townhouse

125 Great Suffolk Street, SE1 (020 7407 1312). Borough or Elephant & Castle tube. **Open** noon-11pm Mon-Sat; noon-6pm Sun. **Food served** noon-3pm Mon-Fri. **Credit** AmEx, DC, MC, V.

This is a surprisingly congenial pub in an area that has yet to feel the developers' wad of cash wash over it. It is clearly a locals' joint, yet it doesn't feel unwelcoming to strangers such as ourselves and music is kept discreetly low enough for conversation to flow. Real ales (all £2.10) include London Pride and Flowers Original. The lunchtime menu suits both the traditionalist (chips and butties) and more adventurous eaters (wild mushroom quiche £4.30) and is cooked to order. *Games (fruit machine). Jukebox. Music (bands 8pm Fri, 2pm Sun). Vegetarian dishes.*

Wheatsheaf

6 Stoney Street, SE1 (020 7407 1514). London Bridge tube/rail. **Open** 11am-11pm Mon-Sat; noon-4pm Sun (first Sun in month only). **Food served** noon-2.30pm Mon-Sat. **No credit cards**.

If you've always fancied being part of a kitchen-sink drama, then the Wheatsheaf is the place to come. It's a pub with a classic '60s working-class feel: wood cladding, wrought-iron decoration and red vinyl on the seats. If you're female, be warned you will feel like a rare species as this is real ale territory and the pub is quite a man's domain. However, if you enjoy experimenting with real ale, then don't let any of this put you off, as the beer list is innovative and constantly changing. Sit and enjoy a pint of Harvey's Best (£1.70) and play a game of cards while the trains rumble overhead. *Babies and children admitted. Games (darts, fruit machine). Music (Irish folk band first Sun in month). Satellite TV. Vegetarian dishes.*

Also in the area...

All Bar One 28-30 London Bridge, SE1 (020 7940 9981); 34 Shad Thames, SE1 (020 7940 9771).
Balls Brothers Hays Galleria, Tooley Street, SE1 (020 7407 4301).
Boot & Flogger (Davys) 10-20 Redcross Way, SE1 (020 7407 1184).
Café Rouge Hays Galleria, Tooley Street, SE1 (020 7378 0097).
Cooperage (Davys) 48-50 Tooley Street, SE1 (020 7403 5775).
Goose & Firkin 47 Borough Road, SE1 (020 7403 3590).
Heeltap & Bumper (Davys) Chaucer House, White Hart Yard, Borough High Street, SE1 (020 7357 7454).
Hop Cellars (Balls Brothers) 24 Southwark Street, SE1 (020 7403 6851).
Mughouse (Davys) 1 Tooley Street, SE1 (020 7403 8343).
Skinkers (Davys) 42 Tooley Street, SE1 (020 7407 9189).
Slug & Lettuce 32 Borough High Street, SE1 (020 7378 9999).

Brixton SW2, SW9/ Streatham SW9

Bar Lorca

261 Brixton Road, SW9 (020 7274 5537/ www.barlorca.com). Brixton tube/rail. **Open** noon-1am Mon-Thur; noon-3am Fri, Sat; noon-midnight Sun. **Food served** noon-11.30pm Mon-Thur; noon-12.30am Fri, Sat; noon-10.30pm Sun. **Happy hour** 6-9pm daily. **Admission** £5 after 10pm Fri, Sat. **Credit** AmEx, DC, MC, V.

The former Old White Horse has been turned into what the illuminated sign outside calls 'barra y music', or what locals would refer to as a 'tapas bar with bleeding salsa music'. The former arrangement of separate bars has been done away with and now the space is basically two connecting rooms littered with tables and chairs, one with a small stage at the blunt end. The decor will be familiar to tapas-bar devotees everywhere: light wood furniture and flooring, white and cream paintwork, with low-hanging blue table lights adding a welcome dash of panache. Service couldn't have been more helpful and, although there's no real beer, the likes of Staropramen, Red Stripe and Guinness (from £2.40 a pint) are on draught, Dos Equis, San Miguel and Estrella in bottles at around £2.50. Fans of Rioja will savour the well-oaked Marqués de Cáceres Crianza (£17 a bottle), while those in the know will plump for Pacharan liqueur at just £1.80 for a lip-wetting. Apart from tapas (from £2.10), there's paella at weekends (£6 a head, £2.90 for children) and vegetarian Mediterranean-style casserole (£4.80). *Babies and children admitted (children's menus, high chairs, nappy-changing facilities, toys). Dance classes £5 hour, £7 two hours 7.30-9.30pm Fri, Sat). Disabled: toilet. Function room. Late licence Fri, Sat. Music (DJs Wed, Thur; world music live band Sun, every other Fri; Salsa band Fri, Sat). No-smoking area. Restaurant. Tables outdoors (terrace yard). Vegetarian dishes.*

Baze 2 Baze

10-12 Tunstall Road, SW9 (020 7737 4797). Brixton tube/rail. **Open/food served** 8.30am-midnight daily. **Happy hour** 4-9pm daily. **No credit cards**.

Another of those Brixton bar-restaurants that can be deathly quiet during the week and then inexplicably full to bursting right through the weekend. Baze 2 Baze is only a stone's throw from the main drag and the bustle of the tube station, but since it's in a half-hidden courtyard, it's nicely secluded (though this probably accounts for the lack of custom). The classy creole-influenced food is worth a try (rigatoni with red pepper purée and sun-dried tomatoes is £6), and there's occasional live jazz in the basement. Staropramen is on tap (at £2.60) and the bar is well stocked for cocktails. A good summer place – chill behind its picture windows and watch the world unfurl. *Babies and children admitted (not weekends). Function room. Tables outdoors (terrace). Vegetarian dishes.*

Brixtonian Havana Club

11 Beehive Place, SW9 (020 7924 9262). Brixton tube. **Open** noon-1am Tue, Wed; noon-2am Thur-Sat. **Food served** 7-10.30pm Tue-Sat. **Happy hour** 5.30-7.30pm Mon-Fri. **Credit** MC, V.

'Hidden' is hardly the word for a building painted bright lavender, but the Brixtonian is tucked well out of sight in an alleyway near the market, giving customers a hint of illicit discovery. Outside there's a rosy-red courtyard (complete

with space heaters), but the main attraction is a wonderful attic loft space with blue and pink plastic blobs decorating the bar, and odd junk-sculptures that hint at Cuban provenance. The restaurant serves excellent Caribbean food, themed monthly to a particular island, and the bar groans under a staggering 300 varieties of rum (£3-£80 a shot) – familiar, exotic, white, dark and killer overproof – and a few bottled beers at £2.50. There are occasional parties here, as well as regular rum-tasting soirées, and your host, the flamboyant Vincent Osborne, is a confirmed booster for his favourite drink. 'Do you like rum?' he'll ask innocently enough, luring you into a heady night of cocktails and connoisseurship.
Function room. Late licence (Tue-Sat). Music ('70s revival Thur; Gospel 2pm Sun; Jazz Wed; Latin American Fri, Sat). Restaurant. Tables outdoors (paved area). Vegetarian dishes.

Bug Bar
The Crypt, St Matthew's Peace Garden, Brixton Hill, SW2 (020 7738 3184/www.bugbar.co.uk).
Brixton tube/rail. **Open/food served** 7pm-1am Mon-Wed; 7pm-2am Thur; 7pm-3am Fri, Sat; 8pm-1am Sun. **Credit** MC, V.
Creep into the crypt and you'll be pleasantly surprised. Here, under St Matthew's church (itself now a nightclub), is the Bug Bar, hedonistic Gothic hangout of Brixton's latest wave of tipplers. Oak pews and angelic frescoes give the ecclesiastical ambience, sofas the necessary low-slung comfort, while a steady supply of DJs play music that's intriguing enough to give the chin-scratchers something to talk about, with a few monthly dance nights that are really worth checking out. Drinks are just less than a club, just more than a pub, with a smallish selection of bottled lagers (Budvar, Red Stripe both £2.50) and a range of cocktails (£4.50-£6) leading the line. It's mainly popular with up-for-it students, although the entrance fee at the weekends after 9pm might deter some. Next door the flavourful and much-praised vegetarian restaurant Bah Humbug lets you indulge in 'decadent dining'.
Disabled: toilet. Late licence Music (DJs Thur-Sun). Restaurant. Tables outdoors (garden). Vegetarian dishes.

Dogstar
389 Coldharbour Lane, SW9 (020 7733 7515/ www.dogstarbar.co.uk). Brixton tube/rail. **Open** noon-2.30am Mon-Thur; noon-4am Fri, Sat; noon-2am Sun. **Happy hour** 5-8pm daily. **Food served** 2-8pm Tue-Sun. **Admission** £3 9-10pm, £4 10-11pm, £5 11pm-4am, Fri; £4 9-10pm, £5 10-11pm, £6 11pm-4am, Sat; £3 after 10.30pm Sun. **Credit** AmEx, DC, MC, V.
After being fire-bombed in its first week of opening, the Dogstar quickly established itself as a fact of Brixton life, its character deriving from a busy schedule of DJ nights and a vaguely crusty take on the designer bar aesthetic. As well as being a regular provider of after-hours drinking and dancing, the Dog – a big corner pub with a capacious upstairs dancefloor – also hosts comedy and cabaret, and you can even watch football or enjoy a quiet vegetarian lunch, depending on when you visit. Friday and Saturday nights are the hottest and sweatiest, when rain drips down the windows on the inside and queues are common after 11pm. There's a handsome display of spirits, particularly flavoured vodkas (double shots £2.80) and a fulsome supply of draught and bottled beers (Hoegaarden, Budvar, Michelob) from £2.40.
Babies and children admitted (until 6pm). Disabled: toilet. Function room. Games (fruit machine, pinball machine, pool table). Late licence. Music (DJs nightly). Satellite TV (big screen). Tables outdoors (garden). Vegetarian dishes.

Duke of Edinburgh
204 Ferndale Road, SW9 (020 7924 0509). Clapham North tube/Brixton tube/rail. **Open** noon-11pm Mon-Sat; noon-10.30pm Sun. **No credit cards.**
Ahh, the Duke, scene of much misbehaviour. Outwardly innocent, a smallish corner pub on quiet Ferndale Road; once inside you find it larger – and occasionally wilder – than you would ever guess. Battered oak panelling covers the walls, a roaring fire is in the grate when needed, and chummy bar staff serve up just what the doctor ordered. Biggest surprise is the Olympian beer garden hidden out back. Here, on summer nights, there are 50 yards of tables and raucous barbecue gatherings that would shame a medieval banquet. Generally, you'll find a crushing population of locals intent on letting loose, and even on a quiet night you may find yourself drinking deep into the evening (John Smith's Smooth £2.25, Boddingtons £2.30, Scrumpy Jack £2.40).
Babies and children admitted. Games (fruit machine, pool table, table football). Jukebox. Music (DJs most weekends). Satellite TV (big screens). Tables outdoors (garden).

Fridge Bar
1 Town Hall Parade, Brixton Hill, SW2 (020 7326 5100/www.fridge.co.uk). Brixton tube/rail. **Open/ food served** (*main bar*) 5.30pm-2am Mon-Thur; 5.30pm-4am Fri, Sat; 7pm-2am Sun, (*chill-out bar*) 5.30am-noon Sat, Sun. **Admission** after 9pm Fri-Sun £5. **Credit** AmEx, DC, MC, V.
It's tucked under the club with which it shares its name, and this narrow bar with its grotesque nudes (is the male one so drastically underendowed to make others feel superior?) was famously the first place in London to revive absinthe, and is still proud to offer the vicious green confection (a cubeful of sugar helps the medicine go down), even though most trend-obsessed Brixtonians would consider that particular drink *so* 1999. Otherwise it's the usual suspects, with Red Stripe and Kronenbourg on tap (£2.50), and Sol, Freedom, Budvar and the full range of Bacardi Breezers all available by bottle for £2.70. The Fridge Bar is also pushing back the boundaries of licensing with its 5.30am weekend opening times, making it a popular after-hours spot as well as a pre-club gathering ground. In any case, once you're inside, thanks to the dark and booming cellar dancefloor, you may not bother going anywhere else.
Dress code. Late licence. Music (DJs nightly). Satellite TV. Tables outdoors (pavement). Vegetarian dishes.

Hope & Anchor
123 Acre Lane, SW2 (020 7274 1787). Clapham North tube/Brixton tube/rail. **Open** 11am-11pm Mon-Sat; noon-10.30pm Sun. **Food served** noon-2.30pm, 6-9pm Mon-Fri; noon-5pm Sat, Sun. **Credit** MC, V.
Despite the fairly bland exterior, and its location on the even duller Acre Lane, this boozer proves to have a cavernous interior with a humming beat. The high-ceilinged ochre and cream room holds a central bar around which plain tables and chairs hug the walls, occasionally interupted by wooden partitions to break up the space. MOR music competes with the healthy buzz of youngish 'Claxton' folk, who sup Young's 'ordinary', Special or Winter Warmer (between £1.90 and £2.15), and tuck into one of a selection of mains (chilli prawn stir-fry £5.50, sandwiches £2.95). In the summer, the huge garden, waterfeatures, shrubberies and all, draws the crowds. In the winter, a friendly warmth ensures its popularity doesn't wane.
Disabled: toilet. Function room. Games (fruit machines, video golf). Satellite TV (big screen). Tables outdoors (garden). Vegetarian dishes.

Hope & Anchor.
See page 169.

Junction Dance Bar

242 Coldharbour Lane, SW9 (020 7738 4000).
Loughborough Junction rail/P4, 35, 45, 345 bus.
Open 4pm-midnight Mon; 4-11pm Tue, Wed; 4pm-2am
Thur, Fri; noon-2am Sat; noon-midnight Sun. **Admission**
after 11pm Fri, Sat £3. **Happy hour** 4pm-midnight Mon;
4-8pm Tue-Sun. **Credit** AmEx, MC, V.
This was where chart stars Basement Jaxx threw their
legendary parties before their fame necessitated a move to
more capacious ballrooms, and back in those heady days of
1998 it was a crumbling old knacker of a pub. There are still
plenty of pack-em-in disc-driven dance nights here, mostly
on the underground house tip, but the Junction has also been
given several coats of very shiny black and red paint, and has
never looked so good. Coupled with admirably dimmed
lighting, the decor magically mutates a regular Edwardian
pub into a flamboyant opium den where the occasional
poetry/cabaret/arts events flourish. Most drinks cost £2.50,
whether draught Guinness and John Smith's Extra Smooth
or bottled Grolsch and Budvar, and there's a good deal on
four-pint pitchers (£5) in the lengthy happy hours.
Babies and children admitted (daytime only). Disabled:
toilet. Function room. Games (board games, table football).
Late licence (Mon, Thur-Sun). Music (DJs Thur-Sun).

Satay Bar

447-450 Coldharbour Lane, SW9 (020 7326 5001/
www.sataybar.co.uk). Brixton tube/rail. **Open** noon-
11pm Mon-Fri; 1pm-midnight Sat; 1-10.30pm Sun.
Happy hour 5-7pm daily. **Food served** noon-3pm,
6-11pm Mon-Fri; 1pm-midnight Sat; 1-10.30pm Sun.
Credit AmEx, DC, MC, V.
A busy place, caught (spiritually and geographically) between
the dodgy dealings of Coldharbour Lane and the more gentrified
feel of the Ritzy cinema next door. This is reflected in the mix
of clientele: a varied cross-section of young(ish) Brixton, all
using it as a high energy hang-out, filled with vaguely modern
decor, lots of tables and booming dance music. Food – fast
Indonesian – is very good (£12-£15 for two courses – no bar
snacks), and service is brisk, with adrenalin-fuelled staff
skilfully manoeuvring their way around to replenish drinks (all
bottled beers, Tiger, Bintang both £2.30). It's a good place for
some pre/post-movie nosh, or even a quiet strung-out lunch.
Babies and children admitted. Disabled: toilet. Restaurant.
Tables outdoors (pavement). Vegetarian dishes.

SW9

11 Dorrell Place, SW9 (020 7738 3116). Brixton tube/
rail. **Open** 9am-11pm Mon-Thur; 9am-1am Fri; 10.30am-
1am Sat; 11am-11pm Sun. **Food served** 9am-10pm
Mon-Thur; 10am-10pm Fri; 10.30am-10pm Sat; 11am-
10pm Sun. **Happy hour** 5-8pm Mon-Fri. **Credit** MC, V.
Somehow this sweet little place, in what was once no doubt
a long-gone corner grocery shop, conjures a feeling of sunny
misspent afternoons regardless of what time you visit, and
of the backstreet car-fixing and railway arches just outside.
Perhaps it's the teashop layout, or maybe the chatty variety
of drinkers, but this is definitely a good, unhurried place to
drink a pint or two of Red Stripe (£1.65) or munch on a light
meal. The food drives a busy lunchtime trade, with soups,
salads and daily specials (£5.95) of the health-conscious
variety. There's a gay presence here (and the music can tend
toward campy hi-NRG pop), but it's far from a gay bar, more
an inclusive one. But don't miss the zippy picture of Morph
and his friends having an omnisexual circle jerk on a sofa.
Babies and children admitted. Late licence (Fri, Sat).
Tables outdoors (patio). Vegetarian dishes.

Trinity Arms

45 Trinity Gardens, SW9 (020 7274 4544). Brixton
tube/rail. **Open** 11am-11pm Mon-Sat; noon-10.30pm Sun.
Food served noon-3pm Mon-Fri. **No credit cards.**

Watch when you come down the stairs because you might find yourself in the flightpath of a game of darts. A recent refurb has smartened it up, but changing little – cosiness is still the name of the game at this popular Young's local. In winter, it's full of people huddling together for radiator-friendly chats, and in summer, it's packed with folk buying pints on trays to take out into the air of the crumbling square (although they're also opening a garden soon). Friends have unfairly labelled it an old man's pub for its lack of booming choons and pill-popping pre-clubbers, but, in fact, the clientele is a full cross-section of the locale. A pint of ESB is £2.25, London Pride £2.15, Chiswick Bitter £2 and there's Guinness and several lagers, too.
Games (fruit machine). Satellite TV. Tables outdoors (garden).

Z Bar & Brasserie
30 Acre Lane, SW2 (020 7501 9001). Brixton tube/rail/ 3, 35, 37, 109 bus. **Open** noon-midnight Tue-Sun. **Food served** noon-11pm Tue-Sun. **Happy hour** 5-7pm daily. **Credit** MC, V.
As you traipse up from McDonald's to catch your bus to Clapham, you'll encounter a small stretch of Acre Lane that somehow resembles the strip in Las Vegas – rude Beemers parked three deep, Jeeps leaking two-step sub-bass, rusty Mercs with dark windows and chrome wheel arches. At the centre of all this action is the Z Bar (its inhabitants prefer the 'zee' pronunciation), a cavernous drinkerie that has taken up where the Brixton Brasserie (in the same location) left off. It's a big raw space with big raw jags of spiky animal-print zig-zags in night-time colours – kind of sophisticated-like. The bar is well stocked with spirits for shots and cocktails (from £3.75) and bottled beers (most are £2.50). It can be quiet during the week, but the mostly black crowd parties hard enough at the weekend to make up for any deficiencies.
Babies and children admitted. Late licence. Music (DJs Thur-Sun). Restaurant. Tables outside (terrace). Vegetarian dishes.

Also in the area...

Babushka 40 St Matthew's Road, SW2 (020 7274 3618).
Flourmill & Firkin 442-444 Brixton Road, SW9 (020 7737 4892).
Furze & Firkin 103-105 Streatham High Street, SW16 (020 8677 8392).
Hobgoblin 95 Effra Road, SW2 (020 7501 9671).

Camberwell SE5

Funky Munky
25 Camberwell Church Street, SE5 (020 7252 5222). Denmark Hill rail/12, 36 bus. **Open** noon-midnight Mon-Wed; noon-1am Thur; noon-2am Fri, Sat; noon-10.30pm Sun. **Food served** noon-3pm, 6-10pm Mon-Fri; noon-5pm Sat, Sun. **Credit** MC, V.
Another converted boozer, this time the end result being a single medium-sized oblong room with large windows on two sides and the customary wooden floor, aimed squarely at Camberwell's arty student types. The beer's pretty standard stuff, featuring the likes of John Smith's Smooth, Foster's and Kronenbourg; shots – a speciality – are £2.50/£4 and a bottle of Beck's will set you back £3. Snacks like burger and fries (£4.25), houmous, salad and toast (£2.95) and Welsh rarebit (£3.50) are extended to brunch at the weekend, and the service is friendly and informal, as are the punters – if you resent

groups plonking themselves down unannounced at your table, you're either in the wrong place, too uptight, or probably both.
Babies and children admitted (daytimes only). Games (board games Sun eve). Late licence (Thur-Sat). Music (DJs Thur-Sun). Tables outdoors (pavement). Vegetarian dishes.

Grove House Tavern
26 Camberwell Grove, SE5 (020 7703 4553). Bus 12, 36, 68, 68A, 171, 176, 185, 345. **Open** 11am-11pm Mon-Sat; noon-10.30pm Sun. **Food served** noon-8pm daily. **No credit cards**.
Ignore the small, dingy front bar – the plasticky seats and oversized TV screen make it look like a fleapit cinema – and head for the large, popular main bar at the rear. Given its location on a beautiful Georgian street, though, even this may come as a slight disappointment: it's a fairly unremarkable bar, but a curiously beguiling one, with well-worn, lumpy upholstery and a choice of board games available behind the counter. In summer, the place really comes into its own, with seating in the cobbled alley at the front or in the large back garden. Burton's and Young's Bitter (both £2.02) are among the beers, while the extensive menu includes pub staples such as scampi and chips (£4.15) and steak and ale pie (£4.95).
Babies and children admitted (3-7pm only). Games (board games, fruit machine, quiz machine). Jukebox. Quiz (Tue). Satellite TV (big screen). Tables outdoors (garden, pavement). Vegetarian dishes.

Hermit's Cave
28 Camberwell Church Street, SE5 (020 7703 3188). Denmark Hill rail/12, 36, 171, 185 bus. **Open** 11am-11pm Mon-Sat; noon-10.30pm Sun. **Food served** noon-3pm daily. **No credit cards**.
At the Hermit's Cave, what you see is what you get: an unpretentious boozer frequented mainly by local musicians and artists. There's no frippery here – no music, no soft lights, no carpet – but, instead, an imaginative range of cask ales (Gravesend Shrimper, Batcombe Bitter both £2.10) and cheap-and-cheerful nosh (shepherd's pie, bangers and mash both £2.95). On a winter's evening, you could do a lot worse than grab a spot near the roaring fire; be aware, though, that the tall tables near the doors are as unstable as they look.
Babies and children admitted. Games (fruit machine). No piped music or jukebox. Satellite TV (big screen). Tables outdoors (pavement). Vegetarian dishes.

Phoenix & Firkin
5 Windsor Walk, SE5 (020 7701 8282). Denmark Hill rail. **Open/food served** 11am-11pm Mon-Sat; noon-10.30pm Sun. **Credit** AmEx, DC, MC, V.
Occupying the old ticket hall of Denmark Hill station on a bridge straddling the railway line, the Phoenix is one of the most pleasing of the Firkin pubs, with a spectacular vaulted ceiling, roaring fire and tons of railway paraphernalia. All it needs is steam rising up outside the windows as a train pulls in, though the persistent juddering under the floorboards is authentic enough. Regular punters include medics from the nearby King's College and Maudsley hospitals, sports fans (there's a huge TV, thunderously amplified) and, for all we know, escapees from the Salvation Army training centre opposite. Among the beers are competitively priced Burton's (£2) and Wadworth (£2.10); among the dishes are Thai chicken curry (£5.45) and roast chicken (£4.95).
Games (fruit machines, quiz machine). Jukebox. Music (bands 9pm Sat). Satellite TV (big screen). Tables outdoors (pavement). Vegetarian dishes.

Sun & Doves

61-63 Coldharbour Lane, SE5 (020 7733 1525/
www.sundoves.com). Brixton or Oval tube/35, 45 bus.
Open 11am-11pm Mon-Fri; noon-11pm Sat; noon-
10.30pm Sun. **Food served** noon-11pm Mon-Sat; noon-
5pm Sun. **Credit** AmEx, DC, MC, V.
Part wine bar, part pub, part restaurant, part art gallery, the
Sun & Doves is a thoroughly independent freehouse,
resolutely ploughing its own farrow at this unpromising (ie
Camberwell) end of Coldharbour Lane. Few bars can boast
such a varied clientele: on our visit, drinkers ranged from
earnest aesthetes sipping wine (20 varieties, £9.95-£23.95 a
bottle) to knackered workmen supping real ales (Directors
£2.30). The seating layout helps: practical school-style tables
and chairs in the main part of the bar, mini-living rooms
(groups of comfy chairs and settees) in the corners. The pub
is renowned for its food, which includes kedgeree (£7.95) and
venison, pearl barley and juniper berry stew (£8.25), and for
its house-speciality hot toddies (£3.75).
No-smoking area (in restaurant). Restaurant. Tables
outdoors (garden). Vegetarian dishes.

Also in the Area...

Babushka 65 Camberwell Church Street, SE5
(020 7277 2601).

Catford SE6

Catford Ram

9 Winslade Way, SE6 (020 8690 6206). Catford or
Catford Bridge rail. **Open** 11am-11pm Mon-Sat; noon-
10.30pm Sun. **Food served** 11am-3pm, 7-10.30pm Mon-
Sat. **No credit cards.**
Hidden in a corner of the Catford Shopping Centre – a
potential setting for the British remake of *Fort Apache, The*
Bronx – the Ram is a Tardis-like space entered though a
single door. You leave behind a world of half-price socks and
bananas (19p a pound) and behold! A glowing cream-and-
wood Young's pub that could have been transported complete
from Wandsworth. Split over two levels, with masses of
comfortable furniture and a solid dark wood bar, it's the
meeting place for workers from the nearby Lewisham Town
Hall and Theatre, plus market traders and real ale buffs. Food
is a feature: hefty portions of home-made beef and ale pie, and
cauliflower cheese can be had for around a fiver. The beer is
good: Special bitter is £2 a pint, with Young's lager at £2.20.
Disabled: toilet. Games (darts, fruit machine, pinball
machine). Vegetarian dishes.

Rutland Arms

55 Perry Hill, SE6 (020 8291 9426). Catford Bridge rail/
54, 185 bus. **Open** 11am-11pm Mon-Sat; noon-10.30pm
Sun. **Food served** noon-2.30pm daily. **No credit cards.**
The Rutland Arms is a large L-shaped one-bar pub of the old
school variety, with neatly arranged tables and chairs, and
six different real ales – including Adnams Broadside (£2) and
Bass (£2.05) – plus the usual selection of lagers and, of course,
Guinness. Trad jazz, swing and R&B bands play on the small
bandstand most evenings, with Jazz FM beamed over the
sound system the rest of the time. The clientele is a mix of
ageing jazz fanatics and twentysomething men plus a
smattering of cosmopolitan couples of all ages.
Function room. Games (fruit machines). Music (trad jazz
Mon, Sat; modern jazz Tue, Sun lunch; R&B Thur;
pianist Wed, Fri, Sun). Quiz (first Sun in month). Satellite
TV. Tables outdoors (pavement). Vegetarian dishes.

Clapham SW4, SW9, SW12

100

100 Clapham Park Road, SW4 (020 7720 8902).
Clapham Common tube. **Open/food served** noon-11pm
Mon-Sat; noon-10.30pm Sun. **Credit** MC, V.
The roar of animated chat hits you square in the chest as
you step off a grey stretch of Clapham Park Road into this
fancifully decorated pub. The volume level of the black-clad
post-uni youngsters inside is driven ever higher by raucous
DJ music from the dancing area at the back. Despite the
hippie nonsense painted on the exterior and a lick of colour
inside, the actual fabric of the pub is nicely untampered-
with, and the elegant central bar dispenses a serviceable
range of lagers (Stella Artois, Staropramen both £2.50),
along with pizzas (£5-£7.50). Friendly and fun, without
being unbearably silly, and with a distinctly pre-club
atmosphere at weekends. The beer-garden fills up in the
summer, as do the few tables on the front patio.
Babies and children admitted (until 7pm). Function room.
Games (table football). Music (DJs 8pm Sat). Satellite
TV (big screen). Tables outdoors (garden, patio).
Vegetarian dishes.

Alexandra

14 Clapham Common Southside, SW4 (020 7627 5102).
Clapham Common tube. **Open** 11am-11pm Mon-Sat; noon-
10.30pm Sun. **Food served** noon-3pm Mon-Sat; noon-
4pm Sun. **No credit cards.**
A grand old dame of a place, which, according to your point
of view, either guards the top of the common with the dignity
of a bygone age, or lurks behind the hordes of people waiting
for a bus to Streatham. Inside it's a bit of a split, too. Upstairs
there's a tall-ceilinged function room with sofas and large
windows that suggest a quiet read of the papers; downstairs
you'll find a multi-level drinkerie with all manner of wooden
booths and cubby holes, weirdly reminiscent of a Tex-Mex
steak house. The Alexandra is big and popular, its chalk
boards are filled with bargains and offers, and it's a much-
favoured place for big-screen football. Drinks offer few
surprises (Foster's, Miller both £2.15, John Smith's Smooth
£2.25), and apart from a Sunday roast (£5.95), the menu
focuses on sandwiches.
Function room. Games (fruit machine, pinball machine).
Jukebox. Satellite TV (big screen).

Arch 635

15-16 Lendal Terrace, SW4 (020 7720 7343). Clapham
North tube/Clapham High Street rail. **Open/food served**
5-11pm Mon-Fri; noon-midnight Sat; noon-10.30pm Sun.
Happy hour 5-8.30pm Mon-Fri; 6-8.30pm Sat; noon-6pm
Sun. **Credit** MC, V.
In its previous incarnation as Trainspotters this railway
arch was more or less a ravey youth club. But now the
fridges full of alcopops have gone, the pool cues and table
football have been relegated to the edges of the action and
the rather slapdash paint job has been updated to
understated decor. In fact, the whole place has grown up
very pleasantly into a relaxing club/bar. It's a definite plus
that, even though music is a key feature, the volume doesn't
overawe the whole place. And a healthy racial mix is
refreshing against the bleached 'a-bar-theid' of Clapham
High Street. There's Grolsch and Staropramen (both £2.50),
Carling (£2.20) and Guinness (£2.40) on tap, with big-screen
football and DJ nights Thursday to Saturday (from Latin
sounds to funky disco).
Games (chess, pool table, table football). Music (DJs Thur-
Sat). Satellite TV (big screen). Vegetarian dishes.

Belle Vue

1 Clapham Common Southside, SW4 (020 7498 9473).
Clapham Common tube. **Open** 5-11pm Mon-Fri; 10am-
11pm Sat, Sun. **Food served** 6.30-10.30pm Mon-Fri;
12.30-4.30pm, 6.30-10pm Sat; 12.30-4pm, 6.30-10pm Sun.
No credit cards.
This is one of those places that has been around long enough
to transcend the continental trendiness with which it was no
doubt conceived, making it a cosy haunt for a fireside gaggle,
with the added benefit of excellent food. Scrubbed wood
panelling forms the decor, together with rustic furniture and
library sofas. The paintings by local artists adorn the walls
and attractive twenty- to thirty-year-olds line the seating.
Eating is usually the focus here, hence the overabundance of
tables, and the fact that drinkers will be moved in favour of
diners, who nosh on simple bistro dishes done very well, with
sausage and mash (£6.95) a particular favourite. The
waitresses bring you what you need, drawn from a basic
range of (mostly bottled) beer (a range of Belle Vue fruit beers
£3.50, Budvar £2.50 and Leffe £3.50).
Restaurant. Vegetarian dishes.

Bierodrome

44-48 Clapham High Street, SW4 (020 7720 1118/
www.belgorestaurants.com). Clapham Common or
Clapham North tube. **Open/food served** noon-midnight
Mon-Wed; noon-1am Thur-Sat; noon-10.30pm Sun. **Credit**
AmEx, DC, MC, V.
Where Islington leads, Clapham will surely follow. That's
Belgo's way of thinking, at least, for this is the second of the
Belgian restaurant chain's concept-bar outposts. And this place
is designed to the back teeth – with its curved planked ceiling
and cleanly illuminated signage, Bierodrome is positively
bursting with the neo-modernist design aesthetic.
Complementing the decor perfectly are plenty of well-heeled,
charcoal-grey young things (the building was previously Hugh
Henry estate agents and Hugh and Henry are here in force). If
you don't fancy Hoegaarden (£2.65 per bottle), Leffe (£2.65 per
bottle), De Koninck or Antoon (on draught: £1.95, £2.25 per
half), all of which are duly served in the correct glass, there's a
menu with hundreds of strange Trappist beers, including one
exotic tipple (La Vieille Bon Secours) priced at £635 for a 15-
litre bottle. And if you can judge an entire bar by one feature,
allow us to point out the 8ft sticks with sockets all along their
length: these are planks for lining up shot-glasses.
Babies and children admitted (restaurant only; children's
menus, high chairs, nappy-changing facilities). Disabled:
toilet. Jukebox. Restaurant. Tables outdoors (pavement).
Vegetarian dishes.

Bread & Roses

68 Clapham Manor Street, SW4 (020 7498 1779).
Clapham Common or Clapham North tube. **Open** 11am-
11pm Mon-Sat; noon-10.30pm Sun. **Admission** every
other Wed comedy £4/£2 concs; Sun folk music £4. **Food**
served noon-3pm, 6.30-9.30pm Mon-Wed; noon-3pm, 6.30-
10pm Thur, Fri; noon-4pm, 6-10pm Sat; 6-10pm Sun
(African buffet 1-4pm). **Credit** MC, V.
Also known as Dunmarchin, this is where Clapham socialists
gather en famille to sympathise/fantasise about the plight of
the working man, as well as to compare their ethical share
portfolios and the outrageous rise in local house prices. New
Labour quips aside, it's an excellent pub – the first
permanent home of the Workers' Beer Company, a trade
union offshoot that has long watered the masses of the
festival circuit. As a result, there's a good selection of beers,
whether their own fine brews (Smile's Workers' Ale £2), or
a guest ale (Adnams Broadside £2.35 on our visit). At

weekends it can get a little too child-friendly, although this
is ameliorated by the fine conservatory area and, in summer,
the garden. There are regular music, comedy, poetry and
theatre events here, including Mwalimu Express, a weekly
chance to investigate the music and cuisine of a particular
part of Africa. The old joke is that the Bread of B&R is
ciabatta (an extensive menu includes sausage and mash
£5.55, Thai chicken curry £6.45) for the Rose is decidedly
Blairite; indeed, the swank lines of its design hardly suggest
flat caps and Kier Hardie. However, lurking under the feet of
Bread & Roses' middle-class professionals, you'll find the
spirit of a surprisingly traditional pub.
Babies and children admitted (until 9pm; colouring books,
games, high chairs, nappy-changing facilities, toys).
Comedy (8pm every other Wed). Disabled: toilet. Function
room. Games (board games, Jenga). Music (African 1-4pm
Sun, folk 8.30pm Sun). No-smoking area (until 6pm). Quiz
(third Mon in month). Tables outdoors (conservatory,
garden, patio). Vegetarian dishes.

Falcon

33 Bedford Road, SW4 (020 7274 2428). Clapham North
tube/Clapham High Street rail. **Open** noon-11pm Mon-Sat;
noon-10.30pm Sun. **Food served** noon-3pm, 6-10pm Mon-
Fri; noon-10pm Sat, Sun. **Credit** MC, V.
The Falcon is near indistinguishable from its beer garden,
its single greatest asset and the scene of many meandering
summer evenings. Space heaters extend the season, but it's
really when the outside shed is serving drinks and the
barbecue is firing on all cylinders that it becomes the place
to be. Some have even attached 'a Mediterranean feel' to the
place, such as the calming power of the surrounding trees.
Once inside, there is a competitive and popular pool table,
cheap Thai food (£5-£6), a fair range of drinks (Grolsch and
Caffrey's both £2.50) and all manner of lusty young things.
Babies and children admitted (until 7pm). Games (fruit
machine). TV. Tables outdoors (garden, patio). Vegetarian
dishes.

Frog & Forget-Me-Not

32 The Pavement, SW4 (020 7622 5230). Clapham
Common tube. **Open** 4-11pm Mon-Fri; noon-11pm Sat;
noon-10.30pm Sun. **Food served** 1-4pm Sun.
Credit MC, V.

Great roast dinners (£6), a bar billiards table and a storming Thursday pub quiz are helpful hints that make this is a hugely popular and unpretentious Clapham pub. Not a whiff of clever decor, just a load of tables, chairs and sofas; not a room full of media professionals, DJs and stylists, just a drinking den buzzing to bursting with local lager-than-life youngsters, mostly under 25. There's a refuge from the smoke and the decibels in a rooftop garden, which overlooks the common, though this gets equally busy in good weather. John Smith's Smooth (£2.30), Foster's and Carling Premier (both £2.20) are on tap, and about ten bottled beers (Beck's, Molson both £2.50) are among the ample selection of drinks on offer. *Games (bar billiards, fruit machine). Quiz (Tue). Satellite TV. Tables outdoors (roof terrace). Vegetarian dishes.*

Kazbar

50 Clapham High Street, SW4 (020 7622 0070/www.the kudosgroup.com). Clapham North tube/Clapham High Street rail. **Open**/food served 4pm-midnight Mon-Fri; noon-midnight Sat, Sun. **Happy hour** 4-9pm Mon-Fri daily. **No credit cards.**
Here goes: 'Save some cash with a well-timed dash, 'cos when Madonna's on, it's two for one.' Drinks promotions are the name of the game in this chirpy gay bar that has a little less cruising and a lot more video equipment than the **2 Brewers** (*see p177*) a block or so yonder. Testament to its fine character is the fact that after enjoying the Brewers' absence (while closed for a refit), Kazbar has positively thrived in the shadow of its reopened neighbour. Added attractions include the new red paint job (the old blue and yellow did nobody any favours), brutal dyke bouncers with hearts of gold, and club vouchers for Salvation. Drinks include Bombardier (£2.40) and Kirin (£2.75) on tap.
Games (fruit machine). Tables outdoors (pavement). Music (video DJs nightly). TV (video screen). Vegetarian dishes.

Landor

70 Landor Road, SW9 (020 7274 4386). Clapham North tube/Clapham High Street rail. **Open** noon-11pm Mon-Sat; noon-10.30pm Sun. **Food served** 5.30-10pm Mon-Sat; 12.30-6.30pm Sun. **Credit** AmEx, DC, MC, V.
Well geeze, that canoe's been on the ceiling for more than a year now and no one's nicked it. But neither has anybody offered a sensible explanation for the Landor's sudden transformation into a nautical pub filled with blistering barnacles and spliced mainbraces. Despite the shiny paint, the lobster pots and the Vicwardian lamplights, the pool tables still await your lost afternoons, and the darts trophies are still on show. Nevertheless, the fringe theatre upstairs hints at a variety of cultural events, and the ever-changing real ales (Spitfire £2.10, Old Speckled Hen £2.20 on our visit) and a Modern British menu have not destroyed the charming unkempt feel to the place.
Games (fruit machine, pool table, quiz machine). Quiz (every other Sun). Satellite TV (big screen). Tables outdoors (garden). Theatre. Vegetarian dishes.

Loaffers

102-104 Clapham High Street, SW4 (020 7720 9596). Clapham Common or Clapham North tube/Clapham High Street rail. **Open** noon-11pm Mon-Fri; 11am-11pm Sat; noon-10.30pm Sun. **Food served** noon-10pm Mon-Sat; noon-9.30pm Sun. **Credit** DC, MC, V.
There have been a succession of failed restaurants on this elegant corner site, but Loaffers looks like it might have beaten the jinx. Its secret weapon has been the canny move of expanding rearwards and making the place much bigger than shop-window sized, giving the High Street yet another classy cocktail lounge/bar/brasserie. The decor is immaculate,

with blue on blue cherubs adorning the prettily curved windows and a chic blue and orange interior frilled with comfy stools and sofas, but as of yet not much of a crowd has evolved for the all-French staff to fuss over. A shot of Stoli is £4.20 so you might as well have a cocktail, most of which come in at £5.50. Hoegaarden (£3.20), Guinness (£2.80) and Kronenbourg (£2.80) on tap with a further clutch of bottled beers at £2.80 each. Food is good (mains upwards from about a tenner) but the meaty menu is a little fussy. We hid in the very secluded dining room right at the back and enjoyed a very nice partridge for £11.50 with, ooh, lots of trimmings. *Restaurant. Vegetarian dishes.*

Manor Arms

128 Clapham Manor Street, SW4 (no phone). Clapham Common or Clapham North tube/Clapham High Street rail. **Open** 11am-11pm Mon-Sat; noon-10.30pm Sun. **No credit cards.**
Don't all rush here in search of a quiet night, because you'll spoil it. In fact, you should arrange with the other readers of this book to visit on different dates, so as not to disturb the Manor Arms' delicate balance. This is not a theme pub, it's not a chain pub and it's certainly not a bar. It's not a bistro, it's not a club'n'pub and there's not a feng shui in sight. What it is, and it is remarkable round here for being nothing else, is a pub. A smallish, cosy, welcoming hostel with all the right things for a quiet pint (London Pride £2.10, Flowers Best £1.50) or a port and lemon. There's a TV but the sound's off, there's a jukebox but you can hardly hear it, and there's a little alcove at the back with some books, but you're probably not meant to even notice them (although the Manor is rumoured to have one of the brainiest pub quiz teams in the land). 'A traditional pub, traditional values' reads a sign outside the door. And to that I'll doff my cap.
Babies and children admitted (garden only). Games (darts, fruit machine, video game). Jukebox. Tables outdoors (garden, pavement). Satellite TV.

Nightingale

97 Nightingale Lane, SW12 (020 8673 1637). Clapham South tube. **Open** 11am-11pm Mon-Sat; noon-10.30pm Sun. **Food served** noon-2.15pm, 7-9.30pm Mon-Fri; 1-3pm Sat, Sun. **Credit** MC, V.
The Nightingale fits in neatly between a rash of old people's homes and the snaking half-timbered semis of Wandsworth. If they turned the lights down a little, it would be a whole lot cosier, but then the atmosphere of well-established suburban bliss might not be so gleamingly evident. Maybe the high illumination is to lessen the risk of wife-swapping and adultery, for who knows what middle-class passions lurk here 'betwixt commons'. Probably few, in fact, other than for a decent pint of Young's (Bitter £1.88, Special £2.03), or a bottle or glass of a wide range of wines to accompany the varied menu (Sunday roast £5.50). There's also a selection of 20 or so bottled beers. Plenty of regulars, most in pairs, so not a place to meet a blind date.
Babies and children admitted (separate area; children's menu Sun only). Games (board games, darts, fruit machine). No piped music or jukebox. No-smoking area. Quiz (First Mon in month). Satellite TV. Tables outdoors (garden, pavement). Vegetarian dishes.

Oblivion

7-8 Cavendish Parade, Clapham Common Southside, SW4 (020 8772 0303). Clapham South tube. **Open** noon-11pm daily. **Happy hour** 5pm-7pm daily. **Food served** noon-10pm Mon-Fri; noon-9pm Sat, Sun. **Credit** AmEx, MC, V
The strip near Clapham South tube is blossoming into a slightly downscale version of the swank yuppery to be found

along Clapham High Street, such that pretty soon all will be bars of varying degrees of trendiness. And Oblivion and the bad poetry on its menus has led the way. We may laugh at its rather gauche attempts at provocative decor (surreal eyes-on-stalks ironmongery and the ugliest figurative sculpture anywhere), but the packs of breezy young Balhamites who ignore its pretensions and gather here nightly consider it a great old place for a noisy get-together. John Smith's Extra Smooth is £2.40, Hoegaarden £3.80, the bottled beers £2.60, and cocktails start at £4.50. A menu of salads, sandwiches and mains (such as asparagus and artichoke risotto) are all under £8.

Function room. Music (DJs Fri-Sun). Satellite TV. Tables outdoors (terrace). Vegetarian dishes.

Polygon Bar & Grill

4 The Polygon, Clapham Old Town, SW4 (020 7622 1199/www.thepolygon.co.uk). Clapham Common tube. **Open/food served** 6-11pm Mon-Thur; noon-3pm, 6-11pm Fri; 11am-5pm, 6-11pm Sat; 11am-5pm, 6-10.30pm Sun. **Happy hour** 6-7.30pm daily. **Credit** AmEx, MC, V.

Rumour has it that Sir T Conran has just bought Budgens halfway down the High Street and is planning another of his famous large-scale eateries there. But, in fact, the Conranian style of doing things arrived in Clapham (albeit not full-scale) a year or two ago with Polygon, a sleek, white, cubic restaurant with an admirable and well-populated cocktail bar thrown in. Dining here isn't quite as good as you want it to be, thanks to cacophonous acoustics, tables slightly too close together and service that's more formal than the food, but pop in for cockers and you'll be well taken care of. A Whisky Sour is £4, a Martini is £4.95 and is crafted confidently to your exact specifications. Other highlights included a Roasted Toasted Almond and a Harlem Superkick, which we shared among a growing gaggle of elegant drinkers, evenly divided between those enjoying an aperitif and those settling in for a night at the bar.

Babies and children admitted (restaurant; high chairs). Disabled: toilet. Restaurant. Vegetarian dishes.

Prince of Wales

38 Clapham Old Town, SW4 (no phone). Clapham Common tube. **Open** 5-11pm Mon-Fri; noon-11pm Sat; noon-10.30pm Sun. **Food served** 1-4pm Sun. **No credit cards.**

If you look hard enough among the clutter, you can see the piece of moonrock with Princess Margaret's face engraved in it, or the giant fossilised leek with a golliwog sitting in its cockpit, or the antique advertisement promising longer teeth in minutes, not to mention the amazing 1867 model of the Navy's first fully submersible cricket bat. You'll have to look very hard for some of these things, but your patience will be rewarded, and time spent in this rather magical pub is never wasted. And even if you never find these fabled objects, there are plenty of equally nutty ones to keep you amused. It's more of a gently camp pub than a gay one: a quiet coccoon of low red lighting, with acres of mysterious junk inside and a constantly changing display of mannequins and other strange things on the roof. A pint of Wadworth 6X is £2.03.

Babies and children admitted (before 7pm). Music. Tables outdoors (pavement). Vegetarian dishes.

Railway

18 Clapham High Street, SW4 (020 7622 4077). Clapham North tube/Clapham High Street rail. **Open** 11am-11pm Mon-Sat; noon-10.30pm Sun. **Food served** noon-3pm, 6-10.30pm Mon-Fri; noon-10.30pm Sat, Sun. **Credit** AmEx, MC, V.

It's the non-dancing **Dogstar**, suggested one source, comparing this busy, boisterous pub with the well-known Brixton hangout (*see p169*). The ground-level bar is a bit of a goldfish bowl, thanks to huge picture windows glaring on to the street (it's often so crowded there's no room to swim), but the upstairs room is usually a little cosier and a touch less crammed. Of the three pubs in this mini-chain – the **Falcon** (*see p174*) and the **Sun** (*see below*) are its giggly partners in crime – this is perhaps the calmest, but it's all strictly relative. It's a place for young Clapham to meet and squeal in great lusty lungfuls at each other. Decent Thai dishes are around £5-£7 and Caffrey's, Guinness and Grolsch (all £2.50) are on tap.

Function room. Tables outdoors (pavement). Vegetarian dishes.

Sand

156 Clapham Park Road, SW4 (020 7622 3022). Clapham Common tube/Brixton tube, then 35 or 37 bus. **Open/food served** 5pm-3am Mon-Fri; noon-2am Sat; noon-1am Sun. **Credit** MC, V.

Helping fill the rapidly closing gap between upwardly mobile Clapham and bohemian Brixton is Sand bar and restaurant. The delightful interior is cleverly and expensively designed: sand-textured walls and pseudo-Islamic screens divide the large space into intimate areas, from leathery sofas where you can play backgammon to secluded dining areas lit by tea-lights. Wall recesses hold elegant objets d'art; tiny LCD screens play movies; and there's a postmodern wit about that wall of 1970s garden breeze blocks (doesn't it look so now?). Decent wines are sold by the glass, and voguish cocktails (including flavoured Martinis) cost around a fiver. The menu's ambitious – mint-cured salmon (£8.50) is served on a salad of black-eyed beans, pak choy and holy basil – and service is genuinely friendly.

Disabled: toilet. Music (DJs Thur-Sun). Vegetarian dishes.

Sequel

75 Venn Street, SW4 (020 7622 4222). Clapham Common tube. **Open** 5-11pm Mon-Fri; 11am-11pm Sat; noon-10.30pm Sun. **Food served** 5-11pm Mon-Fri; 11am-4pm, 5.30-11pm Sat; noon-5.30pm, 6-10.30pm Sun. **Credit** AmEx, DC, MC, V.

If you drink before the movie, would it be a prequel? The name hints that this is the place to head after a leisurely night watching dreams in the dark at the Picture House next door, and it's certainly a classy enough joint to sustain any celluloid fantasies your moviegoing might have engendered. Most of the tables contain diners enjoying the delicate, Modern global menu (ostrich fillet, spinach chick pea mash and paw-paw tamarind chutney, £12.50), but there's usually room at the bar for an unhurried cocktail (£5-£6.50), a glass of wine or a bottle of Leffe Blonde (£2.75) and, if not, there's a rather fine secluded booth atop the stairs. Sequel offers excellent drinks in an atmosphere of quiet class. There are so many bars in Clapham with pretensions to be like this; here's one of the few to get it just right.

Babies and children admitted. Restaurant. Vegetarian dishes. Video screen.

Sun

47 Clapham Old Town, SW4 (020 7622 4980). Clapham Common tube. **Open/food served** 11am-11pm Mon-Sat; noon-10.30pm Sun. **Credit** DC, MC, V.

This booming box of a pub was the first in Clapham to be dressed in tribal Dayglo surfwear designs and packaged up to more exactly match the local needs: drinks include Caffrey's and Grolsch on tap, Corona and Rolling Rock by the bottle, all £2.50; there's Thai food served for around £5, and there's a steady supply of the opposite sex. The decor (and

the rugger shirts) might suggest an Antipodean sun, shining down on blond-streaked surfers, though you are more likely to find young professionals in evidence. Socially, this is Clapham's beach, and you'll find imports from miles around gathering here to quaff, scoff and score. Even in inclement weather the beer garden often spills out into the road (the Sun was reputedly the first pub in town to import space heaters to lengthen its outdoor season), and when summer's actually here the crowds can stretch for days.
Babies and children admitted (until 7pm). Function room. Restaurant. Tables outdoors (garden). Vegetarian dishes.

2 Brewers

114 Clapham High Street, SW4 (020 7498 4971). Clapham Common or Clapham North tube/Clapham High Street rail. **Open** 4pm-2am Mon-Thur; 4pm-3am Fri; 2pm-3am Sat; noon-midnight Sun. **Admission** after 11pm Tue-Thur £2; 9.30-11pm Fri, Sat £3, after 11pm Fri, Sat £4. **Happy hour** 4-9pm Tue-Sat; noon-9pm Sun. **Food served** noon-6pm Sun. **Credit** MC, V.
Supposedly 70% of London's gay men live south of the river; at the weekend you'll find a healthy proportion of them here. And at the 2 Brewers, local doesn't mean less. The bright front bar area has a stage for drag acts, disco dollies and the very popular Monday karaoke, while to the rear, where once was the darkened back room, is a darkened nightclub of near-W1 proportions. A healthy sound system pumps out hard but poppy dance tunes while a room full of guys check each other out. It's cleverly designed so that even though the cruising to dancing ratio is sky-high, the place feels more like a dance club than a meat market. But don't worry, the upstairs bathroom area is as large as the dancefloor and filled with nice gentlemen in no hurry to return to the disco. Grolsch, Staropramen (both £2.80) and Worthington (£2.45) are among those on tap, with Beck's and Tiger part of the bottled beer selection (£2.95).
Cabaret (nightly). Disabled: toilet. Games (fruit machines). Late licence. Music (DJs nightly). Vegetarian dishes.

Windmill on the Common

Clapham Common Southside, SW4 (020 8673 4578). Clapham Common tube. **Open** 11am-11pm Mon-Sat; noon-10.30pm Sun. **Food served** noon-2.30pm, 7-10pm Mon-Fri; noon-9pm Sat, Sun. **Credit** AmEx, DC, MC, V.
On summer days the Windmill is an essential fact of outdoor Clapham, acting as sole beer dispensary and vital bladder repository for the hordes who gather on the grass armed with hacky sacks, frisbees, kites and Sunday papers. The rest of the year it's… well, it's a pub, with a small hotel and restaurant attached, that happens to be in the middle of the common. Unremarkable decor including Edwardian advertising mirrors, solid pub grub, Young's many brews (Bitter £1.92, Special £2.08 and Winter Warmer £2.14), and a mature and variegated clientele ensure that there's little of note to record, although these same factors render it refreshingly different from the excitably trendy hostelries that dominate these parts.
Babies and children admitted (separate area; children's menu, high chairs). Disabled: toilet. Function room. Restaurant. Tables outdoors (garden). Vegetarian dishes.

Also in the area...

Café Rouge 40 Abbeville Road, SW4 (020 8673 3399).
Fine Line 182-184 Clapham High Street, SW4 (020 622 4436).
Friesian & Firkin 87 Rectory Grove, SW4 (020 7622 4666).
Pitcher & Piano 8 Balham Hill, SW12 (020 8673 1107).

Deptford SE8

Bird's Nest

32 Deptford Church Street, SE8 (020 8692 1928). Deptford or New Cross rail/Deptford Bridge DLR/47 bus. **Open** 11am-11pm Mon-Sat; noon-10.30pm Sun. **Food served** noon-3pm, 6-10pm daily. **No credit cards**.
The Bird's Nest is a cosy one-bar freehouse that's busy most nights with an eclectic mix of locals and students. The Thai restaurant that used to occupy the back area has been reclaimed by drinkers. Upstairs is the 80-seat theatre that hosted Scabaret, the mid-'80s starting point for *Vic Reeves' Big Night Out*. The real ale tends to be the uninspiring Theakston Best, but at under £2 a pint no one's complaining too loudly; bottled beers such as Beck's come in at £2.50. A games area to the right of the bar offers pool, video games and darts.
Babies and children admitted (until 7.30pm). Games (fruit machine, pool table, video games). Jukebox. Music (live band every other Sun, 8.30pm). Restaurant. Satellite TV (big screen). Tables outdoors (pavement). Theatre (Tue-Sat). Vegetarian dishes.

Crystal Palace Tavern

105 Tanner's Hill, SE8 (020 8692 0682). New Cross or New Cross Gate tube/rail/St John's rail/21, 36, 36B, 53, 177 bus. **Open/food served** 11am-midnight, Sun-Thur; 11pm-2am Fri, Sat. **No credit cards**.
A recent change of management has added a carpet and some home comforts, but removed most of the Belgian beers on offer at this popular backstreet boozer. But with six real ales usually available, including a rotating selection that includes the likes of Greene King IPA, Courage Best, Old Speckled Hen and Ventnor Kangaroo (from just £1.50 a pint), the pub's real attraction remains. Also, sprucing the place up, adding more seats and moving the pool table has shifted the balance of the clientele to include more women and more couples. Licensing difficulties have so far restricted the late opening and the provision of weekend music, but by the time you read this, everything should be tickety boo. Food is still evolving, but expect home-cooked pub grub at knock-down rates.
Babies and children admitted (until 7pm). Games (darts, fruit machine, pool table). Jukebox. Late licence (Fri, Sat). Music (disco 9.30pm Fri, 8pm Sun; live bands 10.30pm Sat). Satellite TV (big screen). Tables outdoors (garden). Vegetarian dishes.

Dog & Bell

116 Prince Street, SE8 (020 8692 5664). Deptford rail or New Cross tube/rail. **Open** noon-11pm Mon-Sat; noon-10.30pm Sun. **Food served** noon-2.30pm, 6-9pm Mon-Fri. **No credit cards**.
Regulars at this backstreet local include lecturers and students from nearby Greenwich University, musicians, actors, writers, builders and market traders. The pub is divided into three small rooms, with walls painted a pleasant shade of peach and plenty of rustic wood furniture scattered around. At the back, there's a pool table and a shove-ha'penny board, while the unobtrusive music comes from a tinny transistor radio. Being a genuine freehouse, the beer is good. The full range of Fuller's cask ales is available – including London Pride (£1.89) and ESB (£2.25) – together with a trio of guest beers: on our last visit, we sampled a pleasantly bitter Nethergate Umbel Ale (filtered through coriander seeds, £1.75). Food is home-cooked and palatable: two specials that caught our eye were pasta, broccoli and three cheese bake (£3) and Lincolnshire sausages with French stick (£2.50).
Games (bar billiards). Quiz (Sun). Tables outdoors (garden). TV. Vegetarian dishes.

Dulwich SE21

Crystal Palace Tavern

193 Crystal Palace Road, SE22 (020 8693 4968).
East Dulwich or North Dulwich rail/40, 176, 185 bus.
Open 11am-11pm Mon-Sat; noon-10.30pm Sun.
No credit cards.
This boozer doesn't look like much from the outside, but inside, it's that rare beast: a Victorian pub that wasn't reconstructed from plastic in 1984. The delicately curved wooden serving area in the L-shaped saloon bar is to the left as you enter, with a roaring fire opposite. Red velvet banquettes and a smattering of tables and stools sit under a deep maroon ceiling hung with chandeliers, and the tastefully papered walls studded with contemporary pictures and artefacts from the original Crystal Palace. The public bar is similar but less comfortable, attracting a cosmopolitan mix of students, twenty- and thirtysomethings and pensioners. This pub has no links with its namesake in Deptford (*see p177*), but well-kept and cheap real ales are also a speciality here: Burton Ale (£1.80), Marston's Pedigree, London Pride and Young's Special (all £1.90) were available on our last visit. Food is strictly low-key, but with sandwiches starting at £1.30, you can't go wildly wrong.
Babies and children admitted. Games (darts, fruit machine). Quiz (Wed). Satellite TV. Tables outdoors (pavement).

Crown & Greyhound

73 Dulwich Village, SE21 (020 8693 2466). North Dulwich rail. **Open** 11am-11pm Mon-Sat; noon-10.30pm Sun. **Food served** noon-2.30pm, 5.30-10pm Mon-Sat; noon-3pm Sun. **Credit** MC, V.
Around the turn of the last century, two Dulwich pubs – the Crown and the Greyhound – were demolished and replaced with this single pile. And in the Victorian way, it's big, going on huge: there are four bar areas, including a ludicrously unprotected no-smoking area (nice thought, though), as well as a banqueting suite and a restaurant, where you can get upwardly mobile pub food of the steak and mushroom pie/rainbow trout variety (around £5-£7). There's also an expansive garden and a child-friendly conservatory where – if you're lucky – crayons may have been left out for you to play with. The drinking part has ornate dark wood partitions, high ceilings and plenty of good-looking glasswork. Beers are well kept: Tetley's Bitter (£1.10) and Young's 'ordinary' (£1.12) are regulars, while ciders include Dry Blackthorn (£2.40) and Sweet Blackthorn (£1.50 by the bottle).
Babies and children admitted (children's menu, high chairs, nappy-changing facilities). Disabled: toilet. Function rooms. Games (fruit machine). No piped music or jukebox. No-smoking area (in restaurant). Restaurant. Satellite TV (big screen). Tables outdoors (garden). Vegetarian dishes.

Also in the area...

Café Rouge 84 Park Hall Road, SE21
(020 8766 0070).

Forest Hill SE23

Bird in Hand

35 Dartmouth Road, SE23 (020 8699 7417). Forest Hill rail. **Open** 11am-11pm Mon-Sat; noon-10.30pm Sun.
Food served noon-8pm daily. **Credit** AmEx, DC, MC, V.
Not all Wetherspoon pubs are barns, a fact proven by this compact little number. The square-shaped front bar is where the serious drinkers hang out, downing reasonably priced pints

(Courage Best £1.10, Stella £2.27), studying the racing form and pondering Lottery numbers. The narrow central section leads up a couple of shallow steps to a dining room, which doubles as a no-smoking area. Here, earnest young things mull over their theses while grizzled older types brush up on Kerouac and Kesey. Expect the usual Wetherspoon perks: a lack of piped music and video games, and good food for under a fiver.
Babies and children admitted (until 6pm). Games (fruit machines). Music (live 8.30pm Sat). No-smoking area. Satellite TV. Tables outdoors (pavement). Vegetarian dishes.

Railway Telegraph

112 Stanstead Road, SE23 (020 8699 6644). Forest Hill rail/122, 185 bus. **Open** 11am-11pm Mon-Sat; noon-10.30pm Sun. **Food served** noon-2pm Mon-Fri.
Credit AmEx, DC, MC, V.
The Railway Telegraph used to be something of a local, festooned with Southern Region railway imagery and stocking all of Shepherd Neame's fine ales on draught. A recent makeover improved the decor immeasurably – it's now a light and airy yellow, gold and white one-room continental-style bar, and the imagery is more Orient Express than Ivor the Engine – but along the way, some of the beers went walkabout. Now, you'll be lucky to find more than a couple of bitters (Masterbrew £1.85, and an autumn seasonal ale when we last visited), with the rest in bottles. The array of lagers seems unaltered, with Oranjeboom (£2.05) leading the rabble, while the food is a very palatable cross between home-made pub grub and Café Rouge-ish bistro fare; the chunky sandwiches are a bargain (£2.25-£2.45).
Babies and children admitted (until 7pm). Games (darts, fruit machine, quiz machine). Jukebox. Quiz (last Wed of month). Satellite TV (big screen). Tables outdoors (garden, pavement). Vegetarian dishes.

Also in the area...

Hobgoblin 7 Devonshire Road, SE23
(020 8291 2225).

Greenwich SE10

Ashburnham Arms

25 Ashburnham Grove, SE10 (020 8692 2007). Greenwich rail/DLR. **Open** noon-3.30pm, 6-11pm Mon-Sat; noon-3.30pm, 7-10.30pm Sun. **Food served** noon-2.30pm, 6-8.30pm Tue-Fri; noon-2.30pm Sat, Sun.
Credit (food only) MC, V.
Hidden away in a sidestreet within staggering distance of the railway station, this is the sort of pub you thought had been knocked into a Finnegan's Wake (sic) years ago. This is a genuine locals' local: the welcome is friendly, the beer – Shepherd Neame Spitfire (£2.20), Hürlimann lager (£2.40) – is good, and the food, though limited to an array of pasta dishes, is decent value at £4.95 a throw. A bar billiards table lounges in its own space to the left of the bar, and there's a cosy little conservatory at the rear.
Babies and children admitted (conservatory only; children's menu). Games (bar billiards). Quiz (Tue). Tables outdoors (garden, patio). Vegetarian dishes.

Cutty Sark

Ballast Quay, off Lassell Street, SE10 (020 8858 3146). Greenwich rail/DLR/Maze Hill rail. **Open** 11am-11pm Mon-Sat; noon-10.30pm Sun. **Food served** 11am-9pm Mon-Sat; noon-7pm Sun. **Credit** DC, MC, V.

Railway Telegraph

Formerly the Union Tavern, more a seaman's pub then than now, the Cutty Sark is a spacious, split-level establishment. As seems compulsory in Greenwich, nautical knick-knacks line the walls, though real river lovers will enjoy a pleasant view across the Thames. The five real ales are changed on a regular basis, though their price (around £2.20) reflects the fact that this is a tourist haunt as well as a local. Food is good and – as you may have guessed already – tends to be fish-based.
Babies and children admitted (children's menu). Function room. Games (fruit machine). Jukebox. No-smoking area. Restaurant. Tables outdoors (riverside terrace). Vegetarian dishes.

Gipsy Moth

60 Greenwich Church Street, SE10 (020 8858 0786). Greenwich rail. **Open** 11am-11pm Mon-Sat; noon-10.30pm Sun. **Food served** noon-3pm daily. **Credit** (food only) MC, V.
Like its near-neighbour the **Cutty Sark** (*see above*), the Gipsy Moth was not always named after a ship. The former Wheatsheaf has come into its own in recent years, providing standard pub food (roast beef £6.50) and drink to the hordes of tourists that come to ogle the vestiges of a seafaring nation. The beer is good: Adnams Broadside (£2.20) is the pick of the ales, though visitors who prefer lager are well served by Carlsberg Export (£2.40). The pub is large and jangly with the sound of the many machines that occupy most free corners. There's a terrace at the back, where it's almost possible to escape the worst of the piped music that's beamed out to pacify the young locals who congregate by the bar.
Babies and children admitted (before 7pm; colouring books, high chairs, nappy-changing facilities). Disabled: toilet. Games (fruit machines, quiz machine, video game). Tables outdoors (garden). Vegetarian dishes.

North Pole

131 Greenwich High Road, SE10 (020 8853 3020). Greenwich rail/DLR. **Open** 5.30-11pm Mon; noon-11pm Tue-Sat; noon-10.30pm Sun. **Food served** noon-3pm Tue-Sat. **Credit** AmEx, DC, MC, V.
This vast pub near Greenwich station has a bar downstairs and a restaurant upstairs, with each taking on a distinct identity. Below, a zinc bar, curved purple walls and a high noise level create a clubby, style-conscious ambience. The North Pole is a freehouse: draughts include Stella, Murphy's (both £2.50), Boddingtons (£2.30) and Hoegaarden (£1.80 a half). Head up the spiral staircase and you're in a spacious modern country-house dining room. The food is expensive but worth it: roast fillet of red mullet with Jerusalem artichoke mash (£12), or char-grilled beef teriyaki with crispy glass noodles (£14.50). Customers tend to be young students and the better-heeled.
Babies and children admitted (high chairs). Function room. Music (DJs Sun; live jazz Thur). Restaurant. TV. Tables outdoors (pavement). Vegetarian dishes.

Richard I

52-54 Royal Hill, SE10 (020 8692 2996). Greenwich rail/DLR. **Open** 11am-11pm Mon-Sat; noon-10.30pm Sun. **Food served** noon-2.30pm Mon-Fri; 1-3pm Sat; 1-4pm Sun. **No credit cards**.
There are people whose dream it is to escape to a world without muzak and video games, where Young's beer (Bitter £1.90, Special £2.10) flows freely. You'll find many of them here, at this smart two-bar local tucked away behind Greenwich nick. The clientele is mainly young, and a fair few radiate the well-being only a good income can bestow. A large beer garden at the back offers a popular option during the warmer months. Lunchtime food is tasty if unexceptional: expect the likes of fish in parsley sauce and spicy bean burgers (both £3.65).
No piped music or jukebox. Tables outdoors (garden, pavement). Vegetarian dishes.

Time

*7A College Approach, SE10 (020 8305 9767). Greenwich
Maritime DLR.* **Open** noon-11pm Mon-Fri; noon-midnight
Sat; noon-10.30pm Sun. **Food served** 7-10.30pm Mon,
Sat; noon-2pm, 7-10.30pm Tue-Fri; noon-3pm, 7-10pm Sun.
Credit MC, V.
Situated beside the central market, Time resembles an old
Methodist hall: the main bar is on the first floor, with the
restaurant perched on a balcony above. The bar-gallery –
check out the regularly changing paintings and designs –
has tall, white-painted stone walls and comfortable low-slung
metal and padded fabric sofas, occupied, typically, by a
craggily handsome thirtysomething actor out with his long-
legged student girlfriend. Various draught lagers are on offer
at £2.50 a pint, with bottled beers and spirit-mixer combos
similarly priced. The menu may include tiger prawns stuffed
inside baby squid skewered on lemon grass, and tofu and
wild mushroom stroganoff; foodies insist it's much better
than the descriptions would suggest (set dinner £22.50 for
three courses).
*Babies and children admitted (high chairs). Dress code
(weekends). Function room. Music (DJs Fri, Sat; live jazz
9pm Sun). Restaurant. Vegetarian dishes.*

Trafalgar Tavern

*Park Row, SE10 (020 8858 2437/www.gmt2000.co.uk).
Cutty Sark Gardens DLR/Maze Hill rail.*
Open 11.30am-11pm Mon-Sat; noon-10.30pm Sun.
Food served noon-10pm Mon-Sat; noon-3pm Sun, Mon.
Credit MC, V.
This large and stately riverside pub was built in 1837 on the
site of the old George Tavern. In the nineteenth century, it was
customary for members of the Cabinet to pop in for whitebait
dinners, reduced versions of which are still available in the
dining rooms (a mere £5.25). Indeed, the food is upmarket for
a pub, ranging from moules marinière and chips (£6) to
spinach tagliatelle in tomato sauce (£7.95). The three large bar
rooms, meanwhile, retain a stately air, with walls painted in
dark browns, greens and gold. The Courage beer is well kept,
though perhaps the biggest perk is the riverside terrace: it
offers views of the Millennium Dome and, if you crane your
neck past the university buildings, the *Cutty Sark*.
*Babies and children admitted (children's menu, high
chairs). Function rooms. Music (jazz 9pm Sat).
Restaurant. Tables outdoors (riverside terrace).
Vegetarian dishes.*

Also in the area...

Café Rouge 30 Stockwell Street, SE10 (020 8293
6660).
Davys Wine Vaults 161-169 Greenwich High Road,
SE10 (020 8858 3919).
Funnel & Firkin 174 Greenwich High Road, SE10
(020 8305 2088).

Kennington, Lambeth, Oval, SE1, SE11

Bar Room Bar

*111 Kennington Road, SE11 (020 7820 3682). Lambeth
North tube.* **Open** noon-11pm Mon-Wed; noon-midnight
Thur; noon-1am Fri, Sat; noon-10.30pm Sun. **Food
served** noon-10.30pm Mon-Wed; noon-11.30pm Thur;
noon-12.30am Fri, Sat; noon-10pm Sun. **Happy hour** 5.30-
7.30pm Thur-Tue; all day Wed. **Credit** MC, V.

Time

A pub sign is all that remains of the pub, the Tankard, that
once occupied this site. The building has been completely
overhauled and is now a part of the Bar Room Bar chain, a
spacious bar-cum-pizzeria with a shiny metal-and-wood bar
– offering the likes of Heineken (£2.30), Guinness (£2.50) and
Hoegaarden (£3) – and a wood-burning oven cooking tasty,
thin-crust pizzas: try the original feta Greek flatbread (£6.95).
The warm brick walls display modern art, while fairy lights
bead the huge windows. Up the spiral staircase is a roof
garden overlooking the Kennington Road; it's fabulous in the
sunshine, potted palms and all. When the wind whips up,
retreat to the upstairs snug with its tan leather sofas and a
computer offering Internet access. Loud music limits
conversation and ensures a clubby feel in the evenings.
*Babies and children admitted (until 8pm). Disabled: toilet.
Games (board games Sun). Function room. Music (DJs
Tue, Wed, Fri, Sat; live music Thur). Satellite TV. Tables
outdoors (roof terrace). Vegetarian dishes.*

Beehive

*60 Carter Street, SE17 (020 7703 4992). Kennington
tube/12, 68, 68A, 171, 176 bus.* **Open** 11am-11pm
Mon-Sat; noon-10.30pm Sun. **Food served** noon-3pm,
5.30-10pm Mon-Fri; noon-10pm Sat, Sun. **Credit** MC, V.
The trendy young of SE17 are attracted to the Beehive like
bees to a honeypot, not so much by the overflowing hanging
baskets but, rather, by the fine beers on tap: expect to find
such delights as Wadworth 6X (£2.13), Courage Bitter (£1.90)
and Directors (£2.13). The food, despite the cosy candlelit
railway carriage benches of the self-named 'bistro', is not
worth the journey: the special was a three-egg omelette
(£4.50), while the double-decker Beehive burger (£6.20) was

dull. Settle down, instead, with a pint in the library area, where you can admire a *Daily Mail* front page telling of Thatcher's downfall; once hung, no doubt, to inspire the workers at what used to be Labour's HQ along the Walworth Road nearby.
Babies and children admitted. Function room. Satellite TV. Tables outdoors (patio). Vegetarian dishes.

Dog House
293 Kennington Road, SE11 (020 7820 9310). Kennington or Oval tube. **Open** noon-11pm Mon-Fri; 6-11pm Sat; noon-10.30pm Sun. **Food served** noon-3pm Mon, Tue; noon-3pm, 7-10pm Wed, Thur; noon-3pm Sun. **Credit** MC, V.
Given the unprepossessing nature of both its location (on the corner of Kennington Cross) and exterior (sludgy-brown), you'd be forgiven for heading straight past the Dog House. Try not to. The interior is more pleasant than the exterior: the chic bohemian look – distressed brown walls, gilded mirrors, a huge green fireplace dripping with candle wax – attracts south London's twentysomethings, who are found a-grooving and a-shaking here most nights. There are no decent bitters, but the tap beers include Grolsch (£2.50), Guinness (£2.45) and Caffrey's (£2.45), and the food is wholesome: a generous vegetable chilli and tortilla cost £5.95. The traditional roast and the wobbly stack of board games also make this an appealing place in which to settle down for a lazy Sunday.
Babies and children admitted. Function room. Tables outdoors (pavement). Vegetarian dishes.

Greyhound
336 Kennington Park Road, SE11 (020 7735 2594). Oval tube. **Open** 11am-11pm Mon-Sat; 12.15-10.30pm Sun. **Food served** noon-4pm daily. **Credit** AmEx, DC, MC, V.
The Surrey cricket bat and sweater encased in a glass cabinet give away this cosy, unpretentious locals' location: just a lofted straight drive or two from the Oval Cricket Ground. The decor is a mix of suburban sitting room and Victorian pub: olde-style lamps, plates along the painted beams, and a swirling carpet that would hide the most lurid vomit. Leather benches line the thin seating area, which also holds a Heritage jukebox, two small TVs and a fruit machine. The Guinness (£2.20) is popular, although Greene King IPA, Directors (both £2) and Courage Best (£1.90) are all on offer. Food is of the functional variety – sausage, egg and chips (£3.50) and the like – with Sunday lunch served noon-4pm.
Babies and children admitted (until 7pm). Games (fruit machine). Jukebox. Satellite TV. Vegetarian dishes.

Prince of Wales
48 Cleaver Square, SE11 (020 7735 9916). Kennington tube. **Open** noon-3pm, 5-11pm Mon-Wed; noon-11pm Thur, Fri; 5-11pm Sat; noon-10pm Sun. **Food served** noon-2pm, 5.30-7.30pm Mon-Wed; noon-2pm Thur, Fri. **Credit** MC, V.
The Prince of Wales is a delightfully old-school pub: warm fire, real ales, red floor and walls, and *Vanity Fair* prints. Candles in bottles and the friendly, attentive staff ensure a good atmosphere in which to settle down to your Shepherd Neame Spitfire, or the seasonal ale, currently Early Bird (both £2.20) or Oranjeboom (£2.10), or in which to tuck into a beef stew (£5.95) or beer-battered haddock (£5.25). The tables outside look out on to pretty Cleaver Square, with its Georgian houses and French-looking white-gravel gardens, and an area not unfamiliar to previous party leaders Paddy Ashdown and John Major. Good for a relaxed evening of intimate conversation.
Babies and children admitted (dining only). Tables outdoors (pavement). Vegetarian dishes.

Three Stags
67-69 Kennington Road, SE1 (020 7928 5974). Lambeth North tube. **Open** noon-11pm Mon-Sat; noon-10.30pm Sun. **Food served** noon-8.30pm daily. **Credit** AmEx, DC, MC, V.
Guinness barrels remain stacked outside, but otherwise the Irish theme has been abandoned: Brendon O'Grady's has reincarnated as the Three Stags, the bar where Charlie Chaplin's dad reputedly drank himself to death. The wall decorations are a mix of Chaplin memorabilia and fighter pilot photographs, the latter there for the benefit of visitors to the nearby Imperial War Museum. Gone, too, is the Irish folk music and plain English food: pie and mash (£4.85), fish and chips (£3.45) and the like. The quirky booths, though, remain, as does the same chatty barman, who now serves a range of Greene King specialities (IPA £1.90, Triumph £2.05).
Babies and children admitted (until 5pm). Disabled: toilet. Games (fruit machine). Tables outdoors (pavement). Sports TV. Vegetarian dishes.

White Bear
138 Kennington Park Road, SE11 (020 7735 8664). Kennington or Oval tube. **Open/food served** 11am-midnight Mon-Sat; 11am-11pm Sun. **No credit cards.**
The White Bear is a fabulous cross between a flamboyant theatre pub and a smoky dive. The maroon walls are adorned with framed posters of past productions, while beneath the turquoise ceiling is a gilded arch over the double doors marked 'Theatre'. On the opposite wall is a huge TV screen, visible from the high-backed stools at the circular bar and the battered lime-green sofas along the walls. The owner's own German beer mugs fill the shelves, but the beers on tap are unremarkable, such as Greene King IPA (£2.30) and Grolsch (£2.10). There's a quiz on Monday nights with a £65 prize, which, when coupled with a fruit machine, a friendly barman and a meaty all day breakfast (£2.80), adds up to plenty of entertainment.
Babies and children admitted (until 7pm). Games (fruit machines). Jukebox. Quiz (Mon). Satellite TV. Tables outdoors (courtyard, garden). Theatre. Vegetarian dishes.

Lee SE12

Crown
117 Burnt Ash Hill, SE12 (020 8857 6607). Lee rail. **Open** 11am-11pm Mon-Sat; noon-10.30pm Sun. **Food served** noon-2.30pm, 6-9pm Mon-Sat; noon-3pm, 7-9pm Sun. **Credit** DC, MC, V.
A large, comfortable open-plan Young's pub with a long serving area running practically the length of one wall. The bar is backed by a hefty piece of woodwork, decorated with carved ram's heads, with an almost equally solid group of middle-aged locals sitting on stools in front. Younger customers lounge in armchairs and wooden granddad chairs scattered around chunky timber tables in the pub's three linked rooms. The walls are covered in Regency-style wallpaper and dotted with framed pictures of every subject imaginable, from hunting prints to a photograph of a grizzled old seaman to a bowl of fruit. The beer is Young's (Special £2.05), and an extensive wine list runs to 18 and kicks off at £2.25 a glass (£8.95 a bottle). Food caters to most tastes and includes hand-sliced ham and two eggs (£4.75), and mussels in white wine and garlic (£5.25).
Games (fruit machine). Function room. Quiz (Sun). Tables outdoors (garden). Vegetarian dishes.

Lewisham SE13

Hogshead

354 Lewisham High Street, SE13 (020 8690 2054).
Ladywell rail. **Open** 11am-11pm Mon-Sat; noon-10.30pm
Sun. **Food served** noon-2.30pm, 5-7pm Mon-Sat; noon-
6pm Sun. **No credit cards.**
Sitting between Lewisham Hospital and an undertaker's
parlour, this friendly outpost of the Hogshead estate gets
more than its fair share of medical types, who quaff the fine
selection of rotating real ales, country wines and lagers on
offer. They're usually joined by a pretty mixed slice of
Lewisham life, from old codgers mourning their passing
youth over pints of Wadworth 6X (£2.05) and young bucks
aiming their mobile phones at the ceiling as they take careful
sips of their bottled lager (Budweiser £2.30). The two small
drinking areas are connected by a central serving area, and
pictures of a Lewisham long gone dot the ochred walls.
Babies and children admitted (summer only; beer garden).
Games (fruit machine, quiz games). Satellite TV. Tables
outdoors (garden). Vegetarian dishes.

Quaggy Duck

139-141 Lewisham High Street, SE13 (020 8297 8645).
Lewisham rail. **Open** 11am-11pm Mon-Sat; noon-10.30pm
Sun. **Food served** 11am-3pm, 6-9pm Mon-Thur; 11am-
5pm Fri; 11am-6pm Sat; noon-5pm Sun. **Credit** MC, V.
A large, purpose-built one-room bar opposite the Lewisham
Centre, with a high ceiling, a sturdy wooden balcony looking
like something out of *High Noon* along one wall, and a huge,
muted TV screen tuned, inevitably, to Sky Sports. The decor is
clean and bright – plenty of wood, ragged walls peppered with
pictures of old Lewisham and an unhealthy number of duck
motifs – and the crowd is young, smart and mostly studenty.
Drinks include the standard – draught Bass (£1.30) and Foster's
(£2.05) – while there are also selections of guest real ales and
shooters (£2.50, five for £10). The food is typical pub grub – a
towering Sunday roast can be had for £4. The Quaggy,
incidentally, is a neglected local river; a duck is, well… a duck.
Disabled: toilet. Games (fruit machines). Music (DJs Fri,
Sat). Quiz (Sun). Satellite TV. Tables outdoors (pavement).
Vegetarian dishes.

Watch House

198-204 Lewisham High Street, SE13 (020 8318 3136).
Lewisham rail/DLR/122 bus. **Open** 11am-11pm Mon-Sat;
noon-10.30pm Sun. **Food served** 11am-10pm Mon-Sat;
noon-9.30pm Sun. **Credit** AmEx, DC, MC, V.
Named after the nearby Watch House Green, this is a medium-
sized Wetherspoon pub with the now-requisite no-smoking
area, silence (no music or video games) and decent pub grub
at even more decent prices (£4-£7). The real ales change on a
regular basis, but we enjoyed Shepherd Neame Spitfire (£1.55)
and bottled Beck's at a bargain £1.35. The decor is interesting
and seems to change according to where you sit: a portrait of
Marie Lloyd sits alongside Dadd-ish impressions of fairies,
Alice in Wonderland and an outrageously picture of something
resembling an impressionist sea view. The clientele reflects the
area and is a cosmopolitan cross-section of Lewisham society,
with a bias towards fortysomething males downing the bitter.
Disabled: toilet. Games (fruit machines). No piped music or
jukebox. No-smoking area. Tables outdoors (patio).
Vegetarian dishes.

Also in the area...

Fox & Firkin 316 Lewisham High Street, SE13
(020 8690 8925).

New Cross SE14

Hobgoblin

272 New Cross Road, SE14 (020 8692 3193). New Cross
Gate tube/rail/36, 89, 136, 171, 177 bus. **Open** 11am-
11pm Mon-Sat; noon-10.30pm Sun. **Happy hour** 2-8pm
Mon-Fri. **Food served** noon-5pm Mon-Sat; noon-4pm
Sun. **No credit cards.**
The former Rose Inn, a pub located between Goldsmith's
College and New Cross station that once sheathed itself in a
pall of cigarette smoke to repel boarders, has had a welcome
makeover. Emerging as a user-friendly member of
Wychwood Brewery's Hobgoblin chain, it's now a large,
bright, wood-floored, wooden-alcoved, single-bar pub
wrapped in a horseshoe shape around a wood-and-tile central
serving area with a flagged garden to the rear. The
Wychwood goblin motif seems limited to blackboards,
although the skeleton behind the bar may tell a tale. The
beer's good and cheap, with the Wychwood Special at £1.80
a pint and Marston's Pedigree, Directors and a regularly
changing guest ale all £2. Bottled beers and lagers on tap
widen the choice. Food ranges from sausage casserole (veggie
or meat, £3.50) to spicy parsnip soup (£1.80) and brie and
salmon bap (£2.50). Most customers are students
(unsurprising since they're offered 20% discount 2-8pm, Mon-
Fri); the rest are older locals.
Disabled: toilet. Games (fruit machines, quiz machines).
Jukebox. Satellite TV. Tables outdoors (garden).
Vegetarian dishes.

Peckham SE15, SE22

Clock House

196A Peckham Rye, SE22 (020 8693 2901).
East Dulwich or Peckham Rye rail/Elephant & Castle
tube/12, 37, 63, 176, 185, 312 bus. **Open** 11am-11pm
Mon-Fri; 10am-11pm Sat; 10am-10.30pm Sun.
Food served 12.30-10pm Mon-Fri; 10am-10pm Sat, Sun.
Credit MC, V.
You won't find too many pubs with olive trees growing inside
them: this, in fact, is the only one we can find in Peckham.
The tree in question sits underneath a skylight in the centre
of the recently refurbished and extended back room. The
theme here is clocks: the place is full of them, though hardly
any seem to work. Outside, there's a heated terrace with bench
seats, surrounded in summer by masses of award-winning
flowers in tubs and baskets. The beer is Young's (Special
£2.08) and there's the usual wide selection of wines by the
glass and bottle, though food is limited to slices of pies and
salad: chicken and broccoli, vegetable quiche and the like (all
£4.50, £3 just garnish). The customers bear no relation to
those in *Only Fools and Horses*: the last time we visited,
drinkers included a well-known writer/performer and a
notable author. Consider this end of Peckham Rye well and
truly gentrified.
Disabled: toilet. Music (pianist Tue-Thur eve). Tables
outdoors (patio). Vegetarian dishes.

Wishing Well

77 Choumert Road, SE15 (020 7639 5052). Peckham
Rye rail. **Open** 11am-11pm Mon-Sat; noon-10.30pm Sun.
Food served 11am-2.30pm Mon-Fri; 1-5pm Sun. **Happy**
hour 11am-6pm Mon-Fri. **No credit cards.**
Tucked away in a backstreet behind Peckham Rye station,
this comfortable green and gold pub has an ornate
Edwardian wooden ceiling and bar-back that harks back to
the time when it was the Victoria Hotel, a notable commercial

inn. Beer doesn't come much cheaper, even in Peckham – draught Guinness and Flowers are both £1.90 a pint – and despite the over-sentimental songs on the jukebox, the atmosphere is lively and you'll receive a genuine welcome. The banquettes around the walls are slightly past their sell-by date, but that's part of the charm: this is a genuine locals' local (with a slight Irish accent) that's also famed for its £4 Sunday roasts.

Babies and children admitted (until 7pm). Games (fruit machine, pool tables, quiz machine). Jukebox. Quiz (Thur). Satellite TV (big screen). Tables outdoors (pavement).

Putney SW15

Bar Coast
50-54 High Street, SW15 (020 8780 8931). Putney Bridge tube. **Open/food served** noon-midnight Mon-Thur; noon-1am Fri, Sat; 11am-10.30pm Sun. **Happy hour** 5-8pm daily. **Credit** MC, V.
There's nothing particularly subtle about this good-time place, but it delivers the liquid goods to the Putney lads and ladettes whenever they're up for a shouty night out. Black T-shirted staff work the long shiny bar, backed by a glowing blue wall stacked with the usual designer beers (draught Grolsch £2.40, Hoegaarden £3.60; bottled Tiger, Michelob both £2.60) pile-'em in spirits, cappuccino machines and – bizarrely – a selection of plastic dinosaurs and shoes. Armchairs down the far end of the room offer partial sanctuary at peak times (and you'll get served quicker here), otherwise there are precious few seats troubling the scrubbed floorboards. Things are more relaxed during the day, thanks to the high, handsome windows opening on to the street and a more subdued clientele of tired shoppers.
Disabled: toilet. Games (fruit machine). Late licence (Fri, Sat). Music (DJs Thur-Sat). Vegetarian dishes.

Bier Rex
22 Putney High Street, SW15 (020 8394 5901). Putney Bridge tube. **Open** noon-11pm Mon-Sat; noon-10.30pm Sun. **Food served** noon-3pm, 6-9pm daily. **Credit** MC, V.
If you're young, you live in Putney and you don't like pubs or wine bars, then you probably end up in Bier Rex, a modern design bar that comes on like a club at the weekends. A narrow, bare brick entrance, lined with a couple of tables and lashings of neon, opens on to the long side bar – get your Belgian beer here – before revealing the large, dark back room and a bedraggled DJ operating in front of an impressive glass photomontage. It's young, it's loud and it's yellow. And if you can't be arsed to go anywhere better, it'll do.
Disabled: toilet. Games (fruit machine). Music (DJs Thur-Sat). Satellite TV. Tables outdoors (pavement). Vegetarian dishes.

Coat & Badge
8 Lacy Road, SW15 (020 8788 4900). Putney Bridge tube/Putney rail/14 bus. **Open** 11am-11pm Mon-Sat; noon-10.30pm Sun. **Food served** noon-2.30pm, 7-9.30pm Mon-Fri; noon-3pm, 7-9.30pm Sat; noon-4pm, 7-9.30pm Sun. **Credit** MC, V.
Pine tables, pine shelving loaded with aged books, stained-glass windows, oars, art and masks on the walls, a large Welsh dresser and a fine long wooden bar studded with Young's pumps and backed with malts – all add up to an easy, arty atmosphere that's helped by an upfront, late-20s night-time crowd. The high-end pub food is also a draw: moules marinière (£4), pork and spinach sausages (£7.50) and gigot of lamb (£9.50) are well produced and all,

apparently, GM-free. You can eat this indoors or at a pub table on the large, flagstoned courtyard out front – very popular with Waitrose refugees in the summer.
Babies and children admitted (until 7pm). Function room. Tables outdoors (terrace). Vegetarian dishes.

Duke's Head
8 Lower Richmond Road, SW15 (020 8788 2552). Putney Bridge tube/265 bus. **Open** 11am-11pm Mon-Sat; noon-10.30pm Sun. **Food served** noon-2.30pm, 6-10pm Mon-Sat; noon-3pm Sun. **Credit** MC, V.
The Duke's Head was undergoing some minor redecoration on our last visit, but they'll be hard-pushed to improve on this comfortable pub's main asset – a row of huge, high bay windows offering spectacular views of the river. This is in the (currently sparse) main back room, which otherwise flaunts a fine collection of ornate mirrors, art deco uplights and a trim little bar from which Young's ales ('ordinary' £2, Special £2.10) and decent pub grub (sausages and mash £5.50, scampi £6.50) are dispensed by cheery young women. Large groups of local bankers occupy the comfy sofas. The snug front room clings to the main, central bar and is chosen by a more subdued crowd, perhaps tuned into the football on the telly.
Games (table football). No piped music or jukebox. Tables outdoors (riverside patio). Satellite TV. Vegetarian dishes.

Green Man
Wildcroft Road, Putney Heath, SW15 (020 8788 8096). East Putney tube/Putney rail/14, 39, 85, 93, 170 bus. **Open** 11am-11pm Mon-Sat; noon-10.30pm Sun. **Food served** noon-2.30pm daily. **No credit cards.**
The Green Man can justly claim to be the area's one true destination venue, given that the No.14 bus wheezes to a halt just opposite its front door. Inside, what you get is a thoroughly unpretentious and comfortable two-bar pub. The smaller one to the left has wooden benches, a couple of tables and soft-spoken locals supping down the Young's ales (£1.87 a pint of Bitter) and the strong sense of history (Dick Turpin and Algernon Swinburne have both raised a glass here). The larger bar has yet more wood, a marginally more animated clientele, a tiny TV and some cheerful signs stating the times of the next Chelsea game. The place is invariably busier in the summer, given its pleasant courtyard out front, which would look directly on to the heath were it not for the intervening traffic.
Games (board games, darts, fruit machine). No piped music or jukebox. Quiz (Mon). TV. Tables outdoors (children's play area, garden, patio). Vegetarian dishes.

Half Moon
93 Lower Richmond Road, SW15 (020 8780 9383/ www.halfmoon.co.uk). Putney Bridge tube/Putney rail. **Open** noon-11pm Mon-Sat; noon-10.30pm Sun. **Happy hour** 8.30-11pm Mon. **No credit cards.**
What was once Putney's acclaimed acoustic music venue (and the back still plays host to any number of young and eager bands) also happens to offer all the ingredients for an unchallenging big night out: table football and pool, video games, a big screen and a jukebox of rare depth and volume, all arranged round a curved, pillared bar stocking the usual roster of fine Young's ales ('ordinary' £2, Special £2.10) and a standard selection of bottled beers for £2.50. The relaxed, almost nostalgic vibe is further enhanced by the pub's jumble of junk shop clutter – chandeliers, gargoyles, sofas, pots and pans, Victorian wall lamps – and kept breezy by the high ceilings and the deeply unpretentious punters. Candidate for Putney's best pub.
Games (fruit machine, pool table, table football). Music (bands nightly, from £2, 8.30pm; live jazz 1-4pm Sun). Satellite TV (big screen). Tables outdoors (garden).

Parisa Café Bar

146-148 Putney High Street, SW15 (020 8785 3131).
East Putney tube/Putney Bridge rail. **Open/food served**
8am-11pm Mon-Sat; 10am-10.30pm Sun. **Happy hour** 5-
7pm daily. **Credit** AmEx, MC, V.
Coming on like a Café Rouge with attitude, Parisa offers a
pleasant chance for younger Putneyites to enjoy a decent
range of wines and fair food in an untroubled atmosphere
(we're charitably assuming the satanically loud MOR music
was a Friday night aberration). Food goes from the
pleasingly simple (continental platter £6.25) to the more
exotic (Cypriot chicken £9.25), and although wine is Parisa's
main business – every wall is piled high with its 250 bottles,
glasses start at £2.25 – the bar also proudly sports all the
shiny brass fittings of a microbrewery. This is misleading,
in that we're told the beer is brewed elsewhere and shipped
in, but we can still enthusiastically endorse the Parisa Silver
Shadow ale (£2.30).
Babies and children admitted (high chairs). Disabled: toilet.
No-smoking area. Vegetarian dishes.

Putney Bridge

Embankment, 2 Lower Richmond Road, SW15 (020 8780
1811/www.putneybridgerestaurant.com). Putney Bridge
tube. **Open** noon-11pm Mon-Sat; noon-10.30pm Sun.
Food served noon-2.30pm, 7-10.30pm Tue-Sat; 12.30-
3pm Sun. **Credit** AmEx, DC, MC, V.
Whether you're dining or not in the splendidly chic French
restaurant, its satellite bar (which in any case occupies the
entire ground floor) is a fine place in which to while away an
evening. A chunky bronze Elizabeth Frink and a gaggle of
receptionists guard the entrance, but once through you can
enjoy a slickly designed operation: the high, sleek bar curves
down the left side, banquettes and river views sit to the right.
Further down is a smaller, more private room with curious
box wall lights. The clientele can afford to spend £3.10 on
bottled beers (Kirin, Red Stripe), £5.75 or more on any one of
80 cocktails or indulge in a bar menu that includes tempura
vegetables (£4.95) and smoked salmon (£8.50). A word of
caution: Monday evenings, when the restaurant's closed and
the only bar snacks are salted almonds, are sad affairs.
Babies and children admitted (restaurant only). Disabled:
toilet. Restaurant. Tables outdoors (riverside terrace).
Vegetarian dishes.

Also in the area...

Café Rouge 200-204 Putney Bridge Road, SW15
(020 8788 4257).
Slug & Lettuce 14 Putney High Street, SW15 (020
8785 3081).

South Norwood SE25

Alliance

91 High Street, SE25 (020 8653 3604). Norwood
Junction rail. **Open** 11am-11pm Mon-Sat; noon-10.30pm
Sun. **Food served** noon-2pm Mon-Fri. **No credit cards.**
A proper local next to Norwood Junction rail station that
manages to mix the virtues of an old-fashioned pub with fresh
air and decent grub. The patterned carpet matches the
upholstery, brass pots and pans dangling from the ceiling,
and the combining of Gothic wrought-iron ceiling lamps with
art nouveau shades is strangely effective. The customers are
a mixed bunch – in age, sex and background – ranging from
tight groups of late-teens to whiskery old geezers puffing on
pipes; but most are 25-40-year-olds, home from work. Food is

home-cooked and cheap, with the likes of egg and chips,
grilled gammon and shepherd's pie available lunchtimes, for
£2-£3, with O'Hagen's sausages a speciality. Courage Best at
a bargain £1.50 is joined by two or three high-quality guest
ales (Timothy Taylor Landlord included) for £1.75 a pint.
Worth seeking out.
Games (fruit machines). Jukebox. TV. Vegetarian dishes.

Goat House

2 Penge Road, SE25 (020 8778 5752). Norwood Junction
rail. **Open** 11am-11pm Mon-Sat; noon-10.30pm Sun.
Food served noon-3.30pm, 5.30-9.30pm Mon-Fri; noon-
9.30pm Sat; noon-6pm Sun. **Credit** AmEx, DC, MC, V.
A large open-plan Fuller's pub that's recently been converted
into a heavily wooded area, complete with enclosed wooden
platforms and a timber stage for the pool table. On the
Thursday night we popped along it was all but deserted,
except for a gang of youths engaged in a private knockout
pool tournament and a brace of young couples keeping an
eye on the car park. The lone barmaid coped admirably. The
beer is well kept, with London Pride at £1.95 a pint, Chiswick
Bitter £1.60, and a reasonable wine selection kicks off at
£2.35. Food is of the pile it high and sell it cheap school of
catering, with meat by the kilo (even if they haven't yet gone
metric in these parts): 1lb rack of ribs, surf and turf and pig
and hen platter for around £6-£7. Vegetarians have a pretty
hard time, unless they're heavily into cheese sandwiches.
There's a conservatory and a sizeable bench-table garden for
sunny days.
Babies and children admitted (until 9pm; high chairs).
Disabled: toilet. Games (darts, fruit machines, pool table).
Jukebox. Music (live 9.30pm every other Sat). Satellite TV
(big screen). Tables outdoors (patio). Vegetarian dishes.

Stockwell SW8, SW9

Bar Estrela

111-115 South Lambeth Road, SW8 (020 7793 1051).
Stockwell tube/Vauxhall tube/rail. **Open/food served**
8am-midnight Mon-Sat; 11am-9pm Sun. **Credit** MC, V.
If it wasn't for the predictably dull English weather outside,
you could almost imagine you'd stepped into a bar in the
heart of the Algarve, at this authentic Portuguese hangout.
Waist-coated waiters serve bottled beers (Sagres, Cristal
both £2.80) and spirits (Madeira £1.30) to a predominantly
Portuguese crowd who stand chatting around the bar, or
lounge in the adjacent café, watching football from the large
(and blaring) corner TV. The bar also boasts a huge range
of Portuguese wines (from around £7.50 a bottle), including
a selection of fruity, fresh vinhos verdes from the north of
the country. Down a glass with (the rather stolid) tapas
dishes on offer (around £2.50), or opt for something more
substantial from the main menu. There are also desserts to
die for (from around £2). However, the café's a little chilly
and uncomfortable for full-on dining (so try the adjoining
restaurant), but this is a lively place to come for a spot of
Mediterranean spirit.
Babies and children admitted (children's menu,
high chairs). Games (pool table). No-smoking area.
Restaurant. Satellite TV. Tables outdoors (pavement).
Vegetarian dishes.

Circle

348 Clapham Road, SW9 (020 7622 3683). Stockwell or
Clapham North tube. **Open** noon-11pm Mon-Sat; noon-
10.30pm Sun. **Food served** noon-3pm, 7.30-10pm
Mon-Thur; noon-3pm Fri-Sun. **Credit** MC, V.

Spirit

The open fire, dimmed lights and dubby background music make this a relaxed and mellow place to hang out on a Sunday, or for a quiet weekday after-work drink. Shabby-chic furnishings are arranged around the central zinc bar, where affable, attentive staff serve up drinks and New World-style meals (including a delicious Moroccan-style lamb kebab £6.75), as well as light snacks (bruschetta melts £3.20). The vodka and cranberry juice is a bargain at £2.20, and Stella is £2.45 on tap. Table football, games machines, a jukebox, DJs and space for dancing will keep you happily entertained till chucking out time.
Function room. Games (board games, fruit machine, table football). Music (DJs Thur-Sat). Satellite TV (big screen). Tables outdoors (garden). Vegetarian dishes.

The Plug

90 Stockwell Road, SW9 (020 7274 3879). Stockwell tube/ Brixton tube/rail. **Open** noon-midnight Mon-Wed, Sun; noon-2am Thur; noon-3am Fri, Sat. **Admission** after 10pm Fri, Sat £5. **Food served** noon-3pm daily. **Credit** AmEx, DC, MC, V.
Traditional pub trappings – wood panelling, stripped floors and sturdy tables – mix with glitter balls, a luminous lime ceiling and steel-topped bar to create a funky, clubby feel at this spacious venue. On weekend nights, the Plug features an eclectic range of DJs spinning everything from techno to hip hop to rhythm and funk, and heaves with a young, trendy crowd here to dance as much as drink. Weekdays are quiet, with most noise coming from the huge satellite sports screen on one wall. There's also a good-size pool table. Amiable staff serve up Grolsch (£2.60 bottled, £2.50 on tap), Foster's and Caffrey's (both £2.40 on tap) with other bar staples.
Babies and children admitted. Disabled: toilet. Function room. Games (fruit machine, pool table, table football). Late licence (Thur-Sat). Music (DJs Thur-Sun). Satellite TV (big screen).

Priory Arms

83 Lansdowne Way, SW8 (020 7622 1884). Stockwell tube. **Open** 11am-11pm Mon-Sat; noon-10.30pm Sun. **Food served** noon-3pm Mon-Sat; 1-3.30pm Sun. **No credit cards.**
This welcoming pub boasts an extensive selection of continental bottled beers with a strong German contingent, including an organic Meusel (£2.80). Adnams fruit wines (£2.60), Kriek fruit beers, a reasonably priced wine list and a punchy Thatcher's cider are also on offer. Board games scattered over the tables, warm and chatty bar staff and theme night specials (such as a haggis supper for Burns' night) all enhance the lively ambience, and the place attracts a loyal, local professional crowd. Food comes in the form of traditional pub fare such as shepherd's pie and quiche, and Sunday lunch is also served. A cosy, comfortable place to while away an evening.
Babies and children admitted (until 8pm). Function room. Games (fruit machine). Quiz (Sun). Satellite TV. Tables outdoors (patio). Vegetarian dishes.

Surprise

16 Southville, SW8 (020 7622 4623). Stockwell tube/ Vauxhall tube/rail. **Open** 11am-11pm Mon-Sat; noon-10.30pm Sun. **Food served** noon-2.30pm, 5.30-8.30pm Mon-Fri; *Apr-Sept* noon-2.30pm Sat, Sun. **Credit** MC, V.
A snug, homely, backstreet pub, set at the end of a dead-end road, and decked out with traditional old-style furnishings and etchings. There are few surprises on the drinks front: draughts include Young's bitters (from £1.90), Carling (£2.25) and Guinness (£2.30), but there is a substantial lunch menu with regularly changing specials, as well as a Surprise Brunch fry-up (£3.50). The older, mostly male crowd almost did a double take when we (two females) walked in, but the atmosphere is relaxed, and chatty bar staff put us at ease. Probably at its best in the summer, when the pretty trellised

beer garden fills up with locals and students from the nearby South Bank University, and punters spill into Larkhall Park that the garden overlooks.
Games (board games, boule pitch, fruit machine, pinball machine). Satellite TV. Tables outdoors (patio). Vegetarian dishes.

Swan
215 Clapham Road, SW9 (020 7978 9778).
Stockwell tube. **Open** 5-11pm Mon-Wed; 5pm-2am Thur; 5pm-3am Fri; 7pm-3am Sat; 7pm-2am Sun. **Admission** 99p Thur; £2.50 before 9pm, £5 after 9pm Fri; £3 before 9pm, £6 after 9pm Sat; £4 after 9pm Sun. **Credit** AmEx, DC, MC, V.
With nightly live acts such as YB Sober and Celtic folksters Bog the Donkey, it's almost worth a trip to the Swan just to check out the band names. Fake wooden beams, chunky wooden furniture and low ceilings give the place a dated '70s feel, and the atmosphere is down-to-earth and unpretentious. On weekdays, it fills up slowly with a laid-back local crowd, who come for the half-price Guinness on Mondays (£1.20), pinball machines and sports coverage via overhead TVs. At weekends, the pub operates strictly as a club, with admission charged, and comes alive with lively, up-for-it revellers. Budweiser and Carlsberg (both £2.20) are on tap, and Irish coffee is available with a choice of liqueurs (from £2.50).
Dress code (weekends). Function room. Games (fruit machine). Late licence (Thur-Sun). Music (DJs Thur-Sun; bands nightly). Satellite TV.

Sydenham SE26

Dulwich Wood House
39 Sydenham Hill, SE26 (020 8693 5666). Sydenham Hill rail/63, 202 bus. **Open** 11am-11pm Mon-Sat; noon-10.30pm Sun. **Food served** *summer* noon-3pm, 6-9pm Mon-Fri; 11am-11pm Sat; noon-10.30pm Sun; *winter* noon-2.30pm Mon-Fri; noon-3pm Sat, Sun. **Credit** MC, V.
Something of a locals' pub, the Wood House's core clientele are residents from the surrounding housing estates – council and private – who bring their dogs and partners along to sample the rather good Young's beers on offer here. Special is £2.04, 'ordinary', £1.88. You do tend to get the feeling that you're the only stranger in the pub – which could well be true – but service is pleasant and attentive. There are three connecting rooms – including a food servery, dishing up the likes of bangers and mash for £4 and lamb chops for £4.75 – red carpets and Hogarthian prints on the walls. The atmosphere is warm and the conversation lively.
Disabled: toilet. Games (fruit machines, quiz machine). No piped music or jukebox. Quiz (last Wed in month). Satellite TV. Tables outdoors (garden). Vegetarian dishes.

Two Half's
42 Sydenham Road, SE26 (020 8778 4629). Sydenham rail. **Open** 11am-11pm Mon-Sat; noon-10.30pm Sun. **Credit** AmEx, DC, MC, V.
What the apostrophe's doing in the name is anybody's guess, but now that the Pukkabar curry restaurant has gone, a new monicker's needed for this modern-style bar. The old colonial atmosphere of gleaming teak and whirring ceiling fans is tempered by the sight of Sydenham's twentysomethings, who lounge around in the comfortable armchairs and prop up the bar, occasionally tapping a toe to the club-style music bashing out of speakers. Draught Hoegaarden is £3.50 a pint, regular real ales including Young's PA and Greene King are £1.60, while lager, which is what most seem to be drinking,

is £2.40 for Stella or Kronenbourg. After some deliberation they have decided not to offer food, an oddly refreshing decision in the age of the gastropub.
Disabled: toilet. No-smoking area. Quiz (Thur). Restaurant. Satellite TV. Tables outdoors (pavement). Vegetarian dishes.

Tooting SW17

Freedom & Firkin
196 Tooting High Street, SW17 (020 8672 5794). Tooting Broadway tube. **Open** noon-11pm Mon-Sat; noon-10.30pm Sun. **Food served** noon-8.30pm daily. **Credit** MC, V.
Pleasantly busy on a Sunday night, the Freedom remains one of Firkin's less affected outlets. Yes, there are some barrel-based tables, a few 'witty' uses of Firkin as an adjective, and some memorabilia, but otherwise it has an authentic feel. The large central bar looks out on an open plan of pews and tables below large windows at the front, and hides a cosier raised section at the rear. A lighter corridor to the left hosts a pool table and gives access on to the patio fronting the road. Ken's uniform from BBC's *Citizen Smith* is still displayed around the back, and the bar still offers a wide array of bevvies on draught. It's now a Bass concern, but still serves Marston Pedigree (£2.15) and Grolsch (£2.40), while a corporate-looking menu offers a mix of standard pub fare with a Mexican twist (£3-£5.25).
Disabled: toilet. Games (board games, fruit machine, pool table, quiz machine, video games). Jukebox. Satellite TV (big screen). Tables outdoors (garden, patio). Vegetarian dishes.

Spirit
94 Tooting High Street, SW17 (020 8767 3311). Tooting Broadway tube. **Open** 11.30am-11pm Mon-Sat; noon-10.30pm Sun. **Food served** noon-10.30pm Mon-Thur; noon-6pm Fri-Sat. **Happy hour** 5-8pm Mon-Fri. **Credit** AmEx, MC, V.
This friendly, basic bar is a popular draw for the happening folk of Tooting, attracting to its thumping beat the youth of the area. It has a mix of design effects – the front is all glass, the wall opposite the tiny bar is tinsel strips à la tacky nightclub, and the back room beams neon lighting on to glittered walls. Otherwise it's charmingly simple, regular, and small – there are the necessary chairs and tables, about ten bottled beers (Beck's £2, Stella £2.10, Budvar £2.40), wine by the glass (starting at £2.30), and a fine coffee and syrup selection. Bar snacks are also tastefully restrained (sandwiches, chilli, baked potatoes £4-£7). The sound system edges up a notch or two to keep pace with the burgeoning numbers, and although most locals might not have caught on yet, to those in the know there's a lively buzz here just off (Tooting) Broadway.
Babies and children admitted (children's menu, high chairs). Music (DJs Thur-Sat). Satellite TV. Vegetarian dishes.

Wandsworth SW18

Alma Tavern
499 Old York Road, SW18 (020 8870 2537/ www.thealma.com). Wandsworth Town rail. **Open** noon-11pm Mon-Sat; noon-10.30pm Sun. **Food served** 12.30-10.30pm Mon-Sat; noon-4pm Sun. **Credit** AmEx, DC, MC, V.

The Alma is one of the most popular venues in Wandsworth, always brimming with a twenty- and thirtysomething crowd, even when other drinking outlets just down the road are virtually empty. This sister pub to the **Ship** (*see below*) has the same stripped floorboards and central bar look, with Mediterranean greens and oranges and large windows lending a light and airy atmosphere. The well-heeled, broad-shouldered overspill from Chelsea pack the room with collars, brogues and pearls, and received pronunciation chatter. Nevertheless, it's a friendly place, with a dining extension that displays a fine plaster frieze above the picture rail and boasts an extensive menu, from shredded duck with Thai noodles (£8.50) to char-grilled pork cutlet with apple mash (£8), and puddings well worth the indulgence. It's a Young's establishment, but this being nigh on Battersea, its Pilsner and Export cost a relatively hefty £2.45 and £2.55 respectively.
Babies and children admitted (high chairs). Disabled: toilet. Function room. Games (fruit machine, pinball machine). No piped music or jukebox. Restaurant. Satellite TV (big screen). Vegetarian dishes.

B@1
350 Old York Road, SW18 (020 8870 5491/ www.beatone.co.uk). Wandsworth Town rail. **Open/food served** 5-11pm Mon-Fri; 11am-11pm Sat; 11am-10.30pm Sun. **Credit** AmEx, DC, MC, V.
On a strip of four or five drinking options, B@1 offers a rustic alternative to the **Alma** (*see above*) and the All Bar One opposite. Exposed brick walls, open fires, wooden tables and chests, shiny sofas, nightlights illuminating the tables and art deco wall lights are set off against plastic plotted plants and a Led Zep soundtrack, lending a slightly contrived but warm atmosphere. The bar at the front is small but well stocked, with standard cocktails (£2.50-£5), shooters and even ice-cream cocktails (including an enticing chocolate dip strawberry – kahlua, chocolate syrup, cream and strawberries) leading the drinks list. The food menu is a mix of the likes of nachos, steak, burger and Thai fishcakes (£5-£10). It was relatively quiet when we visited (as were neighbouring bars), but as a recent addition to the area, its log-on might yet .com.
Tables outdoors (pavement). Vegetarian dishes.

ditto
55-57 East Hill, SW18 (020 8877 0110).Wandsworth Town rail. **Open** 11am-11pm Mon-Fri; 10.30am-11pm Sat; 10.30am-10pm Sun. **Food served** noon-3pm, 7-9.30pm Mon-Sat; 11.30am-9pm Sun. **Credit** MC, V.
Although mainly a restaurant (which is set off to right), ditto also has an engaging bar area that is worth a visit in this relative desert for homely drinking venues. The simple wood and metal bar is to the left as you enter, by some window seats, but the eye is drawn to the sofa and cushion extravaganza at the end of the long thin seating area. Rough hewn and bolted tables, pot plants, framed photos and oil paintings lend a Wandsworth chic to the interior, while sailing mags and property sections indicate the expected clientele here. Draught Leffe (£2.50 a half-pint) and Boddingtons (£2.60 a pint), alongside a bottled selection (Old Porter £2.60) and a few cocktails (£4.75) are among the drinks, while the bar menu reflects ditto's main function as a restaurant (woodland mushroom and spinach risotto £6.50, shredded duck with Thai noodles £5.50). With the sublime sounds of Nat King Cole and the soothing decor, ditto's sofas are well worth sinking into for a drink or two.
Babies and children admitted (restaurant only). Dress code. Function room. Restaurant. Satellite TV. Vegetarian dishes.

Ship
41 Jew's Row, SW18 (020 8870 9667). Wandsworth Town rail. **Open/food served** 11am-11pm Mon-Sat; noon-10.30pm Sun. **Credit** AmEx, DC, MC, V.
Although situated next to a ready-mix concrete works that has long been a feature of the local landscape, the Ship continues to attract the well-heeled of Wandsworth to its riverside location. During the summer, its outdoor complex of patios, barbecue burner, trellising and river view draws the masses, parking their convertibles nearby and donning their shades in preparation for an evening of Young's beers ('ordinary' £2.05, Special £2.15) and fine food (home-made fishcakes £4.50, lamb shoulder chop with rosemary ratatouille £8.80). The interior comprises a large conservatory that leads to the open-plan kitchen, and a smaller back bar where it is easier to escape the hordes. Bare boards and oak tables add to the spacious feel, but when the sun's out and the weekend arrives, the Ship sinks under the weight of its crew.
Babies and children admitted (high chairs). No piped music or jukebox. Restaurant. Tables outdoors (riverside garden). Vegetarian dishes.

Tír Na Nóg
107 Garratt Lane, SW18 (020 8877 3622). Earlsfield rail. **Open** 11am-11pm Mon-Sat; noon-10.30pm Sun. **Credit** AmEx, DC, MC, V.
This bow-fronted Irish pub is a welcome relief from this busy and charmless road end of Garratt Lane. The walls and ceiling are teeming with bric-a-brac – guns, bedpans, puppets, all things agricultural – and overlook wooden tables and pews at which the young and not so young sup their pints (Guinness, Holsten, Foster's all £2.10), or drain their bottles of beer (all £2.25). The staff are very friendly, usually hosting a posse of compatriots seated at the bar that faces you as you enter, discussing the nation's latest sporting endeavours, or flicking through the pub's copy of the *Irish Times*. The back room offers more space during the Irish music nights and a haven from the big-screen sports events, but this can be as pleasantly quiet as it is authentically Irish.
Babies and children admitted. Games (fruit machine). Music (Irish bands, DJ Sun). Quiz (first Thur in month). Satellite TV (big screen). Tables outdoors (garden).

Also in the area...

All Bar One 527-529 Old York Road, SW18 (020 8875 7941).
Café Med 2 North Side, SW18 (020 7228 0914).
Faith & Firkin 1 Bellevue Road, SW17 (020 8672 8717).
Pitcher & Piano 11 Bellevue Road, SW17 (020 8767 6982).

West Norwood SE27

Southern Pride
82 Norwood High Street, SE27 (020 8761 5200). Brixton tube, then bus 2/West Norwood rail. **Open** 6pm-2am Mon-Thur; 6pm-3am Fri, Sat; noon-midnight Sun. **Food served** noon-4pm Sun. **Credit** MC, V.
Southern Pride wins its merits by the plain truthfulness of its claim to cater for gay girls and boys in equal abundance, when more often the term 'mixed' stems from the reported sighting of a token female. It's an unpretentious boozer: loud and lairy and swamped by the south London gay community. Granted, you won't be tripping over any West End beauties inside, but the emphasis here is on partying, not striking poses. A large

and well-ventilated conservatory bar at the rear serving London Pride (£2.30 a pint) and Beck's (£2.40 a bottle) helps accommodate the drinking, dancing and, of course, cabaret.
Function room. Games (fruit machines, quiz machines). Late licence (Mon-Sat). Music (DJs/cabaret nightly). Quiz (Tue). Satellite TV. Tables outdoors (garden). Vegetarian dishes.

Also in the area...

Fewterer & Firkin 313 Kirkdale, SE26 (020 8778 8521).

Wimbledon SW19/Southfield, Earlsfield, SW18/Raynes Park SW20

Alexandra

33 Wimbledon Hill Road, SW19 (020 8947 7691). Wimbledon tube/rail. **Open** 11am-11pm Mon-Sat; noon-10.30pm Sun. **Food served** noon-3pm, 6-9.30pm daily. **Credit** AmEx, DC, MC, V.
A wine bar, cheesily called the Smart Alex, has grown out of the back of this looming Victorian pub. The Alexandra, however, has little time for its new sibling's airs and graces and has stuck to its slightly stodgy trad decor. An interior of dark wood, stained glass and a beamed ceiling houses a big-screen TV for sports enthusiasts quaffing Young's ales (Special £2.10, 'ordinary' £1.92). On our visit, the punters seemed a bit on the lethargic side, but boisterous long-lunchers fill the place during the week to sample the wine bar-style menu. There's a no-smoking area near the door and a patio and roof garden for warmer times.
Disabled: toilet. Dress code (weekends in wine bar). Games (fruit machine, quiz machine). Music (live band £5 Fri, Sat in wine bar). No-smoking area. TV (big screen). Tables outdoors (garden, pavement). Vegetarian dishes.

Bar 366

366 Garratt Lane, SW18 (020 8944 9591). Earlsfield rail. **Open** 5-11pm Mon-Sat; 7-10.30pm Sun. **Happy hour** 5-7pm Mon-Fri. **Food served** 5-9.30pm Mon-Thur; 5-8pm Fri, Sat; 7-9pm Sun. **Credit** MC, V.
Candlelit tables, orange walls, funky mirrors and modern fixtures make 366 stand out from the majority of Earlsfield's other watering holes. The simple layout and light-hearted appeal of this bar attract a young, post-work crowd, swigging bottled beers (Budvar £2) or cocktails (£2.50-£4.50). Ten decent wines are also available by the glass. Two large TVs beam in MTV, entrancing punters with a three-minute attention span, although music is often supplied from a hi-fi behind the bar. Food-wise, there's nothing too exotic; burgers, chicken wings and nachos (£5). The size of the portions makes up for the menu's lack of imagination.
Games (board games). Satellite TV. Tables outdoors (garden). Vegetarian dishes.

Cavern

100 Coombe Lane, SW20 (020 8946 7911). Raynes Park rail. **Open** 11am-11pm Mon-Sat; noon-10.30pm Sun. **Food served** noon-2.30pm Mon-Fri. **Credit** AmEx, DC, MC, V.
Named after the Fab Four's first venue, this genuine rock 'n' roll pub is littered with rock memorabilia, especially of the Beatles and Rolling Stones. A few tables inlaid with posters are pushed into the corners of the dark bar, and a red phonebox adds another splash of Britishness to the decor. Bands perform occasionally, while the jukebox and bass-

heavy sound system provide air-guitar opportunities at other times. Unspectacular pub fodder is served from a counter next to the bar, where Raynes Park rockabillies sup pints of Flowers and London Pride (both £1.95).
Babies and children admitted (until 6pm). Games (fruit machines). Jukebox. Satellite TV (big screen). Tables outdoors (pavement). Vegetarian dishes.

Country House

2 Groton Road, SW18 (020 8874 2715). Earlsfield rail. **Open** noon-11pm Mon-Sat; noon-10.30pm Sun. **Food served** noon-2.30pm daily. **No credit cards**.
If pubs were packaged along the lines of supermarket produce, then the Country House would be a 'no-frills' product. Under the shadow of the railway line, locals come to this tatty boozer to dull the senses. Choosing their weapon from a selection of uninspiring beers, such as Courage Directors and Kronenbourg (both £2.30), most regulars are on first-name terms with the bar staff. Pool, darts and a jukebox are on hand to liven things up, although the TV by the bar tuned to whatever soap is on may distract from any fun that may be had. Platefuls of traditional pub grub can fill the gap should hunger strike.
Games (darts, fruit machine, pool table). Jukebox. Satellite TV. Vegetarian dishes.

Fox & Grapes

9 Camp Road, SW19 (020 8946 5599). Wimbledon tube/rail. **Open/food served** 11am-11pm Mon-Sat; noon-10.30pm Sun. **Credit** AmEx, DC, MC, V.
Dating back to 1787, the Fox & Grapes nestles in the middle of Wimbledon Common, but is worth the journey if you're a fan of the traditional country pub look. Apart from the open fire in the large open section and snug lower bar, and the buzzy atmosphere that pervades, even on a Sunday, the main draw is the food. Mirroring the pub's off-the-wall individuality, and playing on its bar manager's New Zealand roots, dishes include specials such as 'kiwi' burgers, beer-battered 'orange roughie' alongside ordinary favourites, such as steak and ale pie. Refreshments are more familiar; Bombardier (£2.10) and Directors (£2.20) are the pick of the ales.
Babies and children admitted (high chairs). Function room. No-smoking area. Satellite TV (big screen). Tables outdoors (Wimbledon Common). Vegetarian dishes.

Hand in Hand

6 Crooked Billet, SW19 (020 8946 5720). Wimbledon tube/rail. **Open** 11am-11pm Mon-Sat; noon-10.30pm Sun. **Food served** noon-2.30pm, 7-10pm daily. **Credit** MC, V.
In keeping with the countrified image of this rather twee area of Wimbledon, the Hand in Hand warms the cockles of your heart. It's a pub suited to nothing more strenuous than reading the Sunday papers over a pint and catching up with friends. The oak-lined booths are great places in which to sit and while away the hours, but for those who need flashing lights and trivia with their pint there's a small separate room with pinball and a quiz machine. Ordinary bitter costs £1.84 a pint, and Stella £2.50. Food is low-key, like the atmosphere, but occasionally there are specials, which are usually worth sampling. They also have a welcoming attitude to children.
Babies and children admitted (separate area; children's menu). Games (darts, pinball machine). No piped music or jukebox. Quiz (Tue). Tables outdoors (courtyard). Vegetarian dishes.

Hartfield's

27 Hartfield Road, SW19 (020 8543 9788/ www.winetoyourdoor.co.uk). Wimbledon tube/rail. **Open** noon-11pm Mon-Fri; 6-11pm Sat. **Food served** noon-2.30pm, 6-10pm Mon-Fri; 6-10pm Sat. **Credit** AmEx, DC, MC, V.

Lurking behind Wimbledon's main drag, Hartfield's continues to be a reliable stop for south London's wine lovers. Over 35 wines are served in this brightly coloured wine bar, where the terracotta-yellow walls and tiled floor hint at Mediterranean-taverna ambitions. Wine prices range from £2.50 to £4.50 per glass or £8.95 to £18.95 per bottle If you visit on a Saturday, live music is performed, ranging from flamenco guitarists, a pop-covers band or even Acker Bilk's backing band. It's popular with parties and large groups, so arrive early in the evening to ensure a table and the chance to try the extensive menu and the exotic daily specials, such as swordfish (£9.75). *Babies and children admitted. Disabled: toilet. Music (acoustic guitarist/jazz Sat). No-smoking area. Quiz (last Mon in month). Vegetarian dishes.*

Hogshead

25-27 Wimbledon Hill Road, SW19 (020 8947 9391). Wimbledon tube/rail. **Open** 11am-11pm Mon-Sat; noon-10.30pm Sun. **Food served** noon-9pm Mon-Thur; noon-8pm Fri-Sun. **Credit** DC, MC, V.
Having ditched the tennis memorabilia and Hand & Racket moniker, this is now a prime example of a 'new' Hogshead pub: bright and welcoming, with contemporary design fixtures and furniture. Apart from a salmon and lime-green colour scheme to match the Ikea-style sofas next to the fireplace, little has changed. It remains well populated by local Wombles and, being a Hogshead, has a fine selection of guest ales that are rotated regularly. Wychwood Shires (£2.01 a pint) and Hogsback Winter Lightning (£2.24) were the pick of the bunch on our visit. The menu has a few flourishes, but relies mostly on baked spuds, pies and burgers.
Disabled: toilet, specially adapted low bar. Games (fruit machines). No-smoking area. Vegetarian dishes.

Leather Bottle

538 Garratt Lane, SW17 (020 8946 2309). Earlsfield rail. **Open** 11am-11pm Mon-Sat; noon-10.30pm Sun. **Food served** noon-3pm daily. **Credit** MC, V.
A great Young's pub for outdoor fun. The large garden has several benches and a children's play area and during the summer months a barbecue is kept stoked up. Inside, the decor is decidedly rustic, with an anvil and brick hod complementing the copper pots and kettles. If a quiet drink in a cosy atmosphere is what you're after, then nab a seat in the raised central area. The main bar serves Young's finest (Special £2.02, 'ordinary' £1.90). A light snack menu showed promise with some imaginative dishes, such as spicy chicken kebab with yoghurt (£4.65) and spinach, avocado and bacon salad (£3.75).
Satellite TV. Tables outdoors (garden). Vegetarian dishes.

Old Garage

20 Replingham Road, SW18 (020 8874 9370). Southfields tube. **Open** noon-11pm Mon-Sat; noon-10.30pm Sun. **Food served** noon-9pm daily. **Credit** AmEx, DC, MC, V.
A decent pitstop should you be feeling a bit run down, the Old Garage is less antiquated in appearance than the name suggests. Edwardian trinkets and knick-knacks are dotted throughout, but the furniture at the front of the pub wouldn't look out of place in a sunlit conservatory. It used to get raucous in here with a lively young crowd, but since they stopped booking live bands, you're more likely to find suits unwinding after a hard day's work. An impressive menu of daily specials is worth sampling to accompany a pint of Stella (£2.35) or Abbot ale (£2.15).
Games (fruit machines). Satellite TV. Tables outdoors (garden, pavement). Vegetarian dishes.

Rose & Crown

55 High Street, SW19 (020 8947 4713). Wimbledon tube/rail/93 bus. **Open** 11am-11pm Mon-Sat; noon-10.30pm Sun. **Food served** noon-2.30pm, 6-9.30pm Mon-Sat; noon-3pm Sun. **Credit** MC, V.
An unassuming Young's pub with the usual Victorian prints and old maps adorning the walls, but with a huge local following, due to its broad appeal. Monied Wimbledon youth rub shoulders with suburban couples, thirtysomethings and various local characters, helping to create a lively atmosphere, especially on Friday and Saturday nights. Friendly staff serve the usual range of Young's ales (Triple A is £2.05) and selection of lagers (Stella is £2.55). The charming, low-ceilinged seventeenth-century building has a number of cosy nooks, a sizeable garden that's popular in the summer, and a conservatory where a menu of traditional British fare and more exuberant specials is served.
No-smoking area. Tables outdoors (garden). Vegetarian dishes.

Sultan

78 Norman Road, SW19 (020 8542 4532). Colliers Wood or South Wimbledon tube/Wimbledon tube/rail. **Open** noon-11pm Mon-Sat; noon-10.30pm Sun. **No credit cards.**
The lifeless interior of this obscure local is a study in mid-tones and scrubbed pine furniture. Little to recommend it then, you might think, but the great range of ales from Salisbury's excellent Hogsback brewery makes up for what the decor lacks. Thanks to its offering of hearty Entire Stout (£1.90), Summer Lightning, Thunderstorm (both £2) and the lighter GSB (£1.65), ale aficionados will find this pub well worth a visit. All the award-winning brews are also available for takeaway. The ambience is so laid-back it's almost horizontal, and entertainment, if it can be called that, comes in the form of a fruit machine and an inquisitive pub cat.
Disabled: toilet. Games (fruit machine). Quiz (Tue). Tables outdoors (patio).

Willie Gunn

422 Garratt Lane, SW18 (020 8946 7773). Earlsfield rail. **Open/food served** 11am-11pm Mon-Sat; 11am-10.30pm Sun. **Credit** MC, V.
Earlsfield's beautiful people flock to this light and prettily decorated wine bar, where a large restaurant is tacked on the back. The menu has a fine spread of Modern European dishes that change regularly, although some of the starters remain consistent. Seafood is particularly well covered: octopus marinated with lemon, sweet peppers and paprika (£4.75) and fishcakes with home-made tartare sauce (£7.75) are among the options. Staff have a schmoozing style and are happy to help you choose from the 45-strong wine list (12 are available by the glass). Prices start at £2.50 for a glass of house wine. Bottled beers such as Budvar (£2.70) are offered and draughts, including St Omer (£1.65), are available only by the half-pint.
Babies and children admitted (high chairs). Restaurant. Satellite TV (big screen). Vegetarian dishes.

Also in the area...

All Bar One 37-39 Wimbledon Hill Road, SW19 (020 8971 9871).
Café Rouge 573 Garratt Lane, SW18 (020 8947 9616); 26 High Street, SW19 (020 8944 5131).
Dôme 91 High Street, SW19 (020 8947 9559).
Pitcher & Piano 4-5 High Street, SW19 (020 8879 7020).

EAST

Bethnal Green E2

Approach Tavern

47 Approach Road, E2 (020 8980 2321). Bethnal Green tube. **Open** noon-11pm Mon-Sat; noon-10.30pm Sun. **Food served** 12.45-2.30pm, 7-9.45pm Mon-Sat; 12.45-4pm Sun. **No credit cards.**

An art gallery upstairs (open noon-6pm Thur-Sun) showcases local artists and defines the style at this busy East End pub. A cut above neighbouring boozers, the Approach offers four regular ales (Adnams bitter, London Pride, Pedigree and Wadworth 6X, mostly under £2) plus a couple of guest beers and superior lagers such as Hoegaarden (£3.80) and Budvar (£2.35). The main room at the front has a long bar, bare boards, stuffed animals and chunky wooden furniture; there's also a snug at the rear that pretty much lives up to its name, and out front there's a patio with rows of bench tables (under cover) that get stuffed in warm weather. As might be expected food is way above average, with an ever-changing chalkboard menu including such things as herb-crusted baby chicken and clove-studded ham with colcannon, all for under £10. Customers here cover all age and social groups, but typically will be a couple of young arty types out for a beer and a chat about 1920s German Expressionists, or maybe (not being local) about how Man-U are doing.

Babies and children admitted. Jukebox. Quiz (Tue). Restaurant. Satellite TV. Tables outdoors (pavement). Vegetarian dishes.

Cock & Comfort

359 Bethnal Green Road, E2 (020 7729 1476). Bethnal Green tube/rail/8 bus. **Open** 4-11pm Mon-Thur; 2pm-2am Fri; 1pm-2am Sat; noon-midnight Sun. **Food served** noon-4pm Sun. **Credit** MC, V.

This brightly coloured, hetero-friendly gay pub, ahem, stands out a bit on overtly macho Bethnal Green Road. Inside there's one medium-sized oblong space, with a bar down half of one side, opposite which stands a black, pink-neon-edged stage where performers like Paula Pure cavort. The rest of the place is decorated in bright orange and blue gloss, with shuttered windows and a partly carpeted, partly bare-board floor. A handful of tables and chairs are scattered about – all taken the night we visited – and the music is the usual pounding 'Love To Love You, Baby'-type mix. Staff are friendly and efficient, and it was a surprise to find a decent pint of Courage Directors at a bargain £1.80, as well as Guinness, Grolsch and what-have-you for just over £2. The average drinker appears to be male, thirtysomething and casually dressed.

Cabaret (Fri-Sun). Games (fruit machine, pinball machine, quiz machine). Late licence (Fri, Sat). Satellite TV. Vegetarian dishes.

Royal Oak

73 Columbia Road, E2 (020 7739 8204). Bethnal Green or Old Street tube/26, 48, 55 bus. **Open** 1pm-2am Mon-Sat; 8am-10.30pm Sun. **Food served** 8am-2pm Sun. **No credit cards.**

This friendly little pub comes into its own on Sunday mornings, when the Columbia Road flower market disgorges a mixed crowd of traders, tourists and elderly locals to join the usual trendy and gay twenty- and thirtysomethings who make up its core clientele. The central bar is surrounded by a diverse collection of mismatched wooden furniture: solid tables, chairs and stools, and bench seats that look as if they may have accommodated Lloyd George. The beers are disappointing, being the usual mix of John Smith's Smooth (£2), Guinness (£2.20) and lager, but there's also bottled stuff, and wine from £1.50 a glass. Upstairs is the Crazy Maracas

Tex-Mex café-bar, where you can find bargain-priced cocktails, Mexican beer and Southwestern/Mexish nosh.

Babies and children admitted (until 6pm; high chairs, menus). Function room. Games (fruit machine, pinball machine, quiz machine, pool table). Jukebox. Late licence (Mon-Sat). Quiz (Thur). Restaurant. Satellite TV (big screen). Tables outdoors (pavement; yard in summer). Vegetarian dishes.

Bow E3

Bar Risa

Bow Wharf, 221 Grove Road, E3 (020 8980 7874). Mile End tube. **Open/food served** noon-11pm Mon-Thur; noon-12.30am Fri; noon-1am Sat; noon-10.30pm Sun. **Credit** AmEx, DC, MC, V.

This calls itself a 'cool, sophisticated café-bar', and who are we to disagree? As is the policy with all branches, Bar Risa shares a building with a Jongleurs comedy venue, and is aimed at the same twenty- to thirtysomething budding executives who like to 'eat, drink and laugh their heads off'. Said building is a converted warehouse by the side of the Regent's Canal, and the bar occupies a large, high-ceilinged room with a mezzanine, armchairs, bare floorboards, Miró posters and a large wooden island-style bar. Food is a cross between snack bar and bistro fare, with things like roasted vegetable lasagne (£4.25) nestling next to ham, eggs and chips (£4.50), hot sandwiches and jacket spuds from around £3. There are only a few draught beers, Hoegaarden (£3.70 a pint) and Caffreys (£2.50) among them.

Babies and children admitted (until 9pm). Comedy (8.30pm £12 Fri, Sat). Disabled: toilet. Function room. Games (fruit machine). Late licence (Fri, Sat). No-smoking area. Satellite TV. Tables outdoors (patio). Vegetarian dishes.

Bow Bells

116 Bow Road, E3 (020 8981 7317). Bow Road tube/ Bow Church tube/DLR/25, D8 bus. **Open** 11am-11pm Mon-Sat; noon-10.30pm Sun. **Credit** MC, V.

Just along from Bow Church DLR – and a useful place to pass those 18-minute waits between trains – this is a bright, welcoming Victorian pub that has recently been tarted up. The big, square ground-floor bar is made a U-shape by a hefty wooden serving area, the wood theme continuing around the room with bulky furniture and solid wood flooring that surrounds a bright carpet. Huge blackboards announce the food options, and differentiate between 'home-made dishes' (beef Madras, Quorn and vegetable pie, Thai chicken curry, all £3.95) and others. The DJ was playing 'It's Raining Men' on the Friday night we visited, but it looked rather to be raining under-dressed young women with discreetly tattooed shoulders. The beer's good, with guest ales at £2 a pint as well as London Pride (£1.90) and Adnams Southwold (£1.75), and Stella (£2.20) and Lowenbrau (£2.30) among the lagers. *Babies and children admitted (until 7pm). Function room. Games (darts, fruit machines, pool table). Jukebox. Music (DJ Fri; DJ/Cabaret Sat). Quiz (Wed). Satellite TV. Tables outdoors (pavement).Vegetarian dishes.*

New Globe

359 Mile End Road, E3 (020 8981 4383, ext 24). Mile End tube. **Open** noon-midnight Mon-Wed; noon-2am Thur-Sat; noon-10.30pm Sun. **Food served** noon-3pm Mon-Fri. **Admission** after 11pm Thur-Sat £2. **Credit** MC, V.

The New Globe has had a sizeable facelift, making it unrecognisable from the grim local it used to be. These days it's a tidy-sized, modern-style pub aimed squarely at students from nearby Queen Mary College, and strikingly decorated in dark blue and brown with plenty of exposed wood. Island tables and tall stools housed a high proportion of local student life on our last visit, with a single table of plasterers relaxing after a hard day's labour the only reminder that we were on Mile End Road. The beers are well kept, and include Flowers IPA and London Pride, both for £1.90. Food is a speciality, and the imaginative menu includes a veggie section with vegetable kiev, pasta bake and vegetarian bangers and mash for around £3 each, as well as hot stuffed baguettes and ciabattas (from £2.20), rump steak (£4.95), comforting sausage, beans and chips (£3) and the like for meat eaters. *Disabled: toilet. Games (fruit machine, pool table, quiz machine). Jukebox. Late licence (Thur-Sat). Music (DJs Thur-Sat). Tables outdoors (canalside). Vegetarian dishes.*

Also in the area...

Flautist & Firkin 588 Mile End Road, E3 (020 8981 0620).

Clapton E5

Anchor & Hope

15 High Hill Ferry, E5 (020 8806 1730). Clapton rail/ 653 bus. **Open** 11am-3pm, 5.30-11pm Mon-Sat; noon-3pm, 7-10.30pm Sun. **No credit cards.**

A tiny riverside pub on the banks of the Lea that just might well serve the best-kept Fuller's beers in London. It's a locals' pub with a floor covered in red lino throughout and framed mementos and plates on the two-tone walls. The landlord has been here since Coronation Year (that's 1953, Einsteins), and it looks as if most of the furniture actually preceded him. The 'main' bar is small enough, but the room housing the dartboard and a couple of tables is truly tiny; if more than ten people turn up at once, you won't have room to throw. The view across the river, towards a water filtration plant and an electrified rail line, is as urban as they come. The customers are a complete cross-section of the neighbourhood: male, female and every age from teens to tired pensioners. London Pride is £2, ESB £2.15 and Guinness a cool £2.10. *Games (darts, fruit machine). Tables outdoors (riverside). TV.*

Docklands E14

Blacksmiths Arms

25 Westferry Road, E14 (020 7987 3439). Canary Wharf tube/South Quay DLR/D3, D7 bus. **Open** 11am-11pm Mon-Sat; noon-10.30pm Sun. **Food served** noon-3pm daily. **No credit cards.**

Just a few yards from the **City Pride** (see below), this old-fashioned, smoke-filled boozer couldn't be more different from the corporate money-machine down the road. The decor is based around framed pictures of 'old docklands', red leatherette furniture that's seen better days and mismatched tables and chairs. When we visited a diverse group of people was sitting at the small bar, talking. The clientele includes a percentage of office workers, but this is primarily a locals' pub. Sadly, it no longer carries any real ales, but John Smith's Smooth, Guinness and Carlsberg are all very accessibly priced at around £2. Food is basic pub grub, but at between £2.50 and £5 a plateful, only a Gordon Ramsay would complain. *Babies and children admitted. Games (darts, fruit machine). Vegetarian dishes.*

Cat & Canary

1-24 Fisherman's Walk, Canary Wharf, E14 (020 7512 9187). Canary Wharf tube/DLR. **Open** 11am-11pm Mon-Fri. **Food served** noon-2.30pm Mon-Fri. **Credit** AmEx, DC, MC, V.

The woodwork on the walls is supposed to have come from an old Victorian church in Hornchurch, and the phone kiosk was made out of its pulpit. Built in 1992, but mixing old pub fittings (including, for some reason, pictures of Henry VIII and his wives) with a twist of modernity, this big Fuller's house attracts a complete cross-section of Canary Wharf life. We witnessed a gaggle of secretaries cavorting with a gang of postal workers, while at a nearby table an earnest young journalist was trying to interview a well-known TV actor and in a back room a group of pin-striped financial wizards was discussing the finer points of EMU. Only in Canary Wharf. The bar staff are friendly, and offer the full range of Fuller's beers (at high prices: London Pride is £2.30, ESB £2.40 and Stella lager is £2.70). A separate food counter offers decent pub food at lunchtimes, centred around hot sandwiches and pasta dishes. Expect change from £5. *Babies and children admitted. Disabled: toilet. Function room. Games (darts, fruit machine). No-smoking area. Satellite TV (big screen). Tables outdoors (dockside terrace). Vegetarian dishes.*

City Pride

15 Westferry Road, E14 (020 7987 3516). Canary Wharf tube/DLR/Heron Quays DLR. **Open** noon-11pm Mon-Sat; noon-10.30pm Sun. **Food served** noon-9pm, 6-9.45pm Mon-Fri; 1-7.45pm Sat, Sun. **Credit** AmEx, MC, V.

A pub called the City Pride has existed here since 1823, but the current building dates from the 1950s, and has recently been made over with bare brick, barrels and artefacts that evoke the era of working docks in an attempt to attract local office workers. And it works: they flock here in their hundreds, especially at lunchtime and in the early evening. The beer's cheap (Tetley's Bitter is just £1.80), wines are good and plentiful and there's a cellar-full of tequilas to make the journey home that much more adventurous. The food menu is ambitious, in a corporate kind of way, including such things as paella (with those traditional crab sticks, £5.95), lime and ginger swordfish (£7.95), dim sum (£3.95) and 'fresh' omelettes for £5.95 (cheese, ham or mushroom, 75p extra; eggs included). Presumably 'stale' omelettes would be less. *Function room. Games (fruit machines, pool tables, quiz machines). Tables outdoors (garden). Vegetarian dishes.*

EastEndings

It looks unassuming enough from the outside. Just another pub in an area where the boozer still holds an almost mythic social importance. But then… well, why would it look any different? Every pub has its little histories, after all – incidents that have shaped its character. It just so happens that one of the incidents in this pub's past has made it famous the world over. For it was to this pub on 9 March 1966 that Ronnie Kray journeyed after several hours spent in his own local, **The Lion**. And when he arrived, he shot and killed George Cornell as the Walker Brothers' *The Sun Ain't Gonna Shine Anymore* played on the jukebox. The reason? Cornell had once called Kray a 'poof'.

Walking into the **Blind Beggar** nowadays, you get the feeling that if you threw a similar epiphet at any of the punters they might not get a gun out, but would make pretty bloody sure that the drink in your hand was your last in there that evening. The Beggar is still what it was then: a nice enough East End local with a slightly sinister edge. It goes to great pains not to advertise its dubious heritage; rather, weary middle-aged cockneys and a smattering of younger drinkers sup on a bog-standard range of draught beers beneath the ruby-red glow of wall lamps and bemoan any slumps in West Ham's form. Switch Bobby Moore for Paolo Di Canio, and it can't have been much different when the Krays ruled the roost.

On the other side of Whitechapel tube is a boozer where the Krays spent rather more time, but which didn't get them into anywhere near as much trouble. The **Grave Maurice** was Ronnie and Reggie's local when they lived on nearby Vallance Road, and seems to have barely changed in the 30-plus years since they were locked up. Fans of the Pitcher & Piano and the like would be appalled to find that pubs like this still exist: eerily lit and morgue-ishly silent, it looks like it's not been cleaned since the 1970s.

Of course, Pitcher-ites don't tend to hang around the Whitechapel Road. This is a good thing both for them ('poofs', as George Cornell might have said) and for the rest of us, who can revel in a pub that, while hardly the height of fashion, makes no claims to be anything other than what its shabbily dressed customers want it to be: a place where they can take a break from all their worries and where everybody knows their name. In this respect, it has more in common with *Cheers* than first impressions would seem to indicate.

Jack the Ripper – identity still unknown, despite the best efforts of amateur Poirots the world over – is perhaps the world's most infamous murderer. For a brief time, Whitechapel was his territory: Jack murdered of no fewer than five women in the space of ten weeks in 1888, on what are now Durward Street, Hanbury Street, Henriques Street, Mitre Square and White's Row. On your way west down Whitechapel Road, stop in for a pint at the **Black Bull**: on a small poster by the bar it advertises itself as an essential stop on the Jack the Ripper tour, for no reason other than that it's roughly in the middle of the area where his killings took place. Still, after the Grave Maurice, its modern furniture and sympathetic lighting may come as some relief in what is otherwise an unremarkable boozer.

The **Ten Bells** pub on Commercial Street, however, was where all of Jack's prostitute victims hung out at one time or another. It's strangely reassuring to find that this is the one East End crime boozer still trading off its history. The pub is, of course, a regular stop on the myriad Jack the Ripper tours that scuttle about the East End most nights, and sells Ripper T-shirts, mugs and the like to Americans hungry for a slice of London murderabilia. As well as that, though, it offers what can decorously be described as exotic dancing every weekday lunchtime, and in the early evenings from Wednesday to Friday.

This dual personality – between strip joint and tourist attraction – means it's less sleazy than the many other pubs in the area – the **Nag's Head**, for example, which you'll pass between here and the Black Bull – that offer a similar service without the historical ties. However, if you find this offensive, turn up after 8pm, when the girls depart and the tourists arrive. The Ripper, thankfully, hasn't been seen in here for quite some time.
Will Fulford-Jones

Black Bull (*no review*) 199 Whitechapel Road, E1 (020 7247 6707).
Blind Beggar (*p204*) 337 Whitechapel Road, E1 (020 7247 6195).
Grave Maurice (*no review*) 269 Whitechapel Road, E1 (020 7247 5883).
The Lion (*no review*) 8 Tapp Street, E1 (020 7247 0960).
Nag's Head (*no review*) 17 Whitechapel Road, E1 (020 7377 8005).
Ten Bells (*no review*) 84 Commercial Street, E1 (020 7377 2145).

Davys at Canary Wharf

31-35 Fisherman's Walk, Canary Wharf, E14 (020 7363 6633). Canary Wharf tube/DLR. **Open** 11am-11pm Mon-Fri. **Food served** 11am-9pm Mon-Fri. **Credit** AmEx, DC, MC, V.

Thanks to friendly and efficient staff and the usual Davys high quality in wines and food this is one of Canary Wharf's more relaxing venues. The customers seem a less frenetic version of those at the nearby **Cat & Canary** (*see p193*), with more of an emphasis on pinstripe. The colour scheme is terracotta and cream, with Davys' traditional dark wooden barrel tables and flagstone and sawdust flooring. Beers are limited to Davys' Old Wallop (£2.50) and Ordinary (£2.30) bitters, 1870 lager (£2.60) and a few bottles such as Budvar (£2.70); otherwise you're on to wine, with house white/red at £2.75 a glass, £10.85 a bottle, and on up to £39.95 for the exquisite Château St Pierre 1988. The menu is typical Davys, simple and effective, with such things as Scottish herring marinated in dill (£4.25), seared tuna steak (£8.95) and rib-eye steak with red onion sandwiches at £6.95. The treacle tart with clotted cream (£3.85) is a must.

Babies and children admitted (in restaurant). Disabled: toilet. Function rooms. Tables outside (riverside pavement). Restaurant. Satellite TV (big screen). Vegetarian dishes.

Gun

27 Cold Harbour, E14 (020 7987 1692). Blackwall DLR. **Open** 11am-11pm Mon-Sat; noon-10.30pm Sun. **Food served** noon-2.30pm Mon-Fri; 1-4pm Sun. **Credit** DC, MC, V.

When it comes to Dockland views, the Gun has got it taped: the views of the Dome from its riverside terrace, lounge bar and first-floor 'Lady Hamilton Room' are spectacular – especially at night – and would soften the heart of any detractor. This is a blue-collar riverside pub that seems to cock a snook at the gentrification that's gone on around it. A haunt of sailors for centuries and supposed meeting place for Lord Nelson and Lady Hamilton, it has around its walls an array of nautical relics that extends to flags, hatbands and pictures of famous ships. The big main bar has a stage at one end, a pool table, dartboard and big-screen TV; customers seem an easy mix of local couples of all ages and office workers in suits. The Thursday evening we visited there was no real ale on, but usually a pint of Nelson's Bitter is under £2, with lager only slightly more. The roasts for Sunday lunch (£5.50) are famous, and during the week you can have standard pub fare, plus the odd more complicated dish, for around £3-£5.

Babies and children admitted (until 9pm; children's menus). Function rooms. Games (darts, fruit machine, pool table, quiz machine). Music (live bands Fri, Sat). Satellite TV (big screen). Tables outdoors (large riverside balcony). Vegetarian dishes.

Harry's Bar

21 Pepper Street, E14 (020 7308 0171). Crossharbour DLR. **Open/food served** 11am-11pm Mon-Fri; 5-11pm Sat; 11am-6pm Sun. **Credit** AmEx, DC, MC, V.

The view down Millwall Dock from the large picture windows here is as good as views get in Docklands. This is an upmarket modern bar-diner on two floors, attracting a mixture of well-heeled visiting business people and local office dwellers, half of whom seem to have names like Rupert and Clarissa, the other half being Darrens and Traceys. The decor is modern, and the angular furniture, light wood and black fittings give the place an air of a smart urban hotel. Wines (from £2.50 a glass) and cocktails are the main features

Gun

on the drinks list, but bottled lagers start at £2.60, while draught San Miguel is £1.70 for a half-pint. The high-standard menu encompasses Modern European and traditional English dishes, with starters costing £4-£7, and main courses up to £16.

Babies and children admitted (children's menus, high chairs, nappy-changing facilities, toys). Disabled: toilet. Function room. Music (live jazz, last Fri in month). Tables outdoors (riverside terrace, balcony). Restaurant. Satellite TV. Vegetarian dishes.

Henry Addington

22-28 Mackenzie Walk, Canary Wharf, E14 (020 7513 0921). Canary Wharf tube/DLR. **Open** 12.30-11pm Mon-Sat; 12.30-5pm Sun. **Food served** 12.30-9.30pm Tue-Fri; 12.30-4pm Sat-Mon. **Credit** AmEx, DC, MC, V.
Addington was the Prime Minister who gave permission for Canary Wharf (the dockside, not the office megalith) to be built back in the 1800s, and we think he might rather like the pub that bears his name. It's large, modern and comfortable, with a 100ft bar overlooking Heron Quays through large picture windows. The subtle decor imparts a warm red and golden glow through clever use of fittings and lighting. Customers predictably tend to be office folk, and as the aim here is to be a cut above the local opposition, they tend to be higher-ups rather than the photocopier operatives. Upmarket sandwiches on the menu include 8oz rib-eye (£7.95) and pastrami with mustard (£4.95), while snacks take in moules marinière (£7.25) and six oysters with ciabatta (£7.95). Beers include London Pride (£2.20) and Staropramen (£2.80), and wine starts at £3.90 for a large glass, £12.50 a bottle.
Babies and children admitted. Disabled: toilet. Games (fruit machine, quiz machines, video games). Music (DJs Thur, Fri). Satellite TV (big screen). Tables outdoors (pavement). Vegetarian dishes.

Tollesbury Wine Bar

Millwall Inner Dock, Marsh Wall, E14 (020 7363 1183). South Quay DLR. **Open/food served** 11.30am-11pm Mon-Fri. **No credit cards**.
A hundred years or so ago the Tollesbury was a barge built to haul goods up and down the Thames, and in 1940 it brought soldiers back from Dunkirk. Since 1987 it has been one of Docklands' more characterful bars. The 'wine bar' label is a bit misleading, as on the Friday night we visited none of the score or so twenty- and thirtysomethings present was drinking wine, but just Adnams bitter, straight from the cask, or lager such as Heineken (both £2). Harvey's bitter is usually available, too, also for £2. You enter by means of a gangplank and then a tight staircase down into a wooden hull with no portholes, just the odd skylight, and a large wooden table running down the centre. It's not big, and anyone over 5ft 6in should mind their heads. Lunchtime snacks are limited to the likes of jacket potatoes and sandwiches, from £1.50.
Games (fruit machine). Tables outdoors. Vegetarian dishes.

Via Fossa

West India Quay (opposite footbridge), Canary Wharf, E14 (020 7515 8549). West India Quay DLR. **Open/food served** noon-11pm Mon-Sat; noon-7pm Sun. **Credit** AmEx, DC, MC, V.
There's a Gothic feel to this massive but stylish new bar, in a converted warehouse on the edge of West India Quay. A spectacularly lit footbridge outside the front drawbridge (honest) offers easy access to Canary Wharf. As you'd expect there's plenty of exposed stone and red brick, plus enough chunky wood, beams, boards and wrought iron to stock a Chelsea DIY emporium. The ground floor is where serious

drinking (and eating) goes on; more comfortable alcoved spaces with sofas and armchairs are found in the basement and on the first-floor gallery. The sole real ale (Wadworth 6X £2.55) was expensive and actually warm when we tried it, but most people come here for lager or wine. The menu is tight but well thought out, with bar snacks such as tortilla wraps (£4.25), pasta (£5.25-£6.75), noodles (£5.75), open sandwiches and jacket spuds (around £4), and more substantial dishes in the restaurant. Expect plenty of fruit, as in duck breast pan-fried with ginger and apricot sauce (£9.95), apricot and rosemary lamb (£9.25) and timbale of couscous (£6.95).
Babies and children admitted (weekends only). Disabled: lift, toilet. Function room. Tables outdoors (pavement). No-smoking area. Vegetarian dishes.

Also in the area...

All Bar One 42 Mackenzie Walk, South Colonnade, Canary Wharf, E14 (020 7513 0911).
Café Rouge 29-35 Mackenzie Walk, Cabot Square, Canary Wharf, E14 (020 7537 9696).
Corney & Barrow 9 Cabot Square, Canary Wharf, E14 (020 7512 0397).
Fine Line 10 Cabot Square, Canary Wharf, E14 (020 7513 0255).
Slug & Lettuce 30 South Colonnade, Canary Wharf, E14 (020 7519 1612).

Forest Gate, Stratford, E7, E15

Goldengrove

146-148 The Grove, E15 (020 8519 0750). Stratford tube/DLR/rail. **Open/food served** 11am-11pm Mon-Sat; noon-10.30pm Sun. **Credit** AmEx, DC, MC, V.
This used to be a jeans superstore; now it's a popular mock-Victorian JD Wetherspoon pub, on the edge of the shopping centre. Popular with a wide selection of locals, from bank staff or market traders to actors and staff from the nearby Theatre Royal, it has an excellent beer selection: cask-conditioned ales include Directors (£1.75), Boddingtons (£1.35) and Theakston Best (£1.40), plus some interesting guests. As is expected in JDW pubs, prices are keen and special offers bring selected bottled lagers and draught pints down to under £1.50, with food also available for well under £5 – often two for the price of one. Named after a line in a poem by local lad Gerard Manley Hopkins, this is a comfortable locals' pub that boasts a well-tended large flowery garden and the usual variety of sofas, pub chairs and stools, plus (as in all JDWs) a designated no-smoking/dining area.
Disabled: toilet. Games (fruit machines). No piped music or jukebox. No-smoking area. Tables outdoors (two gardens). Vegetarian dishes.

Ye Old Spotted Dog

212 Upton Lane, E7 (020 8472 1794). Plaistow tube or Stratford tube/DLR/rail. **Open** noon-11pm Mon-Sat; noon-10.30pm Sun. **Food served** noon-2pm Mon-Sat. **Credit** MC, V.
Originally built in the sixteenth century, but much enlarged since, the Spotted Dog (as it was until recently) is a great barn of a place with largely authentic bare boards, wood panelling and bare stone walls. An extension houses a family room and a restaurant, with above-average pub food for around £5-£10. There's a decent range of well-kept beers, headed by Courage Directors and Marston's Pedigree (both £2), plus a regularly changing guest ale, and a similarly good-quality wine selection (from £2 a glass, £7.50 a bottle). City merchants used

the Dog as an exchange in 1603 and during the Great Plague of 1665, and Charles II gave it a 24-hour licence so that he could have a pint on his way back from hunting; Dick Turpin lived nearby and committed his first robbery just outside. Today customers don't quite match such a glamorous past, and seem to fall into three categories: young couples in flash suits and short skirts contemplating forthcoming nuptials, hoary old jumper-wearers slurping ales and middle-aged, off-duty City men in expensive casual clothes. When we visited we had trouble getting served, as the one barmaid was monopolised by groups of regulars competing to buy rounds.
Babies and children admitted (high chairs). Games (darts, fruit machines). Restaurant. Tables outdoors (children's play area, garden). Vegetarian dishes.

Hackney E8, E9

291
291 Hackney Road, E2 (020 7613 5676). Bethnal Green or Old Street tube. **Open** 5pm-midnight Mon-Wed; 5pm-2am Thur, Fri; 11am-2am Sat; 11am-6pm Sun. **Admission** after 10pm Thur-Sat £3-£6. **Food served** 5-11pm Mon-Fri; 11am-11pm Sat; 11am-6pm Sun. **Credit** MC, V.
A remarkable conversion from a neo-Gothic church (St Augustine's by name) with a tall, spacious art gallery in what was the nave, a long thin bar beside it and a small Modern-European restaurant upstairs (starters are around £5, mains £10). The stylish bar – check out the painted altar and font – packs out at weekends, when DJs and live acts appear. On weekdays it's quieter, with plentiful seating available in the row of tables and chairs that runs down the wall opposite the serving area. Hoegaarden (£2 a half-pint) and Kronenbourg (£1.55 a half, £6 for a two-pint jug) are on tap, but most of the young, arty crowd who come here seem to go for bottled beers, while aficionados appreciate the good selection of spirits.
Babies and children admitted (high chairs). Disabled: toilet. Function rooms. Late licence (Tue-Sat). Music (DJs, live bands Tue-Sun; live jazz Sun from 11am). No-smoking area (in gallery). Restaurant. Tables outdoors (garden). Vegetarian dishes.

Dove Freehouse
24-28 Broadway Market, E8 (020 7275 7617). Bethnal Green tube. **Open** noon-11pm Mon-Thur; noon-midnight Fri, Sat; noon-10.30pm Sun. **Food served** noon-3pm, 6-10pm Mon-Thur; noon-3pm, 6-10.30pm Fri; noon-10.30pm Sat; noon-10pm Sun. **Credit** MC, V.
Walk into what from the outside looks like Walt Disney's idea of a London tavern, and you have to be impressed (especially if you're a fire officer) by the rows of neat tables, each with their own candle, and by the range of 20 or so continental beers on offer, including Leffe Brune and Blonde, Hoegaarden and Belle-Vue Kriek (cherry beer), all for around £2 per half-pint. Spirited types will go a bundle over the big choice of single malts, bourbons and vodkas. Decor could be described as Hackney hippie chic, with plenty of pot plants and mock-leopardskin seats that somehow manage not to clash with the rest of the stone and wood structure. The restaurant in a raised area to one side serves hearty, vaguely Belgian-style stews, sausages and what-have-you for £5-£7. The clientele tend to be twentysomethings and studenty types, self-consciously modelling themselves on Emin and McQueen.
Babies and children admitted (in dining area; high chairs, toys). Games (board games). No-smoking area. Tables outdoors (pavement). Vegetarian dishes.

Prince Arthur
95 Forest Road, E8 (020 7254 3439). Hackney Downs rail/38 bus. **Open/food served** noon-11pm Mon-Sat; noon-10.30pm Sun. **No credit cards.**
A friendly local of the old school, comfortable and carpeted, with a scattering of tables, red-upholstered stools and banquettes around a central, horseshoe-shaped bar. Painted wood panels cover the walls up to chest-height, in unfashionable beiges and browns. There are usually two or three ales on offer, including London Pride and Abbot Ale (both £2.15), as well as lagers and Guinness. Simple food is available all day, and includes chicken or vegetable curry (£3.50), home-made pizzas (from £4) and burgers. It's equally popular with older locals and their trendy new neighbours, and both factions seem to coexist in perfect harmony.
Babies and children admitted. Games (darts). Tables outdoors (garden). Vegetarian dishes.

Prince George
40 Parkholme Road, E8 (020 7254 6060). Bus 30. **Open** noon-2.30pm, 5-11pm Mon-Fri; noon-11pm Sat; noon-10.30pm Sun. **Food served** noon-3pm Sun. **No credit cards.**
A popular local that combines three bar rooms, set around a central, curved serving area. The small room to the right has a blazing fire in winter and seems the most cosy option, attracting young couples and book-toting fortysomething loners, while most of the serious drinkers prefer the area to the front. The tiny space on the other side always seems to be the last to fill up. Beers include London Pride (£2.15) and Budvar on tap (£2.50) and a bottled German *weiss*-beer or two, and there's a better-than-average range of wines and spirits. Sunday roasts and a few snacks are the food options.
Babies and children admitted (until 8.30pm). Games (pool table). Jukebox. Quiz (Mon). Sport TV. Tables outdoors (forecourt). Vegetarian dishes (Sun).

Pub on the Park
19 Martello Street, E8 (020 7275 9586). Hackney Central rail. **Open** 11am-11pm Mon-Thur; 11am-midnight Fri, Sat; noon-10.30pm Sun. **Food served** noon-3pm Mon-Sat; noon-4pm Sun. **No credit cards.**
Its proximity to London Fields and the airy tables on its wooden outside decking overlooking the park explain the popularity of this open-plan pub. The patio has recently expanded and now lies alongside a *boules* court. Inside, the bare boards and chunky wood tables are classic turn-of-the-millennium Hackney, the friendliness and efficiency of the bar staff are not. London Pride (£2 a pint) and Hoegaarden (£3.80) are on tap, and most of the customers appear to be the usual trendy young Hackneyites out after a day's work. The blackboard food menu throws up some interesting Modern-European dishes for around £5.
Babies and children admitted. Function room. Late licence (Fri, Sat). No-smoking area. Satellite TV (big screen). Tables outdoors (terrace). Vegetarian dishes.

Railway Tavern
339 Mare Street, E8 (020 8985 4184). Hackney Central rail. **Open** 11am-11pm Mon-Sat; noon-10.30pm Sun. **Food served** noon-3pm Mon-Sat. **No credit cards.**
Possibly the last genuinely Irish pub left in Hackney. Some find its mix of stained-glass windows, elegant pillars, Vegas-style bar stools and tables divided by wooden fretwork over-the-top and kitsch, others regard it as a classic of pub decor. On the night we visited Irish Radio 558 was holding a roadshow, and the air was thick with Daniel O'Donnell, Patsy Cline and nicotine from 100 Carroll and Major

Railway Tavern. *See page 197.*

cigarettes. The drinks are Irish-oriented (so no cask-conditioned beers), but inexpensive: Guinness is £1.40, Foster's £1.95. Simple bar food is served at lunchtimes only. *Babies and children admitted (until 7pm). Games (darts, fruit machines). Jukebox. Quiz (Wed). Satellite TV. Vegetarian dishes.*

Royal Inn on the Park
111 Lauriston Road, E9 (020 8985 3321/ www.theroyalinn.co.uk). Mile End tube/bus 277. **Open** noon-11pm Mon-Wed; noon-midnight Thur-Sat; noon-10.30pm Sun. **Food served** noon-2.30pm, 6-9.30pm Mon-Fri; noon-3pm, 6-9.30pm Sat; noon-4pm Sun. **Credit** MC, V.
A big, impersonal pub that's a strange mix of wooden floor and chunky-wood furniture along with chandeliers, marble pillars and antique fireplaces. The twin accents are on food and on attracting cash-rich twentysomethings, so expect loud music at night and plenty of bottle-toting young locals. The atmosphere is different during the day, especially at weekends, when couples tuck into staples like pie of the day (£6.50) and fresh pasta of the day (£7). Drinks include six real ales, among them Abbot Ale (£2.20), as well as Staropramen (£2.55), and the usual array of bottled beers and wines. *Dance classes (salsa, 7.15-11.15 Thur, £5). Disabled: toilet. Function room. Jukebox. Life-drawing classes (7-9.30pm Wed, 1.30-3.30pm Sat, £10). No-smoking area (in restaurant). Quiz (Tue). Satellite TV. Tables outdoors (garden). Vegetarian dishes.*

Also in the area...

Falcon & Firkin 360 Victoria Park Road, E9 (020 8985 0693).

Leyton, Leytonstone, E10, E11

Birkbeck Tavern
45 Langthorne Road, E11 (020 8539 2584). Leyton tube. **Open** 11am-11pm Mon-Sat; noon-10.30pm Sun. **Food served** 11am-11pm Mon-Sat. **No credit cards.**
Aficionados of late-Victorian hotel architecture will reach orgasm at this comfortable cemetery-side boozer. Two contrasting bars contain ample reminders of its turn-of-the-century splendour: an original Arts and Crafts fireplace, ornate high ceilings and a majestic staircase that leads up to a parquet-floored function room that is now an extension of the snug. The small 'public bar' houses a TV, fruit machine and pool table, and there's a reasonably sized garden outside. Real ale at bargain prices is where it's at here, and the regularly changing selection runs from the pleasant locally brewed Rita's Special (£1.55) to Ridley's ESX, King & Barnes Broadwood and other guest beers for £1.85-£2. Customers on the midweek night we visited stretched from a group of girl students chatted up by a couple of local Jack the Lads to thirty- and fortysomething blokes in quiet conversation. Bargain-priced sandwiches are available at lunchtimes. *Function room. Games (darts, fruit machine, pool table). Jukebox. Tables outdoors (garden). TV. Vegetarian dishes.*

Sir Alfred Hitchcock Hotel
147 Whipps Cross Road, E11 (020 8530 3724/ www.hitchcock.clara.net). Leytonstone or Walthamstow Central tube. **Open** 11am-11pm Mon-Sat; noon-10.30pm Sun. **Food served** 10am-3.30pm, 5-10.30pm daily. **Credit** AmEx, DC, MC, V.
The ivy-covered façade of this majestic building on the edge of Epping Forest has been unfairly compared to the Hammer House of Horror and the Bates Motel: we prefer to think of it

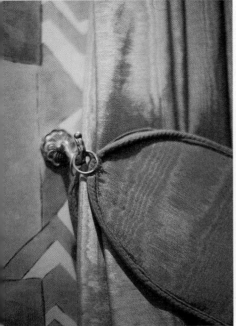

s the location for an Agatha Christie murder mystery. The main room has settle-lined cubby holes and alcoves arranged round a central island bar that offers a wide range of ales – London Pride and Flowers Original, both for £1.78 – as well s lagers and an unusually tasty Murphy's stout. As you might suppose, the walls are decorated with pictures of eytonstone's most famous son and scenes from his movies. 'he restaurant area has been taken over by the Star of India, reasonable Indian restaurant offering the usual suspects for igh street prices. As it's near Whipps Cross Hospital a good roportion of the clientele are young medical staff, with a few rinkled old prospective patients scattered about. Service is riendly and rapid, and the ambience pretty damn congenial. *abies and children admitted. Function room. Games (fruit machine). Quiz (Tue). Restaurant. Satellite TV (big screen). 'ables outdoors (garden). Vegetarian dishes.*

Villiam IV

16 Leyton High Road, E10 (020 8556 2460). Leyton r Walthamstow Central tube/Walthamstow Central rail.)pen 11am-11pm Mon-Sat; noon-10.30pm Sun. Food erved noon-3pm, 5.30-8.30pm Mon-Sat; 12.30-5pm Sun. o credit cards.

gnore the 'wine bar' signs: this is a large, friendly beer rinker's pub on the Leyton High Road. It's a grand dwardian building with two large bars, the front hosting ig-screen football action, the back a quieter affair with a Van Iorrison soundtrack, tasty domed skylight and chess and ackgammon sets available for hire. Both are carpeted and ne unifying colour is deep red – terracotta, you could call it, ut being Leyton we'll stick to deep red – dotted throughout rith framed pictures, clocks and authentic pub mirrors. The ront bar is further hung with copper pots and implements. eers are good: four real ales are on offer, including London

Pride (£1.95), ESB (£2) and Woodforde Wherry (£1.85), and draught Budvar is a reasonable £2.20. Food is better-than-average pub grub, including steak chasseur (£6) and pork spare ribs (£5.95). Customers when we called were chiefly male, thirtysomething and white collar, although a smattering of younger women added to the ambience. *Babies and children admitted (until 7pm). Games (fruit machines, quiz machine). Quiz (Sun). Satellite TV. Tables outdoors (paved area). Vegetarian dishes.*

Limehouse E14

Booty's Riverside Bar

92A Narrow Street, E14 (020 7987 8343). Westferry DLR. Open 11am-11pm Mon-Sat; noon-10.30pm Sun. Food served 11am-8.30pm Mon-Sat; noon-9.30pm Sun. Credit AmEx, DC, MC, V.

Another conversion into a 'typical' riverside pub (it has been known to have an annual flood) this time in 1979 and from an engineer's toolhouse – check out the winch hanging over the water at the rear – Booty's is one of the friendliest pubs in the area. Wine is the speciality: the house Château Belair claret (£2.60 a glass, £11.50 a bottle) and the honeyed Château de Mersault white burgundy are both worth trying, although at £28 a bottle we sadly had to leave the latter on the rack. Bottled beers are available as well – the usual Budweiser/Pils selections – as are draught Bass (£2.10), Tetley's (£2), Caffreys (£2.40) and Staropramen (£2.50). The food is largely own-made nosh of the chilli con carne/beef and ale pie variety, at around £5 a dish. *Babies and children admitted. Games (fruit machine, quiz machine). Tables outdoors (pavement). TV. Vegetarian dishes.*

Grapes

76 Narrow Street, E14 (020 7987 4396). Westferry DLR.
Open noon-3pm, 5.30-11.30pm Mon-Fri; 7-11pm Sat; noon-3pm, 7-10.30pm Sun. **Food served** 7-9pm Mon-Sat; noon-3pm Sun. **Credit** AmEx, DC, MC, V.
The building itself dates back to 1583, and like many a pub in this area, the Grapes has also has a literary past. It claims to be the pub Dickens described in *Our Mutual Friend* as 'the Six Jolly Fellowship Porters', although scholars point to the **Prospect of Whitby** in Wapping (*see p203*) as another possible contender. Either way, it's a long, thin, multi-levelled old pub with wooden floors and panelling, chunky furniture and an eccentric staircase leading up to the toilets, which share the first floor with a pleasing little fish restaurant. Whitebait, cooked to the 'Greenwich recipe', is £4.50; most other main courses are sold at market prices (usually about £10), with sauces an extra £2.25. The bar menu features simpler dishes – fish and chips, bangers and mash – for around a fiver, which many choose to accompany with pints of Burton Ale (£2.25) or Stella Artois (£2.45). Sadly, Max, the lethargic resident Alsatian, may not be around much longer due to a diseased spine.
Function room. Games (board games). Restaurant. Tables outdoors (riverside balcony). Vegetarian dishes.

The House Bar and Restaurant

27 Ropemakers Fields, E14 (020 7538 3818). Limehouse or Westferry DLR/15, 115, 395, D3 bus. **Open/food served** noon-3pm, 6-11pm Mon-Sat; noon-3pm, 6-10.30pm Sun. **Credit** MC, V.
There's been another move upmarket at the former House They Left Behind (even more formerly the Black Horse), with the sad result that they've replaced cask-conditioned beers with Grolsch, Guinness, Caffreys and the like (all £2.50). Still, it's the same long, thin ground-floor room, with a bar along half of the left-hand side. These days the walls are pastel-painted, too, which along with clever lighting effects gives a warm, welcoming sheen to the room. The staff couldn't be more friendly, and even the food has become grander with dishes such as wild mushroom risotto (£11.95) and grilled lobster and clam sauce (£19.95) now on the menu. Good, old-fashioned Sunday lunch – a choice of two roasts – is still available, though, priced at £7.25.
Babies and children admitted. Restaurant. Tables outdoors (basement). Vegetarian dishes.

Queen's Head

8 Flamborough Street, E14 (020 7791 2504). Limehouse DLR. **Open** 11.30am-3pm, 5.30-11pm Mon-Fri; 11.30am-3pm, 8-11pm Sat; 11.30am-3pm, 8-10.30pm Sun. **Food served** 11.30am-3pm Mon-Fri. **No credit cards**.
If you've ever been in a Young's pub, chances are you'll have seen a picture of the Queen's Head: this is where the Queen Mother pulled a pint on 16 July 1987, and there's a plaque on the bar to prove it. Young's has had pubs in the East End for over a century – it used to haul the barrels up the river from Wandsworth – and this is one of its gems. It's very much a locals' pub, situated in the conservation area off gentrified York Square, so expect a diverse mix of regulars. The saloon is the larger of the two bars, with green velvet curtains and velvet banquettes around a central, timbered island bar. The public bar is horseshoe-shaped, redder and dominated by the rare 'Queen's Head Sports and Social Club' London Fives dartboard (ask an aficionado). 'Ordinary' bitter is £1.85 a pint, special £1.95; food (served lunchtimes only) is the usual pub fare (cottage pie, lasagne, baguettes, sandwiches) but it is home-cooked and tasty, with nothing over a fiver.
Games (darts).

Black Lion. *See page 203*.

Babe Ruth's

LIVE

Plaistow E13

Black Lion

59-61 High Street, E13 (020 8472 2351). Plaistow tube.
Open 11am-3.30pm, 5-11pm Mon-Thur; 11am-11pm Fri,
Sat; 11am-10.30pm Sun. **Food served** noon-2.15pm,
5.30-7pm Mon-Fri. **Credit** DC, MC, V.
The Black Lion has been here since the sixteenth century, and
the half-timbering outside makes it look like a country inn
dropped out of the sky. It's a friendly place, with plenty of
bare brick and boards, antique accoutrements and two bars.
The saloon is a gentle little room, devoid of music, while the
main bar, on a raised wooden platform at the front of the pub,
resounds to the sounds of Oasis and Van Morrison. There's
also a beer garden at the rear. It can usually offer three ales
– including Adnams Broadside (£2) and Courage Directors
(£1.95) when we visited – and the food is classic pub stuff
such as shepherd's pie, steak and kidney pudding (both £4)
and filled jacket spuds (£2.50). The clientele varies according
to where you sit, from lively groups in their early twenties to
retired couples sipping their stout.
Babies and children admitted (until 7pm). Function room.
Games (fruit machine). Tables outdoors (garden). TV.
Vegetarian dishes.

Walthamstow E17

Goose & Granite

264 Hoe Street, E17 (020 8223 9951). Walthamstow
Central tube/rail. **Open** 11am-11pm Mon-Sat; noon-
10.30pm Sun. **Food served** 11am-9pm Mon-Sat;
noon-9pm Sun. **Credit** MC, V.
This big, brash pub opposite Walthamstow Central station,
now run by the Just So chain, attracts a lively, young evening
crowd who come here to wine and dine. Real ales include
Bass and Adnams Southwold (both £2 a pint), to go with
Carling and other lagers and Guinness (£2.10). House wine
costs £1.95 a glass or £6.95 a bottle, and on Sundays you can
have a bottle of Blossom Hill red or white with your roast
lunch (beef or chicken, £4.95) for just £5.50. During the week
the food available includes hot sandwiches (sausage and
onions, £3.25), steak pies (£4.50) and burgers (from £3.25).
Although the pub has been knocked into one huge dog-leg-
shaped bar, it's still divided into separate areas by wooden
partitions, and includes a small no-smoking platform.
Disabled: toilet. Function room. Games (fruit machines).
No-smoking area. Vegetarian dishes.

Wapping E1

Babe Ruth's

172-176 The Highway, E1 (020 7481 8181). Shadwell
tube/DLR. **Open/food served** noon-10.30pm Mon-Thur;
noon-1am Fri, Sat; noon-10.30pm Sun. **Credit** AmEx, DC,
MC, V.
A vast, warehouse-sized shrine to the sporting life that falls
down firmly on the side of American games. There's a mini-
basketball court to the right as you walk in, where besuited
blokes attempt to outdo each other (earlier in the day and at
weekends, it's more of a handy place for families to distract
the kids). A long, lozenge-shaped metal bar overlooks an
array of shiny tables and chairs, beyond which there's a
sunken restaurant area where pan-American food can be had
– for a price. The drinks of choice are bottled beers
(Budweiser, Miller and the like, £2.75) for the guys, and under-
a-fiver cocktails for the gals. If you're an aggressively sporty

twenty- or thirtysomething with a bit of dosh who likes to
dress smartly, then Babe Ruth's is for you; although, to its
credit, it also attracts quite a lot of families.
Babies and children admitted (restaurant only; children's
menu, high chairs, nappy-changing facilities). Disabled:
lift, toilet. Function room. Games (basketball pen, fruit
machines, pool table, table football, video games). Late
licence (Fri, Sat). No-smoking area. Restaurant. Satellite
TV (big screen). Vegetarian dishes.

Captain Kidd

108 Wapping High Street, E1 (020 7480 5759). Wapping
tube. **Open** 11am-11pm Mon-Sat; noon-10.30pm Sun.
Food served noon-3pm, 6.30-10.30pm daily. **Credit**
AmEx, DC, MC, V.
This sizeable, open-plan pub themed on the exploits of the
noted pirate is a fairly recent conversion from a warehouse,
given the look of an eighteenth-century tavern. Well, nearly.
The over-loud clubby music played here doesn't quite fit with
the interior of flagstones, oak panelling and beams. However,
judging by the masses that were packed in here the last time
we visited, it's also snared a large number of local office
workers, who quaff the lagers and keg bitters on offer (no
cask ales here) with gusto. Its popularity may be due in part
to Samuel Smith's policy of charging Tadcaster prices in
London, thus making it impossible to spend more than £2 on
a pint. In the upstairs restaurant, bread is £2.50, asparagus
risotto £6.90, and collops of venison with pears £13.20.
Disabled: toilet. Function room. Games (fruit machine,
quiz machine). Restaurant. TV (big screen). Tables
outdoors (garden). Vegetarian dishes.

Prospect of Whitby

57 Wapping Wall, E1 (020 7481 1095). Wapping tube.
Open 11.30am-3pm, 5.30-11pm Mon-Fri; 11.30am-11pm
Sat; noon-10.30pm Sun. **Food served** noon-2.30pm,
6-9pm Mon-Sat; noon-3pm, 6-9pm Sun. **Credit** AmEx,
DC, MC, V.
The former Devil's Tavern was built around 1520 and last
remodelled in 1777, and even today it's something of a river
landmark and tourist attraction. The pewter-topped counter
resting on wooden casks, stone-flagged floors, low ceilings,
giant timbers, fireplaces and pebbled windows are
wonderfully preserved and add to the unique atmosphere,
while the river views from the terrace and rickety balcony are
quite stunning. If only it wasn't such a tourist trap: beers
aren't cheap – Courage Directors is upwards of £2.20 a pint
– and the upstairs restaurant charges premium prices for
quite ordinary food: Whitby pie (fish in a white sauce, topped
with a pastry crust) is £12.75, and fish and chips is £9.95.
Babies and children admitted (in dining area). Function
room. Games (fruit machine, video games). No-smoking
area. Restaurant. Tables outdoors (riverside terrace).
Vegetarian dishes.

Town of Ramsgate

62 Wapping High Street, E1 (020 7264 0001). Wapping
tube/100 bus. **Open** noon-11pm Mon-Sat; noon-10.30pm
Sun. **Food served** noon-2.30pm, 6-9pm Mon-Fri; noon-
6pm Sat; noon-4pm Sun. **Credit** MC, V.
This pleasant old pub has a grisly history. Next to the pub is
Wapping Old Stairs, where Captain Kidd was tarred, tied to
a post and left until three tides had washed over him; in 1688
disgraced Judge Jeffreys, the 'hanging judge', was also
discovered in the bar, and all but lynched by the mob as he
attempted to flee to France (or Hamburg, depending on your
sources) disguised as a sailor. In the cellars, meanwhile, are
dungeons where convicts were chained before being deported
to Australia. These days, the Town of Ramsgate is a well-

preserved old boozer, with a wooden ceiling and a tiny riverside terrace. We've yet to find more than one real ale on at any one time, but if it's the London Pride, it's kept pretty well and costs £1.95. Food is pretty standard pub stuff (steak and ale pie £4.25, rump steak and fried chicken combo £5.45). *Games (fruit machine, quiz machine). Quiz (Mon). Satellite TV. Tables outdoors (riverside courtyard). Vegetarian dishes.*

Whitechapel E1

Blind Beggar
337 Whitechapel Road, E1 (020 7247 6195). Whitechapel tube. **Open** 11am-11pm Mon-Sat; noon-10.30pm Sun. **Food served** noon-3pm daily. **No credit cards.**
Ronnie Kray's fatal shooting of George Cornell at 8.33pm on 9 March 1966 gave the Blind Beggar a certain notoriety, but rest assured: there's not been a murder here since. As you walk into this very traditional East End locals' boozer, you'll be greeted by a comfortable red glow generated by traditional shaded wall lights and deep red carpets, curtains and furnishings. It's a big pub, with two medium-sized rooms linked by a central serving area. Latched on to the side of the pub is a heated conservatory, opening on to a fair-sized garden. The beers are pretty standard (Courage Best £2, Foster's £2.10) – and the food is no-nonsense pub grub. *Babies and children admitted (conservatory only). Games (fruit machine, video game). Restaurant. Tables outdoors (garden). Vegetarian dishes.*

Half Moon
213-223 Mile End Road, E1 (020 7790 6810). Stepney Green tube. **Open** 11am-11pm Mon-Sat; noon-10.30pm Sun. **Food served** 11am-10pm Mon-Sat; noon-9.30pm Sun. **Credit** MC, V.
From 1979 until a couple of years ago this was the home of the Half Moon Theatre Company, and long before that it was a Welsh Calvinist chapel, with pews for 400 Mile End Methodists. Now a large Wetherspoon's outlet in two parts – it won the best conversion category in Camra's year 2000 Pub Design Awards – it is invariably packed. On the Friday night we visited it was busy with a mix of young men and women out on the pull and what looked like a senior citizens' outing. 'The food here's luvverly, son,' said one, and indeed it is: the standard Wetherspoon menu, augmented by local favourites such as pie, mash and liquor (sic) (£3.50). The main room is the former chapel, a massive space with a small gallery overlooking the serving area. Rows of wooden alcoves line one side, with tall tables and stools in the centre, and a big patio lies at the front. Beers are varied, and impossibly cheap: regular cask ales are Theakston Best (99p), Boddingtons (£1.29), Shepherd Neame Spitfire (£1.35) and Courage Directors (£1.67), together with, usually, a pair of guest ales. *Babies and children admitted (until 9pm in no-smoking area). Disabled: toilet. No piped music or jukebox. No-smoking area. Tables outdoors (garden). Vegetarian dishes.*

London Hospital Tavern
176 Whitechapel Road, E1 (020 7247 8978). Whitechapel tube. **Open/food served** noon-1am Mon-Sat; noon-11pm Sun. **Credit** AmEx, DC, MC, V.
As it's right next to the eponymous hospital, you might expect to see a few medical types – student doctors, nurses, porters and the like – in here. You won't be disappointed. The London Hospital Tavern is a handsome pub that has maybe been refurbished a little too strictly, but the wooden alcoves, floorboards, heavy wood furniture and antique paintings

scattered around the walls (and ceiling) still impress. Staff at the T-shaped bar dispense a fair range of real ales, including London Pride (£2.10) and Burton Ale (£2.18). *Babies and children admitted (high chairs, toys). Function room. Jukebox. No-smoking area. Satellite TV (big screen). Tables outdoors (pavement). Vegetarian dishes.*

Pride of Spitalfields
3 Heneage Street, E1 (020 7247 8933). Aldgate East tube. **Open** 11am-11pm Mon-Sat; noon-10.30pm Sun. **Food served** noon-3pm Mon-Fri. **Credit** AmEx, DC, MC, V.
Tucked away just off Brick Lane, the Pride has a clientele that's a microcosm of the area: arty types from the studios next door mix with local Asian businessmen, medical students, builders and slack-jowelled pensioners. The beer's good: Crouch Vale Woodham IPA (£1.65), London Pride (£1.75), a couple of guest ales and the customary lagers, cider and stout. Its decor won't win any design awards, but it's comfortable: plenty of red velvet, some dark wood tables and stools, and a carpet that's typically pub-psychedelic. The walls and ceiling are covered with old photographs of Victorian enterprise set on a coquettish tint of nicotine-cream. Basic home-cooked lunches, such as ham, egg and chips (£2.50) are served from the grandly named Mary's Kitchen. *Babies and children admitted (separate area; children's menus). Satellite TV (big screen). Vegetarian dishes.*

Vibe Bar
The Brewery, 91-95 Brick Lane, E1 (020 7377 2899). Aldgate or Aldgate East tube. **Open** 8.30am-11pm Mon-Fri, Sun; 8.30am-midnight Sat. **Food served** noon-7pm daily. **Credit** MC, V.
The main room at the hyper-cool Vibe Bar is a large, square space in what was once Truman's Black Eagle Brewery, with a serving area in one corner and an almost-too-arty graffiti mural along one of the walls. Add some sofas, four Internet consoles, some battered tables and a Playstation, and it all seems a little, trendily, chaotic. They like their up-to-the-minute dance music loud here, which can make it difficult to order successfully. Thankfully for some, there's a quieter room at the back, as well as a courtyard that fills up quickly in summer. The beers are all pretty much lager-ish, and include draught Grolsch and Staropramen (both £2.50). *Function rooms. Games (Internet terminals, Playstation). Tables outdoors (forecourt). Music (DJs daily). Vegetarian dishes.*

White Hart
1 Mile End Road, E1 (020 7790 2894). Bethnal Green or Whitechapel tube/25 bus. **Open** 11am-midnight Mon-Sat; noon-10.30pm Sun. **Food served** 10am-6pm daily. **Credit** MC, V.
The customers at this one-bar Victorian boozer reflect the character of the area: students rub shoulders with shifty-eyed Jack the Lads, while white-haired locals nurse their slowly-evaporating pints of stout. Pleasingly, the White Hart has been preserved very well: its elegant mirrors, panelling and tiling are all worth more than just a passing glance but not most of the furniture which is past its best. Cover bands play here from time to time, while there are also the usual crowd-pleasers of a pool table, video machines and big-screen TV. Beers include London Pride (£1.90), Young's 'ordinary' (£1.70) and a couple of guest ales, while the food is standard pub fare, and prepared in-house (fish and chips £3.95, shepherd's pie £3.50). *Disabled: toilet. Function room. Games (fruit machines, poker machine). Jukebox. Late licence (Wed, Fri, Sat). Satellite TV (big screen). Music (cover bands Wed, Sat). Tables outdoors (pavement). Vegetarian dishes.*

NORTH

Camden Town, Chalk Farm, Primrose Hill, NW1

Bar Gansa
2 Inverness Street, NW1 (020 7267 8909).
Camden Town tube. **Open** 10am-midnight Mon, Tue;
10am-1am Wed-Sat; 10am-11pm Sun. **Food served**
10am-11.30pm Mon, Tue; 10am-12.30am Wed-Sat; 10am-
10.30pm Sun. **Credit** MC, V.
One of a veritable strip of nu-young bars breeding on pissy
Inverness Street, Bar Gansa promises much on the food front.
'Where the tapas are made with passion and served with love',
they say. Unfortunately, our server happened to be rather
surly and unhelpful – some people take 'relaxed' to extremes.
Still, they do a decent lunch and dinner, based around a tapas
and Mediterranean menu. Hoegaarden (£2.50 half-pint) and
San Miguel (£2.25 half-pint) are on tap, and there's a good
range of bottled beers. The decor in the narrow room is
vibrant without being OTT, peppered with plants and flowers
and intimate lighting. Do note that in the evening it is not
somewhere to go for a quiet drink – the talkative young crowd
have to bellow over the music and you risk an elbow in your
cocktail if you venture in after 9pm. Their slogan is
'Bohemian, wild and fancy free'. Whether that makes you
baulk or bellow for pure joy should be your ultimate guide.
Babies and children admitted. Late licence (Wed-Sat).
Tables outdoors (pavement). Vegetarian dishes.

Bar Harley
2 Castlehaven Road, NW1 (020 7267 7106).
Camden Town or Chalk Farm tube. **Open** noon-11pm
Mon-Sat; noon-10.30pm Sun. **Food served** noon-3pm,
6-9pm Mon-Fri; noon-6pm Sat; noon-5pm Sun.
Credit AmEx, DC, MC, V.
This attractive, sultry bar was half empty on the Tuesday
night we visited, maybe accounted for by its location, slightly
beyond the main Camden strip. The unobtrusive music is
Latin in flavour, and there's an exotic feel to the spacious
room. The decor is vibrant red and yellow, with whirring fans,
laid-back lighting and high ceilings with a core clientele that's
centred around Camden's fresh-faced young things. There's
draught Kronenbourg, Caffrey's and Strongbow for £2.20-
£2.50, while Hoegaarden is £4 a pint. There's a good selection
of wine, champagne, cocktails (£4) and shooters (£2). Food
specials include Mexican bean burger (£4.95), pasta of the
day (£5.50) and Alabama chocolate cake (£2.45).
Tables outdoors (patio). Vegetarian dishes.

Bar Risa
11 East Yard, Camden Lock, NW1 (020 7428 5929).
Camden Town or Chalk Farm tube. **Open** 11am-11pm
Mon-Sat; noon-10.30pm Sun. **Happy hour** 4-7pm Mon-
Fri. **Food served** noon-6pm daily. **Credit** AmEx, MC, V.
The name promises an exotic, dusky Spanish drinking hole,
but in reality Bar Risa is a large barn of a bar with a
generously proportioned balcony area. The music is mellow
(they stress they don't play Nirvana any more!) and the
clientele laid-back young locals, though judging by the
security cameras this probably changes when there are gigs
in Dingwalls downstairs. Both establishments are operated
by Jongleurs/Regent Inns, as is the nearby Avanti bar, and
there's a bit of a loadsamoney feel to the place. Looking
around at the brick walls and wooden roof, it's a shame
Jongleurs chose to daub everything with glaring slogans and
gaudy paint. Still, the brightly coloured armchairs upstairs
are indulgently comfortable, even if one does have to endure
naff sculptures and a lack of ashtrays. There's an average

selection of draught lagers and bitters (Kronenbourg and John
Smith's Extra Smooth both £2.50), as well as some bargains:
ten cocktails are available at £3 each or £12 for a pitcher.
Games (fruit machine). Tables outdoors (roof terrace).
Vegetarian dishes.

Bar Solo
*20 Inverness Street, NW1 (020 7482 4611). Camden Town
tube.* **Open** 8am-1am daily. **Happy hour** 5-8pm Mon-Fri;
5-7pm Sat. **Food served** 9am-1am daily. **Credit** MC, V.
One of the more appealing venues in Camden's emerging 'bar
street', Bar Solo occupies a bright inverted T-shaped ground
floor and basement (open evenings only), the former
decorated in pastel blues and greens, with striking Caribbean-
style pictures and the now compulsory bare wood floor. The
welcome is friendly, the service efficient and the customers
tend to be young and – on our last visit, at least – mostly
female and trendy. Food is good, based around a no-nonsense
Mediterranean-influenced menu, ranging from an all day
breakfast of free range scrambled eggs with smoked salmon
and chives (£4.50), through a lunch of Thai fishcakes with
salad (£6.50) and dinner of slow-baked lamb shank, served
on garlic mashed potatoes (£7.50). All bread is baked on the
premises and generously filled baguettes cost between £3.95
and £4.95 with fries and salad. Draught San Miguel is £2 a
glass (33cl), £7.50 a pitcher (two pints) and bottles of Beck's,
Hoegaarden, Sol, Peroni and the like at £2.50. Cocktails are
£4.50 each and shooters (a house speciality) are £3.50.
Babies and children admitted. Function room. Late licence.
Music (DJs Sat, live music Fri). Tables outdoors (pavement).
Vegetarian dishes.

Bartok
78-79 Chalk Farm Road, NW1 (020 7916 0595).
Chalk Farm or Camden Town tube. **Open/food served**
5pm-midnight Mon-Thur; 5pm-1am Fri; noon-1am Sat;
noon-midnight Sun. **Credit** MC, V.
The main idea at this Mean Fiddler-run bar is to provide a
plush setting in which the area's twenty- and thirtysomethings can enjoy modern classical music that's loud
enough to sway along to, but soft enough to talk comfortably
over. There are also frequent live sessions and readings. The
Habitat-style furniture is strangely at odds with the ultra-
modern decor, but it's easy to sink into the homely sofas and
not get up again until closing time. Lighting is low, baubles
glisten and the walls and curtains are an opulent red, causing
passers-by to press their noses against the windows. There
were enough seats to go around when we attended on a
weekday night, but it did fill up after 9.30pm and it often gets
busy before and after shows at the Roundhouse opposite.
Pints average at £2.60 (Stella, John Smith's, Caffrey's, Dry
Blackthorn), with Hoegaarden a reasonable £3.50. Cocktails
are just £3 between 4pm and 8pm and there's a good wine
selection. Food could be spinach, ricotta and Parmesan ravioli
for a fiver or perhaps a Covent Garden soup for £3.50.
*Babies and children admitted. Music (DJ Tue, Fri; live
music Wed; string quartets Wed, Sun). Vegetarian dishes.*

Bar Vinyl
6 Inverness Street, NW1 (020 7681 7898).
Camden Town tube. **Open/food served** 11am-11pm
Mon-Thur; 11am-midnight Fri, Sat; noon-10.30pm Sun.
No credit cards.
The beautiful young things here are painstakingly dressed
down, and dance or lounge around checking each other out –
there's no point trying to talk over the thumping ultra-hip
music. A cliquey mixture of house, hip hop and funky breaks,
spun by a different DJ every night, is often courtesy of
basement resident and record label Vinyl Addiction. The

Musical lairs

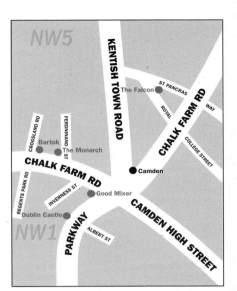

When it's busy, there are few pubs more unpleasant than the **Dublin Castle**: hot, sweaty and cramped, it can also be a nightmare to get served. But that, of course, is exactly how the indie kids like it, which makes it a perfect place in which to start a crawl of Camden's music scene. The music programme at the Castle itself has seen better days, though, and it gets by on past rep – Blur and Madness have both played secret gigs here in the past. These days, you can expect to see a D-list indie celeb or two who's unaware that Britpop is over propping up the bar, while bands with names like God's Todger and Null And Void play in the salubrious backroom.

Speaking of Britpop, just around the corner is the bar where, if you believe the music press, it all began. The **Good Mixer** is right at the hub, and became a home from home to *Parklife*-era Blur, Stranglers-era Elastica and record deal-era Menswear when the B-pop scene was at its height. Damon and Justine have long since parted and stopped coming, but the pub's reputation precedes it and it's still full-ish most evenings with indie kids. However, the Good Mixer T-shirts on sale at the bar give the game away that this is now something of a tourist trap, albeit an unlikely one. Amuse yourself by trying to win a couple of quid from the 'Top of the Pops' quiz game.

The **Camden Falcon**, a ten-minute walk away, was once the one bar on this tour where you may have been able to see someone you'd heard of. Granted, we're not talking monobrowed Mancunian brothers, but for keen readers of the music papers the programme of mostly new bands would usually yield a couple of much-talked-about Next Big Things each week: Muse or New Electrics, for example, who'll either be famous or finished by the time you actually read this.

But no longer. For live music finished – temporarily, we hope – at the Falcon in spring 2000 after the promoters reputedly got fed up of the venue's limited licenced capacity. Hopes, though, are high for live music to return to this Camden stalwart in the future: check *Time Out* magazine for details.

Head back on to the main Camden drag, then wander up Camden High Street towards Chalk Farm. Up on the right you'll find the **Monarch**, arguably the nicest of the NW1 music pubs. Bands – a mix of unknowns called things like Rage, Basinger or Glue Buddha, and some rather more likely, music press-sponsored lads with guitars and the right kind of haircut – play upstairs in a relatively spacious and nicely equipped space. And after the recent difficulties at the Falcon, the Monarch now acts as a home for the Barfly Club, noted promoters of new bands in north London for absolutely donkey's years.

Downstairs, though, the pub is nothing but a nice place for a pint or two, particularly since a welcome redecoration smartened it up no end. As at the Dublin Castle and the Falcon, the list of bands who've played here includes a string of British indie notables, if that's not too much of a contradiction in terms.

None of whom, incidentally, has ever played at **Bartok**, further up towards Chalk Farm tube. As its atrociously punning name would seem to suggest, this is a classical-music-theme boozer. Well, boozer isn't perhaps quite the right word: at this mildly luxuriant, dimly lit establishment customers drink Beck's and Hoegaarden, as opposed to the Foster's and Kronenbourg quaffed at the Mixer and Dublin Castle. The frequent live music and the occasional DJ (whose mixing technique on the night we visited wouldn't have had Fatboy Slim unduly worried) manage to produce an undefinable harmony of styles that might best be described as 'worthy'. Still, after all the noisy posturing found at the assorted watering holes down the street, Bartok comes as blessed and welcome relief.
Will Fulford-Jones

Bartok (*p206*) 78-79 Chalk Farm Road, NW1 (020 7916 0595).
Camden Falcon (*p208*) 234 Royal College Street, NW1 (020 7485 3834).
Dublin Castle (*p209*) 94 Parkway, NW1 (020 7485 1773).
Good Mixer (*p210*) 30 Inverness Street, NW1 (020 7916 7929).
Monarch (*p211*) 49 Chalk Farm Road, NW1 (020 7916 1049).

furnishings are very modern and very uncomfortable, but ten out of ten for the bizarre paintings. The bar is more bottle oriented than draught, with bottled Michelob and Hoegaarden at £2.60 and pints of Budvar and Caffrey's at £2.50. Food is impressively varied, including Thai noodles, bangers and mash, and a full breakfast, all for £4.95. Be warned: it gets stuffed on Friday and Saturday nights, and the presence of burly bouncers may put sensitive souls off.
Babies and children admitted. (DJs nightly; daytime Sat, Sun). Tables outdoors (pavement). Vegetarian dishes.

Bistroteque
4 Inverness Street, NW1 (020 7428 0546). Camden Town tube. **Open/food served** 9am-midnight daily. **Happy hour** 5-7.30pm Mon-Fri. **Credit** MC, V.
The former Café Joe seems to undergo a transformation as often as Italy changes its governments. The latest version features a single sofa on a raised platform as you walk in, leading to a thin corridor-like space opposite a cluttered serving bar, opening out into a square room with a scattering of regimented rows of tables. The walls are dotted with curious modern art representing (we think) leaves and, er, well… it's anybody's guess. Bottled beers seem to be the norm, including Sol, Holsten Pils and Beck's (all £2.30), with a selection of cocktails, from £3.50 to £4.50. Food is centred around reasonably priced bistro basics, such as pan-fried salmon steaks (£5.95) and home-made burgers (£5.95). The clientele when we visited looked as if they were waiting to audition for the Camden Town remake of *Trainspotting*.
Babies and children admitted (high chairs). Music (DJs Fri-Sun). No-smoking area. Satellite TV (big screen). Tables outdoors (garden). Vegetarian dishes.

Black Cap
171 Camden High Street, NW1 (020 7428 2721). Camden Town tube. **Open** noon-2am Mon-Thur; noon-3am Fri, Sat; noon-midnight Sun. **Food served** noon-6pm daily. **Admission** (downstairs £2-£4). **Credit** AmEx, MC, V.
Predominantly a gay bar, but laid-back and good-natured enough to be mixed; one of our party was eyed up by a camp TV personality, but the atmosphere is hardly predatory. The music is of the loud, hi-energy variety, but if that's not your thing you can escape to the pretty outdoor terrace and grab one of the many seats out there. The internal furnishings make it look like a brilliantly coloured hotel lounge, but most people are here to chug back a pint or six, not admire the feng shui. Try Worthington Cream Bitter £2.40; Grolsch £2.70 or Strongbow £2.75. Prices are slightly higher in the cabaret bar and dancefloor downstairs.
Cabaret (most nights). Disabled: toilet. Games (fruit machine). Late licence Mon-Sat. Satellite TV (big screen). Tables outdoors (roof terrace). Vegetarian dishes.

Blakes
31 Jamestown Road, NW1 (020 7482 2959). Camden Town tube. **Open** 11am-11pm Mon-Sat; noon-10.30pm Sun. **Food served** noon-3pm, 7-10.30pm daily. **Credit** AmEx, DC, MC, V.
Tucked off the main Camden drag, this is a fond haunt of the local socialites in the know – indeed, on Friday and Saturday nights it is rammed to the Gothic rafters and there is standing room only. The main room has a medieval dungeon-like feel; clientele, however, more closely resemble upwardly mobile media youngsters straight out of *Cosmo/Esquire*, admiring themselves in the mosaic mirrors. If you can dodge the air-kisses, check out the 'champagne and oyster' menu at the bar, or the well-regarded, cosy

restaurant upstairs, or escape to the gas-lit tables on the pavement outside. Draught Stella, Guinness and Scrumpy Jack are all £2.40, with Hoegaarden at £4.40.
Babies and children admitted (Sun lunch). Restaurant. Tables outdoors (pavement). Vegetarian dishes.

Café Corfu
7-9 Pratt Street, NW1 (020 7424 0203). Camden Town or Mornington Crescent tube. **Open/food served** noon-11pm Mon-Sat; noon-10.30pm Sun. **Credit** MC, V.
This new Greek-themed café-bar, practically midway between Camden Town and Mornington Crescent tubes, is strikingly decorated with walls of bold blue, red and cream, with a raised wooden-floored dining area dotted with generously spread tables and chairs. Check out the devastatingly simple but striking back-lit bottle display in the large cube-shaped back room, sometimes cordoned off for private parties. The welcome is genuinely friendly, service remains cordial, and the clientele seemed a diverse mixture of Camden offices workers and twenty- and thirtysomething residents. Drink prices tend to be very reasonable: cocktails (such as Granita, Santorini Martini and Ionian Sea Breeze) are from £2.95, beers – including Stella and Corfu's own Mythos – are £2.35 a bottle (Anchor Steam £2.95) and a connoisseur selection of ouzos are available at £2.95. Food is Greek-based and includes mezes from £2.25 – the sampler, Corfu platter is £9.95 – brizola (grilled rib steak and Greek salad in pitta with chips (£7.95), Greek sausage omelette in pitta (£3.75), and mixed vegetables in pitta (£6.50). An upmarket Greek experience without the plate-smashing bollocks.
Babies and children admitted (high chairs). Function room. Jukebox. No-smoking area. Restaurant. Satellite TV. Tables outdoors (patio). Vegetarian dishes.

Camden Brewing Co.
1 Randolph Street, NW1 (020 7267 9829). Camden Town tube/Camden Road rail. **Open** noon-11pm Sun-Thur; noon-midnight Fri, Sat. **Food served** noon-3pm Mon-Fri; 2-5pm Sat; 4-8pm Sun. **Credit** MC, V.
Once dismissed as the unremarkable Camden Arms, this building was taken over and revamped into the current wunder-pub. Straight out of an interior design mag, the bar resembles a particularly stylish lounge with beach hut-blue walls set off by cool yellow and spicy paprika splashes. The windows and the ornate winding staircase are lined with fairy lights, completing this unique look. Sink into the comfy sofas around either of the two pretty open fires, and tuck into a variety of real Thai food (stir-fried meat of choice with ginger and vegetables in black bean sauce £4.50) or a bar snack (freshly prepared breast of chicken in a baguette with salad £4.20). The choices on tap include Hoegaarden (£3.50), Adnams Broadside (£2.10) and Scrumpy Jack (£2.20), and there's a fine whisky collection. Ultimately, though, a real effort has been made here and it would be a great shame to pass it up.
Disabled: toilet. Tables outdoors (pavement). Satellite TV. Vegetarian dishes.

Camden Falcon
234 Royal College Street, NW1 (020 7485 3834). Camden Town tube/Camden Road rail. **Open** 2-11pm Mon-Sat; 2-10.30pm Sun. **Admission** after 7pm £5; £4 concessions. **No credit cards.**
Until recently the Falcon has been warmly regarded by gig-goers as having the dodgiest taps in town, but no one seemed to care because the back-room club, the Barfly, was usually packed full of indie kids checking out the latest hopefuls on the Camden music scene, which also includes the **Dublin Castle** (*see below*). The grotty pool table, unpretentious vibe

and range of beers and lagers (Guinness, Dry Blackthorn, Courage Best, John Smith's, Kronenbourg, Beck's, Miller, all at £2.50) keep punters happy enough… it's just really not designed for anyone over 25. However the venue has recently ended hosting live music – temporarily we hope – so its traditional role in the Camden scene is in the balance.
Games (pool table). Satellite TV. Music (bands nightly).

Crown & Goose
100 Arlington Road, NW1 (020 7485 8008).
Camden Town tube. **Open** 11am-11pm Mon-Sat;
noon-10.30pm Sun. **Food served** 11am-3pm, 6-10pm
Mon-Sat; noon-3pm, 6-10pm Sun. **No credit cards.**
One of London's original gastropubs, there are signs that the Goose's gastronomic star is in decline. The sole real ale is London Pride (£2.20), though Beamish Red (£2.20), Guinness (£2.40) and Kronenbourg (£2.30) seemed more popular with the gastronomes the evening we last stepped in. Most of our fellow customers were couples over 30, slumped conspiratorially over tables, deep in conversation. The decor of bare board flooring, lime green rag-washed walls and wooden shutters makes for a café-like atmosphere, which isn't helped by the attitude of the staff, which veers from total indifference to helpfulness. The food menu changes daily but typically will include dishes like baked mackerel fillet, Chinese noodles with chicken and courgette, and leek soup. Starters are just less than a fiver, main courses double that.
Babies and children admitted. Disabled: toilet. Function room. Restaurant. Tables outdoors (pavement). Vegetarian dishes.

Dublin Castle
94 Parkway, NW1 (020 7485 1773). Camden Town tube.
Open 11am-midnight daily. **No credit cards.**
This small Victorian-built pub is two things at once. During the day the shabby front bar, with mock-Tudor trimmings, alcoves with once-red wall seating and a TV sticking out of a hole knocked in the plywood serves as an Irish bar, with the jukebox resounding with the likes of the Dubliners and the Pogues. At night the doors to the back room open (an entry charge is levied), bar prices go up by about 20% a pint and the Dublin turns into a music pub (Madness, Catatonia and Blur all started out here), with earnest young bands playing to their fans at the back and grizzled former punk musicians rolling Old Holborn ciggies at the front.

Critics' choice
live music

Bull's Head (p140)
The capital's oldest jazz pub still attracts fine American imports.

Monarch (p211)
Camden's liveliest indie pub.

Swan (p187)
Up-for-it revellers enjoy Irish influenced music.

Troubadour (p37)
Jazz, folk and blues in a Parisian ambience.

Vortex (p236)
Jazz and literature share civilised surroundings.

The beers are standard keg, with John Smith's Extra Smooth, Beamish Red and Foster's being the favourites (all £2, rising to £2.40 after 7.30pm).
Games (fruit machine). Jukebox. Music (indie/rock bands nightly). Satellite TV.

Edinboro Castle
57 Mornington Terrace, NW1 (020 7255 9651). Camden Town or Mornington Crescent tube. **Open** noon-11pm
Mon-Sat; noon-10.30pm Sun. **Food served** noon-8pm
Mon-Sat; noon-6pm Sun. **Credit** MC, V.
On a summer's night when a baseball game finishes at nearby Regent's Park, you'll find it difficult to get into the large open-plan interior or even the sizeable terrace, so popular is this pub. Floors are wood and the walls painted orange, purple and green and to the right of the main entrance is a raised area decked out with comfortable armchairs and low wooden tables, where Camden's media types hang out. The other clientele tend to be twenty- and thirtysomething locals and it can get noisy – loud conversation competes with pounding drum 'n' bass from the sound system. There is usually a couple of real ales on tap – including London Pride, £2.20 – as well as bottled specialities (all £2.70) such as Duvel and a German *weiss* (wheat) bier. Food is simple: prawn and guacamole sandwich (£3.50) and penne pasta with roasted vegetables (£4.25) are as good as it gets.
Disabled: toilet. Games (fruit machine). Satellite TV. Tables outdoors (garden). Vegetarian dishes.

Edward's
1 Camden High Street, NW1 (020 7387 2749).
Mornington Crescent tube. **Open** 10am-11pm Mon-Sat;
noon-10.30pm Sun. **Happy hour** 5-8pm daily. **Food served** 10am-7pm Mon-Sat; noon-7pm Sun. **Credit** MC, V.
Bass Leisure's attempt to snatch several bites of the same cherry means opening early and offering breakfasts, lunches and teas during the day, before revving up to (in their words) 'a livelier and faster pace at night'. Meals veer from the all day breakfast (£3.95), through hot sandwiches with fries (from £3.35 for a mushroom, red onion and cheese melt) and to delights such as char-grilled steak with tiger prawn and javelin fish skewer (£6.95) and the chemist's favourite, steak and Caffrey's pie (£5.55). The decor is modern in style with plenty of clean lines, exposed brickwork and a raised area laid out with tables and chairs. Newspapers on poles are available for those so inclined. There was no real ale available on the three separate occasions we visited but luckily there's never a shortage of easy-to-serve keg beers such as Caffrey's (£2.40), Staropramen and Grolsch (both £2.50). At night, when the music's cranked up and the pace quickens, most customers appear to be well-heeled twenty- and thirtysomethings out on the pull – there's an over-21s rule at all times.
Babies and children admitted (until 5pm). Disabled: toilet. Music (DJs Thur-Sat). Satellite TV. Tables outdoors (pavement). Vegetarian dishes.

Engineer
65 Gloucester Avenue, NW1 (020 7722 0950).
Camden town or Chalk Farm tube/C2 bus. **Open** 9am-11pm Mon-Sat; 9am-10.30pm Sun. **Food served** 9am-11.30am, 12.30-3pm, 7-10.30pm Mon-Sat; 9am-11.30am, 12.30-3.30pm, 7-10pm Sun. **Credit** MC, V.
Unlike most of its peers, this Primrose Hill gastropub manages just the right balance of countrified charm and unpretentiousness. The surroundings are adorned with huge exotic flower arrangements, furnished with sturdy wooden tables and lit by candles. The atmosphere is laid-back and friendly and, being off the beaten track, it doesn't get too

packed at weekends. A great place to come for a cushy evening with friends or to grab a quiet corner for a bit of romance. On tap are Guinness, Grolsch, Caffrey's (all £2.50), London Pride (£2.20) and Old Speckled Hen (£2.30). Simple soups of the day are £3.75/£4.75 and although restaurant meals hit the £14 mark (with the likes of whole roast sea bass), smaller dishes, such as pasta variations, can be had in the bar for under a tenner, as well as olives and nuts.
Babies and children admitted (crayons, high chairs, nappy-changing facilities). Disabled: toilet. Function rooms. Restaurant. Tables outdoors (garden). TV. Vegetarian dishes.

Freshlands
49 Parkway, NW1 (020 7428 7575). Camden Town tube. **Open** 8am-9.30pm daily. **Food served** 11.30am-2pm daily. **Credit** MC, V. **Unlicensed**.
This large organic warehouse in trendy Parkway is as popular as sugar in an ant colony, the ants in this case being predominantly the well-heeled twenty- and thirtysomethings who live and work in Camden. Just to the right as you walk in, past the 'deli' counter (offering the likes of 'classic veggie' and 'natural ham' sandwiches from £2.95 and organic coffee, 69p/89p), is the juice bar, with a cluster of seats over by the window reserved for snackers and juicers. The style of the place is cosmopolitan, with red lino flooring, high displays of vegetables and provisions on two levels, plenty of bare wood shelving, good lighting and smiling staff in colourful aprons: think David Lynch's idea of a Californian organic warehouse, and you'll not be far off. As with the rest of the place, prices aren't exactly rock bottom: wheat grass cocktails are £3.19 for 8oz, £4.19 for 12oz, smoothies (Purple Haze is our favourite: blueberries, apple, frozen yoghurt) are £2.99/£3.99 and straight juices are £1.89/£2.79).
Babies and children admitted. No-smoking (all areas). Tables outdoors (pavement). Vegetarian dishes.

Good Mixer
30 Inverness Street, NW1 (020 7916 7929). Camden Town tube. **Open/food served** 11am-11pm Mon-Sat; noon-10.30pm Sun. **No credit cards**.
What used to be a pretty nondescript Irish pub has now become a pretty nondescript hangout for cool and trendy twentysomethings following the disclosure that various members of fashionable popular music combos used to come here to play pool. Just so long as no one finds out that they drank in the **Spread Eagle** (*see p214*) and came here for the pool. The pub itself is one of those purpose-built 1950s efforts with a horseshoe-shaped serving area jutting out into a room littered around the edges with low settles, stools and tables. The jukebox cranks out the hits – with special emphasis on the Kinks and Blur when we last visited – and pool is played until 9pm, when the covers come on and the serious drinking begins. We've not seen the keg version of Courage Best for quite a while but they have it here (£1.80), together with real ales such as Marston's Pedigree and Timothy Taylor Landlord (both £2.30). Food seems to have moved on since the old days of Irish stew for a pound and now you can have sausage and chips for a fiver.
Disabled: toilet. Games (fruit machine, pool table, quiz machine). Jukebox. Satellite TV. Vegetarian dishes.

JD Young Sports Bar
2 Lidlington Place, NW1 (020 7387 1495). Mornington Crescent tube. **Open** 11am-11pm Mon-Sat; noon-10.30pm Sun. **Food served** noon-2pm Mon-Fri. **Credit** AmEx, DC, MC, V.
Primarily, it seems, a bar frequented by locals, who make the most of the two pool tables, dartboard and arcade machines or just sit with a pint and stare slack-jawed at one of the many

TV screens dotted around. Drinks are reasonably priced for the area – Stella is £2; Kronenbourg £2.10; John Smith's Smooth £1.90; all spirits £1.50. The spacious bar is filled with sports paraphernalia, neon Americana signs, MTV and children. You can't get away from sport, that's for sure – it does exactly what it says on the tin – so steer clear if testosterone's not your thing.
Babies and children admitted. Disabled: toilet. Function room. Games (fruit machines, pool tables, quiz machines, racing games). Satellite TV (big screens). Tables outdoors (garden). Vegetarian dishes.

Julono
73 Haverstock Hill, NW3 (020 7722 0909/ www.sourcetec.co.uk/julono). Chalk Farm tube. **Open** 6pm-midnight Mon-Sat. **Happy hour** 6-7.30pm Mon-Sat. **Food served** 6-11pm Mon-Thur; 6-11.30pm Fri, Sat. **Credit** MC, V.
Opened late in 1998, this is a bar/restaurant boasting that it combines 'Moorish style with Mediterranean flair'. There are two floors, with a small bar dominating a ground floor decorated in Moroccan chic, with suitably low seating, magnificent Arab carpeting everywhere (especially on the walls), striking terracotta paintwork and a room at the rear that's painted in duck egg blue. Downstairs there's a similarly impressive dining area and outside is a small covered terrace overlooking Havistock Hill for those who enjoy exhaust fumes with their cocktails and couscous. It's the sort of place that likes to encourage you to shed a few pounds – and we don't mean dieting – so it's aimed more at the cocktail crowd (prices from £4.50 to £6.50, including £5.50 for a Green Fairy absinthe cocktail) than at the half-a-lager-a-night crew. Food is ambitious and Mediterranean in flavour with main courses like roast scallops and potato gnocchi priced around the £12-£14 mark.
Function room. Tables outdoors (terrace). Music (live Latin jazz/world music bands 8pm Mon, Wed, Fri). Restaurant. Vegetarian dishes.

Lansdowne
90 Gloucester Avenue, NW1 (020 7483 0409). Chalk Farm tube/31, 168 bus. **Open** 7-11pm Mon; noon-11pm Tue-Sat; noon-4pm, 7-10.30pm Sun. **Food served** 7-10pm Mon-Sat; 1-2.30pm, 7-10pm Sun. **Credit** MC, V.
Always fairly lively, this gastropub fills up with nouveau bohemians in the evenings. It's essentially a popular local where Primrose Hill residents go to chat, so there's no music or other distractions. The no-frills decor is black and white and the tables are sturdy and practical. The real effort has been put into the impressive drinks selection. On tap are Woodford's Wherry (£2.20), Staropramen (£2.60) and Burrow Hill Cider (£2.10); and the ales won definite nods of approval from enthusiasts. Alternatively, there's a comprehensive wine and bubbly list that is worth the visit alone. There's a candle-lit restaurant upstairs, but the tasty morsels prepared in the open-plan kitchen as bar snacks are just as superior: it's not every boozer that serves fried squid in mayo (£4) or braised shank of lamb with mash and spinach (£8.50).
Babies and children admitted (high chairs, nappy-changing facilities). Disabled: toilet. Function room. No piped music or jukebox. Restaurant. Tables outdoors (pavement). Vegetarian dishes.

Liberty's
100 Camden High Street, NW1 (020 7485 4019). Camden Town tube. **Open/food served** noon-11pm Mon-Sat; noon-10.30pm Sun. **Credit** MC, V.
Like so many Camden pubs, this is a former Irish boozer that's been magically transformed into a modern, clean-line bar, likely to attract the zillions of young people who flock to the area like

flies to, er, sugar. The floorboards have been bared, the walls stripped of nicotine stains and chunky furniture has been shipped in. Liberty's has managed to retain a good number of the old clientele – the Guinness is said to be good – as well as bringing in a new bottle-swigging group of twentysomethings and a representative sample of Camden's cosmopolitan mix. The bar service is friendly and swift and the canned music veers towards the commercial side of indie. Beers include Abbot Ale (£2.25) and Heineken Export (£2.45) and the food menu is centred around hot grilled panini sandwiches, from £3.95.
Tables outdoors (pavement). Satellite TV. Vegetarian dishes.

Lord Stanley
51 Camden Park Road, NW1 (020 7428 9488). Camden Town tube/Camden Road rail, then 29, 253 bus. **Open** 6-11pm Mon; noon-11pm Tue-Sat; noon-10.30pm Sun. **Food served** 7-10pm Mon; noon-3pm, 7-10pm Tue-Sun. **Credit** AmEx, DC, MC, V.
A chummy little pub, mainly frequented by locals and by Bobby the cat. Although the punters vary in age, it is very much 'grown-up', filled with animated chatter rather than thumping music. The dark wood surroundings have a cosy feel, but more by coincidence than design, one suspects. The seating surrounding the large central bar is basic, but there are huge leather couches and a fireplace in one corner if you can fight off those sleeping off their hangovers. Wine and bubbly drinkers are adequately catered for, cocktails range from £2 to £2.70 and drinks on tap include Stella (£2.50), Greene King IPA (£2.20) and Marston's Pedigree (£2.30). It's well worth coming here for a quiet meal, too: try grilled lamb chops with mash (£8) or prawns and squid with plantain salad (£9). Although veggies might have to make do with a cheese salad.
Babies and children admitted. Music (occasional two-piece jazz band Sun). Tables outdoors (garden, pavement). Vegetarian dishes.

Monarch
49 Chalk Farm Road, NW1 (020 7916 1049). Camden Town or Chalk Farm tube. **Open** 8pm-midnight Mon-Thur; 8pm-2am Fri, Sat. **Admission** Fri, Sat £5. **No credit cards.**
This is home to a predominantly glamorous indie crowd, whether they're here to see the small bands that play upstairs or not. There are frequent club nights in the main bar, usually with a 1960s-present day pop/indie theme, and even when there isn't, a constant soundtrack blends with the muffled din from upstairs. The latest revamp seems to have paid off, and the Monarch is eye-pleasing and accommodating, with the curvy '60s-influenced furniture, table football, and matches screened on a TV behind the bar. On tap are Hoegaarden (£4; £2 half-pint), Murphy's and Stella (both £2.50). Other favourites include bottled Source and the schnapps mini-bar of exotic flavours, all at £1.50.
Late licence (Fri, Sat). Music (live bands nightly).

Monkey Chews
2 Queen's Crescent, NW5 (020 7267 6406). Chalk Farm tube. **Open** 3-11pm Mon-Fri; noon-11pm Sat; noon-10.30pm Sun. **Credit** AmEx, MC, V.
Is it a bar, is it a pub, is it a restaurant? The answer is that the former Queen's Arms is all three. Although the pub's late-Edwardian façade still peeps out behind the simply pasted posters, stained glass and occasional dangling piece of art, it's been converted into an approximation of how a bar would look if Mervyn Peake has been let loose at the drawing board with a bottle of absinthe. The atmosphere is friendly and the welcome couldn't have been more congenial to a bar scattered with Chalk Farm's arty and theatrical types. The large back bar has been converted into a restaurant that combines the seemingly unlikely match of rotisserie specialising in spit-roast chicken ('the wall of flame' – from £4.70) and Sunday roasts, a Thai menu (most dishes around a fiver) and

The Purple Turtle Camden Town

Camden's Grooviest Bar

The Turtle has at long last crawled into Camden, and if you have been lucky enough to have visited one before you will know Camden will never be the same again. Late night DJs, the coolest jukebox in town and probably the maddest staff around. Check it out, huge space, open from midday, late bar til 12am during the week 1am weekends, NO DOOR CHARGE. Happy Hour all day Sunday & Monday, Cocktail pitchers only £7, selection of bottled beers £1.50 and all week til 7.30pm. Why not try one of 80 different beers from around the globe or sample our chef's Thai food dishes available all day, (traditional food & Sunday lunch also served). Big screen movies and entertainment roll through the evenings, chilled out area with retro games and table football. If you are having a party for any reason think purple and give us a call, DON'T FORGET IT'S CAMDEN'S ONE & ONLY GROOVIEST BAR...

61/65 CROWNDALE ROAD, CAMDEN TOWN TEL: 020 7383 4976 NEXT TO MORNINGTON CRESCENT TUBE STATION

an upmarket shellfish selection. Drinks include Courage Best (£2), Grolsch (£2.30) and a selection of bottles such as Asahi and Budvar (both £2.50). For those needing such things, it would be worth noting that Monkey Chews has a portable oyster bar available for hire.

Babies and children admitted. Function room. Music (DJs Fri-Sun). Restaurant. Satellite TV. Tables outdoors (pavement). Vegetarian dishes.

O'Bar

111-113 Camden High Street, NW1 (020 7911 0667).
Camden Town or Mornington Crescent tube. **Open** noon-midnight Mon-Fri, Sun; noon-2am Fri, Sat. **Happy hour** 5-8pm daily. **Food served** noon-11pm daily. **Admission** after 10pm Fri, Sat £3. **Credit** AmEx, MC, V.

A lively, airy bar for undiscerning cocktail drinkers. All cocktails cost £4.50 and for more traditional types there is a decent selection of bottled beverages, plus a small draught selection. The furnishing is relaxed and comfortable, but it does tend to get very congested in the evenings; on Mondays from 8pm you have dodge the energetic salsa class in order to get to the bar. A Thai kitchen to the rear of the room serves tasty dishes for reasonable prices, such as sweet and sour chicken (£4.95). Outdoor seating by the main crossroad will give you a nice dose of carbon monoxide with your Bacardi.

Babies and children admitted (until 8pm). Dress code (Fri, Sat). Function room. Late licence (Fri, Sat). Music (DJs nightly). Tables outdoors (pavement). Vegetarian dishes.

Odette's Wine Bar

130 Regent's Park Road, NW1 (020 7722 5388).
Chalk Farm tube. **Open** 12.30-3pm, 5.30-11pm Mon-Sat; 12.30-3pm Sun. **Food served** 12.30-3pm, 6.30-11pm Mon-Sat; 12.30-3pm Sun. **Credit** AmEx, DC, MC, V.

In the heart of pretty Primrose Hill, tiny Odette's is snuggled under a French restaurant and offers mouth-watering delicacies itself (roast butternut squash and couscous £4.50; pizzetta of goat's cheese with caramelised onions and potatoes £7.50). It's all very discreet and quiet (except when we were there for a burst of song from a chef who was promptly shushed), and there are nooks and crannies for the romantically inclined. The walls are crammed with framed prints and posters that would make any break in the conversation enjoyable and the low ceilings heighten the sense of intimacy. The house wine is deliciously fruity (£3.15) and there are 23 to chose from by the glass. A charming little den.

Babies and children admitted. No piped music or jukebox. Restaurant. Tables outdoors (roof terrace). Vegetarian dishes.

Pembroke Castle

150 Gloucester Avenue, NW1 (020 7483 2927).
Chalk Farm tube. **Open** 11am-11pm Mon-Sat; noon-10.30pm Sun. **Food served** 11.30am-7pm Mon-Fri; noon-5pm Sat, Sun. **Credit** DC, MC, V.

A bustling, trendy oasis in stiff upper-lipped Primrose Hill… indeed, Oasis themselves have been known to be bustled out on occasion. A loud crowd shout over loud music and swell around the stained-glass, well-stocked bar. Abbot Ale (£2.20), Hoegaarden (£3.90) and Caffrey's (£2.40) are on tap. There's plenty of seating, though, as well as a quieter games room upstairs (with pool table) and what can only be described as a terraced beer pavement. The main room is tastefully if unimaginatively turned out in light and muted colours with red and green pillars. Bar snacks include pannini (£3.30-£3.75) and steak sandwiches (£5.50).

Babies and children admitted (until 7pm). Function room. Games (pool table). Satellite TV. Tables outdoors (garden). Vegetarian dishes.

Queens

49 Regent's Park Road, NW1 (020 7586 0408).
Chalk Farm tube/31, 168 bus. **Open** 11am-11pm Mon-Sat; noon-10.30pm Sun. **Food served** noon-2.30pm, 7-9.45pm Mon-Sat; 12.30-5pm, 6-8pm Sun. **Credit** MC, V.

Kingsley Amis used to be a regular here and the cellar is haunted by the ghost of a murdered barmaid. But don't be put off. This is a classy neo-Georgian Young's pub that manages that tricky win-double of good beer and good food. The Special bitter (£2.20) is extraordinarily tasty, provided you can ease aside the 'resting' thespians and interior decorators to get to the bar. There's a scattering of chunky farmhouse tables and chairs around the place and a raised balcony at one end, with various attempts at art strewn across the blue and cream walls. We'll let the Kings and Queens toilet signs pass. Upstairs they have a good, unpretentious Modern European restaurant that seems to have inadvertently acquired an African theme. Expect dishes like potato, tomato and basil soup (£3.55), Caesar salad (£5.45/£6.55 main), Cumberland sausage with roast garlic and mash (£6.95) and Mediterranean couscous (£7.50).

Babies and children admitted. Restaurant. Satellite TV. Tables outdoors (balcony). Vegetarian dishes.

Queens Tavern

1 Edis Street, NW1 (020 7586 3049). Chalk Farm tube.
Open 11am-11pm Mon-Sat; 11am-10.30pm Sun.
Food served 6-10pm Mon-Sat. **No credit cards**.

An unpretentious and comfortable little pub that places great emphasis on its Thai food menu, available Mondays to Saturdays from 6pm. Starters, such as sateh kai (£3.95), are from £2.75 to £4.75, with mains from £3 for a vegetarian soup to a maximum of £6.95. For drinks, there's a standard selection including a pleasant drop of cask-conditioned Courage Best (£2.20), Kronenbourg, Guinness and Carlsberg. The room is long and narrow, comfortably furnished in a modern version of 1930s style, and decorated in cream and beiges, with a small serving area bulging out from the centre. Customers tend to be down-to-earth Camdenites (a dying breed), with a preponderance of thirtysomething couples.

Tables outdoors (pavement). Vegetarian dishes.

Quinns

65 Kentish Town Road, NW1 (020 7267 8240).
Camden Town tube. **Open/food served** 11am-midnight Mon-Sat; noon-10.30pm Sun. **Credit** DC, MC, V.

Long and thin, with an air of comfortable distress to its alcoved bench seating and crazy-patterned carpet, Quinns is Irish-owned and one of the best places in Camden for Belgian and continental beers, with 22 on the menu. Draught Leffe Gueeze is £1.80 a half, the impossibly strong Bush (12% abv) is £2.75 a bottle. The mix of twenty- and thirtysomething Camdenites who frequent the place – a large proportion of local traders meet here – seem to appreciate the five real ales, which usually include Greene King Abbot and IPA (£2 a pint). Food is home-cooked and centred around such staples as roast lamb, chilli con carne and shepherd's pie, all for a fiver. The taped music varies from Talking Heads and the Kinks to more modern club style, played at medium+ volume.

Satellite TV. Tables outdoors (patio garden). Vegetarian dishes.

Reids

195 Albany Street, NW1 (020 7383 3331). Camden Town or Great Portland Street tube. **Open/food served** 10am-midnight daily. **Happy hour** 5.30-7pm daily. **Credit** DC, MC, V.

A recent conversion has left Reids with a stylish look centred around a bare board floor, overlooked by neo-classical arches, porticos, mighty mirrors and graceful columns, with a scattering of comfortable armchairs and a curious mock-stone fireplace that looks as if it was lifted from a low budget vampire film set. A proliferation of stuttering candles sets the scene off nicely and the rows of tables in the large dining area (empty on the Tuesday night we last popped in) looked ready for anything – or anybody. Food is upmarket pub grub with pretensions: hot baguettes cost from £3.15 to £3.95, a large bowl of mussels with chips (we kid you not) fetches £6.95 and the steak, kidney and Guinness casserole is a steal at £7.30. No proper cask-conditioned beers, but the likes of Grolsch, Carling Black Label and Staropramen are in plentiful supply all at £2.50 a pint.

Babies and children admitted (children's menus, high chairs, toys). Function room. No-smoking area (in restaurant). Restaurant. Tables outdoors (roof terrace). Vegetarian dishes.

Sauce

214 Camden High Street, NW1 (020 7482 0777/ www.sauce-organicdining.co.uk). Camden Town tube. **Open/food served** noon-11pm Mon-Sat; noon-4pm Sun. **Happy hour** 5-7.30pm Mon-Sat. **Credit** MC, V.

For the health conscious, this is an oasis among toxic taverns. Calling itself an all day organic diner, Sauce doesn't ram piety down your throat (smokers will not be stoned on entry, merely asked to be considerate), rather it pours beneficial juices (£2.95-3.55) and tasty alcoholic beverages down it (organic beers £2.90, bottled Beck's and Fisher £2.20). More an airy room than a bar, it's light, calm, soothing and probably feng shui-ed. A large open fire takes pride of place in the centre, there are plants and flowers scattered around and a modest number of thirtysomethings nodding their heads to Macy Gray. The food is rather special: try a roast aubergine, tomato and goat's cheese tart (£4.75) or sesame glazed tofu with stir-fried vegetables and brown rice (£8.50). Meat eaters are more than catered for, but you can bet your last pork chop that it'll be doing you good.

Babies and children admitted (children's menu, colouring books, crayons, high chairs). Restaurant. Vegetarian dishes.

Sir Richard Steele

97 Haverstock Hill, NW3 (020 7483 1261). Belsize Park or Chalk Farm tube. **Open** 11am-11pm Mon-Sat; noon-10.30pm Sun. **Happy hour** all day Mon. **No credit cards.**

The spirit of Bacchus lives on in Chalk Farm in this warmly regarded tavern. The clientele come from miles around and it can get a bit anarchic some evenings, albeit in a jovial sort of a way. The walls and ceilings of the main bar resemble a white elephant stall, groaning with tin signs, quirky paintings, posters and branches, but it's still pretty enough to appreciate over a quiet drink during the day. It's worth a visit just to admire the ceiling painting depicting Judgement Day and starring the diehard punters, but it's probably best just to squint and sprint when visiting the lavs beyond it. A quieter back room has a little stove fire and basic seating. On tap you can find Scrumpy Jack (£2.30), Flowers Original (£1.90), Hoegaarden (£3.50) and Stella (£2.30), and there are deals on Mondays whereby double house spirits are £1.50 and Murphy's and Heineken drop to £1.50 per pint.

Games (fruit machine). Function room. Music (rock duos Sun lunch; trad Irish Sun eve; trad jazz Mon eve; flamenco jazz guitarist or blues duo Wed eve). Satellite TV (big screen). Tables outdoors (patio).

Spread Eagle

141 Albert Street, NW1 (020 7267 1410). Camden Town tube. **Open/food served** 11am-11pm Mon-Sat; noon-10.30pm Sun. **Credit** MC, V.

Sauce

You can see how this busy Young's pub has expanded over the years, taking in shops and a dairy on either side of it until now it's a large, multi-roomed space that's popular with Camden's new elite. There's still a small snug as you walk in where the older customers still sit (we spotted a record company executive and one part of a bookshop co-op), supping their Young's 'original' (£1.91) and wine by the glass (from £2.25) that comes with nearly 20 to chose from. The floor is mostly bare board and the furniture is the standard wood-topped heavy metal affairs Young's specialises in. Outside are a host of bench tables that are seriously fought over in summer. As you'd expect in a media hangout, there's no music, but occasionally the TV will stutter into action for major sporting events.
Games (fruit machines). Satellite TV. Tables outdoors (pavement). Vegetarian dishes.

WKD
18 Kentish Town Road, NW1 (020 7267 1869/ www.wkd.bizhosting.com). Camden Town tube/ Camden Road rail. **Open** noon-2am Mon-Thur; noon-3am Fri, Sat; noon-midnight Sun. **Admission** £1-£7. **Happy hour** 4-8pm Mon-Fri. **Food served** noon-9pm daily. **Credit** MC, V.
Cunningly disguised as part of a supermarket, WKD is always packed with an enthusiastic, metropolitan crowd, grooving on the funky vibes. Every day there's a different club night, playing garage, house, nu disco and '70s-'80s funky soul, plus three jam nights and one singers' night a week. The main bar serves the dancefloor/seating area and there's also another bar on the balcony level. Dismissing draught drinks as archaic, you can buy a bottle of Bud for £2.75 or a Bacardi Breezer for £3, but most prices dive during happy hour from 4pm to 8pm every day. Bar snacks include spring rolls filled with crunchy vegetables (£2.75) and chicken satay with peanut sauce (£2.75). The late licence means it really fills up after the pubs shut.
Disabled: toilet. Function room. Late licence. Music (bands Thur, Sat, Sun; DJs nightly). Tables outdoors (pavement). Vegetarian dishes.

World's End
174 Camden High Street, NW1 (020 7482 1932). Camden Town tube. **Open** 11am-11pm Mon-Sat; noon-10.30pm Sun. **Food served** 11am-3pm Mon-Fri; 6.30-10.30pm daily. **Admission** (club only) £4-£8. **No credit cards.**
A vast cavernous venue that's really several bars in one. The decor is a cross between a Victorian street reconstruction executed by the *Dr Who* scenery department and a stonemason's yard. All parts of the pub are invariably packed with an uneasy mix of tourists and twentysomethings drinking their bottled lager in formation. Despite the enticing (and possibly illegal) signs promising six real ales, we've never encountered anything other than one (usually Courage Best, £2.30) and a wadge of standard lagers and creamflow bitters (Foster's is £2.40, Tetley's Smooth £2). Food is standard pub grub and you can get stuffed for less than a fiver.
Disabled: toilet. Games (fruit machine, pinball machine). Music (in club: live bands most nights). Satellite TV. Vegetarian dishes.

Zodiac Bar
1 Hurdwick Place, NW1 (020 7388 6806). Mornington Crescent tube. **Open** noon-midnight Mon-Sat; 7-10.30pm Sun. **Food served** noon-6pm Mon-Fri. **Happy hour** noon-midnight Mon; 5-7pm Tue-Fri. **Credit** MC, V.
The theme of this small pastel-painted bar is astrology and there's a sign of the zodiac on every table top and on each of

the painted disks that hang from the ceiling. Even the short cocktail list (er, 12) utilises them: Aquarius is tequila, triple sec and 'our special sweet and sour sauce', while Cancer is apple schnapps, sweet and sour, cranberry juice and soda. Cocktails are £3.50 each, £9.95 for a pitcher (£6 during happy hours). Those who don't fancy a glass of Cancer can opt for draught Stella and Heineken or one of a dozen or so bottled beers. Customers tend to be young and trendy, a fact reflected in the canned music that's played at suitably stirring volume. Food is no longer available, not even goat (Capricorn), beef (Taurus) or fish (Pisces), though there is a cigarette machine (Cancer).
Function room. Late licence. Music (DJ Fri). Satellite TV. Vegetarian dishes.

Also in the area...

Café Rouge 18 Chalk Farm Road, NW1 (020 7428 0998).
Camden Tup 2-3 Greenland Place, NW1 (020 7482 0399).
Ha! Ha! Bar & Canteen 273 Camden High Street, NW1 (020 7482 0767).
Ruby in the Dust 102 Camden High Street, NW1 (020 7485 2744).
Fusilier & Firkin 7-8 Chalk Farm Road, NW1 (020 7485 7858).

Crouch End N8

Banners
21 Park Road, N8 (020 8348 2930). Archway or Finsbury Park tube/rail. **Open/food served** 9am-11.30pm Mon-Thur; 9am-midnight Fri; 10am-midnight Sat; 10am-11pm Sun. **Credit** MC, V.
Perennially popular, Banners, with its laid-back staff, multi-coloured paintwork, creaky tables, Cuban flag and steer's skull on the walls, global music tracks, roof fans and little cloth lampshades manages a passing imitation of the tropical-island dinner-house it obviously hopes to evoke. It has something for everyone: parents and kids dropping in for midweek coffee and snacks, Sunday brunchers, dining couples and late-night drinkers at the bar. Food follows a fashionably global line, with such things as Thai vegetable curry (£7.95), monkfish medallions in basil (£10.25), jerk chicken, pasta and so on. The highlight of the drinks range is a globe-trotting beer selection – König Pilsner (£2.80 a pint) and Leffe Blonde (£1.95 a half-pint) on draught, and bottles that include Cuban Cristal (£2.65), Argentinian Quilmes (£2.50) and other lagers, Old Speckled Hen bitter (£2.65), several more Belgian beers, Mexican Negra Modelo (£2.95) and more. There's also fine Breton cider (£1.75 a glass), cocktails (all £4.50, with double spirits), rums, tequilas and vodkas and a decent wine range. For the non-alcoholic, as well as conventional coffees there are spiced and fruit teas and scrumptious fruit cocktails and ice-cream floats.
Babies and children admitted (crayons, high chairs). Games (board games). Satellite TV. Vegetarian dishes.

Florian's
4 Topsfield Parade, Middle Lane, N8 (020 8348 8348). Finsbury Park tube/rail/Highgate tube. **Open/food served** noon-11pm Mon-Sat; 11am-11pm Sun. **Credit** MC, V.
Inside, Florian's contains a highly regarded Italian restaurant. Just as much of a local favourite is the comfortable bar at the front, lined with classic Italian posters and artwork that give it a sense of style without too much effort. People come here to drink wine more than beer, but there are Moretti (£1.90)

and Beck's (£2.30) lagers. The bar wine selection is brief but well chosen (Garda red or white, £2.50 a glass), but if you want to go further you can also pick from the full restaurant list, which offers plenty of fine Italian labels. The bar menu features a similar style of fresh, imaginative modern Italian food as the restaurant range (tomato, basil and shallot salad, Sicilian sausages and celeriac purée, creamy desserts), and, with two courses for £8.50 and daily specials for £5.95, is consistently impressive value. The regular clientele that fills the bar seems to fit one kind of Crouch End archetype: between 20 and 45 years old, professional and often wearing black.
Babies and children admitted (high chairs). Restaurant. Tables outdoors (courtyard). TV. Vegetarian dishes.

Harringay Arms
153 Crouch Hill, N8 (020 8340 4243). Finsbury Park tube/rail, then W3, W7 bus/91 bus. **Open** noon-10.30pm daily. **Food served** noon-3.30pm daily. **No credit cards**.
A curious, old wood-panelled den of a pub, stretching back tunnel-like from the pebble-glass windows to the dartboard beyond the bar, and lined by very comfy, red-plush benches, porcelain plates, other bits and bobs and old photos, maps and posters that make it a bit like a museum of Crouch End. There's nothing special about the beer range (except that it's well kept), with Courage Best and Directors (£2.15), John Smith's Smooth (£1.95), and mainstream lagers (Carlsberg £2.10, Holsten £2.25), and there's not much food (lunchtime snacks only, such as a cheese and ham ploughman's, £2.50) but there's no music of any kind, which is a blessed relief. However, it's precisely the Harringay's quirky, unfussy old-pub character that draws in its many regulars, from fruity-voiced local bohemians of a certain age to a completely mixed crowd of several generations. An ideally relaxing place to drink, chat, read a book or just watch the clock tick, even when it gets packed some nights of the week.
Games (fruit machine). No piped music or jukebox. Quiz (Tue). Satellite TV. Tables outdoors (garden). Vegetarian dishes.

King's Head
2 Crouch End Hill, N8 (020 8340 1028). Finsbury Park tube/rail. **Open** 11am-11pm Mon-Thur; 11am-1am Fri, Sat; noon-10.30pm Sun. **Food served** 11am-9pm Mon-Thur; 11am-9pm Fri, Sat; noon-9pm Sun.
No credit cards.
This is not a pub you'd go to for its character, with a big, open bar that was given a production-line woodwork-and-plush makeover a few years ago, but what keeps the King's Head up among Crouch End's most buzzing bars is the range of entertainment squeezed into its 'Downstairs' cellar. It's one of north London's best comedy venues, especially for catching rising talent, with shows every Saturday and Sunday, try-out nights on Thursdays and sometimes extra shows on Wednesdays that are recorded for the BBC; at other times it hosts the Club Senseless live music/comedy bash (first Friday of each month), salsa nights (Mondays), the Kalamazoo acoustic blues and folk club, live jazz (Sunday midday), second-hand record fairs and other one-offs. Stay in the main bar and you're still likely to find a young, up-for-it crowd most nights, as well as Tetley's bitter for £2 and lagers for £2.10-£2.40. There's a big range of pub nosh, from potato skins with bacon and cheese (£2.50) to a healthy soup of the day (£1.75) and a roast for Sunday lunch.
Babies and children admitted (dining only). Comedy club (8pm nightly £3-£5). Function room. Games (fruit machine). Jukebox. Late licence (Fri, Sat). Satellite TV. Vegetarian dishes.

Railway Tavern
23 Crouch End Hill, N8 (020 8347 2991). Hornsey rail. **Open** noon-11pm Mon-Sat; noon-10.30pm Sun. **Food served** noon-2.30pm Mon-Fri; noon-5pm Sat, Sun. **Credit** MC, V.
Looking a bit like an outsize 1920s mock-half-timbered cottage, the Railway is one of the area's 'old favourite' pubs for meeting up and enjoying a comfortable drink. Inside, there's nothing special about the bar, with satellite TV and a scattering of train-associated knick-knacks to commemorate the railway that once ran nearby, but decent beers are cheap (London Pride £1.90, Carling £2) and the landlords are extremely welcoming, setting the tone for an easygoing atmosphere that draws in a whole mix of punters. If you're hungry, there's a bargain range of pub grub, with hot baguette sandwiches, burgers, jacket potatoes and larger dishes all for around £3-£4 or less.
Babies and children admitted (until 7pm; dining area only). Games (darts, fruit machine, quiz machine). Quiz (Tue). Satellite TV. Tables outdoors (pavement). Vegetarian dishes.

Also in the area...

All Bar One 2-4 The Broadway, N8 (020 8342 7871).
Café Rouge 46-48 Crouch End Hill, N8 (020 8340 2121).

Finchley N3, N12

Catcher in the Rye
317 Regent's Park Road, N3 (020 8343 4369/ www.catcherintherye.co.uk). Finchley Central tube. **Open** 11am-11pm Mon-Sat; noon-10.30pm Sun. **Food served** noon-2.30pm, 6-9pm Mon-Sat; noon-9pm Sun. **Credit** AmEx, DC, MC, V.
A popular local rather than a destination pub, the Catcher gets very busy at the weekends, drawing in a cheery, varied crowd. It's larger than it looks and has a vaguely rural theme, with hoes on the roof and some well-dodgy leather gear on the walls, but don't expect to see JD Salinger: this is more firmly Finchley than existential Americana. The range of beers is generally excellent, usually including Hancock's HB (£1.85) and Catcher in the Rye (£1.50), and the likes of Adnams Bitter and Bass (both £1.95) plus three guest ales; they also have occasional beer festivals, serving 25 different ales for £1.85-£2.10. The number of different seating areas generally allows loud lager drinkers to share the pub with quieter punters. There's a patio out front if you don't mind the traffic thundering down Regent's Park Road.
Games (fruit machine, quiz machine). No-smoking area (11am-3pm). Quiz (Tue). Satellite TV. Tables outdoors (patio). Vegetarian dishes.

Also in the area...

Café Rouge Leisure Way, High Road, N12 (020 8446 4777).

Finsbury Park, Stroud Green, N4

Old Dairy
1-3 Crouch Hill, N4 (020 7263 3337). Crouch Hill rail/Finsbury Park tube/rail, then W2, W7 bus. **Open** 11am-11pm Mon-Sat; noon-10.30pm Sun. **Food served** 11am-10pm Mon-Sat; noon-10pm Sun. **Credit** AmEx, DC, MC, V.

Critics' choice
gardens

Clock House (p183)
Award-winning garden and indoor olive tree.

Drayton Court (p142)
Choose between landscaped garden and wrought-iron patio.

Duke of Edinburgh (p169)
Weekend barbecues now the stuff of legend.

Freemasons Arms (p218)
Hampstead's biggest and best.

White Swan (p151)
Extensive gardens blossom in summer.

The fascinating friezes of life in a Victorian dairy painted on to the outer walls of this ornate building, completed in 1889 when there were still cows in fields alongside, form Stroud Green's most distinguished landmark. In the last few years it's been transformed into a big bar/café, run by Regent Inns, which still retains something of a rustic feel (echoed in its many knick-knacks) despite the TV, and the London punters who often fill the place. A good choice of reasonably priced drinks includes Boddingtons (£2), Wadworth 6X (£2.10) and lagers at £2-£2.35, and wines by the glass; food is of the pub-grub variety (mainly sandwiches, such as brie with cranberry £3.15, and chicken and bacon with tomato salad £4.65). So large is the Old Dairy that you can choose your atmosphere, between the bustle at the bar and quieter spaces for eating and chatting in the side rooms.
Babies and children admitted (children's menus, high chairs). Disabled: toilet. Function rooms. Games (darts, fruit machines, quiz machines, table football). Music (live acoustic guitar Thur). No-smoking areas. Quiz (Tue). Restaurant. Satellite TV. Vegetarian dishes.

Triangle
1 Ferme Park Road, N4 (020 8292 0516). Crouch Hill rail/Finsbury Park tube/rail, then W3 bus. **Open** noon-midnight Tue-Fri; 10am-midnight Sat; 10am-11.30pm Sun. **Food served** noon-midnight Tue-Sat; 10am-11.30pm Sun. **Credit** MC, V.
Triangle has taken over from what was WXD café. And the elaborate new decor conjures images of a Morocco of the future (and is also very comfortable, with plenty of intimate places to sit) accompanied by music, on our visit, that ran from rai through jazz, to eastern European gypsy bands. The menu features an enjoyable, global mix of the likes of Moroccan baïssara soup of mixed pulses (£3.95), Caesar salad (£4.95), jerk chicken with basmati rice (£9.50) and a 'new English breakfast' at weekends. It may be more a restaurant, but at the bar you can sample cocktails (Margarita and Long Island Iced Tea both £4.95), Corona and other bottled beers (all £3), wines (from £9.95 a bottle) and teas and coffees, with an eclectic range of tapas. And service is with a smile. For warmer months, there's a little paved garden at the back.
Babies and children admitted (high chairs, nappy-changing facilities). Disabled: toilet. Function room. Music (jazz 7pm Sun). Tables outdoors (garden, pavement). Vegetarian dishes.

White Lion of Mortimer
125 Stroud Green Road, N4 (020 7281 4773). Crouch Hill rail/Finsbury Park tube/rail, then W3, W7 bus. **Open** 11am-11pm Mon-Sat; noon-10.30pm Sun. **Food served** 3-6pm daily. **Credit** AmEx, DC, MC, V.
A veteran pub that has been part of the JD Wetherspoon's chain for some time, though it's held on to its original pub features, such as blue plush seating, knick-knacks and a dark varnished-wood bar. A well-tended range of ales (guest bitters, such as Lincolnshire Longwood, London Pride and Theakston, all £1.50-£2) served by friendly staff, makes it a favourite for beer fans, and there's a simple, but good-value food menu (veg roast £3.45, soup and a bap £1.95). It has plenty of (fairly elderly) regulars who treat it as their living room, supplemented by a mixed bunch who pass through during an evening.
No-smoking area. No piped music or jukebox. Vegetarian dishes.

World's End
21-23 Stroud Green Road, N4 (020 7281 8679). Finsbury Park tube/rail. **Open** 11am-midnight Mon-Thur; 11am-12.30pm Fri, Sat; noon-10.30pm Sun. **Happy hour** 11am-9pm daily. **No credit cards.**
Anybody thought pub rock was dead? Not in Finsbury Park it ain't, where the Aussie-run World's End hosts tyro indie/rock bands, cover and tribute combos, jams and karaoke sessions, every night of the week. You know the punters like to party when the drinks list consists of shooters (£2.50) with labels like 'quick fuck' or 'Springbok blowjob', and there are loads of high-alcohol-intake-inducing special offers such as four-pint jugs of lager for £3, or vodka 'n' Red Bull jugs for £8. The more discriminating can find an interesting range of guest beers, such as Fuller's Jack Frost, all at £2.02, and there are several kinds of fruit schnapps (£1). On a weekday night the congregation included punkish locals, Kosovar boys, the bands' mates and some dodgy-looking characters probably drawn by the cheap booze; at weekends it gets packed with travelling Antipodeans, students and other grunge-ophiles.
Games (fruit machine, pinball, quiz machine, video games). Music (live bands 9.30pm nightly). Satellite TV. Tables outdoors (pavement).

Hampstead NW3

Bar Room Bar
48 Rosslyn Hill, NW3 (020 7435 0808). Hampstead tube/Hampstead Heath rail. **Open** 11am-11pm Mon-Sat; 11am-10.30pm Sun. **Food served** noon-11pm Mon-Sat; noon-10.30pm Sun. **Credit** MC, V.
This is a really swinging joint – even on a Sunday night the locals were living it large. The space is light and airy with huge front windows and a central dark green wooden bar, and is populated by the young and thrusting of Hampstead, striking poses and enjoying the pleasures of Hoegaarden (£3.90), a good range of bottled beers (from £2.50) and wine by the glass – pretty reasonable with oven-baked pizzas (from £4.50) and salads, too. The sound system was in full effect on our visit, adding a clubby, pick-up feel to the place. Come and watch the Hampstead media babes at play.
Artist (caricatures Mon). Babies and children admitted (until 6pm). Games (board games). Music (DJs Thur, Sat, Sun). Tables outdoors (garden). Vegetarian dishes.

Duke of Hamilton
23-25 New End, NW3 (020 7794 0258). Hampstead tube. **Open** 11am-11pm Mon-Sat; noon-10.30pm Sun. **Food served** noon-2.30pm Mon-Sat. **No credit cards.**

Set above the road, the Duke of Hamilton offers a great place to drink in the summer as it has plenty of tables outside for supping and enjoying the summer air. Inside it's packed with cricketing ephemera and cricket's on the TV, too. It has a devoted group of hardcore locals – old geezers well installed at the bar drinking down Fuller's ESB (£2 a pint) or London Pride along with Budvar (£2.50) on tap (all prices are approximate because staff weren't prepared to confirm them with us). This is a low-key place to sip a quiet pint, although it gets busy before and after performances at the New End Theatre next door. Word has it that this is the favoured watering hole of the Hampstead police, so make sure you're legally entitled to drink from the list of good guest ales and cider.
Disabled: toilet. Function room. Games (darts). No piped music or jukebox. Tables outdoors (terrace). TV. Vegetarian dishes.

Flask
14 Flask Walk, NW3 (020 7435 4580). Hampstead tube.
Open 11am-11pm Mon-Sat; noon-10.30pm Sun.
Food served noon-3pm Mon; noon-3pm, 6-8.30pm Tue-Sat; noon-4pm Sun. **Credit** DC, MC, V.
Flask is the kind of place where you wouldn't be surprised to see someone's teeth soaking while they sup on a pint – the place has a serious old-geezer fraternity that gathers around the front tables. It's a Young's pub so you can enjoy a pint of Special (£2.02) or Winter Warmer (£2.07); however, the Guinness (£2.30) was not great on our visit – end of the barrel stuff. Food is standard, but cheap, with offerings such as carrot and coriander soup (£2) and liver, bacon and onion casserole (£4.50). All said, this is a traditional, average pub in a great location, which has a history for hosting the area's intellectuals and creative types. Our drinking session was greatly improved by some star spotting: John Hurt was at the bar.
Babies and children admitted (until 8pm). Disabled: toilet. Function room (conservatory). Games (fruit machine, quiz machine). No piped music or jukebox. No-smoking area. Quiz (Thur). Restaurant. Satellite TV (big screen). Tables outdoors (pavement, terrace). Vegetarian dishes.

Freemasons Arms
32 Downshire Hill, NW3 (020 7433 6811). Belsize Park or Hampstead tube/Hampstead Heath rail. **Open** noon-11pm Mon-Sat; noon-10.30pm Sun. **Food served** noon-10pm Mon-Sat; noon-9pm Sun. **Credit** MC, V.
Thankfully, not a funny handshake in sight. This pub is situated in a really lovely part of town and benefits from a great beer garden out back. The place itself is the classic modernised pub: pine tables, paint-effect walls, but with old-fashioned pictures on the wall and objects strewn about to give the place a homely feel. There's London Pride (£2.10) and Grolsch (£2.65) on tap and a reasonable selection of whiskies including Laphroaig (£2.05). The food is standard, but cheaper than many pubs in the area – soup of the day (£1.95) and Sunday roasts (£5.95).
Babies and children admitted (in dining area). Disabled: toilet. Games (fruit machine). No-smoking area. Tables outdoors (garden, patio). Vegetarian dishes.

Hollybush
22 Holly Mount, NW3 (020 7435 2892/ www.hollybush.com). Hampstead tube/Hampstead Heath rail. **Open** noon-11pm Mon-Sat; noon-10.30pm Sun.
Food served noon-3pm, 5.30-10.30pm Mon-Fri; noon-10.30pm Sat; noon-10pm Sun. **Credit** MC, V.
People will hate the *Pubs & Bars Guide* for outing this perfect little pub, but it has to be done, because it's a real gem. Tucked up one of Hampstead's tiny backstreets, it's a snug old pub, which is small, intimate and has a real locals brigade. The

building originally housed the stables belonging to George Romney and the pub still has stalls of dark panelling beneath Victorian gas lamps in the public bar and an original stable beam in the carpeted lounge bar. Take advantage of the ever-changing guest list of four or five real ales (all £2.20 and chosen by a Camra member), the Benskins Bitter (£1.90) or order a pint of properly poured Guinness (£2.25). The pub has recently been taken over and will soon upgrade the menu, too.
Babies and children admitted. Disabled: toilet. Function room. Poetry readings (8.30pm Tue £2). No-smoking area. Tables outdoors (pavement). Vegetarian dishes.

Horse & Groom
68 Heath Street, NW3 (020 7435 3140). Hampstead tube.
Open noon-11pm Mon-Sat; noon-10.30pm Sun.
Food served noon-4pm daily. **Credit** MC, V
There isn't anything essentially notable about this pub, but it's extremely central, comfortable and it's a Young's pub so the beer is decent. On our visit it was virtually deserted and the carp swimming in the tank behind the bar made for an eerie sight. Food is bog standard – cod and chips (£4.95) or spotted dick (£1.95) for the schoolboys. However, if the talk is to be believed, the Guinness (£2.30) is good as is the Young's 'ordinary' Bitter (£1.85) and this is a popular spot for watching the Premiership teams battle it out for glory and big bucks. So if your partner can't stand the shops any more, this might make a good male crèche for the afternoon.
Babies and children admitted. Function room. Satellite TV. Vegetarian dishes.

Jack Straw's Castle
North End Way, NW3 (020 7435 8885). Golders Green or Hampstead tube. **Open** 11am-11pm Mon-Sat; noon-10.30pm Sun. **Food served** noon-9pm daily.
Credit MC, V.
This has the dubious honour of being Britain's youngest listed building (built in 1964) and it isn't the most attractive of places. It's huge, though, and has a wonderful beer garden, which makes it a top spot in the summer. Unfortunately, the tourists think so, too, and its proximity to the heath makes this place bustling and busy at all times. Beers on offer include London Pride (£2.40) and Hoegaarden (£3.95). The place really smells like a deep-fat fryer, which is a bit off-putting and a shame, since the food on offer looks tasty: sandwiches made with Neal's Yard organic bread and the classic Sunday roasts (£7.95).
Babies and children admitted (children's menu). Function rooms. Games (fruit machine, pool table). No-smoking area. Tables outdoors (pavement, terrace). Vegetarian dishes.

King William IV
77 Hampstead High Street, NW3 (020 7435 5747). Hampstead tube. **Open** noon-11pm Mon-Sat; noon-10.30pm Sun. **Food served** noon-6pm Mon-Sat; noon-4pm Sun.
Credit AmEx, DC, MC, V.
The rainbow flag flapping outside proudly announces this as Hampstead's premier gay pub, and if the landlord is to be believed, it's the oldest gay pub in London. On our visit, the clientele were pretty much exclusively males listening to the throbbing beat of the Backstreet Boys. The pub itself is very traditional with no modern revamp, and beers on offer include Courage Directors (£2.30) and John Smith's Extra Smooth (£2.40), along with the usual array of lagers. Although this is a gay pub, clientele tends to be very mixed at lunchtime with tourists and office workers, and there's a beer garden in the back, which fills with the yummy smells of the crêpes that are sold by a vendor just outside the pub.
Function room. Music (DJ Fri). No-smoking area. Quiz (Wed). Tables outdoors (garden). Vegetarian dishes.

Jack Straw's Castle

Magdala

2A South Hill Park, NW3 (020 7435 2503). Hampstead Heath rail/24, 168 bus. **Open** 11am-11pm Mon-Sat; noon-10.30pm Sun. **Food served** noon-3pm, 6.30-10pm Mon-Sat; 11am-11pm Sat; noon-10.30pm Sun. **Credit** MC, V.
The Magdala, following a makeover about eighteen months ago, is now less of a locals' local, and more a bar/restaurant and one of the area's hipper joints. The venue is quite large and airy with a separate dining area upstairs but plenty of people eating in the main bar, too. Downstairs is divided into two separate sections, one light and open with pine tables where the young were hanging out listening to Natalie Imbruglia, while on the other side it was dark and quiet and populated with an older fraternity reading the papers and supping on pints. It has somehow lost the aura it held previously, an aura stirred by the fact it was outside this pub is where Ruth Ellis shot her lover, for which she was subsequently hung (the bullet holes are still visible in the tiles on the façade). Brews on offer include Hoegaarden (£3.80) and Stella (£2.40). Foodwise, there's plenty on offer, although it ain't cheap – roast chicken and potatoes (£8.70), seared skate wing and stir-fried veggies (£9).
Babies and children admitted. Function rooms.
Restaurant. Tables outdoors (patio). Vegetarian dishes.

Spaniard's Inn

Spaniards Road, NW3 (020 8731 6571). Hampstead tube/210 bus. **Open** 11am-11pm Mon-Sat; noon-10.30pm Sun. **Food served** noon-9.30pm Mon-Sat; noon-5pm Sun. **Credit** AmEx, MC, V.
It's practically in the middle of nowhere – in the almost rural nether region between Hampstead and Golders Green – but this little bit of history is constantly packed on weekends. Tourists come to see Dick Turpin's musket and to marvel at the olde-worlde charm of tunnels, creaky staircases and a real fire, features that remain from the time when this was the

residence of the Spanish Ambassador to James I's court. Locals also flock here to rest their muddied feet after traipsing around the heath and refuel with proper British comfort food (roasts £7.45). In summer, everyone comes to drink Staropramen (£2.80) and London Pride (£2.26) while wandering around the canary-filled rose garden, which was featured in Dickens's *Pickwick Papers*.
Babies and children admitted (children's menus).
Function room. Games (board games, fruit machine, quiz machine). No-smoking area. Tables outdoors (garden).
Vegetarian dishes.

Toast

First floor, 50 Hampstead High Street, NW3 (020 7431 2244). Hampstead tube. **Open/food served** 6pm-midnight Mon; noon-midnight Tue-Sat; 11am-5pm Sun. **Happy hour** 6pm-midnight Mon. **Credit** AmEx, MC, V.
Straight out of the pages of *Wallpaper** comes the über hip Toast, conveniently located right on top of Hampstead tube. Posing is at a maximum here and that includes the staff, who have the obligatory good looks and pout a lot. The interior is low-lit with lots of muted good-taste shades and smoked glass, there's even a padded wall making this look like a hipster asylum. That said, this place serves very decent cocktails (£5-£6) – strong and properly constructed – along with wine by the glass (from £3.50). There are bar snacks to choose from, too, including pitta bread and humous (£4) or a steak sandwich (£7.50). The punters are definitely trying hard to be noticed and spend too much time looking at themselves in the smoked mirrors, but the atmosphere's crackling. However, a word of warning: Toast is a members' club and the official line is that you can't get in after 6pm unless you are a member. However, we sailed by the doorman on the Sunday we visited so pop on your glad rags and give it a try if you're in the area.
Babies and children admitted (high chairs).
Vegetarian dishes.

Washington Hotel

50 England's Lane, NW3 (020 7722 6118). Belsize Park or Chalk Farm tube. **Open/food served** 10am-11pm Mon-Fri; 11am-11pm Sat; noon-10.30pm Sun. **Credit** MC, V.

It may very well be the home of the Hampstead Rugby Club, but this locals' pub is a mellow, comfortable place to enjoy a pint. The Victorian interior – red patterned carpet, etched glass, big windows, old wood partitions and railway carriage-type snuggery – makes melting into the cushioned booths with a pint of Adnams Southwold (£2.15), Burton Ale (£2) or Young's 'ordinary' (£1.70) easy. Alternatively, there's wine (from £2.60), standard pub grub (English breakfast £3.95) and even a Thai menu. On our Sunday visit the clientele were indulging in a spot of Sunday Premiership action – so stay well clear if you loathe the footie.

Comedy (8pm Sat £6/5 concs). Function room. Games (board games, darts, fruit machines, video games). Jukebox. Quiz (Tue). Satellite TV (big screen). Tables outdoors (pavement). Vegetarian dishes.

Wells Tavern

30 Well Walk, NW3 (020 7794 2806). Hampstead tube/Hampstead Heath rail. **Open** 11am-11pm Mon-Sat; noon-10.30pm Sun. **Food served** noon-3pm daily. **Credit** MC, V.

If you walk across Hampstead Heath from Highgate, this makes a perfect destination: it's a relaxed local full of muddy-booted walkers, dogs, kids and a good showing of locals. It helps that this attractive pub is tucked down one of Hampstead's beautiful residential streets, so summertime drinking at the tables outside is a pleasure and beers are reasonably priced – try a pint of Castle Eden Ale (£2) or Stella (£2.20). The pub is also part of Hampstead history as there's been a drinking house on the site since 1701. Be warned, though, with its plummy location, the place is mobbed during the public school holidays.

Babies and children admitted (daytimes only). Games (darts, fruit machine, quiz machine). Jukebox. Quiz (check with pub). Satellite TV (big screen). Tables outdoors (garden, terrace). Vegetarian dishes.

White Horse

154 Fleet Road, NW3 (020 7485 2112). Belsize Park tube. **Open** 11am-11pm Mon-Sat; noon-10.30pm Sun. **Food served** noon-9pm Mon-Fri; noon-3pm Sat, Sun. **Credit** AmEx, DC, MC, V

Located 100 yards away from the Royal Free Hospital, this attractive pub (its most notable feature is an amazingly ornate gold and black ceiling) is popular with both doctors and locals alike. The curvy, green and cream interior is divided into sections that focus on the fireplace and board games or tables for dining on the cheap Tex-Mex lunches. When they're not trying to pull the med school students, the bar staff pull pints of John Smith's Extra Smooth (£2.15) and Abbot Ale (£2.10). A pleasant, justifiably popular pub.

Comedy (8pm Sat £6). Games (fruit machine, quiz machine, table football). Function room. No-smoking area (daytime only). Sport TV. Tables outdoors (garden). Vegetarian dishes.

Ye Olde White Bear

New End, NW3 (020 7435 3758). Hampstead tube. **Open** 11am-11pm Mon-Sat; noon-10.30pm Sun. **Food served** noon-10pm daily. **Credit** DC, MC, V.

Secreted down one of Hampstead's backstreets is this sleepy local. It's a nice place to creep for a quiet pint of Abbot Ale (£2.10) or Adnams Bitter (£2) and relax. There's a roaring fire and a mishmash of furniture – sofas, pews and the like.

However, this is definitely still a pub in the traditional sense and the walls are studded with prints of locomotives and pen-and-ink drawings of ye olde England. The young and old who drink here appreciate the atmosphere and the low lighting.

Babies and children admitted. Quiz (Thur). Satellite TV. Tables outdoors (garden, pavement). Vegetarian dishes.

Also in the area...

All Bar One 79-81 Heath Street, NW3 (020 7433 0491).
Café Flo 205 Haverstock Hill, NW3 (020 7435 6744).
Café Rouge 38-39 High Street, NW3 (020 7435 4240).
Dôme 58-62 Heath Street, NW3 (020 7431 0399).

Highgate N6

Flask

77 Highgate West Hill, N6 (020 8340 7260). Archway or Highgate tube/143, 210, 214, 271 bus. **Open** 11am-11pm Mon-Sat; noon-10.30pm Sun. **Food served** noon-3pm, 6-9pm Mon-Sat; noon-4pm Sun. **Credit** AmEx, MC, V.

Just off the picture-postcard high street, this cutesy old pub is popular with locals and the hordes of tourists that flock across the heath. Low ceilings and a classic, country-style pub interior with lots of little rooms and nooks and crannies make this a perfect place to slump after a bracing walk around Hampstead Heath. The beer selection is decent, including Adnams Southwold (£2.30) and Abbot Ale (£2.40) and there's wine by the glass (from £2.30). The food list is long and includes such quintessentially British delights as steak and kidney pudding (£6.95), along with more common pub food such as filled baguettes. There's a big space out front with plenty of tables, which gets packed in the summer.

Babies and children admitted. Games (board games, fruit machine). Tables outdoors (garden). Vegetarian dishes.

Idaho

13 North Hill, N6 (020 8341 6633). Highgate tube. **Open** noon-11pm Mon-Sat; 11am-10.30pm Sun. **Happy hour** 6-8pm daily. **Food served** noon-3.30pm, 6.30-11pm Mon-Sat; 11.30-4pm, 6.30-10.30pm Sun. **Credit** AmEx, MC, V.

There's quite a bit of bar space at what must be Highgate's hippest eaterie – with bar stools plus large leather footstools to sit on. The space is light and bright and there's a grand piano if you feel like an impromptu tinkle on the ivories. For the spirit-minded, there's a selection of seven tequilas including the ludicrously expensive Porfidio Cactus Añejo (£12 a glass) and bourbons, too, such as the pleasing Woodford Reserve (£7). Luckily, the wine list is decent and less of a burden on your wallet (£11 a bottle/£3 a glass). The mix of people is eclectic, but generally trendy and the staff are blessed with quite a bit of (sometimes unwelcome) attitude. It's worth checking out the loos for their pervy rubber doors and bondage adornments.

Babies and children admitted (crayons, high chairs). Disabled: toilet. Function room. Music (live jazz 8.30pm daily). Restaurant. Tables outdoors (terrace). Vegetarian dishes.

Also in the area...

All Bar One 1-3 Hampstead Lane, N6 (020 8342 7861).
Café Rouge 6-7 South Grove, N6 (020 8342 9797).

Landseer

Holloway N7

Coronet

338-346 Holloway Road, N7 (020 7609 5014).
Holloway tube. **Open** 11am-11pm Mon-Sat; noon-10.30pm
Sun. **Food served** 11am-10pm Mon-Sat; noon-9.30pm
Sun. **Credit** AmEx, DC, MC, V.
One of London's odder drinking experiences, the Coronet is
housed in a 1930s cinema, transformed by JD Wetherspoon
into a giant pub with one long bar, a block of games
machines and a raised no-smoking area in the middle. The
result is a bit like a bar in an airport terminal, populated by
people whose flights have been delayed at Highbury Corner.
But it's dead cheap – John Smith's Extra Smooth is £1.45,
Theakston Best £1.15, Carling £1.60 and bottled and
'premium' lagers £1.99; all that space also means it's
surprisingly comfy and tranquil, and you can always get a
seat. A large number of old geezers pass the time of day
drinking real ale in the afternoons, giving way later to a
more mixed crowd. Food, from a standard JDW menu, also
comes at bargain prices – particularly the specials, such as
a soup of the day at £1.70, or fish, chips and peas, £2.75. A
good choice if you're on a budget.
Disabled: lift, toilet. Games (fruit machine). No piped
music or jukebox. No-smoking area. Vegetarian dishes.

Landseer

37 Landseer Road, N19 (020 7263 4658). Archway
tube/43, 217 bus. **Open** 5-11pm Mon-Thur; 11am-11pm
Fri; noon-11pm Sat; noon-10.30pm Sun (supper licence Fri,
Sat). **Food served** 6.30-10pm Mon-Thur; 12.30-2.30pm,
6.30-10pm Fri; 12.30-3.30pm, 6.30-10pm Sat; 1-5pm, 6-9pm
Sun. **Credit** MC, V.
Up a quiet street, a few steps from Holloway Road, this old
pub has been attractively gastro-ised with plain, light walls,
big blonde-wood tables, bookshelves and leather chairs and
sofas, making a likeable, laid-back place to hang out, eat, play
board games or otherwise mingle. Big, uncurtained windows
might make it seem cold on slow nights in winter, but give a
fine warm glow in brighter weather. There are good real ales
(Pedigree, Wadworth 6X both £2.10) and other beers
(Guinness £2.35, Stella £2.45) on tap and a short, but
international wine list, with decent bottles from around £9-
£10. The globe-wandering food menu changes regularly, but

might include the likes of chicken stir-fry with black bean
sauce and basmati rice (£7.50), seafood lasagne (£8), polenta
baked with chestnuts and Parmesan (£7.50) and steak (£9.75).
A pleasant combination of gastropub and relaxed local, the
Landseer has quickly established its popularity.
Babies and children admitted. Function room. Games
(board games). Satellite TV. Tables outdoors (pavement).
Vegetarian dishes.

Shillibeer's

Carpenters Mews, North Road, N7 (020 7700 1858).
Caledonian Road tube. **Open** noon-midnight Mon-Thur;
noon-2am Fri; 7pm-2am Sat. **Happy hour** 5-8pm Mon-
Thur. **Food served** noon-3pm, 6-10pm Mon-Sat. **Credit**
AmEx, DC, MC, V.
A big bar-brasserie venue occupying part of the giant
Carpenters Mews factory redevelopment on the gaunt North
Road, Shillibeer's is an attractive place, with lofty windows,
potted plants and stripped-wood floors. It's laid out on three
levels, with a dining area, so despite its popularity, there is
almost always somewhere to sit. Frequented by local
workers and crowds from the Pleasance Theatre above the
bar, it has a mixed clientele. Warsteiner lager (£2.30) is the
only beer on tap, but there's a big line in bottled beers
(Beck's, Budvar, Sol and more, all £2.50) and Bacardi
Breezers and similar are £3. Shillibeer's has greeted the new
millennium with an all-new list of 50 cocktails (around £4-
£5), a revised wine list and an expansion of its 'global' food
menu (new additions include calvados sausages and mash
£7.50, and char-grilled steak sandwich £7.25). The food is
pleasant, if relatively expensive, but would be more
enjoyable if service was less disorganised. As well as its DJ
nights, private parties and other events are a major feature
at Shillibeer's, and the whole venue is available for hire.
Babies and children admitted (dining only; children's
menus, high chairs). Disabled: toilet. Function room. Late
licence (Fri, Sat). Music (DJs Fri, Sat). Restaurant. Tables
outdoors (courtyard). Theatre (Pleasance Theatre
upstairs). Vegetarian dishes.

Also in the area...

Flounder & Firkin 54 Holloway Road, N7
(020 7609 9574).
Hobgoblin 274 Holloway Road, N7 (020 7607 3743).

Since opening last year, Toast has become Hampstead's premier bar and restaurant. Toast's ability to attract a mix of chilled bar goers and more serious diners (and accommodate both groups easily) is unique for not only the local area, but also London as a whole.

The sophisticated New York inspired interior is all burnished wood, sleek leather banquettes and floating mirror discs.

Despite the air of exclusivity, the staff are unremittingly cheerful and welcoming.

The Toast regulars enjoy an extensive choice of classic martinis, fresh fruit daiquiris and champagne cocktails, and can either sample the delicious modern European cuisine of the restaurant carte or choose from an excellent selection of lighter dishes from around the world off the bar menu which is available until midnight.

The normally relaxed tempo steps up a pace on Monday nights, with an eclectic live DJ and an animated crowd of Hampstead's party people.

Bookings	Membership enquiries
T 020 7431 2244	T 020 7431 8000
F 020 7794 2333	F 020 7431 4767

1st Floor, 50 Hampstead High Street, London, NW3 1QG

BARTOK

78-79 Chalk Farm Road, Chalk Farm, NW1, Tel : 020 7916 0595

Bartok is a relaxed and opulent drinking establishment encompassing a wide range of classical music in keeping with the luxury of it's interior. Throughout the week Bartok offers refreshing drinks and delicious food to complement music from the traditional through to the contemporary and innovative. From bellini to Beethoven, Grieg to Glass, and martini to Mendelsson.

Be inspired.

Opening Hours
Monday - Thursday 5pm - 12am, Friday 5pm - 1am, saturday 12pm - 1am, Sunday 12pm - 12am

Islington N1, EC1

25 Canonbury Lane

25 Canonbury Lane, N1 (no phone). Highbury & Islington tube/rail. **Open** 5-11pm Mon; noon-11pm Tue-Sat; noon-10.30pm Sun. **Food served** 5-9pm Mon; noon-4pm, 5-9pm Tue-Sat; noon-4pm Sun. **Credit** DC, MC, V.

You have no idea what you're getting into when you enter this bar – the windows are frosted over and all you can see from outside is the alluring candelabras twinkling from the ceiling. Inside, it's decorated in a mix of dark red, duck egg blue and gold (which works surprisingly well) and the narrow bar extends down one wall surrounded by a small clutch of tables and a couple of leather sofas. There's brunch/tapas on offer including dishes such as pear kebab with Parma ham and potato and coriander roll with mango salsa (both £3). Drinks include the usual Hoegaarden and Guinness alongside some quite extraordinary cocktails (all £5): the bar has chosen to take a 'fresh new direction' with the classics, so a Manhattan is made with whisky, two types of vermouth, sweet syrup and lemon juice, while both White and Black Russians are finished with a dash of Guinness – iconoclastic or unspeakable, we'll leave you to decide.

Babies and children admitted (until 8pm). Vegetarian dishes.

Albion

10 Thornhill Road, N1 (020 7607 7450). Angel tube/Highbury & Islington tube/rail. **Open/food served** 11am-11pm Mon-Sat; noon-10.30pm Sun. **Credit** AmEx, DC, MC, V.

Situated in the Barnsbury area, away from the bustle of Upper Street, this ivy-clad pub is a delight. It's deceptively big with a warren of homely rooms decked out with hunting prints, copper pans, horse brasses and little fringed lamps – a little like a comfortable country hotel. A mixed crowd, from older locals to younger drinkers, take advantage of the peaceful atmosphere and the Theakston Best (£1.93) and Beck's (£2.40), both on tap. Food is robust and reasonably priced (steak and stilton pie £6.45, sausage and mash £4.95). There are tables out front and a lovely pub garden, too, so a visit in the summer will reap extra rewards. A truly charming pub.

Babies and children admitted (dining only; children's menus). Disabled: toilet. Games (fruit machine, quiz machine). No-smoking area. Satellite TV. Tables outdoors (garden). Vegetarian dishes.

Almeida Theatre Bar

1 Almeida Street, N1 (020 7226 0931). Angel tube/Highbury & Islington tube/rail. **Open** 11am-11pm Mon-Sat. **Food served** noon-8.30pm daily. **Credit** AmEx, MC, V.

This understated but stylish bar, attached to the celebrated theatre of the same name, was gently busy with a mixed crowd on our visit. The interior is modern and fairly sparse with raw brick walls, spotlights and a few artfully placed black and white theatre stills. All beers are bottled (Hoegaarden and Beck's both £2.50), but wine is also available by the glass (£2.50). Hot food is available until 8.30pm (the likes of quiche and salad and a daily pasta dish both £4), then cold snacks (slices of pizza and sausage rolls both £2) and bowls of nuts and olives (£1 each) can be nibbled on until closing time. A great place to go if you fancy a quiet chat away from the crowds of hipsters that frequent nearby Upper Street.

Babies and children admitted. Disabled: toilet. Theatre. Vegetarian dishes.

Bar Latino

144 Upper Street, N1 (020 7704 6868). Angel tube. **Open/food served** 6pm-2am Mon-Sat. **Happy hour** 6-7.30pm Sat. **Credit** AmEx, MC, V.

The doorman and velvet ropes that guide the queues may be intimidating, but having passed scrutiny you'll enjoy whiling away an evening at Bar Latino. The interior is relatively sparse and trendy, warmed up by low lighting and Latin beats that emanate from the sound system or from the live bands that often play. Clientele verge on swanky, with a good few post-work people out to play in their suits, supping Caipirinhas (cachaça, fresh lime and sugar over crushed ice, £4.50) and Margaritas (£4.50). Cocktails and bottled beers (£2.70) add to the drinks list, and with tapas as snacks, or full Latin American mains also available (£5.95-£12), you can eat and drink Latino till the early hours.

Dress code. Function room. Late licence (Mon-Sat). Music (DJs/live bands nightly). Tables outdoors (pavement).

Bierodrome

173-174 Upper Street, N1 (020 7226 5835/www.belgo-restaurants.co.uk). Angel tube/Highbury & Islington tube/rail. **Open** noon-midnight Mon-Sat; noon-10.30pm Sun. **Happy hour** 6-7.30pm Mon-Fri. **Food served** noon-3pm, 6-11pm Mon-Fri; noon-11pm Sat; noon-10.30pm Sun. **Credit** AmEx, DC, MC, V.

Belgian beer lovers know they've hit the jackpot when they come to a place where the walls are studded with bottles. And the atmosphere is great, too, perpetuated by the young crowd that's churned through, consuming large quantities of moules, frites and excellent Belgian beers as they go. Bierodrome has a fabulous list: an exhaustive list of Belgian wheat beers, bottle-conditioned Trappist ales, lambic and fruit ales, complemented by 100 types of Belgian schnapps, with flavours taking in anything from chocolate to pineapple. However, this is bar first, restaurant second, so you can pop in for those lovely ales without having to have a meal as well. Try the 12% Bush beer (£3.65 for a 25cl bottle) or a bottle of devilishly good Lucifer (£3.25). Lower down the alcohol scale is the Hoegaarden Grand Cru (£3.35), which is truly delicious. All in all, it's a great place to experiment with different Belgian beers as long as you don't mind the possibility of being in the midst of an office party. The jukebox is pretty good, too. For the Clapham branch *see p174.*

Babies and children admitted. Disabled: toilet. Jukebox. Restaurant. Tables outdoors (pavement). Vegetarian dishes.

Camden Head

2 Camden Walk, N1 (020 7359 0851). Angel tube/19, 38 bus. **Open/food served** 11am-11pm Mon-Sat; noon-10.30pm Sun. **Credit** AmEx, DC, MC, V.

Situated on a winding lane among a cluster of expensive antique shops at the end of Camden Passage, the Camden Head has an appropriately traditional look and an opulent Victorian-style interior. A wooden central bar presides over seating divided by partitions of etched glass, and Corinthian columns and fireplaces date back to its opening in 1806. Trade is thoroughly modern, though, with local stall holders downing pints and traditional pub grub at lunchtime, and the post-work crowd supping the likes of Courage draught Directors (£2.18), Kronenbourg (£2.45) and Beck's (£2.49) and relaxing in the brick-walled beer garden in the summer.

Comedy club (8.30pm Fri, Sat £5). Function room. Games (fruit machines, quiz machines, pool table). Jukebox. Satellite TV (big screen). Tables outdoors (terrace). Vegetarian dishes.

Bierodrome. *See page 223*.

Centuria

*100 St Paul's Road, N1 (020 7704 2345). Highbury &
Islington tube/rail/30, 277 bus.* **Open** 5-11pm Mon-Fri;
noon-11pm Sat; noon-10.30pm Sun. **Happy hour** 5-8pm
Mon-Thur. **Food served** 6-10.45pm Mon-Thur;
12.30-11pm Fri, Sat; 12.30-10.30pm Sun. **Credit** MC, V.
It may be quite a haul to get to Centuria (nearing the wrong
end of St Paul's Road), but once there you'll be welcomed by
a warm and pleasant pub-restaurant. Stripped wood floors,
large windows and an eclectic mix of furniture in the bar
makes for a relaxed environment from which to watch the
world go by. At the back there's a dining room, which was
packed on our visit, and food is also served in the bar: the upmarket pub fare includes the usual Mediterranean infusions
(seafood risotto £7.50, chicken with spinach and mozzarella
£9.50). If you're local, then you're lucky; if not, then take the
hike – it's a relaxed place to lose an evening with a half of
Hoegaarden (£2) or a pint of Stella (£2.80).
Tables outdoors (patio, pavement). Vegetarian dishes.

The Chapel

29A Penton Street, N1 (020 7833 4090). Angel tube.
Open noon-11pm Mon-Wed; noon-midnight Thur; noon-
1am Fri, Sat; noon-10.30pm Sun. **Food served** noon-9pm
daily. **Credit** DC, MC, V.
A bar that certainly lives up to its name: stained-glass
windows, dark red walls, candles burning everywhere and
a bar like a crypt; on our visit even the barman looked like
Dracula. However, there's no pine furniture or sad attempts
at faux Irish heritage and the Chapel is, at least, a themed
pub with a difference and should be commended for trying
to offer the London punter a different environment. (At the
time of publication, the finishing touches were being added
to a pastiche of Micelangelo's Sistine Chapel, featuring a
landlord handing over a pint of Guinness.) Early in the
evening, it's a mellow place to enjoy a pint of Stella (£2.50)
or Boddingtons (£2.50), slumped on the leather chairs or
sofas – its womb-like ambience is most pleasant on a cold
winter's evening.
*Function room. Late licence (Fri, Sat). Music (singer Wed;
live jazz Thur; DJs Fri, Sat). Restaurant. Tables outdoors
(terrace). Vegetarian dishes.*

Compton Arms

*4 Compton Avenue, N1 (020 7359 6883).
Highbury & Islington tube/rail.* **Open** 11am-11pm Mon-
Sat; noon-10.30pm Sun. **Food served** noon-3pm, 6-9pm
Mon, Wed-Sun; noon-3pm Tue. **Credit** MC, V.
Tucked down a little alley, this is the place the yuppies
frequent when they wish they were in the country. The low-
beamed ceiling and hanging baskets offer a homely charm
that many Islington pubs lack, making the Compton Arms
a popular stop: it was heaving on our Friday night visit.
The beers are decent, and include Greene King IPA (£1.95)
and Abbot Ale (£2.15), and there's decent pub grub, too.
For warmer weather, there's a beer garden at the back,
which is large (but less attractive than the pub), reasonably
quiet and provides much-needed respite from the hullabaloo
of Upper Street.
*Babies and children admitted (separate area). No piped
music or jukebox. Satellite TV (big screen). Tables
outdoors (garden). Vegetarian dishes.*

Crown

116 Cloudesley Road, N1 (020 7837 7107). Angel tube.
Open noon-11pm Mon-Sat; noon-10.30pm Sun.
Food served noon-2.45pm, 6-9.45pm Mon-Sat;
noon-3.30pm Sun. **Credit** AmEx, MC, V.

An attractive, busy pub tucked down one of Islington's many
well-to-do streets. The interior is packed full of period features
but has updated itself in fine style – lounge on one of the
comfy leather sofas and admire the multitude of panels of
Victorian etched glass. There's wine by the glass (from £2.60)
or Fuller's London Pride (£2) for the beer drinker. There's also
a huge menu in gastropub-style such as pork, chorizo and
olive casserole (£7.75) or, for the smaller appetite, soup of the
day (£2.50). The tables out front are a welcome addition in
the warmer months when the place is heaving. Clientele is
suitably well heeled and bourgeois.
*Babies and children admitted. Tables outdoors (patio).
Vegetarian dishes.*

Cuba Libre

72 Upper Street, N1 (020 7354 9998). Angel tube.
Open 11am-11pm Mon-Thur; 11am-2am Fri, Sat;
11am-10.30pm Sun. **Happy hour** 5-8pm Mon-Fri;
11am-8pm Sat; 11am-10.30pm Sun. **Food served**
11am-7pm daily. **Credit** MC, V.
With the Gipsy Kings blaring out of the speakers, a couple
snogging at the bar and posses of young women downing
creamy cocktails, you know you've hit a good-time bar. This
place has a serious party-holiday atmosphere and is open late
for boozing and carousing, which is no bad thing. Don't be
put off by thinking at first it's just a restaurant, as the buzzing
bar is stashed at the back. There's food available (£5.95 for
six different tapas dishes), but it's the booze they all come for.
Happy hour offers three drinks for the price of two, choose
your poison from Cuban beers by the bottle (such as Cristal
£2.50) and dangerous rum-based cocktails such as the ever-
popular Mojito (golden rum, lime bitter, soda and fresh mint)
and Zombie (two types of rum, and apricot brandy) both
£3.95). This is an excellent place to carry on your drinking
post-pub for the atmosphere is happy and light – just imagine
you're on holiday and you're halfway there.
*Babies and children admitted (in restaurant). Late licence
(Fri, Sat). Restaurant. Tables outdoors (pavement).
Vegetarian dishes.*

The Dove Regent

65 Graham Street, N1 (020 7608 2656). Angel tube. **Open**
11am-11pm Mon-Wed; 11am-midnight Thur-Sat; 11am-
10.30pm Sun. **Food served** 11am-10pm Mon-Wed; 11am-
10.30pm Thur-Sat; 11am-10pm Sun. **Credit** DC, MC, V.
Off the beaten track but rewarding nevertheless, the Dove
Regent is well stocked with a fab range of Belgian beers and
reasonably priced food. Formally a gay bar, new management
has made it a more mixed, gay-friendly place to socialise with
a more relaxed and intimate atmosphere– clientele, on the
evening we visited, was solely female, but we're told it's
usually a very diverse crowd. With a similar range of beers,
including Leffe, Hoegaarden (both £2 a half) and Bellevue
(£2.10) on tap, this is an excellent alternative to the nearby
Bierodrome (*see p223*). Food on offer includes three tapas
for £5 or a good chorizo, merguez and vegetable stew (£3.95).
The bar is happy to arrange Belgian beer and Trappist cheese
tastings, with specialist breads to boot.
*Comedy (8.30pm Thur £5). Disabled: toilet. Function
rooms. Games (board games). Music (live jazz Sun lunch).
No-smoking area. Satellite TV. Tables outdoors
(pavement). Vegetarian dishes.*

Duke of Cambridge

30 St Peter's Street, N1 (020 7359 3066). Angel tube.
Open 5-11pm Mon; noon-11pm Tue-Sat; noon-10.30pm
Sun. **Food served** 6.30-10.30pm Mon; 12.30-3pm, 6.30-
10.30pm Tue-Fri; 12.30-3.30pm, 6.30-10.30pm Sat; 12.30-
3.30pm, 7-10pm Sun. **Credit** AmEx, MC, V.

London's premier organic gastropub makes a welcome intervention on the Islington scene. A large, relaxed and extremely pleasant place in which to hang out, where everything is organic or additive-free, even the chunky wooden furniture is recycled. A wide range of beer is available on tap and by the bottle: draught ales include St Peter's Organic Ale (£2.80) and, exclusive to the Duke, Singh Boulton (£2.70); also available is the popular London-brewed unpasteurised Freedom lager (£2.80) and a wide selection of wine available by the glass (from £2.60). If you get peckish, try a generous dish of olives (£2.75) or pick at some delicious bread (£1.50 basket). Or try a dish of the excellent (if expensive) food; the menu changes daily and takes in the likes of bruschetta with mozzarella and cherry tomatoes (£6.50) and spicy pork meat balls with rice (£11.50).
Babies and children admitted (high chairs, organic baby food). Function room. No piped music or jukebox. No-smoking areas. Restaurant. Tables outdoors (conservatory, courtyard). Vegetarian dishes.

Embassy Bar

119 Essex Road, N1 (020 7226 9849). Angel tube/ Highbury & Islington tube/rail/38, 56, 73, 171A bus. **Open/food served** 5-11pm Mon-Thur; 5pm-1am Fri, Sat; 3-10.30pm Sun. **No credit cards**.
With its smoked glass windows, from the outside the Embassy looks a bit like a celebrity limousine. Inside, the darkness continues with some seriously trendy interior decoration, drawing parallels with a 1970s pimp's flat. The place has the trendsters flocking in, busy with scenesters nodding their heads to the drum 'n' bass pumping out of the speakers. As this is the über hip place to be, bar staff can be suitably snotty, especially if you don't pass muster. This seemed to be the case with us – in fact, we have no idea how much drinks such as bottled Budvar or draught Guinness cost as the bartender ignored us and wondered off to chat with her friends. Its popularity remains undiminished, although not a place to come for a quiet drink and evening of sophisticated discussion.
Late licence (Fri, Sat). Music (DJs Fri, Sat). Vegetarian dishes.

Euphorium

203 Upper Street, N1 (020 7704 6909). Highbury & Islington tube. **Open** noon-11pm Mon-Sat; noon-3.30pm Sun. **Food served** noon-2.30pm, 6-11pm Mon-Sat; noon-3.30pm Sun. **Credit** AmEx, DC, MC, V.
Somebody's been taking *Elle Decoration* far too seriously – Euphorium is done out with minimal, distressed fixtures and fittings, but the rooms are dominated by huge, long plastic lamps filling the area with an intense Barbie pink glow. We're told it usually does a decent business with plenty of the young and the bold supping on bottled Budvar and Peroni (£2.75) and glasses of wine (£3.25), but the punters were staying away in droves the night we visited. Classy food from the restaurant menu can be had at the bar, from big chips (£3) to king prawns, tomato and chilli (£9).
Babies and children admitted. Restaurant. Tables outdoors (garden). Vegetarian dishes.

Filthy McNasty's

68 Amwell Street, EC1 (020 7837 6067). Angel tube/ Farringdon tube/rail/19, 38, 171A bus. **Open** noon-11pm Mon-Sat; noon-10.30pm Sun. **Food served** noon-3pm Mon-Fri; noon-7pm Sat, Sun. **Credit** MC, V.
You might expect a flea pit when you visit a pub called Filthy McNasty's, yet here you'll be pleasantly surprised. The atmosphere is warm and jovial and it's packed on weekends, which is no surprise as it's a fine place to hunker down and

enjoy a pint of Guinness (£2.20). There aren't any real ales here, so take advantage of a really fine and wide selection of whiskies including Bushmills, Canadian Club or Black Bush (all £1.60). McNasty's attracts a fairly young and happening crew, but this isn't a place for posing – it buzzes with conversation and it's obvious people come here to enjoy a night with their friends. Watch out for literary nights at the pub, too – it's hosted the odd famous face such as John Cage and Jimmy Boyle.
Babies and children admitted (daytime only). Disabled: toilet. Function room. Literary readings (Wed, Thur). Music (Sun). Quiz (Tue). Satellite TV. Tables outdoors (pavement). Vegetarian dishes.

The Finca

96-98 Pentonville Road, N1 (020 7837 5387). Angel tube/73, 241 bus. **Open** noon-11pm Mon-Thur; noon-1.30am Fri, Sat; noon-10.30pm Sun. **Happy hour** 5-7pm Mon-Fri; 6-8pm Sat. **Food served** noon-10.30pm Mon-Thur; noon-1am Fri, Sat; noon-10pm Sun. **Credit** MC, V.
The Finca represents the South American hub of Pentonville Road: downstairs you can sup on a mix of Spanish, Brazilian and Mexican beers and cocktails, upstairs you can learn salsa dancing from the estimable Roger. The bar is in the centre of a large dining area that serves tapas (£2.95-£4.90) and other Spanish fare (paella £7.95). It's quite an ordinary place, apart from a large cart that sits atop the bar for no good reason. The frozen Margarita (£2.80) was less than a pleasure, although the beers are a much better bet with Negra Modelo (£2.75), Estrella (£2.30) and Cruz Campo (£2.30), all at £1.50 during happy hour. But read the fine print before you visit as 'angry hour' falls after midnight on Friday and Saturday when an extra 15% is added to the price of all drinks.
Babies and children admitted. Dance classes (salsa nightly, from £5). Function room. Late licence (Fri, Sat). Music (live jazz/flamenco, ring for details). Restaurant. Vegetarian dishes.

Frederick's

Camden Passage, N1 (020 7359 2888). Angel tube. **Open** 11am-11pm Mon-Sat. **Food served** noon-2.30pm, 5.30-10.30pm Mon-Sat. **Credit** AmEx, DC, MC, V.
The bar at Fred's is really meant for pre-dinner diners to snag a cocktail before heading into the adjoining swanky French restaurant. However, the small, intimate and comfortable space makes a good place for a quiet gin and tonic (£4.40 for a double) or a glass of wine (from £2.75 a glass). There are comfy armchairs, in muted shades, and stools at the bar – the whole place has a thoroughly refined feel, a bit like a modern gentlemen's club. For those who want to linger at the bar, there's a small snack menu – the simple pleasures of chips and mayo (£3) were most satisfying. We'd recommend looking reasonably smart if you're going to hang out here – it's not a place to debut your latest street wear.
Babies and children admitted (children's menu; high chairs). Function rooms. No-smoking area. Restaurant. Tables outdoors (patio garden). Vegetarian dishes.

Hanbury Restaurant & Bar

33 Linton Street, N1 (020 7226 3628). Angel tube/ Highbury & Islington tube/rail. **Open** noon-midnight Mon-Sat; noon-10pm Sun. **Food served** noon-3pm, 7-10pm Mon-Sat; noon-10pm Sun. **Credit** AmEx, MC, V.
Somewhat off the beaten track lies this laid-back and pleasant bar-cum-restaurant. It has very recently had a change of management, but they reassure us that this does not signal a change of 'concept'. So it remains spacious and relaxed with sofas, chairs and tables on one side and a restaurant on the

other. From the bar you can watch the chefs rustle up gastropub fare, such as warm mushroom salad (£3.95) or lamb, dauphenoise potatoes and vegetables (£9.65). For the bored and fidgety there are plenty of games around to distract, or simply sit and sup on a pint of Charles Wells' Bombardier (£2.20) or Red Stripe (£2.50), or choose from the extensive wine list. Whatever your choice, a pleasant evening is in store. *Babies and children admitted (high chairs). Function room. Restaurant. Tables outdoors (pavement). Vegetarian dishes.*

Hemingford Arms

158 Hemingford Road, N1 (020 7607 3303). Caledonian Road tube. **Open** 11am-11pm Mon-Sat; noon-10.30pm Sun. **Food served** 12.30-2.30pm, 6.30-10.30pm Mon-Fri; 6.30-10.30pm Sat, Sun. **Credit** AmEx, DC, MC, V.
The first thing that hits you on entering this pub is the incredible collection of bric-a-brac suspended from the ceiling – as a crick in your neck develops you might spy a stuffed badger, old-fashioned ice skates and a concertina, to name but a few. Elsewhere, the cluttered Victoriana theme continues and the walls are covered with posters of plays past and present that have been performed in the theatre above. The crowd is mixed – hippies, office workers, courting couples and old codgers all seem to enjoy the atmosphere while sampling a pint of Courage Best, Wadworth 6X or Directors (all £1.95), or snacking on the Thai food on offer (all mains, including the likes of stir-fried chicken with chilli, cucumber and noodles, cost £4.50). *Babies and children admitted (until 8pm). Function room. Games (fruit machine, poker machine). Music (bands Mon-Wed, Fri-Sun). Quiz (Thur). Satellite TV. Tables outdoors (pavement). Vegetarian dishes.*

Hope & Anchor

207 Upper Street, N1 (020 7354 1312). Highbury & Islington tube/rail. **Open** *ground floor* noon-1am Mon-Sat; noon-10.30pm Sun; *basement* 8pm-1am Mon-Sat; 8pm-midnight Sun. **Food served** noon-3pm, 5-7pm Mon-Fri. **Credit** AmEx, DC, MC, V.
You can spend a happy evening playing 'spot the *NME* journalist' at the Hope & Anchor, a pub that proudly calls itself 'London's most famous music venue'; with all the Sleeper and Oasis posters on the wall, you'd almost think you were in Camden. If you're not here to see the band, you'll hear it thundering through the floors from the basement below. Clientele is predominantly young and male and beers are pretty decent with Abbot Ale (£1.95) and Greene King IPA (£1.75) on tap. If the noise in the rattle and hum bar gets too much, retire upstairs and play pool on one of the three tables. *Disabled: toilet. Function room. Games (fruit machines, pool tables, video games). Music (bands nightly). Late licence (basement). Vegetarian dishes.*

Island Queen

87 Noel Road, N1 (020 7704 7631). Angel tube. **Open** noon-11pm Mon-Sat; noon-10.30pm Sun. **Food served** noon-3pm daily. **Credit** MC, V.
Tucked down a quiet Islington street is this attractive and popular pub. The interior alone, with acres of etched mirrors stretching right up to the ceiling, makes the place worth a visit – apparently, there used to be ship rigging splayed across the room (as the Island Queen is named after a boat), but this has been removed. Suspended above the bar is a small upper gallery where a bizarre-looking Father Christmas was still hanging on our visit. Take time out from the fast lane of Upper Street and settle in for a night of drinking and gentle chat with a pint of Bass (£2) or Grolsch (£2.35). *Function room. Games (pool table). Tables outdoors (pavement). Vegetarian dishes.*

Islington Bar

342 Caledonian Road, N1 (020 7609 4917). Caledonian Road or King's Cross tube/Caledonian Road & Barnsbury rail. **Open/food served** 5pm-midnight Mon-Wed; 5pm-1am Thur, Fri; 1.30pm-1am Sat; 1.30-10.30pm Sun. **Admission** after 9.30pm Fri £3; after 8pm Sat £3. **No credit cards.**
A truly humongous bar with industrial metal vents on the ceiling and battered leather chairs and sofas scattered at the front; perfect for people who want to slump à la *i-D* photo shoot while aspiring to hipness, slurping Leffe (this year's Hoegaarden at £1.80 half-pint) and Stella (£2.40). Like its clientele, the place has aspirational tendencies: the name Islington Bar is more a hope than a reality, as it's far closer to King's Cross and Pentonville Prison than it is to Upper Street. The back of the bar houses two pool tables and has a permanent DJ booth. The homage to '60s and '70s furniture continues on the walls with illuminated pictures of classic furniture – the *Antiques Roadshow* of the future arcs out in front of us. *Babies and children admitted (weekend daytimes only). Games (board games, pool tables). Late licence. Music (DJs Thur-Sun). Tables outdoors (pavement). Vegetarian dishes.*

Kings Head

115 Upper Street, N1 (020 7226 0364). Angel tube/Highbury & Islington tube/rail. **Open** 11am-midnight Sun-Thur; 11am-2am Fri, Sat. **No credit cards.**
A great example of British eccentricity at its best, the Kings Head is populated by the most diverse of clientele – suits, hipsters, the odd bum and bicycle couriers all sup on a decent array of beers including Adnams Best and Burton (both £2). The dilapidated walls are plastered with posters for shows, past and present, at the theatre above, and the theme continues, as many of the seats in the bar are old theatre seats, too. There's live music most nights and the theatre gives the pub that buzzing feel. Staff still charge in pounds, shillings and pence here, so don't ask for their position on the Euro. *Games (pool table). Late licence. Music (DJs Thur-Sat).*

Lark in the Park

60 Copenhagen Street, N1 (020 7833 3784). Angel tube. **Open/food served** 11am-11pm Mon-Wed; 11am-2am Thur-Sat; 11am-11pm Sun. **Happy hour** 4-7pm daily. **Credit** AmEx, DC, MC, V.
The Lark in the Park did not live up to its name on the night we visited. In fact, it was a bit of a graveyard pub situated next to one of Islington's less attractive estates. The sign outside advertising a '70s disco, with no music to speak of inside, seemed more a reference to the average age of the punters than to a night out. However, word has it that this run-down, utterly generic Irish pub puts on literary evenings that attract a cross-section of Islington's hipper denizens enjoying pints of the black stuff (Guinness £2.20, or John Smith's Extra Smooth £1.90). So check it out if you want to see some genuine Erse culture in action – just make sure you get the right night. *Babies and children admitted (until 7pm). Function room. Games (fruit machines). Late licence (Fri, Sat). Music (Irish band Sun lunch). Satellite TV (big screen). Tables outdoors (garden). Vegetarian dishes.*

Marquess Tavern

32 Canonbury Street, N1 (020 7354 2975). Highbury & Islington tube/rail/Essex Road rail. **Open** 11am-11pm Mon-Sat; noon-10.30pm Sun. **Food served** 11am-9.30pm Mon-Sat. **No credit cards.**

This place is a bit of a hit with the Camra cognoscenti of the area and the beard and anorak quotient was pretty high on our visit. The Camra chaps are right, however. This is a good pub, close to the canal on a quiet street and on a summer evening it's a very pleasant place to while away the time with a pint of well-kept Young's 'ordinary' (£1.91) or Special (£2.06). The interior has a classic pub feel right down to a set of porcelain shire horses pulling a flagon of Young's beer behind the bar. Come here for a mellow night with a mate or when nursing a hangover.
Function room. Games (board games, darts, fruit machine). No piped music or jukebox. Quiz (first Mon of month). Satellite TV. Tables outdoors (patio). Vegetarian dishes.

Matt & Matt
112 Upper Street, N1 (020 7226 6035). Angel tube. **Open** 5pm-midnight Tue, Wed; 5pm-1am Thur; 5pm-2am Fri; 7pm-2am Sat. **Happy hour** 5-8pm Tue-Fri. **Admission** after 9pm Fri, Sat £3. **Credit** MC, V.
If you fancy taking a trip to an Ibiza bar in central London, then Matt & Matt is the place to do it. Rave music in the background, fluorescent lights and a curious amount of basket-work bric-a-brac around the place will bring back memories of Spanish bars aplenty. On offer for the happy boozers are flavoured vodka shots (£1.80) and Hoegaarden (£2 a half-pint); during happy hour bottles of Rolling Rock and Heineken are a very reasonable £1.50. There are guest DJs and the atmosphere is generally laid-back and pleasant. There's none of that snooty members nonsense, either.
Games (pool table). Late licence. Music (DJs Thur-Sat).

Medicine Bar
181 Upper Street, N1 (020 7704 9536/www.liquid-life.com). Angel tube/Highbury & Islington tube/rail. **Open** 4pm-midnight Mon-Thur; noon-1am Fri, Sat; noon-10.30pm Sun. **Food served** noon-5pm Fri, Sat. **No credit cards.**
The lighting is so dark at the Medicine Bar that it would make a good hangout for Goths, but, of course, it's full of Upper Street's finest young things looking moody and drinking pints of Kronenbourg (£2.50) or sipping on a Sea Breeze (£3.90). From the moment you approach, this bar oozes attitude and it comes as no surprise that us lowly mortals are only allowed in during the week because it's members only on Friday and Saturday nights. The lighting is just right, though, for skulking in the corners, giving the place a divey feel that is generally lacking in London's brightly lit pine-filled bars. Drinking in the dark is cool – everybody knows that.
Games (board games). Late licence (Fri, Sat). Music (live jazz 3-6pm Sun; DJs Thur-Sun). Tables outdoors (mews). Vegetarian dishes.

Narrow Boat
119 St Peter Street, N1 (020 7288 9821). Angel tube. **Open** noon-11pm Mon-Sat; noon-10.30pm Sun. **Food served** noon-3pm daily. **Credit** AmEx, DC, MC, V.
The Narrow Boat is a theme pub with a difference – the theme actually bears a connection to the landscape it inhabits – as it's right next to the canal, or if you're part of the gentrification committee for the area, the 'new river'. Either way, the Narrow Boat serves a mixed bag of boozers the delights of London Pride (£2.30) and Guinness (£2.50), and offers billiards, a good selection of board games, plus the attractions of a fine Wurlitzer jukebox, too. In the back of the pub is the theme part – a room that is a reconstruction of the inside of a barge with sloping wood panelled walls and a slightly claustrophobic feel. There's even a winding spiral staircase leading to a couple of tables by the towpath – very romantic.

Babies and children admitted (until 7pm). Games (board games, fruit machine, quiz machine). Jukebox. Music (open mic 7.30pm Sun). Tables outdoors (balcony, towpath). Vegetarian dishes.

nubar
196 Essex Road, N1 (020 7354 8886). Angel tube/Highbury & Islington tube/rail/Essex Road rail. **Open** 4-11pm Mon-Thur; noon-11pm Fri; 11am-11pm Sat; noon-10.30pm Sun. **Happy hour** 4-9pm Mon-Thur; noon-9pm Fri, Sun; 11am-9pm Sat. **Credit** MC, V.
Another genetically modified bar-cum-pub, the nubar is suffused with a pale blue light and a hipster band of clientele. The furniture takes the postmodern a step further with rococo chairs joining the usual mishmash and there's evidence of a past life as a classic boozer, as one wall is covered in beautifully framed mirrors surrounded by dark green decorative tiles. On our visit all bottles or pints were £2 before 9pm and there was Stella, Leffe and Hoegaarden to quench the thirst. The place is huge with lots of floor space to accommodate the trendies who come here for a well-organised range of music, offering everything from lounge to hip hop and house depending on the night you visit.
DJs (nightly).

O'Hanlon
8 Tysoe Street, EC1 (020 7837 4112). Angel tube/19, 38 bus. **Open** noon-11pm Mon-Sat. **Food served** noon-2.30pm Mon-Fri. **Credit** MC, V.
O'Hanlon is a proper Irish pub, not part of the themed breed that comes out of a box, with fake prints on the wall and mediocre Guinness on tap. It's a cosy little place that serves damn good, award-winning ales and stouts. During our visit the pub was packed with a mixed bunch of punters taking advantage of the delicious Dry Stout (£2.40) and Port Stout (£2.20), both of which are brewed in Vauxhall by the proprietor John O'Hanlon himself. Food is classic pub grub in the sausage and mash vein, but it has to be said the booze is the star of the show here, and rightly so. A remarkable pub.
Babies and children admitted (until 4.30pm). Function room. Tables outdoors (patio). TV. Vegetarian dishes.

Old Queens Head
44 Essex Road, N1 (020 7354 9273). Angel tube. **Open** noon-11pm Mon-Sat; noon-10.30pm Sun. **No credit cards.**
The first thing you notice about the Old Queens Head is that it's popular with the biking fraternity – there's a large number of shiny, posey bikes parked ostentatiously out front for all to see. Inside, it's an open-plan pub with a seemingly anachronistic Elizabethan-style, highly ornate fireplace as its centrepiece. Punters are made up of a mixed bunch of trendies and gentrifiers, hanging out with the leather-clad bikers while downing John Smith's Extra Smooth (£2.10) and Beck's (£2.70). In warmer months the hordes spill on to the pavement and strike poses for the Essex Road pedestrians. The bar upstairs is a private members' club called 1559.
Babies and children admitted. Function room. Games (table football). Satellite TV. Tables outdoors (pavement).

Old Red Lion
418 St John Street, EC1 (020 7837 7816). Angel tube. **Open/food served** 11am-11pm Mon-Fri; 11am-3pm, 7-11pm Sat; noon-3pm, 7-10.30pm Sun. **Credit** AmEx, MC, V.
A classic old boozer that attracts a mixed crowd of drinkers knocking back the London Pride (£1.90) and Guinness (£2.20). It's a theatre pub (and has been for the past 21 years),

which always guarantees an interesting clientele, queues at the bar before and after performances, plus, if rumours are to be believed, the odd celebrity, from time to time. The lighting is a bit gruesome, but the interior is attractive with Victorian glass dividers and dark wood. There's a snooker table, too (out of action on weekends), standard pub grub and plenty of room to spread out.
Games (fruit machines, pool table). Satellite TV. Tables outdoors (patio). Theatre. Vegetarian dishes.

Purple Turtle

108 Essex Road, N1 (020 7704 9020). Angel tube/38, 56, 73, 171A bus. **Open** noon-11am Mon-Sat; noon-10.30pm Sun. **Happy hour** noon-7pm daily. **No credit cards.**
If you ever want to step back into a university-style bar, then this is a great place to come. Adorning one wall is a truly terrible, yet amusing mural-tableau of rock stars, including Elvis, Frank Zappa, Hendrix and some so badly rendered you have no idea who they might be. The atmosphere is lively with a young, suitably student-like contingent of locals. But the beer list is what makes the Purple Turtle worth a visit. Try the brackish delights of Kenyan Tusker (£2.30), with its brilliant label, or knock back a bottle of the Danish Elephant (£2.25). The jukebox is reasonable, too – with a suitably eclectic selection to help you while away the evening. In the summer the front doors fold back to give the room more light and air.
Comedy (8pm Mon). Games (fruit machine, pinball machine, video game). Jukebox. Music (acoustic guitar session 5-7pm Sun). Satellite TV.

Rosemary Branch

2 Shepperton Road, N1 (020 7704 2730/ www.rosemarybranch.co.uk). Angel or Old Street tube. **Open** noon-11.30pm Mon-Thur; noon-midnight Fri, Sat; noon-10.30pm Sun. **Food served** noon-3.30pm, 7-9.30pm Mon-Sat; noon-5pm Sun. **Credit** MC, V.
This is the official drinking den of the 'artistes' of this up-and-coming part of north London and, despite some really terrible art on the walls and student-like additions such as metal palm trees and Spitfires hanging from the ceiling, it's a good pub. Even on a Monday night the place was humming and a musical pub quiz was in full swing. Clientele is youngish with a mix of suits, trendies and the odd indie kid for good measure. The selection of beers includes Old Speckled Hen, Brakspear (both £2.20) and Leffe (£2.20 half-pint) and there's reasonable wine by the glass (from £2). The Modern Mediterranean menu falls in the £4-£7 price range.
Babies and children admitted (until 8pm). Function room. Jukebox. Late licence (Mon-Sat). No-smoking area. Quiz (Wed, music quiz Mon). Satellite TV. Tables outdoors (pavement). Theatre. Vegetarian dishes.

Ruby in the Dust

Downstairs, 70 Upper Street, N1 (020 7359 1710). Angel tube. **Open** 8pm-2am Thur-Sat. **Admission** after 9pm Fri, Sat £3. **Credit** MC, V.
It may be a pokey basement room, but the bar at Ruby in the Dust is eternally popular. Perhaps it's the dark lighting and cramped conditions that promote a school disco feel and pull in the crowds. There aren't many places to sit and the decoration is pretty spartan, but the resident DJs pump a good range of grooves and the walls drip with condensation. It can only hold 50 people, so get here early to take advantage of the late-night boozing – and carouse into the early hours chugging bottles of San Miguel or Budvar (both £2.50) as you go.
Late licence (Thur-Sat). Music (DJs Fri, Sat).

Salmon & Compass

58 Penton Street, N1 (020 7837 3891). Angel tube. **Open** 5pm-midnight Mon-Wed; 5pm-2am Thur, Fri, 2pm-2am Sat; 2-10.30pm Sun. **Admission** after 9pm Fri, Sat £3. **No credit cards.**
This pub really should be called the Red Bull, as it's the de rigueur drink of 70% of its inhabitants. And it's a popular haunt, for it was throbbing and lively when we visited. A DJ was spinning some fine tunes and the local young and lovely set were swinging their stuff in fine style. It's a pre-club kind of bar with a definite on-the-pull feel to it. The decor is sparse and modern, apart from copies of old master paintings of horses, and the likes, on the wall. There are sofas to lounge moodily on and, apart from Red Bull, there's Stella (£2.40) and Hoegaarden (£1.80 half-pint) – good for a night on the razzle.
Games (pool table). Late licence (Thur-Sat). Music (DJs Thur-Sat).

Santa fe

75 Upper Street, N1 (020 7288 2288). Angel tube. **Open** 11am-11pm Mon-Sat; 11am-10.30pm Sun. **Food served** noon-10.30pm Mon-Sat; 11am-10pm Sun. **Credit** AmEx, MC, V.
Cashing in on our love for all things American, Sante Fe is a pleasant place to come and hang out. The interior is attractive with muted browns, cobalt blue and cow skulls to summon up the feel of the New Mexico desert. The bar is short but there are tables at the front, too, which you can sometimes snag. Staff are a little posey and, if our experience is anything to go by, the cocktails are woefully weak – a pointless Margarita (£3.95) barely warmed the cockles. The bottled beers make for a better choice (Corona, San Miguel and Negra Modelo from £2.65) or try a shot of tequila (from £2). There's a bar snacks menu with decent munchies including chips and salsa or guacamole.
Babies and children admitted (childrens menu, high chairs, nappy-changing facilities, toys). Disabled: toilet. Function rooms. No-smoking area. Restaurant. Vegetarian dishes.

York

82 Islington High Street, N1 (020 7278 2095). Angel tube. **Open** 11am-11pm Mon-Sat; noon-10.30pm Sun. **Food served** noon-3pm daily. **Credit** MC, V.
An easy to locate, central pub, the York is a good place to meet friends if you're planning an evening in the area. Though it's a generic pub, with few distinguishing features, it's always busy, with suits at lunchtime and a more mixed crowd in the evening. A big-screen TV shows Sky Sports on a regular basis, pleasing the Premiership devotees who knock back pints of Adnams Southwold (£2.10) and Tetley's (£2). For those without the palate for beer there's wine by the glass (from £2.35). Food is nothing special – cheese and pickle sandwiches (£2.35) and sticky toffee pudding (£2.95).
Function room. Games (fruit machines, quiz machines). Tables outdoors (patio, pavement). Satellite TV (big screen). Vegetarian dishes.

Also in the area...

All Bar One 1 Liverpool Road, N1 (020 7843 0021). **Café Flo** 334 Upper Street, N1 (020 7226 7916). **Café Med,** 370 St John Street, EC1 (020 7278 1199). **Dôme** 341 Upper Street, N1 (020 7226 3414). **Finnock & Firkin,** 100 Upper Street, N1 (020 7226 3467). **Islington Tup** 80 Liverpool Road, N1 (020 7354 4440).

Pitcher & Piano 68 Upper Street, N1 (020 7704 9974).
Po Na Na Souk Bar 259 Upper Street, N1 (020 7359 6191).
Puzzle 188-190 New North Road, N1 (020 7226 6307).
Slug & Lettuce 1 Islington Green, N1 (020 7226 3864).

Kentish Town, Gospel Oak, NW5

Bull & Last
168 Highgate Road, NW5 (020 7267 3641).
Kentish Town tube/rail, then C2, 214 bus. **Open** 11am-11pm Mon-Sat; noon-10.30pm Sun. **Food served** noon-10.30pm Mon-Sat; noon-10pm Sun. **Credit** DC, MC, V (over £10).
One of the longest-running ventures in the Kentish Town to Holloway gastropub belt, the Bull & Last has a distinctive mix of chunky wooden furniture and bare wood floors, deep, weathered leather sofas, slightly flouncy lampshades and tulips on the tables in its old pub bar. Simultaneously snug, warm and stylish, this makes it an inviting place to settle into, which helps to keep it busy with a trendy, affluent crowd. Bar snacks are available all day, and a more extensive menu is offered for lunch and in the evening in the bar as well as a large upstairs dining room. The modish, enjoyable modern dishes include vegetable and saffron risotto (£7) or sautéed king prawns with tomato, chilli and salad (£9). Quality is pretty good (and the olive oil placed on our table for dunking fresh bread was excellent), but portions could be more generous for the highish prices. There's a wide range of lagers (Staropramen £2.50, Grolsch £2.40, Hoegaarden £2.90, and more) on tap, Greene King IPA (£2) and Bass bitters, and an interesting, international wine list. Good for meeting up before or after a walk on nearby Parliament Hill.
Babies and children admitted (until 8.30pm). Function room. Restaurant. Tables outdoors (pavement). Vegetarian dishes.

Pineapple
51 Leverton Street, NW5 (020 7485 6422).
Kentish Town tube/rail. **Open** 3-11pm Mon-Fri; noon-11pm Sat; noon-10.30pm Sun. **No credit cards**.
With flowery wallpaper, deep carpets, fresh flowers and fireplaces around its cramped little bar, the Pineapple feels like a rather chintzy hidden drinking den, an impression accentuated by its location sitting on a corner by a cobbled mews in a residential street. Furthermore, you have to push through heavy curtains as you make your way through the front door, and then in the evenings you may have to squeeze in further between the very mixed and friendly crowd of punters. There are as many women as men who frequently fill the place here, gathered around the TV or chatting at tables at the other end. It sticks to what it's best at – no food of any kind, and a regular list of just three bitters (Pedigree, Brakspear, Boddingtons all £2.10), but they're expertly kept, which has made it a favourite among beer aficionados. There's also a good range of lagers on tap (around the £2.20 mark) and an enjoyable wine selection. One final touch of character is provided by the perkily painted pineapples, which were somehow built into the pub's original Victorian exterior.
Babies and children admitted. Disabled: toilet. Games (darts room). Quiz (monthly, check with pub). Satellite TV. Tables outdoors (pavement).

Vine
86 Highgate Road, NW5 (020 7209 0038).
Tufnell Park tube/Kentish Town tube/rail. **Open** 11am-11pm Mon-Sat; noon-10.30pm Sun.
Food served noon-2.30pm, 7-10pm Mon-Sat; noon-10pm Sun. **Credit** AmEx, MC, V.
The style leader among the Kentish Town-to-Holloway foodie pubs, with one of the hipper versions of the de rigueur rustic wood, leather sofa and painted walls decor, and a sophisticated, regularly changing menu. The globe-trotting dishes might include French onion tart on mixed leaves with red pesto (£5.25), Thai curried chicken on wild and basmati rice (£9.75) and seared tuna on roast peppers with quince jam (£14.75); they're finely and imaginatively done, if sometimes a little over-busy. Service is outstanding – friendly, helpful and very efficient. Its success as a restaurant has tended to eclipse its role as a bar, but there's still a drinking area, with a big line in cocktails (Mint Julep is £4.75 a glass, Gin Sling £3.95) and the same carefully selected wine list as the dining area. Beers are a second feature here, but there are Staropramen (£3), Guinness (£2.70) and some bottled beers (Beck's, Red Stripe both £2.60). For brighter days, there's extra seating in a canopied, paved garden at the back, and less attractively on the forecourt out front.
Babies and children admitted. Restaurant. Tables outdoors (conservatory). Vegetarian dishes.

Kilburn NW6

Power's
332 Kilburn High Road, NW6 (020 7624 6026).
Brondesbury rail/Kilburn tube. **Open** noon-11pm Mon-Sat; noon-10.30pm Sun.
Bare brick and dark blue walls and a deep red ceiling give Power's bar a dingy atmosphere that belies its jolly exterior. That said, it's one of the livelier spots on a pretty dismal stretch of Kilburn High Road and on our visit of a wet Monday night was packed with young locals, mostly Irish. Guinness and Caffrey's are both £2.20 a pint, served up with unflagging good humour, and the jukebox pumps out the kind of music that has made owner Vince Power's Mean Fiddler organisation a huge success. The battered church pews, pseudo-tribal artwork and a quieter back room make this a popular place for a party or just a quiet snog.
Babies and children admitted (Sun afternoon only). Jukebox. Music (live Irish band, 4-6pm Sun). Tables outdoors (pavement). TV.

Black Lion
274 Kilburn High Road, NW6 (020 7624 1520). Kilburn tube/Brondesbury rail. **Open** 11am-11pm Mon-Sat; noon-10.30pm Sun. **No credit cards**.
Almost opposite the **Zd Bar** (*see below*) and the Tricycle Theatre and Cinema is this grand, unreconstructed Victorian drinking palace. It's worth dropping in, if only for a look at its extraordinary dark red and gold coffered ceiling, etched glass and beaten-copper wall panels depicting Georgian gentry at their leisure. Now firmly in Irish hands, on the night we visited the public bar was the scene of some overheated pre-millennial shenanigans that threatened to turn into a punch-up, but the large saloon bar remained unperturbed. Large TVs dominate the atmosphere here and drinks include Webster's Green Label and, of course, Guinness, which is a very reasonable £2 a pint.
Babies and children admitted. Function room. Games (darts, fruit machine). Quiz (Thur). Satellite TV. Tables outdoors (garden).

Ha! Ha! Bar & Canteen.
See page 232.

The Salusbury

50-52 Salusbury Road, NW6 (020 7328 3286). Queens Park tube. **Open** noon-11pm Mon-Sat; noon-10.30pm Sun. **Food served** noon-3.30pm, 7-10.30pm Mon-Sat; noon-4pm, 7-10.30pm Sat, Sun. **Credit** MC, V.
If we hadn't frequented the shabby but fun Irish pub it's replaced, we'd never have believed that the Salusbury had been recently made over. Already it seems to have settled into a comfortable ambience that's rare to find in new enterprises. The new Salusbury is a wooden-floored boozer with gastro pretensions that can boast red walls and some etching orange table lamps. It appeared crammed on the Wednesday night we visited, with a predominantly young crowd quaffing pints of Everard Tiger bitter, Bass (both £2.30), Grolsch (£2.40) or holding bottles of Asahi or Freedom Lager (both £2.40). The layout is a squared-off horseshoe shape around a central serving area, with the open kitchens off to the right. It turned out not to be as busy as we'd thought: a bottleneck caused by a single drinker at the bar meant that only a third of the pub was occupied, the rest (including the main dining area) practically deserted. Even so, the food is definitely a draw and the menu is impressive, but we couldn't help thinking that prices may be a little lofty for ever-so 'umble Queen's Park. Starters such as Jerusalem artichoke risotto and grilled prawn with chilli are £7 for a starter, £9 and £11 respectively as a main course, with roast monkfish with mussels available at £12. Mind you, it is good.
Restaurant. Vegetarian dishes.

Zd Bar

289 Kilburn High Road, NW6 (020 7372 2544). Brondesbury rail/Kilburn tube. **Open/food served** 5pm-2am Mon-Thur; 5pm-2am Fri, Sat; 6pm-midnight Sun. **Happy hour** 5-9.30pm. **Admission** 10-11pm Fri, Sat £2; after 11pm £4. **No credit cards**.

The Zd Bar's stylish interior, with its cream, mock-leather seating, funkily lit, bare brick-backed bar and blonde wood floor, is beginning to look a bit tatty. But then again, that's testament to the place's well-established popularity and several years of heavy usage. It's still easily the most hip music bar on the Kilburn High Road. The small, sunken dance-floor with built-in DJ crow's nest is often rammed at weekends, overlooked by a gallery area at the back where drinkers are raised up almost on a level with the DJ and the exposed ventilation pipe running the length of the room. Drinks are largely confined to lagers on draught (Stella £2.50) and bottled beers (Budweiser £2.50), while food is restricted to a range of filled panninis (£2.50-£3). Recently-arrived new management might develop things further, but it shouldn't affect the salsa classes on Mondays and Wednesdays.
Disabled: toilet. Late licence. Music (DJs nightly). Quiz (last Thur of month). Satellite TV. Vegetarian dishes.

Muswell Hill, Alexandra Palace, N10, N22

Fantail & Firkin

87 Muswell Hill Broadway, N10 (020 8883 1183). East Finchley or Highgate tube/43, 134 bus. **Open** noon-11pm Mon-Sat; noon-10.30pm Sun. **Food served** noon-8pm daily. **Credit** MC, V.
The current boozer of choice for young Muswell Hill occupies a huge old Victorian church with a spectacular panelled wood roof, from which there now hangs an appropriately massive model pigeon, a 'theme' that's repeated at many other points in the decor. Bars and tables are spread over many levels, giving it a loopy-Gothic look a bit like Cruella de Vil's mansion, but even so, it often fills up, and the music volume, funnelled into the roof, means that it's no place for

a quiet chat. Footie-watching is a big number here, with one giant screen and many more smaller ones. As in other former Firkin brew pubs, since its recent takeover by the Punch Taverns chain it no longer brews its own ales, and the main beers are London Pride (£2.05), Marston's Pedigree (£2.10) and a range of lagers. Blackboards offer a hefty and intercontinental range of food (beef chimichangas £4.95, lasagne £5.45, ale pie and chips £5.60), but don't expect any subtle ethnic seasonings.

Disabled: toilet. Games (board games, quiz machine, table football). Jukebox. No-smoking area. Quiz (Tue). Sport TV (big screen). Vegetarian dishes.

Ha! Ha! Bar & Canteen
390-392 Muswell Hill Broadway, N10 (020 8444 4722). Highgate tube/43, 134 bus. **Open/food served** 11am-11pm Mon-Sat; 10am-10.30pm Sun. **Credit** AmEx, DC, MC, V.

Silly name, but the Ha! Ha!s are an attractive variation on the minimalist modern bar style, with obviously All Bar One-influenced (but less corporate) decor of steel and blonde wood, but with the added attraction of a scattering of comfy chairs and sofas for sitting over coffee or scanning the papers. To drink, there are more lagers (Stella, Heineken both £2.40) than bitters (Boddingtons £2.20), and an easy-to-handle, fashionably global wine list (from £2.60 a glass). The similarly multinational menu features snacks and larger offerings, and dishes such as chicken Caesar sandwich on focaccia (£5) and home-made fishfingers with chips and braised peas (£7) are full of enjoyable flavours (and come in very ample portions). There's also a Ha! Ha! range of food products – balsamic vinegar (£3), sticky onion relish (£2) – available to buy. A pleasant place for brunch, the Muswell Hill branch is regularly buzzing on weekend afternoons.

Disabled: toilet. Music (live jazz Sun 7.30pm, Tue 8.30pm). No-smoking area. Vegetarian dishes.

Phoenix
Alexandra Palace Way, N22 (020 8365 2121). Wood Green or Turnpike Lane tube/Alexandra Palace rail/W3 bus. **Open/food served** 11am-11pm Mon-Sat; noon-10.30pm Sun. **Credit** MC, V (minimum £5 with food).

This pub in one corner of the beautiful Alexandra Palace (lately refurbished for the nth time) is an airy, spacious, high-ceilinged bar with columns, sofas, pot plants and conservatory windows that make it look as if it should perhaps be in an old-fashioned seaside hotel, especially when there are some elderly ladies up for a Sunday-afternoon antiques fair. The enterprising range of beers includes Crouch Vale IPA (£2.05), some guest ales (£2.10) and Löwenbräu lager (£2.30); coffee and hot chocolate are served, and to eat there's an ample and well-priced range of café/pub grub from full English breakfasts (£3.50) to pasta dishes (£3.50), sandwiches (£1.95) and daily specials. In winter, with sunlight shafting through the high windows, this is a pleasant, tranquil, underused bar (which nevertheless manages to draw a wide mix of people up the hill); it really comes into its own on summer weekends, when you can sit outside on the big front terrace and take in the great view from north London's highest point.

Babies and children admitted (children's menus, nappy-changing facilities). Disabled: toilet. Function room. Satellite TV. Tables outdoors (patio, terrace). Vegetarian dishes.

Also in the area...
Ruby in the Dust 256 Muswell Hill Broadway, N10 (020 8444 4041).

Palmers Green N13

Fox
413 Green Lanes, N13 (020 8886 9674). Southgate or Wood Green tube/Palmers Green rail/329, W2 bus. **Open/food served** 11am-11pm Sat-Thur; 11am-1am Fri. **Credit** AmEx, MC, V.

The Fox is straight out of the golden age of British pub building (1904), with its grand country house-style granite stone entrance, high ceilings and its best feature an elegant circular bar that serves both saloon and lounge. As with Palmers Green High Street, it looks to have gone a little downmarket since its Edwardian heyday. The seats need re-upholstering, its food menu is worryingly cheap – (lasagne or top rump steak and chips are £2.99), Guinness costs £2.10 and Strongbow £1.95. The Fox is the venue for the long-running Bound and Gagged comedy night.

Comedy (Fri £6). Disabled: toilet. Function room. Games (pool tables). Jukebox. Music (karaoke Thur). Quiz (Sun). Satellite TV (big screens). Tables outdoors (garden). Vegetarian dishes.

Woodman
128 Bourne Hill, N13 (020 8882 0294). Southgate tube/W9 bus. **Open** 11am-11pm Mon-Sat; noon-10.30pm Sun. **Food served** noon-3pm, 7-9pm Mon-Sat; noon-3pm Sun. **Credit** AmEx, DC, MC, V.

The title of this pub is not some faux country name for the Barbour jacket brigade, for this is your genuine article country pub stranded in an enveloping London – near its location along the tree-lined Bourne Hill there are the remnants of a sheep pen. Inside the pub there are typically low-beamed rickety rooms, adorned with antique guns, copper kettles and horse saddles, while little, red-shaded lamps throw out a cosy olde-worlde glow. A tastefully added extension dining room has a gourmet menu, including, for example, roasted duckling in citrus brandy sauce (£9.50) and Woodman's mixed game pie (£8.95). On tap are Stella (£2.35 a pint) and Worthington, George Gale HSB (both £2.20) and Theakston Old Peculier (£2.50). A large garden with a climbing frame is an attraction for kids.

Babies and children admitted (high chairs). Games (fruit machine). Music (live guitarist, Sun). Restaurant. Tables outdoors (gardens, patio). Vegetarian dishes.

St John's Wood NW8

Clifton
96 Clifton Hill, NW8 (020 7624 5233). Maida Vale or St John's Wood tube. **Open** 11am-11pm Mon-Sat; noon-10.30pm Sun. **Food served** noon-2.45pm, 6.30-9.30pm Mon-Sat; noon-4pm Sun. **Credit** AmEx, DC, MC, V.

One of the Nicholson chain's 'heritage' pubs, the Clifton largely avoids the characterlessness that that might suggest, attracting a pleasingly varied social mix from some distance around. It's particularly popular with the art crowd from the Saatchi Gallery just down the road. The front garden, hedged in off the street, is usually packed in summer. Inside, a variety of different areas on different levels, including a snug at the front and a conservatory at the back, mean that you can usually find a seat in which to appreciate the vaguely ecclesiastical and Edwardian ambience, the latter justified on the grounds that this was one of the places where Edward VII liked to meet Lillie Langtry. A variety of good beers are on tap, including Adnams (£2.15) and Marston's Pedigree (£2.20), and there's also a small back garden.

Babies and children admitted (conservatory only). Games (fruit machine). Satellite TV. Tables outdoors (garden, patio). Vegetarian dishes.

Clifton

Crocker's Folly

*24 Aberdeen Place, NW8 (020 7286 6608).
Edgware Road or Warwick Avenue tube.* **Open** 11am-
11pm Mon-Sat; noon-10.30pm Sun. **Food served** noon-
2.30pm, 6-9.30pm Mon-Sat; noon-9pm Sun. **Credit** AmEx,
DC, MC, V.

Frank Crocker spared no expense in building this palatial
Victorian boozer in 1898, hoping to catch the trade promised
by the arrival of the railway. Unfortunately, the terminus was
eventually built some distance away at Marylebone, and
Crocker went bust, throwing himself out of an upstairs
window in despair. A shame really, because his pub is now
worth travelling to and does decent trade in the summer
thanks to the proximity of Lord's cricket ground. Everything
is on a grand scale: the large mahogany bar dominates the
main room on the right, where excellent beers are served up
at very reasonable prices (Brakspear IPA is £1.85 a pint, HSB
£1.90) and can be enjoyed with a game of bar billiards or
chess at one of the inlaid tables. Sunday lunches in the vast
Victorian dining room on the left are something of an event.
A new chef promises more vegetarian options as well as the
traditional roast and two veg, on offer from noon to 9pm.
*Babies and children admitted (restaurant only). Disabled:
toilet. Games (bar billiards, darts, fruit machines). Music
live R&B/jazz Sat). No-smoking area. Quiz (Thur).
Restaurant. Satellite TV. Tables outdoors (pavement).
Vegetarian dishes.*

Lord's Tavern

*Grace Gates, St John's Wood Road, NW8 (020 7266
5980). St John's Wood tube.* **Open/food served** 11am-
11pm Mon-Fri; 10am-11pm Sat; 10am-10.30pm Sun.
Credit AmEx, MC, V.

From the outside this place looks like an unattractive adjunct
to Lord's cricket ground, but inside you'll discover a fairly
salubrious modern sports bar. It's roomy and light, with a

vaulted brick ceiling, big tables and a cosier corner
harbouring a clutch of chesterfield-style sofas. Cricket is
obviously the sport in question: pictures of players adorn the
walls and the TVs give preference to coverage of the game
whenever possible. Customers tend to be young and male,
while the after-work crowds keep the bar busy later in the
week. Beers on offer at the long L-shaped bar include the
excellent Charles Wells' Bombardier (£2.30) and Miller
(£2.40). There's also a restaurant to one side.
*Babies and children admitted (until 7pm). Music (live rock
Fri). Restaurant. Satellite TV. Tables outdoors (terrace).
Vegetarian dishes.*

Salthouse

*63 Abbey Road, NW8 (020 7328 6626). St John's Wood
tube.* **Open** 11am-11pm Mon-Sat; noon-10.30pm Sun.
Food served noon-3pm, 6.30-10.30pm Mon-Fri; noon-
4pm, 7-10.30pm Sat, Sun. **Credit** AmEx, DC, MC, V.

A new gastropub on the corner of Abbey Road, the Salthouse
looks set to become a firm favourite with the area's affluent
residents. The bar area is painted an understated battleship
blue-grey, with comfy blue sofas and rugs on bare
floorboards. A few good draught beers, like Greene King IPA
(£2.20), are backed up by an impressive wine list (a glass of
house white is £2.40), although it's the array of cookery books
behind the bar that betrays the main focus of the
management's enthusiasm. The restaurant is tucked away in
a room to the side, but some items on its menu, like marinated
salmon (£5.25) or black pudding and poached egg (£4.75), can
be ordered at the bar. On our lunchtime visit, the restaurant
was busier than the pub, but this is a bright, friendly venture
following confidently in the footsteps of places like the
Engineer (*see p209*) and the **Westbourne** (*see p108*).
*Babies and children admitted (children's room; high
chairs). Function room. Restaurant. Tables outdoors
(pavement). Vegetarian dishes.*

Star

38 St John's Wood Terrace, NW8 (020 7722 1051).
St John's Wood tube. **Open** 11am-11pm Mon-Sat;
noon-10.30pm Sun. **No credit cards**.
New management may have given the exterior a much-
needed facelift, but nothing much else seems to have changed
at the Star since the 1950s, which is clearly why the regulars
at this unpretentious St John's Wood local seem to like it. The
bar staff are friendly and maintain an easy-going atmosphere,
helped along by the music choices made behind the bar (Elvis
was crooning away on our visit). The draught beers are
nothing special, including Worthington Best (£1.90) and Bass
(£2), but it's the place's down-to-earth pubby cosiness that
makes the Star stand out among those in the area that strive
more strenuously after bonhomie.
Games (fruit machine). Tables outdoors (garden). TV.

Also in the area...

All Bar One 60 St John's Wood High Street, NW8
(020 7483 9931).
Café Med 21 Loudon Road, NW8 (020 7625 1222).
Café Rouge 120 St John's Wood High Street, NW8
(020 7722 8366).

Stoke Newington N16

Bar Lorca

175 Stoke Newington High Street, N16 (020 7275 8659).
Bus 73. **Open** noon-1am Mon-Thur; noon-2am Fri, Sat;
noon-midnight Sun. **Food served** noon-11pm Mon-Thur;
noon-midnight Fri, Sat; noon-10pm Sun. **Admission** after
10pm Fri, Sat £3. **Happy hour** 6-9pm Mon, Tue. **Credit**
AmEx, MC, V.
Bar Lorca could be described as the party heart of Stoke
Newington. A big tapas bar-venue that offers live
entertainment (salsa bands and classes, flamenco, lounge
bands and more) most nights of the week. When things are
less hectic it's more like a relaxing local hangout, with lots of
space and big windows for people watching. Wines by the
glass are expensive at £3.50, and are from £10.50 by the
bottle; good Spanish beers (Mahou, Estrella) cost £2.30-£4
and there's also a recently revamped giant cocktail list, with
special offers on hot sellers like Margaritas and Caipirinhas
(£3.50, £4; both £2.50 during happy hour). Food is hit and
miss: classic Spanish tapas, such as calamares and roasted
peppers (mostly £3-£5) and largèr dishes like mixed grill
(£15) can be peppy and well prepared, but not always.
Service, too, can be chaotic when the place is buzzing (which
is often). Just sit back and enjoy it. There's another branch of
Bar Lorca in Brixton (*see p168*)
*Babies and children admitted (until 8pm; clowns, high
chairs, toys). Disabled: toilet. Games (pinball machine,
table football). Late licence. Music (Latin bands Tue,
Wed, Sun; DJs Fri, Sat). Restaurant. Satellite TV.
Vegetarian dishes.*

Coach & Horses

178 Stoke Newington High Street, N16 (020 7254 6697).
Stoke Newington rail/67, 73, 106 bus. **Open** 11am-11pm
Mon-Sat; noon-10.30pm Sun. **Food served** 1-10pm Mon-
Sat; 1-9pm Sun. **No credit cards**.
An amiable, unpretentious chip of old Stokey. You might get
punkish/thrash guitar background music and crusty-ish
regulars, wearing floppy trousers and woolly hats pulled over
pierced eyebrows, but this is also a pub where anyone can
settle into a corner and read a book, should they so wish. The

bar – clad in 1960s-70s tongue-and-groove panelling – is
covered in maps, postcards and other pics of Thailand in
honour of the cooks, who provide simple but enjoyable Thai
snacks, such as chicken or veggie stir-fry, at real bargain
prices (starters from £2, mains from £3.50). To drink, as you
ponder the scene, there are Old Speckled Hen and Pedigree
ales (both £2), although most of the regular faithfuls seem to
go for one of the standard range of lagers (£2-£2.40) or
Blackthorn cider.
*Babies and children admitted. Games (fruit machines).
Jukebox. Satellite TV. Vegetarian dishes.*

Fox Reformed

*176 Stoke Newington Church Street, N16 (020 7254
5975). Arsenal, Finsbury Park or Manor House tube/73
bus.* **Open/food served** 5-11pm Mon-Fri; noon-11pm Sat,
Sun, bank holidays. **Credit** AmEx, MC, V.
Stoke Newington isn't all old pubs and grunge. An
alternative is this long-running, much-enjoyed wine bar, with
its air of genteel, slightly eccentric bohemia. Red walls, old
wood and open fires encourage punters to settle for hours,
playing chess and backgammon (both particular interests of
the owners). A sign recounts the fact that Edgar Allen Poe
went to school on this very spot – adding one more Gothic
touch to the place. The individually selected wine list is
renowned, strongest in traditional French regions but now
open to more global influences: the Montesquieu house claret
(£2.75 a glass) is excellent on a cold night. There is also
draught Stella (£2.70) and some interesting bottled beers
(Chimay Red, Duval both £3.45). The short menu offers an
interesting range of modern dishes, such as onion tart (£3.75)
or grilled tuna with tomato and mango salsa (£9.25), and no
one objects if all you feel like is a bowl of chips. The Fox also
functions as something of a local history centre and stopping
off-point on local walks, and hosts exhibitions of prints
around the bar, all available for sale.
*Babies and children admitted (high chairs). Games (board
games). Tables outdoors (garden). Theme nights
(backgammon Mon; book club monthly, Tue; investment
club every other Sun; wine tasting club every other Thur,
all £30 per year, £5 table fee). Vegetarian dishes.*

Oak Bar

*79 Green Lanes, N16 (020 7354 2791). Manor House
tube/73, 141 bus.* **Open** 5pm-midnight Mon-Thur;
5pm-2am Fri; 1pm-2am Sat; 1pm-midnight Sun.
Happy hour 5-7pm Mon-Fri. **Food served** 1-7pm Sun.
No credit cards.
By reputation, the Oak Bar is the staunch den of the north
London gay women's scene, though these days it's more (gay)
boy-friendly with only Friday evenings and a once-a-month
club night, Liberté, as strictly women-only. A low-lit, red-hued
bar neatly splits the pool area and dancefloor and exudes an
intimate and friendly welcome, particularly when the pub is
quiet (Hoegaarden £3 a pint, Beck's £2.50 a bottle). Its only
drawback, for those who fuss over decor, is that its recent
overhaul looks unfinished. Amid the well-considered lighting
and smart furniture, the cabaret area remains a tatty
regulation navy.
*Babies and children admitted (daytimes). Disabled: toilet.
Games (pinball machine, pool table). Karaoke (Sun). Late
licence. Music (DJs most nights). Quiz (Mon). TV (big
screen). Vegetarian dishes.*

Rose & Crown

*199 Stoke Newington Church Street, N16 (020 7254
7497). Bus 73.* **Open** 11.30am-11pm Mon-Sat;
noon-10.30pm Sun. **Food served** noon-2.30pm Mon-Fri;
noon-4pm Sun. **No credit cards**.

Big bay windows, beautiful floor-to-ceiling 1920s woodwork and stained-glass details mark this fine traditional pub, presiding over the corner of Church Street and Albion Road. Staff are unfussily friendly, and the Rose & Crown is especially welcoming in winter, when there's usually a fire going in the grate. The range of ales includes Adnams Bitter (£1.95), Pedigree (£2.20) and Ruddles County (£2.30); Guinness is £2.30, and Holsten and other good lagers £2.40. Pub grub highlights, served at lunchtimes, are lovely fresh sandwiches (£1.80-£3), plus bigger offerings such as roast beef (£5) and veggie pies (£4.80). An excellent place to settle for a long and cosy chat.

Function room. Games (fruit machine, video games). No piped music or jukebox. Satellite TV. Tables outdoors (pavement). Vegetarian dishes.

Shakespeare

57 Allen Road, N16 (020 7254 4190). Bus 73.
Open noon-2pm, 5-11.30pm Mon-Sat; noon-10.30pm Sun. **No credit cards.**
In one of the back corners of Stoke Newington stands this small and basic (but nonetheless renowned) boho boozer. Well-trodden floorboards and battered church-pew seating adds to its earthy, easygoing intimacy, complemented by a mix of original paintings, French posters and what looks like a grand Victorian sculpture of a Greek goddess standing against one wall. The friendly Stokey clientele matches the decor. The landlord knows his beer, with London Pride (£2.20) and Brakespear among the ales, Budvar on tap (£2.40) and a set of bottled beers that includes Leffe Blonde or Brune (£2.40) and Samuel Adams (£2.30), and there are good wines (from £2.10 a glass) and fine selection of malt whiskies, too (£2.10). A few tables outside provide space to take in the air (and avoid the smoke) in summer. And, how many pubs do you know that have a whole page given over to Jeff Buckley on the jukebox?

Babies and children admitted. Jukebox. Quiz (Mon). Satellite TV. Tables outdoors (garden).

Stoke Newington Tup

132 Stoke Newington Church Street, N16 (020 7254 0959). Stoke Newington rail/Manor House tube/73 bus.
Open 3-11pm Mon-Fri; noon-11pm Sat; noon-10.30pm Sun. **No credit cards.**
Situated in a distinctive and imposing building – which began life as the Red Lion, a name still built into the walls – this Tup remains one of the social hubs of Church Street. It is, perhaps, a tad plain in its present incarnation, with many wooden chairs and tables set off by a few pieces of contemporary artwork on the walls, but the atmosphere is dependably comfortable. A fairly standard range of beer – Courage and Wadworth 6X (£2.20) bitters, Kronenbourg (£2.40), Stella (£2.50) and other lagers – is complemented by an expanding wine selection, but the Tup, surprisingly, still doesn't offer any food beyond crisps and nuts. However, in the quaint rooms upstairs there's now a pool table and even a coin-in-the-slot Net terminal; and a little beer garden can be found at the back.

Games (pool table). Internet. Tables outdoors (garden).

Vortex

139 Stoke Newington Church Street, N16 (020 7254 6516/www.palay.ndirect.co.uk/vortex.jazz). Stoke Newington rail/73 bus. **Open** 10am-midnight daily.
Admission after 9pm £2-£10. **Food served** 11am-10pm daily. **Credit** MC, V.
Unchanging in its chilled-out, alternative style, the Vortex continues to be one of London's best small jazz venues and arguably Stoke Newington's most easygoing refreshment

point. Most nights, the black-painted upstairs room hosts first-rate jazz, and on Sundays (the only time when food isn't available) it welcomes DJ sessions. By day, the Vortex with its creaky chairs and battered wooden tables makes a tranquil place to sit and take stock, read, and have coffee and cake or maybe a vegetarian dish from the chalked-up menu, such as veg chilli with basmati rice (£4.60) or pasta with a choice of sauces (£4.80). You can drink bottled Stella (£2.40) or Czech Ostrava (£2.90), and some decent wines. On a day visit, head downstairs for a browse in the second-hand bookshop (open 11am-6.30pm daily), with a stock that runs from dead-cheap paperbacks to a few modern first editions.

Cabaret (Mon). Karaoke (first Sun in month). Music (jazz/indie rock Mon-Sat). Vegetarian dishes.

Swiss Cottage NW3

Babe Ruth's

The O2 Centre, 255 Finchley Road, NW3 (020 7433 3388/ www.baberuths.com). Finchley Road tube. **Open/food served** 5.30-11pm Mon-Fri; noon-11pm Sat; noon-10.30pm Sun. **Credit** AmEx, MC, V.
Quite possibly the shape of things to come, the O2 Centre is a swanky US-style shopping mall that's home to several chain shops and restaurants. Babe Ruth's, on the first floor, up an escalator past a ladder of rock pools incorporating a jumping waterfeature, is, perhaps, the most unusual of them. As with the other branch in Wapping (see p203), there are endless screens showing only 'major' sporting events. The cocktails are good value at £4.50, and include American favourites like the White Russian (vodka, Kahlúa and cream) and a few more offbeat mixtures like the alcoholic milkshake they call Cool Bananas (rum, banana liqueur, fresh bananas and cream). Only Miller is on draught (£1.76 a half-pint), and a standard bottled beer range are £2.75 each. Off to one side, next to the video game area, the bar is small compared to the restaurant, but you can get the same menu here: an extensive mix of American and global classics. Try spring rolls or crab cakes for starters (£4-£6), or choose from an eclectic mains list (£8-£15) that features, predictably burgers and fillet steak, but also offers red Thai Bream and blackened swordfish.

Babies and children admitted (children's menu, high chairs, nappy-changing facilities). Disabled: toilet. Function room. Games (interactive sports). No-smoking area. Restaurant. Satellite TV (big screen). Vegetarian dishes.

Cube Bar

135 Finchley Road, NW3 (020 7483 2393). Swiss Cottage tube. **Open** 5pm-midnight Thur; 5pm-1am Fri, Sat. **Food served** 6-11pm Thur-Sat. **Happy hour** 5-10pm Thur-Sat. **Credit** DC, MC, V.
True to its name, this conversion of a modern bank building operates in three dimensions. The ground floor – shiny, unadorned surfaces, painted vibrant yellows, blues and purples – is the main bar, where classic cocktails (Bloody Mary £4.50, Long Island Iced Tea £6, Kir Royale £6) are dispensed to fairly loud dance tunes spun by a DJ perched above the bar. Up the industrial staircase, the gallery bar is more mellow with fine views, from tall windows, of headlights flashing by on the expressway. And the basement (available for hire) is small but atmospheric, often becoming a sweaty crush at weekends. Happy hour is good value, with all cocktails at £3.50. Popular with the local twentysomethings.

Babies and children admitted (until 9.30pm). Function room. Late licence (Fri, Sat). Music (DJs Thur-Sat). Vegetarian dishes.

Tufnell Park, Archway, NW5, N7, N19

Dartmouth Arms

35 York Rise, NW5 (020 7485 3267). Tufnell Park tube. **Open** 11am-11pm Mon-Fri; 10am-11pm Sat; 10am-10.30pm Sun. **Food served** 11am-10pm Mon-Fri; 10am-10pm Sat; 10am-4pm Sun. **Credit** DC, MC, V.
One of the latest contenders in the north London foodie pub stakes, the Dartmouth aims to give locals an all-round, morn-till-night facility: big signs outside offer, in no particular order, 'ales, pies, TV, hot chocolate, Sunday lunch, pots of tea, breakfast, cocktails…' and more. Inside, the two large bar areas have maintained their pub look, compared to the more restaurant-ish gastropub, but still have the requisite pine tables, plain paintwork and sofas, as well as candles and potted palms that give it quite a snug feel. There are papers to read, and shelves of books to browse through, or buy. Drinks are well priced, with Adnams Bitter at £2, Young's Special £2.20, Carlsberg £2.20, cocktails £3.60 and a varied list of wines from £8.95 a bottle. Food is more Modern British and less global than in some gastropubs, so the frequently changing menus might include steak (£8.95), veggie pie, mussels in a garlic and white wine sauce and, a regular, sausage and mash (all £5.95). Early weekend opening hours make this a fine and handy place for Sunday brunch, or roast lunch (from £7.95).
Babies and children admitted (until 8pm). Function room. Games (board games). Quiz (every other Tue). Satellite TV. Vegetarian dishes.

Grand Banks

156-158 Fortess Road, NW5 (020 7419 9499). Tufnell Park tube. **Open** 5-11pm Mon-Fri; noon-11pm Sat; noon-10.30pm Sun. **Food served** 6-10pm Mon-Fri; noon-10pm Sat, Sun. **Credit** AmEx, DC, MC, V.
Amid the north London gastrobar boom, the minds behind the Grand Banks – in a former Barclays Bank building – have gone for a distinctive, hipper route, with a look that's less rustic restaurant than chilled out club-bar. Open since October '99, it's now the most happening bar in the vicinity, heaving at weekends with young and trendy folk lounging in the cool modern leather furniture (such as 1960s swivel armchairs). To drink, there are beers from Boddingtons or Heineken (£2.10) to Leffe (£4.80), good wines (from £10) and some 70 cocktails, including Margaritas and Caipirinhas at £4.50. At the back is the smallish dining room where chef Siobhan Belton presents a sophisticated menu: sweet potato, chilli, lemon grass and coconut soup (£3.25) and pearl barley risotto with shiitake mushrooms, leeks, lemon, asparagus and Parmesan (£9) are examples of recent dishes. Note that part of the Grand Banks' cool concept was to have no name outside; they've now relented and are going to put up a small, discreet sign, (however, it's right in front of you as you come out of Tufnell Park tube).
Babies and children admitted (high chairs). Music (live jazz Sun, Mon; DJs Fri, Sat). Restaurant. Vegetarian dishes.

Lord Palmerston

33 Dartmouth Park Hill, NW5 (020 7485 1578). Tufnell Park tube. **Open** 6-11pm Mon; 11am-11pm Tue-Sat; noon-10.30pm Sun. **Food served** 7-10pm Mon; 12.30-3pm, 7-10pm Tue-Sat; 1-4pm, 7-9pm Sun. **Credit** MC, V.
Tufnell Park bohemians, young and old, converge on the Lord Palmerston. Decor is a notably sparse version of the stripped-down gastropub look, with walls half-and-half in chocolate and peppermint and battered wood tables, but the very friendly staff help set off a warm, easygoing atmosphere. The straightforward range of beers – Marston's Pedigree (£2),

Courage Directors (£2.10) and Kronenbourg (£2.30) – is well looked after, and there's a big choice of some 25 quality wines available by the glass. Where the Lord P really stands out, though, is in its food: the chalked-up menu follows a common global style – with the likes of penne with spiced tomatoes and Parmesan (£6.75), a giant grilled chicken sandwich (£7) and loads of vegetarian options – but dishes are given a distinctive zing by skilled cooking and, above all, an exceptional use of fine-quality fresh ingredients. The small conservatory area at the back is an added bonus on bright days.
Babies and children admitted. Function room. No piped music or jukebox. Tables outdoors (garden, pavement). Vegetarian dishes.

St John's

91 Junction Road, N19 (020 7272 1587). Archway or Tufnell Park tube. **Open/food served** 11am-11pm Mon-Sat; noon-10.30pm Sun. **Credit** MC, V.
A veteran Irish pub, on the otherwise-unreformed Junction Road, that's been transformed into one of the area's best new-model gastropubs. The main space at the front contains a big wooden bar with tables to match and simple seating; carry on through to the inner room, where food is served, and there are more pine tables, an open fireplace, venerable sofas and deep red walls lined with a variety of artwork, giving it a kind of Parisian bistro-meets-the-Archway look. The menu features interesting global/Modern British dishes such as Scotch broth with pancetta and rosemary (£4) and pan-fried sea bass with potato cake and red onion and bean salad (£12); service is obliging, although it can get rushed. Drinks options include real ales (Wychwood Special £2.10), Budvar and other lagers (£2.40), excellent Breton cider (£2), fresh juices (£1) and a good wine selection (from £2.50 a glass). If you're eating, it's safer to book, but otherwise it's a relaxing place to settle among the mix of trendsters and elderly Irish regulars.
Babies and children admitted. Games (board games).

West Hampstead NW6

No.77 Wine Bar

77 Mill Lane, NW6 (020 7435 7787). West Hampstead tube/rail/C11, 28, 139 bus. **Open/food served** noon-11pm Mon, Tue; noon-midnight Wed-Fri; 1pm-midnight Sat; 1-10.30pm Sun. **Credit** MC, V.
The 77 opened in 1982, and could be taken as a cliché-model of an '80s wine bar – small wooden tables, potted palms, wine-related bits around the walls, candles and soft lighting in the eating area. The style has been untrendy so long it's probably not worth changing, and the cosy atmosphere and friendly staff are evidently still appreciated by locals. The drinks list contains some unusual plusses such as the rye-based Pig lager from Sussex (£2.45), and there's a good selection of mainly French house wines (from £9.75, and a pleasant Merlot at £11.95). The menu seems as unchanging as that of the bar in general, with dishes such as houmous dips, the '77 burger' (£7.75) and stuffed calamari (£8.25). Lunch is a bargain here, with most dishes at £4.95. Popular with couples for relaxing meals during the week, the 77 becomes more of a party animal at weekends, and a big bash is staged for Burns' night.
Babies and children admitted. Function room. Late licence (Wed-Sat). Music (jazz 1.30pm Sun). Restaurant. Satellite TV. Tables outdoors (pavement). Vegetarian dishes.

Also in the area...

Café Rouge 203 West End Lane, NW6 (020 7372 8177).

Advertisers' Index

Please refer to the relevant sections for
addresses/telephone numbers

Where to go for...

EARLY REFRESHMENT

(open before 11am)

FILM AND TV CONNECTIONS

FOOD

(see also Organic food or drink)

Breakfasts

Gastropubs

Recommended

Traditional Sunday lunch selection

A-Z Index

C

Cactus Blue p96
86 Fulham Road, SW3
(020 7823 7858).
Cadogan Arms p22
298 King's Road, SW3
(020 7352 1645).
Café Baroque p29
33 Southampton Street,
WC2 (020 7379 7585).
Café Bohème p80
13-17 Old Compton Street,
W1 (020 7734 0623).
Café Corfu p208
7-9 Pratt Street, NW1
(020 7424 0203).
Café Flo p61
11 Haymarket, SW1 (020
7976 1313).

Café Flo p27
25-35 Gloucester Road,
SW7 (020 7589 1383).
Café Flo p50
676 Fulham Road, SW6
(020 7371 9673).
Café Flo p53
127-129 Kensington
Church Street, W8 (020
7727 8142).
Café Flo p66
51 St Martin's Lane, WC2
(020 7836 8289).
Café Flo p69
14 Thayer Street, W1 (020
7935 5023).
Café Flo p95
103 Wardour Street, W1
(020 7734 0581).
Café Flo p98
89 Sloane Avenue, SW3
(020 7225 1048).
Café Flo p134
38-40 Ludgate Hill, EC4
(020 7329 3900).
Café Flo p151
149 Kew Road, Richmond,
Surrey (020 8940 8298).
Café Flo p220
205 Haverstock Hill, NW3
(020 7435 6744).
Café Flo p229
334 Upper Street, N1
(020 7226 7916).

Café Kick p114
43 Exmouth Market, EC1
(020 7837 8077).
Café Lazeez p80
21 Dean Street, W1 (020
7434 0022).
Café Med p76
184A Kensington Park
Road, W11 (020 7221
1150).
Café Med p142
320 Goldhawk Road, W6
(020 8741 1994).

Café Med p50
2 Hollywood Road, SW10
(020 7823 3355).
Café Med p95
22-25 Dean Street, W1
(020 7287 9007).
Café Med p120
370 St John Street, EC1
(020 7278 1199).
Café Med p188
2 North Side, SW18 (020
7228 0914).
Café Med p235
21 Loudon Road, NW8
(020 7625 1222).

Café Milan p23
312 King's Road, SW3
(020 7351 0101).
Café Pacifico p29
5 Langley Street, WC2
(020 7379 7728).
Café Rouge p52
2 Lancer Square,
Kensington Church Street,
W8 (020 7938 4200).

Café Rouge p16
Unit 209, Whiteleys,
Queensway, W2 (020
7221 1509).
Café Rouge p27
390 King's Road, SW3
(020 7352 2226).
Café Rouge p36
34 Wellington Street, WC2
(020 7836 0998).
Café Rouge p50
855 Fulham Road, SW6
(020 7371 7600).
Café Rouge p59
27-31 Basil Street, SW3
(020 7584 2345).
Café Rouge p69
46-48 James Street, W1
(020 7487 4847).
Café Rouge p78
31 Kensington Park Road,
W11 (020 7221 4449).
Café Rouge p95
15 Frith Street, W1 (020
7437 4307).
Café Rouge p98
102 Old Brompton Road,
SW7 (020 7373 2403).
Café Rouge p103
Victoria Place Shopping
Centre, 115 Buckingham
Palace Road, SW1 (020
7931 9300).
Café Rouge p134
Hillgate House, 2-3
Limeburner Lane, EC4
(020 7329 1234).
Café Rouge p134
140 Fetter Lane, EC4
(020 7242 3469).
Café Rouge p140
248 Upper Richmond
Road, SW14 (020 8878
8897).
Café Rouge p142
17 The Green, W5 (020
8579 2788).
Café Rouge p142
227-229 Chiswick High
Road, W4 (020 8742
7447).
Café Rouge p142
85 Strand on the Green,
W4 (020 8995 6575).
Café Rouge p142
291 Sandycombe Road,
Kew, Surrey (020 8332
2882).
Café Rouge p144
158 Fulham Palace Road,
W6 (020 8741 5037).
Café Rouge p149
30 Clifton Road, W9 (020
7286 2266).
Café Rouge p149
4-8 Kingston Hill,
Kingston-upon-Thames,
Surrey (020 8547 3229).
Café Rouge p152
98-100 Shepherd's Bush
Road, W6 (0171 603
7732).

Café Rouge p152
7A Petersham Road,
Richmond, Surrey (020
8332 2423).
Café Rouge p161
39 Parkgate Road, SW11
(020 7924 3565).
Café Rouge p164
16-18 Montpelier Vale,
SE3 (020 8297 2727).
Café Rouge p168
Hays Galleria, Tooley
Street, SE1 (020 7378
0097).
Café Rouge p177
40 Abbeville Road, SW4
(020 8673 3399).
Café Rouge p178
84 Park Hall Road, SE21
(020 8766 0070).
Café Rouge p181
30 Stockwell Street, SE10
(020 8293 6660).
Café Rouge p185
200-204 Putney Bridge
Road, SW15 (020 8788
4257).
Café Rouge p190
573 Garratt Lane, SW18
(020 8947 9616).
Café Rouge p190
26 High Street, SW19
(020 8944 5131).
Café Rouge p196
29-35 Mackenzie Walk,
Cabot Square, Canary
Wharf, E14 (020 7537
9696).
Café Rouge p215
18 Chalk Farm Road, NW1
(020 7428 0998).
Café Rouge p216
Leisure Way, High Road,
N12 (020 8446 4777).
Café Rouge p216
46-48 Crouch End Hill, N8
(020 8340 2121).
Café Rouge p220
38-39 High Street, NW3
(020 7435 4240).
Café Rouge p220
6-7 South Grove, N6 (020
8342 9797).
Café Rouge p235
120 St John's Wood High
Street, NW8 (020 7722
8366).
Café Rouge p237
203 West End Lane, NW6
(020 7372 8177).

Cahoots p23
2 Elystan Street, SW3
(020 7584 0140).
Camden
Brewing Co. p208
1 Randolph Street, NW1
(020 7267 9829).
Camden Falcon p208
234 Royal College
Street, NW1 (020 7485
3834).
Camden Head p223
2 Camden Walk, N1 (020
7359 0851).

Camden Tup p215
2-3 Greenland Place, NW1
(020 7482 0399).

Canbury Arms p146
49 Canbury Park
Road, Kingston-upon-
Thames, Surrey (020
8288 1882).

Candy Bar p83
4 Carlisle Street, W1 (020
7494 4041).
Cantaloupe p135
35-42 Charlotte Road,
EC2 (020 7613 4411).
Cantina
Vinopolis p164
1 Bank End, SE1 (020
7940 8333).
Captain Kidd p203
108 Wapping High Street,
E1 (020 7480 5759).
Cardinal p103
23 Francis Street, SW1
(020 7834 7260).
Carpe Diem p66
28 Paddington Street, W1
(020 7935 0556).
Cartoonist p131
76 Shoe Lane, EC4 (020
7353 2828).
Castle p51
100 Holland Park Avenue,
W11 (020 7313 9301).
Castle p131
26 Furnival Street, EC4
(020 7404 1310).
Castle p156
115 Battersea High Street,
SW11 (020 7228 8181).
Cat & Canary p193
1-24 Fisherman's Walk,
Canary Wharf, E14 (020
7512 9187).
Catcher in
the Rye p216
317 Regent's Park Road,
N3 (020 8343 4369).
Catford Ram p173
9 Winslade Way, SE6 (020
8690 6206).
Cave Austin p163
7-9 Montpelier Vale, SE3
(020 8852 0492).
Cavern p189
100 Coombe Lane, SW20
(020 8946 7911).
Central Bar p135
58 Old Street, EC1 (020
7490 0080).
Centuria p225
100 St Paul's Road, N1
(020 7704 2345).
Champagne
Charlie's (Davys) p36
17 The Arches, Villiers
Street, WC2 (020 7930
7737).
Champion p39
12-13 Wells Street, W1
(020 7323 1228).
Chandos p61
29 St Martin's Lane, WC2
(020 7836 1401).
The Chapel p225
29A Penton Street, N1
(020 7833 4090).
Chapel p66
48 Chapel Street, NW1
(020 7402 9220).
Charlie Wright's
International Bar p135
45 Pitfield Street, N1 (020
7490 8345).
Château Bar p69
Mayfair InterContinental
Hotel, Stratton Street, W1
(020 7629 7777).
Che p98
23 St James's Street,
SW1 (020 7747 9380).

Cheers p61
72 Regent Street, W1
(020 7494 3322).
Chelsea Bar p56
Chelsea Hotel, 17 Sloane
Street, SW1 (020 7235
4377).
Chelsea Ram p23
32 Burnaby Street, SW10
(020 7351 4008).
Chequers p98
16 Duke Street, SW1 (020
7930 4007).
Chez Gérard p127
64 Bishopsgate, EC2 (020
7588 1200).
Chez Gérard at the
Opera Terrace p30
First Floor Opera Terrace,
Covent Garden Central
Market, WC2 (020 7379
0666).
Chocolate Bar p69
59 Berkeley Square, W1
(020 7499 7850).

Chopper
Lump (Davys) p76
10C Hanover Square, W1
(020 7499 7569).

Churchill Arms p52
119 Kensington Church
Street, W8 (020 7727
4242).
Churchill Bar
& Cigar Divan p66
Churchill InterContinental,
Portman Square, W1
(020 7486 5800).
Cicada p114
132-136 St John
Street, EC1 (020 7608
1550).
Circle p185
348 Clapham Road, SW9
(020 7622 3683).
Circus p83
1 Upper James Street, W1
(020 7534 4000).
Cittie of Yorke p50
22 High Holborn, WC1
(020 7242 7670).

City Boot (Davys) p127
7 Moorfields Highwalk,
EC2 (020 7588 4766).
City Flogger (Davys) p130
Fenn Court, 120
Fenchurch Street, EC3
(020 7623 3251).
City FOB (Free On Board)
(Davys) p130
Lower Thames Street, EC3
(020 7621 0619).

City Limits p120
16-18 Brushfield Street,
E1 (020 7377 9877).

City Pipe (Davys) p123
Foster Lane, off
Cheapside, EC1 (020
7606 2110).

City Pride p193
15 Westferry Road, E14
(020 7987 3516).

City Tup (Davys) p127
66 Gresham Street, EC2
(020 7606 8176).
City Vaults (Davys) p123
2 St Martin's le
Grand, EC1 (020 7606
8721).

Time Out
2000/2001 Pubs & Bars Guide
Please let us know what you think.

Your feedback is invaluable to us! Please take a few minutes to let us know what you think of London's pubs & bars and of this guide – you could win £100 worth of Time Out guides and merchandise. Just send in this card by 30 November 2000, and if yours is the first out of the hat in our prize draw, you'll get the goodies.

1. How often, on average, do you visit pubs & bars?
Four or more times per week ❑
Two to three times per week ❑
Once a week ❑
Once/twice a month ❑
Less than once/twice monthly ❑

2. Which of the following do you most often drink when visiting pubs & bars? (please tick only one box)
Wine ❑
Spirits ❑
Draught lager ❑
Bottled lager ❑
Canned lager ❑
Draught ale ❑
Bottled ale ❑
Canned ale ❑
Cocktails ❑
Alcopops ❑
Mineral water ❑
Soft drinks ❑

3. How many people use your copy of the *Time Out Pubs & Bars Guide*?
Just me ❑
One other ❑
Two others ❑
Three others ❑
Four others ❑
More than five others ❑

4. Have you ever bought/used Time Out magazine?
Yes ❑   No ❑

5. Have you ever bought any Time Out City Guides?
Yes ❑   No ❑

If yes, which ones?
....
....

....
....

6. Have you ever bought/used other Time Out publications?
Yes ❑   No ❑

If yes, which ones?
....
....
....

7. Are you...?
Single ❑
Living with partner ❑

8. Are you ...?
Employed full-time ❑
Employed part-time ❑
Self-employed ❑
Unemployed ❑
Student ❑
Home-maker ❑

(BLOCK CAPITALS PLEASE)
9. Title (Mr, Ms etc)................................

First name...

Surname...

Address..
....
....

Postcode...

Email...

Daytime telephone................................

10. Year of birth..

11. Sex...

12. At the moment do you earn ...?
Under £10,000 ❑
Over £10,000 up to £14,999 ❑
Over £15,000 up to £19,999 ❑
Over £20,000 up to £24,999 ❑
Over £25,000 up to £39,999 ❑
Over £40,000 up to £49,999 ❑
Over £50,000 up to £59,999 ❑
Over £60,000 ❑

13. Where did you first hear of/see this guide?
Advertising in Time Out magazine ❑
Other press advertising ❑
Advertising on London Underground ❑
Bookshop/newsagent ❑
Other (write in) ❑
....
....

14. Your recommendations
I wish to recommend for future inclusion ❑
Recommend for non-inclusion ❑

Name of pub/bar
....

Address of pub/bar
....
....
....
....

Phone no. of pub/bar
....

Comments
....
....
....
....
....
....
....
....

Please tick here if you want to receive information on related products and services. ❑

Now fold your completed report and questionnaire in half, tape together (no staples please) and return to us FREEPOST. Thanks very much.

✂

Time Out
This voucher entitles the bearer to a free glass of Davy's Bordeaux Claret or Bordeaux Sauvignon at participating Davy's Wine Bars. See page 15 for details.

Terms & Conditions
This offer is valid from April 1 until November 30, 2000 inclusive. One voucher per person. Not valid in conjunction with any other offer or discount. Value £0.001p. Voucher to be redeemed

Time Out Magazine
Universal House
251 Tottenham Court Road
LONDON
W1E 0DQ

Fold here and tape together

For a free glass of wine courtesy of *Time Out* & Davy's,
see page 15 for details.